THE ROUGH GUIDE TO

Mallorca & ~~WITHDRAWN~~ Menorca

written and researched by

Phil Lee

ROUGH GUIDES

roughguides.com

Contents

INTRODUCTION   4

| Where to go | 6 | Things not to miss | 12 |
| When to go | 10 | Itineraries | 18 |

BASICS   20

Getting there	21	Festivals	32
Getting around	23	Sports and outdoor activities	34
Accommodation	26	Shopping	35
Food and drink	28	Travel essentials	36
The media	32		

THE GUIDE   42

1 Palma and around	42	4 Southern Mallorca	158
2 Western Mallorca	86	5 Menorca	194
3 Northern Mallorca	126		

CONTEXTS   244

History	245	Language	276
Flora and fauna	264	Glossary	285
Books	272		

SMALL PRINT & INDEX   287

Introduction to
Mallorca & Menorca

As he approached Mallorca in 1888, the British traveller Charles Wood was all but overwhelmed, exclaiming "Nothing could be more beautiful than the views of sea and land. The island rounded in a succession of curves and bays, one headland after another opening out magnificently". Very few English-speaking travellers ventured to Mallorca and Menorca in the nineteenth century, but those who did were suitably impressed by the beauty of the landscape if not by the islanders themselves, who were generally disparaged as disagreeable and unruly. The same conflicting attitudes survive today: millions of tourists count Menorca and Mallorca as favourite holiday destinations, though surprisingly few know much about the islanders. In fact, this easterly section of the Balearic archipelago – which also includes Ibiza and Formentera – has a rich cultural history, and many of its inhabitants still live in the most charming of country towns – Sineu, Artà and Ciutadella to name but three – at a (safe) distance from the teeming resorts of the coast.

The islands' image embraces extreme ends of the spectrum: on one level, **Mallorca** is a popular haunt of the rich and famous; on the other it has an unenviable reputation for tacky tourism built on sun, sex, booze and high-rise hotels. The truth is that Mallorca manages to be both at the same time: at 5pm you can be carousing with the Brits in Magaluf and half an hour later you can be sipping a coffee in a quiet mountain village. The good news is that the ugly development of the 1960s, which submerged tracts of coastline beneath hotels, villas and apartment blocks, is essentially constrained to the Bay of Palma and a handful of mega-resorts notching the east coast, and for the most part Mallorca remains handsome and frequently fascinating, from the craggy mountains and medieval monasteries of its north coast to the antique towns of the central plain.

To the east of Mallorca lies **Menorca**, the second largest and most agricultural of the Balearic islands, with a population of just 94,000. Menorca's rolling fields, wooded ravines

ABOVE VALLDEMOSSA OLIVE GROVE, MALLORCA; DEIÀ, MALLORCA; TAPAS

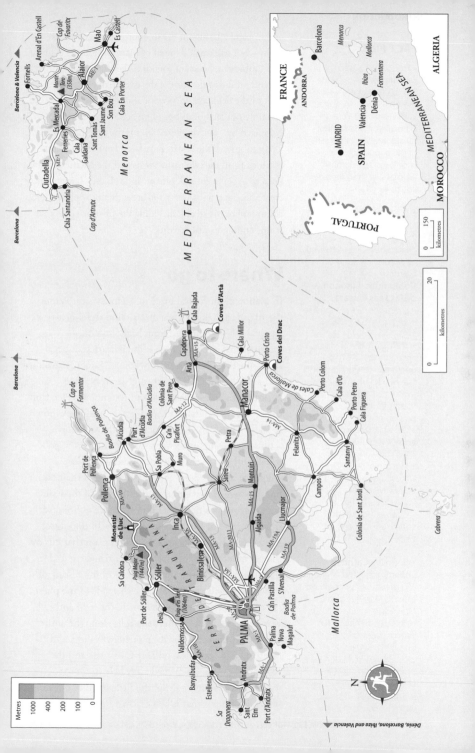

Metres
1000
400
200
100
0

MEDITERRANEAN SEA

Menorca

Fornells
Arenal d'En Castell
Cap de Favàritx
Maó
Es Castell
Alaior
Monte Toro (358m)
Es Mercadal
Ferreries
Cala Galdana
Sant Tomàs
Sant Jaume
Son Bou
Cala En Porter
Ciutadella
ME-1
Cala Santandria
Cap d'Artrutx

Barcelona & Valencia
Barcelona

Mallorca

Cap de Formentor
Badía de Pollença
Port de Pollença
Pollença
Alcúdia
Port d'Alcúdia
Badía d'Alcúdia
Colònia de Sant Pere
Artà
Capdepera
Cala Rajada
Coves d'Artà
Cala Millor
Porto Cristo
Coves del Drac
Manacor
Cales de Mallorca
Porto Colom
Cala d'Or
Porto Petro
Cala Figuera
Felanitx
Santanyí
Colònia de Sant Jordi
Campos
Llucmajor
Algaida
Montuïri
Petra
Sineu
Muro
Sa Pobla
Ca'n Picafort
Inca
Monestir de Lluc
Sa Calobra
Puig Major (1445m)
Sóller
Port de Sóller
Puig d'es Teix (1064m)
Binissalem
Deià
Valldemossa
SERRA DE TRAMUNTANA
Banyalbufar
Estellencs
Andratx
Sa Dragonera
Sant Elm
Port d'Andratx
Palma Nova
Magaluf
Ca'n Pastilla
S'Arenal
Badía de Palma
PALMA

MA-10
MA-13
MA-12
MA-15
MA-14
MA-19
MA-19A
MA-15
MA-3011
MA-13A
MA-3A
MA-11A
MA-1A
MA-1
MA-20

Cabrera

Dénia, Barcelona, Ibiza and Valencia

N

0   20 kilometres
0   kilometres (Menorca scale)

Dénia, Barcelona, Ibiza and Valencia

Inset map

FRANCE
ANDORRA
SPAIN
MADRID
Barcelona
Valencia
Dénia
PORTUGAL
MEDITERRANEAN SEA
Menorca
Mallorca
Ibiza
Formentera
MOROCCO
ALGERIA

0   150 kilometres

FACT FILE

• The Balearic islands have a **population** of just under 1,200,000; Mallorca weighs in with 870,000, Menorca with just 94,000. Foreign-born inhabitants account for around twenty percent of the population; the largest group are from Germany, with an average age of 48.

• The **Spanish parliament** – the Cortes Generales – sits in Madrid, but many of its powers have been devolved to 17 autonomous regions, one of which – the **Comunidad Autónoma de las Islas Baleares** – covers the Balearics, whose capital is Palma.

• The mountains of Mallorca are home to the islands' ornithological star turn, the rare **black vulture** (*Aegypius monachus*), a dark and solitary bird of striking proportions, standing 130cm tall, weighing anywhere between 7 and 14kg and with an adult wingspan of nearly 3m. They almost died out in the 1970s, but a well-executed conservation scheme seems to have saved the day – there are now about 120 birds.

• Spain is a **Catholic** country, though only about 15 percent of its population attends Mass every week. One result of the decline in religious observance has been a shortage of monks and nuns: all the monasteries on Mallorca are now deconsecrated, with several offering inexpensive lodgings (see p.27).

and humpy hills fill out the interior in between its two main – but still small – towns of **Maó**, the island's capital, and **Ciutadella**. Much of Menorca's landscape looks pretty much as it did at the turn of the twentieth century, though a lot of the fields are no longer cultivated, and many – but certainly not all – of its beguiling beachy coves have been colonized by villa complexes. Nor is the development likely to spread: the resorts have been kept at a discreet distance from the two main towns and the Menorcans are keen to avoid overdevelopment. Indeed, they have recently created a chain of conservation areas that now protect about half of the island, including the pristine coves that count among its real delights.

Where to go

In **Mallorca**, the logical place to begin a visit is **Palma**, the island capital, which arches around the shores of its bay just a few kilometres from Mallorca's busy international airport. Palma is the Balearics' one real city, a bustling, historic place whose oligarchic mansions and magnificent Gothic cathedral serve as a fine backdrop to an excellent café and restaurant scene, from the hipster hangouts of the Sa Gerreria neighbourhood to the chef-led, chichi restaurants of the Old Town – plus everything in between. Add to this lots of good hotels and you've got a city that deserves at least a couple of days. Indeed, many visitors spend their entire holiday here, day-tripping out to the rest of the island – an easy proposition as it's only a couple of hours' drive from one end of Mallorca to the other. To the east of Palma stretches **Es Pla**, an agricultural plain that fills out the centre of the island, sprinkled with ancient and seldom-visited country towns, the most interesting of which are **Sineu** and **Petra**. On either side of the plain are coastal mountains. To the north, the wild and wonderful **Serra de Tramuntana** rolls along the entire coastline, punctuated by deep sheltered valleys and beautiful cove **beaches**, notably Cala Deià and the Platja de Formentor. Tucked away here in the mountains is **Sóller**, a delightful little town of old stone merchant houses that is best reached from Palma on the

antique **railway**, an extraordinarily scenic journey. The mountains also camouflage a string of picturesque villages, most memorably **Estellencs**, **Banyalbufar**, **Deià** – the long-time haunt of Robert Graves – and **Fornalutx**, as well as a pair of intriguing monasteries at **Valldemossa**, where Chopin and George Sand famously wintered, and **Lluc**, home to a much-venerated statue of the Madonna. For walkers, the range is crisscrossed with footpaths and makes for ideal **hiking**, particularly in the cooler spring and autumn. Beyond Lluc, the mountains roll down to a coastal plain that holds the lovely little town of **Pollença** and one of the island's most appealing medium-sized resorts, **Port de Pollença**, which is itself just along the bay from the sprawling but well-kept resort of **Port d'Alcúdia**. In the north, Mallorca finishes with a final scenic flourish in the rearing cliffs of the **Península de Formentor**.

Mallorca's second mountain range, the gentler, greener **Serres de Llevant** shadows the coves of the **east coast** and culminates in the pine-clad headlands and medieval hill towns of the island's northeast corner. Many of the east-coast resorts are overblown, but the pick are **Cala Rajada**, close to several fine beaches, and pint-sized **Porto Petro**. There are also a couple of easily visited cave systems – the most diverting is the **Coves del Drac** – and the comely, artsy hilltop town of **Artà**, close to the substantial prehistoric remains of **Ses Paisses**. Different again is the **south coast**, where a long and rocky shelf jags out into the ocean – though this part of the island is redeemed by the charming resort and seaport of **Colònia de Sant Jordi** and its accompanying beaches.

Smaller, flatter **Menorca**, the most easterly of the Balearics, boasts two attractive towns, the island capital of **Maó**, just 5km from the airport, and **Ciutadella**, 45km to

FABULOUS FINCAS

The Balearics are dotted with old stone **fincas** (or farmhouses), many of which have been turned into holiday homes and hotels. The largest – for example *La Granja* (see p.118) and *Raixa* (see p.102) – are effectively rural palaces that have become tourist attractions in their own right, but the bulk offer lodgings, mostly at the top end of the market. Prime examples include *Ca's Xorc* (see p.95) in the mountains near Sóller; *Can Llenaire* (see p.144), still part of a working farm and with panoramic coastal views; *Es Castell* (see p.136), a wonderful hotel in the foothills of the Serra de Tramuntana; and the *Biniarroca Hotel*, near Sant Lluís in Menorca (see p.215). The charm of staying in a *finca* lies at least in part in the solidity and simplicity of its architectural form: a stone or stone-and-rubble exterior, a flagged exterior courtyard, shuttered and grilled rectangular windows, and high, wood-beamed ceilings. It's also usual to find *fincas* surrounded by a raft of specialist agricultural buildings, from olive presses and workshops through to barns and store houses.

the west. Both have preserved much of their eighteenth- and early nineteenth-century appearance, though Ciutadella has the aesthetic edge, the many lanes and alleys of its ancient centre shadowed by fine old mansions and monasteries. Linking the two, the island's only main road, the **Me-1**, slips across the rural interior, passing the pleasant market towns of **Es Migjorn Gran**, **Es Mercadal** and **Ferreries**. A series of sideroads branches off to the island's **resorts**, the best appointed of which are **Cala Galdana** and the one-time fishing village of **Fornells**, as well as a string of wind-battered headlands and remote **cove beaches**. The highway also squeezes past **Monte Toro**, Menorca's highest peak and the site of a quaint little convent with panoramic views. Menorca's other claim to fame is its smattering of prehistoric remains – two of the most important being **Talatí de Dalt**, outside Maó, and the **Naveta d'es Tudons**, near Ciutadella.

OPPOSITE ILLA DE CABRERA **ABOVE** ES CASTELL, MENORCA

BEST BALEARIC BEACHES

MALLORCA

Cala Deià Crystal-clear waters and a narrow pebbly beach in a hoop-shaped cove at the end of a lovely wooded gulch. Great setting; great beach bar-restaurant. See p.108

Cala Tuent Not much sand here – it's all shingle and pebble – but the mountain setting is a delight and the beach is rarely crowded. See p.132

Es Trenc Whichever way you cut it, most of Mallorca's beaches are crowded, but not this one – a long, sandy strand on the south coast. See p.185

Platja de Palma Roast and pose among the muscle-flexing, oiled pecs and abs. See p.84

Port d'Alcúdia A long and immaculately maintained stretch of golden sand on the north coast. See p.154

Port de Pollença A bucket-and-spade family affair, with safe bathing and sandcastle building. See p.142

Sant Elm Cosy, sandy beach in a charming setting on the western tip of the island. See p.122

MENORCA

Cala Macarella A real treat, the cove's band of white sand is flanked and framed by handsome limestone cliffs. See p.242

Cala Pregonda It takes a good deal of effort to get here, but the reward is a wide slice of sand in a beguiling setting. See p.221

Cala Turqueta Exquisite and beautiful beach, comprising a handsome horseshoe of white sand set beneath limestone cliffs. See p.242

Platja de Cavalleria A slender arc of pristine sand is framed by grassy dunes at this delightful north-coast beach. See p.221

When to go

There's little difference between the **climates** of Mallorca and Menorca. **Spring** and **autumn** are the ideal times for a visit, when the weather is comfortably warm, with none of the oven-like temperatures that bake the islands in late June, July and August. It's well worth considering a **winter** break too: even in January temperatures are usually high enough to sit out at a café in shirtsleeves. Both islands see occasional rain in winter, however, and the Serra de Tramuntana mountains, which protect the rest of Mallorca from inclement weather and the prevailing northerly **winds**, are often buffeted by storms, while Menorca, where there's no mountain barrier, can be irritatingly windy. Reflecting their agricultural past, the islanders have names for the four main winds that blow across their land: Tramuntana, Ponent, Migjorn and Llevant, respectively northerly, westerly, southerly and easterly.

Author picks

Our author has made countless trips to Mallorca and Menorca over the years, but there are some things he likes to do, or places he just has to visit, every time he returns. Here's a selection of his favourites.

Prettiest villages Both Menorca and Mallorca are threaded with pretty villages, but three of the best are Estellencs (see p.121), where the tourist presence is noticeably thin, Biniaraix (see p.99), the trailhead for some dramatic mountain walks, and Orient (see p.103), a place so quiet that you can hear the softest of bird calls.

Mallorcan Primitives Not Primitive Mallorcans, but rather a school of medieval artists who produced a brigade of exquisite devotional paintings, on display in Palma at the cathedral (see p.51) and at the Museu Diocesà (see p.53).

Mountain roads Not for the faint-hearted, or the poor-of-steering, some of Mallorca's mountain roads offer superb views: try the hairpins of the Castell d'Alaró (see p.104) and the lane up to the Ermita de Nostra Senyora del Puig (see p.139) for starters.

Palma cathedral No question, this is one of the finest Gothic churches in Europe – absolutely unmissable, both for the stunning beauty of its medieval architecture and for the later additions made by no less a figure than Antoni Gaudí (see p.47).

Great hikes Both Mallorca and Menorca offer the adventurous – and not so adventurous – hiker some wonderful experiences: the circular hike from Valldemossa on the Archduke's Path is a particular favourite (see p.116), as is the hike from Es Grau to Sa Torreta on Menorca (see p.216).

Seaside R&R The sandy beach at Sant Elm (see p.122) is a favourite spot for some downtime, as are the quiet strands near the resort of Colònia de Sant Jordi (see p.189). With kids in tow, head for the family-friendly beach at either Port de Pollença (see p.142) or Port d'Alcúdia (see p.154).

> Our author recommendations don't end here. We've flagged up our favourite places – a perfectly sited hotel, an atmospheric café, a special restaurant – throughout the guide, highlighted with the ★ symbol.

OPPOSITE CALA TURQUETA, MENORCA **RIGHT FROM TOP** BINIARAIX, MALLORCA; EN ROUTE TO CASTELL D'ALARÓ, MALLORCA; SANT ELM, MALLORCA

17

things not to miss

It's not possible to see everything that Mallorca and Menorca have to offer in one trip – and we don't suggest you try. What follows is a selective taste of the islands' highlights: gorgeous beaches and magnificent scenery, quaint towns and great places to eat and drink. All entries are colour-coded by chapter and have a page reference to take you straight into the Guide, where you can find out more.

1 PALMA–SÓLLER TRAIN
Page 93
Take a trip on the vintage train that wends its way over the mountains from Palma to Sóller providing wonderful views and serving as a fine introduction to Mallorca's best landscapes.

2 SÓLLER
Page 91
Sóller is an appealing country town of old stone mansions surrounded by orange and lemon groves, not to mention mountains.

3 TALATÍ DE DALT
Page 206
In an attractive rural setting close to Maó, this extensive site is one of the most satisfying of Menorca's many prehistoric remains.

4 VALLDEMOSSA
Page 111
Sitting pretty in the hills, the ancient town of Valldemossa is home to a fascinating monastery whose echoing cloisters and shadowy cells once accommodated Chopin and George Sand.

5 MONESTIR DE LLUC
Page 133
This rambling monastery holds the Balearics' most venerated icon, La Moreneta, and is also a great base for mountain hikes.

6 THE MALLORCAN PRIMITIVES
Pages 51, 53 & 59

A medieval school of painters who produced strikingly naive devotional works – Joan Desi being one of its most talented practitioners.

7 PENÍNSULA DE FORMENTOR
Page 146

The knobbly peaks and sheer cliffs of this spectacular peninsula backdrop one of Mallorca's best beaches and ritziest hotels.

8 HIKING IN THE SERRA DE TRAMUNTANA
Pages 91 & 131

Rolling along the west coast, this rugged mountain range holds scores of exhilarating hiking trails.

9 EATING IN PALMA
Page 73

Palma has the liveliest café and restaurant scene in the Balearics, with a hatful of first-rate places both in the Old Town and Sa Gerreria; and be sure to try the islanders' favourite nibble – a spiralled flaky pastry known as an *ensaimada*.

10 CIUTADELLA
Page 231

The prettiest town on Menorca, the island's former capital cuddles up to a narrow harbour, its network of cobbled lanes flanked by a string of handsome mansions.

11 DEIÀ
Page 105

No wonder Robert Graves made his home in the coastal village of Deià – a beguiling huddle of old stone buildings set against a handsome mountain backdrop.

6

7

12 SANTUARI DE SANT SALVADOR, ARTÀ
Page 172
The sun-bleached roofs of small-town Artà clamber up the steepest of hills to this shrine, one of Mallorca's most important, with the prehistoric village of Ses Païsses close at hand.

13 PALMA CATHEDRAL
Page 47
Dominating the waterfront, the monumental bulk of Palma's magnificent cathedral offers one of Spain's finest examples of the Gothic style, its interior flooded with kaleidoscopic shafts of light.

14 CAP DE FAVÀRITX
Page 218
This windswept cape, with its bare, lunar-like rocks, is a scenic highlight of Menorca's north coast.

15 MAÓ
Page 200
Menorca's modest capital has an amiable small-town feel, its tiny centre a labyrinth of ancient lanes and alleys graced by old and appealing townhouses and churches.

16 CABRERA
Page 192
Now a national park, this austere, scrub-covered islet is home to a battered hilltop castle, a wealth of birdlife – and the rare Lilford's wall lizard.

17 JARDINS D'ALFÀBIA
Page 100
The lush, oasis-like Jardins d'Alfàbia are the finest gardens on Mallorca, their watered trellises and terraces dating back to green-fingered Moors.

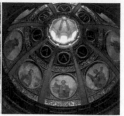

Itineraries

Mallorca and Menorca's attractions are myriad – our three itineraries guide you round Mallorca's must-see sights, Menorca's unique prehistoric remains, and – for those on a budget – Mallorca's most authentic and relatively inexpensive places to stay.

GRAND TOUR OF MALLORCA

Spend a few days in Palma before threading your way along the island's invigorating, surf-battered north coast, via quiet villages and wondrous scenery.

❶ Palma Allow three days to explore the capital's ancient nooks and crannies and enjoy its first-rate cafés and restaurants. **See p.47**

❷ Estellencs Some say this is Mallorca's prettiest village, a huddle of ancient houses clinging gingerly to steep, sea-facing slopes. **See p.121**

❸ Valldemossa A hilltop town with the island's most fascinating monastery, where Chopin spent an unforgiving winter. **See p.111**

❹ Deià Between mountain and sea, chichi Deià has a scattering of old stone houses perched high above the ocean. **See p.105**

❺ Sóller Wandering the narrow cobbled streets of this beguiling town gives you a real flavour of island life. **See p.91**

❻ Port de Sóller Arced around a horseshoe-shaped bay, this recently upgraded resort has a superb selection of restaurants. **See pp.96–99**

❼ Lluc The monks may have gone, but the monastery and its shrine remains, making it one of the island's key sights. **See p.133**

❽ Pollença A cosy town with a low-key feel in the prettiest of settings. **See p.136**

❾ Port de Pollença Safe bathing and a long sandy beach are the key to this resort's family-friendly appeal. **See p.142**

TAULAS AND TALAYOTS: A TOUR OF MENORCA'S PREHISTORY

Menorca is world-famous for its prehistoric remains, which lie scattered across the whole island. They date from the so-called Talayotic period and are named for the distinctive conical rock mounds – *talayots* – found at most key sites. The *talayots* are often lie cheek-to-jowl with Menorca's most mysterious artefacts, T-shaped *taulas* of around 4m high.

❶ Talatí de Dalt This delightful prehistoric site features a *taula*, a large *talayot* – and a tribe of free-range hogs. **See p.206**

❷ Torralba d'en Salord A rural setting and one of the best-preserved *taulas* on the island makes this a worthwhile diversion. **See p.223**

❸ Torre d'en Gaumés One of the largest prehistoric settlements on the island, with three *talayots*, a *taula* and the remains of a water collection system. **See p.223**

❹ Torrellafuda A well-preserved *talayot* in a lovely, rustic setting. **See p.230**

ABOVE ESTELLENCS; THE MONASTERY AT LLUC

⑤ Naveta d'es Tudons The island's most intact *naveta*, or stone ossuary. **See p.230**

AUTHENTIC MALLORCA: FROM HOSTAL TO HOSTAL

In recent years, Mallorca has sprouted a veritable battalion of deluxe hotels as the island as a whole has moved upmarket, and though many are great places to stay, they are expensive, and often reflect little of the island's heritage. But there remains a scattering of well-kept, traditional *hostales* and hotels which offer a taste of an older, less homogenized Mallorca – with the added bonus that they are all relatively inexpensive.

❶ Hotel Born, Palma In a big old townhouse, this enjoyable hotel with its lovely courtyard has a great city-centre location. **See p.72**

❷ Hostal Dragonera, Sant Elm Unpretentious, inexpensive *hostal* with a prime seashore location in this tidy little resort. **See p.123**

❸ Hostal Miramar, Deià Handsome Deià may be a trustafarian paradise, but the *Miramar* bucks the trend, being a simple and traditional *hostal* with grand views out across the coast. **See p.109**

❹ El Guía, Sóller Long-established and very traditional lodgings, just footsteps from the train station. **See p.95**

❺ Pension Bellavista, Pollença Perhaps the funkiest place to stay on the island – these Spanish hipsters must have Franco turning in his grave. **See p.144**

❻ Hostal Condemar, Cala Mondragó A small slice of the east coast has been conserved and protected by the creation of Mondragó Parc Natural – and this *hostal* is at the heart of it. **See p.187**

❼ Hostal Playa, Colònia de Sant Jordi Low-key *hostal* perched tight against the seashore of this appealing resort. **See p.191**

HIKING IN THE SERRA DE TRAMUNTANA

Basics

21 Getting there

23 Getting around

26 Accommodation

28 Food and drink

32 The media

32 Festivals

34 Sports and outdoor activities

35 Shopping

36 Travel essentials

Getting there

Hundreds of flights shuttle back and forth between Britain and Ireland and Mallorca and Menorca during the summer season, and although the pace slackens in winter, there is still a wide choice of flights to Mallorca, if somewhat fewer to Menorca. Visitors from North America, Australasia and South Africa, on the other hand, will need to fly to a European hub airport, such as London, Madrid or Barcelona, before catching an onward flight to the islands. It's also possible to reach Mallorca and Menorca by ferry and catamaran from Spain's east coast, but obviously this takes much longer.

Flights from the UK

From the UK, Mallorca and Menorca are readily reached from London and a veritable raft of regional airports. Flying times from London to either island are a little over 2hr (2hr 45min from Manchester). Fierce competition tends to keep fares way down on flights from London to Palma, but from regional airports fares are more variable. If you strike lucky, a return fare can cost as little as £100, though £250 is more normal, whereas a standard, fully flexible return can cost upwards of £500.

Flights from Ireland

There is a good range of flights from Ireland to both Mallorca and Menorca during the summer, but out of season you may have to travel via London, Madrid or Barcelona. The flying time from Dublin direct to either island is just under 3hr. Prices are highest in August – reckon on around £250 return from Belfast, €300 from Dublin – but drop a little in the months either side.

Flights from the USA

There are no direct nonstop flights from the USA to Mallorca or Menorca, but there are direct nonstop flights from several US cities to Madrid and Barcelona, from where it's a short and easy hop to either island. Often, it's cheaper to travel to London (or an alternative hub city) and pick up an onward flight from there. As sample fares, a return, nonstop flight from New York to Barcelona with American Airlines (Ⓦaa.com) costs upwards of US$1600, US$1700 from Atlanta to Madrid; from both there are regular flights on to the islands (see p.22). The flying time on a direct, nonstop service from New York to Madrid is just over 7hr.

Flights from Canada

There are no nonstop/direct flights from Canada to Mallorca or Menorca. However, you can fly there from any of Canada's major cities by using a combination of airlines and travelling via a European hub airport. Return fares from Toronto to a European hub city with Air Canada (Ⓦaircanada.com) go for around Can$800, Can$1000 from Vancouver. T he flying time nonstop from Toronto to Madrid is 7hr 30min.

Flights from Australia and New Zealand

There are no nonstop/direct flights to Spain from Australia or New Zealand, and you'll need to change planes once or twice to reach Madrid or Barcelona, from where there are regular flights on to Mallorca and Menorca. For flying times, count on 24hr via Asia or 30hr via the USA, not including time spent on stopovers. Fares with the likes of Emirates Airlines (Ⓦemirates.com) from Sydney or Melbourne to Madrid or Barcelona begin at around A$1800, NZ$2500 from Christchurch or Wellington. Another option is to pick up a cheap ticket to London, and then continue your journey to Mallorca or Menorca with a budget airline.

A BETTER KIND OF TRAVEL

At **Rough Guides** we are passionately committed to travel. We believe it helps us understand the world we live in and the people we share it with – and of course tourism is vital to many developing economies. But the scale of modern tourism has also damaged some places irreparably, and climate change is accelerated by most forms of transport, especially flying. All Rough Guides' flights are carbon-offset, and every year we donate money to a variety of environmental charities.

Flights from South Africa

There are no direct/nonstop flights to Spain **from South Africa** – you have to fly to a European hub to catch an onward plane to Mallorca or Menorca. As for **fares**, flights from Cape Town to a European hub cost around ZAR10,000; from Johannesburg, ZAR8000. The **flying time** on a direct, nonstop flight from South Africa to London is just over 11hr.

Flights from mainland Spain

Menorca and more especially Mallorca are easily reached by plane **from mainland Spain** with regular scheduled flights departing from a number of Spanish cities, including Valencia, Barcelona and Madrid. Journey times are minimal (Barcelona to Palma takes just 40min) and **ticket prices** modest, starting out at just €60 for the one-way flight from Barcelona to Palma, €120 from Madrid. The principal carrier is Iberia (Ⓦ iberia.com).

Flights between the Balearic islands

Three of the **Balearic islands** have international airports – Ibiza, Mallorca and Menorca – and there are frequent **inter-island flights**, though flights linking Ibiza and Menorca are often routed via Mallorca. There's usually no problem with seat availability, but you need to book ahead during the height of the season and on public holidays. The two main carriers are **Iberia** (Ⓦ iberia.com) and **Air Europa** (Ⓦ aireuropa.com), both of which operate about six inter-island flights daily. One-way **fares** between any of the islands start at €60, but average €90. The **flying time** between Ibiza and Mallorca and between Mallorca and Menorca is 40min.

By train from the UK

Travelling **by train from London St Pancras**, it takes between 12hr and 18hr to reach Barcelona, from where there are regular ferries to Palma and Maó (see below). Round-trip **fares** from London to Barcelona begin at around £250. For through-ticketing, contact **Rail Europe** (Ⓦ raileurope.co.uk).

By car and ferry from the UK

If you intend to travel to either Mallorca or Menorca **by car and ferry from the UK**, you'll need lots of time – a couple of days, maybe more. The quickest route is across the Channel via **Eurotunnel** (Ⓦ eurotunnel.com), followed by the long drive across France and Spain to one of the ferry ports that serve the Balearics (see below). To save driving time – if not overall journey time – you could also take a car ferry direct from the UK to Spain. There are three main options: Plymouth or Portsmouth to Santander, and Portsmouth to Bilbao. All are operated by **Brittany Ferries** (Ⓦ brittany-ferries.co.uk).

Ferries and catamarans from mainland Spain

Three companies – Trasmediterranea, Iscomar and Baleària (see below) – operate a network of **car ferry** and **catamaran services** from **three ports on the Spanish mainland** (Valencia, Dénia and Barcelona) to two ports on Mallorca (Palma and Port d'Alcúdia) and two ports on Menorca (Maó and Ciutadella). All three ferry companies apply a complex **fare** structure depending on the time of year, length of stay, accommodation on board and any accompanying vehicle; prices peak in June, July and August. Ferries from Dénia only go to Mallorca, but Valencia and Barcelona have ferries to both islands with the latter usually being the less expensive port of embarkation. As **sample fares**, a Baleària passenger **ticket** (without a cabin) from Barcelona to Maó or Palma costs from €50 on a car ferry and €60 on a catamaran; cars up to 4m in length on the same routes and including the driver cost from €170; and return tickets cost about twice as much as a single.

As regards **sailing times**, a regular car ferry takes 8hr to get from Barcelona to Palma, just over half that on a catamaran; and 30min or so less for Maó. Most services run all year, others have a winter break (usually Jan–March).

In all cases, **advance booking** is recommended and is well-nigh essential if you're taking a vehicle or need a cabin. **Tickets** can also be purchased at the port of embarkation, though note that ticket offices are only open near/around ferry departure times. The best price-comparison website for ferry bookings is operated by **Direct Ferries** (see below).

FERRY AND CATAMARAN CONTACTS

Baleària ☏ 902 16 01 80, Ⓦ balearia.com
Direct Ferries Ⓦ directferries.co.uk
Iscomar ☏ 902 11 91 28, Ⓦ iscomar.com
Trasmediterranea ☏ 902 45 46 45, Ⓦ trasmediterranea.es

Ferries and catamarans between the Balearic islands

Three ferry companies – Trasmediterranea, Iscomar and Baleària (see p.22) – operate **inter-island car ferries and catamarans**. There are frequent sailings between Mallorca and Menorca, and Mallorca and Ibiza, but vessels linking Menorca and Ibiza are usually routed via Mallorca. Once again, **fares** are complicated, but peak in June, July and August. As a sample fare, a one-way passenger ticket on a car ferry from Port d'Alcúdia to Ciutadella with Iscomar can cost as little as €35 in October, twice that in August, with cars up to 4m in length costing a further €35 in October, again much more in August. Fares on the much longer journey from Palma to Maó cost about twice as much.

Journey times are manageable: Ibiza to Palma is 3hr 30min by car ferry, about 2hr by catamaran; Maó to Palma 6hr, 3hr 30min by catamaran; and Port d'Alcúdia to Ciutadella 2hr by ferry and just 1hr by catamaran. Most services run all year, others have a winter break (usually Jan–March).

BALEARIC AGENTS AND TOUR OPERATORS

Balearic Discovery ☎ 971 87 53 95, ⓦ balearicdiscovery.com. Friendly and efficient, this Mallorca-based company offers tailor-made trips and holidays both on and off the usual tourist trail. The owners know the island like the back of their hands and have some charming *fincas* to rent.

Balearic Outdoor Holidays ☎ 0800 072 4832, ⓦ balearic outdoorholidays.com. Family-run company offering an excellent range of guided walking holidays and guided day-hikes in Menorca (see p.223).

Mallorcan Walking Tours (MWT) Port de Pollença, Mallorca ☎ 668 54 22 74, ⓦ mallorcanwalkingtours.puertopollensa.com. Small, excellent, Mallorca-based company operating an outstanding range of hikes (see p.142).

Nature Trek UK ☎ 01962 733 051, ⓦ naturetrek.co.uk. Wildlife/natural world specialist offering 8-day birdwatching tours of both Menorca and Mallorca.

North South Travel UK ☎ 01245 608 291, ⓦ northsouthtravel .co.uk. Friendly, competitive travel agency, offering discounted fares worldwide. Profits are used to support projects in the developing world, especially the promotion of sustainable tourism.

Tramuntana Tours c/Sa Lluna 72, Sóller ☎ 971 63 24 23, ⓦ tramuntanatours.com. Small but highly recommended company offering guided walks and an extensive programme of adventurous activities (see p.94).

Getting around

On both Menorca and Mallorca you're spoiled for choice when it comes to transport. There's a reliable bus network between all the major settlements, plus a multitude of taxis, a plethora of car rental firms, plenty of bicycles to rent, plus a couple of very useful train lines on Mallorca. Distances are small and conse-quently the costs of travel low, whether in terms of petrol or the price of a ticket: on Mallorca, for example, it's only 60km from Palma on the south coast to Alcúdia on the north shore, while Menorca has only one major road, which traverses the island from Ciutadella in the west to Maó in the east, a distance of just 45km.

Hopping from one island to the other is easy and economical too, as there are regular and inexpen-sive **inter-island flights and ferries** (see p.22 and p.23) – though it's advisable to book ahead in July and August. Note, however, that car hire companies will not allow you to take their vehicles from one island to another.

By bus

Both Menorca and Mallorca have an extensive network of reliable **bus services**. The three main towns – Palma, Maó and Ciutadella – serve as the hubs of the bus system and have fast and frequent links with most villages and resorts, both inland and on the coast, though in winter (Nov–April) and on public holidays buses to most resorts are scaled back, and in Menorca some resorts have no services at all. These principal bus routes are supplemented by a brigade of more intermittent local services. **Ticket prices** are very reasonable: the one-way fare from Palma to Port de Sóller, for instance, is just €3.25, from Maó to Ciutadella €5.10. In addition, Palma has its own public transport system, with buses linking the centre with the suburbs and surrounding beach resorts (see p.71).

On all island bus services, **destinations** are marked on the front of the bus. Passengers enter at the front and buy tickets from the driver, though you can also buy tickets in advance at a bus station. **Bus stops** are clearly marked in bright yellow and red colours. A baffling variety of **bus companies** operate the various routes on Mallorca and Menorca, but their efforts are coordinated by

Transports de les Illes Balears (TIB). Timetables are available at major bus stations, while most tourist offices carry local timetables. All the islands' bus timetables – with details of routings and bus stop locations – are available online (see below).

BUS CONTACTS

Palma EMT buses Ⓦ emtpalma.es
Mallorca buses Ⓦ tib.org
Menorca buses Ⓦ menorca.tib.org

By train

Mallorca has its own narrow-gauge **train network**. One line, which has vintage rolling stock and is especially popular with tourists, travels through magnificent mountain scenery on its way from Palma to Sóller (see p.93); the second, a modern line geared up for local use, shuttles across the flatlands of the interior, travelling from Palma to Binissalem and Inca, where it forks, with one branch nudging south to Sineu, Petra and Manacor, the other pushing on to Muro and Sa Pobla. Plans to extend the rail network to Alcúdia and Artà have, however, been shelved.

Both these train lines have their terminus train stations adjoining Plaça Espanya in Palma (see p.70). The **return fare** from Palma to Sóller on the vintage line is €21, €15 one-way, whereas fares on the more modern line are trifling – it's just €3.25, for instance, from Palma to Inca. The stations on the modern line also serve as starting points for buses to the surrounding towns and villages.

ADDRESSES

Addresses are usually abbreviated to a standard format. For example, "c/Bellver 7" translates as Bellver Street (*carrer*) no. 7; and "Plaça Rosari 5, 2è" means the second floor at Plaça Rosari no. 5 (*Plaça* means square). "Passeig d'es Born 15, 1–C" means suite C, first floor, at no. 15; and "s/n" (*sense número*) indicates a building without a street number. In Franco's day, most avenues and boulevards were named after Fascist heroes and, although nearly all were relabelled years ago, there's still some confusion in remoter spots. Another source of bafflement can be house numbers: some houses carry more than one number (the by-product of half-hearted reorganizations), and on many streets the sequence is impossible to fathom.

RAIL CONTACTS

Mallorcan trains (Inca line) Ⓦ tib.org
Mallorcan trains (Sóller line) Ⓦ trendesoller.com

By car

Getting around by public transport is easy enough, but you'll obviously have more freedom if you have **your own vehicle** – most of the more secluded beaches are, for example, only accessible under your own steam. Major and minor roads are very good on both islands, but country byroads are variable, ranging from middling dirt-and-gravel tracks to the most precarious of dirt trails, which are particularly lethal after rain, much more so on Mallorca than on (flatter) Menorca. Traffic is generally well behaved, but noisy, especially in Palma, where the horn is used as a recreational tool as well as an instrument of warning. **Fuel** (*gasolina*) comes in three main grades. Different companies use different brand names, but generally *Super Plus* is 98-octane fuel, selling at about €1.65 per litre, and *Super* is 95-octane, selling at about €1.55 per litre; both are without lead (*sense plom/sin plomo*). Diesel (*gasoleo* or *gasoil*) costs about €1.45 per litre. Both Menorca and Mallorca are well supplied with petrol stations; a few are open 24 hours a day, seven days a week, though most close around 9pm or 10pm and on public holidays.

Most foreign **driving licences** are honoured in Spain, including all EU/EEA, US, Australasian and Canadian ones. If you're bringing **your own car**, you must have adequate insurance, preferably including coverage for legal costs, and it's advisable to have an appropriate **breakdown policy** from your home motoring organization too.

Some rules of the road

Speed limits are posted throughout the Balearics: the maximum in built-up areas is 50km/h, sometimes 40km/h. Outside of built-up areas, it's 90km/h or 100km/h, on motorways 110/120km/h. Speed traps are fairly frequent and if you're stopped for any violation, the Spanish police can (and usually will) levy a stiff on-the-spot fine of up to €1500 before letting you go on your way. Most **driving rules and regulations** are pretty standard: seat belts are compulsory; "Stop" signs mean exactly that; drink-driving will land you in big trouble; zebra crossings are strictly observed; and you yield to traffic coming from the right at all junctions, whether or not there's a "give way" sign. A single, unbroken white line in the middle of the road means no overtaking, even if the rule is frequently ignored, and note that drivers often sound their horns when overtaking. On major trunk roads, turnings that take vehicles across oncoming traffic are being phased out and replaced by semicircular minor exits that lead round to traffic lights on the near side of the major road. In towns and villages, **parking spaces** are usually marked in blue and a single yellow line means no parking.

Car rental

On both islands, there are scores of companies offering **car rental** (often still rendered in Castilian as *coches de alquiler*) and their offices throng the islands' resorts, larger towns and airports. All the major international players have outlets, and there are also dozens of small companies. Comprehensive lists of car rental companies are normally available from the islands' tourist offices.

To **rent a car**, you must be 21 or over (and have been driving for at least a year), and you'll probably need a credit card – though some places will accept a hefty deposit in cash and some smaller companies simply ignore all the normal regulations altogether. However, no car rental firm will allow you to transport their vehicles **from one Balearic island to another**. If you're planning to spend much time driving on rougher tracks, you'll be better off with a **four-wheel drive** (about thirty percent more expensive than the average car and available from larger rental agencies).

Rental charges vary enormously: out-of-season costs for a standard car can fall to as little as €20 per day with unlimited mileage; in July and August, by comparison, the same basic vehicle could set you back €80 a day if not more – though weekly prices are usually less expensive. Shopping around is really worthwhile – Affordable Car Hire (ⓦ affordable carhire.com) is a good place to start, with reasonable rates. That said, **local rental firms** often give the best deals, though you should always check the policy for the excess applied to claims, and ensure that it includes CDW (collision damage waiver) and adequate levels of financial cover. Finally, all car rental companies charge you an arm and a leg for a **SatNav** (think €12 a day), so if you have a portable version, bring it. Equally – and this is really annoying – some companies charge for the full tank of petrol that is in your car when you collect it (€90 or so), whether it is used or not: legend has it that disgruntled tourists now drive round and round the airport until all the fuel is consumed.

Taxis

The excellence of the islands' bus and train services means it's rarely necessary to take a **taxi**, though they are a convenient way of getting back to your hotel after a day's hiking, in which case you should fix a collection point before you set out – there's no point wandering round a tiny village hoping a taxi will show up. The taxis of each town and resort area have their own livery: Palma's, for example, are black with a cream-coloured roof and bonnet. **Local journeys** are metered, though there are supplementary charges for each piece of luggage and for travel at night and on Sundays. For **longer journeys** there are official prices, which should be displayed at the airport and at some taxi stands. Naturally, you're well advised to check the price with the driver *before* you get going. **Fares** are reasonable, but not inexpensive: the journey from the airport to downtown Palma, a distance of around 11km, will cost you in the region of €20, while the fare from Sóller to Deià is €22, Port de Sóller to Port d'Andratx €70.

Cycling

Cycling can be an enjoyable way of exploring the islands, though the quiet(er) roads of Menorca are more suitable for easy outings than the busier roads of Mallorca. Menorca is also a good deal flatter, which means the going is much easier – though ardent cyclists will probably prefer the mountain challenges of Mallorca. The Spanish are keen cycling fans, and many of the roads are signed for cyclists, even though bicycle lanes per se are rare. However, drivers are not necessarily obliging on the roads and neither is information readily forth-coming – local tourist offices rarely have much in the way of route information.

For **route planning**, you might check out ⓦ bikemap.net and/or consult *Bike Mallorca*, the best **bike map** for Mallorca, which is clearly marked with colour-coded cycle routes and includes a list of major bike shops too, though it was published in 2010, which means that some of the information is out of date; you can order it from Amazon. There is no similar publication for Menorca. If you're heading for Mallorca, bear in mind that cyclists are not permitted into the Sóller tunnel at the end of the Palma–Sóller road because of the accumulated fumes. More positively, bicycles are transported free on the Palma–Inca train line and either free or at minimal cost on ferries from the mainland (and between the Balearic islands); you can't, however, take bikes on the Palma–Sóller train and, although some buses allow cycles, most do not.

On both islands, **renting a bike** costs about €12 to €15 a day for an ordinary bike, about thirty percent more for a mountain bike. Renting is straightforward: there are dozens of suppliers (usually several at every resort) and tourist offices can provide a list or advise you of the nearest outlet.

Accommodation

Menorca and more especially Mallorca muster a veritable army of hotels and hostales and until recently a majority of their rooms were block-booked by the tour operators months in advance. Things are much more fluid today: bargain-price flights mean that the old stranglehold pattern of week- and fortnight-long holidays has pretty much shattered. This is good news for the independent traveller, who can now find vacancies just about anywhere for any length of time, though advance reservations at the height of the season (broadly June to early September) are still strongly advised.

Outside peak season, it's often worth bargaining over room prices – though note that closure in winter is commonplace in Menorca and frequent in Mallorca. Most hoteliers speak or read at least a modicum of English, so you can usually book online or by phone.

Many hotels and *hostales* have rooms at different **prices**, and tend to offer the more expensive ones first. Some places also have rooms with three or four beds at not much more than the price of a double room, though people travelling alone invariably end up paying over the odds.

In **Mallorca** the easiest place to get a **high-season**, **last-minute room** is Palma, with Sóller not far behind, though you might also consider staying

---

TOP 5 HOSTALES – AUTHENTIC AND INEXPENSIVE

Bellavista Port de Pollença. See p.144
Dragonera Sant Elm. See p.123
Miramar Deià. See p.109
Playa Colònia de Sant Jordi. See p.191
S'Engolidor Menorca. See p.227

ACCOMMODATION SIGNAGE

In theory at least, every place offering accommodation in the Balearics has to carry a **square blue sign** on the outside, which is inscribed with its category and number of stars. These are as follows:

F	*fonda*
CH	*casa de huéspedes*
P	*pensió*
H	*hostal*
HR	*hostal-residencia*
H	*hotel*

at one of the island's former monasteries (see opposite), where there's nearly always a vacancy and prices are very low. In **Menorca**, accommodation is thinner on the ground, with only Maó, Ciutadella and maybe Fornells likely to have last-minute, high-season vacancies.

Accommodation prices

Throughout the Guide we give a **headline price** for all accommodation reviewed. This indicates the lowest price you're likely to pay for a double or twin room with breakfast in high season (usually June to September), barring **special deals**. **Single rooms**, where available, usually cost between 60 and 80 percent of a double or twin. At Mallorca's **hikers' hostels**, we give the price of a dormitory bed (few have doubles), and at **campsites** we give the cost of two people plus car and tent pitch.

Hostales and hotels

Traditionally, Balearic accommodation has been divided into five categories – **fondas**, **casas de huéspedes**, **pensions**, **hostales** and **hotels**. Today, however, the first three categories, which were the least expensive, have almost completely disappeared and you are largely left with *hostales* and hotels. **Hostales** are categorized with one to three stars, and many offer good, functional, en-suite rooms, mostly with showers and not baths. Some *hostales* are designated **hostal-residencias**, again categorized from one to three stars. The *residencia* designation means that no meals other than breakfast are served, but that does not mean that all *hostales* without the *residencia* tag serve anything more than breakfast. No matter the star classification, **prices** at this end of the market start at around €80 for a double room.

Hotels are also graded by stars, ranging from no

stars to five stars, though the distinction between hotels and *hostales* is often rather blurred. One- and no-star hotels cost no more than three-star *hostales* (sometimes less), but three-star hotels cost a lot more, and at four or five stars you're in the luxury class with prices to match. There are also a handful of **hotel-residencias**, where the only meal provided is breakfast, and an increasing number of (un-starred) **hotels d'interior**, mostly bijou family-run hotels away from the coast (hence "interior"). On average, a double room in a two-star hotel should cost in the region of €80–120.

It's safe to assume that bedrooms will be of a decent standard in all the higher categories, but among the **budget places** you'd be advised to ask to see the room before you part with any money: standards vary greatly (even between rooms in the same establishment) and it does no harm to check that there's hot water if there's supposed to be, or that you're not stuck at the back in an airless box.

By law, each establishment must **display its room rates**, and there should be a card on the room door showing the prices for the various seasons. If you think you're being overcharged, complain there and then.

Mallorcan monasteries

Mallorca's monasteries have run out of monks, so five of them now let out empty cells – or rather modernized former cells – to visitors of both sexes (see box below). All occupy delightful settings in the hills or on hilltops, and the majority are dotted across the interior of the island. At all five, you can just turn up and ask for a room, but

> ### MALLORCA'S MONASTERY AND MOUNTAINTOP ACCOMMODATION
> **Ermita de la Victòria** near Alcúdia. See p.152
> **Ermita de Nostra Senyora de Bonany** near Petra. See p.167
> **Ermita de Nostra Senyora del Puig** outside Pollença. See p.140
> **Hostatgeria Castell d'Alaró** outside Alaró. See p.105
> **Monestir de Lluc.** See p.135
> **Santuari de Nostra Senyora de Cura** on Puig Randa. See p.170
> **Santuari de Sant Salvador** near Felanitx. See p.186

> ### MALLORCA'S HIKERS' HOSTELS
> **Can Boi** Deià. See p.109
> **Muleta** Port de Sóller. See p.98
> **Pont Romà** Pollença. See p.140
> **Son Amer** near Lluc. See p.135
> **Tossals Verds** east of the Embassament de Cúber. See p.132

it's a better idea to reserve ahead either online (in three cases) or by phone: if your Spanish isn't up to it, local tourist offices will make reservations for monastery rooms on your behalf. A **double room** at the more rough-and-ready monasteries costs around €25 per night, rising to €60–70 at Lluc, Sant Salvador and the Santuari de Cura; easily the most popular monastery is Lluc. Reasonably priced **food** is usually available, but check arrangements when you book. In the same vein, the former **monastic lodgings** above the **Ermita de la Victòria** (see box below) have been turned into a small budget hotel/*hostatgeria*, while the **Hostatgeria Castell d'Alaró** provides simple accommodation within the walls of a hilltop fortress near Alaró (see box below).

Mallorca's mountain refuges

Mallorca's principal long-distance hiking route is the **Ruta de Pedra en Sec** (Dry-stone Route), the **GR221** (see p.34), which threads its way across the Serra de Tramuntana mountains. It begins in Sant Elm and passes through Sóller before continuing onto Pollença. To assist hikers, Mallorca's governing council has constructed – and in some cases then franchised out – **five refugis** (hikers' hostels) on the GR221. Plans to build a sixth hostel at La Trapa, near Sant Elm (see p.122), are currently stalled. Each of these offers simple but adequate lodgings in dormitory-style rooms with bunk beds and shared bathrooms. The **rate** is just €11 per person per night, with breakfast €4.50, a two-course lunch €10.50, and a main meal at dinner €8; picnic lunches are also available (€6.50). Advance reservations are required a minimum of five days and a maximum of two months beforehand, either direct with the hostel concerned or on the website ⓦconselldemallorca.net.

Agrotourism and fincas

Old stone **fincas** (farmhouses; see box, p.28) are a prominent feature of the Balearic landscape. Some

---

TOP 5 FINCA-HOTELS

Ca's Xorc near Sóller, Mallorca. See p.95
Es Castell Binibona, Mallorca. See p.136
Llenaire Port de Pollença, Mallorca.
See p.144
Rural Morvedrà Nou near Ciutadella,
Menorca. See p.235
Rural Son Palou Orient, Mallorca.
See p.104

---

have been converted into holiday homes and are leased out to package-tour operators and lettings agencies, while others can be booked direct or through the government agency responsible for developing rural tourism, the **Associació Agroturisme Balear** (☎971 72 15 08, ⓦrusticbooking.com). They are not, however, cheap: prices range from €80 to €200 per person per night, and a minimum length of stay of anything between two nights and two weeks is often stipulated.

Camping

Menorca has two **official campsites**: the well-appointed *Son Bou* (see p.224) and the plainer but very pleasant *S'Atalaia* (see p.230), near the resort of Cala Galdana. The *Son Bou* can accommodate about four hundred campers, the *S'Atalaia* just one hundred – and both take tents, trailer caravans and motor caravans. Although neither has a seashore location, they're both very popular, and in the summer it's best to make a reservation well ahead of time. Prices and specific details of each site are given in the relevant chapters. There are currently no recommendable campsites on **Mallorca**.

Camping rough is legal, but not encouraged, and has various restrictions attached: you're not allowed to camp in urban areas, military zones, parks and tourist resorts. Neither are you allowed to camp on beaches – though there is some latitude if you're discreet – and if you want to camp out in the countryside you'll need to ask locally and/or get permission from the landowner.

Food and drink

Traditional Balearic food, which has much in common with Catalan cuisine, is far from delicate, but its hearty soups and stews, seafood dishes and spiced meats can be delicious. In common with other areas of Spain, this regional cuisine has, after many years of neglect, experienced something of a Renaissance, and nowadays restaurants offering Cuina Mallorquína (and to a lesser extent Cuina Menorquína) are comparatively commonplace and should not be missed. Neither should a visit to one of the islands' many pastry shops (pastisserias or pastelerias), where you'll find the tastiest of confections and the Balearics' gastronomic pride and joy – the ensaimada (a spiralled flaky pastry).

While scores of touristy restaurants dish up bland and overpriced pizza, burgers and pasta, or sanitized versions of local favourites, there are still plenty of places where the food is more distinctive and flavoursome. **Fresh fish and seafood** can be excellent, though it's almost always expensive, partly because much of it is imported – despite the best efforts of the local fishing industry. Nevertheless, you're able to get hake, cod (fresh or salted) and squid at very reasonable prices, while fish stews and soups are often truly memorable, as is the *caldereta de llagosta*, a Menorcan lobster stew that's the speciality of Fornells (see p.219). **Meat** can be outstanding too, usually either grilled and served with a few fried potatoes or salad, or – like ham – cured or dried and served as a starter or in sandwiches. Veal is common, served in large stews, while poultry is often mixed with seafood (chicken and prawns) or fruit (chicken/duck with prunes/pears).

Vegetables rarely amount to much more than a few chips or boiled potatoes with the main dish, though there are some splendid vegetable concoctions to watch out for, such as *tumbet*, a pepper, potato, pumpkin and aubergine stew with tomato purée. It's usual to start a full lunch or evening meal with a salad, either a standard green or mixed affair, or one of the islands' own salad mixtures, which come garnished with various vegetables, meats and cheeses. **Dessert** is often fruit, ice cream or *flam*, the local version of *crème caramel*, though the pricier places have all sorts of fancier concoctions.

Opening hours vary considerably. As a general rule cafés open from around 9am until at least early in the evening, and many remain open till late at night. Restaurants open from around noon until sometime between 2pm and 4pm, before reopening in the evening from around 7/8pm until 10/11pm. Those restaurants fixed firmly on the tourist trade often stay open all day and can be relied upon on Sundays, when many local spots close. On both islands, **multilingual menus** are the order of the day, and we have also provided a **menu reader** and a list of popular **Balearic dishes** in Contexts (see p.283).

Breakfast and snacks

The more bargain-priced hotels and *hostales* usually serve a basic **continental breakfast** and only at the pricier places is there much more on offer. Consequently, it's often less expensive and more enjoyable to eat out at a local café or café-bar. A traditional Balearic breakfast (or lunch) dish is *pa amb tomàquet* (*pan con tomate* in Castilian): a massive slice of bread rubbed with tomato, olive oil and garlic, which you can also have topped with ham – washed down with a flagon of wine. *Pa amb oli* (bread rubbed with olive oil) arrives in similar style, but dispenses with the tomato. If that sounds like gastronomic madness, other breakfast standbys include *torradas* (*tostadas*; toasted rolls) with oil or butter and jam, and *xocolata amb xurros* (*chocolate con churros*): long, fried tubular doughnuts that you dip into thick drinking chocolate. Most places also serve *ou ferrat* (*huevo frito*; fried egg) and cold *truita* (*tortilla*; omelette).

Coffee, bread rolls and **pastries** (*pastas*), particularly croissants and doughnuts, are available at some bars and cafés, but for a wider selection, head for a *pastisseria* (pastry shop) or *forn* (bakery). Some bars specialize in **sandwiches** (*bocadillos*), usually outsize affairs in baguettes served either hot or cold, or you can get them prepared – or buy the materials to do so – at grocery shops. Menorcan cheese (*formatge*), commonly known as *Queso Mahón*, is a popular filling – the best is hard and has a rind.

Tapas and racions

Traditionally, **tapas** are small snacks of three or four chunks of fish, meat or vegetables, cooked in a sauce or served with a dollop of salad. In many cafés and café-bars, tapas are lined up along the counter, so you can see what's available and order by pointing without necessarily knowing the names; other places have blackboards. The confusion is that many places (including restaurants) sell tapas that are in effect full (regular) meals with prices to match. "Proper" tapas should cost about €5, €10 at the most. Other variations of tapas are **racions** (*raciones* in Castilian), which are bigger portions of the same, and **pinxtos**, which are smaller versions.

Full meals

Full meals are usually eaten in a **café** or **restaurant**, though the distinction between the two is often blurred, the main difference being the price: a main course at a restaurant costs in the region of €20–25, a third less in the average café. Many restaurants and cafés have a daily set menu for €15–20 – the lunchtime **menú del día** is often a really good deal, comprising two, three or four courses, including bread and a third- to a half-litre of wine per person. The other thing to take account of is **IVA**, a sales tax of ten percent, which is either included in the prices (in which case it should say so on the menu) or added to your bill at the end.

Vegetarians and vegans

Palma has a couple of **vegetarian** restaurants and most of the resorts are accustomed to having vegetarian guests, but elsewhere the choice isn't so great and is essentially confined to large salads, fried eggs and chips or omelettes. If you eat fish, however, you'll find seafood almost everywhere.

If you're a **vegan**, you'll no doubt come prepared to cook your own food at least some of the time. That said, some restaurant salads and vegetable dishes are vegan – like *espinacs a la Catalana* (spinach, pine nuts and raisins) and *escalivada* (aubergine/eggplant and peppers) – but they're few and far between. Fruit and nuts are widely available, and most pizza restaurants will serve you a vegetarian pizza without cheese: ask for *vegetal sense formatge* (in Castilian, *vegetal sin queso*).

Drinking and drinks

As you might expect, **bars** and **café-bars** are legion in both Mallorca and Menorca. Bars situated in old

---

I'M A VEGETARIAN

If you're a **vegetarian**, try in Catalan "Sóc vegetarià/ana – es pot menjar alguna cosa sense carn?" (I'm a vegetarian – is there anything without meat?). In Castilian, that's "Soy vegetariano/a – hay algo sin carne?" Alternatively, you may be better understood if you simply resort to the Catalan "No puc menjar carn" (I can't eat meat).

TOP 10 MALLORCAN WINES

James Hiscock, of the outstanding *Es Castell* and *Son Ametler* hotels (see p.136), has selected his ten top tipples.

RED WINES

Aia Miquel Oliver, Petra. Merlot. Full and fruity, complex, potent aroma with hints of toast from fine woods and fruity, earthy tones. Guide price €15.

Son Negre Anima Negre, Felanitx. In the late 1990s this special wine was given 94/100 by the Parker Wine Guide and achieved international recognition. Made with 95 percent Callet grapes, it's described by Parker as having "a compelling nose of oak, minerals, Asian spices, lavender, black cherry and black raspberry." It's very expensive, at a guide price of €150.

Pedra José Luis Ferrer, Binissalem (Organic). Ferrer is the biggest wine producer on the island and Pedra was its first foray into organic wines. A mixture of Mantonegro and Cabernet Sauvignon, it's a deep violet red, with balsamic and ripe fruit notes, plus smooth, long and lingering fragrances. Guide price €8.50.

Añada Macia Batle, Santa Maria. A young wine, like a Beaujolais. With some tannins, it has a freshness on the palate, with gentle tones to keep drinking till the small hours. Works well chilled, and eaten with barbecued meat. Guide price €5.

L'Ú, Mortix. From the heights of the Serra Nord mountains comes the treasure that is L'Ú. This is a wine with a deep first taste: friendly, smooth, but strong on the palate. Drink it with roast meats, game, fish or chicken. Guide price €28.

WHITES AND ROSÉ

Novell Pere Seda, Manacor. A great value-for-money white wine: crisp, medium dry, clean citrus fruit aromas, with floral hints. Deceptively drinkable when chilled, and well priced. Guide price €3.50.

Moli de Vent Blanc Jaume Mesquida, Porreres. A very dry, light "Sauvignon-blanc-y" white, with Doradillo, Martorell and Chardonnay grapes, perfect for white fish. Guide price €7.50.

Son Prim Merlot Blanc Peach in colour, with real "body", the white wine for those who normally drink red. Good with veal and seafood. Guide price €11.

Ecologic Rosé Binigrau (Organic). Made with Mantonegro and Merlot grapes from some of the region's oldest vines. Perhaps in common with many organic wines from Mallorca, "when it's good, it's very very good…". A bright, cherry-coloured wine with fruit aromas, full and ripe. Drink with suckling pig. Guide price €10.

Butibalausi Rosado Can Majoral, Algaida (Organic). Named after the Christianization of a Moorish hamlet near Algaida, this rosé has intense red fruit aromas and is crisp on the palate, with a rich and persistent ending. Great for paellas. Guide price €7.50.

wine cellars are sometimes called **cellers** or **tavernas**, while a **bodega** traditionally specializes in wine. **Opening hours** vary, but you should have little trouble getting a drink in Palma between noon and 2am or even 3am, and until at least 11pm, sometimes midnight, elsewhere. Nightclubs tend to close by 3am or 4am, while some bars close on Sundays; don't expect much to be open in the resorts out of season.

Wine

Wine (*vi* in Catalan, *vino* in Castilian) is the invariable accompaniment to every meal and remains, as a general rule, inexpensive whether it be red (*negre/tinto*), white (*blanc/blanco*) or rosé (*rosada/rosado*). The thing to check for on a bottle of Spanish wine is that it carries either of the top two appellations – **Denominació d'Origen (DO)** or

Denominació d'Origen Qualificada (DOQ) – as this indicates it has passed muster with the industry's national watchdog. Sixty-eight regions of Spain currently carry DO/DOQ status, including two on Mallorca: Pla i Llevant and Binissalem. Overall, Mallorca has around sixty vineyards and Menorca just half a dozen, and together they produce several million bottles annually. A good selection of these wines is available at most good cafés and restaurants on Mallorca and to a lesser extent on Menorca.

Spain's **sparkling wines** are big sellers too, their popularity built on the performance of two producers, Freixenet and Codorniú, which hail from a small area west of Barcelona. Local grape varieties are used and the best examples, known as **cava**, are made by the same double-fermentation process as is used in the production of champagne. For a detailed introduction to Spanish wines, consult Ⓦ foodswinesfromspain.com.

Mallorcan wine

The Balearics became a major **wine producer** in classical times, but it was the Moors who finessed the sweet "Malvasia" wine – akin to Madeira – that was long one of the islands' main exports. This all ended in the late nineteenth century when the islands' vineyards were devastated by **phylloxera**, an aphid-like insect which arrived in Spain from North America in 1878, and within twenty years had destroyed Spain's existing vine stock and made thousands bankrupt. Indeed, vine cultivation has never re-established itself on Ibiza or, until very recently, Menorca, and Mallorcan wines, produced from newly imported vines, were long regarded as being of only average quality.

During the late 1980s, however, a concerted effort was made to raise the standard of Mallorcan wine-making, driven on one side by the tourist industry and on the other by local producers who realized that they could prosper by producing wine of international quality. This meant new methods and new equipment, and the investment began in earnest, especially in and around **Binissalem**, a small town northeast of Palma (see p.163). The results were encouraging and, following vigorous local campaigning, Binissalem was awarded its Denominació d'Origen credentials in 1991. Binissalem remains Mallorca's leading wine, but its success has inspired others and in 2000 a second Denominació d'Origen was granted, **Pla i Llevant**, covering the central and eastern part of the island from Algaida to Felanitx.

Widely available throughout Mallorca, **red Binissalem** is a robust and aromatic wine made predominantly of the local mantonegro grape. It is not unlike Rioja, but it has a distinctly local character, suggesting cocoa and strawberries. The biggest producer of the wine is **Franja Roja**, who make the **José Ferrer** brand, with prices starting at around €8 per bottle, €15 for the superior varieties; you can also visit their Binissalem winery (see p.164). Names to look out for with the Pla i Llevant designation kick off with the white wines of **Miquel Oliver** from Petra. Also around the island are various country wineries making inexpensive and unpretentious wine predominantly for local consumption. The best place to sample these coarser wines is in the *cellers* and bars of the country towns of the interior. The pick carry the designation **Vin de la Terra** (*Vino de la Tierra*) with labels that indicate the year of production and the grape varieties used.

Spirits and sherry

When ordering **spirits** in the Balearics, you'll usually get an international brand unless you specify otherwise – ask for *nacional* if you want the cheaper Spanish varieties: Larios **gin** from Málaga, for instance, is about half the price of Gordons, but around two-thirds the strength and a good deal rougher. Gin is also made in Menorca: the Menorcans learned the art of gin-making from the British and still produce their own versions, in particular the waspish **Xoriguer**. Sherry – *vino de Jerez* – is the classic Andalucian fortified wine, served chilled or at room temperature. The main distinctions are between *fino* or *jerez seco* (dry sherry), *amontillado* (medium), and *oloroso* or *jerez dulce* (sweet).

In mid-afternoon – or even at breakfast – many islanders take a *copa* of **liqueur** with their coffee. The best – certainly to put *in* your coffee – is **coñac**, excellent Spanish brandy, mostly from the south and often deceptively smooth. If you want a brandy from Mallorca, try the mellow but hard-hitting Suau.

Almost any **mixed drink** seems to be known as a *Cuba libre* or *cubata*, though strictly speaking this only refers to rum and Coke. For mixers, ask for orange juice (*suc de taronja* in Catalan), lemon juice (*llimona*) or tonic (*tònica*).

Beer and sangría

Pilsner-type beer, **cervesa** (more usually seen in Castilian as *cerveza*), is generally pretty good, though more expensive than wine. The two brands you'll see everywhere are San Miguel and Estrella. Beer generally comes in 300ml bottles or, slightly cheaper, on tap: a small glass of draught beer is a *caña*, a larger glass a *caña gran*. Equally refreshing, though often deceptively strong, is **sangría**, a wine-and-fruit punch, which you'll come across at *festas* and in tourist resorts.

Soft drinks

Soft drinks are much the same as anywhere in the world, but one local favourite to try is *orxata* (*horchata* in Castilian), a cold milky drink made from tiger nuts. Also, be sure to try a *granissat*, or iced fruit squash; popular flavours are *granissat de llimona* or *granissat de café*. You can get these from **orxaterias** and **gelaterias** (ice-cream parlours; *heladerías* in Castilian).

Although you can drink the **water** almost everywhere, bottled water – *aigua mineral* – is ubiquitous, either sparkling (*amb gas*) or still (*sense gas*).

Coffee and tea

Coffee is invariably espresso, slightly bitter and, unless you specify otherwise, served black (*café sol*). A slightly weaker large black coffee is called a *café americano*. If you want it white ask for *café cortado* (small cup with a drop of milk) or *café amb llet* (*café con leche* in Castilian) made with hot milk. For a large cup ask for a *gran*. Black coffee is also frequently mixed with brandy, cognac or whisky, all such concoctions termed *carajillo*; a liqueur mixed with white coffee is a *trifásico*. **Decaffeinated coffee** (*descafeinat*) is increasingly available, though in fairly undistinguished sachet form.

Tea (*te*) comes without milk unless you ask for it, and is often weak and insipid. If you do ask for milk, chances are it'll be hot and UHT, so your tea isn't going to taste much like the real thing. Better are the infusions that you can get in some bars, such as mint (*menta*), camomile (*camamilla*) and lime-flower (*tiller*).

The media

English-language newspapers and magazines are widely available in both Mallorca and Menorca, and most hotel (if not hostal) rooms have satellite TV.

Newspapers and magazines

British and other European **newspapers**, as well as the *International Herald Tribune*, are widely available in the resort areas and larger towns of Mallorca and Menorca. These are supplemented by a hotchpotch of locally produced English papers and journals, easily the most informative of which is the enjoyably chatty **Majorca Daily Bulletin**. The online edition is available at ⓦ majorcadailybulletin.es.

Spain is awash with glossy **magazines**, both native to the country and Spanish versions of international periodicals. And, of course, Spain is the home of *Hola* – the original of the UK's glossy gossip mag, *Hello*.

Television and radio

Spaniards love their **television**, and consequently you'll catch more of it than you might expect sitting in bars and cafés. On the whole it's hardly riveting, the bulk being a mildly entertaining mixture of kitsch game shows and foreign-language films and TV series dubbed into Spanish. **Soaps** are a particular speciality, either South American *culebrones* ("serpents" – they go on and on) or well-travelled British or Australian exports, like *EastEnders*

(*Gent del Barri*). **Sports fans** are well catered for, with regular live coverage of football (soccer) matches. The number of TV stations is increasing all the time, but the main national channels are operated by TVE. Most Balearic hotel rooms have satellite TV, which gives access to some or all of the international channels – CNN and so forth.

Frequencies and schedules for the BBC World Service (ⓦ bbc.co.uk), Radio Canada (ⓦ rcinet.ca) and Voice of America (ⓦ voanews.com) are listed on their respective websites.

Festivals

Every town and village in Mallorca and Menorca takes at least one day off a year to devote to a festival. Usually it's the local saint's day, but there are also celebrations for the harvest, deliverance from the Moors, of safe return from the sea – any excuse will do. Each festival is different, with a particular local emphasis, but there is always music, dancing, traditional costume and an immense spirit of enjoyment. The main event of most festas is a parade, either behind a revered holy image or a more celebratory affair with fancy costumes and gigantones, giant carnival figures that rumble down the streets to the delight, or terror, of children. While festas take place throughout the year, Easter Holy Week (Setmana Santa) stands out, its passing celebrated in many places with elaborate processions. For a summary (in Catalan) of what's on where and when, check out ⓦ conselldemallorca.cat.

JANUARY

Revetla de Sant Antoni Abat (Eve of St Antony's Day) Jan 16. Celebrated by the lighting of bonfires (*foguerons*) in Palma and several of Mallorca's villages, especially Sa Pobla and Muro. In these two villages, the inhabitants move from fire to fire, dancing around in fancy dress and eating *espinagades*, traditional eel-and-vegetable patties. Also takes place in Sant Lluís on Menorca.

Beneides de Sant Antoni (Blessing of St Antony) Jan 17. St Antony's feast day is marked by processions in many of Mallorca's country towns, notably Sa Pobla and Artà, with farmyard animals herded through the streets to receive the saint's blessing.

Processó d'els Tres Tocs (Procession of the Three Knocks) Jan 17. Held in Ciutadella, Menorca, this procession commemorates the victory of Alfonso III over the Muslims here on January 17, 1287. There's a Mass in the cathedral first and then three horsemen lead the way to the old city walls, where the eldest of the trio knocks three times with his flagstaff at the exact spot the Catalans first breached the walls.

Revetla de Sant Sebastià (Eve of St Sebastian's Day) Jan 19. Palma has bonfires, singing and dancing for St Sebastian.

Festa de Sant Sebastià Jan 20. This feast day of medieval origin is celebrated in Pollença, Mallorca, with a procession led by a holy banner (*estenard*) picturing the saint. It's accompanied by *cavallets* (literally "merry-go-rounds"), two young dancers each wearing a cardboard horse and imitating the animal's walk. You'll see *cavallets* at many Mallorcan festivals.

FEBRUARY

Carnaval Towns and villages throughout the islands live it up during the week before Lent with marches and fancy dress parades. The biggest and liveliest is in Palma, where the shindig is known as *Sa Rua* (the Cavalcade).

MARCH/APRIL

Setmana Santa (Holy Week). On **Maundy Thursday**, a much-venerated icon of the crucified Christ, *La Sang*, is taken from the eponymous church on the Plaça del Hospital (off Passeig de la Rambla) in Palma and paraded through the city streets. There are also solemn **Good Friday** (*Divendres Sant*) processions in many towns and villages around Mallorca, with the more important taking place in Palma and Sineu. Most holy of all, however, is the Good Friday **Davallament** (the Lowering), the culmination of Holy Week in Pollença, Mallorca. Here, in total silence and by torchlight, the inhabitants lower a figure of Christ down from the hilltop Oratori to the church of Nostra Senyora dels Àngels.

During Holy Week there are also many **romerias** (pilgrimages) to Mallorca's holy places, with one of the most popular being the climb up to the Ermita Santa Magdalena, near Inca. The Monestir de Lluc, home to Mallorca's most venerated shrine, is another focus, with the penitential trudging round its Camí dels Misteris del Rosari (The Way of the Mysteries of the Rosary).

In Menorca's Ciutadella, there's also the **Matança dels bruixots** (the Slaughter of the Wizards), in which puppets representing well-known personalities are hung in the streets.

MAY

Festa de la Verge del Toro (The Festival of the Virgin of the Bull) May 8. The day of the patron saint of Menorca begins with a special Mass at the hilltop shrine of Monte Toro and continues with a shindig down in the little town of Es Mercadal.

Sa Fira i Es Firó Mid-May. This Mallorcan knees-up in Port de Sóller and Sóller features mock battles between Christians and infidels in commemoration of the thrashing of a band of Arab pirates in 1561. Lots of booze and firing of antique rifles (into the air).

JUNE

Corpus Christi Early to mid-June. At noon in the main square of Pollença, Mallorca, an ancient and curious dance of uncertain provenance takes place – the *Ball de les Àguiles* (Dance of the Eagles) – followed by a religious procession.

Festa de Sant Joan June 23–25. This midsummer festival has been celebrated in Ciutadella, Menorca, since the fourteenth century. There are jousting competitions, folk music, dancing and processions following a special Mass held in the cathedral on the 24th. Another highlight is on the Sunday before the 24th, when the *S'Homo d'es Bé* (the Man of the Lamb) leads a party of horsemen through the town. Clad in animal skins and carrying a lamb in honour of St John the Baptist, he invites everyone to the forthcoming celebration.

JULY

Día de Virgen de Carmen July 15–16. The day of the patron saint of seafarers and fishermen is celebrated in many of Mallorca's coastal settlements – principally Palma, Maó, Port de Sóller, Colònia de Sant Pere, Porto Colom and Cala Rajada – as well as in Maó, Menorca, with parades and the blessing of boats.

Festa de Sant Martí Third Sun. The feast day of St Martin is celebrated in Es Mercadal, Menorca, with a popular religious procession followed by dancing and all sorts of fun and games.

Festa de Sant Jaume Last Sunday. This festival in Mallorca's Alcúdia and Menorca's Es Castell celebrates the feast day of St James with a popular religious procession followed by folk dances, fireworks and the like.

AUGUST

Mare de Déu dels Àngels Aug 2. Moors and Christians battle it out again, this time in Pollença, Mallorca.

Festa de Sant Llorenç Second weekend. High jinks on horseback through the streets of Alaior, Menorca.

Cavallet Aug 20. Knees-up in Felanitx, Mallorca, featuring *cavallets*, dancers wearing a cardboard horse and imitating the animal's walk.

Festa de Sant Bartomeu Last week. Three days of festivities in Ferreries, Menorca.

SEPTEMBER

Festa de la Mare de Déu de Gràcia Sept 7–9. This three-day festival in Maó, Menorca, celebrates the Virgin of Grace, the city's patron saint, and begins with a pilgrimage to the chapel of the Virgin. Thereafter, there are processions and parades along with horseback games.

Nativitat de Nostra Senyora (Nativity of the Virgin) Second week. In Alaró, Mallorca, honouring the Virgin with a pilgrimage to a hilltop shrine near the Castell d'Alaró.

OCTOBER

Festa d'es Butifarra (Sausage Festival) Third Sun. Of recent origin, this festival follows on from tractor and automobile contests held in the village of Sant Joan, Mallorca. It features folk dancing and traditional music as well as the eating of specially prepared vegetable pies (*coca amb trampó*) and sausages (*berenada de butifarra*).

DECEMBER

Nadal (Christmas). Christmas is especially picturesque in Palma, Mallorca and Ciutadella, Menorca, where there are Nativity plays in the days leading up to the 25th.

Sports and outdoor activities

During the day at least, tourist life on Mallorca and Menorca is centred on the beach. There are long and generous strands at several of the major resorts – including Port d'Alcúdia, Port de Pollença, S'Arenal and Son Bou – and several dozen smaller cove beaches; we have also picked out some of the best beaches in western Mallorca (see box, p.109), northern Mallorca (see box, p.154) and Menorca (see box, p.224). At all the larger resorts, a veritable army of companies offer equipment for hire for a wide range of beach sports and activities, from sailing and pedalo pedalling through to jet-skiing, windsurfing and scuba diving, not to mention sandcastle-building competitions.

Away from the coast, **cycling** (see p.25) is a popular pastime as is **horseriding**, with a clutch of stables and many kilometres of bridle path. The most popular riding areas on Mallorca are the low hills of the Serres de Llevant in the east and the foothills of the Serra de Tramuntana, while Menorca's stables are mostly inland close to the (one) main road. For a list of outlets in Mallorca, see ⓦ mallorcaonline.com/sport/equitau.htm; for Menorca, begin with Cavalls Son Àngel (see p.238). A wide range of **adventure sports** is offered by Mallorca's Tramuntana Tours (see p.23), including **canyoning**, **sea kayaking** and **deep-sea fishing**.

Hiking

Hiking is a major deal on both islands, with hundreds of hikers arriving here every year. On both Mallorca and Menorca, the prime **hiking seasons** are spring – March, April and May – and autumn, from late September to mid-November. The islands are also warm enough to allow for pleasant hiking in the depths of winter, though there's more rain at this time of year, temperatures can drop dramatically, snow is fairly common on the high peaks of Mallorca, and the number of daylight hours is, of course, more restricted. In summer, by comparison, the heat makes all but the shorter hikes unpleasant and very tiring, plus you'll have to haul a large quantity of water around with you. Bear in mind also that the mountains are prone to mists, though they usually lift at some point in the day, and for obvious safety reasons, lone mountain walking is not recommended.

On **Mallorca**, the prime hiking area is the Serra de Tramuntana mountain range that bands the northern coast. Until the early 1990s, the assorted foot, mule and cart tracks that lattice the range were poorly signed and difficult to navigate. Things are much better today – though far from perfect – and the mountains now boast a network of reasonably well signposted **hiking trails**, largely thanks to the endeavours of the island's ruling council. Equipped with several strategically placed **hikers' hostels** (see p.27), the most popular long-distance trail is the **GR221 Ruta de Pedra en Sec** (Dry-stone Route), which runs right across the mountains from Sant Elm to Pollença, though only three sections are in tip-top condition: Es Capdellà to Estellencs; Deià to Sóller; and Sóller to Pollença. In addition, we have described a number of **day-long hikes** on Mallorca (see p.116, p.145 & p.153) and recommended two Mallorcan companies that organize **guided hikes** – Mallorcan Walking Tours (see p.142) and Tramuntana Tours (see p.23).

Menorca is sufficiently rural to offer pleasing walks almost everywhere, though it's the island's wild and windswept northern coast that offers the most dramatic scenery, its craggy capes and headlands sheltering a clutch of beautiful cove beaches. Although Menorca has no high mountains, it does possess deep wooded gorges that attract hikers too. As for **hiking trails**, the

---

PARKS AND CONSERVATION AREAS

In **Mallorca**, most of the Serra de Tramuntana mountain range is now protected and conserved, and the island also possesses a number of **Parcs Natural** (Natural Parks; ⓦ en .balearsnatura.com). These include Mondragó on the east coast (see p.187); Sa Dragonera (see p.123); S'Albufera (see p.156); and the Península de Llevant, just north of Artà and including the Ermita de Betlem (see p.174). **Menorca** has one natural park, S'Albufera des Grau (see p.218), but most of the rest of the island is protected to some extent or another, hence its UNESCO designation as a "Reserva de la Biosfera" (Biosphere Reserve). Finally, Cabrera island (see p.192) and its surrounding waters are a **Parc Nacional**.

island's pride and joy is the **Camí de Cavalls** (see box, p.241), a long-distance footpath that circumnavigates the whole island, bringing together a network of old mule and military trails. We have also described two **day-long hikes** on Menorca (see p.216 & p.226).

Hiking guides and maps

The best **hiking guides and maps** to Mallorca and Menorca are not available on the islands. These are produced at 1:40,000 by **Discovery Walking Guides**, whose most recent publications are detailed in Contexts (see p.275). Alternatively, the long-established Cicerone *Walking in Mallorca* guide (4th ed. 2006) covers all the island's classic walks and has a GR221-specific companion guide, *Trekking through Mallorca* (see p.275).

On **Mallorca**, both La Casa del Mapa bookshop in Palma (see p.77) and Sóller's Tramuntana Tours (see p.94) sell a good range of hiking guides with maps, including those produced by **Triangle Postals** (Ⓦtriangle.cat), whose *GR221 Serra de Tramuntana* publication provides detailed route descriptions. The main rival to Triangle Postals is **Editorial Alpina** (Ⓦeditorialalpina.com), which produces a number of hiking guides and maps, including one to the Serra de Tramuntana and another to Mallorca as a whole. Editorial Alpina's publications can, however, be difficult to track down on Mallorca with the exception of their widely available *Walking Paradise: Sóller* with around fifty route descriptions and an accompanying map at 1:15,000. Both La Casa del Mapa bookshop in Palma and Sóller's Tramuntana Tours sell this last publication.

On **Menorca**, Maó's quayside tourist office (see p.207) sells an excellent range of hiking guides and maps, including a very detailed, government-produced guide to the *Camí de Cavalls* with nice photos and pretty average maps; they also sell an accompanying box set of maps, but again these lack topographical details. Slightly better maps are included in Triangle Postals' *Camí de Cavalls* (1:60,000) – and this is on sale here too. For road maps, see p.38.

Windsurfing

Windsurfing is common in lots of resorts on both islands, but one of the prime spots is the windswept coast and wide, wave-less bay of Fornells on Menorca (see p.219), home to one of the best windsurfing companies in the Balearics, **Wind Fornells** (Ⓦwindfornells.com).

Scuba diving

By and large, **scuba diving** off **Mallorca** is something of an anticlimax: there may be lots of companies offering this service, but the island's underwater world lacks colour and clarity, with the exception of the clear and reefy waters around the island of Sa Dragonera (see p.123). **Menorca**, on the other hand, offers first-rate diving with visibility averaging around 30m, lots of reefs and a scattering of shipwrecks. Some divers swear by Menorca's north coast, but others prefer the west.

DIVING CONTACTS

Diving Center Fornells Fornells, Menorca ☎ 971 37 64 31, Ⓦ divingfornells.com
Divecenter Poseidon Ciutadella, Menorca ☎ 971 38 26 44, Ⓦ bahia-poseidon.de
Scuba Activa Sant Elm, Mallorca ☎ 971 23 91 02, Ⓦ scuba-activa.com

Shopping

Big-city Palma has its share of chain and department stores as well as a scattering of specialist outlets (p.77), but everywhere else – on both Mallorca and Menorca – is too small to offer much of a shopping "scene". That said, open-air markets (see p.36), mostly selling fresh fruit and vegetables as well as tourist trinkets, are extremely popular and lots of towns have one, either once or twice weekly; go early – at about 8am – to get the best deals.

As for **island specialities**, look out for **artificial pearls** from Manacor; **Camper shoes**; fancy green-tinted glass **chandeliers**; and **siurells** (see p.77), white clay whistles flecked with red and green paint and shaped to depict a figure, an animal or rural scene. There's also Mallorcan wine (see p.31) and Menorcan cheese, gin and honey, all of which come highly recommended, and you shouldn't leave the Balearics without sampling an **ensaimada** (spiralled flaky pastry).

Shopping hours are normally Monday to Friday 9.30/10am to 1.30/2pm and 5 to 7/8pm, plus Saturday morning 9.30/10am to 1.30/2pm, though big department stores operate longer hours, typically Monday to Saturday 9.30am to 9.30pm and Sunday 11am to 8pm. In the resorts, many shops and stores are open daily from 9.30am till late.

PRINCIPAL OPEN-AIR MARKETS (MERCATS)

Palma (Mallorca) has a wide range of markets (see p.78).

Mondays Calvià and Manacor (Mallorca).

Tuesdays Alcúdia and Artà (Mallorca); Maó (Menorca).

Wednesdays Andratx, Capdepera, Deià, Petra; Port de Pollença, Selva and Sineu (Mallorca).

Thursdays Alaior (Menorca); Inca (Mallorca).

Fridays Algaida, Binissalem and Port d'Alcúdia (Mallorca); Ciutadella (Menorca).

Saturdays Alaró, Bunyola, Cala Rajada, Manacor, Santanyí and Sóller (Mallorca); Ciutadella and Maó (Menorca).

Sundays: Alcúdia, Felanitx, Muro, Pollença, Porto Cristo and Valldemossa (Mallorca).

Travel essentials

Costs

In both Mallorca and Menorca, hotel and restaurant prices are on a par with most of the rest of Europe. On **average**, if you buy your own picnic lunch, stay in inexpensive *hostales* and hotels, and stick to cheaper bars and restaurants, you could get by on around €70 per person per day, assuming you're sharing a room. If you stay in three-star hotels and eat at quality restaurants, you'll need more like €120 a day per person, with the main variable being the cost of your room – and bear in mind that room prices rise steeply in peak season. On €200 a day and upwards, you'll be limited only by your energy reserves, unless you're planning to stay in a five-star hotel, in which case this figure won't even cover your bed.

A sales tax, **IVA**, is levied on most goods and services at anywhere between four and twenty-one percent. Most necessities (basic foods, books, medicines) attract a tax of four percent, and most tourist stuff (meals and hotels, for instance) ten percent. Check in advance to see if IVA is included in the price of your bigger purchases, otherwise you may be in for a bit of a shock. As for **tipping**, taxi drivers, restaurant and bar staff anticipate a tip of between ten and fifteen percent.

Crime and personal safety

Setting aside the ETA bombings of 2009, Mallorca and Menorca have very low **crime rates**. In the islands' villages and small towns petty crime is unusual, and serious offences, from burglary to assault and beyond, extremely rare. Of the three

EMERGENCY PHONE NUMBER

For medical, fire and police emergencies, call ☎ 112.

larger towns, only Palma presents any problems, and that's mostly low-key stuff such as the occasional fight and minor theft. Taking common-sense precautions and steering clear of the noisy and **aggressive males** who commonly colonize some late-night bars at the seedier resorts – S'Arenal and Magaluf have the worst reputations – should keep you out of trouble. **Theft from parked cars** is also a problem, especially at major tourist attractions, so don't leave anything in view when you park.

If you are a victim of crime, you'll need to report it to the police (see below), not least because your insurance company will require a **police report** or number. Many police officers speak English, especially in the towns and resort areas, but you can't bank on it. While the police are generally polite, they can become unpleasant if you get on the wrong side of them, so keep your cool at all times.

The police

There are three main types of **police** in the Balearics, all of them armed. The **Guardia Civil**, who are dressed in green, police the highways and the countryside; the brown-uniformed **Policía Nacional**, who are mainly seen in Palma, guard key installations and/or personnel and control crowds and demonstrations; and the **Policía Local**, who wear blue uniforms, operate in the towns. The Policía Local are generally reckoned to be the most sympathetic.

Electricity

Spanish **electricity** runs at 220 volts AC, with standard European-style two-pin plugs. Brits will need a plug adaptor to connect their appliances; North Americans should bring both an adaptor and a transformer.

Entry requirements

Citizens of the EU/EEA, including the UK and Ireland, plus citizens of Australia, New Zealand, Canada and the USA do not need a **visa** to enter Spain if staying for three months or less, but they do need a current **passport**. Travellers from

South Africa, on the other hand, need a passport and a tourist visa for visits of less than three months; visas must be obtained before departure and are available from the Spanish embassy (see below).

For stays of **longer than three months**, there are few hindrances for EU/EEA residents, but everyone else needs a mix of **visas and permits**. In all cases, consult your Spanish embassy at home before departure.

SPANISH EMBASSIES ABROAD

All the embassies below are on the Spanish government website ⓦ exteriores.gob.es.

Australia 15 Arkana St, Yarralumla, Canberra, ACT 2600 ☎ 02 6273 3555. Also consulates in Melbourne and Sydney.

Canada 74 Stanley Ave, Ottawa, Ontario K1M 1P4 ☎ 1 613 747 2252.

Ireland 17A Merlyn Park, Ballsbridge, Dublin 4 ☎ 01 269 1640.

New Zealand Level 11, i Center, 50 Manners St, Wellington 6011 ☎ 04 802 5665.

South Africa Lord Charles Complex, 337 Brooklyn Rd, Pretoria 0181 ☎ 012 460 01 23.

UK 39 Chesham Place, London SW1X 8SB ☎ 0207 235 5555. Also consulates in London and Edinburgh.

USA 2375 Pennsylvania Ave NW, Washington DC 20037 ☎ 01 202 452 0100. Also consulates in Boston, Chicago, Houston, Los Angeles, Miami, New York and San Francisco.

Health

Under reciprocal health-care arrangements, all citizens of the EU (European Union) and EEA (European Economic Area) are entitled to **free medical treatment** within Spain's public health-care system. Non-EU/EEA nationals are not entitled to free treatment and should, therefore, take out their own medical insurance. EU/EEA citizens may want to consider private health insurance too, to cover the cost of items not within the EU/EEA scheme, such as dental treatment and repatriation on medical grounds. No **inoculations** are currently required for Mallorca or Menorca.

The **public health-care system** in the Balearics is of an excellent standard and widely available, with clinics and hospitals in all the larger towns. If you're seeking treatment **under EU/EEA reciprocal health arrangements**, check that the medic who treats you is seeing you as a patient of the public system, so that you receive free treatment just as the locals do. You may be asked to show your passport and **European Health Insurance Card (EHIC)** to prove that you are eligible for EU/EEA healthcare – sometimes no one bothers, but always have it with you just in case.

If you have an insurance policy covering **medical expenses**, you can seek treatment in either the public or private health sectors, the main issue being whether – at least in major cases – you have to pay the costs upfront and then wait for reimbursement or not. Note that in the larger resorts your hotel will probably be able to arrange an appointment with an **English-speaking doctor**, who will almost certainly see you as a private patient; elsewhere, you'll be lucky if the medic speaks English.

Minor complaints can often be remedied at the ubiquitous **pharmacy** (*farmàcia*): pharmacists are highly trained, willing to give advice (often in English), and able to dispense many drugs which would only be available on prescription in many other countries. **Condoms** are available from most *farmàcias* and from all sorts of outlets in the resorts, such as bars and vending machines. It's a good job: a recent survey of 18- to 30-year-old visitors found that the average time between arrival and first sexual contact was 3hr 42min.

Insurance

Even though EU/EEA health-care privileges apply in Spain, it's still a good idea to take out an **insurance policy** to cover against theft, loss and illness or injury. For non-EU/EEA citizens, insurance is a must. A typical policy usually provides cover for the loss of

---

ROUGH GUIDES TRAVEL INSURANCE

Rough Guides has teamed up with WorldNomads.com to offer great **travel insurance** deals. Policies are available to residents of over 150 countries, with cover for a wide range of adventure sports, 24hr emergency assistance, high levels of medical and evacuation cover and a stream of travel safety information. Roughguides.com users can take advantage of their policies online 24/7, from anywhere in the world – even if you're already travelling. And since plans often change when you're on the road, you can extend your policy and even claim online. Roughguides.com users who buy travel insurance with WorldNomads.com can also leave a positive footprint and donate to a community development project. For more information, go to ⓦ roughguides.com/travel-insurance.

TEMPERATURES, SUNSHINE AND RAINFALL											
	Jan	Feb	Mar	Apr	May	Jun	Jul	Aug	Sep	Oct	Nov	Dec
Max/min (°C)	15/5	15/5	17/6	19/7	23/10	27/15	31/17	31/18	28/16	24/13	19/8	16/6
Max/min (°F)	59/41	59/41	63/43	66/45	73/50	81/59	88/63	88/64	82/61	75/55	66/46	61/43
Sunshine	4	6	6	7	9	10	11	11	8	5	4	4
Rainfall	11	8	8	9	7	5	3	4	8	11	12	12

baggage, tickets and – up to a certain limit – cash or cheques, as well as cancellation or curtailment of your journey. Private health insurance also covers the cost of items not included in the EU medical scheme, such as dental treatment and repatriation on medical grounds. In the case of major expense, the more worthwhile policies promise to sort matters out before you pay rather than after, but if you do have to pay upfront, make sure you always keep full doctors' reports, signed prescription details and all receipts. In the event that you have anything stolen, you must obtain an official statement from the police (see p.36).

Internet and email

Almost all hotels and *hostales* provide **internet access** for their guests either free or for a small charge. Failing that, head for the nearest library, where internet access is almost always free, if sometimes for a fixed period only – usually about an hour.

LGBT travellers

The **gay and lesbian scene** is fairly low-key in Mallorca and almost invisible in Menorca – in striking contrast to neighbouring Ibiza. Most of the action takes place in Palma on Avinguda Joan Miró, just south of Plaça Gomila. In 2005, Spain became the fourth country (after Canada, the Netherlands and Belgium) to legalize same-sex marriage, and there is now a battery of laws against discrimination on the grounds of sexual preference/orientation.

Mail

On both islands, there is a **post office** (*correu*) in every town and most larger villages; the majority are handily located on or near the main square. Opening hours are usually Monday to Friday 9am to 2pm, though the post offices in Palma, Maó and Ciutadella are open longer; all close on public holidays. The post is slow but reasonably reliable, with letters or cards taking about a week to reach Britain and Ireland, up to two weeks to North America and Australasia. You can buy **stamps** (*segells*) at tobacconists (look for the brown-and-yellow *tabac* or *tabacos* sign) and at scores of souvenir shops as well as at post offices. **Post boxes** are yellow; where you have a choice of slots, pick the flap marked *províncies i estranger* or *altres destinos*. **Postal rates** are inexpensive, with postcards and small letters attracting two tariffs: one to anywhere in Europe, the other worldwide.

Maps

Detailed **road maps** of Mallorca and/or Menorca are widely available from newsagents, tourist offices, petrol stations, souvenir shops and bookshops; for the most part they cost €3–7. The quality varies enormously and many are out of date, so before you buy a map check the **road numbers**: all Balearic road numbers were changed in 2006, so – for example – the main road along Mallorca's north coast was the C710, but is now the Ma-10, while Menorca's only main road is now the Me-1 (not the C721). You're also better off buying a **Catalan** map rather than a Castilian (Spanish) or even an English or German map. Check the spelling of Port de Pollença on Mallorca's north coast – if it reads "Puerto de Pollensa", you've got a Castilian map; similarly, on Menorca, check the capital is marked Maó, not the Castilian "Mahón".

Currently, the most accurate **road map** of **Menorca** is the *Mapa de Menorca* (1:75,000), produced by the island's ruling council and on sale at the tourist office in Maó (see p.207) and Ciutadella (see p.238). For **Mallorca**, the equivalent is **Kompass Mallorca** (1:75,000), sold online and at most larger bookshops on the island. Both mark major hiking routes and have large-scale inset city maps, one of Maó and Ciutadella, the other of Palma. Hiking maps are covered in our Sports and outdoor activities section (see p.34).

Money and exchange

Spain's currency is the **euro** (€), which is made up of 100 cents. The **exchange rate** at time of writing was €0.74 to the British pound; €1.13 to the US dollar; €1.47 to the Canadian dollar; €1.55 to the Australian dollar; €1.69 to the New Zealand dollar; and €15.13 to the South African Rand. Euros come in notes of €500, €200, €100, €50, €20, €10 and €5, and coins of €2, €1, 50c, 20c, 10c, 5c, 2c and 1c, though many retailers will not accept the €500 and €200 notes – you have to break them down into smaller denominations at the bank. All well-known brands of **travellers' cheque** in all the major currencies are widely accepted in Mallorca and Menorca, and you can change them as well as foreign currency into euros at most Balearic banks and savings banks, which are ubiquitous. **Banking hours** are usually Monday to Friday from 9am to 2pm, with many banks opening on Saturday mornings from 9am to 1pm from October to April. **ATMs** are commonplace in Palma, Maó, Ciutadella and all the larger resorts. Almost all ATMs give instructions in a variety of languages, and accept a host of **debit cards** without charging a transaction fee. **Credit cards** can be used in ATMs too, but in this case transactions are treated as loans, with interest accruing daily from the date of withdrawal. All major credit cards, including American Express, Visa and Mastercard, are widely accepted.

Opening hours and public holidays

Although there's been considerable movement towards a northern European **working day** in Menorca and Mallorca – especially in Palma and the

---

INTERNATIONAL CALLS

PHONING HOME FROM SPAIN

To make an **international phone call from Spain**, dial the appropriate international access code as below, then the number you require, omitting the initial zero where there is one.

Australia ☏0061
Canada ☏001
New Zealand ☏0064
Republic of Ireland ☏00353
South Africa ☏0027
UK ☏0044
USA ☏001

---

major tourist resorts – many shops still close for a **siesta** of at least two hours in the hottest part of the afternoon. There's a lot of variability, but core working hours are typically Monday to Friday 9am to 1/2pm and 4pm to 7pm, Saturday 9am to 1/2pm; notable exceptions are the extended hours operated by the largest department stores, some major tourist attractions and most tourist and souvenir shops. In winter (Nov–March), Menorca's tourist industry pretty much shuts up shop, and although things aren't so clear-cut in Mallorca, most of the resorts scale right down.

Local festivals (see p.32) are a prominent feature of island life and they work in tandem with **public holidays**, whose precise dates and details are fixed annually – so there may be some (minor) variations to the list in our box (see above). The island's resorts are generally oblivious to public holidays, as are hotels and most restaurants, but almost all businesses and shops close and public transport is reduced to a skeleton service.

Phones

The **international phone code** for Spain is 34. Note that most Balearic landline phone numbers begin with ☏971, but this is an integral part of the number, not an (optional) area code. You'll get **mobile phone** reception in all but the remoter corners of Mallorca and Menorca, with the network fixed at GSM900/1800, the band common to the rest of Europe, Australia and New Zealand. Mobile/cell phones bought in North America will need to be able to adjust to this GSM band. If you intend to use your mobile/cell phone in the Balearics, note that call charges can be excruciating – particularly irritating is the supplementary charge you often have to pay on incoming calls –

PUBLIC HOLIDAYS

January 1 New Year's Day (*Cap d'Any*)
January 6 Epiphany (*Reyes Magos*)
Maundy Thursday (*Dijous Sant*)
Good Friday (*Divendres Sant*)
May 1 Labour Day (*Día del Treball*)
August 15 Assumption of the Virgin (*Assumpció*)
October 12 Spanish National Day (*Día de la Hispanidad*)
November 1 All Saints (*Tots Sants*)
December 6 Constitution Day (*Día de la Constitució*)
December 8 Immaculate Conception (*Inmaculada Concepción*)
December 24 Christmas Eve
December 25 Christmas Day (*Nadal; Navidad in Castilian*)
December 26 Boxing Day/St Stephen's Day (*Dia de Sant Esteban*)

so check with your supplier before you depart. You may find it cheaper to buy a **local SIM card**, though this can get complicated: many mobiles/cells will not permit you to swap SIM cards and the connection instructions for the replacement SIM card can be in Spanish only. If you overcome these problems, you can buy SIM cards at high-street phone companies, which offer myriad deals beginning at about €5 per SIM card. **Text messages**, on the other hand, are normally charged at ordinary or at least bearable rates – and with your existing SIM card in place. The **Spanish phone directory** is available (in Spanish) at ⓦ paginas-amarillas.es.

Smoking

On January 1, 2006, smoking became **illegal** in Spain inside all theatres, bars and restaurants as well as on public transport, though scores of restaurants and bars managed to avoid the ban through local exemptions. Follow-up legislation, passed in 2011, removed most of these exemptions, and today, all bars and restaurants are smoke-free inside – though smoking is still allowed outside on the terrace.

Time zones

Spain is on **Central European Time** (**CET**) – one hour ahead of Greenwich Mean Time, six hours ahead of US Eastern Standard Time, nine hours ahead of US Pacific Standard Time, nine hours behind Australian Eastern Standard Time and eleven hours behind New Zealand. There can, however, be minor variations during the change-over periods involved in **daylight saving**. In Spain, the clocks go forward an hour on the last Sunday of March and back an hour on the last Sunday of October.

Tipping

Taxi drivers, restaurant and bar staff anticipate a tip of between ten and fifteen percent.

Tourist information

In **Mallorca**, there's a helpful **provincial tourist office** at the airport (see p.69) and another in the centre of Palma (see p.71). Both will provide free road maps of the island and leaflets detailing all sorts of island-wide practicalities. In addition, most towns and almost every resort has its own **tourist office**. These vary enormously in quality,

and while they are generally useful for local information, they cannot be relied on to know anything about what goes on outside their patch. In **Menorca**, there are extremely efficient year-round **tourist offices** in the two main towns, Maó and Ciutadella, and an island-wide tourist information office at the airport.

USEFUL WEBSITES

ⓦ **en.balearsnatura.com** Official website that gives a detailed lowdown on all the islands' natural parks.

ⓦ **conselldemallorca.net** Extensive, multilingual government site that includes details of – and allows you to make reservations for – Mallorca's hikers' hostels (*refugis*; see p.27).

ⓦ **descobreixmenorca.com** The best source of online information on Menorca's prehistoric sites.

ⓦ **illesbalears.es** The Balearic government's official, multilingual tourist site with separate sections for all of the islands. It covers a wide range of topics – from shopping to nature – and is clearly laid out; a useful introduction.

ⓦ **majorcadailybulletin.com** Mallorca's leading English-language newspaper runs this offshoot website, offering a lively mix of news and gossip.

ⓦ **mallorcaweb.com** and ⓦ **menorcaweb.com** Compendious websites dedicated to many aspects of island life.

ⓦ **menorca.es** First-rate multilingual government-run website illuminating every aspect of Menorcan tourism.

ⓦ **spain.info** The official website of the Spanish National Tourist Office (SNTO) provides an excellent introduction to the country, and its myriad synopses – on everything from national parks to accommodation – are concise, clear and temptingly written.

ⓦ **tib.org** and ⓦ **menorca.tib.org** Outstanding sites carrying all the details of public transport systems on Mallorca and on Menorca.

Travelling with children

Most Balearic *hostales*, pensions and hotels welcome **children** and many offer rooms with three or four beds. Restaurants and cafés almost always encourage families too. Many package holidays have **child-minding facilities** as part of the deal and many more organize a programme of kids' activities. Younger children will, of course, be quite happy to play around on the beach, but pre- and early teens may want more excitement, which is available on Mallorca at three water/theme parks: Hidropark in Port d'Alcúdia (see p.155); Western Water Park in Magaluf (see p.82); and Aqualand in S'Arenal (see p.85). **Concessionary rates** for children under 14/15 years are commonplace and infants go free. At restaurants, some places will prepare food specially for babies, though you might want to bring powdered milk – babies, like most Spaniards, are pretty contemptuous of the UHT stuff generally available. Disposable nappies and other basic supplies are widely available in the resorts and larger towns.

Travellers with disabilities

Despite their popularity as holiday destinations, facilities for **travellers with disabilities** on both Mallorca and Menorca lag some way behind most of the EU. That said, things are improving. Hotels with wheelchair access and other appropriate facilities are increasingly common and, by law, all new public buildings in Spain are required to be fully accessible. On the other hand, toilet facilities for people with disabilities are rare; car rental firms are very ill-stocked with adapted vehicles, even though there are designated disability parking bays; and few buses outside Palma's EMT services have low-floor access. More positively, **flying** to the islands should pose few problems as almost all the scheduled airlines are more than willing to assist.

Palma and around

47 Palma

69 Arrival and departure

71 Getting around

71 Information

71 City tours

71 Accommodation

73 Eating and drinking

75 Nightlife and entertainment

77 Shopping

78 Directory

78 Around Palma

HARBOURFRONT AND CATHEDRAL

1

Palma and around

Palma is an ambitious city. In 1983 it became the capital of one of Spain's newly established autonomous regions, the Balearic islands, and since then it has developed into a go-ahead and cosmopolitan commercial hub of over 400,000 people. The new self-confidence is plain to see in the city centre, a vibrant and urbane place of careful coiffures and well-cut suits, and one which is akin to the big cities of the Spanish mainland – but a world away from the heaving tourist enclaves of the surrounding bay. Neither has the city ever looked better: a long-term programme of reinvention and reconstruction has restored the architectural delights of the Old Town and equipped the centre with a raft of inviting shops, hotels, restaurants, cafés and bars, all enclosed by what remains of the Renaissance city walls and their replacement boulevards.

The boulevards that zigzag round the city centre encourage downtown Palma to look into itself and away from the sea, but its **harbour** has always been the city's economic lifeline. The Romans were the first to recognize the site's strategic value, establishing a military post here known as Palmaria, but real development came with the Moors, who made their **Medina Mayurka** a major seaport protected by no fewer than three concentric walls. Jaume I of Aragón captured the Moorish stronghold in 1229 and promptly started work on the **Cathedral**, whose mellow sandstone still towers above the waterfront, presenting from its seaward side – in the sheer beauty of its massive proportions – one of Spain's most stunning sights.

As a major port of call between Europe and North Africa, Palma boomed under both Moorish and medieval Christian control, but its wealth and prominence came to a sudden end with the Spanish exploitation of the New World: from the early sixteenth century, Madrid looked west across the Atlantic and Palma slipped into Mediterranean obscurity. One result of its abrupt decline has been the preservation of much of the **Old Town**, its beguiling tangle of narrow, labyrinthine streets and high-storeyed houses holding the Gothic **Basílica de Sant Francesc** at its core.

Yet for most visitors, Palma's main appeal is its sheer vitality: at night scores of excellent **restaurants** offer the best of Spanish, Catalan and Mallorcan cuisine, while the city's **cafés and tapas bars** buzz with purposeful chatter. Palma also boasts **accommodation** to match most budgets, making it a splendid base from which to explore the island. In this respect, the city is far preferable to the string of resorts along the neighbouring **Badía de Palma** (Bay of Palma), although, if it's sun and sea you're after, bear in mind that the more agreeable of the bay's resorts lie to the west of the city, where a hilly coastline of rocky cliffs and tiny coves is punctuated by small, sandy beaches. Development is ubiquitous, but **Cala Major** is of interest as the site of the former home and studio of Joan Miró; well-to-do **Illetes** has a couple of lovely cove

Orientation p.47
Gaudí lets in the light p.50
Scandal and intrigue: the strange
   career of Joan March p.55
A Catholic hero: the life and times of
   Ramon Llull p.61

The aristocracy at home: Palma's
   mansions p.64
Palma's top 5 hotels p.72
Siurrels p.77
Top 5 sandy beaches around Palma p.81

Highlights

❶ Palma Cathedral One of Spain's finest Gothic cathedrals, whose honey-coloured buttresses dominate the waterfront from the crest of a hill. **See p.47**

❷ Mallorcan Primitives Both the Museu de la Catedral and the Museu Diocesà hold a superb selection of medieval paintings by the so-called Mallorcan Primitives. **See p.51, p.53 & p.59**

❸ The Old Town The most intriguing part of the city, the Old Town's narrow lanes and labyrinthine alleys are flanked by a handsome medley of Gothic churches and Renaissance mansions. **See p.58**

❹ Palma's hotels Palma has the island's finest selection of hotels, from modernist-chic to fine old townhouses – and the *Dalt Murada* is among the best. **See p.71**

❺ Fundació Pilar i Joan Miró, Cala Major Joan Miró hunkered down in Mallorca partly to avoid the attentions of General Franco, creating some of his finest paintings here during his long exile. **See p.80**

❻ Platja de Palma, S'Arenal Probably the most self-conscious beach in Mallorca, awash with preening pecs and abs, slowly roasting on a 4km-long band of fine white sand stretching around the Bay of Palma. **See p.84**

HIGHLIGHTS ARE MARKED ON THE MAP ON P.46

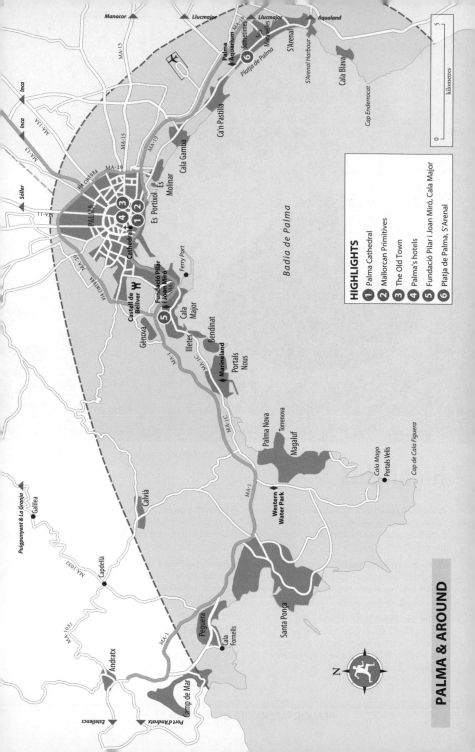

PALMA & AROUND

1

ORIENTATION

Almost everything of interest in **Palma** is located in the **city centre**, a roughly circular affair whose southern perimeter is defined by the Cathedral and the remains of the old city walls, which in turn abut the coastal motorway (the **Ma-19**) and the harbour. The city centre's landward limits are determined by a zigzag of wide **boulevards** built beside or in place of the Old Town walls. Two of these boulevards, Avinguda de la Argentina and Avinguda Gabriel Alomar i Villalonga, connect with the **coastal motorway**, thereby completing the circle. The **Ma-20** ring road around the suburbs loops off from the coastal motorway to create a much larger outer circle. Both the Ma-19 and Ma-20 become the **Ma-1** on the west of the city centre.

The city centre itself is crossed by four interconnected avenues: **Passeig d'es Born**, **Avinguda Jaume III**, **c/Unió** (which becomes **c/Riera** at its eastern end) and **Passeig de la Rambla**. Your best bet is to use these four thoroughfares to guide yourself around the centre – Palma's jigsaw-like side streets and squares can be very confusing. Central Palma is about 2km in diameter, a walk of roughly 30min from one side to the other.

beaches; and pint-sized **Cala Fornells** has a fine seashore setting, and is also within easy reach of the spacious sandy shorelines of family-oriented **Peguera**. Places to avoid include lager-swilling **Magaluf** and all the larger resorts to the east of Palma, where the pancake-flat shoreline is burdened by a seamless band of high-rises stretching from **Ca'n Pastilla** to **S'Arenal** – behind what is, admittedly, one of the island's longest and most impressive beaches, the **Platja de Palma**.

Palma

There's not much argument as to where to start a tour of Palma – it's got to be the **Cathedral**, which dominates the waterfront from the crest of a hill. Central Palma's other landmark is the **Palau de l'Almudaina** next door, an important royal residence from Moorish times and now, much modified, the repository of an engaging assortment of municipal baubles. Spreading northeast behind the cathedral are the narrow lanes and ageing mansions of the most intriguing part of the **Old Town**. A stroll here is a pleasure in itself, and – tucked away among the side streets – are three top-ranking diversions: the ecclesiastical treasures of the **Museu Diocesà**, the Baroque **Basílica de Sant Francesc** and (when it reopens), the **Museu de Mallorca**, the island's most extensive museum. North of the Old Town lies the heart of the early twentieth-century city, where the high-sided tenements are graced by a sequence of flamboyant buildings in the *Modernisme* (Art Nouveau) style, particularly on and around **Plaça Weyler** and **Plaça Major**.

The Cathedral

Plaça Seu • April, May & Oct Mon–Fri 10am–5.15pm, Sat 10am–2.15pm; June–Sept Mon–Fri 10am–6.15pm, Sat 10am–2.15pm; Nov–March Mon–Fri 10am–3.15pm, Sat 10am–2.15pm • €7, includes entrance to the museum • ☎ 902 02 24 45, ⊕ catedraldemallorca.org

Legend has it that when the invasion force of Jaume I of Aragón and Catalunya stood off Mallorca in 1229, a fierce gale threatened to sink the fleet. The desperate king promised to build a church dedicated to the Virgin Mary if the expedition against the Moors was successful. It was, and Jaume fulfilled his promise, starting construction work the following year. The king had a political point to make, too – he built his cathedral, a gigantic affair of golden sandstone, bang on top of the Great Mosque inside the Almudaina, the old Moorish citadel. The Reconquista – the expulsion of the Moors by the Christians – was to be no temporary matter. As it turned out, the **Cathedral** ("La Seu" in Catalan) was five hundred years in the making, but while there are architectural bits and bobs from several different eras, the church remains essentially

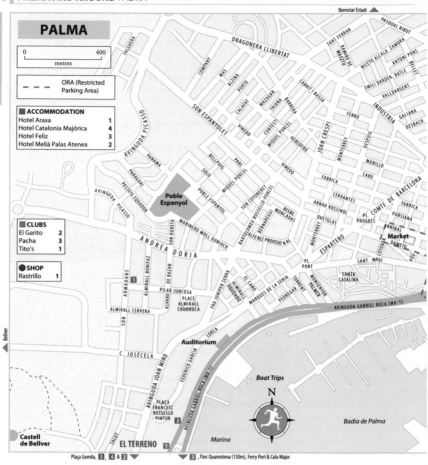

Gothic, with massive exterior buttresses – its most distinctive feature – taking the weight off the pillars within. The whole structure derives its effect from its sheer height, impressive from any angle, but startling when viewed from the waterside esplanade.

The exterior

The finest of the cathedral's three main doors is the **Portal del Mirador** ("Lookout Door"), which overlooks the Bay of Palma from the south facade. Dating from the late fourteenth century, the recently buffed and scrubbed Mirador features a host of Flemish-style ecclesiastical and biblical figurines set around a tympanum where heavily bearded disciples sit at a Last Supper. In contrast, the west-facing **Portal Major** ("Great Door"), across from the Palau de l'Almudaina, is a neo-Gothic disaster, an ugly reworking – along with the 60m-high flanking turrets – of a far simpler predecessor that was badly damaged by an earthquake in 1851. On the north side is a third door, the **Portal de l'Almoina**, whose delicately carved Gothic design dates from 1498. Above rises the solid squareness of the **bell tower** (closed to the public), an incongruous, fortress-like structure that clearly did not form part of the original design. When the largest of the bells, the 5700kg N'Eloi, was tolled in 1857, it shattered most of the cathedral's windows.

1

Sóller & Deià

FRANCESC MARTI I MORA
BALANGUERA
MIQUEL DELS SANTS OLIVER
PAU PIFERRER
JESÚS
ANTONI MARQUES
COMTE DE SALLENT
31 DE DESEMBRE
ARNDIC
LLUIS
SALVADOR
JAVION CRESQUES
EUSEBI ESTADA
FEMENIES
GUAL
RAFAEL RODRIGUEZ MENDEZ
GOETHE
PARELLADES
FRANCESC DE BORJA MOLL
Sóller Train Station
Estació Intermodal
SALVA
BERNAY AMER
ARGENTINA
RAMON I CAJAL
BARO DE PINOPAR
JOAN JERONIM ANTIC
LLUIS ESTELRICH
CECILI METEL
SANT MIQUEL
PL. ESPANYA
MARQUES DE LA FONTSANTA
JOAN MAURA BISBE
RODRIGUEZ DE ARIAS
CIMA
FRIEDRICH HOLDERLIN
PASSEIG MALLORCA
PASSEIG MALLORCA
Hospital General
PASSEIG DE LA RAMBLA
OMS
Mercat de l'Olivar
VINYASSA I LLOBERA
GILABERT DE CENTELLES
ALEXANDRE ROSSELLO
Inca
POU MURILLO
CARO
BONAIRE
Sant Miquel
Museu Fundación Juan March
SINDICAT
ARAGÓ
AVINGUDA JAUME III
Gran Hotel
UNIO
Teatre Principal
MANACOR
Manacor
ARGENTINA
EL PUIG DE SANT PERE
ESVALUARD
Can Solleric
PASSEIG D'ES BORN
La Feixina
Es Baluard Museu
PL. DRAÇANA
Santa Eulalia
Can Vivot
Basílica de Sant Francesc
GABRIEL ALOMA R I VILLALONGA
CONTRAMOLL MOLLET
AVGDA GABRIEL ROCA
Sa Llotja
Ajuntament
Fishing Boats
Palau de l'Almudaina
Cathedral
Can Oleza
PLAÇA PORTA D'ES CAMP
Parc de la Mar
Museu de Mallorca
Museu Diocesà
Banys Àrabs
MA-19
J. MARAGALL
Airport & S'Arenal
P
Customs

SEE 'CENTRAL PALMA' MAP FOR DETAIL

The nave

The cathedral **entrance**, beside the Portal de l'Almoina, leads straight to the museum (see p.51); beyond this is the **nave**, whose majestic proportions are seen to best advantage from the western end – from the Portal Major. In the central aisle, fourteen beautifully aligned, pencil-thin pillars rise to 21m before their ribs branch out, like fronded palm trees, to support the single-span, vaulted roof. The nave, at 44m high, is one of the tallest Gothic structures in Europe, and its 121m length is of matching grandeur. This open, hangar-like construction, typical of Catalan Gothic architecture, was designed to make the high altar visible to the entire congregation and to express the mystery of the Christian faith, with kaleidoscopic floods of light filtered in through the **stained-glass windows**. Most of the original glass was lost long ago, but recent refurbishment has returned a number of windows to their former glory and, now that some others have been un-bricked, the cathedral has re-emerged from its neo-Gothic gloom. There are seven rose windows, the largest of which crowns the triumphal arch of the apse towards the east end and boasts more than 1200 individual pieces of glass; providing the morning sun is out, it showers the nave with a wonderful, dappled light. The cathedral's designers also incorporated a specific, carefully orchestrated artifice: twice a year, at 6.30am on

1

Candlemas and St Martin's Day, the sun shines through the stained glass of the eastern window onto the wall immediately below the rose window on the main, western, facade.

The Capella del Corpus Christi

The aisles to either side of the nave are flanked by a long sequence of **chapels**, dull affairs for the most part, dominated by dusty Baroque altars of gargantuan proportions and little artistic merit. The exception, and the cathedral's one outstanding example of the Baroque, is the **Capella del Corpus Christi**, at the head of the aisle to the left of the high altar. Begun in the sixteenth century, the chapel's tiered and columned altarpiece features three religious scenes, cramped and intense sculptural tableaux depicting – from top to bottom – the temptations of St Anthony, the presentation of Jesus in the temple, and a superb Last Supper, which is exquisitely detailed, right down to the food on the table.

The high altar

Just in front and across from the Capella del Corpus Christi is a massive stone **pulpit** that was moved here by Gaudí, a makeshift but seemingly permanent location for this excellent illustration of the Plateresque style. Dated to 1531, the pulpit's intricate floral patterns and bustling biblical scenes cover a clumsy structure, the upper portion of which is carried by telamons, male counterparts of the more usual caryatids (supporting columns draped in female clothing). By these means, Gaudí made room for a new **high altar**, a medieval alabaster table of plain design above which he installed a phantasmagorical **baldachin**, a giant canopy enhanced by hanging lanterns which was supposed to symbolize the Crown of Thorns. It's not a

---

GAUDÍ LETS IN THE LIGHT

At the beginning of the twentieth century, an inspired local bishop – Pere Joan Campins – commissioned the *Modernista* Catalan architect **Antoni Gaudí** (1852–1926) to direct a full-blown restoration of Palma cathedral. It is not entirely clear what Campins had in mind, but Gaudí was renowned for his fancifully embellished metalwork and although his functionalist extrapolation of Gothic design was still evolving, it is a safe bet that both men were eager to return the cathedral to something like its original Gothic splendour. Gaudí's experimentation led ultimately to his most famous and extravagant opus, the church of the Sagrada Familia in Barcelona, but here in Palma his work was relatively restrained – though still deeply controversial. Indeed, a platoon of Catholic dignitaries objected to the revamp and when, in 1926, a Barcelona tram flattened Gaudí, they must have thought their prayers had been answered.

Gaudí worked on Palma's cathedral intermittently between 1904 and 1914, during which time he shifted the ornate choir stalls from the centre to the side of the cathedral, placing them flat against the walls, and removed the High Baroque altar, replacing it with the alabaster table and baldachin of today (see above). Other examples of Gaudí's distinctive workmanship are dotted around the cathedral: the **railings** in front of the high altar are twisted into shapes inspired by Mallorcan window grilles and the wall on either side of the **Bishop's Throne**, at the east end of the church, sports ceramic inlays with brightly painted floral designs. Yet Gaudí's main concern was to revive the Gothic tradition by allowing extra light. To this end, he introduced **electric lighting**, bathing the apse in bright artificial light and placing lamps and candelabra throughout the church. This was all very innovative: at the time, no Spanish choir had ever been removed and electric lighting was a real novelty. The artistic success of the whole project was undeniable, and it was immediately popular with the congregation. Like the rest of his work, however, it did not bring Gaudí much international acclaim: it was only in the 1960s that his techniques were championed and copied across western Europe, and that his crucial role in the development of modernism was finally acknowledged.

great success, though to be fair Gaudí never had time to complete it – he wanted it to be made of wrought iron, but what you see today is in fact a trial piece fashioned from cork, cardboard and brocade.

The Capella del Santíssim

At the east end of the church, to the right of the high altar, the walls of the **Capella del Santíssim** are covered by a bizarre plaster-and-ceramic dreamscape by the prolific Mallorcan artist Miquel Barceló (b.1957). At the back of the chapel – but currently out of bounds – are the outer and main sacristy, which lead through to the tiny **Capella de la Trinitat** (Trinity Chapel) at the far end of the church. Completed in 1329, this chapel houses the remains of Jaume II and Jaume III, two notable medieval kings of Mallorca. Initially, the bodies were stored in a tomb that operated rather like a filing cabinet, allowing the corpses to be venerated by the devout. They were viewed in 1809 by the first British traveller to write an account of a visit to Mallorca, the unflappable Sir John Carr, who calmly observed that, "considering the monarchs had been dead for five hundred years…they were in a state of extraordinary preservation". This gruesome practice was finally discontinued during the nineteenth century, and alabaster sarcophagi now enclose the royal bones.

The Museu de la Catedral

The ground floor of the bell tower and two adjoining chapterhouses have been turned into the **Museu de la Catedral**, which holds an eclectic assortment of ecclesiastical knick-knacks, gathered here by whim and accident but fascinating all the same. In the glass cabinet in the middle of the **first room** is a gilded silver **monstrance** of extraordinary delicacy, its fairy-tale decoration dating from the late sixteenth century. On display around the walls is a hotchpotch of chalices and reliquaries and a real curiosity, the portable altar of Jaume I, a wood-and-silver chessboard with each square containing a bag of holy relics.

Room two: the Mallorcan Primitives

The museum's second room is devoted to the Gothic works of the **Mallorcan Primitives**, a school of painters that flourished on the island in the fourteenth and fifteenth centuries, producing strikingly naïve devotional works of bold colours and cartoon-like detail. The work of two of the school's leading fourteenth-century practitioners is displayed here, beginning with the so-called **Master of the Privileges**, noted for his love of warm colours and minute detail. His work is shown to good advantage in a large (though unlabelled), cartoon-like panel painting of *The Life of St Eulalia*, whose martyrdom fascinated and excited scores of medieval Mallorcan artists. A Catalan girl-saint, Eulalia defied the Roman emperor Diocletian by sticking to her Christian faith despite all sorts of ferocious tortures, which are depicted here in ecstatic detail. She was eventually burned at the stake and at the moment of her death white doves flew from her mouth, but she somehow managed to end up as the patron saint of sailors. The Master of the Privileges was greatly influenced by Italian painters, but his contemporary, the **Master of Montesión**, looked to his Catalan contemporaries for his sense of movement and tight draughtsmanship – as seen in two panels displayed here, one of the *Crucifixion*, the other of the *Virgin Mary*. Later, the work of the Mallorcan Primitives shaded into the new realism of the Flemish style, which was to dominate Mallorcan painting throughout the sixteenth century. **Joan Desi**'s (unlabelled) *Panel of La Almoina* illustrates the transition – it's the large panel showing St Francis, complete with stigmata, at the side of Christ. One of Desi's pupils was **Alonso de Sedano**, who adopted a similar style in his *Martyrdom of St Sebastian*, which has the saint pierced by so many arrows that he looks like a sort of pin cushion.

1

Room three: the Baroque chapterhouse

The museum's third and final room, the **Baroque chapterhouse**, is entered through a playful Churrigueresque doorway, above which lively cherubic angels entertain a delicate Madonna. Inside, pride of place goes to the High Baroque **altar**, a gaudy, gilded affair surmounted by the Sacred Heart, a gory representation of the heart of Jesus that was very much in vogue during the eighteenth century. Some imagination went into the designation of the reliquaries displayed round the room, comprising an unlikely collection of bits and pieces of various saints. Of more appeal is a pair of finely carved Baroque **crucifixes**, each Christ a study in perfect muscularity swathed in the flowing folds of a loincloth.

The Palau de l'Almudaina

Plaça Seu • April–Sept daily 10am–8pm; Oct–March daily 10am–6pm • €7, audioguide €4 • Free to EU citizens showing their passport on Wed & Thurs pm (April–Sept 5–8pm; Oct–March 3–6pm) • ☎ 971 21 41 34, ⓦ patrimonionacional.es

Opposite the cathedral, the **Palau de l'Almudaina** (Almudaina Palace) was originally the palace of the Moorish *walis* (governors), and later of the Mallorcan kings. Built around a central courtyard, the present structure owes much of its appearance to Jaume II (1276–1311), who spent the last twelve years of his life in residence here. Jaume converted the old fortress into a lavish palace that incorporated both Gothic and Moorish features, an uneasy mixture of styles conceived by the Mallorcan Pedro Selva, the king's favourite architect. The two most prominent "Moorish" attributes are the fragile-looking outside walls, with their square turrets and dainty crenellations, and the delicate arcades of the main loggia, which can be seen from the waterside esplanade below.

Once Mallorca was incorporated within the Aragonese kingdom, the Palau de l'Almudaina became surplus to requirements, though it did achieve local notoriety when the eccentric Aragonese king Juan I (1387–95) installed an **alchemist** in the royal apartments, hoping he would replenish the treasury by turning base metal into gold. He didn't succeed. Today the palace serves a variety of official functions, has a small garrison to protect it, and holds a series of state apartments kept in readiness for visiting dignitaries and the king. When royalty or some other bigwig is in residence, parts of the palace are cordoned off.

The Salón de Consejos

A visit begins with a series of medieval corridors and rooms whose rough stonework is largely devoid of ornamentation, but things pick up in the **Salón de Consejos** (Hall of Councils), where the walls sport a quartet of admirable Flemish tapestries, all fifteenth- and sixteenth-century imports devoted to classical themes. Among them is a Roman Triumph, a blood-curdling war scene and, best of the lot, the suicide of Cleopatra, showing a particularly wan-looking queen with the guilty asp slithering discreetly away.

Comedor de Oficiales

The **Comedor de Oficiales** (Officers' Mess) possesses a handful of Flemish genre paintings, fine still-life studies including one by the Antwerp-based artist Frans Snyders (1579–1657) – there's no label, but it's the painting with the man, the woman, the cat and several carcasses. Snyders was a contemporary of Rubens and odd-jobbed for him, painting in the flowers and fruit on many of his canvases. Next door to the Comedor, there are charming views out across the city and harbour from the **terraza** (terrace), which holds a small formal garden.

Sala de Guardia

Inside the **Sala de Guardia** (Guard Room) are several dire eighteenth-century Spanish tapestries. Crude and inexact, these are in striking contrast to the Flemish tapestries exhibited elsewhere, but by then Spain had lost control of the Netherlands and the Spanish court could no longer acquire pieces from its traditional suppliers. In 1725, the Spanish king founded a tapestry factory in Madrid, but its products – as demonstrated here – were poor, and there must have been some aesthetic gnashing of teeth when the Spanish court took delivery.

Baños Árabes
Better preserved than the Arab baths in Palma's Old Town (see p.58), the **Baños Árabes** (Arab Baths) here are a rare survivor from Moorish times, comprising three stone-vaulted chambers, one each for cold, tepid and hot baths. Enough remains to see how this sophisticated setup worked and why the Christian kings who supplanted the Moors adopted them lock, stock and barrel.

Salón Mayor
Beyond the Arab baths, you soon reach the **central courtyard**, from where the **Escalera Real** (Royal Staircase), installed by Philip II, leads up to the **state apartments** that fill out the palace's upper level. These apartments are really rather sterile, but there are several splendidly ornate Mudéjar wooden ceilings and one architectural peculiarity: extra floors were inserted into the original structure and the result is most clearly visible on the top floor, where the **Salón Mayor** (Main Hall) is framed by heavy stone arches. In this room also is a magnificent seventeenth-century tapestry, *The Siege of Carthage*, which covers most of the back wall. The adjoining **Despacho de Su Majestad el Rey** (Study of the King), with its attractive Gothic gallery, was where the Moors surrendered to Jaume I in 1229.

Capella de Santa Ana
Adjoining the courtyard is the **Capella de Santa Ana** (Chapel of St Anne), a largely fourteenth-century Gothic structure – the Romanesque marble carving above the entrance may suggest an earlier date, but is in fact a deliberate use of what was by then an archaic tradition. The intimate interior has a fine vaulted and embossed ceiling and a conspicuous side chapel, the **Capella de St Praxedis**, which, with its medieval effigy and bony reliquary, is devoted to a much venerated saint, Praxedis. A second-century figure, Praxedis survived the massacre of her Christian companions and had the presence of mind to mop up their blood with a sponge and preserve it for later worship; Jaume III brought the reliquary back with him from Rome.

The Museu Diocesà
C/Mirador 5 • April, May & Oct Mon–Fri 10am–5.15pm, Sat 10am–2pm; June–Sept Mon–Fri 10am–6.15pm, Sat 10am–2pm; Nov–March Mon–Fri 10am–3.15pm, Sat 10am–2pm • €3 • ☏ 971 71 31 33, ⓦ catedraldemallorca.org
The smartly turned out **Museu Diocesà** (Diocesan Museum) occupies part of the old bishop's palace, a handsome courtyard complex round the back of the cathedral, directly above the old city walls. The museum's highlight is the city's largest collection of **Mallorcan Primitive art**, displayed on the ground floor alongside an assortment of religious statuary and a scattering of reliquaries.

The ground floor
Behind the museum's reception desk is an intriguing *St Paul* retable by the **Master of Bishop Galiana**, whose tight lines are very much in the Catalan tradition. This particular panel painting is a didactic cartoonstrip illustrating the life of St Paul, who is shown with his Bible open and sword in hand – a view of the Church militant that must have accorded well with the preoccupations of Mallorca's powerful bishops. Look out also for the way Galiana portrays the Conversion on the road to Damascus, with Saul/Paul struck by a laser-like beam of light.

1

Beyond, in the first room, is another fine work, **Pere Niçard**'s large and dramatic *St George and the Dragon*, a late fifteenth-century panel painting in which the fortifications of Palma appear in the background. Below the saint, to either side of Christ emerging from his tomb, are smaller paintings depicting the conquest of Mallorca by Jaume I – the storming of Palma on the right and the administering of (rough) justice to the left. Here also is the striking *Passion of Christ* by an unknown artist dubbed the **Master of the Passion of Mallorca**. Dated to the end of the thirteenth century, the painting consists of a series of small vignettes outlining the story of Christ, but the artistry is in the warm and gentle detail: the Palm Sunday donkey leans forward pushing his nose towards a child; one of the disciples reaches out across the Last Supper table for the fish; and two of Jesus' disciples slip their sandals off in eager anticipation during the Washing of the Feet.

Close by are several paintings by **Pere Terrencs**, but it is his *Crucifixion* that catches the eye, a sophisticated, early sixteenth-century work of strong, deep colours set within a triangulated structure. Above is the blood-spattered, pale-white body of Christ, while down below – divided by the Cross – are two groups, one of hooded mourners, the other a trio of nonchalant Roman soldiers in contemporary Spanish dress. Terrencs has chosen to ignore the two thieves who were crucified with Christ, showing him suffering alone on a bare and barren hill.

Beyond the Mallorcan Primitives, the museum's paintings hit the Catholic skids, sliding into the sentimental religiosity of the Counter Reformation.

The first floor

Upstairs, the museum's first floor has a lively, semi-interactive display outlining **Gaudí**'s work on the cathedral. There are also a few bits of furniture designed by Gaudí, who lodged here at the palace during some of the renovations, and a **graffiti wall** where generations of bored priests dawdled and doodled.

The Palau March

C/Palau Reial 18 • April–Oct Mon–Fri 10am–6pm, Sat 10am–2pm; Nov–March Mon–Fri 10am–5pm, Sat 10am–2pm • €4.50 • ☏ 971 71 11 22, ⓦ fundacionbmarch.es

Footsteps from the cathedral, the arcaded galleries and imperious Italianate bulk of the **Palau March** fill out the entire block between c/Palau Reial and c/Conquistador. The *palau* was built between 1939 and 1945 in the general style of the city's earlier Renaissance mansions on behalf of **Joan March**, long the island's most powerful citizen (see box opposite). A visit begins with the palace's most enjoyable feature, its splendid **Italianate courtyard**, which offers attractive views over the city centre and displays a potpourri of modern **sculpture** drawn from the March collection. Among the twenty or so pieces exhibited, there are two Henry Moores, a Rodin torso and two small marbles by Barbara Hepworth.

Beyond the courtyard, the **interior** of the *palau* is an anticlimax, its cold stone walls displaying an odd and unsatisfying mix of curios. As you enter the building on the right-hand side of the courtyard, the first mini-room gives some background information on the kitsch, eighteenth-century **Neapolitan figurines** that are the villa's main exhibit – as displayed in several subsequent rooms and culminating in a **Nativity Scene**, complete with a veritable army of small models packed into a large glass cabinet. It's difficult to know quite what to make of all this – and things get worse on the first floor, where the Spanish painter **Josep Maria Sert** (1874–1945) was responsible for both the brutal muscularity of the ceiling painting at the top of the stairs and the March family's one-time **music room** just beyond. The latter is decorated with racist murals depicting New Orleans jazz scenes of frolicking "Negroes" – Sert did much better elsewhere. The only modest lights in the cultural gloom are several coldly opulent ersatz nineteenth-century period rooms.

1

SCANDAL AND INTRIGUE: THE STRANGE CAREER OF JOAN MARCH

Joan March (1880–1962), one of the most controversial figures in Mallorca's recent history, was born a peasant's son in the small town of Santa Margalida on the east side of the island. At school, he showed his entrepreneurial flair by loaning money to his classmates at a high rate of interest and deciding, so the story goes, to start a trade in cigarettes, charging by the puff. March's father was a pig herder and at the age of 20 Joan negotiated the first of his major business deals, supplying meat direct to a sausage factory in Barcelona. In the next few years he allegedly established a dominant position in the **tobacco smuggling** trade with Algeria, displaying a ruthlessness that made him feared and loathed in equal measure.

March made more money in World War I, when both the British and the Germans paid him for his services, and took advantage of the difficulties experienced by the island's landed aristocracy to make yet more. For a variety of reasons, including the phylloxera infestation of the vineyards (see p.31), many of Mallorca's large estates had become uneconomic. March bought them up for a song and then sold them back to the farm hands who had previously worked them. The profit on each transaction was small, but there was the economy of scale: March sold no less than forty thousand land titles, an enormous number for a small island, and by these means transformed the structure of Mallorcan society as an accidental corollary to his greed.

During the Spanish Civil War, it seems likely that March loaned **Franco** money on generous terms and helped the Fascists with military supplies. Whatever the truth, March did become the richest man in Franco's Spain and was much favoured by the regime, though he was not averse to playing it both ways: recently declassified documents have revealed that during World War II the British paid him handsomely for his efforts in keeping Spain neutral. In 1955, for reasons that remain obscure, he decided to reinvent himself, becoming a **patron of the arts**, buying up dozens of sculptures and paintings and giving millions of pesetas to a new charitable foundation, the **Fundación Juan March**. In Palma, the *fundación* runs a major art gallery (see p.67) and March's old house, the Palau March (see p.54), is open to the public. However, the man is now mainly recalled by the bank he set up in 1926, the **Banca March**, which has branches right across the island.

The city walls

A wide flight of steps leads down from between the cathedral and the Palau de l'Almudaina to a handsomely restored section of the **Renaissance city walls**, whose mighty zigzag of bastions, bridges, gates and dry moats once encased the whole city. These replaced the city's **medieval walls**, portions of which also survive – look back up from the foot of the steps and a large chunk is clearly visible beneath the cathedral. Constructed of sandstone blocks and adobe, the earlier fortifications depended for their efficacy on their height, with a gallery running along the top from which the defenders could fire at the enemy. By the middle of the fifteenth century, however, the development of more effective artillery had shifted the military balance in favour of offence, with cannons now able to breach medieval city walls with comparative ease. The military architects of the day soon evolved a new design in which walls were built much lower and thicker to absorb cannon shot, while four-faced bastions – equipped with artillery platforms – projected from the line of the walls, providing the defenders with a variety of firing lines. The whole caboodle was protected by a water-filled **moat** with deep, sheer sides. The costs of refortifying the major cities of western Europe were astronomical, but every country joined in the rush. In Palma, the Habsburgs ordered work to start on the new (Renaissance) design in the 1560s, though the chain of bastions was only completed in 1801.

The city walls' walkway

A wide and pleasant **walkway** runs from the foot of the steps below the cathedral along the top of the Renaissance walls, providing delightful views of the city and harbour plus an insight into the tremendous strength of the fortifications. Heading **west**, the walkway leads to the **tiered gardens** of a lush Moorish-style park, which tumbles down

1

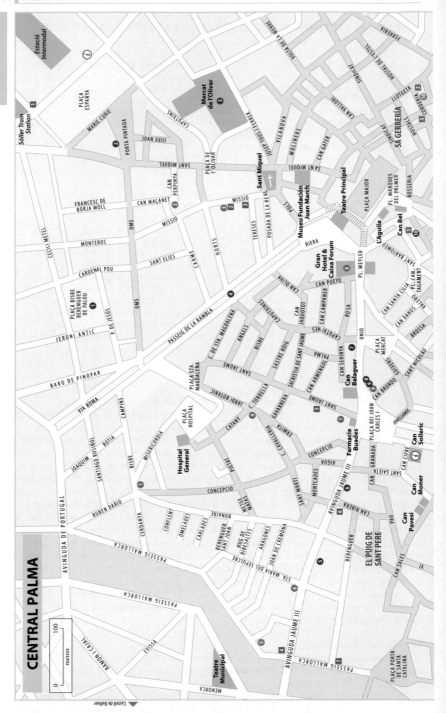

CENTRAL PALMA

0 100 metres

Castell de Bellver

Estació Intermodal

Sóller Train Station

PLAÇA ESPANYA

Mercat de l'Olivar

Sant Miquel

Museu Fundación Juan March

Teatre Principal

PLAÇA MAJOR

SA GERRERIA

Gran Hotel & Caixa Forum

L'Aguila

Can Rei

Can Balaguer

PLAÇA MERCAT

Can Solleric

Farmacia Buades

PLAÇA REI JOAN CARLES I

Can Moner

Can Pavesi

EL PUIG DE SANT PERE

Hospital General

PLAÇA HOSPITAL

PLAÇA STA. MAGDALENA

Teatre Municipal

PLAÇA PORTA DE SANTA CATALINA

AVINGUDA DE PORTUGAL

PASSEIG MALLORCA

AVINGUDA JAUME III

VIA ROMA

PASSEIG DE LA RAMBLA

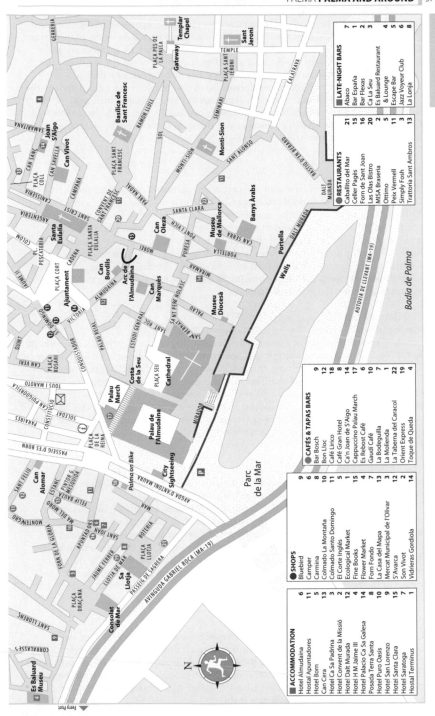

ACCOMMODATION

Hotel Almudaina	6
Hostal Apuntadores	11
Hotel Born	5
Can Cera	13
Hotel Ca Sa Padrina	3
Hotel Convent de la Missió	2
Hotel Dalt Murada	12
Hotel H M Jaime III	4
Hotel Palacio Ca Sa Galesa	14
Posada Terra Santa	8
Hotel Puro Oasis	10
Hotel San Lorenzo	9
Hotel Santa Clara	15
Hotel Saratoga	7
Hostal Terminus	1

SHOPS

Bluebird	9
Camper	6
Carmina	8
Colmado La Montaña	10
Colmado Santo Domingo	11
El Corte Inglés	5
Ecological Market	1
Fine Books	12
Flower Market	4
Forn Fondo	7
La Casa del Mapa	13
Mercat Municipal de l'Olivar	3
S'Avarca	12
Son Vivot	15
Vidrieras Gordiola	2

CAFÉS & TAPAS BARS

Bar Bosch	9
Bon Lloc	12
Café Lírico	18
Café Gran Hotel	8
Ca'n Joan de S'Aigo	14
Cappuccino Palau March	17
Es Rebost Café	6
Gaudí Café	10
La Bodeguilla	7
La Molienda	3
La Taberna del Caracol	22
Orient Express	19
Toque de Queda	4

RESTAURANTS

Caballito del Mar	21
Celler Pagès	15
Forn de Sant Joan	16
Las Olas Bistro	20
MISA Braseria	2
Ottimo	5
Peix Vermell	11
Simply Fosh	3
Trattoria Sant Ambros	13

LATE-NIGHT BARS

Abaco	7
Bar España	1
Bar Flexas	2
Ca La Seu	3
Es Baluard Restaurant	4
& Lounge	
Escape Bar	5
Jazz Voyeur Club	6
La Lonja	8

1

to – and runs along beside – **Avinguda d'Antoni Maura**, an extension of the tree-lined Passeig d'es Born (see p.62). Heading **east**, the walkway passes above the planted trees, concrete terraces and ornamental lagoon of the **Parc de la Mar**, an imaginative and popular redevelopment of the disused land that once lay between the walls and the coastal motorway. Indeed, it has proved so popular that the municipality are considering shoving the highway underground so that they can extend the park to the seashore. Wall and walkway eventually fizzle out at Plaça Llorenç Villalonga, but long before that – just a couple of minutes from the cathedral – you reach the double **Portella gateway**, where you go down one of the wide stone ramps to reach the foot of c/Portella near the Banys Àrabs (see below).

The Old Town

The medina-like maze of streets to the rear of the cathedral constitutes the heart of the **Old Town**, which extends north to Plaça Cort and east to Avinguda Gabriel Alomar i Villalonga. Long a neglected corner of the city, most of the district has now been refurbished in an ambitious and massively expensive project that has restored its antique charm. The area's general appearance is its main appeal, and you can spend hours wandering down narrow lanes and alleys, loitering in squares and gazing at Renaissance mansions. It's also worth seeking out the district's two finest churches – the **Església de Santa Eulalia** and the **Basílica de Sant Francesc** – plus the city's most extensive museum, the **Museu de Mallorca**.

The Banys Àrabs

C/Can Serra 7 • Daily: June–Sept 9.30am–7pm; Oct–May 9.30am–6pm • €2.50 • ☎ 971 72 15 49

North of the Portella gate (see above), the first turning on the right leads to the **Banys Àrabs** (Arab Baths), one of the few genuine reminders of the island's Moorish presence. Dating back to the tenth century, this brick *hammam* (bathhouse) consists of a small horseshoe-arched and domed chamber that was once heated through the floor. The arches rest on stone pillars, an irregular bunch thought to have been looted from the remains of the island's Roman buildings. The baths are reasonably well preserved, but if you've been to the baths in Girona or Granada, or even the Baños Árabes in the Palau de l'Almudaina (see p.53), these are really rather dull. The lush garden outside, with tables where you can picnic, is perhaps nicer.

The Museu de Mallorca

C/Portella 5 • Currently closed for refurbishment, but scheduled to reopen in 2016 when opening hours are likely to be Mon–Fri 11am–6pm, Sat 11am–2pm • ☎ 971 17 78 38, ⓦ museudemallorca.caib.es

The expansive **Museu de Mallorca** occupies **Can Aiamans**, a rambling Renaissance mansion, whose high-ceilinged rooms make a delightful setting for an enjoyable medley of Mallorcan artefacts. The earliest exhibits date from prehistoric times, but there's also a superb assortment of Gothic paintings and some excellent examples of *Modernista* fittings and furnishings. The labelling is patchy but hopefully the **major revamp**, which is currently underway, will rectify matters; it's also possible that the layout of the museum will change – so the description below should be treated with caution.

Prehistory, the Romans and the Moors

Currently, the collection begins in the **basement**, on the right-hand side of the entrance courtyard, with a series of rooms that track through the island's early history. Here you'll find a ragbag of **archeological finds** and displays on the *navetas* and *talayots* typical of the Balearics' early Talayotic culture (see p.246). The **Late Talayotic Period** (500/400 BC–123 AD) is when the islanders either made – or possibly imported – the finely detailed and extremely **bellicose statuettes** that are some of the museum's most

1

prized artefacts. Of the dozen or so statuettes, most are of nude aggressive men, helmeted and armed, and representative of a warlike culture: indeed, such was the islanders' reputation as warriors that the Carthaginians recruited hundreds of them to fight in their armies during the Punic Wars against Rome in the third century BC. Equally striking is the **Bou de Talapí**, an angular carving of a bull's head that exudes a brutish strength of almost disconcerting proportions.

The museum also possesses a number of finely worked funerary tablets from **Roman Mallorca**, while highlights of the **Moorish** period include some ornate Mudéjar wooden panelling and an exquisite selection of Arab and Moorish jewellery.

The Mallorcan Primitives

On the left-hand side of the entrance courtyard, an old stone stairway leads up to a section devoted to the city's second-largest collection of **Mallorcan Primitive painters** after the Museu Diocesà (see p.53). On display are works by the Masters of Montesión and Castellitx and an especially fine panel painting entitled *Santa Quiteria*, whose lifelike, precisely executed figures – right down to the king's wispy beard – are typical of the gifted **Master of the Privileges** (possibly Joan Loert). There's also a curious thirteenth-century work by an unknown artist dedicated to St Bernard of Clairvaux, the founder of the Cistercian order, with the saint on his knees devotedly drinking the milk of the Virgin Mary.

One of the most talented of the Mallorcan Primitives was **Francesc Comes** (1379– 1415), whose skill in catching subtle skin textures both matched his Flemish contemporaries and represents a softening of the early Mallorcan Primitives' crudeness. The museum exhibits several of his paintings, including a striking *St George*, in which the saint – girl-like, with typically full lips – impales a lime-green dragon with more horns/hooks than could possibly be useful.

Active around 1500, the **Master of the Predellas** – probably a certain Joan Rosató – was one of the last talented exponents of Mallorcan Gothic. He is well represented by his Bosch-like triptych of the *Life of Santa Margalida*, with each group of onlookers a sea of ugly, deformed faces and cruelly curious eyes. The work outlines the life of **Margaret of Antioch**, the patron saint of pregnant women. During the reign of the Roman emperor Diocletian (284–305 AD) she refused to marry a pagan prefect and was consequently executed after being tortured with extravagant gusto. As if this weren't enough, Satan, disguised as a dragon, swallowed her, but couldn't digest her holiness, so his stomach opened up and out she popped unharmed.

The Counter-Reformation

The stodgy art of the **Counter-Reformation** was a poor successor to the Mallorcan Primitives, but Palma's own Miquel Bestard (1590–1633) redeems some of the artistic bacon with his whopping *Feeding of the Five Thousand*. Miraculously, Jesus feeds the hungry crowd from a meagre supply of loaves and fishes, but the subtext is much more revealing: Bestard's crowds are well behaved and respectful of authority – just what the Catholic hierarchy had in mind.

Modern art and the *Modernista* school

The museum possesses a mildly engaging assortment of nineteenth- and early twentieth-century **paintings** by both native artists and foreign artists once resident in Mallorca. This includes a neat sample of works by Mallorca's own **Juli Ramís** (1909– 90), whose striking style is illustrated by his oil-on-fabric *Tres Cavalls* (Three Horses) and the radiant blues of *Tardor en blau* (Blue Autumn). A native of Sóller, Ramis left the island when he was nineteen to spend the next sixty years abroad, travelling widely and becoming acquainted with some of the leading artistic lights of his day. Ramis mixed his styles, but was essentially an Expressionist with Surrealist leanings. He returned to Mallorca in the last years of his life and died in Palma.

The museum also possesses a substantial collection of **Modernista** fittings and furnishings, mostly retrieved from shops and houses that have since been demolished. Of particular interest are the charming wall tiles manufactured at the island's **La Roqueta** works. The pottery was in production for just twenty years (1897–1918), but this coincided with the vogue for the *Modernista* pieces in which La Roqueta excelled.

Carrer Morei and around

Up the hill from the Museu de Mallorca, c/Portella leads into **Carrer Morei** where, at no. 9, you'll find **Can Oleza** (no public access), a sixteenth-century mansion with an elegant shaded courtyard embellished by a handsome balustrade and a set of Ionic columns. Nearby, in c/Almudaina, are the chunky remains of the old east gate, the **Arc de L'Almudaina**, a rare survivor from the Moorish fortifications.

Església de Santa Eulalia

Plaça Santa Eulalia • Mon–Fri 9.30am–noon & 6.30–8.30pm, Sat 10.30am–1pm & 6.30–8.30pm, Sun 9.30am–1.30pm & 6.30–7.30pm • Free • ☎ 971 71 46 25

Large and imposing, the **Església de Santa Eulalia** was built on the site of a mosque in the mid-thirteenth century. It took just 25 years to complete and consequently possesses an architectural homogeneity that's unusual for ecclesiastical Palma, though there was some later medieval tinkering, and nineteenth-century renovators added the belfry and remodelled the main (south) facade. The church is typically Gothic in construction, with a yawning nave originally designed – as in the cathedral – to give the entire congregation a view of the high altar. The bricked-up windows of today – as well as the darkness of the stained glass – keep out much of the light and spoil the effect, but suggestions that they be cleared have always been ignored. Framing the nave, the aisles accommodate twelve shallow **chapels**, one of which (the first on the right) sports a delightful Gothic panel painting in the finely observed Flemish style, its figures including St Barbara (with her symbolic tower) and St Lucia (the eyes on a plate). In kitsch contrast, the other chapels are standard-issue Baroque, though they pale into insignificance when compared with the hourglass-shaped **high altarpiece**, a flashy Baroque extravagance of colossal proportions. This holy ground witnessed one of the more disgraceful episodes of Mallorcan history. During Easter week, 1435, a rumour went round that **Jewish** townsfolk had enacted a blasphemous mock-up of the Crucifixion. There was no proof, but the Jews were promptly robbed of their possessions and condemned to be burnt at the stake unless they adopted Christianity. The ensuing mass baptism was held here at Santa Eulalia.

The Basílica de Sant Francesc

Plaça Sant Francesc • Mon–Sat 9.30am–12.30pm & 3.30–6pm, Sun 9.30am–12.30pm • €3 • ☎ 971 71 26 95

Anchoring this part of the Old Town, the **Basílica de Sant Francesc** is a domineering pile plonked on the site of the old Moorish soap factory. Built for the Franciscans towards the end of the thirteenth century, the original church was a vast Gothic edifice that benefited from royal patronage after King Jaume II's son, also named Jaume, became a member of the monkish order in 1300. Subsequent remodellings replaced the initial wooden ceiling with today's single-span, vaulted stone roof of imposing dimensions and added grandiloquent chapels to the nave and apse. The Basílica became the most fashionable church in medieval Palma and its friars received handsome kickbacks for entombing the local nobility within its precincts. Increasingly eager to enrich themselves, the priests came to compete for possession of the corpses, while the various aristocratic clans vied with each other in the magnificence of their sarcophagi. These tensions exploded when a certain Jaume Armadams had a jug of water emptied over his head inside the church on All Saints' Day, 1490. The congregation went berserk and more than three hundred noblemen fought it out in the nave before the priests finally restored order – and the scandal caused the Basílica to be closed by decree

A CATHOLIC HERO: THE LIFE AND TIMES OF RAMON LLULL

The life of **Ramon Llull** (1235–1315) – a figure much beloved of Catholic propagandists – was an exercise in redemption through carnal excess. As a young man, Llull was an ebullient rake in the retinue of the future Jaume II. His sexual adventures were not impeded in the least by his marriage, but they ground to a dramatic halt when a certain Ambrosia de Castillo, his latest amatory target, whom he had pursued into the church of Santa Eulalia on horseback, revealed to him her diseased breasts. A deeply shocked Llull devoted the rest of his life to the Catholic faith, becoming a fearless missionary and dedicated scholar of theology, philosophy and alchemy. Exemplifying the cosmopolitan outlook of thirteenth-century Mallorca, Llull learned to read, write and speak several languages, including Arabic, and travelled to France, much of Spain and North Africa. He also founded a monastery and missionary school on **Puig Randa** (see p.170), east of Palma, where he spent ten years in seclusion, writing no fewer than 250 books and treatises. It was Llull's scholarship that attracted the attention of his old friend Jaume II, who summoned him to court in 1282. With royal patronage, Llull then established a monastic school of Oriental languages in the mountains near Valldemossa, and it was here he trained his future missionary companions. Llull was **killed** on his third evangelical excursion to Algeria in 1315, his martyrdom ensuring his subsequent beatification.

for several decades. In the seventeenth century the church was badly damaged by lightning, prompting a thoroughgoing reconstruction, which accounts for most of its present-day appearance.

The main facade

Dating from the seventeenth century, the church's **main facade** displays a stunning severity of style, with its great rectangular sheet of dressed sandstone stretching up to an arcaded and balustraded balcony. It's pierced by a gigantic rose window of Plateresque intricacy and embellished by a **Baroque doorway**, the tympanum of which features a triumphant Virgin Mary engulfed by a wriggling mass of sculptured decoration. Above the Madonna is the figure of St George and to either side and below are assorted saints – look out for the scholar and missionary Ramon Llull (see above), shown reading a book. The strange statue in front of the doorway of a Franciscan monk and a young Native American celebrates the missionary work of **Junipero Serra** (see p.166), a Mallorcan priest despatched to California in 1768, who subsequently founded the cities of San Diego, Los Angeles and San Francisco – not bad going by anyone's standards.

The interior

Approached through a neat and trim Gothic cloister, the church's **interior** is distinguished by its monumental **high altar**, a gaudy Baroque affair featuring balustrades, lattice-work and clichéd figurines beneath a painted wooden statue of *St George and the Dragon*. It's heady stuff, as are the rolling scrollwork and trumpeter-angel of the **pulpit** on the wall of the nave, and the ornate Gothic-Baroque frontispiece of the **organ** just opposite. Beside the high altar, recessed chapels enclose the ambulatory with the first chapel on the left holding the **tomb of Ramon Llull**, whose bones were brought back to Palma after his martyrdom in Algeria in 1315. Considering the sanctity of the man's remains, it's an odd and insignificant-looking memorial, with Llull's alabaster effigy set high up on the wall to the right of the chapel altarpiece at a disconcertingly precarious angle.

The Templar chapel

C/Temple • In theory, Mon–Fri 9.30am–1pm & 3.30–7pm, Sat 9.30am–1pm • Free

At the end of c/Ramon Llull, a large and distinctive thirteenth-century fortified **gateway** marks what was once the entrance to the castle-like compound of the **Knights**

1

Templar, a military order founded to support the Crusades. The knights established bases right across the Mediterranean and this was one of the more important – though they were ultimately dispossessed: the order was rich and secretive, its independence resented by the papacy and just about every secular ruler in Europe. In 1312, following trumped-up charges of heresy, sorcery and bestiality, the pope disbanded the order and their Palma compound passed into the hands of the Hospitallers of St John, a rival knightly order. The Knights Hospitallers survived until 1802, when the Spanish king disbanded them and confiscated their property.

An alley leads through the gateway to the only other surviving part of the military compound, the **Templar chapel**, whose gloomy, rib-vaulted, Gothic-Romanesque nave is supported by a set of narrow columns and flanked by arcaded galleries.

Església de Sant Jeroni

Plaça Sant Jeroni s/n • No set opening hours • ☎ 971 72 73 98

South of the Templar gateway, along c/Temple, **Plaça Sant Jeroni** is a pretty little piazza set around a dinky water fountain. The severe stone walls of a former convent, now a college, dominate one side of the square, while the **Església de Sant Jeroni** fills out another. The church facade is mostly a plain stone wall, but it is broken up by two doorways, the one on the left displaying a swirl of carved foliage and garlands of fruit. The door's tympanum portrays the well-known story of Saint Jerome in the desert, during which the saint endures all sorts of tribulations and temptations, but still sticks true to the faith; above, two heraldic lions stand rampant. The **interior**, with its heavy stone vaulting, is mostly seventeenth century, but it's rarely open to the public – a shame, given that the church holds several good paintings by the Mallorcan Primitives.

Plaça Cort and around

Bustling **Plaça Cort**, with its elegant nineteenth-century facades and grizzled olive tree, was named after the various legal bodies – both secular and religious – which were once concentrated here. Along with the rest of Spain, Mallorca possessed a truly Byzantine legal system until the whole caboodle was swept away and rationalized during the Napoleonic occupation. Today, one side of the square is dominated by the **Ajuntament** (Town Hall), a debonair example of the late Renaissance style: pop in for a peek at the grand and self-assured foyer, which mostly dates from the nineteenth century, and the six folkloric *gigantones* (giant carnival figures) stored here – four in a corner, the other two tucked against the staircase.

From Plaça Cort, it's a pleasant five-minute stroll to the Passeig d'es Born via **c/Sant Domingo**, which meanders down the hill lined by attractive nineteenth-century townhouses. Alternatively, it's a short walk from Plaça Cort along c/Palau Reial to the Palau March (see p.54) and the cathedral (see p.47).

The Passeig d'es Born

The **Passeig d'es Born** is distinguished by its long line of plane trees and by the stone sphinxes at its top and bottom. The avenue has been the city's principal promenade since the early fifteenth century, when the stream that ran here was diverted following a disastrous flash flood. In recent years, it has suffered badly from traffic congestion, but newly imposed restrictions have restored some of its more pleasing features and a concerted effort has also been made to clean up its decaying mansions, large and decorous affairs that once housed the island's most powerful families. Two of the mansions to receive the treatment are Can Solleric (see p.64) and **Can Alomar**, an imposing stone extravagance at the corner of c/Sant Feliu that now accommodates luxury shops.

1

Can Solleric

Passeig d'es Born 27 • Tues–Sat 11am–2pm & 5.30–8.30pm, Sun 11am–2.30pm • Free • ☏ 971 72 20 92, ⓦ casalsolleric.palmademallorca.es

Built for a family of cattle and olive-oil merchants in 1763, **Can Solleric** is one of the grandest mansions on the Passeig d'es Born, a lavish affair of heavy wooden doors, marble columns, metal grilles and vaulted ceilings with an elegant double stone stairway leading up from an internal courtyard. The house now displays moderately interesting temporary exhibitions of art and local history – and there is a small tourist information desk, too.

Plaça de la Reina

At the south end of the Passeig d'es Born is **Plaça de la Reina**, a tiny, leafy square set beside the **Costa de la Seu**, a wide and good-looking flight of steps that leads up beneath the spiky walls of the Palau de l'Almudaina to both the cathedral and the Palau March (see p.54). The *palau* originally extended right down to the Plaça de la Reina, incorporating what is now the *Cappuccino* café as well as the tiny Biblioteca March Servera (library), but these parts were hived off years ago.

Avinguda d'Antoni Maura

South of Plaça de la Reina, **Avinguda d'Antoni Maura** slices down to the wide breakwater that marks the start of Palma harbour (see p.68). Until recently, the avenue was a traffic-clogged mess, but it's been prettied up with a long line of cafés on one side and tiered gardens on the other. It takes its name from **Antoni Maura** (1853–1925), a Mallorcan who served as prime minister of Spain four times between 1903 and 1921. An outstanding orator and extraordinarily forceful personality, Maura was a conservative who saw universal suffrage – in place from 1887 – as "the politics of the mob", preferring a limited franchise and a constitution that gave power to the middle classes, as long as they marched to the tune of Church and Crown. In a backward, largely agrarian, society, most Spaniards were largely indifferent to national issues and

---

THE ARISTOCRACY AT HOME: PALMA'S MANSIONS

Much of medieval Palma was destroyed by fire, so the **patrician mansions** that characterize the Old Town today mostly date from a **Renaissance** reconstruction programme that began in the late seventeenth century and finished a few decades later. This building bonanza spawned a high degree of uniformity, with columns and capitals, loggias and arcades tucked away behind outside walls of unadorned stone three or four storeys high. Entry to almost all of these mansions was through a great arched **gateway**, which gave onto a rectangular courtyard around which the house was built. Originally, the **courtyard** would have been cheered by exotic trees and flowering shrubs, and equipped with a fancy stone and ironwork wellhead, where visitors could water their horses. From the courtyard, an **exterior staircase** led up to the main public rooms – with the servants' quarters below and the family's private apartments up above. For the landed gentry, it was a very comfortable life indeed: as one British gentleman stated in the 1840s, "The higher classes lead a life of perfect inactivity – doing little, but eating occasionally … It is difficult to imagine a less agitated or more objectless existence."

Very few of these mansions are open to the public, and all you'll see for the most part is the view from the gateway – the municipality actually pays people to leave their big wooden gates open. Several have, however, passed into the public domain, with **Can Aiamans**, now the home of the Museu de Mallorca (see p.58), being the prime example. Others that merit a gander are **Can Vivot**, an especially opulent mansion with a spacious main courtyard, set behind the church of Santa Eulalia at c/Can Savella 4; **Can Bordils**, c/Almudaina 9, now housing municipal offices but with two splendidly carved windows and a thick stone doorway arch left to recall its better days; **Can Oleza** (see p.60); and **Can Solleric** (above); only the last one of these is open to the public.

power was concentrated in the hands of district bosses, or *caciques*, who would bring out the vote for any candidate provided they kept control of political patronage. Some bosses ruled by intimidation, others by bribery, but the end result was a dense mixture of charity and jobbery, dubbed *caciquismo*, which made national government well-nigh impossible. Maura struggled against this chicanery, and his assertive nationalism was quite enough for Franco to have this avenue named after him; no one has bothered to change the name since.

El Puig de Sant Pere

The ancient neighbourhood of **El Puig de Sant Pere** (St Peter's Mount) covers the area west of the Passeig d'es Born and north to Avinguda Jaume III. The district comprises a cobweb of narrow lanes and alleys that shelter a sprinkling of old stone mansions, though most were divided up years ago to cater for the district's sailors, dockers and fishermen. It's the general flavour of Sant Pere that appeals rather than specific sights, but it's still worth seeking out two late Renaissance facades on **c/Sant Feliu**, which runs off Passeig d'es Born. At no. 8 is **Can Moner**, whose ornate doorway sports telamons, cherubs and cornucopia, while no. 10, **Can Pavesi** – now home to the ultra-exotic Gerhardt Braun gallery – offers a mythical beast with its tongue stuck right out.

There's a gruesome story behind the name of a lane off nearby c/Estanc: **Mà del Moro**, "The Hand of the Moor", harks back to Ahmed, an eighteenth-century slave who murdered his master in a house on this alley. Ahmed was executed for the crime, and his hand was chopped off and stuck above the doorway of the house where the murder was committed – "pour encourager les autres" as Voltaire would have it.

Avinguda Jaume III and around

Avinguda Jaume III marches west from the top of Passeig d'es Born flanked by a matching set of long and sturdy stone arcades, which encase some of the island's chicest clothes shops and downtown's biggest department store, **El Corte Inglés** (see p.77). Dating from the 1940s, this is Francoista architecture at its most appealing – very symmetrical and self-consciously Spanish – and there's something very engaging about the airs and graces of the avenue, with its jostle of be-shorted tourists and be-suited Spaniards. Furthermore, the web of ancient alleys immediately to the north of the avenue, focused on **c/Concepció**, is another attractive corner of the city, all high stone walls and dignified old mansions.

Passeig Mallorca

At the top of Avinguda Jaume III, the **Passeig Mallorca** is a busy boulevard bisected by the deep, walled watercourse that once served as the city moat – and is now an especially handsome feature of the city. Peer down into its walled depths and you'll spy a greenish, slow-moving stream which becomes a swirling torrent after rain.

Es Baluard museu d'art modern i contemporani

Plaça Porta Santa Catalina • Tues–Sat 10am–8pm, Sun 10am–3pm • €6 • ☎ 971 90 82 00, ⓦ esbaluard.org

Es Baluard museu d'art modern i contemporani (Es Baluard Modern and Contemporary Art Museum) has a spectacularly handsome setting, nestled within the stern lines of a mighty stone bastion that looks out over the harbour. Outside, the museum begins with a series of large, geometric **sculptures** carefully positioned across the top of the fortification in a perfect match of style and setting. Inside, the museum, which spreads over three floors, does not quite live up to its location, but it does host a lively programme of temporary exhibitions, which affect exactly what parts of the permanent collection are on display – and where. That said, the ground floor usually has one section devoted to **Joan Miró**, with examples of his early landscape paintings through to his more characteristic cartoon-like squiggles. On the first floor, you can also expect to see Es Baluard's pride and joy, a rare and unusual sample of **Picasso** ceramics, most memorably a striking white, ochre and black vase-like piece entitled *Big Bird Corrida*. There are more sculptures on the museum's rooftop walkway, complemented by panoramic views over the harbour and the city.

La Feixina

Near Es Baluard, a footbridge spans the Passeig Mallorca to reach **La Feixina**, a pleasant terraced **park**, whose trees, lawns, flower beds and fountains step south to the foot of **Avinguda Argentina**, just east of the fenced-off jetties where the fishing boats come in. The park's only scenic blot is the whopping **column** erected by Franco to honour those sailors who died when the Nationalist heavy cruiser *Baleares* was sunk by torpedo off Cartagena in 1938 during the Spanish Civil War.

Carrer Unió and around

Running east from Plaça Rei Joan Carles I, **Carrer Unió** is a new if rather unimaginative appellation – it means "unity" – for a street Franco had previously named after **General Mola**, one of the prime movers of the Nationalist rebellion of 1936. Mola was killed in a plane accident during the Civil War, possibly to Franco's relief. Hitler, for one, thought that Mola was the more competent, remarking that his death meant that "Franco came to the top like Pontius Pilate in the Creed". Near the start of c/Unio, at no. 3, is **Can Balaguer**, a sprawling Renaissance mansion with imposing doors and a grand cobbled courtyard. A mouldy sort of place, it has long been in need of a major refurbishment – and one has at last just started; the plan is to turn the place into an art gallery.

Plaça Mercat

Flanking c/Unió is **Plaça Mercat**, an agreeable little square that is overseen by two identical *Modernista* buildings commissioned by a wealthy baker, Josep Casasayas, in 1908. Each is a masterpiece of flowing, organic lines tempered by graceful balconies and decorated with fern-leaf and butterfly motifs.

Plaça Weyler

Plaça Weyler is home to a number of *Modernista* extravagances, with the **Forn des Teatre** (theatre bakery), at no.9, boasting floral motifs and a gaily painted wooden doorway. The bakery is downright playful, but across the street is a much more imposing *Modernista* edifice, the **Gran Hotel** of 1903. Recently cleaned and buffed, the hotel's facade boasts a dinky turret-tower, balconies, columns and bay windows enlivened with intricate floral trimmings and brilliant polychrome ceramics inspired by Hispano-Arabic designs. The *Gran Hotel* now houses a café on the ground floor (see p.74) and the Caixa Forum art gallery up above.

Caixa Forum art gallery

Plaça Weyler 3 • Tues–Sat 10am–9pm, Sun 10am–2pm • €4 • ☎ 971 17 85 00

Spread over two floors of the *Gran Hotel*, the **Caixa Forum art gallery** organizes an excellent programme of temporary exhibitions on its top floor – Floor 2 – with its permanent collection down below on Floor 1. The latter is essentially confined to a large sample of work by **Hermen Anglada Camarasa** (1871–1959), a Catalan Impressionist-Expressionist best known for the evocative Mallorcan land- and seascapes he produced during his longest sojourn on the island, from 1914 to 1936. Disappointingly, the gallery only possesses one or two of these

1

scenes, but it does have a couple of Camarasa's sombre and finely executed women's portraits as well as two huge and drearily folkloric canvases entitled *Valencia* and *El Tango de la Corona*.

Plaça Major and around

Built on the site of the former headquarters of the Inquisition (see p.255), **Plaça Major** is a large and pleasant pedestrianized square with a symmetrical portico running around its perimeter. It once housed the fish and vegetable market, but today it's mainly popular for its pavement cafés. Feeding off to the south, the much smaller **Plaça Marquès del Palmer** is a cramped setting for two fascinating *Modernista* edifices. The more dramatic is **Can Rei**, a six-storey apartment building splattered with polychrome ceramics and floral decoration, its centrepiece a gargoyle-like face set between a pair of winged dragons. The facade of the adjacent **L'Àguila** building is of similar ilk, though there's greater emphasis on window space, reflecting its original function as a department store. Close by, the shopping area stretching south from Plaça Marquès del Palmer to Plaça Cort retains an agreeably old-fashioned air, with the three- and four-storey buildings that frame its main streets – principally pedestrianized **c/Jaume II** – embellished with an abundance of fancy iron-grilled balconies.

Carrer Sant Miquel

A popular and agreeable shopping street, **Carrer Sant Miquel** cuts north from Plaça Major, running up past the main city market, on Plaça Olivar (see p.78), en route to Plaça d'Espanya. Near the start of the street, at no. 11, a branch of the **Banca March** occupies a fine Renaissance mansion whose *Modernista* flourishes date from a tasteful refurbishment in 1917. The building has two entrances, one to the bank, the other leading upstairs to the Museu Fundación Juan March.

Museu Fundación Juan March
C/Sant Miquel 11 • Mon–Fri 10am–6.30pm, Sat 10.30am–2pm • Free • ☎ 971 71 35 15, ⓦ march.es

The **Museu Fundación Juan March** showcases a prime sample of modern and contemporary art drawn from the collection of the March family (see p.55). The collection, which spreads over two floors, features works by most leading twentieth-century Spanish artists, the intention being to survey the country's contribution to modern art – a theme which is further developed by temporary exhibitions. The displays are regularly rotated, but you can expect to see a room devoted to paper drawings by Picasso and a particularly interesting early piece by the same artist, his *Tête de femme* (1907). This was one of the first of Picasso's works to be influenced by the primitive forms that were to propel him, over the following decade, from the re-creation of natural appearances into abstract art. Miró and Dalí are also well represented, and there's a still life by the Spanish Cubist Juan Gris, as well as a number of harsh abstractions by the influential Catalan artist Antoni Tàpies (1923–2012). Rather harder to negotiate are the allegedly "vigorous" abstractions of both the El Paso (Millares, Feito, Canogar) and the Parpalló (Sempere, Alfaro) groupings of the late 1950s.

Església Sant Miquel
C/Sant Miquel 21 • Mon–Sat 8am–1.30pm & 4.30–7.30pm; Sun 10am–1pm & 6–8pm • Free • ☎ 971 71 54 55

From the Museu Fundación Juan March, it's a brief stroll north along c/Sant Miquel to the **Església Sant Miquel**, whose sturdy exterior is the result of all sorts of architectural meddlings. Inside, the barrel-vaulted nave is almost entirely windowless, a dark and gloomy space where the one highlight is the high altarpiece, a Baroque classic with a central image celebrating St Michael in smiting mode. The altarpiece is a good example

1

of the intricate work of **Francesc Herrara** (1590–1656), a much-travelled Spanish painter of religious and genre subjects known for his purposeful compositions and tangy realism.

Along the harbourfront

The various marinas, shipyards, fish docks and ferry and cargo terminals that make up Palma's **harbourfront** extend west for several kilometres from the bottom of Avinguda d'Antoni Maura to the edge of Cala Major (see p.80). The harbour is at its prettiest along its eastern, city-centre-skirting stretch, where a cycling and walking path hugs the seashore, with boats to one side and bars, restaurants, apartment blocks and the smart hotels of the **Avinguda Gabriel Roca** – often dubbed the Passeig Marítim – across the main road on the other.

Sa Llotja

Plaça Llotja s/n • Hours vary with exhibitions • Free • ☎ 971 71 17 05

A harbourfront landmark, the fifteenth-century **Sa Llotja** once housed the city's stock exchange, but now hosts regular art exhibitions. Designed by Mallorca's own **Guillermo Sagrera**, one of the most original European architects of his day, the exterior of this carefully composed, late Gothic structure is distinguished by its four octagonal turrets, ornate windows and, above the front door, fierce-looking gargoyles and muscular angel with feathery wings – appropriately the Guardian Angel of Commerce. The interior is, if anything, even more striking, its six slender, spiralling columns and magnificent vaulting providing an exhilarating sense of space – perfect for art displays.

Consolat de Mar

Passeig de Sagrera s/n

The stolid **Consolat de Mar**, next door to Sa Llotja, was built in the 1660s to accommodate the Habsburg officials who supervised maritime affairs in this part of the empire. Today, as the home of the president of the Balearic islands, it's closed to the public, but the outside is worth a second look for its pair of crusty old cannons and elegant Renaissance gallery. The large gate between the Consolat and Sa Llotja – the **Porta Vella del Moll** – originally stood at the end of Avgda d'Antoni Maura, where it was the main entrance into the city from the sea; it was moved here when portions of the town wall were demolished in the 1870s.

Parc Quarentena

A 20min walk west of Avgda Argentina along the harbourfront • Daylight hours • Free

The delightful **Parc Quarentena** is one of the city's best-kept parks, a verdant tangle of flowering shrubs and plants spread beneath a canopy of palm trees, its cool and shaded terraces clambering up the hillside from the harbourfront. You can exit at the top on c/Patrimoni, metres from Plaça Gomila and Avgda Joan Miró.

Castell de Bellver

C/Camilo José Cela s/n • April–Sept Mon 8.30am–1pm, Tues–Sat 8.30am–8pm, Sun 10am–8pm; Oct–March Mon 8.30am–1pm, Tues–Sat 8.30am–6pm, Sun 10am–6pm • €4 • ☎ 971 73 50 65, Ⓦ castelldebellver.palmademallorca.es • Served by Citysightseeing double-decker buses (see p.71), or take EMT bus #3 to Plaça Gomila, from where it's a stiff, 30min uphill walk

Boasting superb views over Palma and its harbour from a wooded hilltop some 3km west of the city centre, the **Castell de Bellver** is a handsome, strikingly well-preserved fortress built for Jaume II at the beginning of the fourteenth century. Of canny circular design, the castle's immensely thick walls and steep ditches encircle a central

1

keep that incorporates three imposing towers. In addition, an overhead, single-span stone arch connects the keep to a massive freestanding **tower**, built as a final refuge. To enhance defence, the walls curve and bend and the interconnecting footbridges are set at oblique angles to each other. It's all very impressive – and looks well-nigh impregnable – but the castle was also intended to serve as a royal retreat from the summer heat, and so the austere outside walls hide a genteel-looking **circular courtyard**, surrounded by two tiers of inward-facing arcades that were once living quarters. The whole construction is ingenious, incorporating many skilful touches: the flat roof, for example, was designed to channel every drop of rainwater into a huge underground cistern. Soon after its construction, however, improvements in artillery rendered the original fortress obsolete, and although modifications were made, they were never very convincing. Neither did it last long as a royal residence. As early as the 1350s the keep was in use as a prison, a function it performed until 1915, before finally becoming a **museum**.

The museum

Inside the castle, the ground floor houses a plodding exhibition on the history of the city, along with a small display on the castle's most distinguished prisoner, the eighteenth-century reformer Gaspar Jovellanos. Much better, however, is the delightful collection of **Roman statuary** on the floor above. A local antiquarian and ecclesiastical bigwig by the name of **Cardinal Antonio Despuig** (1745–1817) gathered together these classical pieces and bequeathed the whole lot to the city on his death. The only problem is that there's no labelling, so unless you're a classical expert it's impossible to know quite what you're looking at. Nevertheless, among the miscellany of busts and effigies, there's no mistaking a rare and perfectly preserved column of strikingly patterned *cippolino* marble and, most extraordinary of all, a small and exquisite alabaster of a sleeping **hermaphrodite**, apparently troubled by a confusing dream, half-in but mainly out of her toga. Other exhibits include carved seals, marble inscriptions, first-century medallions, a funeral stele, and a fearsome bust of **Medusa**, her head crawling with snakes.

ARRIVAL AND DEPARTURE	PALMA

BY PLANE

Mallorca international airport Mallorca's airport (☎971 78 90 00, ⓦmallorcaairport.com) is 11km east of the city centre, immediately behind the resort of Ca'n Pastilla. It has one enormous terminal which handles both scheduled and charter flights, with Arrivals downstairs and Departures upstairs. On the Arrivals floor, a flotilla of car rental outlets jostles for position by the luggage carousels. Beyond, through the glass doors, is the main Arrivals Hall, with 24hr ATMs and currency exchange facilities, dozens of package-tour agents plus a provincial tourist office.

AIRPORT INFORMATION

Tourist information In the Arrivals Hall, the provincial tourist office (Mon–Sat 8.30am–8pm, Sun 9am–1.30pm; ☎971 78 95 66, ⓦvisitpalma.com) is beside Exit 3. It has a wide range of brochures, public transport timetables, maps and lists of hotels and *hostales*, but very few of them are on display – and the more specific your question, the more useful the reply is likely to be. Note that they do not arrange accommodation.

TRANSPORT FROM THE AIRPORT

By car The airport is linked to Palma by a busy highway – the Ma-19 – which shadows the shoreline from S'Arenal in the east to Cala Major in the west, where it becomes the Ma-1, which continues on to the resorts of the Bay of Palma – Palma Nova, Magaluf and so forth. The outer ring road – the Ma-20 – forks off from the Ma-19 on the east side of the city and then loops right round to join the Ma-1, also at Cala Major.

By bus The least expensive way to reach downtown Palma from the airport is by EMT bus #1 (daily every 15min 6am–1am; €3), which leaves from outside the main entrance of the terminal building, just behind the taxi rank. They reach the city's inner ring road near the foot of Avgda Gabriel Alomar i Villalonga, at the c/Joan Maragall junction, and then proceed to Plaça d'Espanya, Passeig Mallorca, Avgda Jaume III and ultimately the port, stopping frequently en route. Traffic depending, the journey from the airport to Plaça d'Espanya takes about 40min, and 1hr or so to the port.

By taxi A taxi from the airport to the city centre costs about €20 and takes around 25min, depending on

1

traffic; taxi rates are controlled and a list of island-wide fares is available from the provincial tourist office in the Arrivals Hall.

BY FERRY

Operators and bookings Palma's car ferry and catamaran terminal is about 4km west of the city centre: Trasmediterranea (☎ 902 45 46 45, ⓦ trasmediterranea .es) and Iscomar (☎ 902 11 91 28, ⓦ www.iscomar.com) boats arrive at Terminal 2; Balearia boats (☎ 902 16 01 80, ⓦ balearia.com) at Terminal 3, about 150m away. Ferry and high-speed catamaran tickets can be bought online, by phone, and at the ferry port, though the ticket offices at the port are only open before and just after sailings. EMT bus #1 (daily every 15min 6am–1am) runs from outside Terminal 2 to Plaça d'Espanya (20min) – and continues on to the airport (1hr). There are also taxi ranks outside both terminal buildings; the fare to the city centre is about €10 and takes about 10min. For ferry routes and fares, see Basics (p.22, p23).

BY BUS

Estació Intermodal Almost all long-distance buses arrive at and depart from Palma's combined bus and train station, the Estació Intermodal, adjoining Plaça d'Espanya. There's an information desk at the Estació (June–Oct Mon–Fri 7am–9pm, Sat 8am–9pm, Sun 9am–9pm; Nov–May Mon–Fri 7am–9pm, Sat 9am–7pm), where you can get public transport timetables. There's also an all-embracing, multilingual website, covering both train and bus services on ⓦ tib .org, or call ☎ 971 17 77 77 (though you'll probably need to speak Spanish or Catalan). Long-distance buses are operated by a variety of companies, but EMT has a monopoly on Palma buses (see opposite).

Destinations (long-distance buses) Alcúdia (every 1–2hr; 1hr); Andratx (1–2 hourly; 1hr); Artà (5–8 daily; 1hr 20min); Banyalbufar (4–8 daily; 1hr); Cala d'Or (Mon–Sat 6 daily, 3 on Sun; 1hr 15min); Cala Figuera (May–Oct Mon–Sat 2 daily; 1hr 45min); Cala Major (every 30min–1hr; 20min); Cala Millor (Mon–Sat every 1–2hr, 3 on Sun; 2hr); Cala Rajada (5–8 daily; 1hr 50); Colònia de Sant Jordi (4–8 daily; 1hr 20min); Coves del Drac (May–Oct Mon–Sat 4 daily, 1 on Sun; 1hr 15min); Deià (4–7 daily; 1hr); Estellencs (4–8 daily; 1hr 15min); Lluc (2 daily; 1hr 10min); Magaluf (1–2 hourly; 1hr); Peguera (1–2 hourly; 1hr); Pollença (Mon–Fri hourly, Sat & Sun 7 daily; 45min); Port d'Alcúdia (every 1–2hr; 1hr); Port d'Andratx (1–2 hourly; 1hr 10min); Port de Pollença (every 1hr–2hr; 1hr 15min); Port de Sóller, via the tunnel (Mon–Fri hourly, Sat 8 daily, Sun 5 daily; 40min); Port de Sóller, via Valldemossa (4–7 daily; 1hr 30min); Porto Cristo (May–Oct Mon–Sat 8 daily, 3 on Sun; Sept–April 2–3 daily; 1hr 15min); Sóller, via the

tunnel (Mon–Fri hourly, Sat 8 daily, Sun 5 daily; 35min); Sóller, via Valldemossa (4–7 daily; 1hr 15min); Valldemossa (4–7 daily; 30min).

BY TRAIN

Services and information Mallorca has two train lines. One is the vintage tourist line between Palma and Sóller (see box, p.93), the other is the modern commuter line running east from Palma across the interior of the island to the likes of Binissalem, Inca, Manacor and Muro. Trains on this modern line arrive at and depart from the Estació Intermodal, adjoining Plaça d'Espanya, where the information desk (June–Oct Mon–Fri 7am–9pm, Sat 8am–9pm, Sun 9am–9pm; Nov–May Mon–Fri 7am–9pm, Sat 9am–7pm) issues train timetables. Alternatively, check out the multilingual ⓦ tib.org, or phone ☎ 971 17 77 77 (if you speak Spanish or Catalan). Mallorca's vintage train line departs Palma from a separate station a few metres from the Estació Intermodal.

Destinations (standard trains) Binissalem (every 20min; 30min); Inca (every 20min; 40min); Manacor (hourly; 1hr); Muro (hourly; 50min); Petra (hourly; 55min); Sineu (hourly; 50min).

Destinations (tourist trains) Sóller (April–Oct 5–6 daily; Nov–March 4 daily; 55min).

BY CAR

Driving in Palma Driving into the city is straightforward enough, though you would do well to avoid the narrow lanes and complicated one-way system of the Old Town, sticking instead to the zigzag of boulevards that encircle the centre from Avgda Gabriel Alomar i Villalonga in the east to the Passeig Mallorca in the west.

PARKING

Car parks Trying to find an on-street parking space in downtown Palma can be a nightmare, and you're well advised to either leave your vehicle on the city's outskirts, or head for one of several car parks – the Parc de la Mar near the cathedral often has spaces when others do not. Car parks charge around €1.80/hr. If you're staying downtown, choose a hotel which either has its own car park or has an arrangement with a local one (some hotels offer parking discounts).

ORA tickets On-street parking in the city centre requires an ORA ticket during busy periods (Mon–Fri 9am–2.30pm & 4.30–8pm, Sat 9am–2.30pm); outside these hours parking is free. Tickets are available from ORA meters but parking is limited to just 2hr; costs are reasonable (currently €2.65/2hr), but note that fines for over-staying your time are immediate and steep. Note also that if the time allowed overlaps into a free period, your ORA ticket is still valid when restricted time begins again.

GETTING AROUND

BY BUS

Information, routes and tickets Frequent and efficient, Palma's buses are operated by EMT (Empresa Municipal de Transports; ☎971 21 44 44 in Spanish or Catalan, ⓦemtpalma.es). Nearly all their services pass through Plaça d'Espanya and together they combine to link the centre with the suburbs and the nearer tourist resorts; several of the more useful services also pass through Plaça de la Reina. In the city centre, each downtown EMT bus stop displays a schematic route map and timetable for the buses that stop there, as well as an electronic display showing when the next bus will arrive. Tickets are available from the driver and cost €1.50 per journey within the city limits.

Destinations Airport (#1: daily every 15min; 25–45min); Cala Major (#3: every 10–20min; 15min); Illetes (#3; every 10–20min; 20min); S'Arenal (#15; every 10–20min; 45min).

BY BIKE

Bike rental Palma on Bike, centrally located at Avgda d'Antoni Maura 10 (☎971 70 86 02, ⓦpalmaonbike.com), rents out city and mountain bikes from €12/day. Reservations, at least 24hr in advance, are advised.

BY CAR

Car rental Mallorca's airport (see p.69) heaves with international car rental companies, and there's a concentration of both large and small companies west of Palma's centre along the harbourfront on Avgda Gabriel Roca. The city's two main tourist offices (see below) can supply a complete list, or try Europcar, at Avgda Gabriel Roca 19 (☎971 45 68 50; airport ☎971 74 65 49; ⓦeuropcar.com), or Hertz, at Avgda Gabriel Roca 13 (☎971 73 47 37; airport ☎971 78 96 70; ⓦhertz.com).

BY TAXI

Companies and fares Taxi fares are reasonable, metered at €0.55 per km during normal working hours, €0.85 on the weekend and after 9pm; there is also an initial charge of €1.80 and a small supplement for luggage. There are several city-centre ranks, with one on Plaça d'Espanya, another on Avgda Jaume III, a third on Avgda d'Antoni Maura, and a fourth on Passeig d'es Born; alternatively, phone Taxis Palma (☎971 40 14 14).

INFORMATION

Tourist offices There's a provincial tourist office in the centre of Palma just off Passeig d'es Born at Plaça de la Reina 2 (Mon–Fri 8.30am–8pm; Sat 8.30am–2pm; ☎971 17 39 90). The main municipal tourist office is on the north side of Plaça d'Espanya (daily 9am–8pm; ☎902 10 23 65). These both provide city- and island-wide information, free maps, accommodation lists, bus schedules, lists of car rental firms and a range of specialized leaflets. Another, smaller, municipal office is inside Can Solleric, at Passeig d'es Born 27 (daily 9am–8pm; ☎902 10 23 65), but this only provides a

limited range of city information. There's also a provincial tourist office at the airport (see p.69).

Website Palma's official website is ⓦwww.visitpalma .com.

City pass Introduced in 2015, the Palma Pass (ⓦpalmapass.com) entitles holders to free entry to almost all the city's museums and sights and also gives discounts at a variety of shops and stores. A booklet detailing these benefits is issued when you buy the pass. It's on sale online and at the municipal tourist office on Plaça d'Espanya – either 2 days for €34, or 3 days for €43.

CITY TOURS

By bus Palma Citysightseeing (☎902 10 10 81, ⓦcity -sightseeing.com) operates double-decker hop-on/hop-off bus trips round the major sights (daily: May–Sept 9.30am–8pm; Oct–April 10am–6pm; every 20–30min). Tickets (€15) are available on board all their buses, and are valid for 24hr. The most popular departure point is at the top of Avgda d'Antoni Maura, near the cathedral. Citysightseeing buses are particularly useful for visiting the Castell de Bellver (see p.68), which is not served by EMT

bus, otherwise EMT buses (see above) are a much better and less expensive bet.

By horse and carriage One popular way to see central Palma is by horse and carriage. These line up in front of the cathedral with tours costing €30 per carriage for 30min, €50/hour; confirm the price before you canter off. They are not universally popular, however: many feel that the horses get a rough deal.

ACCOMMODATION

Palma's **hotel** scene is experiencing something of a boom, with a string of new, deluxe hotels opening up in the last couple of years. The **Old Town** is the most enticing part of the city and it's here you'll find several of the most distinctive places housed within handsomely converted Renaissance mansions. There's also a cluster of places, both budget and deluxe, along the narrow, cobbled side streets off the **Passeig d'es Born** and a number of more modern mid-range hotels on the **Passeig Mallorca**, an attractive boulevard bisected by a deep and walled watercourse-cum-moat. Finally, modern

1

high-rise hotels, including several plush places, line up to the west of the centre, overlooking the waterfront along **Avgda Gabriel Roca** (also known as the Passeig Marítim).

BOOKING A ROOM

Despite the substantial number of hotels and *hostales*, you still need to book ahead in peak periods, most notably June, early July and September. Surprisingly, things are not usually as busy from the middle of July to late August, when many Spaniards avoid the searing heat of the city, but even so vacant rooms can still be sparse. The city's tourist offices (see p.71) can provide a full list of hotels and *hostales*. Note that many of the budget hotels and *hostales* may have some ropey rooms as well as good ones – if you are not satisfied, insist on a transfer.

CENTRAL PALMA

Hotel Almudaina Avgda Jaume III, 9 **☎**971 72 73 40, **ⓦ**hotelalmudaina.com; map pp.56–57. Dapper modern rooms in one of the attractive 1940s blocks overlooking the city's premier shopping street. It's popular with Spanish business folk, and has great rooftop views from the uppermost floors. **€130**

Hostal Apuntadores c/Apuntadors 8 **☎**971 71 34 91, **ⓦ**hostalapuntadores.com; map pp.56–57. A long-established *hostal* with simple, straightforward rooms in a centrally located old house just off Passeig d'es Born. Some rooms are en suite (€15 extra), others have shared facilities, but light sleepers should bag a room at the back as c/Apuntadors can get very noisy at night. **€60**

★ Hotel Born c/Sant Jaume 3 **☎**971 71 29 42, **ⓦ**hotelborn.com; map pp.56–57. Appealing hotel in an excellent downtown location, set in a refurbished mansion with big wooden doors and a lovely courtyard, where you can have breakfast under the palm trees. The rooms, most of which face onto the courtyard, are not luxurious, but they are comfortable and decorated in a traditional style. It's a popular spot, so book early in high season. **€110**

Can Cera c/Convent Sant Francesc 8 **☎**971 71 22 77, **ⓦ**palausafont.com; map pp.56–57. Deluxe hotel in an immaculately renovated Renaissance mansion in the heart of the Old Town. Each of the thirteen rooms has been kitted out in country-house style, all smooth pastel shades with the occasional piece of period furniture adding character. **€220**

Hotel Ca Sa Padrina c/Tereses 2 **☎**971 42 53 00, **ⓦ**casapadrina.com; map pp.56–57. Run by the owners

of the *Hotel Dalt Murada* (see below), this six-room budget hotel occupies a late nineteenth-century townhouse complete with beamed ceilings and antique Spanish furniture. It's all very pleasant and competitively priced – but there are no staff on site (access is via a pin-coded entry panel) and no breakfast. The location is good, right in the centre of town, albeit in the (sometimes noisy) side streets off the Passeig de la Rambla. **€80**

Hotel Convent de la Missió c/de la Missió 7A **☎**971 22 73 47, **ⓦ**conventdelamissio.com; map pp.56–57. Über-cool, 27-room hotel, whose slick minimalism has been intelligently shoehorned into the wide spaces of a former convent. The location, however, is really rather drab – on a dull side street off c/Sant Miquel. Also home of the headline-hitting *Simply Fosh* restaurant (see p.75). **€180**

★ Hotel Dalt Murada c/Almudaina 6 **☎**971 42 53 00, **ⓦ**daltmurada.com; map pp.56–57. Undoubtedly one of the most characterful hotels in the city, this family-run place occupies a splendid old mansion down a cobbled alley metres from Plaça Cort. The house retains many of its original eighteenth-century – and even earlier – features, and there is a lovely roof terrace with views of the cathedral. The 23 guest rooms are all large and well appointed, and most hold antique furnishings, such as age-old chandeliers and paintings. The pick have balconies overlooking the courtyard, where breakfast is served. **€100**

Hotel H M Jaime III Passeig Mallorca 14 **☎**971 72 59 43, **ⓦ**hmjaimeiii.com; map pp.56–57. Four-star hotel with smart modern rooms kitted out in crisp, minimalist style. The public areas are a little overdone, but that's hardly a major drawback. The guest rooms at the front, overlooking the Passeig Mallorca, have the advantage of a balcony, but try to keep to the upper floors away from the noise of the traffic. **€110**

Hotel Palacio Ca Sa Galesa c/Miramar 8 **☎**971 71 54 00, **ⓦ**palaciocasagalesa.com; map pp.56–57. Charmingly refurbished seventeenth-century mansion set among the narrow alleys of the oldest part of town, with just twelve luxurious and tastefully furnished rooms and suites. There's an indoor heated swimming pool (set in a renovated Roman bath) and fine views of the city from the rooftop terrace. Opened in the early 1990s, this was one of the first deluxe hotels to occupy an old island mansion and its success has set something of a trend. **€250**

Posada Terra Santa c/Posada Terra Santa 5 **☎**971 21 47 42, **ⓦ**posadaterrasanta.com; map pp.56–57. Chi-chi four-star hotel in a sympathetically modernized Renaissance mansion on the northern edge of the Old Town. The rooms are decorated in crisp modern style – and the hotel has all mod cons, including a spa. Great beakfasts, too. **€250**

PALMA'S TOP 5 HOTELS

Hotel Araxa See opposite
Hotel Born See above
Hotel Dalt Murada See above
Hotel Santa Clara See opposite
Hotel Saratoga See opposite

Hotel Puro Oasis Montenegro 12 ☎971 42 54 50, ⓦpurohotel.com; map pp.56–57. Self-conscious designer hotel in an old house among the narrow side streets west of the Passeig d'es Born. Aimed at the "hip" city dweller, it has details such as rugs on the ceiling, cushions on the floor, and ambient music in the public areas. As you might expect, the guest rooms are similarly slick and modish. **€270**

Hotel San Lorenzo c/Sant Llorenç 14 ☎971 72 82 00, ⓦhotelsanlorenzo.com; map pp.56–57. Among the somewhat careworn lanes of what was once the fishermen's quarter of Sant Pere, this chichi four-star hotel has been cleverly squeezed into a seventeenth-century mansion. The antique details have been lovingly preserved, while all mod cons, including a swimming pool in the garden, have been tastefully added. **€170**

★**Hotel Santa Clara** c/Sant Alonso 16 ☎971 72 92 31, ⓦsantaclarahotel.es; map 000–000. In an intriguing corner of the Old Town, this four-star hotel occupies an old stone mansion, but the interior has been remodelled to accommodate ultra-modern rooms of sharp and crisp design with the occasional flourish from what went before – wooden beams and stone walls etc. **€180**

★**Hotel Saratoga** Passeig Mallorca 6 ☎971 72 72 40, ⓦhotelsaratoga.es; map pp.56–57. Bright, modern, centrally located hotel in a tidy seven-storey block complete with a garden and rooftop swimming pools. The rooms are neat and trim, with marble floors and balconies either overlooking the boulevard (which can be noisy) or an interior courtyard (much quieter). Substantial banquet-breakfasts too. **€150**

Hostal Terminus Plaça d'Espanya 5 ☎971 75 00 14, ⓦterminushostal.com; map pp.56–57. Two-star establishment with a quirkily old-fashioned foyer and reasonably large but distinctly frugal rooms beyond – en-suite rooms cost an extra €10. Very handy for the Palma–Sóller train station, but also within earshot of the traffic-clogged inner ring road. **€55**

OUTSIDE THE CENTRE

★**Hotel Araxa** c/Pilar Juncosa 22 ☎971 73 16 40, ⓦhotelaraxa.com; map pp.48–49. Attractive four-storey, three-star modern hotel with pleasant gardens and an outdoor swimming pool, located in a quiet residential area about 2km west of the centre, not far from the Castell de Bellver. Most of the rooms, which are decorated in comfortable modern style, have balconies. To get there by public transport, take EMT bus #3 from Plaça d'Espanya and get off at c/Marquès de la Sènia, just before the start of Avgda Joan Miró; it's a 10min walk from the bus stop. **€100**

Hotel Catalonia Majórica c/Garita 3 ☎971 40 02 61, ⓦhoteles-catalonia.com; map pp.48–49. Big, modern four-star hotel overlooking the coast, with some 170 rooms kitted out in brisk and efficient chain-hotel style – ask for a room with a sea view. About 4km west of the centre, it's handy for the ferry port and reasonably priced. **€130**

Hotel Feliz Avgda Joan Miró 74 ☎971 28 88 47, ⓦhotelfeliz.com; map pp.48–49. The *Feliz* occupies a well-kept, tastefully kitted-out modern block 3km west of the centre, at the junction of Avgda Joan Miró and c/Patrimoni. There are forty-odd guest rooms, some with sea-facing balconies, and each is decorated in shades of white and cream interspersed with bold splashes of colour. The hotel also has a cool lounge-bar, an outside pool, a rooftop sun terrace and a mini-library. On EMT bus route #3, giving access to several points in the city, including Plaça Joan Carles I. **€100**

Hotel Melià Palas Atenea Avgda Gabriel Roca 29 ☎971 28 14 00 or ☎0808 234 1953, ⓦmelia.com; map pp.48–49. A vast, really rather classy 1960s-style foyer, which looks like it has been imported from Las Vegas, leads to attractively furnished, comfortable rooms with balconies overlooking the bay. **€160**

EATING AND DRINKING

There's more gastronomic variety in Palma than anywhere else in Mallorca, with **cafés**, **tapas bars** and **restaurants** liberally distributed around the city centre and its immediate suburbs. There's a particular concentration in the main tourist zone, among the side streets just to the west of the **Passeig d'es Born** and **Avgda d'Antoni Maura**, and others in the **Old Town** and on and around the Passeig Mallorca.

PRICES

There's often little distinction between these cafés, tapas bars and restaurants – after all, put a couple of tapas together and you've got a full meal – and the differences often have more to do with appearance than food: if you've got a tablecloth, for instance, you're almost certainly in a restaurant. At all but the most expensive restaurants, €20/€25 should cover the price of a main course in the evening, and you can usually cut costs by opting for a lunchtime *menú del día*. Tapas can cost as little

as €5 per dish, and should never be more than €14. Multilingual menus are commonplace, though we have also provided a menu reader at the back of the Guide to help you identify some of the dishes you may come across (see pp.281–284).

CAFÉS AND TAPAS BARS

Bar Bosch Plaça Rei Joan Carles I, 6 ☎971 72 11 31, ⓦbarbosch.es; map pp.56–57. One of the most popular and inexpensive tapas bars in town, the traditional haunt of the city's intellectuals and usually humming with conversation. At peak times you'll need to be assertive to get served. Tapas from €5. Daily 8am–1am.

Bon Lloc c/Sant Feliu 7 ☎971 71 86 17, ✎bonlloc restaurant.com; map pp.56–57. One of the few vegetarian café-restaurants on the island, with good food at low prices – and an informal, homely atmosphere in old and pleasant wood-beamed premises; mains at around €11. Mon–Sat 1–4pm & Thurs–Sat 8–11pm.

Café Lirico Avgda d'Antoni Maura 6 ☎971 72 11 25; map pp.56–57. For better or worse, most of Palma's downtown cafés have been modernized, but this old stalwart has kept progress pretty much at bay, its old photos, mirrors, imitation marble and weather-beaten clientele reminiscent of Spanish cafés of yesteryear. A good place for coffee and a Spanish brandy. Daily 8am–midnight.

Café Gran Hotel Plaça Weyler 3 ☎638 38 23 33; map pp.56–57. Set on the ground floor of the eponymous hotel, a handsome *Modernista* building of 1903, this trim, modern café makes a good spot for coffee and a snack, with tables inside or out on a pleasant little square. Tapas from €5. Mon–Wed 9am–9pm, Thurs–Sat 9am–11pm, Sun 9am–3pm.

★**Ca'n Joan de S'Aigo** c/Can Sanç 10 ☎971 71 07 59, ✎www.canjoandesaigo.webs-sites.com; map pp.56–57. Long-established coffee house offering wonderful, freshly baked *ensaimadas* (spiral pastry buns), the thickest, richest hot chocolate imaginable, and the best fruit-flavoured mousses south of Barcelona. Charming decor too, from the kitschy water fountain to the traditional Mallorcan green-tinted chandeliers. On a narrow alley near Plaça Santa Eulalia. Daily 8am–9pm.

Cappuccino Palau March c/Conquistador 13 ☎971 71 72 72, ✎grupocappuccino.com; map pp.56–57. Occupying the lower part of the Palau March, this attractive terrace café (one of a small but growing island chain) offers nicely presented burgers and sandwiches (€10–15) and salads. Service is attentive, the furnishings and fittings slick and the soundtrack jazzy and housey, all of which contribute to making this a very popular spot. Daily 8.30am–midnight.

Es Rebost Café Avgda Jaume III, 20 ☎971 71 00 00, ✎es-rebost.com; map pp.56–57. Straightforward self-service café offering authentic Balearic cuisine, made from local ingredients wherever possible – try the *Panzanella Mallorquina* of tomatoes, roasted red peppers, olives and cheese. Tapas from €7. Daily 9am–9pm.

Gaudí Café Plaça de la Quartera 5 ☎606 45 79 00; map pp.56–57. Plain and straightforward Sa Gerrería haunt with a graffiti wall and an über-casual-meets-careworn look. Also serves tapas (from €6), which you can devour either inside or outside on the pavement terrace. Mon–Fri noon–11pm, Sat noon–4pm.

★**La Bodeguilla** c/Sant Jaume 3 ☎971 71 82 74, ✎la-bodeguilla.com; map pp.56–57. Located in a glossily refurbished old townhouse just off Avgda Jaume III, this smart and intimate esablishment is divided into a restaurant and a wine-cum-tapas bar. It's the tapas bar you want, offering a tasty range of tapas from €10: try, for example, the oxtail cannelloni in a red wine sauce. Daily noon–11pm.

La Molienda c/Bisbe Campins 11 ☎661 73 40 92, ✎lamolienda.es; map pp.56–57. On the north side of the city centre, this bright and modern café sells what many think is the best coffee in town. Does a good line in cakes and teas too. Mon–Fri 8am–8pm, Sat 10am–3pm.

★**La Taberna del Caracol** c/Sant Alonso 2 ☎971 71 49 08, ✎tabernacaracol.com; map pp.56–57. Deep in the Old Town, this intimate tapas bar-cum-restaurant occupies charming old premises, all wooden beams and ancient arches. Choose from thirty different sorts of tapas at €5–20 – and look out for the daily market specials. The meatballs are especially tasty and cost just €6.40. Reservations recommended. Mon 7.30–11pm, Tues–Sat noon–3pm & 7.30–11pm.

Orient Express c/Llotja de Mar 6 ☎971 71 11 83; map pp.56–57. Beside Sa Llotja, this idiosyncratic, split-level café-restaurant justifies its name by having an interior like a railway carriage, festooned with a platoon of vintage French advertising posters. Crêpes are the speciality – served every which way and costing €4–10. Mon–Sat 1–4pm & 8pm–midnight.

Toque de Queda c/Can Cavalleria 15B ☎971 21 38 10; map pp.56–57. On the north side of the city centre, in old premises that once served as a bakery, this excellent tapas bar specializes in local platters of meat and cheese (from €8) with a variety of breads. Mon–Fri 5.30–11.30pm, Sat 12.30–4.30pm & 6.30–11.30pm.

RESTAURANTS

Caballito del Mar Passeig de Sagrera 5 ☎971 72 10 74, ✎caballitodemar.info; map pp.56–57. There was a time when this harbourside restaurant served the best seafood in town; this isn't really the case today, but it does excel with its house speciality – the *daurada amb sal al forn* (sea bream baked in salt) – and it continues to attract well-heeled holidaymakers. The terrace is the place to eat here as the interior is surprisingly glum. Metres from Sa Llotja. Main courses average €25, but the extras soon mount up. Reservations well-nigh essential. Daily 1–11pm.

★**Celler Pagès** c/Felip Bauza 2, off c/Apuntadors at ☎971 72 60 36; map pp.56–57. Small, intimate and well-established restaurant in a pleasantly decorated, two-room basement with an easy-going family atmosphere. It serves traditional Mallorcan food – try the stuffed marrows with home-made mayonnaise on the side, the delicious roast leg of duck with dried plums and grilled vegetables or the tongue with capers. Mains are a real bargain here, from just €12. Reservations advised. Mon–Sat 1–3.30pm & Tues–Sat 8–11pm.

Forn de Sant Joan c/Sant Joan 4 ☎971 72 84 22, ⓦforndesantjoan.com; map pp.56–57. Set in an old bakery, this extremely popular restaurant may be something of a tourist trap, but it does offer a wide-ranging menu – anything from cannelloni to kangaroo. Main courses average about €25, the tapas €15 – try the red peppers stuffed with shellfish, followed by a lemon and cinnamon mousse. It's bang in the centre of the city's nightlife area, so get ready for the crowds. Daily 1–4pm & 6.30–11.30pm.

Las Olas Bistro c/Can Fortuny 5 ☎971 21 49 05, ⓦlasolasbistro.com; map pp.56–57. Cosy, very informal family-run restaurant that serves an inventive mix of Vietnamese/Cambodian and French/Mediterranean dishes: try, for example, the wonton soup followed by bream in a rich sauce with beans and rice. Main courses cost as little as €10, tapas €6. Mon–Sat 12.30–4pm & Wed–Sat 8.30–11pm.

MISA Braseria Can Maçanet 1 ☎971 59 53 01, ⓦmisabraseria.com; map pp.56–57. In the deluxe *Mision de San Miquel Hotel*, this smart, brasserie-style restaurant – part of the Marc Fosh group – offers a shortish but creative menu with a Spanish twist; try the hake with saffron parmentier and tomato compote. It's all first rate – but the portions are a bit stingy. Mains range from €18–28. Mon–Sat 1–3.30pm & 7.30–10pm.

Ottimo Passeig Mallorca 16 ☎871 71 34 09, ⓦottimo -restaurante.com; map pp.56–57. In a prime location, with an attractive pavement terrace beneath the arches of the *passeig*, this neat and modern Italian restaurant offers a creative menu covering all the classics – spaghetti and so forth – and then some: try, for example, the oxtail ravioli or the octopus carpaccio. The fish of the day costs €25. Mon–Sat noon–4pm & 7–11pm, Sun noon–4pm.

★**Peix Vermell** c/Montenegro 1 ☎971 07 93 74, ⓦpeixvermell.com; map pp.56–57. Make no mistake, this is the city's finest seafood restaurant, a noticeably friendly place in tastefully converted old premises – one room is stone-vaulted, the other wood-beamed. Starters average €8, mains €22 – choose from hake, wolffish, turbot, sole and all their friends. Daily 1–11pm.

Simply Fosh Hotel Convent de la Missió, c/de la Missió 7A ☎971 72 01 14, ⓦsimplyfosh.com; map pp.56–57. Taking its name from one of Mallorca's leading chefs, Marc Fosh, this top-notch restaurant has garnered lavish praise from all and sundry. The premises are super-cool/very minimalist and you can eat either inside or on the shaded terrace. Food is light, well balanced and finely flavoured with local, seasonal ingredients to the fore. Try such delights as smoked ham in a pea and truffle broth or pork belly with orange and rosemary. A three-course set lunch costs an affordable €24, but in the evenings you'll have to stump up much more. Great service too. Reservations essential. Daily 1–3.30pm & 7.30–10.30pm.

Trattoria Sant Ambros Plaça Coll 11 ☎971 72 52 26; map pp.56–57. There's a *Sant Ambros* café on one side of this little square, the trattoria on the other. The trattoria menu covers all the Italian classics, and although the food isn't great, it is inexpensive (pizzas from €9), and Plaça Coll, on the edge of the Sa Gerrería neighbourhood, is a great place to savour the city. Mon–Sat noon–4pm & 7.30–11pm.

NIGHTLIFE AND ENTERTAINMENT

LATE-NIGHT BARS

Most of the cafés and tapas bars that we've reviewed are happy to ply you with drink until midnight or beyond, but there is also a cluster of lively late-night bars – mostly with music as the backdrop rather than the main event – among the narrow and ancient side streets backing onto Plaça Llotja. This is, however, the main tourist zone, and if you're after close encounters with the Catalans, then one good bet is the huddle of bars in the Sa Gerrería neighbourhood, just southeast of Plaça Major. Sa Gerrería has a relaxed, informal vibe – the area is popular with students, but if it's high heels and bronzed pecs you're after, there are a number of much more modish bars west of the centre, dotted along Avgda Gabriel Roca in the vicinity of the Jardins La Quarentena.

Abaco c/Sant Joan 1 ☎971 71 49 39, ⓦbar-abaco.es; map pp.56–57. Set in a charming old mansion in the city centre, just off c/Apuntadors, this is Palma's most unusual bar, with an interior straight out of a Busby Berkeley musical: fruits cascading down its stairway, caged birds hidden amid patio foliage, elegant music and a daily flower bill you could live on for a month. Drinks, as you might imagine, are expensive (cocktails cost as much as €20), but you're never hurried into buying one. It is, however, rather too sedate to be much fun if you're up for a big night out. Mon–Thurs & Sun 8pm–1am, Fri & Sat 8pm–3am.

Bar España c/Can Escursac 12 ☎971 72 42 34; map pp.56–57. In the side streets just southwest of the Plaça Major – and a little hard to find – this funky café-bar serves a good line in tapas, and spicy tapas (Mexican, Thai) to boot. A popular spot, so best to arrive early or late. Mon–Sat 7.30pm–12.30am.

Bar Flexas c/Llotgeta 12 ☎971 42 59 38, ⓦbarflexas .com; map pp.56–57. Enough to make Franco turn in his grave, this might well be the most idiosyncratic – even weird – bar in the Sa Gerrería neighbourhood. The tiled bar is a vintage relic; the furniture rickety-rackety; the modern paintings on the wall are eye-catching – but the phallic toys are perhaps a step too far. Snacks and light meals, but this is really a place to drink. Great website too. Mon–Sat noon–12.30am.

1

Ca La Seu c/Corderia 17 ☎871 57 21 57; map pp.56–57. One of the grooviest spots in the Sa Gerrería neighbourhood, this café-cum-bar occupies high-ceilinged premises that were formerly an ever-so-traditional rope and twine shop. The tapas are cheap and filling, at just €2–5 each. Mon–Fri 8pm–1am.

Es Baluard Restaurant & Lounge Plaça Porta Santa Catalina s/n ☎871 23 49 54, ⓦrestaurantesbaluard.com; map pp.56–57. In a spectacular setting, overlooking the waterfront from the top of the bastion it shares with the Es Baluard gallery (see p.65), this combined lounge and restaurant looks great – but the restaurant isn't and you're better off coming here for a drink. Sink into a rattan chair and admire the view. Daily 10am–1am.

Escape Bar Plaça Draçana 13 ☎971 72 49 68; map pp.56–57. Friendly little café-bar, and always lively, located just off a square that gets busier and groovier every year. Has a boho, international feel from breakfast time through to the wee hours. Mon 5pm–1am, Tues–Thurs 10am–1am, Fri & Sat 10am–3am, Sun 10am–1am.

Jazz Voyeur Club c/Apuntadors 5 ☎971 72 07 80, ⓦjazzvoyeur.com; map pp.56–57. Pocket-sized jazz club in the heart of the city, metres from Sa Llotja. Live sounds most nights – check the website for who's coming when. Daily 8.30pm–1am.

La Lonja c/Llotja de Mar 2 ☎971 72 27 99; map pp.56–57. A popular, well-established haunt, with revolving doors and pleasantly old-fashioned decor; the background music caters for (almost) all tastes and you can sit outside in the square – right in front of one of the city's most handsome buildings, Sa Llotja. Mon–Sat 8am–1am.

CLUBS

Along the waterfront, a kilometre or two west of the centre, Avgda Gabriel Roca hums at night with fashionable locals dressed to the nines, the main pull being its several nightclubs (*discotecas*). Clubs are not perhaps Palma's forte, but there are certainly enough to be going on with, though they are rarely worth investigating until around 1am. Entry charges cost anything up to €20, depending on the night and what's happening, although admission is sometimes free. The door staff mostly operate an informal dress code of one sort or another – if you want to get in, avoid beach gear and (heaven forbid) white trainers. There is a modest range of gay clubs and bars in the somewhat careworn suburb of El Terreno, about 3km west of the centre below the Castell de Bellver, but the scene is something of a moveable feast, so check out ⓦmallorcagaymap.com for the latest news.

El Garito Dàrsena de Can Barbarà s/n ☎971 73 69 12, ⓦgaritocafe.com; map pp.48–49. Cool club that caters for all musical tastes, from house to disco classics, with regular live bands too. West of the centre, just off Avgda Joan Miró. June–Sept daily 8pm–4am; Oct–May Thurs–Sat 8pm–4am.

Pacha Avgda Gabriel Roca 42 ☎687 57 01 02, ⓦpachamallorca.es; map pp.48–49. This loud, popular and raucous superclub has a gyrating dancefloor and several bars inside, as well as a bar outside in the garden. A 10min walk west of the Jardins La Quarentena – and 800m east of the ferry terminal. July & Aug daily 11pm–6am; rest of the year Thurs–Sat 11pm–6am.

Tito's Avgda Gabriel Roca 31 ☎971 73 00 17, ⓦtitos mallorca.com; map pp.48–49. With its stainless-steel and glass exterior, this long-established nightspot looks a bit like something from a sci-fi film. Outdoor lifts carry you up from the entrance on Avgda Gabriel Roca to the dancefloor, which pulls in huge crowds from many countries – or you can go in through the entrance on Plaça Gomila. The music (anything from house to mainstream pop) lacks conviction, but it's certainly loud. The Avgda Gabriel Roca entrance is just on the city-centre side of the Jardins La Quarentena. June to early Sept daily 11.30pm–5am; rest of the year Fri & Sat 11.30pm–6am.

PERFORMING ARTS

Palma puts on a busy cultural programme during the summer, staged both in the open air and in the city's brace of major performing arts venues. Top spots for open-air performances are the Parc de la Mar, just below the cathedral, and the Castell de Bellver (see p.68). Ask at the tourist office (see p.71) for details of upcoming events.

Auditorium de Palma Avgda Gabriel Roça 18 ☎971 73 47 35, ⓦauditoriumpalma.com; map pp.48–49. Large, modern harbourfront auditorium used both for conferences and for a range of performing arts – opera, ballet, theatre, etc – often by visiting troupes from far and wide.

Teatre Principal c/Riera 2A ☎971 21 96 96, ⓦteatreprincipal.com; map pp.56–57. Housed in a grand nineteenth-century building, whose tympanum sports a relief dedicated to the nine Muses of Greek mythology, Palma's main performing arts venue offers a mixed bag of classical concerts, opera, theatre, dance and cabaret. Gala nights here are some of the biggest social events on the island.

SPECTATOR SPORTS: FOOTBALL

Mallorca's premier football team is Real Club Deportivo Mallorca (ⓦrcdmallorca.es), but they aren't having a good time at the moment – they were relegated from La Liga (the First Division) after the 2012–13 season. They play at the Iberostar Estadi on the north side of town. Check the website for fixture details.

1

SIURRELS

Though somewhat out of favour today, **siurells** are a Palma speciality. White clay whistles flecked with red and green paint and shaped to depict a figure, an animal or a scene (a man sitting on a donkey, for instance), *siurells* were traditionally given as tokens of friendship in Mallorca. Although the custom has faded away, you might want to pick up one as a souvenir – after all, Miró is said to have been inspired by them. You'll come across them all over the place, but mostly in more traditional shops, and they only cost a few euros each.

SHOPPING

Like every other big city in Spain, Palma has its share of multinational stores and most of them have extended opening hours, whereas the smaller, more local companies sometimes still stick to the traditional norm and close for a siesta in the afternoon. Two of the city's perennial favourite purchases are **Mallorcan wine**, which is sold at most large supermarkets and a number of specialist stores, and **artificial pearls**, an island speciality (see p.171). The largest manufacturer of these pearls is Majorica (w majorica.com), whose products are on sale at scores of outlets across the city, including El Corte Inglés (see below). A third favourite is **shoes** – Mallorca and Menorca have had a shoe industry since the early twentieth century, and the most famous local manufacturer is Camper.

ARTS AND CRAFTS
Vidrieras Gordiola c/Victoria 2 ☎ 971 71 15 41; map pp.56–57. Glass-making is a traditional island craft and *Vidrieras Gordiola*, near the Ajuntament, has a fine range of clear and tinted glassware, from bowls, vases and lanterns through to some wonderfully intricate chandeliers. Mon–Fri 10.15am–1.45pm & 4.30–8pm, Sat 10.15am–1.45pm.

BOOKS AND MAPS
Fine Books c/Morei 7 ☎ 971 72 37 97; map pp.56–57. There's nothing quite like this English-owned and -run bookshop elsewhere in Palma – or for that matter in the whole of the Balearics: a secondhand bookshop whose interior heaves with dishevelled tomes on every subject under the sun. Great for browsing. Mon–Fri 9am–7pm, Sat 9am–4pm, Sun 9am–1pm.
La Casa del Mapa c/Sant Domingo 11 ☎ 971 22 59 45; map pp.56–57. In the mini-arcade below c/Conquistador, this is easily the best map shop in town, part funded by the city council and with a wide selection of town, cycling and hiking maps covering every corner of Mallorca. Mon 9.30am–2pm, Tues–Fri 9.30am–7pm.

CLOTHES AND SHOES
Apart from the more individual shops described below, there's also a gaggle of international-brand and designer clothes shops on and around Avgda Jaume III and the Passeig d'es Born – Plaça Rei Joan Carles I, for example, has two Zaras, an H&M and a Loewe.
Bluebird c/Unió 2A ☎ 971 71 69 90, w bluebird-palma .com; map pp.56–57. Nicely turned out women's store selling a wide range of designer clothes, often at discount prices. Mon–Sat 10am–6pm.
Camper Avgda Jaume III, 5 ☎ 971 71 46 35, w camper .com; map pp.56–57. Fashionable and extremely popular, Camper shoes are made in Mallorca, but the company now

has an international reach, with outlets all over the world. They have several stores in Palma, but this is the most central and it carries a wide range of their footwear. Mon–Sat 10am–8.30pm.
Carmina c/Unio 4 ☎ 971 22 90 47, w carmina shoemaker.com; map pp.56–57. Mallorca has a long tradition of shoe-making. The Carmina company is at the top end of the men's market, with shops in several European capitals and one here, right in the city centre. The shoes begin at €250, which is a fair old heft, but there's no disputing the quality. Mon–Sat 10am–6pm.
S'Avarca Sant Domingo 14 ☎ 971 712 058; map pp.56–57. Neat and trim little shop located in the mini-arcade below c/Conquistador and offering a wide selection of S'Avarca, the simple but stylish leather sandals made in Menorca. Mon–Sat 10.30am–8.30pm.

DEPARTMENT STORE
★ **El Corte Inglés** Avgda Jaume III, 15 ☎ 971 77 01 77, w elcorteingles.es; map pp.56–57. The biggest and best department store in the city centre, selling just about everything you can think of, including all the familiar fashion and electronic brands. In the basement, there is a first-rate food and drinks section with an especially wide range of both Spanish and Mallorcan wine, all at competitive prices – a top-notch Binissalem red costs about €16. The book section sells a small and rather eccentric assortment of English-language titles from Ken Follett to Anne Frank alongside a modest selection of Mallorca guidebooks and maps. Mon–Sat 9.30am–9.30pm, Sun 11am–8.30pm.

FOOD AND DRINK
Colmado La Montaña c/Jaime II, 27 ☎ 971 71 25 95; map pp.56–57. Aladdin's cave of a place, a little more adventurous than the Colmado Santo Domingo (see p.78), with an excellent range of Mallorcan produce: garlic,

1

honey, *ensaimadas*, cheeses and, of course, sausage. Mon–Sat 10am–6pm.

Colmado Santo Domingo c/Sant Domingo 1 ☏ 971 71 48 87, ⓦ colmadosantodomingo.com; map pp.56–57. This tiny, cave-like, old-fashioned store is packed with hanging sausages and local fruit and veg; it's right in the city centre, metres from Plaça Cort. The sausages to try carry the "Sobrasada de Mallorca de Cerdo Negro" label, which guarantees they are made from the island's own indigenous black pig. Mon–Sat 10.30am–8pm.

Forn Fondo c/Unió 15 ☏ 971 71 16 34; map pp.56–57. Palma has a platoon of good cake and pastry shops (*pastelerías*) and this is certainly one of the best – the fig cake (*higos* in Castilian) is especially delicious for starters. They also sell tasty chocolates and the freshly baked *ensaimadas* (spiral pastry buns) that are so much a feature of island life. Daily 8am–8pm.

★**Son Vivot** Plaça Porta Pintada 1 ☏ 971 72 07 48, ⓦ sonvivotpalma.com; map pp.56–57. Exemplary shop specializing in Balearic produce and products; more than 300 items, from honeys and jams to olives, cheeses, Sobrasada black pork sausages and liqueurs. Also has an especially fine selection of Mallorcan wines. Mon–Sat 9.45am–8.30pm.

MARKETS

Ecological market Plaça Bisbe Berenguer de Palou; map pp.56–57. A showcase for local producers, this busy and flourishing market is loaded up with organic fruit, vegetables, oils, jams and so forth. Health-food stalls, too. Sat 8am–2pm.

Flower market Passeig de la Rambla; map pp.56–57. Shaded by plane trees, this open-air flower market stretches out along the *passeig*, its long line of stalls popular with locals and expats alike. Mon–Fri 8am–2pm & 5–8pm, Sat 8am–2pm.

★**Mercat Municipal de l'Olivar** Plaça de l'Olivar ☏ 971 72 03 14, ⓦ mercatolivar.com; map pp.56–57. The city's main covered market is a flourishing affair, jam-packed with good-quality stalls selling all the island's varied produce, from sausages to cheese, olives to tomatoes. The separate fish section is simply superb. Mon–Thurs & Sat 7am–2pm, Fri 7am–8pm.

Rastrillo Avgda Gabriel Alomar i Villalonga, between Plaça Porta d'es Camp and c/Manacor; map pp.56–57. Palma's biggest open-air flea market takes place weekly, but nowadays it's the atmosphere that appeals rather more than the stalls, which mainly sell tat. Sat 8am–2pm.

DIRECTORY

Banks and exchange There are plenty of banks on and around the Passeig d'es Born and Avgda Jaume III. ATMs are similarly commonplace – there is one on Passeig d'es Born at the foot of c/Estanc and another near the top of Passeig d'es Born at the foot of c/Can Brondo.

Consulates Ireland, c/Sant Miquel 68A ☏ 971 71 92 44; UK, c/Convent dels Caputxins 4 ☏ 971 71 24 45.

Doctors and dentists Most hotel receptions will be able to find an English-speaking doctor or dentist. For complete lists look under *metges* (Castilian, *médicos*) or *clíniques dentals* (*clínicas dentales*) in the Yellow Pages (ⓦ paginasamarillas.es).

Emergencies ☏ 112.

Library There's a quaint old municipal library inside the Ajuntament (Town Hall) on Plaça Cort (Mon–Fri 8.30am–8.30pm, Sat 9am–1pm).

Pharmacies Farmacia Buades, Plaça Rei Joan Carles I, 3 (daily 8.30am–10.30pm; ☏ 971 71 15 34), is centrally located. For a full list of pharmacies, see Yellow Pages (ⓦ paginasamarillas.es) under *farmàcies* (Castilian *farmacias*).

Post office The central *correos/correu* is at c/Constitució 5 (Mon–Fri 8.30am–8.30pm, Sat 9.30am–1pm).

Around Palma

Spread around the sheltered waters of the **Badía de Palma** are the package tourist resorts that have made Mallorca synonymous with the cheap and tacky. In recent years the Balearic government has done its best to improve matters – greening resorts, restricting high-rise construction and redirecting traffic away from the coast – but their inherited problems remain. In the 1960s and 1970s, the bay experienced a **building boom** of almost unimaginable proportions as miles of pristine shoreline sprouted concrete-and-glass hotel towers, overwhelming the area's farms and fishing villages. There were few planning controls, if any, and the legacy is the mammoth sprawl of development that now extends, almost without interruption, for 30km along the coast from **S'Arenal** in the east to **Magaluf** in the west – with Palma roughly in the middle. To make matters worse, it is also debatable as to whether the recent move away from high-rise construction is well conceived. The villa complexes that are now the fashion gobble up

PLATJA DE PALMA, S'ARENAL (P.84) >

1

the land at an alarming rate and multiply traffic. Furthermore, although the new villas are rarely more than three storeys high and built in a sort of pan-Mediterranean style, they end up looking remorselessly suburban. As a consequence, although this stretch of coast is divided into a score or more resorts, it's often impossible to pick out where one ends and the next begins. That said, most of the resorts have evolved their own identities, in terms of the nationalities they attract, the income group they appeal to, or the age range they cater for. And, amid the aesthetic gloom, there are a couple of noteworthy attractions – primarily the one-time home and studio of **Joan Miró** – as well as a clutch of appealing hotels and a string of excellent **beaches**.

West of Palma

West of Palma, the coast bubbles up into the low, rocky hills and sharp coves that prefigure the mountains further west. The sandy **beaches** here are very small – and some are actually artificial – but the terrain makes the tourist development seem less oppressive. **Cala Major**, the first stop, was once the playground of the jet set. It's grittier today, but some of the grand old buildings have survived and the **Fundació Pilar i Joan Miró**, which exhibits a fine selection of Miró's work, makes an enjoyable detour. The neighbouring resort of **Illetes** is more polished, boasting comfortable hotels and attractive cove beaches, and is the best place to stay in the area, especially when compared with its westerly neighbours: **Portals Nous**, known hereabouts for its swanky marina; **Palma Nova**, a major package holiday destination popular with Brits; and **Magaluf**, where the modern high-rise hotels, thumping nightlife and substantial sandy beach cater to a youthful and very British crowd. West of Magaluf, the coastal highway leaves the Badia de Palma for large and sprawling **Santa Ponça** before pushing on to **Peguera**, a rambling resort with attractive sandy beaches and a relaxed family atmosphere. Next door – and much more endearing – is tiny **Cala Fornells**, where pretty villas thread along the coastal hills and a brace of first-rate hotels overlooks a wooded cove – and concrete-slab beaches, which are not (quite) as bad as they sound. The development is fairly restrained here and, if you're after a straightforward resort holiday on this part of the coast, this is as good as it gets. From Cala Fornells, it's another short hop to the good-looking bay that encloses the burgeoning resort of **Camp de Mar**.

Cala Major

Beginning just a couple of kilometres to the west of Palma's ferry port, cramped and crowded **CALA MAJOR** snakes its way along a hilly stretch of coastline bisected by its main street (the Ma-1C). This modest, modern pile-up is brightened by the occasional *Modernista* building, reminders of halcyon days when Cala Major was a byword for elegance – hence the ritzy, coast-hugging *Hotel Nixe Palace* (see p.84), restored after years of neglect and now the finest hotel hereabouts by a long chalk. There's also a royal palace, the **Palacio de Marivent**, and although it's not open to the public, you can glimpse it from the main street – it's beside the Ma-1C at the east end of the resort.

Fundació Pilar i Joan Miró

C/Joan de Saridakis 29, Cala Major • Mid-May to mid-Sept Tues–Sat 10am–7pm, Sun 10am–3pm; mid-Sept to mid-May Tues–Sat 10am–6pm, Sun 10am–3pm • €6 • ☎ 971 70 14 20, ⓦ miro.palmademallorca.es • The Fundació is signed off the main Ma-1C road as it weaves through Cala Major, and EMT bus #46 from central Palma (every 20–30min) stops 100m below the entrance

One of Mallorca's most enjoyable attractions, the **Fundació Pilar i Joan Miró** was where the painter **Joan Miró** (1893–1983) lived and worked for much of the 1950s, 1960s and 1970s. Initially – from 1920 – the young Miró was involved with the **Surrealists** in Paris and contributed to all their major exhibitions: his wild squiggles, supercharged with bright colours, prompted André Breton, the leading theorist of the movement, to describe Miró as "the most Surrealist of us all". In the 1930s he adopted a simpler style, abandoning the decorative complexity of his earlier work for a more minimalist use of

---

TOP 5 SANDY BEACHES AROUND PALMA

Camp de Mar 83
Magaluf See p.82
Palma Nova See p.82

Peguera See p.83
Platja de Palma See p.84

---

symbols, though the highly coloured forms remained. Miró returned to Barcelona, the city of his birth, in 1940, where he continued to work in the Surrealist tradition, though as an avowed opponent of Franco his position was uneasy. In 1957 he moved to Mallorca, its relative isolation offering a degree of safety. His wife and mother were both Mallorcan, which must have influenced his decision, as did the chance to work in his own purpose-built studio with its view of the coast. Even from the relative isolation of Franco's Spain he remained an influential figure, prepared to experiment with all kinds of media, right up until his death here in Cala Major in 1983.

The Edifici Moneo

The expansive hillside premises of the Fundació fan out from the **Edifici Moneo**, an angular modern gallery which displays a rotating and representative sample of the artist's work. Miró was nothing if not prolific, and the Fundació owns 134 paintings, 300 engravings and 105 drawings, as well as sculptures, gouaches and preliminary sketches – more than six thousand works in all. There are no guarantees as to what will be on display, but you're likely to see a decent selection of his paintings, most notably the familiar dream-like squiggles and half-recognizable shapes that are intended to conjure up the unconscious, with free play often given to erotic associations. The gallery also hosts temporary exhibitions of modern and contemporary art, which are often well reviewed.

Taller Sert

From the Edifici Moneo, it's a brief stroll up to the **Taller Sert** (Sert Workshop), a striking Modernist structure with a roof partly shaped like seagull wings. The workshop takes its name from the architect who designed it, Josep Sert, but this was very much Miró's studio, and was where he spent a large slice of his life. The interior has been left pretty much as it was at the time of the artist's death and it certainly gives the flavour of how the man worked – tackling a dozen or so canvases at any one time.

Son Boter

Just beyond the Taller Sert, **Son Boter** is a traditional Mallorcan farmhouse dating from the seventeenth century. Miró bought the place in 1959 and used it as a reserve studio for some of his larger compositions. He also doodled on the walls and his graffiti has survived intact – and a delightful sample of his work it is too.

Illetes

Busy **ILLETES**, just off the Ma-1C immediately to the west of Cala Major, spreads along the coast, its ribbon of restaurants, hotels and apartment buildings bestriding the steep hills that rise high above a rocky shoreline. A string of tiny cove beaches punctuates the coast here, the most attractive being the pine-shaded **Platja Cala Comtesa**, right at the southern end of the resort.

Portals Nous

Nudging tight against the coast to the west of Illetes, **PORTALS NOUS** is a ritzy settlement where polished mansions fill out the green and hilly terrain between the coast and the dull and drab main street (Ma-1C). There's a tiny **beach**, set beneath the cliffs and reached via a flight of steps at the foot of c/Passatge del Mar, but the main draw is the **marina**, one of Mallorca's most exclusive, where the boats look more like

1

ocean liners than pleasure yachts. What you make of all this glitz and the flock of celebrities that it attracts is very much a matter of taste (and politics), but the marina is certainly a lively spot.

Marineland Mallorca

C/Garcilaso de la Vega 9, Costa d'en Blanes • Late March to Oct daily 9.30am–5.30pm • €24, children (1.1–1.4m) €14, children (0.9–1.1m) €10 • ☎ 971 67 51 25, ⓦ marineland.es/mallorca

All the fun of the fair – or to be more accurate a nautical theme park – is here at **Marineland**, from performing dolphins and seals to a shark aquarium, penguins, stingrays and pelicans. Young children love the place; adults mostly suffer in silence. Marineland is in Costa d'en Blanes, the westerly extension of Portals Nous.

Palma Nova

Old Mallorca hands claim that **PALMA NOVA**, 4km west of Portals Nous, was once a beauty spot, and certainly its wide and shallow bay, with its excellent beaches and pine-clad headlands, still has its moments. Nevertheless, for the most part, the bay has simply been engulfed by a broad, congested sweep of tourist facilities – and with the development has come a vigorous (mainly British) nightlife, its participants issuing out from a platoon of hotels on or near the seashore.

Calvià

Tucked away in the hills behind the coast, about 7km north of Palma Nova, is the tiny town of **CALVIÀ**, the region's administrative centre – hence the oversized town hall, paid for by the profits of the tourist industry. The parish church of **Sant Joan Baptista** is the town's key building, a large and much modified thirteenth-century structure whose Gothic subtleties mostly disappeared during a nineteenth-century refurbishment – hence the crude bas-relief carving of the Garden of Gethsemane above the main door. There are pleasant views across the surrounding countryside from outside the church, and the adjacent square is home to a modern mural showing a neat depiction of the island's history.

Magaluf

Torre Nova, on the chunky headland at the far end of Palma Nova, is a cramped and untidy development that slides into **MAGALUF**, whose high-rise towers march across the next bay down the coast. For years a cheap-as-chips package holiday destination, Magaluf finally lost patience with its youthful British visitors in 1996. The local authorities won a court order allowing them to demolish twenty downmarket hotels in an attempt to end the annual binge of "violence, drunkenness and open-air sex" that, they argued, characterized the resort. The high-rise hotels were duly dynamited and an extensive clean-up programme freshened up the resort's appearance. These draconian measures have brought some improvement, but the resort's British visitors remain steadfastly determined to create, or at least patronize, a bizarre caricature of their homeland: it's all here, from beans on toast with Marmite to endless supplies of lager.

Western Water Park

Carretera Cala Figuera a Sa Porrasa (Ma-1, Exit 14) • Late May, June & Sept daily 10am–5pm; July & Aug daily 10am–6pm • Adults €26.50; children (1.1–1.4m) €18.50, children (0.9–1.1m) €10 • ☎ 971 13 12 03, ⓦ westernpark.com

Stuck on the western edge of Magaluf, **Western Water Park** contrives to weld together a replica Wild West town – one of the most incongruous sights in Spain – with a platoon of water rides and water chutes. It's all very odd, but very popular.

Santa Ponça

West of Magaluf, the Ma-1 trims the outskirts of **SANTA PONÇA**, one of the less endearing of the resorts that punctuate this stretch of coast. Mostly a product of the 1980s, this sprawling conurbation has abandoned the concrete high-rises of yesteryear for a pseudo-vernacular architecture that has littered the hills with suburban-looking villas. More positively, the setting is attractive, with rolling hills flanking a broad bay, and the resort's white sandy beaches offer safe bathing.

Peguera
PEGUERA, about 6km northwest of Santa Ponça, strings out along a lengthy, partly pedestrianized main street – the Avinguda Peguera – immediately behind several generous sandy beaches. There's nothing remarkable about the place, but it does have an easy-going air and is a favourite with families and older visitors. The Ma-1 loops right round Peguera, and the easiest approach, if you're just after the **beach**, is from the south. Head into the resort along the main street and park anywhere you can before you reach the pedestrianized zone, where the town's baffling one-way system sends you weaving through the resort's side streets – best avoided, if possible.

Cala Fornells
Next door to Peguera, the much prettier – and much smaller – resort of **CALA FORNELLS** is reached via either of two signed turnings on the Avinguda Peguera just to the west of the pedestrianized centre. Take the more easterly turning – along Carretera Cala Fornells – and the road climbs up to a string of chic, *pueblo*-style houses that perch on the sea cliffs and trail round to the tiny centre of the resort, where a wooded cove is set around a minuscule beach and concreted sunbathing slabs. Although Cala Fornells tends to be overcrowded during the daytime, at night the tranquillity returns, and it makes a good base for a holiday, especially as it has a particularly appealing hotel (see p.84).

Camp de Mar
Mushrooming **CAMP DE MAR**, which flanks a hilly cove just 3km west of Peguera, has an expansive beach and fine bathing, though the scene is marred by the presence of several thumping great buildings dropped on the seashore. Camp de Mar and its surroundings are also in the throes of a massive expansion, with brand-new villa complexes trailing back from the beach in an all-too-familiar semi-suburban sprawl. All the same, the **beach** is an amiable spot to soak up the sun, and it's hard to resist the eccentric café stuck out in the bay and approached via a rickety walkway on stilts. A minor road twists a scenic route west from Camp de Mar over wooded hills to **Port d'Andratx** (see p.123).

ARRIVAL AND DEPARTURE   WEST OF PALMA

By bus Bus services along the coast west from Palma are fast and frequent. The nearer resorts (Cala Major and Illetes) are served by EMT (see p.71), with buses departing from several points in central Palma. The resorts to the west of Illetes are served by several other bus companies, but almost all services start and terminate at Palma's main bus station, the Estació Intermodal, off Plaça d'Espanya. There's a transport information desk at the Estació. Alternatively,

check ⓦ tib.org, or call ☎ 971 17 77 77 (Spanish or Catalan only).

Destinations Palma to: Cala Major (EMT #3: every 10–20min; 15min); Calvià (every 2hr; 40min); Camp de Mar (1–2 hourly; 1hr); Illetes (EMT #3; every 10–20min; 20min); Magaluf (1–2 hourly; 1hr); Palma Nova (1–2 hourly; 55min); Peguera (1–2 hourly; 1hr 30min); Portals Nous (1–2 hourly; 45min); Santa Ponça (1–2 hourly; 1hr 15min).

ACCOMMODATION

Taken together, the Badía de Palma resorts have scores of **hotels**, as well as *hostales* and apartment buildings, but it's still a good idea to book ahead of time in the peak season – say June to early September; out of season, many places simply close down. We've selected five of the more interesting and enjoyable hotels, but really the options seem almost limitless.

BENDINAT
Hotel Bendinat c/Andrés Ferret Sobral 1, off Avinguda de Bendinat ☎ 971 67 57 25, ⓦ hotelbendinat.es. Once the country estate of Spanish aristocrats, Bendinat is now a

well-heeled residential area, much quieter than its neighbours – Portals Nous to the west and Illetes to the east. It's also home to the three-star *Bendinat*, dating from the 1950s and built in the traditional *hacienda* style with a

1

charming arcaded terrace overlooking a secluded rocky cove, a spa and multiple pools. In decor, the 54 rooms vary from the traditional to the modern – and are, perhaps, not quite as good as the lovely coastal setting. March to Oct. **€250**

CALA FORNELLS
Cala Fornells Carretera Cala Fornells 76 ☏ 971 68 69 50, ⓦ calafornells.com. In a handsome location on a hill looking straight out to sea, this charming, modern hotel has around a hundred well-appointed guest rooms as well as indoor and outdoor pools, fitness facilities and a sauna. Be sure to get a room with sea view and balcony. **€160**

CALA MAJOR
Hotel Nixe Palace Avgda Joan Miro 269 ☏ 971 70 08 88, ⓦ hotelmallorcanixepalace.com. There was a time when this grand hotel was the chichi haunt of socialites, and although those days are long gone – and the furnishings and fittings now lack a little élan – it's still a

handsome building with Art Nouveau flourishes, wide sun terraces and its very own sandy cove beach. **€250**

ILLETES
Hotel Bon Sol Passeig de Illetes 30 ☏ 971 40 21 11, ⓦ hotelbonsol.es. This popular, long-established hotel spreads down the hillside in the heart of Illetes in a sort of pan-Andalucian style that is really rather appealing. The interior has a stately, country-house feel, the gardens are lush and the hotel's assorted terraces tumble down the cliffs to the seashore – and its own little cove beach. **€180**

PORTALS NOUS
H10 Punta Negra c/Punta Negra 12 ☏ 971 68 07 62, ⓦ h10hotels.com. Spread over two rugged coves beside crystal-clear waters, this deluxe, four-star, 135-room resort boasts a fine location and every modern facility. It's just south of the old coastal road, the Ma-1C, 3km west of Portals Nous. **€270**

East of Palma

The **Ma-19** coastal motorway clips **east** out of Palma, with tourist resorts on one side and the airport on the other. The flatlands backing onto the coast were once prime agricultural land, hence the multitude of ruined **windmills**, built to pump water out of the marshy topsoil and now gaunt reminders of earlier, more pastoral, times. The alternative route, along the **old coastal road**, is a bit more interesting and a lot slower: take the turning off the motorway just beyond the city walls (signposted to Ca'n Pastilla) and follow the road as it tracks through a series of resorts, beginning with **Es Portixol**, once down at heel but now really rather pleasant. Thereafter, things get distinctly dull – and the route east is easy to lose – but ultimately you reach **Ca'n Pastilla**, the first substantial tourist resort on this part of the coast, its fifty-odd hotels and apartment buildings set in a rough rectangle of land pushed tight against the seashore. The place is short on charm and certainly too close to the airport for sonic comfort, but it does herald the start of the fine **Platja de Palma beach**, which stretches round to **S'Arenal** in a great sandy arc. Make no mistake, the **beach** is superb, but the flat shoreline behind it accommodates an unprepossessing, seemingly interminable strip of cheap restaurants and souvenir shops with dozens of pounding bars and all-night clubs mainly geared up for young German tourists.

Es Portixol
ES PORTIXOL, just a couple of kilometres east of Palma Cathedral, was once the preserve of local fishermen, who docked their boats at its brace of sheltered coves. The district hit the skids in the 1960s, but is now championed as an exemplar of urban renewal, its terrace houses all cleaned and dusted, one cove turned into a marina, the other into a tiny beach resort.

The Platja de Palma
Beyond Ca'n Pastilla lies the **Platja de Palma**, the 4km stretch of sandy beach that defines the three coterminous (and indistinguishable) resorts of **SOMETIMES**, **SES MARAVELLES** and **S'ARENAL**. The beach here is crowded with serious sun-seekers, a sweating throng of bronzed and oiled bodies slowly roasting in the heat. It's also a busy pick-up place, the spot for a touch of verbal foreplay before the night-time bingeing begins. It is, as they

say, fine if you like that sort of thing – though older visitors can't help but look marooned. A wide and pleasant walkway lined with palm trees runs behind the beach and this, in turn, is edged by a long sequence of bars, restaurants and souvenir shops. A toy-town tourist "train" shuttles up and down the walkway, but there's so little to distinguish one part of the beach from another that it's easy to become disoriented. To maintain your bearings, keep an eye out for the series of smart, stainless-steel beach bars, each numbered and labelled "*balneario*", that are dotted along the seashore.

Palma Aquarium

C/Manuela de los Herreros i Sorà 21, Ca'n Pastilla (Ma-19, Exit 10) • Daily 10am–6pm • €24, children (4–12yrs) €14 • ☎ 902 70 29 02, ⓦ palmaaquarium.com • EMT bus #23 stops outside

A watery world with bells and whistles, **Palma Aquarium**, at the western end of the Platja de Palma, has around fifty tanks displaying sea creatures in various marine habitats, including a Tropical Sea, a Mediterranean Sea, a tank full of jellyfish and the "Big Blue", the deepest shark tank in Europe. In addition, there's a jungle area, a mock-up of an old sailing ship, and a play area that will appeal to most young children.

Aqualand

Ma-19, Exit 13 • Daily: late May, June & late Sept 10am–5pm; July & Aug 10am–6pm • €28, children (1.1–1.4m) €18.50, children (0.9–1.1m) €8 • ☎ 971 44 00 00, ⓦ aqualand.es • EMT bus #23 stops outside

A huge leisure complex of swimming pools, water flumes and children's playgrounds, **Aqualand** is Mallorca's largest waterpark, and is located on the eastern edge of S'Arenal, about 15km east of Palma. One of the chutes resembles a wriggling snake, another features a giant dragon – and it's all great fun for the kids.

ARRIVAL AND DEPARTURE   **EAST OF PALMA**

By bus EMT (see p.71) bus #15 runs every 10–20min from central Palma to Es Portixol (25min) and S'Arenal (45min).

ACCOMMODATION

ES PORTIXOL

Hotel Portixol c/Sirena 27 ☎971 27 18 00, ⓦ portixol.com. This high-rise, seafront hotel in the creatively revamped former fishing village of Es Portixol is a very urban and urbane spot, with all sorts of finessed details, from creative backlighting through to guest-room TV cabinets that look like mini beach huts. It's all good fun, but if you're paying this much, it's worth splashing out the extra €90 for a room with a sea view. There's an outside swimming pool and a restaurant, where you can dine either inside or outside looking out over the ocean. **€290**

Western Mallorca

91 Sóller

96 Port de Sóller

99 Biniaraix

99 Fornalutx

100 Jardins d'Alfàbia

102 Raixa

103 Bunyola to Alaró

105 Deià

109 Son Marroig

111 Miramar

111 Valldemossa

118 Port de Valldemossa

118 La Granja

119 Esporles

120 Banyalbufar

121 Estellencs

122 Andratx

122 Sant Elm and around

123 Port d'Andratx

DEIÀ

Western Mallorca

2

Western Mallorca "Presents to the delighted eye a charming blend of savage wilderness and fertile cultivation. In no part of the world can one behold a more complete picture gallery of all the varieties of natural scenery," wrote Captain Clayton as he wandered the region in the 1860s. And no wonder: few would argue that Mallorca is at its scenic best in the gnarled ridge of the Serra de Tramuntana, the imposing mountain range that stretches the length of the island's northwestern shore, its rearing peaks and plunging sea cliffs intermittently punctuated by valleys of olive and citrus groves.

Midway along and cramped by the mountains is **Sóller**, an antiquated merchants' town that serves as a charming introduction to the region, especially when reached on the vintage narrow-gauge **train line** from Palma. From Sóller, it's a short hop down to the coast to **Port de Sóller**, a one-time port and fishing village that has become a popular resort set around a deep and handsome bay: this geographical arrangement – the town located a few kilometres inland from its port – is repeated across Mallorca, a reminder of more troubled times when marauding corsairs forced the islanders to live away from the coast. Nearby, the mountain valleys in the vicinity of Sóller were once remote and isolated, but today they shelter three bucolic stone-built villages – **Biniaraix**, **Fornalutx** and **Orient** – and two of the island's finest gardens, the oasis-like **Jardins d'Alfàbia** and the Italianate terraces of **Raixa**.

Southwest of Sóller, the principal coastal road, the **Ma-10**, threads up through the mountains to the amenable village of **Deià**, tucked at the base of formidable cliffs and famous as the former home of Robert Graves, whose old house and studio are now open to the public. Beyond lies the magnificent Carthusian monastery of **Valldemossa**, whose shadowy cloisters briefly accommodated George Sand and Frédéric Chopin in the 1830s; and the *hacienda* of **La Granja**, another compelling if perhaps over-visited stop. Continuing southwest, the Ma-10 wriggles high above the shoreline, slipping through a sequence of mountain hamlets, of which **Banyalbufar** and **Estellencs** are the most picturesque, their tightly terraced fields tumbling down the coastal cliffs. A few kilometres further and you leave the coast behind, drifting inland out of the mountains and into the foothills that precede the market town of **Andratx**. Beyond, on Mallorca's western tip, lies the underrated mini-resort of **Sant Elm**, where you can hike out into the mountains or catch the boat to **Sa Dragonera**, a humpy island nature reserve with both hiking trails and an abundant bird life. Nearby are the safe waters of **Port d'Andratx**, a medium-sized resort and sailing centre draped around a handsome inlet, its villas announcing the start of the intense tourist development that eats up the coast eastwards to Palma.

Vintage trains and trams: Palma to
  Sóller and Port de Sóller p.93
Sa Fira i Es Firó p.95
Walks around Biniaraix p.99
Irritated islanders p.103
Robert Graves in Deià p.107
Western Mallorca's best beaches p.109

The ups and downs of the Archduke
  Ludwig Salvator p.110
George Sand at Valldemossa p.113
A circular hike from Valldemossa to Puig
  d'es Teix by the Archduke's path p.116
The hike to La Trapa p.122

Highlights

❶ Sóller This delightful town boasts handsome stone mansions, a dinky main square and an exquisite setting amid craggy mountains. **See p.91**

❷ Palma-Sóller train Ride the antique train over the mountains from Palma to Sóller for a charming introduction to the island's jagged, rearing mountains. **See p.93**

❸ Jardins d'Alfàbia First established by the Moors, these are the finest gardens in Mallorca, with lush trellises and terraces leading to the sweetest of lily-choked pools. **See p.100**

❹ Deià One of Mallorca's most engaging villages, where a huddle of ancient stone houses

is set against a spectacular mountain backdrop. **See p.105**

❺ Valldemossa Monastery The old stone town of Valldemossa zeroes in on its splendid medieval monastery, whose echoing cloisters once sheltered George Sand and Frédéric Chopin. **See p.111**

❻ Hiking in the Serra de Tramuntana Crisscrossed by scores of exhilarating trails, the rugged mountains that range along the length of the island's northwest shore offer the finest hiking in the Balearics. **See p.99, p.116 & p.122**

HIGHLIGHTS ARE MARKED ON THE MAP ON P.90

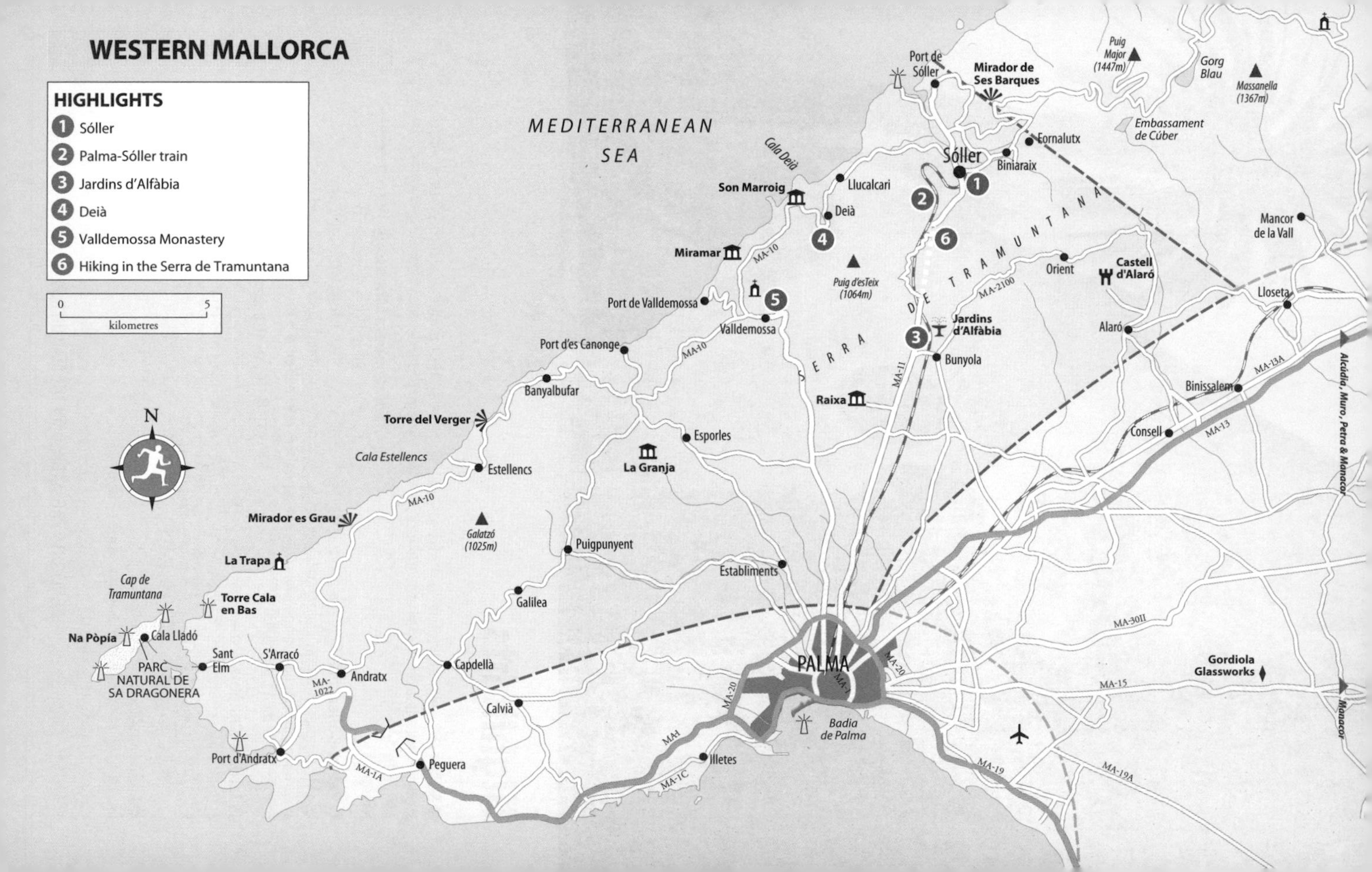

WESTERN MALLORCA

HIGHLIGHTS

1. Sóller
2. Palma–Sóller train
3. Jardins d'Alfàbia
4. Deià
5. Valldemossa Monastery
6. Hiking in the Serra de Tramuntana

N

0   5
kilometres

MEDITERRANEAN SEA

Alcúdia, Muro, Petra & Manacor

Manacor

Massanella (1367m)

Gorg Blau

Embassament de Cúber

Puig Major (1447m)

Mancor de la Vall

Lloseta

Binissalem

Consell

Gordiola Glassworks

Castell d'Alaró

Alaró

Orient

Fornalutx

Biniaraix

Mirador de Ses Barques

Sóller

Port de Sóller

Jardins d'Alfàbia

Bunyola

PALMA

Badia de Palma

Illetes

Lluc-alcari

Deià

Puig des Teix (1064m)

Raixa

SERRA DE TRAMUNTANA

Cala Deià

Son Marroig

Miramar

Valldemossa

Port de Valldemossa

Establiments

Esporles

La Granja

Puigpunyent

Galilea

Calvià

Capdellà

Peguera

Port des Canonge

Banyalbufar

Estellencs

Galatzó (1025m)

Andratx

Torre del Verger

Cala Estellencs

Mirador es Grau

La Trapa

Torre Cala en Bas

Sant Elm

S'Arracó

Port d'Andratx

Cap de Tramuntana

Cala Lladó

Na Popia

PARC NATURAL DE SA DRAGONERA

MA-10

MA-11

MA-13

MA-13A

MA-2130

MA-20

MA-1

MA-19

MA-19A

MA-15

MA-3011

MA-1C

MA-1A

MA-1032

MA-10

GETTING AROUND
WESTERN MALLORCA

By car Several fast roads link Palma with the northwest coast. The prettiest – the Ma-1110 – runs to Valldemossa, and a delightful network of country roads patterns the foothills, but the key sights and the best scenery are most readily reached along the main coastal road, the Ma-10. Distances are small – from Andratx to Sóller via the Ma-10 is only about 60km – and the roads are good.

Parking Right along the coast, parking can be a real pain: all the villages hereabouts have small car parks, but in summer finding a space between about 10am or 11am and 5pm can be problematic. Parking is easier in Sóller, the largest town on this stretch of the coast, though its one-way system is tricky to negotiate.

By train Vintage trains run along the line from Palma to Sóller (see box, p.93).

By bus There is a regular bus service from Palma to Sóller and Port de Sóller via either the tunnel or Valldemossa and Deià. Another bus runs from Palma to Esporles, La Granja, Banyalbufar and Estellencs. There are also fast and frequent buses from Palma to Andratx and Port d'Andratx. The only major gaps are along the Ma-10 coast road between Estellencs and Andratx and between Banyalbufar and Valldemossa. For timetable details, check ⓦ tib.org.

By taxi Distances between destinations are short, so taxis can be a reasonable proposition, especially if you're in a group. Fixed-rate tariffs apply – for example, Deià to Valldemossa costs €20, Sóller to Deià €22, and Port de Sóller to Port d'Andratx €70.

HIKING

The Serra de Tramuntana mountains provide the finest hiking on Mallorca, with scores of hiking trails latticing the mountains. There are trails to suit all aptitudes and levels of enthusiasm, from the easiest of strolls to the most gruelling of long-distance treks, and generally speaking paths are reasonably well marked, though apt to be clogged with thorn bushes.

Trails The region is crossed by Mallorca's main long-distance hiking trail, the Ruta de Pedra en Sec (Dry-stone Route, the GR221), which begins in Sant Elm and threads its way through the mountains to Sóller before proceeding on to Pollença (see p.136). Note, however, that the GR221 varies in quality, with only two sections in Western Mallorca currently in tip-top condition: Deià to Sóller and Es Capdellà to Estellencs.

Hostels There are two hikers' hostels (*refugis*; ⓦ consellde mallorca.net) on the Sant Elm–Sóller section of the GR221 – one each at Deià (see p.109) and Port de Sóller (see p.98).

Guides and maps Hiking guides and maps are best purchased before you arrive (see p.35), though you can buy Editorial Alpina's *Walking Paradise: Sóller*, with trail notes and map (1:15,000) in Sóller (see p.94).

Sóller

One of the most laidback and enjoyable towns on Mallorca, beguiling **SÓLLER** lies at the end of the vintage train line from Palma, and makes an ideal and inexpensive base for exploring the Serra de Tramuntana. Rather than any specific sight, it's the general flavour of the town that appeals, with its narrow, sloping lanes cramped and crimped by eighteenth- and nineteenth-century **stone houses** adorned with fancy grilles and big wooden doors – the former dwellings of the area's wealthy fruit merchants. A scattering of low-key attractions fills out a stroll around the town, though hikers will soon want to head off into the surrounding mountains, often via **Biniaraix**, a picturesque hamlet just a short walk east of town.

Sóller train station

Plaça Espanya • Exhibition rooms daily 10.30am–6.30pm • Free

Sóller **train station** is a handsome building, its imposing, *hacienda*-like facade and wide stone staircases witnessing the days when it was crucial to the town's merchants. One of the station's most famous visitors was **Joan Miró** – his maternal grandfather came from Sóller – and the main station hall sports a couple of large **photos** of the artist in the company of **Picasso**, the former looking rather crumpled when compared with his handsome friend, surely one of the few men in the world to be able to wear sandals and socks and still look ineffably groovy. Five of the station's rooms have been turned into **exhibition areas** – two displaying a selection of cheery, sometimes tongue-in-cheek ceramics by Picasso and three for the flamboyant squiggles of his friend, Miró.

2

Plaça Constitució

St Bartomeu June–Oct Mon–Fri 11am–6pm, Sat 11am–1.30pm & Sun noon–1pm; Nov–May Mon–Fri 11am–1.15pm & 3–5pm, Sat 11am–1.30pm • Free

In Sóller, all streets lead to the main square, **Plaça Constitució**, an informal, pint-sized affair of big old plane trees, crowded cafés and grouchy mopeds – all within shouting distance of the train station. The square is dominated by the hulking mass of the church of **St Bartomeu**, a crude but somehow rather fetching neo-Gothic remodelling of a medieval original, with a couple of Art Nouveau flourishes thrown in for good measure. Its most appealing features are the enormous and precisely carved rose window stuck high in the main facade and the heavy-duty but apparently pointless balustrade above it. Inside, the cavernous, barrel-vaulted nave is suitably dark and gloomy, the penitential home of a string of gaudy Baroque altarpieces.

Next door, and almost equally striking, is the **Banco de Sóller**, now the Banco Santander, which occupies a *Modernista* extravagance, sheathed in a coat of roughly dressed stone and adorned by miniature balconies and wrought-iron grilles. It was designed by the prolific **Joan Rubió** (1870–1952), a Gaudí acolyte, who was responsible for a string of buildings in Barcelona as well finding time to be an archeologist and politician. Also of interest, and close by at c/Sa Lluna 16, is **Can Prohom** (no access), a grand eighteenth-century mansion with massive wooden doors and overhanging eaves; it was here in this traditional townhouse that the district's landed gentry used to bed down when they dropped into town.

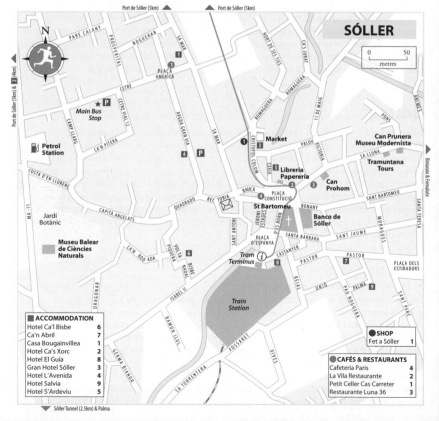

■ ACCOMMODATION	
Hotel Ca'l Bisbe	6
Ca'n Abril	7
Casa Bougainvillea	1
Hotel Ca's Xorc	2
Hotel El Guía	8
Gran Hotel Sóller	3
Hotel L'Avenida	4
Hotel Salvia	9
Hotel S'Ardeviu	5

● SHOP	
Fet a Sóller	1

● CAFÉS & RESTAURANTS	
Cafeteria Paris	4
La Vila Restaurante	2
Petit Celler Cas Carreter	1
Restaurante Luna 36	3

VINTAGE TRAINS AND TRAMS: PALMA TO SÓLLER AND PORT DE SÓLLER

The 28km **train journey** from Palma to Sóller is a delight, dipping and cutting through the mountains and fertile valleys of the **Serra de Tramuntana**. The line was completed in 1911 on the profits of the orange and lemon trade: the railway was built to transport the fruit to Palma, at a time when it took a full day to make the trip by road. The rolling stock is tremendously atmospheric too, with narrow carriages – the gauge is only 914mm – that look like something from an Agatha Christie novel, though frankly it is rather a clanky, bumpy ride. Once past the scratchy suburbs of Palma, the train runs across pancake-flat farmland with the impenetrable-looking peaks of the Serra de Tramuntana dead ahead. After a short stop at **Bunyola**, the train threads upwards to spend five minutes tunnelling through the mountains, where the noisy engine and dimly lit carriages give the feel of a roller-coaster ride. Beyond, out in the bright mountain air, are the steep valleys and craggy thousand-metre peaks at the heart of the Serra de Tramuntana, and everywhere there are almond groves, vivid with blossom in January and February. From the terminus at Sóller train station, **vintage trams**, some of which date from 1912, grind their way down to the coast at Port de Sóller, 5km away. For tram and train schedule and prices, see below.

Can Prunera Museu Modernista

c/Sa Lluna 86 • March–Oct daily 10.30am–6.30pm; Nov–Feb Tues–Sun 10.30am–6.30pm • €5 • ☎ 971 63 89 73, ⓦ canprunera.com

As well as Sóller's Banco de Sóller (see opposite), Joan Rubió was responsible for the fanciful stone facade of **Can Prunera**. Finished in 1911, this is another fine example of **Modernista** architecture, built for a well-heeled family of fruit growers named, appropriately enough, the Plums. In private hands until 2006, the mansion has now been turned into a museum, whose two lower floors are distinguished by their graceful *Modernista* furnishings and fittings, with a splendid circular stairway rounding things off. The top floor holds paintings by a wide range of artists, both foreign and Spanish – though for the most part they are lesser pieces.

Museu Balear de Ciències Naturals and Jardí Botànic

Carretera Palma–Port de Sóller s/n • March–Oct Mon–Sat 10am–6pm; Nov–Feb Tues–Sat 10am–2pm • €8 • ☎ 971 63 40 14, ⓦ museucienciesnaturals.org & ⓦ jardibotanicdesoller.org

In an old merchant's villa, the mildly diverting **Museu Balear de Ciències Naturals** (Balearic Museum of Natural Sciences) hosts a series of modest displays, with the **permanent collection** on the first two floors and temporary exhibitions on the top floor up above. The former begins with a fairly good section on the leading botanists of yesteryear, including Archduke Ludwig Salvator (see p.110), and continues with an assortment of island fossils and rocks. The labelling is in Catalan, but English leaflets are available in each room.

Outside, the neat and trim **Jardí Botànic** rolls down the hillside, divided into a dozen or so small areas, half of which (M1–M6) are dedicated to Balearic species, including dune and sea-cliff species in M2, shade-loving plants in M4, and mountain plants in M5. A free English-language brochure identifying and illustrating many of the plants is issued at the main gate for both the house and the gardens.

ARRIVAL AND DEPARTURE   SÓLLER

BY TRAIN

Sóller train station The station is in the centre of town on Plaça d'Espanya. From April to October, there are 6 vintage trains daily from Palma to Sóller, and 5 back from Sóller to Palma; from November to March, there are 4 trains daily in each direction. The journey takes just under 1hr and a one-

way ticket costs €15, a return €21. For further information, call ☎ 971 75 20 51, or check ⓦ trendesoller.com.

BY TRAM

Sóller tram terminus Trams terminate outside the train station, on Plaça d'Espanya. Vintage trams link Sóller and

2

Port de Sóller every 30min (daily 8am–8.30pm), a clanking 20min journey that costs an exorbitant €5.50 each way – pay the conductor.

BY BUS

Sóller's main bus stop Almost all long-distance buses pull in to the mini-bus station on the northwest side of the centre, just off the Ma-11 on c/Cetre; from here, it's a 5- to 10min walk to Plaça Constitució. Note that buses travelling east along the coast to LLuc or Pollença are often full; to be sure of a seat, it's best to get on down in Port de Sóller, where the service originates. Note also that the fastest Palma–Sóller buses use the Ma-11 – and its tunnel – while the slower, more scenic service runs via Deià and Valldemossa. And finally, note that there are no buses from Sóller to points west along the coast beyond Valldemossa. Bus timetables are online at ⓦ tib.org.

Destinations Biniaraix (Mon–Fri 4 daily, Sat 2 daily; 10min); Deià (5–7 daily; 25min); Fornalutx (Mon–Fri 4 daily, Sat 2 daily; 15min); Lluc (April–Oct Mon–Sat 2 daily; 1hr); Palma (via the tunnel: Mon–Fri hourly, Sat 8 daily, Sun 5 daily; 30min); Palma via Valldemossa (5–7 daily; 1hr 30min); Pollença (April–Oct Mon–Sat 2 daily; 1hr 35min); Port de Pollença (April–Oct Mon–Sat 2 daily; 1hr 50min);

Port de Sóller (Mon–Fri hourly, Sat & Sun every 1–2hr; 10min); Valldemossa (5–7 daily; 55min).

BY CAR

The Ma-11 Fast and straight, the Ma-11 cuts across Mallorca from Palma to Sóller, tunnelling straight through the mountains as it approaches its destination. The 27km journey takes about 30min, and the tunnel, which is 3023m long and ends 2.5km from the centre of Sóller, costs €5 per car. Note that cyclists are not allowed to use the tunnel on account of the vehicle fumes.

The Ma-11A You can avoid the tunnel – and the toll – by taking the scenic route over the mountains: as you near the tunnel entrance, follow the signs for the Ma-11A, a minor road that hairpins its way up and over the mountains in fine style. En route, there are splendid views out along the coast at the Coll de Sóller, a rocky pass with a lookout point – the whole detour only adds 7km to the journey, and takes about 20min.

Parking On-street parking in Sóller is almost impossible – especially as the town's streets are very narrow and the one-way system byzantine. There's a car park behind the main bus stop on c/Cetre and a more central (unpaved) car park off Avgda Gran Via. There's rarely a problem finding a vacant slot at either.

GETTING AROUND

By taxi There's a taxi rank beside the tourist office, – and outside the train station on Plaça d'Espanya; alternatively, call ☏ 971 63 84 84. The fixed-rate tariff to Port de Sóller is €8, the same to Biniaraix.

By bike Bike rental is available from Tramuntana Tours,

c/Sa Lluna 72 (☏ 971 63 24 23, ⓦ tramuntanatours.com). They have several different types of bike, with the least expensive costing €14 per day; advance reservations are recommended. They also have an outlet in Port de Sóller (see p.97).

INFORMATION

Tourist office Sóller's cramped tourist office is in an old train carriage just outside the train station in the middle of Plaça d'Espanya (Mon–Fri 10am–2pm & 3–5pm, Sat & Sun 10am–1pm; ☏ 971 63 80 08, ⓦ www.ajsoller.net). They have a limited range of local information, including bus

and train timetables, and issue free town maps.

Maps For local hiking maps, go to the Libreria Papereria bookshop, on Plaça Constitució. The latest and best map is Editorial Alpina's *Walking Paradise: Sóller* (1:15,000), which costs about €12.

ACTIVITIES

Outdoor pursuits Tramuntana Tours, c/Sa Lluna 72 (Mon–Fri 9.30am–1.30pm & 3.30–7.30pm, Sat 9.30am–1.30pm; ☏ 971 63 24 23, ⓦ tramuntanatours .com), runs mountain-bike tours, canyoning, fishing trips, sea-kayaking and a range of guided day-hikes to suit most aptitudes. There are, for example, medium-to-difficult guided walks to the Puig d'es Teix (16km) and up

the Barranc de Biniaraix (17km); a difficult clamber down the Torrent de Pareis gorge (8km); and an easy jaunt round the Sóller valley (7km). Costs vary, but reckon on a minimum of €25 per trip per person. Transport is provided to and from the trailhead as required and the operators will, within reason, collect hikers from where they are staying.

ACCOMMODATION

★**Hotel Ca'l Bisbe** Bisbe Nadal 10 ☏ 971 63 12 28, ⓦ hotelcalbisbe.com. This appealing, four-star hotel occupies a creatively refurbished former bishop's palace, complete with beamed ceilings, pool and garden. Each of the 25 guest rooms is generously appointed, unfussily decorated

in a bright modern style and with every mod con. The best rooms also have smashing views out towards the mountains. Reservations well in advance are advised. **€150**

Ca'n Abril c/Pastor 26 ☏ 971 63 35 79, ⓦ hotel-can -abril-soller.com. In a sympthetically modernized old town-house on a side street just to the east of the main square, this competitively priced hotel has family rooms, suites and ordinary doubles in a variety of attractive modern designs. Breakfast can be taken outside in the garden patio. €125

Casa Bougainvillea c/Sa Mar 81 ☎971 63 31 04, Ⓦcasa-bougainvillea.com. An enjoyable B&B that occupies an old and intelligently refurbished three-storey terrace house on a busy side street a short walk from Plaça Constitució. There are eight guest rooms, all en suite, and each is decorated in a pleasingly straightforward style. Weather permitting, breakfast is served in the garden, where guests can idle away their time reading and relaxing. €120

★**Hotel Ca's Xorc** Carretera Sóller–Deià (Ma-10: Km 56.1) ☎971 63 82 80, Ⓦcasxorc.com. Located high in the hills, about 4km west of Sóller, this superb hotel occupies a renovated old olive mill in which each of the fifteen guest rooms has been decorated in sleek modern style. There's an outside pool and handsome terraced gardens, and the food is fabulous, featuring local ingredients and variations on traditional Mallorcan dishes. Reservations well nigh essential. €210

Hotel El Guía c/Castanyer 2 ☎971 63 02 27, Ⓦsollernet.com/elguia. This long-established, family-run place is really rather engaging. Set behind a pretty little courtyard, the hotel's layout and decor are very traditional, and although the guest rooms are a tad spartan, they are perfectly adequate and spotlessly clean. Great location, too – just 2min from the train station: turn right at the station entrance. Closed mid-Nov to late March. €95

Gran Hotel Sóller c/Romaguera 18 ☎971 63 86 86, Ⓦgranhotelsoller.com. There are four good things about this five-star hotel: the central location; the rooftop pool and breakfast bar; the garden; and the building itself, a grand structure whose *Modernista* flourishes date back to the 1880s – amazingly enough, considering its size, the building started out as a private house. Less positively, the interior has been kitted out in a plush but pedestrian modern style, and although the guest rooms have every convenience, they hardly stir the imagination. €240

Hotel L'Avenida Gran Via 9 ☎971 63 40 75, Ⓦavenida -hotel.com. Swish, deluxe hotel in an extravagant Art Nouveau mansion on what was once the ritziest street in town. The rooms offer every luxury – though the period stuff ends up looking a little gloomy – and there is a pool, a garden and that harbinger of high room rates, a wellness centre. €245

★**Hotel Salvia** c/Palma 18 ☎971 63 49 36, Ⓦhotel salvia.com. The *Salvia* is one of Sóller's smartest small hotels, its six guest rooms cleverly inserted into a fine old stone mansion complete with period furnishings and fittings. There's an outside pool, gardens, a shaded terrace and long views of the surrounding mountains. It's a luxurious spot – and you pay for it. €230

Hotel S'Ardeviu c/Vives 14 ☎971 63 83 26, Ⓦhotel sardeviu.com. Down an unbecoming alley a stone's throw from the main square, the S'Ardeviu is a small, family-run hotel in an intelligently revamped old mansion. Many of the house's original features have been maintained and the bedrooms are smart, comfortable and well appointed. €105

EATING AND DRINKING

Sóller's main square and its immediate surroundings heave with **cafés** and **café-bars**, but although prices are reasonable, the quality of the food on offer is often disappointing. The **restaurant** scene is similarly constrained and although there are one or two good spots, by and large you're much better popping down to Port de Sóller, where there is a whole gaggle of excellent restaurants (see p.98).

Cafeteria Paris Plaça Constitució 4 ☎971 63 19 51. This family-run café may be in standard-issue modern premises, but it serves up the best coffee in town, plus filling snacks and above-average salads from €9. Daily 7am–10pm.

SA FIRA I ES FIRÓ

If you're around Sóller and Port de Sóller in the **second week of May**, be sure to catch the **Sa Fira i Es Firó**, which commemorates the events of May 1561, when a large force of Arab pirates came to a sticky end after sacking Sóller. The Mallorcans had been taken by surprise, but they ambushed and massacred the Arabs as they returned to their ships and took grisly revenge by planting the raiders' heads on stakes. The story – bar decapitations – is played out in chaotic, alcoholic fashion every year at the festival. The re-enactment begins with the arrival of the pirates by boat and continues with fancy-dress Christians and Arabs battling it out through the streets of the port, to the sound of blanks being fired in the air from antique rifles. On the days preceding this knees-up, there are also sporting and cultural events as well as a large, open-air market. The tourist office (see opposite) can give you a rough idea of the schedule of events, plus details of the dances and parties that follow.

La Vila Restaurante Plaça Constitució 14 ☎ 971 63 46 41, ⊕ lavilahotel.com. Occupying the ground floor of a handsome *Modernista* building on the main square, the inside dining area of this restaurant may be a tad gloomy, but the patio seating is more agreeable. The menu is short, but well chosen, the Spanish dishes given an international twist, and there is a good-value fish of the day too. Patchy service − take something to read, just in case. Mains average €20, less at lunch times. Daily: noon−6pm & 7−10.30pm.

Petit Celler Cas Carreter c/Cetre 4 ☎ 971 63 51 33, ⊕ cascarreter.net. Long-established, family-run restaurant in a cleverly recycled old wheelwright's workshop − the large and conspicuous wine-barrel bottoms were added later. Offers a mixture of well-presented Spanish and Mallorcan dishes − try the snails − with mains averaging €15. Daily noon−4pm & 7.30−11pm; closed Dec & Jan.

★ **Restaurante Luna 36** c/Lluna 36 ☎ 628 67 00 02, ⊕ luna36.es. In a narrow-fronted old building that was once a chocolate factory, this excellent restaurant is Sóller's best, and should not be missed. Kitted out in an attractive modern rustic style and with a garden terrace, the *Luna* offers a creative range of tapas as well as traditional Spanish food: the fish of the day is particularly recommended and costs around €25. Mon−Sat 12.30−3pm & 6−10pm.

SHOPPING

Fet a Sóller c/Romaguera 12 ☎ 971 63 50 08, ⊕ fetasoller.com. Sweet little shop, part of a community initiative, selling all things local, including nuts, olives, wine, fruit juices and jam. Attached to an ice-cream parlour, where they sell locally made ice cream in a variety of alarming colours. Daily 10am−9pm.

Port de Sóller

One of the west coast's most popular resorts, family-oriented **PORT DE SÓLLER** has a lovely setting, its wide, horseshoe-shaped bay ringed by forested hills. A decade ago, the place looked tired and sad, but today Port de Sóller is on the up. Traffic has been directed away from the waterfront by means of a tunnel (1290m), private investment has followed in the slipstream of government subsidy, and a string of classy hotels and restaurants has been grafted onto the old fishing jetty and naval base. The only fly in the ointment is the **beach**: a narrow strip of imported sand encircling most of the bay, it's a scrawny affair except at the south end, where the **Platja d'en Repic** just about passes muster.

Port de Sóller makes for a pleasant wander and the **vintage tram** (see p.93), which gambols round the east side of the bay, provides an appealing backcloth. It's also worth making the enjoyable hour-long hike − or brief drive (1.7km) − west to the **lighthouse** (*far*) guarding the cliffs of Cap Gros above the western entrance to the bay. From here, the views out over the wild and rocky coast and back across the harbour are truly magnificent, especially at sunset. There's a narrow surfaced road all the way: from the tram terminus, walk round the southern side of the bay past Platja d'en Repic and keep going, following the signs.

ARRIVAL AND INFORMATION   PORT DE SÓLLER

By bus At present, Port de Sóller does not have a proper bus station, so buses pull in at the stops beside the roundabout at the east end of Camí de Sa Figuera; from here, it's a 5min walk to the waterfront.

Destinations Biniaraix (Mon−Fri 4 daily, Sat 2 daily; 10min); Deià (5−7 daily; 30min); Fornalutx (Mon−Fri 4 daily, Sat 2 daily; 15min); Lluc (April−Oct Mon−Sat 2 daily; 1hr 10min); Palma (via the tunnel: Mon−Fri hourly, Sat 8 daily, Sun 5 daily; 35min; via Valldemossa: 5−7 daily; 1hr 35min); Pollença (April−Oct Mon−Sat 2 daily; 1hr 40min); Port de Pollença (April−Oct Mon−Sat 2 daily; 1hr 50min); Sóller (Mon−Fri hourly, Sat & Sun every 1−2hr; 10min); Valldemossa (5−7 daily; 1hr).

By tram The vintage tram from Sóller (every 30min; 20min; daily 8am−8.30pm) travels along the east side of Port de Sóller bay; the tram terminus is right on the waterfront beside the ferry jetties. The tram costs a pricey €5.50 each way; pay the conductor.

By taxi There are fixed tariffs for taxi fares across the island. From Port de Sóller, these include Deià at €22; Lluc €52; Sóller €8; Palma €44; and Port de Pollença €88.

Tourist information Port de Sóller tourist office is located on the ferry jetty, the Muelle Comercial (Mon−Fri 9.30am−1pm & 3−6pm, Sat 10am−1pm; ☎ 971 63 30 42, ⊕ ajsoller.net).

TOURS AND ACTIVITIES

Boat trips The main boat company is Barcos Azules (☎971 63 01 70, ⓦbarcosazules.com) and their most popular excursion is to Sa Calobra (April–Oct Mon–Sat 2–3 daily in each direction; €25 return). Boats leave from the Muelle Comercial – the boat (not ferry) dock beside the tram terminus.

Inflatables Nàutic Sóller, c/Marina 4 (☎609 35 41 32, ⓦnauticsoller.com), rents out speedboats and kayaks, but their most distinctive offering is their children's inflatables – dig those brightly coloured cars; endless fun.

Tours Tramuntana Tours, Passeig Es Través 12 (mid-Feb to mid-Nov daily 9am–7.30pm; ☎971 63 27 99, ⓦtramuntana tours.com). This well-regarded company has a seasonal outlet here in the port and a larger branch in Sóller (see p.94), and offers mountain-bike tours, canyoning, fishing trips, sea-kayaking and a range of guided day-hikes.

ACCOMMODATION

Most of the port's hotels and *hostales* overlook the bay, and although **rooms** are hard to find in high season, there are usually lots of vacancies the rest of the year. Pleasingly, there are no massive hotel tower blocks round the bay, but rather a ring of 1960s three- to four-storey blocks, several of which have benefited from a recent upgrade.

★**Hotel Aimia** c/Santa Maria del Camí 1 ☎971 63 12 00, ⓦaimiahotel.com. In a low modern block just off the main waterfront promenade, this immaculately maintained, medium-sized four-star hotel has the most comfortable of guest rooms, each with the unmistakeable signs of a designer's touch, starting with the flush ceiling lights. There's a spa, a gym and a garden pool – and it's all reassuringly smart and relaxing. Closed Nov–March. **€190**

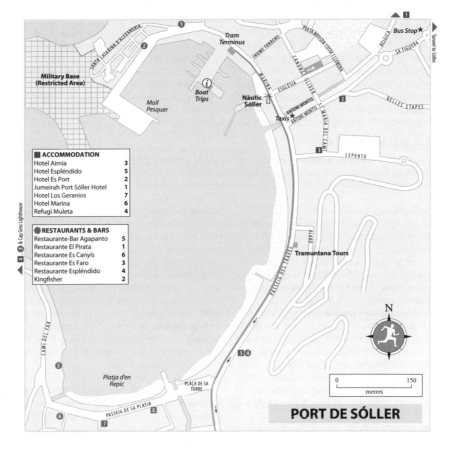

PORT DE SÓLLER

2

Hotel Espléndido Passeig des Través 5 ☎971 63 18 50, ⓦesplendidohotel.com. The self-styled "pride of Port de Sóller" comprises a remodelled and refashioned five-storey 1950s hotel block peering out across the bay. There are all the facilities you might expect – terraced gardens to the rear, a spa, pools and so forth – but the rooms do vary in quality: the pick have sea-facing balconies and a pleasant feel, but some of those with a "garden view" are cramped and mundane (but still not cheap). Closed Nov–March. **€230**

★**Hotel Es Port** c/Antoni Montis s/n ☎971 63 16 50, ⓦhotelesport.com. In its own lush gardens at the back of the port, a few minutes' walk from the waterfront, this is one of the resort's more distinctive hotels. Most of the public areas are in a seventeenth-century country house, whose interior displays many charming original features, including a Baroque family chapel. The guest rooms in the old section are commodious and have an antique feel, with wood-beamed ceilings, but most of the rooms are housed in a modern annexe at the back. There are also indoor and outdoor pools. Closed Nov–March. **€170**

Jumeirah Port Sóller Hotel c/Bélgica s/n ☎971 63 78 88, ⓦjumeirah.com. The last word in luxury, this super-duper, deluxe hotel perches high above the resort on the crest of a hill with exquisite views over bay and coast. No expense has been spared in its construction, from the neo-baronial stone staircase to the wonderfully positioned outside pool. There are more panoramic vistas from many of the guest rooms, which are large and über-modern with

every facility. And, of course, there's a spa too, plus bars and a restaurant. The only irritant is navigation: the hotel rooms are spread out in different blocks and getting from one to the other is far from straightforward, given the architect's decision to dispense with ordinary internal stairways. Closed Nov to early March. **€500**

Hotel Los Geranios Passeig de Sa Platja 15 ☎971 63 14 40, ⓦhotel-losgeranios.com. Straightforward sea-front hotel with four stars that overlooks the Platja d'en Repic, and has twenty-odd rooms on four floors, mostly with sea views. The place is independently managed, but the rooms are equipped in standard chain style. Closed Nov–March. **€140**

Hotel Marina Passeig de Sa Platja 3 ☎971 63 14 61, ⓦhotelmarinasoller.com. Large, long-established and competitively priced hotel overlooking the Platja d'en Repic. The rooms are decorated in standard-issue modern style, but most of them are spacious with balconies, and many have cooking facilities. Recently upgraded with a new spa. Closed Nov–March. **€90**

Refugi Muleta Camí del Far s/n, Cap Gros s/n ☎971 63 42 71, ⓦconselldemallorca.net. Government-owned hikers' hostel in an old stone building beside the lighthouse up on the headland immediately to the west of Platja d'en Repic. The hostel is also within easy walking distance of the GR221 long-distance hiking trail (see p.91). Offers dormitory accommodation for 30 in bunk beds; breakfast is €4.50 extra. Open all year; advance reservations required. Dorms **€11**

EATING AND DRINKING

Port de Sóller is awash with **restaurants** and standards are generally very high – indeed the port has some of the best restaurants in Mallorca. Most of the prime places have bayside locations and the majority mix Mallorcan and Spanish dishes, with seafood, some of it caught by local fishermen, being an especially big deal.

★**Kingfisher** San Ramon de Penyafort 25 ☎971 63 88 56, ⓦkingfishersoller.com. Outstanding restaurant, the best in the resort, with a small but extremely well-chosen menu featuring the likes of black seafood spaghetti or mussels and shrimp pasta in squid ink. In an old-ish stone house at the back of the harbour and with a pleasant terrace. Mains average €20. Reservations recommended. Mon–Sat noon–4.30pm & 7–11.30pm.

Restaurante-Bar Agapanto Camí del Far 2 ☎971 63 38 60, ⓦagapanto.com. At the west end of Platja d'en Repic, right beside the seashore, the *Agapanto* is a modish restaurant with a stylish, inventive menu featuring subtle sauces and imaginatively prepared vegetables. Try, for example, the scallops and pea purée followed by the fish of the day (from €26). Outstanding service too, plus an "ambient" soundtrack. Daily: kitchen noon–4pm & 7–11pm; bar 7pm–1am.

Restaurante El Pirata Santa Catalina d'Alexandria 8 ☎971 63 14 97, ⓦchilimontes.com. The decor of this

busy café-restaurant is a little off-putting – it's much too garish for most tastes – but they do serve a good line in grilled seafood as well as home-made pastas and salads, both inside and outside on their bayfront terrace. Mains average €17. Daily noon–11pm.

★**Restaurante Es Canyís** Passeig de Sa Platja 21 ☎971 63 14 06, ⓦescanyis.es. Bright and cheerful bistro-style restaurant offering an excellent and extensive range of Spanish dishes from its bayside premises behind the Platja d'en Repic. The snails are a house speciality, but the paella is also tempting, as is the chicken breast in almond sauce. Main courses begin at €15. Tues–Sat 1–4pm & 8–11pm, Sun 1–4pm.

Restaurante Es Faro Cap Gros s/n ☎971 63 37 52, ⓦrestaurantesfaro.es. This well-known restaurant has a wonderful location, high up on the cliffs at the entrance to the harbour (and a 1.6km drive – or stiff walk – up from Platja d'en Repic). However, the spectacular views often exceed the quality of the evening meal, so it's perhaps a safer bet for lunch when the *menú del día* is really very good – and a lot cheaper. Reservations essential in the evening. Daily: March–Oct noon–4pm & 6.30–9.30pm; Nov–Feb noon–4pm.

Restaurante Espléndido Passeig des Través 5 ☎971 63 18 50, ⓦesplendidohotel.com. In the hotel of the same name, this fast-moving bistro sits by the bay and offers an all-purpose menu featuring everything from fish and chips to classic Spanish dishes. A little pricey for what you get, with salads, for example, kicking off at around €15. Daily noon–midnight.

Biniaraix

Nestling among the foothills of the Serra de Tramuntana, Sóller's immediate neighbour is the tiny and extraordinarily pretty hamlet of **BINIARAIX**, whose cluster of old stone houses cuddle up to a dilapidated church and the smallest of central squares. It takes about an hour to walk there from Sóller along **c/Sa Lluna** (and its several continuations), a little longer via the much quieter GR221 which loops round the northern edge of Sóller past orchards and farmland. Biniaraix also makes a useful starting point for **hikes** into the surrounding mountains (see box below). Incidentally, try to avoid driving here – walk or catch the bus – as Biniaraix's streets are incredibly narrow and there is hardly anywhere to park.

ARRIVAL AND DEPARTURE
BINIARAIX

By bus Buses to and from Biniaraix pull in beside the main through-road, just east of the main square on c/Fornalutx.
Destinations Fornalutx (Mon–Fri 4 daily, Sat 2 daily; 5min); Port de Sóller (Mon–Fri 4 daily, Sat 2 daily; 10min); Sóller (Mon–Fri 4 daily, Sat 2 daily; 5min).

Fornalutx

Good-looking **FORNALUTX**, about 6km northeast of Sóller, is often touted as the most attractive village on Mallorca, and it certainly has a superb location, its honey-coloured stone houses huddling against a mountainous backdrop with the surrounding valley perfumed by orange and lemon groves. Matching its setting, the quaint centre of Fornalutx fans out from the minuscule main square, the **Plaça d'Espanya**, its narrow cobbled streets stepped to facilitate mule traffic – though nowadays you're more likely to be hit by a hikers' rucksack than obstructed by a mule: tourists and expats love the

---

WALKS AROUND BINIARAIX

From Biniaraix, the most popular hiking route is the stiff, but particularly scenic, 2hr haul up to the L'Ofre farmhouse at the top of the **Barranc de Biniaraix**, a beautiful ravine of terraced citrus groves set in the shadow of the mountains. To get to the Biniaraix **trailhead**, walk uphill from the main square along c/Sant Josep. After about 200m you'll reach a spring and a cattle trough, where a sign offers a choice of hiking trails, including the one east up the *barranc*, on (one small part of) the **GR221** long-distance footpath (see p.91). Sections of the trail up the *barranc* use the old **cobbled roadway** that was once part of the pilgrims' route between Sóller and the monastery at Lluc (see p.133). Built in the fifteenth century, the roadway proved a real headache to maintain for a long line of bishops: sometimes they had to threaten the peasantry with fines to keep the road in good order, sometimes they offered indulgences, but the snail hunters who regularly broke down the retaining walls to collect these tasty creatures proved indifferent to both. At the top of the ravine, you can extend your walk by clambering west up to the **Es Cornadors** viewpoint – allow 45 minutes each way – or by heading northeast to the Cúber reservoir (see p.131), a comparatively easy walk across even ground on the GR221 – allow about two hours. Otherwise, the quickest way to get back to Biniaraix is by returning the way you came.

place and flock here in their droves. Fornalutx does not have a tourist office, but there is a pair of appealing **hotels** a stone's throw from the main square.

ARRIVAL AND DEPARTURE | FORNALUTX

By bus Buses to Fornalutx stop at the foot of c/Sant Bartomeu (the Ma-2120), on the southwest edge of the village, a 3min walk from the Plaça d'Espanya.
Destinations Biniaraix (Mon–Fri 4 daily, Sat 2 daily; 5min); Port de Sóller (Mon–Fri 4 daily, Sat 2 daily; 20min); Sóller

(Mon–Fri 4 daily, Sat 2 daily; 15min).
By car If you're driving from Sóller, the easiest way to get to Fornalutx is to take the Ma-10 east and watch for the turn; this will bring you straight to the car parks at the north end of the village.

ACCOMMODATION

Ca'n Reus c/Alba 26 ☎ 971 63 98 66, ⓦ canreushotel .com. In a sympathetically modernized former fruit grower's house, this family hotel has a likeable rustic-chic-meets-country-house decor, offers long valley views and has a garden and a pool. To get to c/Alba, walk down the main street from Plaça d'Espanya (in the Sóller direction) and take the first left just beyond the conspicuous railings – a minute's stroll. **€130**

★**Fornalutx Petit Hotel** c/Alba 22 ☎ 971 63 19 97, ⓦ fornalutxpetithotel.com. Charming hotel in an immaculately furnished and maintained old stone house in the middle of the village. The rooms are kitted out in the best of modern taste with terracotta-tiled floors and cream-painted walls, and there's a terraced garden and pool. Smart and appealing, the hotel also offers splendid views down the valley below. Reservations are essential. **€200**

EATING

★**Ca N'Antuna** c/Arbona Colom 14 ☎ 971 63 30 68. Well-regarded restaurant where the emphasis is on island dishes. Baked lamb is the house speciality, though the lemon tart is a close rival – and is famous from one end of Mallorca to the other. Has a lovely shaded terrace with views down the valley. Mains begin at €15. Tues–Sun 12.30–4pm & 7.30–11pm.

Es Turó c/Arbona Colom 12 ☎ 971 63 08 08, ⓦ restaurante-esturo-fornalutx.com. The homely *Es Turó* offers good-quality Mallorcan cuisine at very reasonable prices – mains begin at about €15. The restaurant has a pleasant outside terrace with valley views and is located just a couple of minutes' walk uphill from the main square. Daily except Thurs 8.30am–11pm; closed Dec & Jan.

Jardins d'Alfàbia

Carretera Palma–Sóller Km17 • April–Oct daily 9.30am–6.30pm; Nov–March Mon–Fri 9.30am–5.30pm, Sat 9.30am–1pm • €6.50 • ☎ 971 61 31 23, ⓦ jardinesdealfabia.com • The Palma–Sóller bus stops right outside the entrance to the gardens (every 1–2hr; 25min), a few metres from the south end of the Palma/Sóller tunnel on the Ma-11

The lush terraced gardens of the **Jardins d'Alfàbia** are one of Mallorca's most enjoyable attractions, and have an interesting history too. Shortly after the Reconquista, Jaume I granted the estate of Alfàbia to a prominent Moor by the name of **Benhabet**, the one-time governor of Pollença. Seeing which way the historical wind was blowing, Benhabet had given his support to Jaume, provisioning the Catalan army during the invasion. There was no way Jaume I could leave his Moorish ally in charge of Pollença (and anyway it was already pledged to a Catalan noble), but he was able to reward him with this generous portion of land. Benhabet planned his new estate in the Moorish style, channelling water from the surrounding mountains to irrigate the fields and fashion oasis-like gardens. Generations of island gentry added to the estate without marring the integrity of Benhabet's original design, thus creating the lovely gardens of today.

The gardens

From the roadside **entrance**, you follow a stately avenue of plane trees towards the gatehouse. In front of the gatehouse is the **ticket office** and a sign here directs visitors up a wide flight of stone steps. These lead to the **gardens**, where the footpath meanders through trellises of jasmine and wisteria, creating patterns of light and shade. Near the

CLOCKWISE FROM TOP JARDINS D'ALFÀBIA (ABOVE); HIKERS IN THE SERRA DE TRAMUNTANA (P.91); SÓLLER TRAIN (P.93) >

start there's even a visitor-operated water feature – press the button and retire. Thereafter, brightly coloured flowers cascade over narrow terraces to the sound of gurgling watercourses, and at the end of the path lies a verdant jungle of palm trees, where bulrushes crowd in on a tiny pool choked with water lilies. It's an enchanting spot, especially on a hot summer's day, with an outdoor **bar** (usually) selling glasses of freshly squeezed orange juice – a snip at just €2.

2 The house and gatehouse

Metres from the pool is the **house**, a modest *hacienda* with a wide veranda and a handful of high-ceilinged rooms that hold an eccentric mix of antiques and curios, including paintings of local bigwigs and exotic animals, most memorably a particularly odd-looking elephant. Pride of place, however, goes to a superb **oak chair** adorned with delightful bas-relief scenes depicting the legend of **Tristan and Isolde**. There were several versions of this well-known medieval tale, but the one on the chair is all about jealousy: on the front the two protagonists are shown playing chess, an innocent enough pastime, but one that stirs the jealousy of Isolde's husband, the king. On the back of the chair, the king's head appears in the tree peering anxiously down at the two of them as they walk in the garden – and you know it will all end in tears. The chair has been in the house for centuries and local legend asserts that the uncrowned Jaume IV ordered it, but never had the chance to take possession: in 1349, the Aragonese captured Jaume at the battle of Llucmajor and he spent the rest of his days in exile. Unfortunately, it's all poppycock as the chair was actually made in the fifteenth century in Flanders. The other curiosity is the dark-red, chintzy bedroom prepared specially for **Queen Isabella II of Spain** (1830–1904), who stayed the night here in 1860. Even for a Spanish royal, Isabella had a troubled reign, subject to endless conspiracies and sexual speculation – she had nine children, but hardly anyone believed the king had anything to do with any of them.

At the front of the house, the cobbled **courtyard** is shaded by a giant plane tree and surrounded by good-looking, rustic outbuildings. Beyond lies the **gatehouse**, an imposing structure sheltering a fine coffered ceiling of Mudéjar design, with an inscription praising Allah.

Raixa

Carretera Palma–Sóller (Ma-11) Km 12 • Tues–Sat 10am–5pm • Free • ☎ 971 23 76 36, ⓦ conselldemallorca.net • Signed from the Ma-11 (4.7km south of the Jardins d'Alfàbia) & down a short (1km), partly unpaved lane

Recently restored and reopened, **Raixa** was the country estate of the Despuig family from the middle of the seventeenth century until (relative) hard times forced them to sell up in 1910. Like most of the island's gentry, the Despuigs were keen to demonstrate their wealth, so over the years they built themselves a capacious, four-storey *hacienda* graced by a handsome arcaded gallery at the front, with the estate's agricultural buildings tucked away around a courtyard to the rear. The most prominent member of the clan was **Cardinal Antonio Despuig** (1745–1813), an antiquarian whose collection of classical sculptures can be seen in the Castell de Bellver in Palma (see p.68) – they were actually meant to end up here in Raixa, but Despuig's last wishes were ultimately frustrated. Despuig saw himself as a leading light of the Enlightenment, but beneath his cultured cassock lurked medieval piety: he died in Italy and on his deathbed he left instructions for his heart to be cut out and buried close to the body of Mallorca's favourite saint, Catalina Thomàs (see p.114).

The **estate buildings** have survived in good fettle, but the **museum** inside the *hacienda* is a disappointment, comprising, for the most part, a few inconclusive period rooms and several modest displays on the Serra de Tramuntana mountains. Much more diverting are the **terraced gardens** carved out of the hill beside the house, which are still in the process of reconstruction. It was the self-same Cardinal who began work on the gardens, organizing the water supply and decorating them with Neoclassical statues, water fountains and bits of old masonry recovered from medieval buildings in Palma – all in the fashionable Italian style of his day. After his death, several other Despuigs warmed to the scenic theme, adding, for example, the monumental staircase, the false ruins and the grotto in the 1850s.

Bunyola to Alaró   2

On the landward side of the Serra de Tramuntana, a few kilometres south of Sóller, a country road (the **Ma-2100**) forks east off the Ma-11 to loop past the sun-bleached walls of **Bunyola** before negotiating the range's forested foothills. It's a beautiful drive, with mountains to either side, and after about 12km you reach **Orient**, a tiny and extraordinarily pretty little hamlet that makes a perfect spot for lunch or an overnight stay. Thereafter, there's more fine scenery as the road wriggles along the valley to pass beneath the stern hilltop ruins of the **Castell d'Alaró**, with the attractive little towns of **Alaró** and then Binissalem (see p.163), the centre of Mallorca's wine industry, just beyond.

Bunyola

Almost entirely untouched by the tourist hullabaloo, **BUNYOLA**, just east of the Ma-11, is a neat and trim little village lying in the shadow of the mountains, its old stone houses fanning out from an attractive main square. The vintage Palma-Sóller train stops here, but few passengers now alight or embark, whereas in earlier days it was an economic lifeline, making it easy for the locals to get their wine, olives and almonds to market – indeed the name of the place may be derived from the Arabic *bujola* (small vineyard). The liveliest time to be here is on **Saturday morning** (8am–1pm), when there's a fruit and produce market in the main square.

ARRIVAL AND DEPARTURE   BUNYOLA

By bus Buses to and from Palma pull into the centre of Bunyola, beside Sa Plaça, the main square, where they connect with the onward service to Orient (see below). Buses to and from Sóller keep to the Ma-11, with the nearest bus stop being about 1km west of Plaça de l'Església.

Destinations Orient (2 daily; 20min); Palma (hourly; 45min); Sóller (every 1–2hr; 15min).
By train The vintage Palma–Sóller train (see p.93) stops in Bunyola; the train station is a short walk west of the centre.

Orient

With a resident population of around thirty, **ORIENT** is the tiniest of hamlets, its scattering of old houses straddling a wooded gulch on the edge of the Vall d'Orient, a

---

IRRITATED ISLANDERS

When plans for the construction of the Palma–Sóller railway first surfaced, the merchants of Sóller were enthusiastic about the **railway**, but the country folk hereabouts were less convinced – after all, they had history when it came to accepting technological change. In the 1860s, **telegraph poles** were erected between Sóller and Palma in an effort to improve communications. At first, groups of farm labourers in the vicinity of **Bunyola** snipped the wires and chopped down the poles, but when they heard that messages could be sent along the wires, they concluded that the same applied to goods. As a result, according to a visiting British captain, one J. W. Clayton, "bundles of clothes, pairs of knickerbockers, petticoats, baskets of edibles, and even wigs…[were] neatly ticketed and addressed" and hung on the wires for onward transmission. When they stayed put, there were more attacks on the poor old telegraph poles.

slender valley where steep hills crimp and crowd olive and almond groves. The main part of the village slopes up the hill from the road; at the top is a sturdy little **parish church** named in honour of Sant Jordi (St George), whose effigy cuts a striking pose on the high altar. For most of its long history, Orient's isolation made life hard hereabouts, but tourism has transformed the place and now the locals share their bucolic retreat with cyclists, hikers, second-home owners and a pair of smart, rural-chic hotels.

ARRIVAL AND DEPARTURE — ORIENT

By bus Buses from Bunyola (2 daily; 20min) stop in the centre of Orient. Seats need to be reserved ahead of time on ☏ 617 36 53 65.

ACCOMMODATION AND EATING

Hotel L'Hermitage Carretera Alaró-Bunyola ☏ 971 18 03 03, ⓦ hermitage-hotel.com. Smooth and polished, *L'Hermitage* is a combined hotel and spa, where lush gardens surround a complex of old stone buildings, some of which date back to its earliest incarnation as a monastery, others to its days as a manor house – and including an attractively modernized old olive mill. Has twenty rooms, with a handful in the old buildings and the rest in the surrounding chalets. It's located about 1km east of Orient on the Ma-2100. **€150**

★ **Restaurante Orient** c/Orient s/n ☏ 971 61 51 53. At the west end of the village, beside the Ma-2100, this enjoyable restaurant is a low-key, informal affair with a relaxing outside terrace. Few would praise the decor, but who cares when the food is this good, featuring a range of Mallorcan favourites, including snails, suckling pig, partridge with mushrooms and rabbit with prawns; mains average €18. Mon & Wed–Sat 10am–10pm, Sun 10am–7pm; closed in July.

★ **Hotel Rural Son Palou** Plaça de l'Església s/n ☏ 971 61 36 22, ⓦ sonpalou.com. First impressions of this lovely hotel are really rather misleading: the entrance is narrow, almost cramped, squeezed into the square at the top of the village beside the church. In fact, the hotel comprises a series of immaculately restored old farm buildings and the surrounding estate. The gardens are lovely; the dozen or so guest rooms are comfortable and well appointed; and the outside pool is delicious – and so are the views. It's a popular spot – so book early. **€200**

Castell d'Alaró

Beyond Orient, the Ma-2100 zigzags up to slip along the narrow valley of the **Torrent d'en Paragon** for around 3km, before veering south to pass between a pair of molar-like hills whose bare rocky flanks tower above the surrounding forest and scrub. The more westerly of the two sports the sparse ruins of the **Castell d'Alaró**, originally a Moorish stronghold but rebuilt by Jaume I. Visible for miles around, the castle looks impregnable on its lofty perch, and it certainly impeded the Aragonese invasion of 1285: when an Aragonese messenger suggested terms for surrender, the garrison's dual commanders responded by calling the Aragonese king Alfonso III "fish-face", punning on his name in Catalan (*anfos* means "perch"). When the castle finally fell, Alfonso had the two roasted alive – goodness knows what he'd have done if they'd called him something really rude.

Access to the Castell

The **side road** that leads up towards the castle branches off the Orient-Alaró road just to the north of the town of Alaró – watch for the signposted right turn just south of the Kilometre-18 stone marker. The first 3km of the side road are bumpy and narrow but reasonably easy, whereas its last 1.3km are gravel and dirt with a perilously tight series of hairpins negotiating a very steep hillside – especially hazardous after rain. The road emerges at a car park and an old **farmstead**, which now holds the *Es Verger* restaurant (see opposite), from where the views down over the plain are sumptuous. From the restaurant, the ruins of the **castle** are clearly visible above, about an hour and a half's walk away along a clearly marked track. The trail leads to the castle's stone gateway, beyond which lies an expansive wooded plateau accommodating the fragmentary ruins of the fortress, a hikers' hostel (see opposite) and the tiny **pilgrims' church** of Mare de Déu del Refugi.

ACCOMMODATION AND EATING

CASTELL D'ALARÓ

Hostatgeria Castell d'Alaró ☎971 18 21 12, ⓦcastellalaro.cat. This straightforward hikers' hostel occupies a recently upgraded old building in the precincts of the castle. It says a lot for the determination of the local council that it ever got finished at all – much of the heavier tackle had to be lifted in by helicopter. The hostel has thirty bunk beds in several dormitories and there is a café too. Reservations are not required, but you'd be pretty crazy to climb up here without booking first – or checking when they serve food. Half-board costs €24 per person per day. Dorm bed including breakfast **€15.50**

Restaurante Es Verger Castell d'Alaró ☎971 18 21 26. High up on the mountain, on the way to the castle, this oh-so-rustic restaurant, with its wooden benches and long tables, is famous for its lamb (*cordero*), slow-cooked in beer in a wood-fired oven and served with *patatas bravas* (Spanish-style potatoes). Tues–Sun 9am–9pm.

2

Alaró

Just to the south of the Castell d'Alaró turn-off stands the town of **ALARÓ**, a sleepy little place of old stone houses blossoming out from an attractive main square, **Plaça de la Vila**. An elegant arcaded gallery flanks one side of the square, a second is shadowed by the **church**, a fortress-like medieval affair of honey-coloured sandstone embellished by a fancy Baroque doorway. The town was once at the centre of the trade between the mountains and the plain, with farm produce going one way, animal skins and charcoal the other, but it really hit the headlines in 1901 when it became the first place on the island to install electric street lighting – ahead even of Palma, much to the chagrin of that city's ruling council. Just south of Alaró, you leave the foothills of the Serra de Tramuntana and slip down onto the central plain, Es Pla, near to Binissalem (see p.163).

ARRIVAL AND DEPARTURE

ALARÓ

By bus The main bus stop in Alaró is on the main drag, Avgda de la Constitució (Ma-2022), about 350m southeast of the main square, Plaça de la Vila. There are no buses from Alaró to Orient or Bunyola.
Destinations Consell train station, on the Palma–Binissalem–Inca train line (every 30min to hourly; 15min).

ACCOMMODATION AND EATING

Can Xim Hotel Plaça de la Vila 7 ☎971 87 91 17, ⓦcanxim.com. On Alaró's main square, this small, family-owned hotel with eight guest rooms occupies an attractive old stone building. It's a pleasant place to stay and the rooms are neat and modern, if a tad frugal. **€120**

Traffic Restaurante Plaça de la Vila 7 ☎971 87 91 17, ⓦcanxim.com. Alaró's main square holds several cafés and restaurants where local families gather at the weekend, and the pick of the bunch is *Traffic*, part of the *Can Xim Hotel*. Here, Mallorcan specialities – notably casseroles – are served either inside or in the spacious poolside garden at the back. Mains average €15. Mon & Thurs–Sat noon–4pm & 7–11pm, Tues & Wed 7–11pm.

Deià

DEIÀ, 10km west of Sóller, is beautiful. An ancient mountain village glued to the steep terraced slopes that rise high above the seashore, this is where the mighty Puig d'es Teix (1064m) meets the coast, its crumbly mass retaining a formidable, almost mysterious presence, especially in the shadows of a moonlit night. Deià's long main street, **c/Arxiduc Lluis Salvador** – which doubles as the coastal highway (Ma-10) – introduces the village, skirting the base of the Teix and showing off the bulk of the village's hotels and restaurants to fine advantage. It was Robert Graves (see box, p.107) who made Deià famous, holed up in his den, **Ca N'Alluny**, and at its peak in the 1960s and 1970s, the village heaved with writers and poets, painters and musicians. For the most part, the literati have moved on and the affluent have moved in, but enough of a scene remains to sustain the much-lauded **Deià International Music Festival** (see p.108). At times, Deià's popularity can render the main street too congested to be much fun,

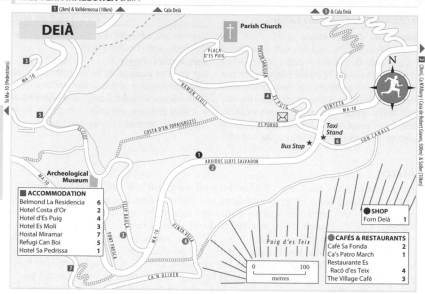

but the tiny heart of the village, tumbling over a high and narrow ridge on the seaward side of the Ma-10, still retains a surprising tranquillity, as do the Deià's several deep, wooded ravines.

Deià church

Plaça d'es Puig s/n • No fixed opening hours • Museum €2

On Deià's seaward side, a lattice of old peasant houses curls up to a pretty **parish church**, in the precincts of which – on the left hand side of the graveyard – lies **Robert Graves**, his headstone marked simply "Robert Graves: Poeta, E.P.D." (*En Paz Descanse*, "Rest In Peace"). From the graveyard, there are memorable views out over the coast and of the Teix, with banks of tightly terraced fields cascading down from the mountain towards the sea. The gloomy, barrel-vaulted church is itself unremarkable except perhaps for the gaudy altarpiece, but one of its side-rooms does hold a modest **Museu Parroquial**, which possesses a folksy assortment of religious bric-a-brac.

Ca N'Alluny: La Casa de Robert Graves

Carretera Deià–Sóller s/n • April–Oct Mon–Fri 10am–5pm, Sat 10am–3pm; Nov–March Mon–Fri 9am–4pm, Sat 9am–2pm • €7 • ☎ 971 63 61 85, ⓦ lacasaderobertgraves.com

Robert Graves put Deià on the international map and his old home, **Ca N'Alluny** (the "Far House" in Catalan), is a substantial stone building overlooking the coast about 500m east of the village. Opened to the public in 2006, the house has been returned to something like its 1940s appearance and comes complete with the family's own furnishings and fittings. A visit begins with a short and well-made film introducing the author's life and times, and then it's on to the house, where the living rooms seem surprisingly modest and very homely. The study, where Graves produced much of his finest work, is of modest proportions too, and beyond is an exhibition area with yet more biographical information, old photographs, letters and manuscripts, plus a recording of Graves reading a poem – *The Face in the Mirror*. In his pomp, Graves had an extensive range of contacts and there are photos of him here in Deià with a long list of the famous, from Kingsley Amis to Alec

Guinness and Ava Gardner. Finally, you emerge into the small but well-kept garden, where there are olive, carob, fruit and almond trees.

Deià Archeological Museum

Es Clot s/n • April–Sept Sat 5–7pm & Sun 11am–1pm, and by appointment; call ahead • Free • ❶ 699 95 79 02

Deià's fascinating **Archeological Museum** is tucked away in a leafy ravine below the main road. The archeologists William and Jacqueline Waldren founded the museum in 1962 to display the items they had retrieved from a number of local prehistoric sites. In particular, the couple had just hit the archeological headlines with their investigations into a prehistoric cave dwelling near Deià. Here they found a great hoard of bones, the remains of a veritable herd of *Myotragus balearicus*, a small species of goat unique to the Balearics, whose precise prehistoric importance has sparked much debate. The Waldrens asserted

2

ROBERT GRAVES IN DEIÀ

The English poet, novelist and classical scholar **Robert Graves** (1895–1985) spent two periods living in Deià, the first in the 1930s, and the second from the end of World War II until his death. During his first stay he shared a house at the edge of the village with **Laura Riding**, an American poet and dabbler in the mystical. Riding had arrived in England in 1926 and, after she became Graves's secretary and collaborator, the two of them began an affair that was to break up both of their marriages. Their relationship created such a furore that they decided to leave England, settling in Mallorca on the advice of Gertrude Stein in 1930. The fuss was not a matter of morality – most of their friends were indifferent to adultery – but more to do with the self-styled "**Holy Circle**" they had founded, a cabalistic and intensely self-preoccupied literary-mystic group. The last straw came when Riding, in her attempt to control the group, jumped out of a window, saying "Goodbye, chaps", and the besotted Graves leapt after her. No wonder his friend T.E. Lawrence (of Arabia) wrote of "madhouse minds" and of Graves "drowning in a quagmire".

Both recovered, but the dottiness continued once they'd moved to Deià, with Graves acting as doting servant to Riding, whom he reinvented as a sort of all-knowing matriarch and muse. Simultaneously, Graves thumped away at his prose: he had already produced *Goodbye to All That* (1929), his bleak and painful memoirs of army service in the trenches of World War I, but now came his other best-remembered books, **I, Claudius** (1934) and its sequel **Claudius the God** (1935), historical novels detailing the life and times of the Roman emperor. Nonetheless, to Graves these "potboilers", as he styled them, were secondary to his poetry – usually carefully crafted love poems of melancholic tenderness in praise of Riding – which were well received by the critics of the time.

At the onset of the Spanish Civil War, Graves and Riding left Mallorca, not out of sympathy for the Republicans – Graves was far too reactionary for that – but to keep contact with friends and family. During their exile Graves was ditched by Riding, and he subsequently took up with a mutual friend, **Beryl Pritchard**. After Graves had returned to Deià in 1946, he worked on *The White Goddess*, a controversial study of prehistoric and classical myth that argued the existence of an all-pervasive, primordial religion based on the worship of a poet-goddess. Pritchard joined him in the midst of his labours (the book was published in 1948), and in 1950 they were married in Palma. They were not, however, to live happily ever after. Graves had a predilection for young women, claiming he needed female muses for poetic inspiration, and although his wife outwardly accepted this waywardness, she did so without much enthusiasm.

Meanwhile, although Graves's novels became increasingly well known and profitable, his poetry, with its preoccupation with romantic love, fell out of fashion, and his last anthology, *Poems 1965–1968*, received a muted response. Nevertheless, Graves's international reputation as a writer still attracted a steady stream of visitors to Deià from the ranks of the literati, with the occasional film star dropping by to add to the self-regarding stew. There was a further boost to Graves's fortunes in the 1970s, when an acclaimed BBC TV production of *I, Claudius* brought his books to the attention of a wider public, but by then he had begun to lose his mind, ending his days in sad senility. The house where Graves lived in Deià from 1946 onwards is now open to the public (see opposite).

that the animal was a dietary mainstay and that there had been attempts to domesticate it. What's more, they claimed that the goat bones were found at a level in the subsoil that pushed back the date at which the earliest islanders settled here by several hundred years – to 4000 or even 5000 BC. Few experts now agree with these conclusions and many believe that the goat was actually extinct before humans arrived, but there's still some heat in the argument. The museum displays many of the key finds retrieved by the Waldrens, who carried on with their explorations after their important discovery – with Jacqueline keeping the archeological flame burning after William's death in 2003.

Cala Deià

Much loved by Graves, **Cala Deià** is the nearest thing the village has to a beach, comprising some 200m of seaweed and shingle at the back of a handsome, hoop-shaped cove of jagged cliffs, boulders and white-crested surf. It's a great place for a swim – the water is clean and cool, and there are two summer-only beach bar-restaurants (see opposite). It's a popular spot, especially at weekends, and parking is often a nightmare – so get there early (by 11am). To drive, head northeast along the main road out of Deià and watch for the (easy-to-miss) sign about 700m beyond the *Belmond La Residencia*. To walk, the most obvious route is signed from the bend in the road 80m or so northeast of the bus stop; this leads down a wooded ravine and takes about thirty minutes. Even more bucolic, however, is the path that threads down through the wooded gulch that lies between the old centre of the village and the *Hotel Es Molí*; this takes about forty minutes.

ARRIVAL AND DEPARTURE   DEIÀ

By bus Buses scoot through Deià along the Ma-10. The handiest bus stop is at the east end of the village near the *Belmond La Residencia* hotel; it takes about 10min to walk from one end of the village to the other along the main street. Destinations Palma (4–7 daily; 1hr); Port de Sóller (4–7 daily; 30min); Sóller (4–7 daily; 25min); Valldemossa (4–7 daily; 30min).

By taxi There's a two-berth taxi stand on the south side of the main road, a few metres from the bus stop. To call a cab, ring ☏ 609 38 61 68. Fixed-rate taxi fares from Deià include: Banyalbufar at €50; Cala Deià €12; Palma €40; Sóller €22; and Valldemossa €20.

INFORMATION

Tourist information There's no tourist information office as such, but most of the hotels and *hostales* can provide advice on local walks and have bus timetables.
Deià International Music Festival ☏ 678 98 95 36, ⓦ dimf.com. Deià is the haunt of long-term expats, who club together to sustain several cultural festivals, most notably this one, whose assorted classical concerts begin in May and end in September.

ACCOMMODATION

IN THE VILLAGE

Belmond La Residencia c/Son Canals s/n ☏ 971 63 90 11, ⓦ belmond.com. Models with nannies, big cars and flash clothes are the order of the day here in one of Mallorca's ritziest hotels. The decor is minimalist-meets-rustic and the hotel itself is an extended extrapolation of two old stone manor houses overlooking the main village drag. Currently owned by Belmond, formerly Orient-Express, it has facilities aplenty – pools, bars, restaurants, tennis court, a spa and so forth. Also has an enterprising programme of sponsoring local artists, whose work adorns the hotel's walls. **€700**

★ **Hotel d'Es Puig** c/Es Puig 4 ☏ 971 63 94 09, ⓦ hoteldespuig.com. A smart and tastefully furnished hotel with eight bedrooms in an elegantly converted, four-storey old stone house located in the centre of the village – between the Ma-10 and the church. It's worth paying a few euros more for a room with a balcony. Closed Jan. **€160**

Hotel Es Molí Carretera Deià-Valldemossa s/n ☏ 971 63 90 00, ⓦ esmoli.com. Overlooking the main road from wooded slopes, this long-established, four-star hotel has an excellent reputation. Inside, the public areas are smart and spacious, with around ninety well-appointed, a/c bedrooms and suites divided between the main building, some of which dates from the seventeenth century, and an annexe at the back. The rooms are decorated in a comfortable, reassuring style and most have a balcony with wide coastal views. The lovely terraced gardens provide a lush setting for the pool, and the breakfast terrace is charming. The hotel minibus takes guests – the majority of whom are British – to a private (rocky) beach, a 20min drive to the east. The better deals are on longer (at least

WESTERN MALLORCA'S BEST BEACHES

Cala Deià A shingle strip, great for swimming. See opposite
Port de Valldemossa A handsome shingle strip of a beach in a wild setting. See p.118
Cala Estellencs Remote, surf-battered shingle beach. See p.121
Sant Elm A pleasant, sandy strip – and the best beach on this part of the island. See p.122

seven nights) bookings. Closed Nov to March. **€200**

★**Hostal Miramar** c/Ca'n Oliver s/n ☎971 63 90 84, ⓦpensionmiramar.com. You don't get many good deals in Deià, but this is one of them: a family-run *hostal* in a traditional stone *finca* perched high above the main road. There are nine pleasant rooms here – some en suite, some with shared facilities – and each is decorated in a plain and unfussy style. The views over the village from the courtyard in front of the house are stunning. On foot, it's a stiff 10min walk up from the village. **€90**

Refugi Can Boi c/Es Clot 5 ☎971 63 61 86, ⓦrefugicanboi.com. Well-run hikers' hostel in a neat and trim old stone building, with 32 bunk beds in four rooms, including one double. It's handily located in the valley below the church and is on the GR221 long-distance footpath. Advance reservations required. Breakfast €4.50. Dorm beds **€11**

OUTSIDE THE VILLAGE

Hotel Costa d'Or Llucalcari ☎971 63 90 25, ⓦhoposa.es. This four-star hotel enjoys a wonderful setting, overlooking an undeveloped slice of coast and surrounded by pine trees and olive groves. There's a shaded terrace bar and an outdoor swimming pool. The rooms are kitted out in slick modern style, with the best looking over the ocean. The hotel – and the hamlet of Llucalcari – are located 2km east of Deià along the Ma-10 coast road. Closed Nov–March. **€200**

Hotel Sa Pedrissa Carretera Valldemossa s/n ☎971 63 91 11, ⓦsapedrissa.com. This hotel, in a solitary setting about 2km west of Deià on the Ma-10, occupies an immaculately revamped old stone farmhouse, perched high above – and with wide views over – the coast. Stone-and-marble floors, exposed wooden beams and oodles of white paint set the tone, and each of the nine bedrooms is impeccably turned out. There's also a terrace pool. **€330**

EATING AND DRINKING

You're spoiled for choice when it comes to eating out in Deià. Dotted along the main street are several smart and polished **restaurants** plus a number of more modest **café-bars**, ideal for nursing a drink in the heat of the midday sun. The village also has a good grocery-store-cum-bakery, Forn Deià, about 200m west of the main bus stop.

Café Sa Fonda c/Arxiduc Lluís Salvador 5 ☎971 63 93 06. If you're looking for island simplicities, Deià is the wrong place, but this busy café-bar – up a flight of steps off the main drag – is the nearest thing you'll get to a locals' favourite. There's a large shaded terrace and although drinks are the main event, they serve snacks and light meals too (from €9). Tues–Sun noon–midnight; closed Feb.

★**Ca's Patro March** Cala Deià ☎971 63 91 37. The better of the two café-bars down in Cala Deià, this lovely place occupies a rustic-looking tumble of old stone buildings that culminate in a shaded terrace perched on the edge of the ocean. Their speciality is seafood (mains from €20) caught and brought here by the owner's son. Daily: May–June & Sept to late Oct 12.30–8pm; July & Aug 12.30–10pm.

★**Restaurante Es Racó d'es Teix** c/Vinya Vella 6 ☎971 63 95 01, ⓦesracodesteix.es. Delightful, much-lauded restaurant in an old stone house with an attractive shaded terrace; it's a steep 30m or so above the main road, about halfway into the village – watch for the sign. The Mediterranean cuisine features local ingredients and is strong on island dishes, but it doesn't come cheap, with main courses at around €35. Reservations well-nigh essential. Wed–Sun 1–3pm & 8–10.30pm; closed mid-Nov to Jan.

The Village Café c/Felip Bauçà 1 ☎971 63 91 99. Lively café with an enterprising range of dishes and an appealing shaded terrace overlooking the coastal hills. The menu is fairly short but very enticing – try, for example, the Caesar salad with chorizo. Mains are competitively priced at around €12. Daily except Tues noon–11pm.

Son Marroig

Carretera de Valldemossa–Deià (Ma-10) • April–Sept Mon–Sat 9.30am–6pm; Oct–March Mon–Sat 9.30am–1pm & 3.30–5.30pm • €4 • ⓦsonmarroig.com

Three kilometres west of Deià, **Son Marroig** is an imposing L-shaped mansion, perched high above the seashore and just below the Ma-10. The house dates from late medieval times, but was refashioned in the nineteenth century to become the favourite residence of the Habsburg archduke **Ludwig Salvator** (see box below). Dynastically insignificant but extremely rich, the Austrian aristocrat first visited Mallorca aged 19, fell head over heels in love with the place, and returned to buy Son Marroig along with a sizeable slice of the west coast between Deià and Port de Valldemossa.

The house and garden

The Son Marroig estate comprises the house, its gardens and the headland below. Despite its setting and long history, the **house** is actually rather dull, with all its key exhibits piled into the first of two large and gloomy first-floor rooms. Here you'll find a small sample of Hispano-Arabic pottery; a handful of classical Greek figurines; a beautifully carved, medieval bas-relief diptych; and a display featuring some of the archduke's manuscripts and pamphlets alongside several ducal photographs and portraits – which show the duke ballooning up from a regular-sized young man to a real heavyweight. More appealing, however, is the **garden**, whose terraces are graced by a Neoclassical belvedere of Tuscan Carrara marble that provides gorgeous views along the jagged, forested coast.

Sa Foradada

Below the house is a slender shank of a promontory known as **Sa Foradada**, "the rock pierced by a hole", where the archduke used to park his yacht. The hole in question is a strange circular affair sited high up in the rock face at the end of the promontory. It takes about forty minutes to **walk** the 3km down to this rock, a straightforward excursion to a delightfully scenic spot, though the estate itself is a little scruffy and ill-kempt. The walk

THE UPS AND DOWNS OF THE ARCHDUKE LUDWIG SALVATOR

Cousin to the Habsburg Emperor Franz Josef of Austria, no less, the young **Ludwig Salvator** (1847–1915) was supposed to join the imperial army, but he cleared off and took his sea captain's certificate instead. Mightily miffed at this insubordination, the emperor decided a carrot was better than a stick and appointed him the Governor of Bohemia, hoping it would settle him down. It might have worked, too, but for a freak accident: Salvator's young wife, **Mathilde**, was watching the archduke inspect his soldiers from a balcony, until, bored out of her brains, she decided to have a furtive cigarette. It was a bad decision. The cigarette set her dress on fire and she burnt to death in double-quick time. Out of sympathy, his family now indulged Salvator's wanderlust and the archduke headed south to the Mediterranean in 1866. It was on his travels that Salvator first visited Mallorca, which made such an impression on him that he returned to live here, buying a chunk of the west coast and building (or at least adopting) no fewer than **three homes** – Son Marroig (see p.109), Miramar (see opposite) and S'Estaca, formerly owned by the actor Michael Douglas.

Once in residence, Ludwig immersed himself in all things *Mallorquín*, learning the dialect and chronicling the island's topography, archeology, history and folklore in astounding detail. He churned out no fewer than **seven volumes** on the Balearics and, perhaps more importantly, played a leading role as a proto-environmentalist, conserving the coastline of his estates and paying for a team of geologists to chart the Coves del Drac (see p.183). Salvator may have been hardworking, but he also squeezed in a lot of R&R, allegedly sleeping with a brigade of local women and fathering a merry (and not so merry) band of children. Back at Habsburg HQ, rumours of Salvator's antics – both in and out of the sack – went down badly: it was not so much that "Don Balearo", as he was nicknamed, slept with peasant girls, but more that he recognized them and their (his) children, giving them money and land. To add grist to the mill, Salvator even brought one of his women – **Catalina Homar** – back to the Habsburg court in Vienna and, after her untimely death, publicly dedicated one of his books to her. It was, however, World War I rather than Vienna's disapproval that brought a sudden end to the archduke's stint in Mallorca. In 1914, at the outbreak of war, Salvator was summoned back to the Austro-Hungarian Empire to do his royal duty; he died within a year.

begins at the gate just up the slope and to the left of the house: you usually have to clamber over the gate's stile – though sometimes the gate is left open – and then, about 100m further on, you need to keep right at the fork in the track; as you approach the tip of the promontory, think carefully before deciding to attempt the precarious climb beyond the old jetties. On your return, you can slake your thirst at one of the two **café-bars** overlooking the coast from beside the car park, metres from the house.

Miramar

Carretera de Valldemossa–Deià (Ma-10), 2km southwest of Son Marroig · Mon–Sat 10am–5.30pm · €4

In between Son Marroig and Valldemossa is **Miramar**, once the site of a medieval monastery – hence the signs for the "**Monestir de Miramar**" – and the last of the three houses bought by the Archduke Salvator. The house and its grounds hold an enjoyable – albeit improbable – assortment of remains and memorials, beginning with a line of thirteenth-century **stone pillars**, which, marooned in the garden, are all that is left of the original monastery built for the scholar-missionaries of Ramon Llull (see p.61). Beyond the pillars is the **house**, whose handful of rooms holds a mock-up of part of the archduke's yacht, the *Nixe II*, two rooms devoted to the life of Ramon Llull, a re-creation of a monk's cell, and a ridiculously romantic stone memorial to the archduke's first secretary (and maybe lover) Vratislav Vyborny, who died in Palma when he was in his twenties. Outside, in the **grounds** are some strange geometric shapes allegedly laid out by Llull, as well as a fancy stone shrine built by the archduke in Llull's honour, though the high point is the short **path** that meanders down through the olive groves to a fine vantage point offering tremendous views along the coast.

Valldemossa

Inordinately pretty, the tiny hill-town of **VALLDEMOSSA** is celebrated for its ancient **monastery**, which has made it one of the most visited places on Mallorca. The origins of Valldemossa date from the early fourteenth century, when the asthmatic **King Sancho** built a royal palace here in the hills where the air was easier to breathe. Later, in 1399, the palace was gifted to Carthusian monks from Tarragona, who converted and extended the original complex into a monastery, which has survived in prime condition. An enjoyable place to spend the night, especially as the tourist hordes leave the town by early evening, Valldemossa has two appealing hotels as well as a couple of good restaurants. It's also within easy striking distance of its old seaport, **Port de Valldemossa**, whose gaggle of modern villas and tiny beach are reached along the dramatic hairpins of a narrow country road.

Valldemossa Monastery

Plaça de la Cartoixa · Feb, March, Oct & Nov Mon–Sat 9.30am–5.30pm, Sun 10am–1pm; April–Sept Mon–Sat 9.30am–6.30pm, Sun 10am–1pm; Dec & Jan Mon–Sat 9.30am–3.30pm, Sun 10am–1pm · €8.50, Cell no. 4 €4 extra · ☎ 971 61 29 86, ⌨ cartujadevalldemossa.com

Remodelled and restructured on several occasions, most of Valldemossa's **Real Cartuja de Jesús de Nazaret** (Royal Carthusian Monastery of Jesus of Nazareth) is of seventeenth- and eighteenth-century construction. It owes its present fame almost entirely to the novelist and republican polemicist **George Sand** (1804–76) who, with her companion, the composer **Frédéric Chopin** (1810–49), lived here for four months in 1838–39. They arrived just three years after the last monks had been evicted during the suppression of the monasteries, and so were able to rent a comfortable set of vacant cells. Their stay is commemorated in Sand's *A Winter in Majorca*, a sharp-tongued and sharp-eyed epistle (see p.272) that expresses Sand's frustration with the ossified social

2

structures on the island, though her diatribes against reaction sometimes merge into a mean-spirited contempt for her Spanish neighbours. Ungraciously, Sand explains that her nickname for Mallorca, "Monkey Island", was coined for its "crafty, thieving and yet innocent" inhabitants, who, she asserts, are "heartless, selfish and impertinent". Quite what the islanders made of Sand is unknown, but her trouser-wearing, cigar-smoking image – along with her "living in sin" – could hardly have made her popular in the rural Mallorca of that period. There's an obvious though limited curiosity in looking around Sand and Chopin's old quarters, but the monastery boasts far more interesting diversions, and it's easy to follow the signs around the place.

The monastery church and pharmacy

A visit begins in the gloomy **church**, a square and heavy construction, which is distinguished by its late Baroque ceiling paintings and barrel vaulting. It also possesses a kitsch high altar and a fanciful bishop's throne, which somehow manages to look a little self-conscious. Beyond the church lie the shadowy **cloisters**, where the first port of call is the **pharmacy**, which survived the expulsion of the monks to serve the town's medicinal needs well into the twentieth century. Its shelves are crammed with a host of beautifully decorated majolica jars, antique glass receptacles and painted wooden boxes, many carefully inscribed with the name of a potion or drug.

The prior's cell

Despite its name, the **prior's cell** is a comfortable suite of bright, sizeable rooms, enhanced by access to a private garden with splendid views down the valley. The cell incorporates a chapel, a library, an audience chamber, a dining room and a bedroom – all graced by a potpourri of religious *objets d'art*. These include a number of handsome majolica pieces and two unattributed medieval **triptychs** displayed in the library. The triptychs are the *Adoration of the Magi*, a charmingly naive painting in the Flemish style, and an intricate marble sculpture celebrating the marriage of Pedro II of Aragón (1174–1213), who died in battle outside Toulouse fighting the army of Simon de Montfort. This degree of luxury was clearly not what the ascetic **St Bruno** had in mind when he founded the **Carthusian order** in the eleventh century. Nevertheless, it's hard to blame the monks at Valldemossa for lightening what must have been a very heavy burden. Bruno's rigorous regime, inspired by his years as a hermit, had his monks in almost continuous isolation, gathering together only for certain church services and to eat in the refectory on Sundays. At other times, lay brothers fed the monks through hatches along the cloister corridors: three days a week the monks had only bread and water, and they never ate meat. The diet and the mountain air, never mind the celibacy, seem to have suited them: the longevity of the Valldemossa monks was proverbial.

2

Cells no. 2 and 4

Along the cloister corridor in Cell no. 2, the **Chopin and Sand Collection** exhibits miscellaneous curios relating to the famous duo, from portraits to musical scores and letters; it was in this cell that the composer wrote his *Raindrop* Prelude. Next door is **Cell no. 4**, which now charges an exorbitant €4 to enter either from the cloisters or from a separate entrance outside the monastery. Pride of place here goes to Chopin's piano, which was finally installed just three weeks before the couple left for Paris. Considering the hype, these incidental Chopin mementos are something of an anticlimax and you'll soon be moving on to the ground-floor galleries of the adjacent Museu Municipal.

Museu Municipal

Just along the cloister corridor from Cell no. 4 is the **Museu Municipal**, whose first main room has a large and laudatory feature on the Archduke Ludwig Salvator (see box, p.110). On display are his letters and books plus a particularly interesting selection of old island photos (including one of his favourite mistress, Catalina Homar), a couple of photos of the island's hermit-monks, and several photos of the archduke's Mallorcan properties, principally Son Marroig (see p.109) and S'Estaca,

---

GEORGE SAND AT VALLDEMOSSA

In the nineteenth century, Mallorca was the subject of many foreign jottings, but the most celebrated were those of **George Sand** (1804–76), the pen name of the French aristocrat Armandine Lucile Aurore Dupin, the Baroness Dudevant. Sand married the eponymous baron in 1822, then left him nine years later for the literary life of Paris, where she embraced the Republican cause. A prolific author, dramatist and journalist, Sand became a well-known figure in French political circles and her occasional travels included an extended stay in Valldemossa (1838–39) with her partner, the pianist and composer **Frédéric Chopin**. Sand was not overly impressed with the islanders, but she did take a liking to Valldemossa, as she recorded in her **memoir** of the time, *A Winter in Majorca*:

"To reach the Cartuja [Valldemossa monastery] you have to leave the coach, for it is impossible for any vehicle to clamber up the stony track that leads to it. It is a fascinating approach with its sudden twists and bends among magnificent trees, and with wonderful views that are unfolded at every step, and increase in beauty the higher one rises. … At the head of the valley …[the Carthusian monks]… have made a vast garden … [which occupies]… the whole inclined background of the valley, and rises in a succession of wide terraces on the lower slopes of the mountain. By moonlight, and when its irregularity is masked by the darkness, it could be taken for an amphitheatre carved out for the battles of giants…

The Cartuja, situated at the highest point of this gorge, looks on the north side over an extensive valley, which widens out and rises in a gentle slope to the coastal cliffs, whose base is battered and eroded by the sea. … It is a surpassing picture, framed in the foreground by dark, pine-covered crags; beyond that by the sharply outlined profiles of mountains set off by superb trees; and in the background by the rounded humps of hills, which the setting sun gilds with the warmest shades, and on whose crests one can still distinguish, from a distance of a league, the microscopic outlines of the trees, as fine as the antennae of butterflies, as black and distinct as a trace of Chinese ink on a backdrop of sparkling gold."

formerly the property of actor **Michael Douglas**. The museum's second main room is devoted to a modest collection of local landscape paintings, among which the bright, cheerful and very folksy canvases of **Joan Fuster** (1870–1943) are the pick.

Museu Municipal Art Contemporani

Upstairs, the **Museu Municipal Art Contemporani** has a small but surprisingly good collection of modern art. There's a platoon of characteristic squiggles by Joan Miró, works by international artists such as Max Ernst and Francis Bacon, and a substantial collection of paintings by the Spanish modernist **Juli Ramís** (1909–90), from geometric abstractions through to forceful, expressionistic paintings like *The Blue Lady* (*Dama Blava*).

Palau Sancho

From near the prior's cell a doorway leads outside the cloisters and across the courtyard to the back entrance of the **Palau Sancho** (Palace of King Sancho). It's not the original medieval palace – that disappeared long ago – but this fortified mansion is the oldest part of the monastery complex. Within its imposing walls, which mostly date from the sixteenth century, lies a string of appealing period rooms cluttered with faded paintings and other curios, from fans, vintage engravings and a head of a suffering Christ to old halberds and muskets. The palace was the first home of the monks, but it has also seen service as the residence of local bigwigs and as a political prison, its most celebrated internee being the liberal reformer **Gaspar de Jovellanos**, a victim of the royal favourite Manuel de Godoy, who had him locked up here from 1801 to 1802. To get a better sense of the layout of the palace, take a peek at the front entrance – back outside and a couple of minutes' walk away on c/Jovellanos. The Palau Sancho is also used to stage fifteen-minute **Chopin concerts**, included in the monastery entrance fee.

Valldemossa town

The monastery is very much the main event in Valldemossa, though there are a couple of minor attractions among the cobbled lanes and old stone houses of the **town centre**, which tumbles prettily down the hillside beneath it. First is the church of **Sant Bartomeu**, an imposing Gothic edifice with a handsome Baroque bell tower that lords it over a tiny piazza. Nearby, round the back along a narrow alley at c/Rectoria 5, is the humble birthplace of **Santa Catalina Thomàs**, a sixteenth-century nun revered for her piety. The interior of the house has been turned into a simple little **shrine**, with a statue of the saint holding a small bird with a saintly reliquary down below.

ARRIVAL AND INFORMATION

VALLDEMOSSA

By car The prettiest approach to Valldemossa is from the south from Palma, along the Ma-111/1110, which squeezes through a narrow defile, passing high above terraced orchards as it clambers up towards the town's sloping jumble of houses and monastic buildings. The Ma-10, meanwhile, dodges Valldemossa by a kilometre or two, with the final approach being through the town's workaday western outskirts.

Parking There are several car parks beside the ring road – Avgda Palma – but spaces can get thin on the ground

between about 10am and 4pm.

By bus The main bus stop is beside the most westerly of the car parks flanking the ring road.

Destinations Deià (4–7 daily; 30min); Palma (4–7 daily; 30min); Port de Sóller (4–7 daily; 1hr); Sóller (4–7 daily; 55min).

Tourist information The town tourist office is beside the ring road (Mon 9am–1pm & 3–5pm; Tues–Fri 9am–6.30pm, Sat 10am–1pm & 2.30–6.30pm; Sun 10am–2pm; ☎971 61 21 06, ⓦvalldemossa.com).

ACCOMMODATION

★**Ca's Papa** c/Jovellanos 8 ☎971 61 28 08, ⓦhotelcaspapa.com. Charming independent hotel in a great location, metres from the monastery, in a brightly

painted old stone-terraced house. Has just thirteen cosily decorated rooms – no chain lookalikes here. Very friendly, with great breakfasts too. **€120**

VALLDEMOSSA (P.111) >

2

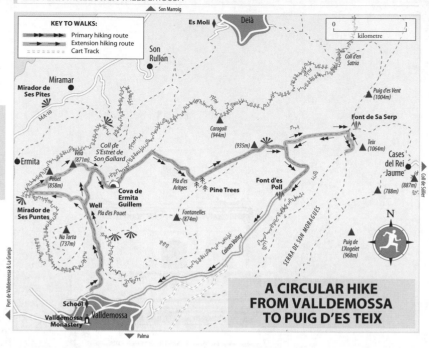

A CIRCULAR HIKE
FROM VALLDEMOSSA
TO PUIG D'ES TEIX

A CIRCULAR HIKE FROM VALLDEMOSSA TO PUIG D'ES TEIX BY THE ARCHDUKE'S PATH

12.5km • 674m of ascent • 4hr 30min–5hr • Medium difficulty • Trailhead: N39.71089°, E002.62091° • Optional extensions: the Mirador de Ses Puntes & Veià (an additional 1.5km; 116m of ascent; 45min); and Puig d'es Teix (2.5km; 186m of ascent; 60min).

The terrain between **Valldemossa and Deià** is mountainous and wild, abounding in steep cliffs and rocky summits; the lower slopes are wooded but the tops are almost devoid of vegetation, with numerous dramatic viewpoints, many of them overlooking the ocean. The land may be rough, but it's still crisscrossed by footpaths, originally made by the charcoal burners, olive growers and hunters who once hunkered down here in the mountains. These tracks can be stony, but the archduke **Ludwig Salvator** (see box, p.110) modified matters by having some wonderful paths constructed so that he could ride around on horseback admiring the scenery. This **circular walk** – which can be lengthened or shortened to suit – is a classic, showing the area to best advantage.

THE ROUTE

From near the monastery on Valldemossa's bypass (Avgda Palma), proceed along **c/Venerable Sor Aina** past the **car park** and take the first right up to the **school**. Climb the **steps** at the left-hand side of the school, then turn right and almost immediately left onto c/Alzines. Follow this road round, turn right onto c/Oliveres and then continue through a chained entry next to **Son Gual Petit** (a house), along a stony path that leads into the woods, entered by a ladder over a locked gate. The path winds uphill steeply through the woods to reach an opening in the wall at the edge of a wooded plain, the **Pla d'es Pouet**, where there is a crossroads. Continue straight ahead here until you reach an old **well** (now polluted) in a large clearing. This well is a vital reference point in a confusing area and it is essential that you take your bearings carefully here.

At this point you can extend the walk to take in the Mirador de Ses Puntes (see below), or take the path from the well that bears slightly right and leads easily up to the **Coll de S'Estret de Son Gallard**. At a T-junction, turn right past some V-shaped stone seats. The main path continues uphill. South of this path lies the **Cova de Ermita Guillem**, a hermit's cave with a shrine and assorted icons – look for a branch path on the right, which leads to the enclosure in front of the cave. From the cave, retrace your steps back to the main path and continue. A short stiff climb takes you to the stone **Archduke's path**. Here, turn left uphill, winding up to the edge of the cliffs for breathtaking views across the island and of the coastline below; this is a great place for a picnic.

Continue along the path and as you skirt the summit of **Puig de Caragolí** (944m) you can spy Port de Sóller down on the coast and the mountains Major, Teix and Galatzó rising high above the seashore. The descent is gentle, over the sloping, arid plain of **Pla d'es Aritges**. A clearly signposted junction at an isolated group of **pine trees** offers a short cut, heading right, back to Valldemossa via Fontanelles. To stay on the main route, continue straight on, heading northeast, which brings you over a 935m top and, shortly after, to a viewpoint overlooking Deià. After this the path swings southeast and begins to descend to the Teix path junction.

A 1m-high **cairn** and waymark clearly identifies the **Teix path junction**, where those heading for the Teix summit (see below) steer left. Otherwise, continue straight ahead to follow the seemingly interminable cement track's descent into the **Cairats valley**. First you'll come to an old "snowhouse" (a deep hole used for storing ice in winter), then a stone mountain refuge, the *Refugi de Son Moragues*, and below that a spring and picnic site, the **Font d'es Poll** (Well of the Poplar). The wide track beyond is stony but you'll have no trouble finding the route. On the way down the valley you'll see the remains of a *sitja*, a charcoal-worker's shelter, and a lime kiln. Keep on the main track down the Cairats valley, going over a wall via stone steps. The main path bends round to the left to lead down to the main road to the east of Valldemossa.

The **more direct route** back to town is to head down a path to your right, before vineyards, where the dirt track eventually leads down to join c/Xesc Forteza. From here, bear left into c/Lluis Vives, at the end of which is a large old house with a square tower. Take a moment to stop here and admire the splendid views over the old part of Valldemossa. Then, continue on down c/San Gual, turn left into c/Mas and right onto Avgda Palma, which will bring you directly into the town centre.

MIRADOR DE SES PUNTES EXTENSION

From the well (see above), take the path to your left, which leads northwest before zigzagging uphill and swinging west. Fork left shortly after passing an old and long-defunct bread oven to reach the **Mirador de Ses Puntes**. From this superb viewpoint, return to the fork and take the left branch, which rises through the trees to the top of **Pouet** (858m) and, after a little dip, **Veià** (871m). For much of the way, the path is the wide bridleway built by the archduke and from it you can look down on Sa Foradada, a rocky headland near his old house, Son Marroig (see p.109). From the ruined shelter on Veià the path descends to the **Coll de Son Gallard**, where you rejoin the main path a little up from the well. You'll need to re-orientate yourself at the well.

PUIG D'ES TEIX SUMMIT EXTENSION

For the hour-long detour to the **Puig d'es Teix summit**, turn left at the waymarked Teix path junction, taking a path that scrambles up a little gully and then continues over a sandy plateau towards a high stone wall. Cross this using the ladders provided and walk on to the **Pla de Sa Serp**, a plain where there is a spring – the **Font de Sa Serp**. A well-used path then leads up to the col between the two summits and on to the main west summit of **Puig d'es Teix** (1064m). From here the views over the Sóller valley and the western summit of Puig Major are especially fine, while the tops of Cornadors, L'Ofre and the Alfàbia ridge form a stunning skyline. Return to the Teix path junction by the same route (avoid the difficult-to-follow route southwest from Teix towards Sa Bussa) and turn left to continue the walk as described above.

2

Es Petit Hotel c/Uetam 1 ☎971 61 24 79, ⓦespetit hotel-valldemossa.com. This small hotel occupies a tastefully renovated old stone house metres from the monastery. There are eight en-suite guest rooms, each decorated in a pleasant, unfussy style with creams and browns to the fore; two also have smashing outside terraces with views down the valley. **€130**

Hotel Valldemossa Carretera Vieja de Valldemossa s/n ☎971 61 26 26, ⓦvalldemossahotel.com. A grand Italianate stairway climbs up to what was originally a pair of nineteenth-century hilltop farmhouses, but is now the sleek, rural-chic *Valldemossa* hotel, with a heated indoor pool, a restaurant and an expansive terrace. Luxurious gardens tumble down the hillside and the twelve rooms – three doubles and nine suites – come with every mod con. All very chichi. **€300**

EATING AND DRINKING

The centre of Valldemossa is packed with **cafés** and **restaurants**, but most are geared up for the day-trippers and offer pretty dire food at inflated prices. That said, there are one or two exceptions, as detailed below, and/or you can enjoy locally made ice cream from the kiosk opposite the monastery entrance.

Ca'n Mario c/Uetam 8 ☎971 61 21 22, ⓦhostal canmario.net. In an old and handsome terraced house, the first-floor *Ca'n Mario* is a family-run place with engagingly old-fashioned decor. They serve traditional Mallorcan food, with main courses averaging around €15. Daily except Tues 1.30–3.30pm & 8–10pm.

Casa de Sa Miranda Plaça Miranda des Lladoners 3 ☎971 61 22 96. Arguably the best restaurant in Valldemossa, offering a wide-ranging menu including Asian fusion, South American and Spanish dishes, from

such delights as octopus with miso sauce to *sobrasada* croquettes. In an old stone bastion with views down the valley. Tapas average €8, main courses from €15. Daily except Tues noon–9.30pm.

Restaurante Es Roquissar Plaça Cartoixa 5 ☎971 61 62 08. In a prime location beside the monastery, this small and cosy restaurant serves up a tasty range of freshly prepared tapas and main meals – try, for example, the spinach and ricotta ravioli. Tapas from €10, main courses from €15. Daily except Wed noon–9.30pm.

Port de Valldemossa

Valldemossa may not have a beach, but you can paddle and swim at **PORT DE VALLDEMOSSA**, where a handful of seaside villas huddle together in the shadow of the mountains at the mouth of a narrow, craggy cove. There's no public transport, but the drive down to the port, once Valldemossa's gateway to the outside world, is stimulating: head west out of Valldemossa to rejoin the Ma-10 and, after about 1.5km, turn right at the sign and follow the twisty side road for 6km down through the mountains. Port de Valldemossa's **beach** is small and shingly, and tends to get battered by the surf, but the scenery is stunning.

EATING AND DRINKING   PORT DE VALLDEMOSSA

Es Port c/Ponent s/n ☎971 61 61 94, ⓦrestaurante sport.es. The only restaurant here in Port de Valldemossa, *Es Port* has a handsome setting, its terrace jutting out into the ocean, and has a good reputation for the quality of its

seafood – try the shellfish paella at just €17 per head. Opening hours may vary, so ring ahead to confirm. Daily: late Feb–mid-May & late Oct 10am–6pm; mid-May to mid-Oct 10am–9pm.

La Granja

Carretera Banyalbufar, Km 1.5 · Daily: May–Sept 10am–7pm; Oct–April 10am–6pm · €15 · ☎971 61 00 32, ⓦlagranja.net · The Palma/Estellencs bus (4–8 daily) stops by the entrance to La Granja

The house and grounds of **La Granja**, a grand *hacienda* in a wooded and terraced valley 9km from Valldemossa, are a popular package-tourist, but, despite the many visitors, the estate just about manages to maintain a languorous air of old patrician comfort. La Granja was occupied until fairly recently by the Fortuny family, who took possession in the mid-fifteenth century; after about the 1920s it seems that modernization never crossed their minds. Pick up the leaflet outlining the numbered **self-guided tour** just before you reach the ticket office.

The house

From the ticket office, which is immediately in front of the main forecourt, signs direct you up round the back of the house, past a gathering of farmyard animals and well-weathered agricultural tackle. At the back of the house, you then proceed up to the old bathhouse, which offers a wide view over the estate, and continue down to the **house** itself, where a sequence of rooms is strewn with domestic clutter. Among much else, there's a games room, an ironing room, a graceful first-floor loggia and a dining room which, with its faded paintings and tapestries, has a real touch of country elegance. A particular highlight is the delightful little theatre, where plays were once performed for the household in a manner common among Europe's nineteenth-century rural landowners.

2

The workshops

Tagged onto the house, a series of **workshops** recalls the days when La Granja was a profitable and almost entirely self-sufficient concern. A wine press as well as almond and olive-oil mills prepared the estate's produce for export, while plumbers, carpenters, cobblers, weavers and rope makers all kept pace with domestic requirements. After the workshops, you can either go for a twenty-minute **walk** through the surrounding woods, or head directly to the **cellars**, the site of the farm kitchen. The Fortunys were one of Mallorca's more enlightened landowning families, and employees were well fed by the kitchen staff, who made cheeses, bread and preserves. Also in the cellars are three entirely unauthentic additions – a display of torture instruments, a torture chamber and an Inquisition tribunal chamber.

The chapel and forecourt

After the cellars, you reach the family **chapel**, a diminutive affair with battered religious paintings and sculptures; and then the expansive **forecourt**, shaded by plane trees and surrounded by antiquated workshops where costumed artisans "practise" traditional crafts such as wood-turning and candle-making. This part of the visit is more than a little bogus, but fun all the same – and the doughnuts (*bunyols*) are a greasy treat.

Esporles

ESPORLES, a couple of kilometres from La Granja, is an amiable, leafy little town whose elongated main street runs parallel to the line of an ancient stone watercourse. This is Mallorca away from the tourist throng, and although there's no strong reason to stop, you might drop by the town's finest building, its thirteenth-century **church**. A massive, heavily buttressed affair, it sits at the top of the town centre overlooking Plaça d'Espanya – though here the *plaça* is not a square but a street. Esporles certainly wasn't the place to be in 1452, when local landowners finally managed to crush a peasants' revolt that had spread across the island from the Esporles district. The leader of the insurrection, a certain Miquel Forns, was tortured to death on Plaça d'Espanya and his body left swinging on a gibbet to hammer home the point.

By bus Buses to and from Esporles pull in on c/Jaume I, just west of the main street (the Ma-1100), towards the north end of town, and three blocks south of Plaça d'Espanya.

Destinations Banyalbufar (4–8 daily; 20min); Estellencs (4–8 daily; 35min); Palma (every 1–2hr; 35min).

Banyalbufar

2

Approaching from the east, the Ma-10 offers spectacular views as it nears **BANYALBUFAR**, a drowsy little village whose terraced fields cling gingerly to the coastal cliffs. The land here has been cultivated since Moorish times, with a spring above the village providing a water supply that's still channelled down the hillside into open storage cisterns, the unlikely-looking home for a few carp. The village is bisected by the Ma-10, also its main street, with ancient houses and steep cobbled lanes to either side. The cute main square, **Plaça de la Vila**, perches above the Ma-10, overlooked by a chunky, barrel-vaulted parish **church** dating from the fifteenth century. Banyalbufar is a fine place to unwind, and there's a rough and rocky **beach** a steep fifteen-minute walk down the hill – just follow the signs to the *Hotel Sa Coma* and keep going. The village does not have a tourist office, but considering its size, it has a good range of reasonably priced accommodation and a competent café and restaurant scene.

Torre del Verger

Heading west from Banyalbufar on the Ma-10, it's about 1.5km to the **Torre del Verger**, a medieval watchtower that offers stunning views out along the coast. The tower was built as a sentinel against pirate attack, but not so much to protect the much-oppressed locals, but more to guard the property of the local lord, the Baron of Banyalbufar, who owned the land and controlled every facet of the local administration – a common state of affairs in rural Mallorca up until the twentieth century.

ARRIVAL AND DEPARTURE BANYALBUFAR

By bus Buses to and from Banyalbufar travel the length of the main street. Services to Estellencs stop about 20m west of – and just round the corner from – the main square; those heading east stop across from the square.

Destinations Esporles (4–8 daily; 20min); Estellencs (4–8 daily; 15min); Palma (4–8 daily; 1hr 10min).

ACCOMMODATION

Hotel Mar i Vent c/Major 49 ☎971 61 80 00, ⓦhotelmarivent.com. In a conspicuous 1940s building on the main street towards the east end of the village, this traditional hotel has thirty rooms, the best of which are reasonably large and have sea-facing balconies with fantastic views along the coast. There's also an outside pool and staff will park your car for you – a blessing given the village's steep and narrow lanes. **€100**

Hotel Sa Baronia c/Baronia 16 ☎971 61 81 46, ⓦwww.hbaronia.com. Traditional – some would say old-fashioned – hotel, parts of which inhabit an ancient fortified house. The forty-odd guest rooms are simple and straightforward, all white walls and varnished furniture, and have sea-facing balconies. It has a large outside pool and is handily located at the west end of the village, beside the main street. Closed Nov–March. **€80**

★**Hotel Sa Coma** Camí des Molí 3 ☎971 61 80 34, ⓦhotelsacoma.com. Banyalbufar has a clutch of traditional, family-run hotels and this is the pick. In a straightforward, three-storey modern block, it has fittings and furnishings reminiscent of the 1970s, but the whole ensemble is engaging and most of the rooms have mini-balconies with sea views. There's an outdoor pool, too. The hotel is located down below the main drag on the way to the beach – just follow the signs. Closed Nov–April. **€130**

Hotel Son Borguny c/Borguny 1 ☎971 14 87 06, ⓦsonborguny.com. A short walk up from the main street, this hotel occupies a creatively modernized three-storey stone house that dates from the fifteenth century. The seven guest rooms are kitted out in a cheerful version of modern-meets-traditional style, though few have sea views. **€100**

EATING AND DRINKING

★**Pegasón y el Pajarito Enmascarado** c/Pont 2 ❶971 14 87 13. The liveliest place in town, this informal bar and restaurant is in cellar-like premises almost underneath the main street across from the main square. Its twin rooms are adorned with bizarre-cum-Baroque furnishings and fittings and it has a short but well-chosen menu that includes traditional Mallorcan dishes from €18 as well as pizzas and the like. Check out, too, the *menú del día* (€15) or the tapas (€8). No cards. Mon–Wed & Sat–Sun 12.30–4pm & 7.30–11pm, Fri 7.30–11pm.

Restaurante 1661 Cuina de Banyalbufar c/Baronia 1 ❶971 61 82 45. Bang on the high street, this well-turned-out restaurant offers a temptingly varied menu with Spanish/Catalan dishes at its core: main courses average €20. Daily 10am–11.30pm.

★**Restaurante Son Tomas** c/Baronia 17 ❶971 61 81 49. At the west end of the village, this agreeable restaurant occupies modern premises with a large, sea-facing terrace. Service is punctilious and the steaks are good, but the seafood is even better – look out for the fish of the day. Main courses average €15. Mon & Wed–Sun: April to late Oct 12.30–4pm & 7–9.30pm; late Oct to March 12.30–4pm.

Estellencs

Delightful **ESTELLENCS**, some eight kilometres west of Banyalbufar, is similar to its neighbour, with steep coastal cliffs and tight terraced fields. If anything, though, it's even prettier, its narrow, winding alleys shadowed by old stone houses and one-time agricultural buildings. The village has one notable structure, a sturdy stone **church**, dating from the fifteenth century and built like a fortress to ward off pirate attacks; attached to it are the ruined walls – and bull's-eye windows – of its predecessor. From the west side of the village, a steep and narrow but driveable 2km lane leads down past olive and orange orchards to **Cala Estellencs**, a rocky, surf-buffeted cove that shelters a rough shingly beach, a fishing jetty and a summertime bar. Alternatively, you can walk down to the beach from the centre of the village along the serpentine c/Mar in about fifty minutes. Finally, there's a superb vantage point over the coast 3.5km southwest of Estellencs on the Ma-10 at the **Mirador Es Grau**, where a flight of stone steps climbs up to an ancient tower.

ARRIVAL AND DEPARTURE ESTELLENCS

By bus Buses stop on the main street in the centre of the village, near the church.

Destinations Esporles (4–8 daily; 35min); Banyalbufar (4–8 daily; 15min); Palma (4–8 daily; 1hr 15min).

ACCOMMODATION AND EATING

Hotel Maristel c/Eusebi Pacscual 10 ❶971 61 85 50, ⓦhotelmaristel.com. Straddling the main road at the west end of the village, this substantial, four-star hotel comprises two modern blocks with fifty or so large and well-appointed rooms. Many rooms have sea-facing balconies with superb coastal views, and there's a pool and spa, too. **€120**

★**Montimar** Plaça Constitució 7 ❶971 61 85 76. The pick of the village's restaurants, up a flight of steps from the main street near the church. The menu here bristles with beautifully prepared Mallorcan favourites like suckling pig, snails and rabbit, and every effort is made to source things locally. The building is attractively ancient, too, and there's a pleasant outside terrace; mains average €15. Tues–Sun noon–3.30pm & 7–10pm.

★**Hotel Nord** Plaça d'es Triquet 4 ❶971 14 90 06, ⓦhotelruralnord.com. Below the main street in the middle of Estellencs, this is a charming family-run place in a cleverly reworked and modernized old stone house and olive press. There are eight guest rooms, two with a private terrace and one with a balcony, each decorated in ochres and whites but featuring the original architecture – especially the wooden beamed ceilings; it's all in the most immaculate of tastes. They serve evening meals here as well and there's a lovely courtyard patio for drinks. It's clearly signed from the main road, but use the car park on the west side of the village as the lanes around the hotel are too narrow to negotiate easily by car. Closed Nov–Jan. **€110**

SHOPPING

Vall Hermós c/Eusebi Pascual s/n ❶971 61 86 10, ⓦvallhermos.com. Attached to a café that bears the same name, this tiny little shop offers a good range of Mallorcan wines and other assorted products. Daily except Wed 10am–11pm.

2

Andratx

An ancient town founded by the Romans, **ANDRATX**, just 20km from Estellencs, is a busy if rather modest little place, whose importance as an agricultural centre amid orchards and almond groves has been pretty much washed away by the tide of tourism. The town is at its prettiest among the aged houses and narrow streets of the **old centre** and these struggle up to the fortress-like walls of the thirteenth-century church of **Santa Maria**, built high and strong to deter raiding pirates, its balustraded precincts offering panoramic views down towards the coast. Andratx hosts a popular **Wednesday morning market**, but is perhaps better known for something much less savoury – the corrupt sale of building permits, which came to light in 2006 and resulted in the arrest of the mayor, Eugenio Hidalgo.

CCA Andratx Art Centre

c/Estanyera 2, 1km east of Andratx on the Ma-1031 to Capdellà · March–Oct Tues–Fri 10.30am–7pm, Sat & Sun 10.30am–4pm; Nov–Feb Tues–Sun 10.30am–4pm · €8 · ☎ 971 13 77 70, ⓦ www.ccandratx.com

Mallorca's largest centre of contemporary art, the **CCA Andratx** occupies a whopping modern structure, built in the style of a *hacienda* complete with an expansive, internal courtyard. The gallery runs an enterprising artists-in-residence programme – the complex incorporates a set of apartments – but the key note is its temporary exhibitions of contemporary art (three or four a year), featuring an international crew of artists. These are often billed as "challenging" – and indeed they are.

ARRIVAL AND DEPARTURE   **ANDRATX**

By bus Andratx, which is just 23km from Palma, is easy to reach by bus, with most services weaving through the centre. One of the more central stops is on Carretera Estellencs (the Ma-10), near its junction with c/Moner.

Destinations Palma (1–2 hourly; 1hr); Peguera (1–2 hourly; 15min); Port d'Andratx (1–2 hourly; 10min); Sant Elm (7 daily; 40min).

Sant Elm and around

Three kilometres west of Andratx, the hillside hamlet of **S'Arracó** is the prelude to a pretty, orchard-covered landscape that buckles up into wooded hills and dipping valleys as it approaches the seashore, another 4km or so away. At the end of the road is the low-key resort of **SANT ELM**, whose main street strings along the shoreline with a pretty, sandy cove **beach** at one end and a **harbour** at the other – and, mercifully, no tower blocks in between. Indeed, one of the pleasures of Sant Elm is its relative lack of development: there are, it's true, a fair number of second homes and holiday apartments, but it is all pretty inconspicuous and there are only two hotels and a small platoon of cafés and restaurants.

THE HIKE TO LA TRAPA

The rugged coastal district just to the north of Sant Elm is almost entirely devoid of development and boasts several enjoyable **hikes**. The most popular is the hour-long (5km) hike along the GR221 (see p.91) to **La Trapa**, a small monastery built by Trappist monks, who arrived here in 1810 having fled from Revolutionary France. Part of the hiking route is along a steep and narrow path that offers superlative views over the coast, though the final ascent involves some rock scrambling. The hike begins from the north side of Sant Elm: follow the shoreline until you reach Plaça Mossen Sebastia Grau (where buses terminate). From this square, take Avgda La Trapa and keep going. Sant Elm tourist office (see opposite) issues free, if rudimentary, hiking maps.

Parc Natural de Sa Dragonera

Daily: April–Sept 10am–5pm; Oct–March 10am–2.30pm • Free • ⓦ en.balearsnatura.com • Passenger boats operated by Cruceros
Margarita (☏ 639 61 75 45, ⓦ crucerosmargarita.com) make the 15min journey from Sant Elm to Sa Dragonera (Feb, March & Oct Mon–
Sat 8 daily, 4 daily return; April–Sept Mon–Sat 10 daily, 6 daily return; €12 return); check the times of return boats on the
outward journey

From Sant Elm's tiny harbour, **passenger boats** shuttle across to the austere offshore islet that comprises the **Parc Natural de Sa Dragonera**. This uninhabited hunk of rock, some 4km long and 700m wide, lies at an oblique angle to the coast, with an imposing ridge of sea cliffs dominating its northwestern shore. Behind the ridge, a rough road/path runs the length of the island, linking a pair of craggy capes and their lighthouses. The boat docks at a tiny cove-harbour – **Cala Lladó** – about halfway up the east shore, which puts both ends of the island within comfortable walking distance, though the excursion north to **Cap de Tramuntana** is both shorter and prettier – allow about an hour each way. There's also a much more challenging, three- to four-hour trail that clambers up to the **Puig de Na Pòpia** (352m) lighthouse on the northwest coast. Most people visit Sa Dragonera for the scenic solitude, but the island is also good for **bird life** – ospreys, shags, gulls and other seabirds are plentiful, and you may also see several species of raptor.

ARRIVAL AND INFORMATION

By bus Buses thread their way through the resort, but the main bus stop is at the south end of the main street, metres from the beach.

Destinations Andratx (7 daily; 40min); Port d'Andratx (7 daily; 30min).

By car The large, partly shaded dirt car park at the south end of the main street – and across from the beach – usually has spaces, but things can get tight after 10am on summer weekends; a flat-rate ticket costs €3.80.

By ferry From Sant Elm, Cruceros Margarita (☏ 639 61 75 45, ⓦ crucerosmargarita.com) runs both the ferry service

SANT ELM AND AROUND

to Sa Dragonera (see above) and another to Port d'Andratx (Feb & March 1 daily Mon–Sat; April–Oct 1 daily; 30min; €8 each way). They also operate cruises round Sa Dragonera (April–Sept 4 daily; €20).

Tourist information Sant Elm tourist office, Avgda Jaume I, 28 (May–Sept Mon–Thurs 9am–4pm, Fri 9am–3pm, Sat 9am–2pm, Sun 9am–4pm; ☏ 971 62 80 08), is on the main street, roughly halfway between the beach and the harbour. They have information on local hikes and hiking maps, issue bus timetables, and have the sailing times of the boat to Sa Dragonera (see above).

ACCOMMODATION AND EATING

Hotel Aquamarín c/Cala Es Conills s/n ☏ 902 02 02 40, ⓦ universalhotels.es. Overlooking the beach at the south end of the resort, this package-tour favourite occupies a distinctive concrete structure built in the style of an old watchtower. Rooms tend to be block-booked, but it's worth a try. Closed Nov–April. **€100**

★ **Hostal Dragonera** c/Jaume I, 5 ☏ 971 23 90 86, ⓦ hostaldragonera.es. An extremely well-kept, modern *hostal* in a prime location, halfway along the main drag and with views over the sea. The rooms are clean and neat, with the pick having sea-facing balconies. Top-notch breakfasts too. At peak times, the minimum stay is one week. Excellent value. Closed Nov–Feb. **€70**

Restaurante de Na Caragola c/Jaume I, 23 ☏ 971 23 90 06, ⓦ restaurantenacaragola.com. Right by the harbour, this long-established restaurant has a long and particularly attractive sea-facing terrace. Seafood is its forte, simply served with a minimum of fuss. Mains cost around €20. Daily 1–4pm & 7–11pm.

Restaurante Vista Mar c/Jaume I, 46 ☏ 971 23 75 47. Straightforward, modern restaurant down by the harbour and with a pleasant seashore terrace. Offers a wide range of fresh fish – the sardines and the fish soup are especially tasty. Main courses from around €20. Feb–Oct daily 10am–11pm.

Port d'Andratx

In recent years, a splash of low-rise shopping complexes and Spanish-style villas has rung the changes in the picturesque port and fishing harbour of **PORT D'ANDRATX**, 6km southwest of Andratx. Nevertheless, it's not all developmental gloom: the heart of the **old town**, which slopes up from the south side of the bay, preserves a cramped

2

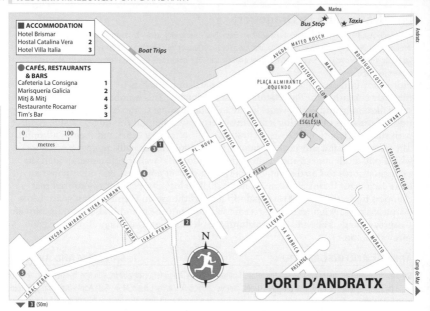

■ ACCOMMODATION	
Hotel Brismar	1
Hostal Catalina Vera	2
Hotel Villa Italia	3

● CAFÉS, RESTAURANTS & BARS	
Cafeteria La Consigna	1
Marisquería Galicia	2
Mitj & Mitj	4
Restaurante Rocamar	5
Tim's Bar	3

PORT D'ANDRATX

network of ancient lanes; the fishing fleet is in good if somewhat diminished fettle; and there's no denying the prettiness of the setting, with the port standing at the head of a long and slender inlet flanked by wooded hills. Sunsets show the place to best advantage, casting long shadows up the bay, and it's then that the old town's gaggle of restaurants crowds with nautical holidaymakers and expats. Port d'Andratx lacks a sandy **beach**, however – the nearest is east over the hills at Camp de Mar (see p.83).

ARRIVAL AND DEPARTURE
PORT D'ANDRATX

By bus Port d'Andratx is easy to reach by bus, with the main bus stop at the back of the bay at the northerly end of the old town and a brief stroll from the marina.

Destinations Andratx (every 30–60min; 10min); Camp de Mar (every 30–60min; 20min); Palma (every 30–60min; 1hr 10min); Sant Elm (7 daily; 30min).

By ferry Cruceros Margarita (📞639 61 75 45, Ⓦ crucerosmargarita.com) runs a ferry between Port d'Andratx and Sant Elm (Feb & March 1 daily Mon–Sat; April–Oct 1 daily; 30min; €8 each way).

By taxi There's a taxi rank at the back of the bay at the northerly end of the old town; alternatively, call Radio Taxi Andratx (📞971 13 63 98). The fare to Camp de Mar is about €8, €12 to Sant Elm.

ACCOMMODATION

Hotel Brismar Avgda Almirante Riera Alemany 6 📞971 67 16 00, Ⓦ hotelbrismar.com. A 1960s block of modest proportions in a prime harbourside location, this long-established three-star hotel has 50-odd plain and straightforward en-suite rooms. The pick have port-facing balconies (though avoid these if you're a light sleeper – there are a couple of bars nearby). Closed Dec–Feb. **€90**

Hostal Catalina Vera c/Isaac Peral 63 📞971 67 19 18, Ⓦ hostalcatalinavera.es. This enjoyable *hostal* is the best place to stay in Port d'Andratx. There are 15 guest rooms, a couple in a building at the back, but the majority are in a neatly shuttered and whitewashed 1950s two-storey house in a quiet but central location. Each room is kitted out in a

traditional albeit frugal version of Spanish style and has its own balcony: those at the front have a sea view. A small orchard and a lovely garden surround the *hostal* – there is even a selection of cacti on the rear stairway – and the foyer is packed with house plants. Nice breakfast; no wi-fi. **€85**

Hotel Villa Italia Camí Sant Carles 13 📞971 67 40 11, Ⓦ hotelvillaitalia.com. Set behind a steeply terraced garden just beyond the west end of the old town, this opulent hotel occupies a handsome and immaculately modernized 1950s twin-towered Italianate mansion. Features include an outdoor pool, a spa and gorgeous views over the bay. There are rooms and suites both in the old villa and in the more modern annexe. Substantial off-season discounts. **€220**

EATING AND DRINKING

Cafeteria La Consigna Avgda Mateo Bosch 19 ☎971 67 16 04. Down by the harbourside, this popular coffee house-cum-patisserie is a straightforward modern affair whose cakes and breads are made nearby at Andratx. Daily 9am–9pm.

Marisquería Galicia c/Isaac Peral 37 ☎971 67 27 05, ⓦmarisqueriagalicia.es. Bistro-style Galician place, where the seafood is the main event – vegetables are second-class citizens. Here you can sample everything from hake to octopus, barnacles to monkfish, at prices that are significantly lower than those down on the harbour. Mains average €22. Daily noon–11pm.

Mitj & Mitj c/Almirante Riera Alemany 9 ☎971 67 27 20. Nice views over the bay from the pavement terrace of this funky little bar in the heart of the resort. Try the cucumber lemonade – or for something a little stronger, add vodka. Daily noon–11pm, sometimes later.

Restaurante Rocamar c/Almirante Riera Alemany 27 ☎971 67 12 61, ⓦrocamar.eu. Well-established restaurant at the very west end of the harbourfront, just away from the crowds. The interior is nothing special, but the ocean-facing terrace is a lovely spot and they serve a good range of seafood. Main courses around €25. Mid-March to mid-Nov daily noon–11pm.

Tim's Bar c/Almirante Riera Alemany 7 ☎971 67 18 92. Cosy, even intimate, little bar down on the harbourfront that attracts a mixed and frequently well-oiled bunch. The cocktails go down a storm and there are occasional DJ nights too. Daily noon–11pm, sometimes later.

2

Northern Mallorca

131 The northern coast

136 Pollença

141 Cala Sant Vicenç

142 Badía de Pollença

148 Alcúdia

151 Badía d'Alcúdia

CAP DE FORMENTOR FROM POLLENÇA

Northern Mallorca

The magnificent Serra de Tramuntana mountains reach a precipitous climax in the rearing peaks of northern Mallorca. This is the wildest part of the island, long the haunt of brigands and monks, and even today the ruggedness of the terrain forces the main coastal road, the Ma-10, to duck and weave inland, scuttling past the once-remote monastery at Lluc – one of Mallorca's real highlights – but offering only the occasional glimpse of the sea. The mountains fade away as they near Pollença – perhaps Mallorca's prettiest town, and within easy striking distance of the region's two prime resorts, Port de Pollença and Port d'Alcúdia, as well as the island's top-ranking birdwatching site, the Parc Natural de S'Albufera.

3

Heading northeast from Sóller, the **Ma-10** soon snakes its way up into the mountains, threading round the stern flanks of **Puig Major** before passing the remarkable sideroad that wiggles and wriggles down to both overcrowded **Sa Calobra** and the attractive beach at **Cala Tuent**. Nonetheless, it's the charming monastery of **Lluc** that remains the big draw hereabouts, for tourists as well as religious islanders, who venerate an effigy of the Virgin known as La Moreneta. To the east of Lluc, the Ma-10 slides out of the mountains near **Pollença**, a handsome old town of honey-coloured stone mansions clustered around a fine, cypress-flanked Way of the Cross. From Pollença, it's a hop, skip and a jump to the **Badía de Pollença**, whose northern flank is guarded by the extravagantly wild and beautiful **Península de Formentor**, the northernmost spur of the Serra de Tramuntana, while the back of the bay is occupied by the low-key, family-orientated beach resort of **Port de Pollença**. Nearby, the pretty little town of **Alcúdia** lays claim to a set of good-looking stone walls and the rubbly remains of the old Roman settlement of Pollentia, and is only a couple of kilometres from the **Badía d'Alcúdia**, which has its own dramatic headland in the bony **Alcúdia peninsula**. Here, also, is the sprawling holiday resort of **Port d'Alcúdia** with its splendid stretch of golden sand, and the **Parc Natural de S'Albufera**, quite simply the best birdwatching wetland in the Balearics.

GETTING AROUND | NORTHERN MALLORCA

By bus Bus services around northern Mallorca are generally excellent between April and October, but are scaled right back in winter. The most popular long-distance route is seasonal bus #354, which runs from Port de Sóller to Ca'n Picafort via Sóller, Lluc, Pollença, Cala Sant Vicenç, Port de Pollença, Alcúdia and Port d'Alcúdia (April–Oct Mon–Sat 2 daily); note that this bus service is very popular and – travelling northeast – you have a better chance of a seat if you get on at Port de Sóller rather than the second stop, Sóller. All the area's tourist offices carry bus timetables – or go to the island's official public transport website, ⓦ tib.org.

By taxi Town-to-town taxi fares are fixed and are very reasonable, especially if you're travelling in a group. Sample fares are: Port de Sóller to Port de Pollença €88; Lluc to Pollença €35; Palma to Pollença €70.

Hiking, hikers' hostels and monastery accommodation p.131
Northern Mallorca: top 5 places to stay p.132
Lluc's choir p.134
The ceramic delights of Majolica p.135
Mallorcan walking tours p.142
A valley hike from Port de Pollença to Cala Bóquer p.145
A circular hike on the Alcúdia peninsula p.153
Northern Mallorca's top 5 beaches p.154

PORT DE POLLENÇA BEACH

Highlights

❶ Monestir de Nostra Senyora de Lluc Home to the Balearics' most venerated icon, La Moreneta, this intriguing monastery also makes an ideal base for mountain hikes. **See p.133**

❷ Pollença Wandering the narrow lanes and alleys of this beguiling little town of ancient stone houses is a real pleasure. **See p.136**

❸ Ermita de Nostra Senyora del Puig A rambling assortment of old stone buildings, this is one of the most appealing of Mallorca's several hilltop monasteries. **See p.139**

❹ Port de Pollença beach A long arc of sand and safe shallows make this one of Mallorca's best beaches. **See p.142**

❺ Península de Formentor This tapered promontory of bleak sea cliffs and pine-clad hills offers gorgeous views and excellent birdwatching. **See p.146**

❻ Parc Natural de S'Albufera A slab of wetland offering the best birdwatching on the island – especially in spring. **See p.156**

HIGHLIGHTS ARE MARKED ON THE MAP ON P.130

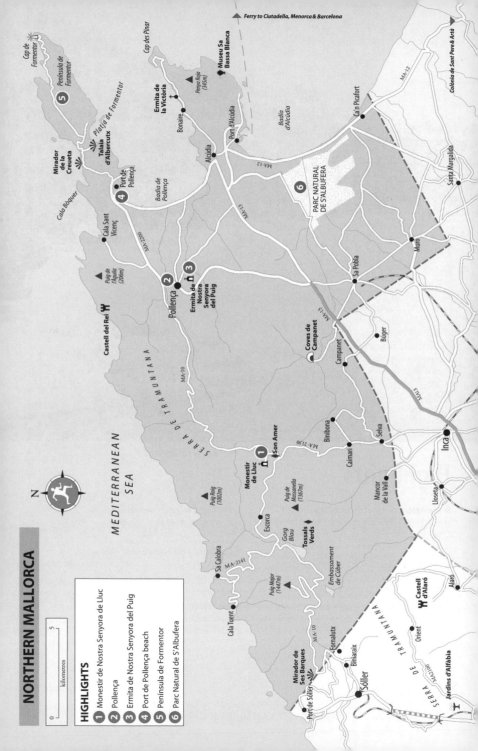

By car & parking If you have your own vehicle, be aware that in summer parking can be a real pain in most villages and resorts between 10 or 11am and 5pm; one exception is Lluc, where there is a huge car park.

The northern coast

Beyond Sóller, the **Ma-10** forges through the highest and harshest section of the **Serra de Tramuntana**, where the mountains drop straight into the ocean, pushing the road inland with barely a cove in sight. The accessible exceptions are the appealing beach at **Cala Tuent** and the overly commercialized hamlet of **Sa Calobra** next door, though it's the mountains that are the real magnet hereabouts, with the **Gorg Blau** (Blue Gorge) a handy place to start any one of several hikes. Popular for its hiking also is **Lluc monastery**, which sits in a wide, inland valley with mountains on all sides, but Lluc is better known for its fascinating church and reliable supply of inexpensive rooms.

3

Gorg Blau and around

Heading northeast from Sóller, the **Ma-10** zigzags up into the mountains, weaving past the steep turning down to Fornalutx (see p.99) before offering a last lingering view along the coast from the **Mirador de Ses Barques** vantage point. Thereafter, the road snakes inland to tunnel through the western flanks of **Puig Major** (1447m), the island's highest mountain. Beyond the tunnel is the **Gorg Blau**, a bare and bleak ravine that was a well-known beauty spot until a hydroelectric scheme scarred the gorge with a trio of puddle-like reservoirs. The second of the three – about 3km east of the tunnel – is the **Embassament de Cúber** (Cúber reservoir), an unappetizing expanse of water redeemed by its abundant birdlife, notably several different types of raptor. For a better look, stop at the lay-by to follow the easy **footpath** that circumnavigates the reservoir – it only takes a couple of hours to complete. The reservoir is also an obvious starting point for the four-hour hike west to the Barranc de Biniaraix along (part of) the **GR221** long-distance footpath; alternatively, it's a two-hour hike southeast to the *Refugi Tossals Verds* **hikers' hostel** (see p.132), in a remote spot high in the mountains. The *refugi* is also on the GR221, but getting there involves a detour from the main route between Biniaraix and Lluc.

To the immediate north of the reservoir rear the bare and craggy flanks of **Puig Major**, but the dramatic trail that twists up to the summit from the military base beside the main road remains off-limits on account of its radar station. This makes **Puig de Massanella** (1367m), which looms over the Gorg Blau to the east, the highest climbable mountain on the island.

HIKING, HIKERS' HOSTELS AND MONASTERY ACCOMMODATION

This part of the Serra de Tramuntana offers superb **hiking** and is home to the island's best hiking company, Mallorcan Walking Tours (see box, p.142). Suggestions for several comparatively easy and/or short walks are given in the text, and we have also described in detail a half-day hike beginning in Port de Pollença (see p.145) and a longer, tougher hike near Alcúdia (see p.153). The region is also traversed by Mallorca's main **long-distance hiking trail**, the **Ruta de Pedra en Sec** ("Dry-stone route"; officially known as the **GR221**), which runs in from Sóller and worms its way through the mountains on its way to Pollença. Not all of the GR221 is in prime condition, but this stretch certainly is, its route punctuated by three **hikers' hostels** (*refugi*): Tossals Verds (see p.132) in the mountains east of the Embassament de Cúber; Son Amer, near Lluc (see p.135); and Pont Romà in Pollença (see p.140). You can also stay in two of the region's **monasteries**, either comfortably at Lluc (see p.135) or more frugally at the Ermita de Nostra Senyora del Puig, just outside Pollença (see p.140).

By bus Buses stop beside the Cúber reservoir. Destinations Lluc (April–Oct Mon–Sat 2 daily; 40min); Pollença (April–Oct Mon–Sat 2 daily; 1hr); Port de Sóller (April–Oct Mon–Sat 2 daily; 50min); Sóller (April–Oct Mon–Sat 2 daily; 30min).

ACCOMMODATION

Refugi Tossals Verds ☎971 18 20 27, reservations ☎971 17 37 00, ⬤www.conselldemallorca.net. Up in the mountains, a 2hr hike southeast of the Embassament de Cúber reservoir, this hikers' hostel is one of several owned and operated by the state. There are thirty bunk beds here at €11 per person per night, with breakfast costing a further €5, and one double room; reservations must be made at least five days beforehand. Dorm €̄11, double €̄40

Cala Tuent

In between Gorg Blau and Escorca, a dramatic sideroad – the **Ma-2141** – slips over the mountains to both Sa Calobra (see below) and Cala Tuent. It's an exhilarating, ear-popping detour with the well-surfaced road zigzagging its way over terrain so severe that at one point it actually turns 270 degrees to run under itself.

About 10km down this road, there's a fork: head left over the hills for the 5km journey to **CALA TUENT**, where a smattering of villas clings to the northern slopes of Puig Major as it tumbles down towards the ocean. Ancient orchards temper the harshness of the mountain, and the gravel-and-sand beach is one of the quietest on the north coast. It's a lovely spot and – provided you stay close to the shore – the swimming is safe.

By car There's no public transport to Cala Tuent – and neither is there anywhere to stay. Parking can be a bit of a hassle too, especially at the weekend, with cars squeezed into unlikely angles where the road nears the beach.

EATING AND DRINKING

★Es Vergeret Cala Tuent ☎971 51 71 05, ⬤esvergeret.com. On the far side of the cove, this excellent restaurant has a gorgeous location, its long, shaded terrace nudging out into the sea. It serves up a tasty range of fish and meat dishes from €15 – all accompanied by the rolling sound of the ocean. March–Oct daily 12.30–4.30pm, plus July & Aug Sat 8.30–10.30pm.

Sa Calobra

The Ma-2141 continues beyond the Cala Tuent turning, wriggling its way down to the seashore at **SA CALOBRA**, where a scattering of houses occupies a pint-sized cove in the shadow of the mountains. The setting is gorgeous, but tour operators deposit busloads of tourists here every day in summer and the crush can be unbearable. The reason so many people come is to visit the impressive box canyon at the mouth of the **Torrent de Pareis** (River of the Twins). It takes about ten minutes to follow the partly tunnelled walkway round the coast from the village to the mouth of the canyon. Here, with sheer cliffs rising on every side, the milky-green river trickles down to the thick bank of sandy shingle that bars its final approach to the sea – though the scene is transformed after heavy rainfall, when the river crashes down into the canyon and out into the ocean.

NORTHERN MALLORCA: TOP 5 PLACES TO STAY

Monestir de Lluc See p.135
Es Castell See p.136
Posada de Lluc See p.140
Hotel Llenaire See p.144
Petit Hotel Hostatgeria la Victòria See p.152

By bus Buses stop in the large car park just up the road from the village.

Destinations Alcúdia (April–Oct Mon–Sat 1 daily; 2hr 30min); Lluc (April–Oct Mon–Sat 1 daily; 1hr 30min); Pollença (April–Oct Mon–Sat 1 daily; 2hr); Port d'Alcúdia (April–Oct Mon–Sat 1 daily; 3hr); Port de Pollença (April–Oct Mon–Sat 1 daily; 2hr 20min).

Escorca and the Torrent de Pareis

A poorly defined scattering of houses, **ESCORCA** strings along the Ma-10 in between the Cala Tuent/Sa Calobra turning and Lluc, its most conspicuous feature being the *Restaurant Escorca*. Directly opposite the restaurant, a sign marks the starting point for the descent of the **Torrent de Pareis**, a formidable, 7km-long, limestone river gorge which drops down to Sa Calobra (see opposite). It's a well-known, very testing and potentially dangerous hike-cum-climb which requires some basic rock-climbing skills, and takes about five hours to negotiate. The descent is not practicable in winter, spring, or after rainfall, when the river may be waist-high and the rocks dangerously slippery. The gorge is always hotter than its surroundings, so take lots of water.

Monestir de Nostra Senyora de Lluc

Just off the Ma-10 about 23km west of Pollença and 8km east of Escorca • Daily: April–Sept 10am–9pm; Oct–March 10am–8pm • Parking €4.50 with a monastery visit, €6 without • ☎ 971 87 15 25, ⓦ lluc.net

Tucked away in a once-remote valley, the austere, high-sided dormitories and orange-flecked roof tiles of the **Monestir de Nostra Senyora de Lluc** (Monastery of Our Lady of Lluc) stand out against the greens and greys of the surrounding mountains. It's a magnificent setting for what has been Mallorca's most important place of pilgrimage since the middle of the thirteenth century, though its religious significance goes back much further: the valley's prehistoric inhabitants were animists, who deified the local holm-oak woods, and the **Romans** picked up on the theme, naming the place from *lucus*, the Latin for "sacred forest". Later, the **monks** who settled here after the Reconquista were keen to coin a purely Christian etymology, so they invented the story of a shepherd boy named Lluc (Luke) stumbling across a tiny, brightly painted **statue** of the Virgin in the woods. Frightened by his discovery, the lad collared the nearest monk and, lo and behold, when the pair returned bright lights dazzled their eyes and celestial voices declared the statue to be an authentic heaven-sent image.

Basílica de la Mare de Déu de Lluc

Daily: April–Sept 10am–9pm; Oct–March 10am–8pm • Free

The **monastic complex** is an imposing and formal-looking affair mostly dating from the eighteenth and early nineteenth centuries. At its centre is the main shrine and architectural high point, the **Basílica de la Mare de Déu de Lluc**, which is graced by an elegant Baroque facade. To reach it, pass through the monastery's stately double-doored entrance and keep straight on till you reach the second – and final – courtyard, where there's a dreary statue of Bishop Campins (1859–1915), who overhauled Lluc in the early part of the last century and is shown kneeling and facing the entrance to the church. Dark and gaudily decorated, the interior of the church is dominated by heavy jasper columns, the stolidity of which is partly relieved by a dome over the crossing. On either side of the nave, stone steps extend the aisles round the back of the Baroque high altar to a much smaller chapel. This is the holy of holies, built to display the statue of the Virgin, which has been commonly known as **La Moreneta** ("the Little Dark-Skinned One") ever since the original paintwork peeled off in the fifteenth century to reveal brown stone underneath. Just 61cm high, the Virgin looks innocuous, her face tweaked by a hint of a smile and haloed by a much more modern jewel-encrusted crown. In her left arm she cradles a baby Jesus, who holds the "Book of Life" open to reveal the letters alpha and omega.

Museu de Lluc

Daily 10am–2pm & 2.30–5pm • €4.50, residents €2 • Entry either via the main entrance – turn right and keep going along the corridor; or through the small door just inside and to the right of the basilica's main entrance, from where you follow the corridor

The entertaining **Museu de Lluc** begins with a section devoted to archeological finds from the Talayotic and Roman periods, and continues with the **Sala del Tresor** (Treasure Room), packed with all manner of folkloric items brought here to honour La Moreneta, from painted fans, medallions, rosaries and crosses through to walking sticks discarded when the supplicants found they were no longer lame. A further room displays examples of traditional island costume as well as sections devoted to religious carvings and **majolica** (see box oppsite), glazed earthenware mostly shaped into two-handled drug jars and show dishes or plates. Some two or three hundred majolica pieces are on display, the pick coming from the eighteenth century, when the designs varied from broad and bold dashes of colour to carefully painted naturalistic designs. The colours, however, remained fairly constant, restricted by the available technology to iron red, copper green, cobalt blue, manganese purple and antimony yellow. There is also a good sample of Catalan and Valencian **lustreware**, brown earthenware with a sheen – or lustre – and manufactured between the sixteenth and the eighteenth centuries. The final rooms on this floor are, by comparison, rather tame, focused on the uninspiring peasant scenes and land- and village-scapes of the prolific **José Coll Bardolet** (1912–92).

The upper floors

Upstairs, the next floor holds an excellent cross section of **Mallorcan art**, either by native artists or artists once resident here. Among them are the Goya-esque works of Salvador Mayol (1775–1834); the romantic landscapes of Bartomeu Sureda (1769–1851); the neo-Impressionist canvases of Llorenç Cerdà Bisbal (1862–1955); and the finely observed mountain landscapes and village scenes of Antoni Ribas Oliver (1845–1911). Oliver is arguably the most talented artist on display here; and look out for his *Gorg Blau*, painted long before the gorge's rugged beauty disappeared under the waters of a reservoir (see p.131). Finally, the top floor is given over to small-scale temporary exhibitions.

Camí dels Misteris del Rosari

About 30m west of the monastery's main entrance • Open access • Free

A large and conspicuous, rough-hewn column marks the start of the **Camí dels Misteris del Rosari** (Way of the Mysteries of the Rosary), a broad pilgrims' footpath that winds its way up the rocky hillside directly behind the monastery. Dating from 1913, the solemn granite stations marking the way are of two types: simple stone pediments and, more intriguingly, rough trilobate columns of Gaudí-like design, each surmounted by a chunky crown and cross. The prettiest part of the walk is round the back of the hill, where the path slips through cool, green woods with rock overhangs on one side and views out over the bowl-shaped **Albarca valley** on the other. It takes about ten minutes to reach the top of the hill, where a wrought-iron *Modernista* cross stands protected by ugly barbed wire.

LLUC'S CHOIR

Nicknamed *Els Blauets* ("The Blues") for the colour of their cassocks, the monastery's choir, the **Escolania de Lluc**, was founded in the early sixteenth century. Originally, the choir had to be "composed of natives of Mallorca, of pure blood, sound in grammar and song", but there has been some backsliding if for no other reason than to keep the numbers up: today the choir consists of about forty boys and girls, some resident, others not. The choir usually sings in the basilica during the 12.45pm daily Mass (but not on Saturdays or during school holidays), and on Sundays at 11am. The timetable does, however, change, so check the Lluc website for details.

THE CERAMIC DELIGHTS OF MAJOLICA

In the fifteenth century, boatloads of decorative pottery were dispatched from Spain to Italy via Mallorca. The Italians coined the term "**majolica**" to describe this imported Spanish pottery after the medieval name for the island through which it was traded, but thereafter the name came to be applied to all tin-glazed pottery. The process of **making majolica** began with the mixing and cleaning of clay, after which it was fired and retrieved at the "biscuit" (earthenware) stage. The biscuit was then cooled and dipped in a liquid glaze containing tin and water. The water in the glaze was absorbed, leaving a dry surface ready for decoration. After painting, the pottery was returned to the kiln for a final firing, which fused the glaze and fixed the painting. Additional glazings and firings added extra lustre. Initially, majolica was dominated by greens and purples, but technological advances in the fifteenth century added blue, red, yellow and ochre. Majolica of one sort or another was produced in bulk in Mallorca up until the early twentieth century.

Jardí Botanic

Daily 10am–5pm • Free • About 70m or so to the right of the main monastery entrance – just follow the signs

The work of a dedicated monk during the 1990s, Lluc's **Jardí Botanic** (Botanical Gardens) are laid out with local plants as well as exotics, plus small ponds and waterfalls, little footbridges and even a windmill. There is also an area devoted to aromatic and medicinal plants and the gardens hold examples of all the island's traditional fruit trees. It takes about twenty minutes to walk through the gardens on a well-defined path.

ARRIVAL

By bus Buses stop right outside the main entrance to the monastery.

Destinations Alcúdia (May–Oct Mon–Sat 2 daily; 1hr); Binissalem (2 daily; 50m); Inca train station (2 daily; 40min); Palma (2 daily; 1hr 15min); Pollença (May–Oct Mon–Sat 2 daily; 30min); Port d'Alcúdia (May–Oct

MONESTIR DE NOSTRA SENYORA DE LLUC

Mon–Sat 2 daily; 1hr 10min); Port de Pollença (May–Oct Mon–Sat 2 daily; 40min); Port de Sóller (April–Oct Mon–Sat 1 daily; 1hr 30min); Selva (2 daily; 25min); Sóller (May–Oct Mon–Sat 2 daily; 1hr 10min).

By taxi Taxi Escorca (☎ 608 631 707) operate a reliable local taxi service.

INFORMATION

Tourist information There's an information desk inside the monastery (April–Sept daily 10am–9pm; Oct–March 10am–8pm) and a small Serra de Tramuntana information office, Ca S'Amitger, beside the main car park (daily 9.30am–4pm). The latter sells mountain-hiking leaflets and mini-guides.

ACCOMMODATION AND EATING

The obvious place to stay in Lluc is at the monastery, which also has the best restaurant. If you don't fancy a sit-down meal, however, you could try any of several cafés between the monastery and the car park: the nearest to the monastery serves fresh and tasty meat and pea pies – *empanadas* – to eat in or take out.

★**Monestir de Lluc** ☎ 971 87 15 25, ⊚ lluc.net. Accommodation here is highly organized, with 81 simple, modern en-suite cells and 39 slightly more comfortable apartments (for up to four people), which offer self-catering but do not provide any utensils. Book ahead in summer; at other times simply ask at the monastery's information office on arrival. Note also that getting back into the place late at night (after about 11pm) can be difficult: if you are planning a big night out (though quite where you would go is another matter), discuss with the information office first. During the day (till about 5pm) residents also get access to an outside pool. Rates include breakfast. Singles €44; doubles €68; apartments €112

Refugi Son Amer Escorca ☎ 971 51 71 09, reservations ☎ 971 173 700, ⊚ www.conselldemallorca.net. The main alternative to the monastery is this *Refugi*, an all-year hikers' hostel in an attractively restored old farmhouse on a hillside close to the Ma-10, just west of the Lluc turn-off. It's also a 15min walk from the monastery on the GR221 long-distance hiking route (see box, p.131). The hostel has a dining room and several bunk-bed dormitories with shared facilities. Breakfast is available for €4.50, dinner for €8. There are no double rooms. Flat rate per person €11

Sa Fonda Lluc ☎ 971 51 70 22, ⊚ lluc.net. Lluc's gastronomic star turn is the monks' former refectory, *Sa Fonda*, a large and pleasantly restored old hall complete with wooden beams, wide stone arches and marble pillars.

3

The food is traditional Spanish, served in walloping portions and with main courses from around €15; the meat dishes – especially the kid (young goat) – are much better than the fish. Opening hours are a tad unpredictable. March–Oct daily 1–4pm & 7–9pm; Nov–Feb Mon 1–4pm, Wed–Sun 1–4pm & 7–9pm.

Selva and around

South of Lluc, the **Ma-2130** drifts its way up and over the mountains in what is one of the island's most beautiful journeys. After about 12km, the road slips through **SELVA**, an amiable country town set among the foothills of the Serra de Tramuntana. The main square – Plaça Major – is especially pleasant and is overlooked by a fortress-like church, whose frontispiece appears to have been glued to the Gothic nave as an afterthought. The oldest part of town nudges up to the church, its narrow lanes crowded by the old stone buildings where the local peasantry once rested after their long days in the surrounding olive groves. From Selva, the Ma-2130 continues on to Inca (see p.165), but it's more enjoyable to head east along the narrow country lanes that traverse the foothills in what is one of the quietest parts of the island. There's no obvious target, however, unless you're lucky enough to be staying at **Binibona's** *Es Castell* (see below).

ARRIVAL AND DEPARTURE   SELVA AND AROUND

By bus Buses travel through Selva on the main drag (the Ma-2130); there's a bus stop beside the main street on c/Font, from where it's a 5–10min walk to Plaça Major.

Destinations Binissalem (2 daily; 25min); Inca train station (2 daily; 15min); Lluc (2 daily; 25min); Palma (2 daily; 50min).

ACCCOMMODATION AND EATING

★**Son Ametler** c/Son Riera s/n ☎971 51 54 19, ⓦ hotelsonametler.com. In an attractive rural setting with the foothills of the Serra de Tramuntana in full view, this new and extremely well-run hotel offers eight (eventually twelve) guest rooms in a sympathetically modernized, nineteenth-century *finca*. All are bright, cheerful and tastefully decorated, with terracotta floors and über-comfortable beds, and most have large balconies. There's an outside pool and a residents' restaurant (dinner Mon–Sat), where the outstanding food showcases local produce – from figs and olive oil to oranges and lemons. The hotel is a signed 3km or so from Selva's main street. Closed mid-Dec to mid-Feb. **€155**
★**Es Castell** c/Binibona s/n ☎971 87 51 54,

ⓦ fincaescastell.com. Deep in the countryside, with the mountains behind and the plains stretching out below, the outstanding *Es Castell* occupies a tastefully restored stone *finca*, parts of which date back to the fourteenth century. Entered via a delightful antique courtyard, the public areas are immensely comfortable, and the twelve guest rooms beyond are similarly smart and tasteful, each making the most of their rustic stonework. Add to this an outside pool and an excellent restaurant, where they highlight home-grown ingredients – oranges, lemons, honey, figs and a superb olive oil – and you could stay here for days. Follow the signs along country lanes from Selva's main street, a journey of about 6.5km. Closed mid-Dec to mid-Feb. **€165**

Pollença

Founded in the thirteenth century, the pretty little town of **POLLENÇA** nestles among a trio of bulging hillocks where the Serra de Tramuntana mountains fade into coastal flatland. Following standard Mallorcan practice, the town was established a few kilometres from the seashore to militate against sudden pirate attack, with its harbour, Port de Pollença (see p.142), left as an unprotected outpost. For once the stratagem worked. Unlike most of Mallorca's old towns, Pollença successfully repelled a string of piratical onslaughts, the last and most threatening of which was in 1550, when the notorious Turkish corsair Dragut came within a hair's breadth of victory. In the festival of **Mare de Déu dels Àngels** on August 2, the townspeople still celebrate their escape with enthusiastic street battles, the day's events named after the warning shouted by the hero of the resistance, a certain Joan Más: "Mare de Déu dels Àngels, assistiu-mos!" ("Our Lady of Angels, help us!").

Lined by lovely old houses, Pollença's maze of streets attracts a well-heeled, mainly British crowd in sufficient numbers to support several first-rate **restaurants** and **hotels**.

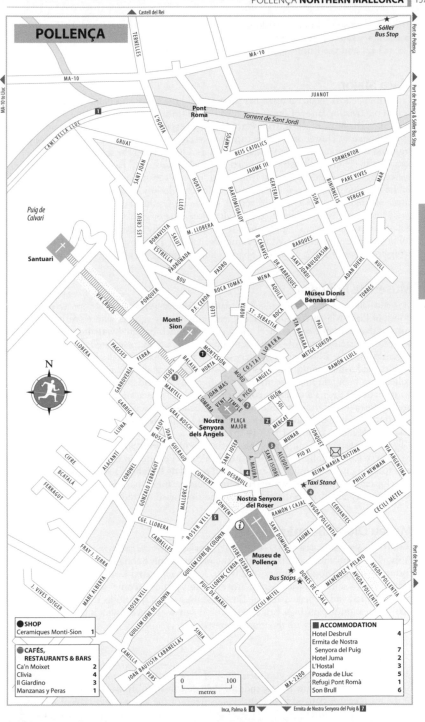

POLLENÇA

Castell del Rei

Sóller
Bus Stop

Puig de
Calvari

Santuari

Monti-Sion

Pont
Roma

Torrent de Sant Jordi

**Museu Dionís
Bennàssar**

**Nostra
Senyora
dels Àngels**

PLAÇA
MAJOR

**Nostra Senyora
del Roser**

**Museu de
Pollença**

Bus Stops

Taxi Stand

● **SHOP**
Ceramiques Monti-Sion 1

● **CAFÉS,
RESTAURANTS & BARS**
Ca'n Moixet 2
Clivia 4
Il Giardino 3
Manzanas y Peras 1

■ **ACCOMMODATION**
Hotel Desbrull 4
Ermita de Nostra
 Senyora del Puig 7
Hotel Juma 2
L'Hostal 3
Posada de Lluc 5
Refugi Pont Romà 1
Son Brull 6

0   100
metres

Inca, Palma & 6   Ermita de Nostra Senyora del Puig & 7

The town is also within easy striking distance of Cala Sant Vicenç (see p.141), a brisk and solitary modern resort on the island's northern shore, and both Port de Pollença (see p.142) and the Península de Formentor (see p.146).

Plaça Major

Little of Pollença's medieval town has survived, and the handsome stone houses that now cramp the twisting lanes of the centre mostly date from the seventeenth and eighteenth centuries. The heart of the town is **Plaça Major**, an especially amiable main square, which accommodates a cluster of laidback cafés and restaurants and is also the site of a lively fruit and veg market on most Sunday mornings. Overlooking the square is the severe facade of the church of **Nostra Senyora dels Àngels**, a sheer cliff face of sun-bleached stone pierced by a rose window. Dating from the thirteenth century, but extensively remodelled in the Baroque style five centuries later, the church's gloomy interior, with its mighty single-vaulted nave, has a mildly diverting sequence of ceiling and wall paintings, as well as a whopping, tiered and towered high altarpiece. The original church was built for the Knights Templar (see p.61) and passed to another knightly order, the Hospitallers of St John, after the pope suppressed the Templars in 1312. The Hospitallers of St John struggled on until 1802, when the Spanish king appropriated all they owned.

Museu de Pollença

c/Guillem Cifre s/n • Theoretically, June–Sept Tues–Sat 10am–1pm & 5.30–8.30pm; Oct–May Tues–Sat 10.30am–1pm • €2 • ☎ 971 53 11 66

South of Plaça Major, c/Antoni Maura leads into a leafy square, whose greenery surrounds an antique water wheel and a stumpy, much battered **watchtower**. Behind looms the austere facade of Nostra Senyora del Roser, a deconsecrated church which, together with the adjoining monastery complex, now makes up the **Museu de Pollença**. Inside, the former **monks' quarters** hold a surprisingly good and regularly rotated collection of contemporary paintings, photography and video art, including pieces by winners of the town's annual art competition. There's also a modest assortment of local archeological finds, though these are poorly labelled, and a room of **Mallorcan Primitive paintings**, most memorably a warm, tender and exquisitely detailed *Virgin and Musical Angels* by Francesc Comes (1379–1415).

In the **cloisters**, look out for the memorial to **Philip Newman** (1904–66), the Manchester-born violinist who took a real shine to Pollença in the 1950s, founding and fostering its main musical festival, the **Festival de Pollença** (see opposite). Next to the cloisters is the **church**, whose truncated, barrel-vaulted nave is a gloomy affair with an enormous gilded altar; the church is sometimes used for temporary exhibitions.

Museu Dionís Bennàssar

c/Roça 14 • May–Sept Tues–Sun 10am–2pm • €2 • ☎ 971 53 09 97, ⓦ museudionisbennassar.com

A short stroll northeast of Plaça Major, the **Museu Dionís Bennàssar** occupies the former home of Dionís Bennàssar (1904–67), who recovered from a wound he sustained as a soldier in the Spanish army in Morocco to become one of the island's most talented and respected artists. The museum holds a tidy collection of his neo-Impressionist paintings, brightly coloured canvases among which the Mallorcan land- and village-scapes are the most interesting.

Puig de Calvari

Pollença's pride and joy is its **Via Crucis** (Way of the Cross), a long, steep and singularly beautiful stone stairway, which ascends the **Puig de Calvari** (Calvary Hill) on the north side of the town centre, flanked by ancient cypress trees. At the top, a much-revered thirteenth-century statue of **Mare de Déu del Peu de la Creu** (Mother of God at the Foot of the Cross) is lodged in a simple **santuari** (sanctuary), whose whitewashed walls sport some of the worst religious paintings imaginable, though the views out over coast and town are sumptuous. On Good Friday, a figure of Jesus is slowly carried by torchlight down from the *santuari* to the church of Nostra Senyora dels Àngels, a procession known as the **Davallament** (Lowering), one of the most moving religious celebrations on the island.

Pont Roma

Although it doesn't merit a huge detour, the **Pont Roma**, on the northern edge of town, is worth a peep. This old Roman bridge spans the Torrent de Sant Jordí, though in summer you'll be lucky to spot a stream, never mind a river. The finely worked stone bridge consists of two slightly different arches, and although in itself it's not a remarkable structure, it has at least survived intact despite all the historical odds.

Ermita de Nostra Senyora del Puig

There are magnificent views over Pollença and its environs from the **Ermita de Nostra Senyora del Puig**, a rambling, mostly eighteenth-century monastery perched on top of the Puig de Maria, a 330m-high hump facing the south end of town. The monastic complex, with its fortified walls, courtyard, chapel, refectory and cells, has had a chequered history, alternately abandoned and restored by both monks and nuns. The Benedictines now own the place, but the monks are gone and today a custodian supplements the order's income by renting out cells to tourists (see p.140). There's nothing specific to see, but the setting is extraordinarily serene and beautiful, with the mellow honey-coloured walls of the monastery surrounded by ancient carob and olive trees.

It takes around an hour to **walk** to the monastery from the centre of town: head for the main Pollença–Inca road (Ma-2200), where a signed turning leads up a steep lane that fizzles out after 1.5km to be replaced by a cobbled footpath winding up to the monastery's entrance. It's possible to drive to the top of the lane, but unless you've got nerves of steel, you're better off parking elsewhere. Note that there have been reports of cars left at the foot of the lane overnight being vandalized; although this is unusual, you might prefer to park in town instead.

ARRIVAL AND DEPARTURE   POLLENÇA

By car To avoid Pollença's baffling one-way system, enter the town from the south, turning off the main Palma road – the Ma-2200 – onto Avgda Pollentia (where there is almost always parking).

By bus Buses to Pollença from Palma, Inca, Port de Pollença and Cala Sant Vicenç pull in on the south side of the centre on c/Cecili Metel, a 5min walk from Plaça Major. Less conveniently, buses from Port de Sóller, Sóller and Lluc pick up and drop passengers on the north side of town, beside the Ma-10, a good 1km from Plaça Major.

Destinations Alcúdia (May–Oct 1–4 hourly; Nov–April hourly; 15min); Cala Sant Vicenç (5 daily; 20min); Inca

(Mon–Fri hourly, Sat & Sun 7 daily; 25min); Lluc (May–Oct Mon–Sat 2 daily; 25min); Palma (Mon–Fri hourly, 7 on Sat & Sun; 1hr); Port d'Alcúdia (May–Oct 1–4 hourly; Nov–April hourly; 20min); Port de Pollença (May–Oct 1–4 hourly; Nov–April hourly; 15min); Port de Sóller (May–Oct Mon–Sat 2 daily; 1hr 45min); Sóller (May–Oct Mon–Sat 2 daily; 1hr 35min).

By taxi The centre of Pollença is best explored on foot, but for the more outlying hotels, you'll mostly need a taxi: there's a rank in the centre at the corner of Avgda Pollentia and c/Reina Maria Cristina, or call Taxi Pollença on ☎971 86 62 13.

INFORMATION

Tourist information The tourist office is a 3min walk from Plaça Major, in the walls of the old convent on c/Guillem Cifre (Nov–April Mon–Fri 8am–3pm; May–Oct Mon–Sat 9am–1.30pm & 2–4pm Sun 10am–1pm; ☎971 53 50 77, ⌨pollensa.com).

Festivals The Festival de Pollença is staged every year throughout July and August (⌨festivalpollenca.org), with the likes of flamenco star Diego El Cigala and Catalan folk legend Joan Manuel Serrat appearing in recent years.

ACCOMMODATION

Hotel Desbrull c/Marquès Desbrull 7 ☎ 971 53 50 55, ⓦ desbrull.com. Small and smart, this family-owned hotel occupies an old stone villa in the centre of town. It has six double rooms, each kitted out in an attractive modern style but with the house's older features – like beamed ceilings – still on show. **€100**

Ermita de Nostra Senyora del Puig de Maria 2km south of town (see p.139) ☎ 971 18 41 32. At this hilltop monastery, the original monks' quarters have been renovated to provide simple rooms with shared facilities. A single room costs €14, triples €30. To be sure of a room, book ahead, but be warned that it can get cold and windy at night, even in the summer. There's a refectory on site, but the food is only average. Doubles **€22**

Hotel Juma Plaça Major 9 ☎ 971 53 50 02, ⓦ pollensa hotels.com. Right in the middle of town, overlooking the main square, this enjoyable small hotel occupies an old stone merchant's house that functions rather like a traditional *pension*, with reception on the first floor, a café down below and the a/c rooms up above. The rooms are bright and cheerful and the best (€10 extra) have balconies with views over the centre. **€130**

L'Hostal c/Mercat 18 ☎ 971 53 52 82, ⓦ pollensahotels .com. In a lavishly updated old stone house, this appealing hotel has six en-suite rooms decorated in a bright and breezy modern style with flashes of the old – beamed ceilings and bare stone walls. The central courtyard is a good place to unwind, and you are just metres from the main square. **€130**

★**Posada de Lluc** c/Roser Vell 11 ☎ 971 53 52 20, ⓦ posadalluc.com. This small and extremely comfortable hotel occupies an attractively restored old stone house in the centre of town. The monks from Lluc monastery (see p.133) used to lodge here when they popped into Pollença to pick up supplies – hence the statue of the Madonna over the front door – and many of the original features have been kept, notably the deep stone arches and masonry walls. There's a small outside pool and each of the a/c guest rooms has been equipped in a traditional style but with modern comforts. **€140**

Refugi Pont Romà Camí Can Gulló s/n ☎ 971 53 36 49, ⓦ www.conselldemallorca.net. After a long period of closure for building repairs, this all-year hikers' hostel on the northern edge of town has reopened, albeit to mixed reviews. The no-frills dormitory accommodation is in half a dozen four- to twelve-bunk bedrooms with shared facilities, and there's also a café area. It's on the GR221 Serra de Tramuntana hiking route (see box, p.131), and is a moderately difficult five-hour hoof from the *Refugi Son Amer* near Lluc (see p.135). Breakfast €4.50, dinner €8.50. Reservations advised. Dorms **€11**

Son Brull Crta. Palma-Pollença, km 49.9 ☎ 971 53 53 53, ⓦ sonbrull.com. Lavish by any standard, this deluxe hotel and spa occupies a handsomely restored eighteenth-century convent, whose honey-coloured stonework has an idyllic setting overlooking vineyards and citrus groves. There are just 23 rooms, each of which is a canny amalgamation of modern design with original features, from the beamed ceilings and shuttered windows to the extremely comfortable beds. Family-owned, the hotel has a bar in the former olive press, an outside pool and a first-rate restaurant. It's about 3km south of Pollença on the Palma road, the Ma-2200. **€700**

EATING AND DRINKING

Pollença does very well for restaurants, which are sustained by the villa owners who gather in the town each and every summer evening. The café and bar scene is less convincing, but there are several reasonably lively spots on and around Plaça Major. Almost all the cafés and bars serve food of some description, mostly tapas.

Ca'n Moixet Plaça Major 2 ☎ 971 53 42 14. Every other place on the main square may heave with the well-heeled and the well-tanned, but the renegades – or at least the semi-renegades – gather here at this old-fashioned, locals' favourite under the sign "Café Espanyol". Drinks are the big deal, but they also serve filling and inexpensive snacks. Daily 10am–midnight.

★**Clivia** Avgda Pollentia 5 ☎ 971 53 36 35. Very hospitable restaurant (and long-time expat favourite) offering an excellent range of Spanish dishes – try the squid in ink. If you choose fish, the waiter brings the uncooked version to the table so you can inspect it before buying/eating. It's a smart place and it attracts an older clientele. Mains average €25. Reservations advised. Daily except Wed 1–3pm & 7–10.30pm.

Il Giardino Plaça Major 11 ☎ 971 53 43 02, ⓦ giardinopollensa.com. One of the best restaurants in town, this smart bistro-style place offers a tip-top range of Italian dishes from about €15, and pastas from €12, all prepared with vim and gusto and featuring the best of local ingredients; the ravioli stuffed with wild mushrooms is particularly good. To be sure of a seat on the terrace – where you will probably want to eat – either come early or book ahead. Great house wines too. Mid-March to Oct daily 12.30–3pm & 7–11pm.

★**Manzanas y Peras** c/Martell 6, Plaça Seglars ☎ 971 53 22 92, ⓦ manzanasyperas.eu. In an attractive location, on a little square at the foot of the Via Crucis, this excellent and mildly boho café-restaurant has every reason to be proud of its fresh and tasty menu, featuring a delicious range of home-made tapas, from Asian spiced chickpea and date purée to roasted chicken and red pepper. Their "Tapas Feast" set menu costs €30. Mon–Sat 6.30–10pm, Sun 10am–4pm.

SHOPPING

Ceramiques Monti-Sion c/Monti-Sion 19 ☎971 53 35 00, ⓦceramicasmontision.com. Arguably the best ceramic shop on Mallorca, offering an excellent range of hand-crafted pieces in both traditional and modern designs. Jugs, cups, tiles, vases and plates – though the biggest plates may prove hard to transport safely home. April to early Nov daily 10am–2pm & 4–8.30pm.

Cala Sant Vicenç

There's no denying that **CALA SANT VICENÇ**, a burgeoning, modern resort just 7km northeast of Pollença, boasts an attractive setting among a set of bare rocky outcrops that nudge gingerly out into the ocean. The only problem – if indeed there is one – is the resort itself: some visitors like the modern villas that spill over and around the wooded ravine at its heart, others think they are dreary, but most are agreed that the *Hotel Don Pedro*, plonked on the minuscule headland separating two of the resort's beaches, is crass in the extreme. If you are staying in Cala Sant Vicenç, it may be comforting to know that it's easy enough to escape all the development by **hiking north** out onto the wild and wind-licked seashore. The obvious targets are the remote *calas* that punctuate the coastline, but you could also undertake the moderately strenuous hoof up to the top of **Puig de l'Àguila** (206m), from where there are grand views. This 6km hike takes around three hours; the first part uses a rough dirt-and-gravel road, the second follows a well-defined path that leads to the base of Puig de l'Àguila – but you'll still need a proper hiking map to find your way. If that sounds too much like hard work, you could simply enjoy the resort's four sandy **beaches**: two on either side of the *Hotel Don Pedro* and two more on the east side of Cala Sant Vicenç on the far side of a dividing headland.

ARRIVAL AND INFORMATION   CALA SANT VICENÇ

By bus Buses to and from Cala Sant Vicenç stop in the centre of the resort on both Avgda Cavall Bernat and on c/Temporal.
Destinations Lluc (May–Oct Mon–Sat 2 daily; 40min); Pollença (May–Oct 8 daily, Nov–April 3 daily; 20min); Port de Pollença (May–Oct 8 daily, Nov–April 3 daily; 15min);

Port de Sóller (May–Oct Mon–Sat 2 daily; 1hr 50min).
Tourist information The tourist office is in a little wooded dell just back from the beach on Plaça Sant Vicenç (June–Sept Mon–Fri 9am–1.30pm & 2–4pm, Sat 10am–1pm; ☎971 53 32 64, ⓦpollensa.com).

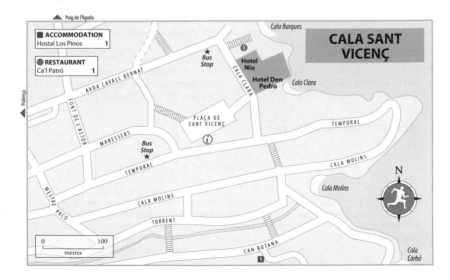

Ca'l Patró c/Cala Clara s/n ☎ 971 53 33 89. Among the resort's several cafés and restaurants, this is the pick – just down the steps to the left of the *Hotel Don Pedro*. The focus is firmly on seafood: the catch of the day is usually first-rate and costs in the region of €25. Daily except Tues noon–3pm & 6–10pm.

Hostal Los Pinos c/Can Botana s/n ☎ 971 53 12 10,

✇ hostal-lospinos.com. Cala Sant Vicenç is a popular resort, so on-spec, vacant rooms can be thin on the ground, but you might try this two-star *hostal*, which occupies an attractive modern villa with Art Deco flourishes on a wooded hillside on the south side of the resort. The rooms here are furnished in a spick-and-span version of traditional Spanish style, and there's an outside pool. Closed mid-Oct to April. **€75**

Badía de Pollença

Pollença is but a few kilometres from the **Badía de Pollença**, a wide U-shaped bay fringed by a long sandy beach, which gets wider and much more enticing as you near **Port de Pollença**, a laidback and low-key resort that's especially popular with Brits. The waters of the bay are sheltered to the south by the Alcúdia peninsula (see p.151) and to the north by the wild and extravagantly beautiful **Península de Formentor**, which pokes its bony finger out into the ocean as the northernmost spur of the Serra de Tramuntana. There are fast and frequent **buses** between Port de Pollença and the surrounding towns, but nothing along the Península de Formentor beyond the Platja de Formentor, near the start of the promontory and reachable by both bus and passenger ferry.

Port de Pollença

With the mountains as a shimmering backcloth, **PORT DE POLLENÇA** is a pleasantly informal, family-orientated resort that arches through the flatlands behind the Badía de Pollença. The **beach** is the focus of attention here, a narrow, elongated sliver of sand, which is easily long enough to accommodate the crowds, while its sheltered waters are ideal for swimming. A rash of apartment buildings and hotels blights the edge of town, but there are no high-rises to speak of and the resort is dotted with attractive whitewashed and stone-trimmed villas. Altogether it's quite delightful, especially to the north of the marina, where a portion of the old beachside road has been pedestrianized – and there are plans to extend the pedestrianization to the south of the marina, too. When – or if – you get bored by the beach, you can also rent a bike and **cycle** out into the surrounding countryside, make the enjoyable hike across to Cala Bóquer (see p.145), or head off to the wondrous mountain scenery of the neighbouring Península de Formentor (see p.146).

By bus Buses to Port de Pollença stop right in the centre of the resort by the beach and at the foot of the main drag, c/Joan XXIII.

Destinations Alcúdia (May–Oct every 15min; Nov–April hourly; 15min); Artà (Mon–Sat 2 daily; 1hr); Cala Sant Vicenç (May–Oct 8 daily, Nov–April 3 daily; 15min); Ca'n

---

MALLORCAN WALKING TOURS

Port de Pollença is home to the island's best hiking company, the small, independent **Mallorcan Walking Tours** (MWT; ☎ (0034) 668 54 22 74, ✇ mallorcanwalkingtours.puertopollensa.com), which runs an outstanding range of **day-long guided hikes** from September to June. There is something to suit most levels of fitness and they cover the whole of the Serra de Tramuntana as well as the hilly uplands north of Artà (see p.172) and Sant Elm (see p.122). Costs vary depending on the hike but begin at €20 per person including transport to the trailhead, though walkers need to take their own food and water. MWT also leads a **week-long traverse of the Serra de Tramuntana** from Valldemossa to Pollença for around €790 per person. You need to book (by phone or online) a minimum of 24 hours beforehand, much more for the longer hikes. MWT also provides route advice and moves luggage between destinations for **self-guided treks**.

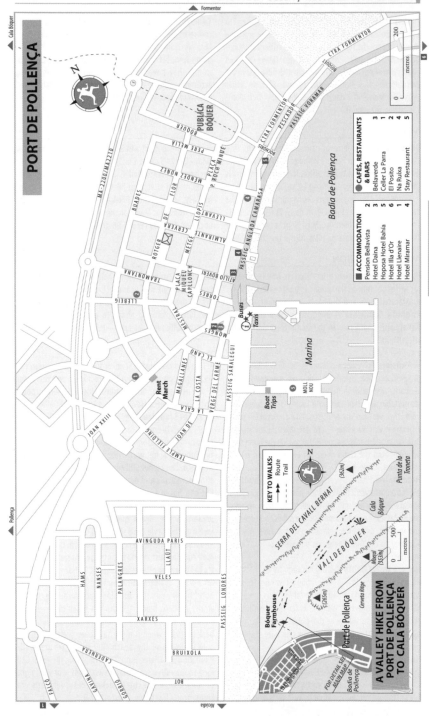

PORT DE POLLENÇA

PUBLICA BÓQUER

Badia de Pollença

3

■ ACCOMMODATION
Pension Bellavista	2
Hotel Daina	3
Hoposa Hotel Bahia	5
Hotel Illa d'Or	6
Hotel Llenaire	1
Hotel Miramar	4

● CAFÉS, RESTAURANTS & BARS
Bellaverde	3
Celler La Parra	1
El Posito	2
Na Ruixa	5

Marina

MOLL NOU

Boat Trips

Rent March

Buses
Taxis

KEY TO WALKS:
→ Route
--- Trail

SERRA DEL CAVALL BERNAT

VALLDEBÓQUER

Bóquer Farmhouse

Port de Pollença

Cala Bóquer

Punta de la Troneta

Cavall Bernat

Badia de Pollença

FOR DETAIL SEE MAIN MAP

A VALLEY HIKE FROM PORT DE POLLENÇA TO CALA BÓQUER

Picafort (May–Oct every 15min; Nov–April hourly; 1hr 15min); Lluc (May–Oct Mon–Sat 2 daily; 45min); Palma (hourly to 2 hourly; 1hr 15min); Platja de Formentor (May–Oct Mon–Sat 4 daily; 20min); Pollença (May–Oct 1–4 hourly; Nov–April hourly; 15min); Port d'Alcúdia (May–Oct every 15min; Nov–April hourly; 30min); Port de Sóller (May–Oct Mon–Sat 2 daily; 2hr); Sóller (May–Oct Mon–Sat 2 daily; 1hr 50min).

Tourist information The tourist office is bang in the centre of the resort at Passeig Saralegui 1 (May–Sept Mon–Fri 9am–8pm, Sat 9am–4pm; Oct–April Mon–Fri 9am–3pm, Sat 9am–1pm; ☎971 86 54 67, ⓦpollensa .com). They have lots of local information, including accommodation lists, bus- and boat-trip timetables and details of car rental companies.

ACTIVITIES

Boat trips Excursions of various descriptions are extremely popular in Port de Pollença, and depart from the jetties behind the tourist office. The main company is Lanchas La Gaviota (☎971 86 40 14, ⓦlanchaslagaviota .com), which runs regular excursions out into the Badía de Pollença (May–Sept Tues–Fri 1 daily; 2hr 30min; €23) and to Cap de Formentor (May–Sept 3 weekly; 2hr 30min; €25). The most popular trip is the 20min hop over to the golden sands of the Platja de Formentor (May–Oct 2–5 daily; €13.50 return).

Cycling The rusticated flatlands edging the Badía de Pollença and stretching inland as far as Pollença make for easy, scenic cycling. Bikes and mountain bikes can be rented from Rent March, in the centre of Port de Pollença at c/Joan XXIII, 89 (☎971 86 47 84, ⓦrentmarch.com).

ACCOMMODATION

Though Port de Pollença has sixteen hotels, three *hostales* and a small army of holiday apartment blocks, vacancies get thin on the ground in high season, when it's advisable to book well in advance. In the shoulder seasons substantial deals and discounts are commonplace. The part of town you want is the pedestrianized **Passeig Anglada Camarasa** running north from the tourist office, but if plans go ahead to pedestrianize **Passeig Saralegui**, which runs to the south, then this will become an equally pleasant area – but for now the traffic is off-putting.

★**Pension Bellavista** c/Monges 14 ☎971 86 46 00, ⓦpensionbellavista.com. Funkiest place in town with a laidback vibe and a handful of straightforward but comfortable and clean en-suite rooms, set a brief walk from the seafront in a 1930s house. Breakfasts are vegetarian extravaganzas – and are taken in the shaded *Bellaverde* café-bar (see opposite) adjoining the hotel. Very different from the chain hotels all around – and all the better for it. A snip. €60

Hotel Daina c/Atilio Boveri 2 ☎971 86 62 50, ⓦhoposa .es. Straightforward tower-block hotel with four stars, seventy-odd rooms and an excellent seashore location beside Passeig Anglada Camarasa. The public areas are slick and modern, as are the bedrooms, with shades of white and grey to the fore. There's an outside pool too. Closed Nov–Feb. €200

Hoposa Hotel Bahía Passeig Voramar 29 ☎971 86 65 62, ⓦhoposa.es. In a great location a few minutes' walk north of the marina along the seashore, this three-star hotel occupies one of the town's older villas, with many period details surviving in the public areas. The thirty rooms are bright and breezy and the pick have sea-facing balconies. Closed Nov–March. €160

Hotel Illa d'Or Passeig Colon 265 ☎971 86 51 00, ⓦhotelillador.com. This well-equipped, four-star hotel sits by the waterfront on the northern edge of the resort. Set in its own grounds, with a private jetty and beach, it's built in traditional Spanish style and dates from the 1920s though the interior is ultramodern and the decor a tad pedestrian. Good facilities include saunas, pools and a gym. Closed Nov–March. €200

★**Hotel Llenaire** Camí de Llenaire s/n ☎971 53 52 51, ⓦhotelllenaire.com. Just 5km from the town centre, this handsome Mallorcan manor house sits on the brow of a hill with wide views over the Badía de Pollença. The owner still runs a farm here – with sheep chomping away and groves of almond and olive trees – but the house is now a charming country hotel with most of its eighteenth-century features sympathetically revamped. The eleven guest rooms are decked out in lavish period style, and there's an outside infinity pool and a sauna. The hotel is signposted from the inner ring road running just inland from the seashore. €260

Hotel Miramar Passeig Anglada Camarasa 39 ☎971 86 64 00, ⓦhotel-miramar.net. Pleasant, three-star hotel in two adjacent buildings: one a routine, seven-storey modern block, the other a much more elegant structure, all iron grilles and stone lintels, that dates back to 1912, when it must have been pretty much the only building on the beach. The rooms are standard-issue modern affairs, but it's worth paying the extra €30 for a room with a sea view and a balcony – or you might be plonked at the back looking out over Carretera Formentor. Closed Nov–March. €150

EATING AND DRINKING

Port de Pollença heaves with **cafés and restaurants**. Many of them offer run-of-the-mill tourist fodder, but others skilfully blend Catalan and Castilian cuisines and serve the freshest of seafood. As a general rule, competition keeps prices down to affordable levels, with around €18 covering a main course at all but the ritziest establishments.

★ **Bellaverde** c/Monges 14 ☎ 675 60 25 28. Outstanding vegetarian and vegan café-restaurant, with a delightful shaded courtyard and a simply superb menu: try, for example, the pumpkin lasagne with goat's cheese or the

---

A VALLEY HIKE FROM PORT DE POLLENÇA TO CALA BÓQUER

6km • Linear • 107m of ascent • 45min to 1hr each way • Easy • Trailhead: N39°54.602, E03°05.201

The walk through the sheltered **Vall de Bóquer** is an attractive, easy stroll over the gently undulating, verdant ground that lies between the Serra del Cavall Bernat and the Cerveta Ridge, across the neck of the **Península de Formentor**. The headland at the end of the walk offers splendid views of the severe sea cliffs that characterize the northern coast, with the cove and beach below. The walk is suitable for most ages and abilities – though the last leg down to the beach is uneven and can be difficult for young children. The hike is especially popular with birdwatchers, who favour early morning or evening visits. You'll also see lots of feral goats in the valley.

THE ROUTE

Start by heading north along the seafront from Port de Pollença's marina and then turn left up **Avinguda Bocchoris** until you reach the four-lane ring road. Cross this main road at the roundabout (which has a small car park on its right and provides an alternative start to the walk) and continue up the dirt track with the ridge of the Serra del Cavall Bernat straight ahead. Approximately 300m further on, the path goes through an **iron gate**, passing the **Bóquer farmhouse** on the right. There's a splendid view of the Badía de Pollença from here and some fine examples of the *Agave americana*, a succulent whose flower spikes reach heights of 3m.

Beyond the farmhouse, the path turns round to the right, heading north through a small **iron gate**, then ascends steadily for about 500m, passing between large rocks. Niches in the rocks are occupied by clumps of dwarf fan palms, and you'll probably see the blue rock thrushes that inhabit the area. Here and further along the walk, you may also spot wheatears, black-eared wheatears, black redstarts, rock sparrows and wrynecks, as well as buzzards, peregrines, kestrels, booted eagles, the occasional osprey, Eleonora's falcons in spring and, in summer, stonechats and goldfinches. Various warblers pass through this area during migration too, but the big ornithological thrill is the **black vulture**, with a wingspan of around 2m, which glides the air currents of the north coast. There's a fairly good chance of spotting one from the Vall de Bóquer – and if you're really lucky you'll get a close view, its large, black body contrasting with a brownish head, beak and ruff.

Beyond the boulders the path descends, becoming less rocky, then passes through a gap in a dry-stone wall before ascending gently for about 150m – a scattering of pine trees 50m to the left offers a shady spot for a picnic. The valley's feral goats have grazed the area, leaving the vegetation sparse and scrubby. The most noticeable plant is *Asphodelus microcarpus*, which grows up to 2m high, bearing tall spikes of white flowers with a reddish brown vein on each petal. Not even the goats like it. Other common shrubs are the *Hypericum balearicum*, a St John's Wort whose yellow flowers are at their best in spring and early summer, and the narrow-leaved cistus and spurges, whose hemispherical bushes bear bright yellow glands. At the top of the next incline the path passes through another wall. About 50m off to the right of the junction of wall and path, more or less due south, is a 1.5m-high **tunnel**, inside which is a spring. Be careful, however, if you venture in, as it's popular with goats, who like the water and shade.

Further on, at some carved stone seating, the **path forks**, with the route to the **beach** to the left, while the right path, to the **headland**, splits into as many paths as there are goats. The beach route runs alongside a dried-up watercourse amid the cries of sea birds and the whispering of the tall carritx grass. Patches of aromatic blue-flowered rosemary line the path. The beach at **Cala Bóquer** is disappointing, being predominantly shingle, but the water is clean and it's a good place for a swim. To return to Port de Pollença, simply retrace your steps.

3

beetroot fusili. Great soundtrack – the whole place has a boho feel, as does the adjoining *Pension Bellavista* (see p.144). Mains only cost €11. Tues–Sun 8.30am–midnight; kitchen 8.30am–noon, 12.30–3.30pm & 6–11pm.

★ **Celler La Parra** c/Juan XXIII, 84 ☎ 971 86 50 41, ⓦ cellerlaparra.com. Distinctive, family-run restaurant with a rustic feel – it's in an old *celler* (warehouse) where wine was once bought and sold. The menu pretty much sticks to all things Mallorcan (which is no bad thing) and everything is freshly prepared. They have wood-burning ovens, and main courses start at around €15. April–Oct daily 8am–11.30pm; kitchen 1–3pm & 7.15–11pm. Nov–March Tues–Sun same hours.

El Posito c/Llebeig 8 ☎ 971 86 54 13. On a side street, this modest but very good restaurant, with old sepia photos on the wall, offers a mixed bag of a (Spanish) menu, featuring such delights as suckling pig or rabbit with lobster. Mains around €20. Daily 12.30–4pm & 7–10.30pm.

Na Ruíxa c/Mendez Nunez 3 ☎ 971 86 66 55. On a pedestrianized side street just off the beach, this pleasant restaurant, with its traditional Spanish decor and large terrace, is especially strong on seafood. Mains average €18. Mid-March to mid-Oct daily except Tues 1.30–3.30pm & 7–10.30pm.

Stay Restaurant Moll Nou jetty ☎ 971 86 40 13, ⓦ stayrestaurant.com. This long-established restaurant is known for its wide-ranging menu and the quality of its seafood – though the main courses tend towards the small size. The decor is crisp and modern, and prices a bit above average, though well worth it for the setting out on the pier; there's a top-notch wine list too. It's a popular spot, so reservations are advised in the evening when mains are anywhere between €16 and €50. Prices are much lower in the daytime. Daily noon–11pm.

Península de Formentor

Port de Pollença has been popular with middle-class Brits for decades – witness Agatha Christie's story *Problem at Pollensa Bay* – but the hoi polloi were kept away from the adjoining **Península de Formentor** by an Argentine swank called Adan Diehl. In 1928, Diehl bought the whole peninsula, a wild and stunningly beautiful 20km spur of the Serra de Tramuntana, and then built the *Hotel Formentor* (see p.148) for his friends and contacts. Since then, the Diehl family and then the government have permitted almost no development and you can now drive along the narrow, twisting road to the rugged cape at the end without a villa in view. In summer, however, the road can heave with cars and buses and you're best travelling before 10am or after 6pm.

Mirador de la Creueta

Heading northeast out of Port de Pollença, the ring road clears the far end of the resort before weaving up into the hills at the start of the peninsula. At first, the road travels inland, offering grand views back over the port, but then, after about 3.5km, it reaches a wonderful viewpoint, the **Mirador de la Creueta**, where a string of lookout points perch on the edge of plunging, north-facing sea cliffs. There are further stunning views over the southern shore from the **Talaia d'Albercuix** watchtower, though you'll have to brave the wiggly side road that climbs the ridge opposite the Mirador.

Platja de Formentor

Beyond the Mirador, the road cuts a handsome route as it threads its way along the peninsula, somehow negotiating the sheerest of cliffs before slipping down to a fork in the road, where it's straight on for the cape (see below) and right for the 900m detour to the *Hotel Formentor* (see p.148). The fork is a couple of hundred metres from the start of the **Platja de Formentor**, a narrow strip of golden sand that stretches east for about 1km beneath a low, pine-clad ridge. It's a beautiful spot, with views over to the mountains on the far side of the bay, though it can get crowded in peak season.

Cap de Formentor

Beyond the turn-off for the *Hotel Formentor*, the main peninsula road runs along a wooded valley before climbing up to tunnel through Mont Fumat. Afterwards, it emerges on the rocky mass of **Cap de Formentor**, a tapering promontory of bleak sea cliffs, which offers magnificent views and top-notch **birdwatching**. The silver-domed

lighthouse stuck on the cape's windswept tip is out of bounds, but you can explore the rocky environs, where the sparse vegetation offers a perfect habitat for lizards and small birds, especially the deep-blue feathered rock thrush and the white-rumped rock dove. You can also see the steep, eastward-facing sea cliffs that shelter colonies of nesting Eleonora's falcons from April to October, while ravens, martins and swifts circle overhead. During the spring and summer migrations, thousands of sea birds fly over the cape, Manx and Cory's shearwaters in particular. For a closer look at the cape, take the steep but clearly marked **footpath** leading along the east coast from the lighthouse to the **Moll des Patronet viewpoint**; allow fifteen minutes each way.

ARRIVAL AND DEPARTURE

By car Most visitors drive to and along the peninsula; there is a small car park on the final cape (free) and a much larger one (€9) at the start of the Platja de Formentor, beside the turning for the *Hotel Formentor*.

By bus There's no public transport to the far end of the peninsula, but buses do run as far as the Platja de Formentor car park.

PENÍNSULA DE FORMENTOR

Destinations Alcúdia (May–Oct Mon–Sat 4 daily; 35min); Port d'Alcúdia (May–Oct Mon–Sat 4 daily; 50min); Port de Pollença (May–Oct Mon–Sat 4 daily; 20min).

By boat Lanchas La Gaviota (☎971 86 40 14, ⓦlanchaslagaviota.com) runs a regular passenger ferry service from Port de Pollença to the Platja de Formentor (May–Oct 2–5 daily; €13.50 return).

ACCOMMODATION AND EATING

Hotel Formentor c/Playa de Formentor 3 ☎971 89 91 00, ⓦbarcelo.com. Opened in 1930, the *Formentor* was once the haunt of the rich and fashionable – Charlie Chaplin and F. Scott Fitzgerald both stayed here – and although its socialite days are long gone, the hotel preserves an air of understated elegance befitting its *hacienda*-meets-Art-Deco architecture. Breakfast is taken on the splendid upper-floor loggia with spectacular views over the bay, and you can stroll around the wonderful terraced gardens and up the hillside behind. Now owned by the Barceló chain, the hotel has every facility, and while the

rooms are not quite as grand as you might expect, they are still charming – and about as expensive as you might expect. **€450**

Restaurant Platja Mar c/Playa de Formentor 3 ☎971 89 91 00. Perhaps predictably, there is a standard-issue café-bar down on the Platja de Formentor beach, but you might consider stumping up the extra to eat here at its more upmarket neighbour, an outpost of the *Hotel Formentor*; the restaurant occupies a brisk, modern, two-storey building and serves up delicious grilled fish and tasty paella, with main courses around €30. April–Oct daily noon–8pm.

Alcúdia

To pull in the day-trippers, pint-sized **ALCÚDIA** holds one of the largest open-air markets on Mallorca, a sprawling, bustling affair held on Tuesdays and Sundays, its assorted tourist trinkets taking over the entire east end of the old centre. Otherwise, the town's salient feature is the **crenellated wall** that encircles its centre, and although this is, in fact, a modern restoration of the original medieval defences, the sixteenth- to eighteenth-century stone houses within are the genuine article. It only takes an hour or so to explore the ancient lanes of Alcúdia's compact centre and to check out the town wall and its fortified gates, but this pleasant stroll can be extended by a visit to a series of minor sights, which combine to make an enjoyable whole.

A brief history

Situated on a neck of land separating two large and sheltered bays, **Alcúdia** had a strategic value that was first recognized by the **Phoenicians**, who settled here in around 700 BC and used it as a staging post for the sea trade between northwest Africa and Spain. A few Phoenician baubles have been unearthed here – including several fine examples of delicate, coloured-glass jewellery – but their town disappeared when the Romans razed the place and built their island capital, **Pollentia**, on top of the earlier settlement. In 426 AD, Roman Pollentia was, in its turn, destroyed by the Vandals and lay neglected until the **Moors** built a fortress in about 800 AD, naming it Al Kudia (On the Hill). After the

Reconquista, the Christians began again, demolishing much of the Moorish town and establishing Alcúdia as a major trading centre for the western Mediterranean, a role it performed well into the nineteenth century, when the town slipped into a long and impoverished decline. And what a decline it was: "There is no difficulty in finding a place for shelter in Alcúdia both for man and beast", wrote E.G. Bartholomew in the 1860s, "for by far the greater number of houses are tenantless and doorless." This sorry state of affairs persisted until mass tourism revived the town's economy.

Plaça Constitució and around

The best place to start a visit is **Plaça Carles V**, the old town's eastern entrance, where the ancient stone gateway leads through to the main drag – here c/Moll – and then the slender **Plaça Constitució**, a pleasant square lined with pavement cafés. Just beyond, on c/Major, is Alcúdia's best-looking building, the **Ajuntament** (Town Hall), a handsome, largely seventeenth-century structure with an elegant balcony, a fancy bell tower and overhanging eaves.

Museu Monogràfic

c/Sant Jaume 30 • Tues–Fri 10am–3.30pm, Sat & Sun 10.30am–1.30pm • €3, including admission to Pollentia (see p.150) • ☏ 971 54 70 04

In the southwest corner of the old town, the **Museu Monogràfic** is the most diverting of Alcúdia's sights. The museum consists of just one large room, but it's stuffed with a satisfying collection of archeological bits and bobs, primarily Roman artefacts from Pollentia, including amulets, miniature devotional objects, tiny oil lamps and some elegant statuettes.

Sant Jaume

c/Sant Jaume s/n • Tues–Sat 10am–1pm • Free, museum €1 • ☎ 971 54 86 65

Across the street from the Museu Monogràfic and dominating this portion of the old town, is the heavyweight – and heavily reworked – Gothic church of **Sant Jaume**, part of which holds a modest religious museum. Among the museum's assorted vestments, chalices and crucifixes are a few medieval **panel paintings** illustrative of the Mallorcan Primitives (see p.51). The paintings on display are of unknown provenance, but two sixteenth-century panels stand out: one depicting the Archangel Michael standing on a devil, who is painted red; the second of St John the Baptist, shown – as painterly fashion dictated – with almond-shaped eyes and full lips.

Pollentia

Avgda dels Princeps d'Espanya s/n • Tues–Fri 10am–4pm, Sat & Sun 10.30am–1pm • €3, including admission to the Museu Monogràfic (see p.149) • ☎ 971 89 71 02

Beside Alcúdia's ring road lie the broken pillars and mashed-up walls of Roman **Pollentia**, the disappointingly meagre remains of what was once the island capital. Nearly all the stone was looted by the locals years ago, so you'll need lots of imagination to picture the Roman town, though at least the ruins are clearly labelled and the site is partly redeemed by the substantial, open-air remains of the **Teatre Romà** (Roman Theatre). Dating from the first century BC, this is the smallest of the twenty Roman theatres to have survived in Spain. Nonetheless, despite its modest proportions, the builders were able to stick to the standard type of layout with eight tiers of seats carved out of the rocky hillside and divided by two gangways, though the stage area, which was constructed of earth and timber, has of course disappeared. It's a pleasant spot, set amid fruit and olive trees, though you do have to put up with the rumble of the traffic from the main road nearby.

ARRIVAL AND DEPARTURE   ALCÚDIA

By bus Buses to Alcúdia stop on the south side of the centre beside the ring road, Avgda del Prínceps d'Espanya, and metres from the tourist office.

Destinations Artà (Mon–Sat 2 daily; 50min); Ca'n Picafort (May–Oct every 15min; Nov–April hourly; 1hr 15min); Lluc (May–Oct Mon–Sat 2 daily; 1hr); Palma (every 1–2hr; 1hr); Platja de Formentor (May–Oct Mon–Sat 4 daily; 35min); Pollença (May–Oct 1–4 hourly; Nov–April hourly; 15min); Port d'Alcúdia (May–Oct every 15min; Nov–April hourly; 10min); Port de Pollença (May–Oct every 15min; Nov–April hourly;15min); Port de Sóller (May–Oct Mon–Sat 2 daily; 2hr 15min); Sóller (May–Oct Mon–Sat 2 daily; 2hr).

INFORMATION

Tourist information Alcúdia tourist office is in a flashy new building just off the ring road on Passeig Pere Ventayol s/n (May–Sept Mon–Sat 9.30am–8.30pm, Sun 9.30am–4pm; Oct–April Mon–Fri 9.30am–3pm; ☎ 971 54 90 22, ⓦ alcudiamallorca.com).

Cultural centre Alcúdia's ultra-modern cultural centre, the Auditori d'Alcúdia, Plaça de la Porta de Mallorca (☎ 971 89 71 85, ⓦ alcudiamallorca.com), includes a library, theatre and arts centre; it's just outside – and to the west of – the city wall.

ACCOMMODATION AND EATING

Hotel Ca'n Simó c/Sant Jaume 1 ☎ 971 54 92 60, ⓦ cansimo.com. Smart hotel occupying a substantial, creatively refurbished nineteenth-century stone townhouse. It has seven double bedrooms, each with deluxe furnishings and fittings that complement the building's original features. **€110**

Restaurant S'Arc c/Serra 22 ☎ 971 54 87 18, ⓦ restaurantesarc.com. An ambitious menu featuring local, seasonal ingredients is the hallmark of this attractive restaurant, which occupies part of a cleverly modernized old stone house and its lovely shaded terrace; the rest of the house holds the *Hotel Ca'n Simó* (see above). Mains average €17. April–Sept daily noon–11pm; Oct–March restricted opening hours.

Sa Plaça Plaça Constitució 1 ☎ 971 54 62 78, ⓦ alcudia restaurantes.com. There are mixed reviews for this smart restaurant at the heart of the old town, but at its best the traditional Mallorcan/Catalan cuisine can be very good indeed – try the house speciality, salted fish (*bacalao*). Main courses average €17. Daily 11am–11pm.

Badía d'Alcúdia

The wide arc of the **Badía d'Alcúdia** is framed to the east by the mountains of the Massis d'Artà headland (see p.172) and in the west by the rugged **Alcúdia peninsula**, whose further recesses hold a fine old chapel, the **Ermita de la Victòria**, and the idiosyncratic private art collection of the **Museu Sa Bassa Blanca**. The peninsula also boasts some spectacular mountain scenery and this can be sampled on the four-hour **hike** we have described (see p.153), though you will need a car to get to the trailhead. In between these mountainous flanks lies the mega-resort of **Port d'Alcúdia**, whose glistening sky-rises sweep around a glorious sandy beach – arguably the island's best. In summer the resort is packed, but shoulder seasons are more relaxing and the beach comparatively uncrowded. Port d'Alcúdia's assorted hotels, villas and apartment blocks stretch around the bay to the resort of **Ca'n Picafort**, 10km away, almost without interruption. The developers drained the swampland that once extended behind this coastal strip years ago, but one chunk of wetland has been protected as the **Parc Natural de S'Albufera**, a real birdwatchers' delight. Further behind the coast lies a tract of fertile farmland dotted with country towns, among which **Muro**, with its imposing church and old stone mansions, is the most diverting.

3

GETTING AROUND
BADÍA D'ALCÚDIA

By bus From May to October, a flotilla of buses links Port d'Alcúdia (see p.154) with all the neighbouring towns and resorts, including Muro, Pollença, Port de Pollença, Alcúdia and Ca'n Picafort, as well as Palma. There is also a useful seasonal bus service along the north coast from Port d'Alcúdia to Port de Sóller via Sóller and Lluc (May–Oct Mon–Sat 2 daily). In the wintertime, services are scaled right back – and there are no bus services at any time of the year along the Alcúdia peninsula to the Ermita de la Victòria.

By train Regular trains connect Palma with Muro (see p.157), though Muro train station is a few kilometres out of town; there are plans to extend the rail line to Alcúdia from its present terminus in Sa Pobla, but nothing has yet happened.

The Alcúdia peninsula

The **Alcúdia peninsula**, a steep and rocky promontory to the east of Alcúdia town, pokes a wild finger out into the ocean, its **northern shore** traversed by a country road that begins at the easternmost intersection of Alcúdia's ring road. After about 2km, this promontory road runs past the turning for both the Museu Sa Bassa Blanca (see p.152) and the day-hike trailhead (see p.153) before it loops round the suburban villas of **Bonaire**. Thereafter, the road emerges into more scenic terrain, offering fine sea views as it struggles over the steep, pine-clad ridges that fringe the coast on the way to the Ermita de la Victòria.

Ermita de la Victòria

Perched on a wooded hillside, about 5km from Alcúdia town, the chunky, fortress-like **Ermita de la Victòria** was built in the seventeenth century to hold and protect a crude but much-venerated statue of the Virgin. It was a necessary precaution: this part of the coast was especially prone to attack and, even with these defences, pirates still stole the statue from the church twice, though on both occasions the islanders managed to ransom it back. The Virgin is displayed in the simple, single-vaulted chapel on the ground floor of the Ermita, but this plays second fiddle to the panoramic views out across the bay.

The Ermita is also a popular starting point for **hikes** along the promontory, whose severe peaks are dotted with ruined defensive installations, including a watchtower and an old gun emplacement. An obvious target is the **Talaia d'Alcúdia watchtower** (446m), from the top of which there are great panoramic views: it's a one-hour walk each way.

ACCOMMODATION AND EATING   **ERMITA DE LA VICTÒRIA**

Mirador de la Victòria Camí de la Victòria s/n ☎ 971 54 71 73, ⓦ miradordelavictoria.com. This first-rate restaurant, which offers sweeping sea views from its expansive, shaded terrace, specializes in traditional Mallorcan dishes – try the snails, the suckling pig or the guinea fowl. Main courses cost €15. Feb to mid-April Tues–Sun 12.30–4pm; mid-April to Oct daily 1–3.30pm & 7–11pm.

★**Petit Hotel Hostatgeria la Victòria** ☎ 971 54 99 12, ⓦ lavictoriahotel.com. The old monastic quarters in the Ermita, directly above the chapel, have been turned into a delightful hotel, whose beamed ceilings, ancient stone arches and exposed masonry walls hold twelve en-suite guest rooms decorated in a suitably frugal but highly buffed and polished style. Singles €45, doubles €70

Museu Sa Bassa Blanca

Es Mal Pas, Alcúdia 07400 • Tues 9.30am–12.30pm & 2.30–5.30pm, Wed–Sat pre-booked guided tours only at 11am & 3pm • Gardens and children's gallery free, guided tours €9 • ☎ 971 54 98 80, ⓦ fundacionjakober.org • From Alcúdia, take the Ermita de la Victòria road and turn sharp right at the *Bodega del Sol* bar onto Camí de la Muntanya; after 2km or so, you'll reach the Alcúdia Peninsula trailhead (opposite), from where it's a further 2km along a bumpy dirt road

The **Museu Sa Bassa Blanca** (formerly Fundació Yannick i Ben Jakober) is a bespoke art gallery housed in the subterranean water cistern of a sprawling mansion. Dating from

3

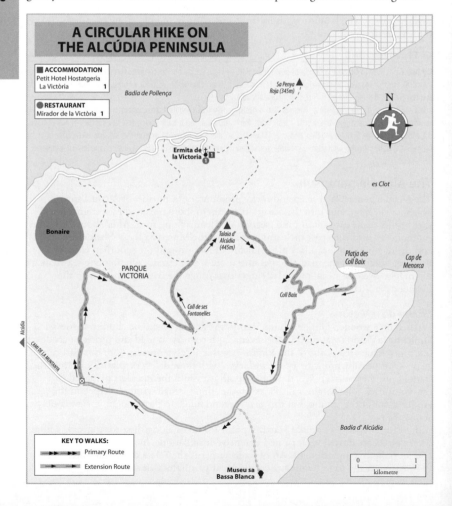

A CIRCULAR HIKE ON THE ALCÚDIA PENINSULA

10km • 450m of ascent • 5hr round trip, plus 1hr for diversion to Platja des Coll Baix • Moderately difficult • Trailhead N39.85133°, E003.15736°

This trek through the heart of the **Alcúdia peninsula** offers stunning sea views, including a 360° panoramic vista from the **Talaia d'Alcúdia**, at 445m the peninsula's highest point. The first part of the walk has moderate ascents on tracks, changing to a more strenuous ascent over exposed ground and a rock scramble to reach the Talaia peak. The second half of the walk steadily descends to the Coll Baix and returns through pine woods to the starting point. If time permits, a diversion can be made from the Coll Baix to the **Platja des Coll Baix**, a small, secluded and unspoilt beach, returning by the same route. There is **parking** at the trailhead.

THE ROUTE

Leave Alcúdia on the road to Bonaire. After about 2km, turn sharp right at the *Bodega del Sol* bar onto **Camí de la Muntanya** and continue straight on until you reach, after another 2km or so, Parque Victoria, a nature reserve administered by ICONA (National Institute for Nature Conservation). Leave your car just inside the park near the battered remains of the **iron gates**. The walk starts at this point: take the path on the uphill side of the gates, ignoring any signposts leading off right. Look and listen out for hoopoes in this area: these striking birds will appear as flashes of salmon-pink with black-and-white-striped wings and crest in woodland glades, making a distinctive hoop-hoop-hoop call. The path climbs gently upwards and then drops into a shallow valley dotted with pine trees. Passing a row of newly built villas, head towards the large white **columned house** on the skyline. Pass this house on your left and descend for about 400m, ignoring the ladder stile on your left which heads into the housing estate, and instead following the path until you reach a T-junction with an information board. Turn right at this point to begin your **ascent to Coll de ses Fontanelles**. After 2–3 minutes you will arrive at a stream, partly dammed with a concrete wall. Ignore the uphill path straight ahead and take the path to the right signposted **Coll de na Benet**. Continue along this and wind your way up the stone path to the valley head (Coll de ses Fontanelles).

The **Coll de ses Fontanelles** is populated by a stand of trees including a large olive tree. These offer valuable shade on a hot day and make this a good spot to stop, rest, take a drink and get your bearings. At the signpost, take the unsigned path to the left. At this point you start the, at first, gradual climb to the Talaia **summit**. The ground here is exposed and rocky on what is the most arduous part of the walk. From here to the summit there's no clear path, and the best way up is to follow dabs of red paint marked on the rocks. Aim for the left-hand side of the stone building at the Talaia summit as the ridge on which it stands is too steep to tackle. At this stage, the scrambling and clambering may seem daunting but reaching the summit is easier than it seems. Nevertheless, you do need to negotiate a steep and short, if relatively easy, rock face. Once on the top, don't be disconcerted by the patrolled military hut but head for the **Trig Point** (stone column) and be rewarded with superb panoramic views of the peninsula with the sea in every direction.

To descend, take the path at the other side of the Trig Point, which drops down to a path signposted "**Collet des Coll Baix**". The well-defined path provides a gentle descent, zigzagging past views of valleys to the left and right and eventually reaching the headland with views of the secluded beach of **Platja des Coll Baix** on the left. Continue your descent until, at the bottom, you reach a wooded area scattered with picnic tables, a water fountain (not drinking water) and much-needed shade. This is a popular spot for the wild Mallorcan goat, which gathers here in numbers to search for picnic leftovers. The beach is also signposted at this point and worth a visit, although **swimming is not encouraged** due to strong undertows.

From the picnic area, it's a fairly long haul on the easily graded **dirt road** to the walk's starting point by the gates. En route you will pass through pine woods, which have an undergrowth of lentiscs, narrow-leaved cistus, carritx, dwarf fan palms, euphorbias, asphodels and the occasional giant orchid; there are also almond and carob groves.

the 1970s, the **house**, Finca Sa Bassa Blanca, has wide views over the ocean and was built in the manner of a Moroccan fortified palace to a design by the Egyptian architect Hassan Fathy. The owners, the eponymous Jakobers, are art-loving sculptors and the house's **gardens** are dotted with large, modern works. The **gallery** itself holds a substantial collection of modern art, hosts temporary exhibitions and is home to a charming selection of **children's portraits** dating from the seventeenth to the nineteenth century. It was Yannick who began the collection in the 1970s, when she picked up a striking *Girl with Cherries* by the nineteenth-century Mallorcan artist Joan Mestre i Bosch. None of the artists represented is particularly well known – and neither are the children – but together they provide an intriguing insight into the way the aristocracy of early modern Spain saw their children as miniature adults. Indeed, many of the portraits were hawked around the courts of Europe in search of a suitable bride or groom.

3 Port d'Alcúdia

PORT D'ALCÚDIA, just 2km south of Alcúdia, is easily the biggest and busiest of the resorts in the north of the island, a seemingly interminable string of high-rise hotels and apartment buildings serviced by myriad restaurants and café-bars. Despite the superficial resemblance, however, Port d'Alcúdia is a step up from the seamy resorts on the Badía de Palma. The tower blocks are relatively well distributed, the streets are comparatively neat and tidy and there's an easy-going air, with families particularly well catered for. Predictably, the daytime focus is the **beach**, a superb arc of pine-studded golden sand that stretches south for 10km around the Badía d'Alcúdia from the jetties of Port d'Alcúdia's combined marina, cruise boat and fishing harbour. The beach and the sky-rises fizzle out as they approach **CA'N PICAFORT**, once an important fishing port, but now an uninteresting suburban sprawl. In the other direction, about 500m east of the marina, lies the commercial and **ferry port**, Mallorca's largest container terminal after Palma and the departure point for car ferries and catamarans over to Ciutadella, on Menorca (see p.231).

The beach

From June to September, a tourist "**train**" (on wheels, with clearly marked roadside stops) runs up and down Port d'Alcúdia every hour or so during the daytime, transporting sun-baked bodies from one part of the **beach** to another. Not that there's very much to distinguish anywhere from anywhere else – the palm-thatched **balnearios** (beach bars) are a great help in actually remembering where you are. There's also a **boardwalk** running along the back of much of the beach, which is usually less crowded the further south you venture.

ARRIVAL AND DEPARTURE   PORT D'ALCÚDIA

By bus Port d'Alcúdia acts as northern Mallorca's summertime transport hub, with fast and frequent buses up and down the coast between Ca'n Picafort and Port de Pollença as well as regular buses to and from Palma. There's no bus station as such, but instead most local and long-distance buses travel the length of the Carretera d'Artà, the main drag, dropping off passengers at clearly signed stops along the way.

Destinations Alcúdia (May–Oct every 15min; Nov–April hourly; 15min); Artà (Mon–Sat 6 daily; 30min); Ca'n Picafort (May–Oct every 15min; Nov–April hourly; 40min); Lluc (May–Oct Mon–Sat 2 daily; 1hr 10min); Palma (every 1–2hr; 1hr); Platja de Formentor (May–Oct Mon–Sat 4 daily; 50min); Pollença (April–Oct 3 daily; 20min); Port de Pollença (May–Oct every 15min; Nov–April hourly; 30min); Port de Sóller (May–Oct Mon–Sat 2 daily; 2hr 30min); Sóller (May–Oct Mon–Sat 2 daily; 2hr 20min).

NORTHERN MALLORCA'S TOP 5 BEACHES

Cala Tuent See p.132
Cala Sant Vicenç See p.141
Port de Pollença See p.142
Platja de Formentor See p.146
Port d'Alcúdia See above

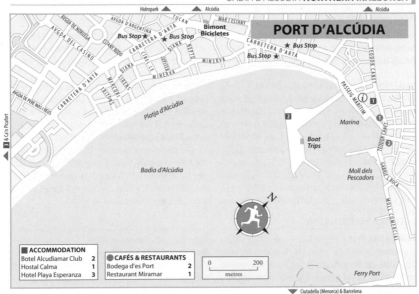

By ferry Balearia (☎ 902 16 01 80, ⓦ balearia.com) operates a fast-ferry catamaran service (1–2 daily; 1hr 30min) from Port d'Alcúdia to Ciutadella on Menorca (see p.231). One-way passenger fares start at about €35 (driver and car €90). In addition, Iscomar (☎ 902 11 91 28, ⓦ www.iscomar.com) operates regular car ferries from Port d'Alcúdia to Ciutadella once or twice daily except in the depths of winter; the journey time is 2hr 30min and fares are about the same as for the catamaran service. Note that Balearic car rental firms do not allow their vehicles to leave the island they were rented on.

GETTING AROUND

Car, moped and bike rental There's a superabundance of car, moped and bike rental companies strung out along the main drag, Carretera d'Artà. The best of the bike shops is Bimont Bicicletes, near the large Eroski store at Carretera d'Artà 38 (☎ 971 54 49 64, ⓦ bimont.com).

INFORMATION

Tourist information The main tourist office occupies a distinctive kiosk in what is effectively the centre of the resort, just behind the marina on Passeig Marítim (May–Sept Mon–Fri 8am–8.30pm, Sat & Sun 8.30am–3.30pm; rest of year Mon–Fri 10am–1.30pm & 3–5.30pm, Sat 9am–1pm; ☎ 971 54 72 57, ⓦ alcudiamallorca.com). They have all sorts of local information, including useful free maps marked with all the resort's hotels and apartments.

ACTIVITIES

Boat trips Several companies operate boat trips from the marina in Port d'Alcúdia, with the prime targets being the rocky, mountainous coastlines of the Alcúdia and Formentor peninsulas. The main company is Brisa (☎ 971 54 58 11, ⓦ tmbrisa.com), whose least expensive excursion is to the Cap des Pinar at the tip of the Alcúdia peninsula (May–Oct 2–3 daily; 2hr; €19). Longer cruises continue round the Cap des Pinar and cross the bay to the Platja de Formentor (May–Oct 1 daily; 4hr, including 1hr on Platja de Formentor; €24).

Water park Hidropark, 1km or so inland from the seashore on Avinguda del Tucá, is a major kids' attraction with assorted water slides, water tubes and so forth (May–Oct daily 10am–5pm; ☎ 971 89 16 72, ⓦ hidroparkalcudia .com; adults and children 12 and over €23; 3–11 years €17; ten percent discount if booked online ahead of time).

Watersports Watersports Mallorca, Avgda S'Albufera s/n (☎ 606 35 38 07, ⓦ watersportsmallorca.com) is a watersports specialist, operating from two beachside locations to the south of Port d'Alcúdia near the national park, and offering windsurfing, sailing, kitesurfing and stand-up paddleboarding.

ACCOMMODATION

In season, you'd be well advised to book ahead as vacant **rooms** can be few and far between – even at the bargain-basement *hostales* that cluster behind the marina in the oldest and least appealing part of the resort. In winter, most of the **hotels** and **hostales** close, but in the shoulder seasons it's often possible to get a good deal at one of the plusher hotels.

Botel Alcudiamar Club Passeig Marítim 1 ☎ 971 89 72 15, ⊛ botelalcudiamar.es. The prime selling point of this modern hotel is its location – right at the end of a jetty with water (almost) all around. There are sea-view terraces, an outdoor pool and a mini-spa. The rooms are decoratively uninspiring, but the best have sea-facing balconies. **€220**

Hostal Calma c/Teodor Canet 25 ☎ 971 54 84 85, ⊛ hostalcalma.com. Few would say this thirty-room, family-run *hostal* was especially endearing, but it is in a central location – close to the marina and a short hop from the beach – and the rooms are perfectly adequate if compact. All are en suite and have a/c, but light sleepers may find the streets outside rather noisy. Bike rental is available too. A snip, with breakfast included. **€48**

Hotel Playa Esperanza Avgda S'Albufera s/n ☎ 971 89 05 68, ⊛ playaesperanzaresort.com. Whopping four-star hotel in a grand location away from the crowds and directly behind the beach, about 5km south of the marina. Has a full range of facilities, splendid, well-tended gardens and a large self-service restaurant. **€180**

EATING AND DRINKING

Bodega d'es Port c/Teodor Canet 8 ☎ 971 54 96 33, ⊛ bodegadesport.com. Set on the waterfront, between the marina and the port, and decked out in an appealing version of traditional *bodega* style with wide windows, wooden chairs and a stone facade, this is one of the resort's better restaurants. The prime offering here is the first-rate selection of tapas from as little as €10. Daily 8am–11.30pm. Closed Nov & Dec.

Restaurant Miramar Passeig Marítim 2 ☎ 971 54 52 93, ⊛ restaurantmiramar.es. Well-established seafront restaurant with an expansive pavement terrace. It serves a top-notch range of seafood – try the hake with spinach – with dishes costing anywhere between €20 and €30. Daily noon–10.30pm, but restricted hours in winter.

Parc Natural de S'Albufera

Avgda S'Albufera s/n • The clearly signed park entrance is beside the Ma-12, about 6km round the bay from Port d'Alcúdia's marina • April–Sept daily 9am–6pm; Oct–March daily 9am–5pm • Free, but visitor permit required, issued for free at the Sa Roca Information Centre (see opposite), about 1km from the entrance along a country lane • ☎ 971 89 22 50, ⊛ en.balearsnatura.com

Given all the high-rise development strung along the Badía d'Alcúdia, the pristine wetland that makes up the 2000-acre **Parc Natural de S'Albufera**, between Port d'Alcúdia and Ca'n Picafort, is a welcome relief. Swampland once extended round most of the bay, but large-scale reclamation began in the nineteenth century, when a British company dug a network of channels and installed a steam engine to pump the water out. These endeavours were prompted by a desire to eradicate malaria – then the scourge of the local population – as much as by the need for more farmland. Further drainage schemes accompanied the frantic tourist boom of the 1960s, and only in the last decades has the Balearic government recognized the ecological importance of the wetland and organized a park to protect what little remains.

From the park's **Sa Roca reception centre**, footpaths and cycle trails fan out into the reedy, watery tract beyond, where a dozen or so well-appointed **hides** and observation decks allow excellent **birdwatching** – the best on the island. More than two hundred different types of bird have been spotted here, including resident wetland-loving birds from the crake, warbler and tern families; autumn and/or springtime migrants such as grebes, herons, cranes, plovers and godwits; and wintering egrets and sandpipers. Such rich pickings attract birds of prey in their dozens, especially kestrels and harriers. The open ground edging the reed beds supports many different wild flowers, the most striking of which are the orchids that bloom during April and May.

ARRIVAL AND DEPARTURE | PARC NATURAL DE S'ALBUFERA

By car Visitors are not allowed to drive down the 1km-long lane from the park entrance to the Sa Roca information centre, but there is a small car park just south of the entrance beside the Ma-12.

By bus Buses running between Port d'Alcúdia and Ca'n Picafort stop close to the entrance.

Destinations Alcúdia (May–Oct every 15min; Nov–April hourly; 45min); Ca'n Picafort (May–Oct every 15min; Nov–April hourly; 10min); Port d'Alcúdia (May–Oct every 15min; Nov–April hourly; 30min); Port de Pollença (May–Oct every 15min; Nov–April hourly; 1hr).

By bike In summer, there's usually a bike rental kiosk at the start of the lane leading to Sa Roca.

INFORMATION

Sa Roca information centre At this information centre (daily 9am–4pm), you can pick up a free map of the park and a list of birds that you might see. The map is marked with four colour-coded walking/cycling trails; the shortest is 725m, the longest 11km. Note, however, that the map is not especially accurate and, although it's perfectly adequate for these four routes, anything more ambitious – say, walking to Ca'n Picafort – is not advised as you would almost certainly get lost. Sa Roca also sells birdwatching guides and there is a small wildlife display in an adjacent building, Can Bateman.

Muro

Perched on a hill in the midst of a pancake-flat, windmill-studded landscape, **MURO** is a sleepy little place whose old stone townhouses date back to the early nineteenth century. The town is at its liveliest on January 16 during the **Revetlla de Sant Antoni Abat** (Eve of St Antony's Day), when locals gather round bonfires to drink and dance, tucking into specialities like sausages and eel pies (*espinagades*), made with eels from the nearby marshes of S'Albufera. Quite what St Antony – an Egyptian hermit and ascetic who spent most of his long life in the desert – would have made of these high jinks it's hard to say, but there again he certainly wouldn't have been overwhelmed by temptation if he had stuck around Muro for the rest of the year.

Plaça Constitució

Muro's main square, **Plaça Constitució**, is an attractive, airy piazza overseen by the domineering church of **St Joan Baptista**, a real hotchpotch of architectural styles, its monumental Gothic lines uneasily modified by the sweeping sixteenth-century arcades above the aisles. A slender arch connects the church to the adjacent **belfry**, an imposing seven-storey construction partly designed as a watchtower; it's sometimes possible to go to the top, from where the views out over the coast are superb. The church's cavernous interior holds a mighty vaulted roof and an immense altarpiece, a flashy extravaganza of columns, parapets and tiers in a folksy rendition of the Baroque.

Museu Etnològic

c/Major 15 • Wed–Sat 10am–3pm, Thurs 5–8pm; Sun 10am–2pm; closed Aug • €3 • ☎ 971 86 06 47

A five-minute walk south of the main square is the **Museu Etnològic**, though it's poorly signed and the town centre is labyrinthine – ask around to find your way. This one of the least-visited museums on the island, and the custodians seem positively amazed when a visitor actually shows up. It occupies a rambling old mansion and showcases a motley assortment of local bygones, from old agricultural implements, pottery and apothecary jars through to Mallorcan bagpipes and traditional costumes.

ARRIVAL AND DEPARTURE — MURO

By train Muro train station is about 4km west of the town centre; there is a bus service between the two (every 2hr; 5min).
Destinations Binissalem (hourly; 20min); Inca (hourly; 15min); Palma (hourly; 50min).

By bus Buses halt at Plaça del Convent, a 5min walk from Plaça Constitució via the dead straight c/Joan Carles I.
Destinations Ca'n Picafort (every 2hr; 35min); Inca train station (every 2hr; 20min).

EATING AND DRINKING

Sa Fonda c/Sant Jaume 1 ☎ 971 53 79 65. On a hot summer's day you'll be glad of a drink at one of the cafés around the main square, and this traditional little place, which also serves a range of inexpensive tapas, is as good as any. Located just off Plaça Constitució across from the church. Daily except Tues 6.30am–8pm.

Southern Mallorca

163 Binissalem
165 Inca
165 Sineu
166 Petra
167 Els Calderers de Sant Joan
168 Gordiola glassworks
169 Algaida
169 The Massís de Randa
171 Manacor
172 Artà and around
176 Colònia de Sant Pere
177 Capdepera
178 Cala Rajada
181 Coves d'Artà
181 Canyamel
181 Porto Cristo
184 Felanitx and around
186 Porto Petro
187 Mondragó Parc Natural
188 Santanyí and around
188 Cap de Ses Salines
189 Colònia de Sant Jordi and around
192 Cabrera National Park

CALA RAJADA

Southern Mallorca

Most of southern Mallorca comprises the island's central plain, Es Pla, a fertile tract bounded to the west by the mountainous Serra de Tramuntana and to the east by the hilly range that shadows the coast, the Serres de Llevant. Although Es Pla may seem today like a sleepy backwater, it pretty much defined Mallorca until the twentieth century: the majority of the island's inhabitants lived here, it produced enough food to meet almost every domestic requirement, and Palma's gentry were reliant on Es Pla estates for their income. This persisted until the 1960s, when the tourist boom turned everything on its head and the developers bypassed Es Pla to focus on the picturesque coves of the east coast.

Still largely ignored by the tourist industry, the **towns of Es Pla** provide the full flavour of an older, agricultural Mallorca, whose softly hued landscapes are patterned with olive orchards, chunky farmhouses and country towns of low, whitewashed houses huddled beneath outsized churches. Admittedly, there's precious little to distinguish one settlement from another, but there are exceptions, most notably wine-growing **Binissalem**, with its streets of handsome old houses; **Sineu**, once the site of a royal palace and now one of the plain's prettiest towns; and **Petra**, with its clutch of sights celebrating the life and times of the eighteenth-century Franciscan monk and explorer Junipero Serra. Other key sights are the impressive monastery perched on the summit of **Puig Randa** and, in the Serres de Llevant, the hilltop shrine at **Artà** plus the delightful medieval castle at **Capdepera**. All these destinations are readily accessible from either the **Ma-13** motorway – the island's busiest and fastest road, which links Palma with Alcúdia – or the Ma-15, which runs the 70km from Palma to Artà, via **Manacor**, noted for its artificial pearl factories.

The ancient fishing villages of the **east coast** have mostly been swallowed up within mega-resorts, whose endless high-rises and villa complexes blemish the land for miles – **Cala Millor and Cala d'Or** being two cases in point. A couple of enjoyable seaside spots have, however, avoided the worst excesses of concrete and glass: **Cala Rajada**, a lively resort bordered by fine beaches and a beautiful pine-dusted coastline, and pint-sized **Canyamel**, which edges a lovely, sweeping cove. The former fishing village of **Porto Petro** has also managed to retain some of its original charm, as has the ramshackle old port of **Porto Cristo**. Different again is tiny **Cala Mondragó**, where a slice of coast has been protected by the creation of a park – and here you can appreciate exactly how charming the shoreline once was. The east coast also boasts the cave systems of **Coves del Drac**, justifiably famous for their extravagant stalactites and stalagmites. On the **south coast**, the scenery changes again, with hills and coves giving way to sparse flatlands, which precede the long and low rocky shelf that jags into the ocean with barely a decent beach in sight. The star turn here is the port-cum-resort of **Colònia de Sant Jordi**, which has a brace of sandy beaches and from where boat trips leave for the bleached remoteness of **Cabrera** island, now a national park.

Porto Cristo's Republican landing p.183   Birdlife of the saltpans p.191

COVES DEL DRAC

Highlights

❶ Sineu The most attractive of central Mallorca's ancient agricultural towns, home to the island's finest parish church and a bustling Wednesday market. **See p.165**

❷ Cala Rajada Perched on the edge of a bumpy headland, this popular resort is within easy striking distance of several excellent, pine-clad sandy beaches. **See p.178**

❸ Coves del Drac Perhaps the finest of the island's cave systems, with fantastically shaped stalactites and stalagmites, as well as one of the world's largest subterranean lakes. **See p.183**

❹ Cala Mondragó Protected within a natural park, this beguiling cove boasts a pair of beautiful cove beaches – and two unassuming hotels to match. **See p.187**

❺ Colònia de Sant Jordi Charming, low-key resort with several sandy beaches, smashing seafood restaurants and easy-going hotels and *hostales*. **See p.189**

❻ Cabrera The bleak and hostile terrain of this offshore islet makes for an unusual day's excursion – and lots of rare Lilford's wall lizards will help you with your sandwiches. **See p.192**

HIGHLIGHTS ARE MARKED ON THE MAP ON P.162

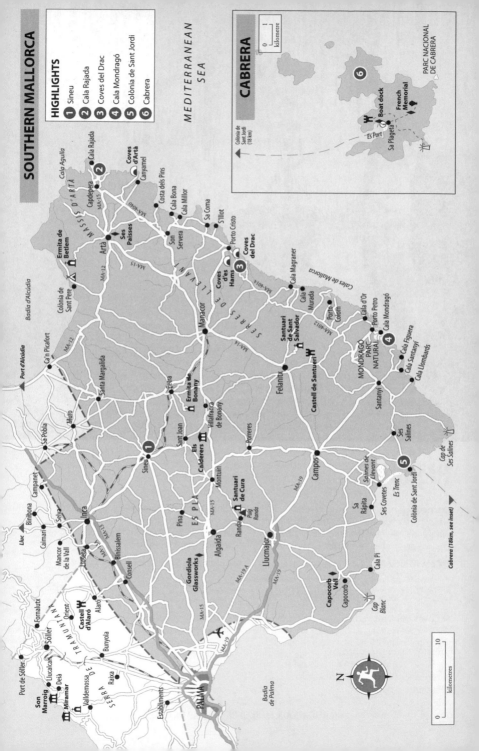

SOUTHERN MALLORCA

HIGHLIGHTS

1. Sineu
2. Cala Rajada
3. Coves del Drac
4. Cala Mondragó
5. Colònia de Sant Jordi
6. Cabrera

CABRERA

PARC NACIONAL DE CABRERA

Boat dock
French Memorial
Es Port
Sa Plageta
Colònia de Sant Jordi (18 km)

MEDITERRANEAN SEA

Badia d'Alcúdia

Port d'Alcúdia

Ca'n Picafort
Colònia de Sant Pere
Ermita de Betlem
Artà
Ses Païses
Capdepera
Cala Rajada
Coves d'Artà
Canyamel

MASSÍS D'ARTÀ

Santa Margalida
Son Serra
Cala Bona
Cala Millor
Sa Coma
S'Illot
Porto Cristo
Coves del Drac
Coves d'es Hams

Manacor

SERRES DE LLEVANT

Cala Magraner
Cala Murada
Porto Colom
Cala d'Or
Porto Petro
Cala Mondragó
Cala Figuera
Cala Santanyí
Cala Llombards

Cales de Mallorca

Santuari de Sant Salvador
Castell de Santueri
Felanitx

MONDRAGÓ PARC NATURAL

Santanyí

Ses Salines
Cap de Ses Salines

Petra
Ermita de Bonany
Vilafranca de Bonany
Sant Joan
Els Calderers
Porreres
Montuïri
Campos

Sineu

ES PLA

Sa Pobla
Muro
Sa Rápita
Ses Covetes
Es Trenc
Salines de Llevant
Colònia de Sant Jordi

Campanet
Binibona
Biniamar
Selva
Inca
Consell
Binissalem
Mancor de la Vall
Caimari
Lluc

Santuari de Cura
Puig Randa
Randa
Algaida
Pina

Gordiola Glassworks

Llucmajor
Capocorb Vell
Capocorb
Cap Blanc

Cabrera (18km, see inset)

Port de Sóller
Son Marroig
Miramar
Valldemossa
Lluc-Alcari
Deià
Fornalutx
Sóller
Bunyola
Raixa
Orient
Alaró
Castell d'Alaró

SERRA DE TRAMUNTANA

Establiments

PALMA

Badia de Palma

N

kilometres 0 10

GETTING AROUND

By public transport Direct buses link Palma with almost every resort and town in southern Mallorca, but services between the towns of Es Pla and along the east coast are patchy. The region also has a train line with frequent services linking Palma, Binissalem, Inca, Sineu, Petra and Manacor. For public transport services and times, consult ⓦ tib.org.

SOUTHERN MALLORCA

ACCOMMODATION

Finding a room Given the difficulty of finding a room in the coastal package resorts on spec and the general dearth of accommodation in the interior, advance reservations are a good idea – and pretty much essential in the height of the season. Towns with a healthy supply of hotels and *hostales* include Artà, Cala Rajada and Colònia de Sant Jordi. In addition, three of the region's former monasteries offer simple, inexpensive lodgings and usually have space at any time of year (see p.167, p.170 & p.186).

Binissalem

First impressions of **BINISSALEM**, about 25km northeast of Palma, are rarely positive, but in fact the careworn semi-industrial sprawl that encases the town camouflages an antique centre of some architectural distinction, its narrow streets flanked by a proud ensemble of old stone mansions dating from the seventeenth and eighteenth centuries. It was the Romans who first settled here, and they were succeeded by the Moors – Binissalem could be derived from the Arabic "Bani Salaam" (Sons of Peace) – but the town's commercial heyday began in the sixteenth century, boosted by its stone quarries and vineyards: indeed, Binissalem has been the centre of Mallorca's wine-growing industry ever since. These days the old centre maintains a sleepy calm particularly attractive to those wanting to escape the bustle of Palma.

4

Església Nostra Senyora de Robines

Binissalem's main square, the **Plaça Església**, is a pretty, stone-flagged piazza where old-timers shoot the breeze in the shade of the plane trees. The northeast side of the square is dominated by the fortress-like **Església Nostra Senyora de Robines**, whose clumpy, medieval nave is attached to a soaring neo-Gothic bell tower added in 1908. Inside, the single-vaulted nave is dark and gloomy, its most distinctive features being its glitzy Baroque altarpiece and the grooved stonework that appears above and beyond the high altar. This grooved stonework pops up all over town, representing the cockleshell emblem of **St James the Greater**. James was the first of the apostles to be martyred, in 44 AD, but despite his early demise Spanish legend insists that he visited Spain and lies buried at Santiago de Compostela in Galicia. These legends may be far-fetched, but they have made James one of the country's most venerated saints.

Casa Museu Llorenç Villalonga

c/Bonaire 25 • Tues–Fri 9am–3pm, plus Tues & Thurs 4–8pm • Free • ☎ 971 88 60 14, ⓦ fundaciocasamuseu.cat • The museum is a 5min walk from Plaça Església via c/Concepció

One of the town's most distinguished patrician mansions, **Can Sabater** was once the home of the writer Llorenç Villalonga (1897–1980), whose most successful novel was *The Dolls' Room*, an ambiguous portrait of Mallorca's nineteenth-century landed gentry in moral decline. In his honour, the house has been turned into the **Casa Museu Llorenç Villalonga**, where a series of exhibits (in Catalan) explores the man's life and times and you can admire his library and study, which have been left much as they were at the time of his death. The house is typical of its type, with elegant stone arches and

BINISSALEM

CAFÉS & RESTAURANTS
| Bar-Restaurante Robines | 1 |
| Terra di Vino | 2 |

4

high-ceilinged rooms redolent of oligarchic comfort. It also has its own chapel: the island's richer families usually had their own live-in priests.

Bodega José Luis Ferrer

c/Conquistador 103 (Ma-13A) · **Tastings & tours** Mon–Fri 11am & 4.30pm, Sat 11am; 45min · €10 · **Shop** April–Oct Mon–Fri 10am–7pm, Sat 10am–6pm, Sun 10am–2pm; Nov–March Mon–Fri 10am–7pm, Sat 10am–2pm · ☎ 971 51 10 50, ⓦ vinosferrer.com

Although there is more competition than ever before, most critics agree that Binissalem's **Bodega José Luis Ferrer** produces Mallorca's best red wines. If you book ahead, you can tour parts of the winery during the working week, but most visitors are content to visit the **shop**, which stocks the full range of the company's wines.

ARRIVAL AND INFORMATION   BINISSALEM

By bus Buses to Binissalem stop beside c/Conquistador (Ma-13A), a few metres to the west of c/Bonaire, which leads straight up towards Plaça Església.
Destinations Lluc (2 daily; 45min); Palma (2–6 daily; 30min); Selva (2 daily; 20min).
By train Binissalem train station is on the northern edge of the town centre, a 10min walk from Plaça Església: head straight down c/S'Estació, turn right at the end and then left at the end of this second street.
Destinations Inca (every 20min; 10min); Manacor (hourly;

40min); Muro (hourly; 20min); Palma (every 20min; 30min); Petra (hourly; 30min); Sineu (hourly; 20min).
Festivals An especially good time to visit Binissalem is in the third week of July, during the week-long festivities that precede St James' feast day on July 25. A second calendar highlight is the Festa d'es Vermar (Festival of the Grape Harvest) at the back end of September, when the town's cordoned-off streets are lined with trestle tables weighed down with all sorts of local wines and foods, proudly presented by their makers.

EATING AND DRINKING

Bar-Restaurante Robines Plaça Església 25 ☎ 971 51 11 36. Binissalem is short of good restaurants, but this old-fashioned place does something to fill the gastronomic gap, serving all the Spanish classics with main courses averaging about €16. Daily except Tues 1–4pm & 7–11pm.

Terra di Vino c/Sa Creu 3 ☎ 871 91 02 26. Head and shoulders the best restaurant in town, this modern and cosy Italian place offers an excellent range of pasta dishes from around €12. Just off the main square. Daily except Tues 1–4pm & 7–11pm; closed Sun July & Aug.

Inca

Some 30km northeast of Palma, sprawling **INCA**, Mallorca's third city, has long had a bad press as an industrial eyesore. In medieval times, one of the few ways to keep out of the clutches of the island's landowners was to practise a craft and then join the appropriate guild. As early as the fifteenth century, Inca had attracted enough **shoemakers** to become the centre of a flourishing shoemaking industry – and so it remains today, with Camper's HQ and main factory-warehouse firmly ensconced here. This may not sound too enticing, but today it's a pleasant enough place with a re-energized and revamped old centre; the **walk** across its pedestrianized core, from the **train station** in the west to Plaça d'Orient in the east, is an agreeable way to spend an hour or so. Along the way, you'll spy a scattering of immaculate *Modernista* buildings and the town's main church, **Santa Maria la Major**, an imposing sandstone pile with all sorts of Baroque flourishes.

ARRIVAL AND DEPARTURE   INCA

By bus and train The bus and train stations are next to each other on the western edge of the city centre on c/des Tren.

Destinations (buses) Lluc (2–3 daily; 35min); Palma (every 1–2hr; 35min); Pollença (every 1–2hr; 25min); Port de Pollença (every 1–2hr; 40min).

Destinations (trains) Binissalem (every 20min; 10min); Manacor (hourly; 30min); Muro (hourly; 15min); Palma (every 20min; 30min); Petra (hourly; 25min); Sineu (hourly; 15min).

EATING AND DRINKING

Celler Ca'n Amer c/Pau 39 ☎971 50 12 61, ⓦcellercan amer.es. As you might expect, Inca has oodles of cafés and restaurants, with one of the best being the long-established *Ca'n Amer*, a wonderfully old-fashioned cellar restaurant a short walk west of the main church. Main dishes cost around €15. Mon–Sat 1–4pm & 7.30–11pm, Sun 1–4pm.

Joan Marc Plaça del Blanquer 10 ☎971 50 08 04, ⓦjoanmarcrestaurant.com. The locals' choice for the best restaurant in town, the excellent *Joan Marc*, named after the restaurant's owner, offers a chic but affordable take on classic Mallorquin dishes. Almost all ingredients and many of the wines are locally sourced, and the à la carte menu of three to four courses, including a drink, comes in at around €30. Plaça del Blanquer is on the north side of the centre, in between the train station and Plaça d'Orient. Tues–Sat 1–3.30pm & 8–10.30pm, Sun 1–3.30pm.

4

Sineu

Handsome **SINEU**, 14km southeast of Inca, is perhaps the most interesting of Es Pla's ancient agricultural towns. Glued to a hill at the geographical centre of the island, with winding, narrow streets cascading down into the valley, the town had obvious strategic advantages for the independent kings of fourteenth-century Mallorca. Jaume II built a royal palace here; his asthmatic successor, Sancho, liked the place for its upland air; and the last of the dynasty, Jaume III, slept in Sineu the night before he was defeated and killed at the battle of Llucmajor by Pedro of Aragón. The new Aragonese monarchs had no need of the Sineu palace, which disappeared long ago, but former pretensions survive in the form of Mallorca's grandest **parish church**, Nostra Senyora de los Angeles.

The best time to visit Sineu is on Wednesdays, when the cafés around the main square are packed and the town fizzes with one of Mallorca's liveliest fresh produce and clothes **markets** (the only one still licensed to sell large livestock). Replete with live gypsy jazz bands and bushels of garlic and chilli peppers hanging from hooks on medieval walls, the market sprawls up and down much of the old centre.

Nostra Senyora de los Angeles

Sa Plaça • Daily 9.30–4.30pm • Free

With its medley of old stone buildings, **Sa Plaça**, Sineu's main square, is overlooked by the severe stone facade of **Nostra Senyora de los Angeles**. Built in the thirteenth century, the church was extensively remodelled three hundred years later, but the majestic simplicity of the original Gothic design is still plain to see. At the side, a single-span arch connects with the colossal freestanding **bell tower**, and close by, at the top of the church steps, a big, modern and aggressive **statue** of a winged lion – the emblem of the town's patron, St Mark – stands guard, courtesy of Franco's cronies.

ARRIVAL AND DEPARTURE · SINEU

By train From Sineu train station, it's about 500m west up the lightly sloping hill to Sa Plaça, the main square; there are no signs, you just follow your nose.

Destinations Binissalem (hourly; 25min); Inca (hourly; 10min); Manacor (hourly; 15min); Palma (hourly; 50min); Petra (hourly; 5min).

ACCOMMODATION AND EATING

Hotel Celler de Ca'n Font Sa Plaça 18 ☎971 52 02 95 (hotel), ☎971 52 03 13 (restaurant), ⓦcanfont.com. Located right on the main square, *Ca'n Font* has just seven fairly basic rooms, and an excellent restaurant in its cellar, with main courses costing around €15. Restaurant open daily 9am–4pm & 7–11pm. **€70**

Celler Es Grop c/Major 18 ☎971 52 01 87. The best place to eat in Sineu is this friendly place, a few metres from Sa Plaça, whose cavernous interior doubles as a wine vault (hence the wooden barrels), and serves first-rate Mallorcan meals, with main courses averaging around €15. Tues–Sun 10am–2pm & 7–11pm, plus Mon on festival days.

Sa Rota d'en Palerm Lloret de Vistalegre ☎654 13 13 31, ⓦsa-rota.com. Around 6km southeast of Sineu, this charming rural retreat is set in a tastefully restored,

eighteenth-century mansion with a large pool and period(ish) guest rooms. Breakfast features home-made products and you can pre-order traditional Mallorquín dinners (made with produce from the hotel's gardens and orchards). From Sineu, take the road towards Lloret de Vistalegre. About 500m before you reach that village, turn left towards Montuïri and after about 800m there's a sign to the hotel on the left, a further 2.5km away. **€156**

Hotel Son Cleda Plaça Es Fossar 7 ☎971 52 10 27, ⓦhotelsoncleda.com. In a handsome old mansion about 100m from Sa Plaça, the agreeable *Hotel Son Cleda* has friendly owners, views over the town, bikes for hire and just eight bedrooms, each of which is kitted out in an attractive modern version of traditional Spanish style. **€100**

Petra

Nothing very exciting happens in **PETRA**, 11km southeast of Sineu, but it was the birthplace of **Junipero Serra**, the remarkable eighteenth-century Franciscan friar who played such an important role in the settlement of Spanish North America. Serra's missionary endeavours began in 1749 when he landed at Veracruz on the Gulf of Mexico. For eighteen years, Serra thrashed around the more remote parts of Mexico until, entirely by chance, political machinations back in Europe saved him from obscurity. In 1768, King Carlos III claimed the west coast of the North American continent for Spain and dispatched a small expeditionary force of soldiers and monks north from Mexico to lay his claim. Serra was made leader of the priests and the royal force proceeded to complete the daunting walk from Mexico City to California, reaching the Pacific Ocean somewhere near the present US–Mexico border in early 1769. Over the next decade, Serra and his small band of priests set about converting the Native Americans of coastal California to the Catholic faith, and established a string of nine missions along the Pacific coast, including San Diego, Los Angeles and San Francisco. Pope John Paul II beatified Serra in 1988.

Junipero Serra Museum

C/Barraca Alta 2 • Mon, Wed, Fri & Sat 10.30am–12.30pm • Donation requested • ☎971 56 11 49

In the upper part of town, on c/Major, is the chunky church of **Sant Bernat**, behind which – down a narrow side street – lies a modest sequence of majolica panels honouring Junipero Serra's life and missionary work. At the end of the side street, further Serra tributes can be found inside the self-effacing **Junipero Serra Museum**, where several rooms are devoted to the Serra cult: the honours paid to him, books written about him, and paintings of him. Another room focuses on Serra's work in California, with photos and models of his foundations. Incidentally, the humble house where Serra was born is just along the street at no. 6.

Ermita de Nostra Senyora de Bonany

Puig de Bonany s/n • Daily dawn to dusk • Free • ☎ 971 82 65 68 • About 5km southwest of Petra: take the Felanitx road and look out for the sign on the edge of the village

Offering extensive views over Es Pla, the hilltop **Ermita de Nostra Senyora de Bonany**, just outside Petra at the end of a bumpy and steep country lane, takes its name from events in 1609 when desperate locals gathered here at the chapel to pray for rain. Shortly afterwards, the drought broke and the ensuing harvest was a good one – hence *bon any* ("good year"). The prettiest feature of the complex is the **chapel**, which is approached along an avenue of cypress and palm trees and comes complete with a rose window, twin towers and a little cupola. The monastery's conspicuous stone cross was erected in honour of Junipero Serra, who left here bound for the Americas in 1749.

ARRIVAL AND DEPARTURE   PETRA

By train Petra's train station is on the northern edge of town, about 700m from Sant Pere, the large church at the north end of c/Major – and a further 500m or so from the church of Sant Bernat.

Destinations Binissalem (hourly; 20min); Inca (hourly; 20min); Manacor (hourly; 10min); Palma (hourly; 50min); Sineu (hourly; 5min).

ACCOMMODATION AND EATING

Ermita de Nostra Senyora de Bonany, 5km southwest of Petra ☎ 971 82 65 68. This hilltop monastery (see above) rents out five simple double rooms: there's one shared bathroom with hot water and cooking facilities, but you'll have to bring your own food and bedding. **€30**
Hotel Sa Plaça Plaça Ramon Llull 4 ☎ 971 56 16 46, ⓦ petithotelpetra.com. Central Petra's accommodation is limited to the *Hotel Sa Plaça* on the main square, which has

just three double rooms with big, old furniture and a mix of whitewashed and rough-stone walls. It is also home to the town's best restaurant, an attractively old-fashioned place, where you can eat traditional Mallorcan cuisine either in the antique-filled interior or on the terrace outside; main courses average around €18. Restaurant open daily 11am–2pm & 7–11pm. **€85**

Els Calderers de Sant Joan

Camí Els Calderers s/n • Daily: April–Oct 10am–6pm; Nov–March 10am–5pm • €9 • ☎ 971 52 60 69, ⓦ elscalderers.com • The house is between the villages of Sant Joan and Vila Franca de Bonany, 2km north of – and signed from – the Ma-15, and 8km or so west of Petra

Dating mostly from the eighteenth century, **Els Calderers de Sant Joan** is an engaging country house that bears witness to the wealth and influence once enjoyed by the island's landed gentry – in this case the **Veri family**. The house was the focus of a large estate whose main cash crop was originally grapes. The phylloxera aphid destroyed the vineyards and the Veris switched to cereals, before subsequently experimenting with a variety of other crops. Indeed, at the beginning of the twentieth century the Veris were at the forefront of efforts to modernize Mallorcan agriculture, much to the consternation of some of their more stuck-in-the-mud neighbours.

The house

Flanked by a pair of crumpled-looking lions, the entrance to the **house** leads to a sequence of handsome period rooms surrounding a cool and verdant courtyard. All are kitted out with antique furniture, *objets d'art* and family portraits, while the hunting room comes with an assortment of stuffed animal heads. There is no mistaking the self-assured authority of the **master's office** with its big armchairs and polished desk, and you can also visit the family's tiny chapel – like every landowning family on the island, the Veris had a live-in priest. Attached to, but separate from, the family house are the living quarters of the *missatge* (farm manager), the barn and the farmworkers' kitchen and eating area. To complete your visit, take a stroll round the **animal pens**. The animals are breeds traditionally used on Mallorcan farms – especially black pigs, from which Mallorcan *sobrasada* (sausage) is derived – though they're here to illustrate the past rather than to be of any practical use.

EATING	ELS CALDERERS DE SANT JOAN

Els Calderers Café Els Calderers ☎ 971 52 60 69, ⓦ elscalderers.com. Simple little café within Els Calderers, where they serve traditional Mallorcan snacks: the *pa amb* *oli* (bread rubbed with olive oil) with ham and cheese is simply delicious and costs just a few euros. Daily: April–Oct 10am–5.30pm; Nov–March 10am–4.30pm.

Gordiola glassworks

Carretera Palma–Manacor Km19 (Ma-15) • June–Sept Mon–Sat 9am–7pm, Sun 9am–1.30pm; Oct–May Mon–Sat 9am–6pm, Sun 9am–1.30pm • Free • ☎ 971 66 50 46, ⓦ gordiola.com

Some 19km from Palma and just 2km from Algaida, stuck beside the Ma-15 in a conspicuous – and conspicuously ugly – castle-like building dating from the 1960s, the **Gordiola glassworks** is not the popular attraction it once was, but is still well worth a visit. For starters, you can watch highly skilled **glassblowers** in action, practising their precise art in a gloomy hall designed to resemble a medieval church and illuminated by glowing furnaces. Staff are usually on hand to explain the techniques involved – the fusion of silica, soda and lime at a temperature of 1100°C – although this is really part of a public relations exercise intended to push you towards the adjacent **gift shops**. These hold a massive assortment of glass and ceramic wares, everything from the most abysmal tourist tat to works of great delicacy, notably green-tinted **chandeliers** of traditional Mallorcan design costing anything from €2000 upwards; more affordably, a simple jug will cost you about €15.

Museu del Vidre

The gift shops are one thing, but the **Museu del Vidre**, hidden away on the top floor, is quite another. The owners of the glassworks, the Gordiola family, have been in business in Mallorca since the early eighteenth century, when the first of the line, **Gordiola Rigal**, arrived from the Spanish mainland. Since then, successive generations have accumulated an extraordinary collection of glassware, now exhibited in thirty-odd cabinets, each devoted to a particular theme or country, and although the museum is dusty and neglected, there's no gainsaying the quality of the items on display. Unfortunately, the labelling is rudimentary and so, to make much more than a cursory sense of what you see, you'll need to invest in a **guidebook** (€7; on sale at the gift shops).

The Gordiola glassware

The **earliest Gordiola pieces** are transparent jugs, whose frothy consistency – provided by trapped air bubbles – was unwanted. Heated by wood and coal, the original hoop-shaped furnaces had windows through which works in progress could be rotated. With such limited technology, it was, however, impossible to maintain a consistently high temperature, so the glass could not be clarified or cleared of its imperfections. Aware of these deficiencies, the next of the line, **Bernardo Gordiola** (1720–91), spent years in Venice gaining knowledge from the leading glassmakers of the day, and the results of what he learned can be seen in the same display case. He greatly improved the quality of the glass and also developed a style of Mallorcan-made jugs decorated with *laticinos*, glass strips wrapped round the object in the Venetian manner. Among **later Gordiola work**, kitchen- and tableware predominate – bottles, vases, jugs and glasses – in a variety of shades, of which green remains the most distinctive. There's also a tendency to extrapolate functional designs into imaginative ornamental pieces, ranging from hideous fish-shaped receptacles designed for someone's mantelpiece to the most poetic of vases.

International glassware

The Gordiola glassware is just a fraction of the collection. Other cabinets feature pieces from every corner of the globe, beginning with finds from **Classical Greece**, the **Nile** and the **Euphrates**. There's also an exquisite sample of early medieval **Islamic** glassware, Spanish and Chinese **opalescents**, and superb **Venetian vases** dating from the seventeenth and eighteenth centuries. The museum also exhibits decorative items from cultures where glass was unknown – principally an eclectic ensemble of **pre-Columbian** pieces worked in clay, quartz and obsidian, along with the zoomorphic and anthropomorphic basalt figures characteristic of the Sahara. More **modern items** include goblets from Germany and Poland, traditional Caithness crystal from Scotland, and a striking melange of Swedish Art Nouveau glasswork.

Algaida

ALGAIDA, just off the Ma-15 about 25km east of Palma, is typical of the small agricultural towns that dot Mallorca's central plain, with low, whitewashed houses fanning out from an old Gothic-Baroque church. There's nothing remarkable about the place, but it is a veritable metropolis compared with some of its neighbours: as late as the 1980s, a young British anthropologist, who was sent here to research rural communities, spent several months living in the hamlet of **Pina**, just north of Algaida. It was an eye-opener: she was criticized for having her light on late at night (she should have been sleeping) and for wanting to live on the edge of the village (she must have something to hide), but the final straw was the anonymous letters she received suggesting that she was only there to entice a young man back to the UK.

To get the flavour of Algaida today, aim for the main square, **Sa Plaça**, a leafy little piazza with a scattering of cafés, and pop into the neighbouring **church of Sant Pere i Sant Pau**, on c/Rei, a timeworn edifice with a Baroque bell tower and an arcaded nave. But really Algaida's redeeming feature is its proximity to a hilltop monastery, the **Santuari de Nostra Senyora de Cura** (see p.170).

ARRIVAL AND DEPARTURE   ALGAIDA

By bus Buses to Algaida pull in about 400m north of the village: to get to Sa Plaça, just follow the main street (c/Tanqueta and its continuation, c/S'Aigua).

Destinations Felanitx (every 1–2hr; 35min); Palma (every 1–2hr; 35min).

The Massís de Randa

The slim band of scenic hills – the **Massís de Randa** – that stretches south from Algaida towards **Llucmajor** reaches its highest point at **Puig Randa**, whose summit, at 543m, offers wondrous views over the central plain and holds a delightful former monastery, the **Santuari de Nostra Senyora de Cura**, which offers simple and inexpensive accommodation. The road to the top is a well-surfaced but serpentine affair, some 5km long, that starts by clambering up through the tiny village of **Randa**.

Santuari de Nostra Senyora de Cura

Puig Randa s/n • **Monastery & chapel** Open access during daylight hours; free • **Museum** No set opening hours – you have to ask a member of staff to let you in • €2.50 • ☎ 971 12 02 60, ⊛ santuariodecura.com

The table-top summit of **Puig Randa** is easily large enough to accommodate a substantial walled complex, the **Santuari de Nostra Senyora de Cura** (Hermitage of Our Lady of Cura), with Cura being the name of the upper part of the mountain. Entry is through a seventeenth-century portal, but most of the buildings beyond are more modern – the work of the last incumbents, Franciscan monks who arrived in 1913 after the site had lain abandoned for decades. The scholar and missionary **Ramon Llull** (see p.61) founded the original hermitage in the thirteenth century, and it was here that he prepared his acolytes for their missions to Asia and Africa. Succeeding generations of Franciscans turned the site into a centre of religious learning, and the scholastic tradition was maintained by a grammar school, which finally fizzled out in 1826. The Llull connection makes the monastery an important place of pilgrimage, especially for the **Benedicció del Fruita** (Blessing of the Crops), held on the fourth Sunday after Easter.

Nothing remains of Llull's foundation and the oldest surviving building today is the quaintly gabled **chapel**, parts of which date from the 1660s. Situated to the right of the entrance, the chapel is homely and familiar, its narrow, truncated nave spanned by a barrel-vaulted roof. Next door, in the old school, there's a modest **museum** with a collection of ecclesiastical bric-a-brac, religious paintings and a few interesting old photos taken by the Franciscans before they rebuilt the place.

Santuari de Sant Honorat and Santuari de Gràcia

Below the Santuri de Nostra Senyora de Cura lie two less significant sanctuaries. Heading back down the hill, past the radio masts, it's 2.4km to the easy-to-miss sharp left turn that leads to the **Santuari de Sant Honorat**, comprising a tiny church and a few stone buildings of medieval provenance. Back on the main summit road, it's a further 1km or so down the hill to the rather more substantial third and final monastery, the **Santuari de Gràcia**, which is approached through a signposted gateway. Founded in the fifteenth century, the whitewashed walls of this tiny sanctuary are tucked underneath a severe cliff face, which throngs with nesting birds. The simple barrel-vaulted church boasts some handsome majolica tiles, but it's the panoramic view of Es Pla's rolling farmland that holds the eye.

Llucmajor

On the south side of the Massís de Randa, just 10km from Algaida, the town of **LLUCMAJOR** has little to detain you, despite its medieval origins as a market town and its long association with the island's shoemakers. It was here in 1349, just outside the old city walls, that Jaume III, the last of the independent kings of Mallorca, was defeated and killed by Pedro IV of Aragon. The **memorial** to Jaume III, on Passeig Jaume III, commemorates the event.

ACCOMMODATION AND EATING
THE MASSÍS DE RANDA

★**Santuari de Cura** Puig de Randa ☎ 971 12 02 60, ⊛ santuariodecura.com. The hotel at the Santuari de Cura has 31 sparse but agreeable double rooms and four suites, all with basic facilities. Four of the rooms come with their own balcony (these cost an extra €20 per person per night). The sanctuary's terrace café offers average food and good coffee – but both are accompanied by superb views out across the island in what is a superb and atmospheric location. **€66**

Es Reco de Randa c/Font 21, Randa ☎ 971 66 09 97,

⊛ esrecoderanda.com. This luxurious but affordable hotel has 25 rooms decorated in traditional Spanish style, plus an outdoor swimming pool on a balustraded terrace with panoramic views. The place gets booked up months in advance in summer, but there are often vacancies out of season. There's also a very good and surprisingly large restaurant (daily 12.30–4pm & 7–11pm), where they specialize in Mallorcan dishes such as roast lamb and suckling pig; you can eat à la carte, but the *menú del día* is a snip at €18. **€100**

Manacor

Home town of the tennis star Rafael Nadal, industrial **MANACOR** declares its business long before you arrive, with vast roadside hoardings promoting its furniture, wrought-iron and artificial pearl factories. On the strength of these, Manacor has risen to become Mallorca's second city, much smaller than Palma but large enough to have spawned unappetizing suburbs on all sides. Locals, however, insist that Manacor is "a big town, not a city", and in keeping with this, its **old centre** has been attractively restored, its more important buildings polished and scrubbed, its avenues and piazzas planted with shrubs and trees.

Església Nostra Senyora Verge dels Dolors

Plaça Rector Rubí • Daily 8.30am–12.45pm & 5–7.30pm • Free, but donations requested • ☎ 971 55 43 48

Lording it over the centre of town is Manacor's principal architectural attraction, the sprawling **Església Nostra Senyora Verge dels Dolors**. The original church was plonked on the site of what had been the Moors' main mosque in the thirteenth century, but the present structure is almost entirely neo-Gothic, built to a design by the modernizing architect Gaspar Bennàssar (1869–1933), who had been hired by an ambitious local priest, Rector Rubí: the railway had just reached Manacor (in 1879) and Rubí thought it was time his church shed its dusty medievalism.

Convent de Sant Vicenç Ferrer

Plaça Convent • Mon–Fri 8am–2pm & 5–8pm • Free

From Plaça Rector Rubí, it's a short walk northwest to Manacor's other main sight, the **Convent de Sant Vicenç Ferrer**, a good-looking Baroque complex dating from the late sixteenth century. The convent **church** is a cavernous affair adorned by some especially intricate stone carving and the adjacent **cloister** is flanked by an comely set of pillared arches.

Perlas Majorica artificial pearl factory

Via Palma 9 (Ma-15C) • Shop & exhibition: Feb & Nov Mon–Fri 9am–5pm, Sat–Sun 9am–1pm; March–Oct Mon–Fri 9am–6pm, Sat–Sun 9am–1pm; Dec & Jan Mon–Fri 9am–2pm, Sat 9am–1pm • Free • ☎ 971 55 09 00, ⓦ majorica.com

Most visitors skip Manacor's centre and stick instead to the north side of town, where the **Perlas Majorica artificial pearl factory** – signposted as the Pearl Centre – offers a somewhat perfunctory **factory tour** and a general insight into the manufacturing process. The core of the imitation pearl is a glass globule onto which are painted many layers of a glutinous liquid primarily composed of fish scales. Artificial pearls last longer than, and are virtually indistinguishable from, the real thing and are consequently expensive – as you will discover if you visit the showroom.

ARRIVAL AND INFORMATION   MANACOR

By train Manacor train station is located on the northwest edge of the old centre, about 1km from Plaça Rector Rubí.
Destinations Binissalem (hourly; 40min); Inca (hourly; 30min); Palma (hourly; 1hr); Petra (hourly; 10min); Sineu (hourly; 20min).
By bus Most long-distance buses arrive at and depart from the stops on Plaça Sa Mora, just outside (and to the east of) the train station.
Destinations Artà (every 1–2hr; 1hr); Cala Rajada (every

1–2hr; 50min); Capdepera (every 1–2hr; 40min); Colònia de Sant Jordi (Mon–Fri 3 daily; 1hr 30min); Felanitx (Mon–Fri 4 daily; 15min); Porto Cristo (Mon–Sat 7 daily, Sun 3 daily; 1hr); Santanyí (Mon–Fri 3 daily; 1hr 10min).
Tourist information The tourist office is in the town centre at Plaça Convent 3 (Mon–Fri 9am–2pm; ☎ 662 35 08 91, ⓦ visitmanacor.com). They have a useful selection of local information, including a map marking the town's high points.

4

ACCOMMODATION, EATING AND DRINKING

Bar Mingo Plaça Ramon Llull 12 ☎ 971 55 26 62. For a taste of real Manacor, head to the locals' favourite: the down-to-earth *Bar Mingo* is well known for its *Bocadillo Mingo* (Mingo Sandwich), a delicious but stomach-busting baguette stuffed with lamb, bacon, cheese and onions. Daily 7am–late.

Ca'n Guixa Hotel c/Gerrers 15 ☎ 971 55 36 97, ⓦ canguixa.es. Centrally located, a 5min walk west of the Convent de Sant Vicenç Ferrer, this two-star hotel has just fifteen straightforward rooms decorated in a style that looks rather like a traditional British B&B. **€50**

El Café Palau Plaça Rector Rubí 8 ☎ 608 83 43 68. This café in the centre of town is a good place to sample the local speciality, *sobrasada de cerdo negro*, a spicy pork sausage made from black pig. Daily 7am–4pm.

La Reserva Rotana Camí de Bendris Km3 ☎ 971 84 56 85, ⓦ reservarotana.com. Four kilometres or so north of Manacor's ring road (Ma-15), *La Reserva Rotana* is a luxury resort in a much extended and tastefully modernized old manor house. Facilities include a pool, spa and a nine-hole golf course. The hotel offers especially opulent lodgings: suites are decorated with unusual antiques, and there's a top-notch restaurant where the menu is firmly Mediterranean. **€325**

Artà and around

The northerly end of the **Serres de Llevant** mountain range bunches up to fill out Mallorca's eastern corner, providing a dramatic backdrop to **ARTÀ**, an ancient hill town of sun-bleached roofs clustered beneath a castellated chapel-shrine. It is a handsome setting and the town's antique charms are complemented by a bohemian, artistic atmosphere – art and artists are everywhere – and there's a lively **market** on Plaça del Conqueridor every Tuesday and on Friday evenings. Artà's cobweb of cramped and twisted alleys are a pleasure to explore and there are two specific targets, the hilltop **Santuari de Sant Salvador**, from where there are panoramic views back over the central plain, and the intriguing prehistoric village of **Ses Països**. It's also a short drive or cycle ride northwest to the **Ermita de Betlem**, in a handsome setting high up in the hills of the **Massís d'Artà**, as this particular portion of the Serres de Llevant is usually known.

Santuari de Sant Salvador

The ten-minute haul up to Artà's **Santuari de Sant Salvador** is a must. It's almost impossible to get lost – just keep going upwards from the foot of the town – and on the way you'll thread your way through the **Plaça de L'Ajuntament**, a pretty little piazza that holds the capacious town hall. Beyond, a short stroll through streets of gently decaying mansions brings you to the gargantuan parish church of **Sant Salvador**. From this unremarkable pile, the steep stone steps and cypress trees of the **Via Crucis** (Way of the Cross) cut up to the **santuari**, which, in its present form, dates from the early nineteenth century, though the hilltop has been a place of pilgrimage for much longer. During the Reconquista, Catalan soldiers demolished the Moorish fort that stood here and replaced it with a shrine accommodating an image of the Virgin Mary. This edifice was, in its turn, knocked down in 1820 in a superstitious – and ultimately fruitless – attempt to stop the spread of an epidemic that was decimating the local population. The present chapel, built a few years later, is hardly awe-inspiring – the curious statue of Jesus behind the altar has him smiling as if he has lost his mind – but the views are exquisite, with the picturesque town below and Es Pla stretching away to distant hills.

Ses Països

Camí Corballa s/n • Mon–Fri 10am–5pm, Sat 10am–2pm • €2 • ☎ 619 07 00 10, ⓦ tourism-mallorca.com/sespaisses • The site is 900m from the Artà ring road – follow the signs down the well-surfaced country lane

On the southern peripheries of Artà, tucked away in a grove of olive, carob and holm-oak trees, lie the substantial and elegiacally rustic remains of Ses Països, a prehistoric village dating back to around 1300 BC if not before. A clear footpath explores every nook and cranny of the site, and its numbered markers are thoroughly explained in the English-language leaflet available at the entrance. The village is entered through an impressive monolithic **gateway**, whose heavyweight jambs and lintels interrupt the Cyclopean **walls** that still encircle the site. These outer remains date from the second phase of the Talayotic era (c.1000–800 BC), when the emphasis was on

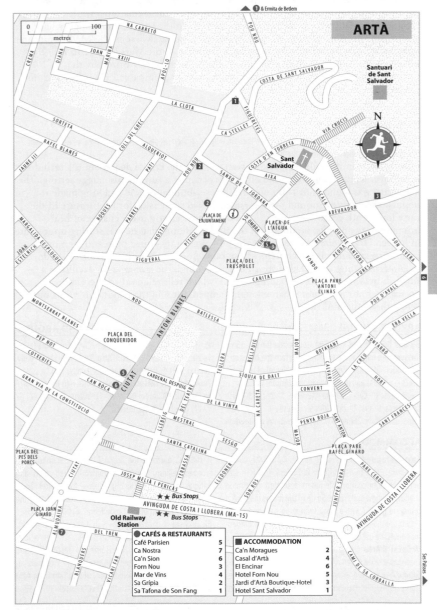

● CAFÉS & RESTAURANTS		■ ACCOMMODATION	
Café Parisien	5	Ca'n Moragues	2
Ca Nostra	7	Casal d'Artà	4
Ca'n Sion	6	El Encinar	6
Forn Nou	3	Hotel Forn Nou	5
Mar de Vins	4	Jardi d'Artà Boutique-Hotel	3
Sa Grípia	2	Hotel Sant Salvador	1
Sa Tafona de Son Fang	1		

consolidation and defence; in places, the walls still stand at their original size, around 3.5m high and 3m thick. Beside the gate, there's also a modern **plinth** erected in honour of Miquel Llobera (1854–1922), a local writer, poet and priest who penned romantic verses about the place.

Beyond the gateway, the central **talayot** is from the first Talayotic period (c.1300–1000 BC), its shattered ruins flanked by the foundations of several rooms of later date and uncertain purpose. Experts believe the horseshoe-shaped room here was used – at least towards the end of the Talayotic era – for cremations, while the three rectangular rooms were probably living quarters. In the rooms, archeologists have discovered iron objects and ceramics imported from elsewhere in the Mediterranean. Some of them were perhaps brought back from the Punic Wars (264–146 BC) by mercenaries – the skills of Balearic stone slingers were highly prized by the Carthaginians, and it's known that several hundred accompanied Hannibal and his elephants over the Alps in 218 BC.

Ermita de Betlem

Open access in daylight hours • Free • To get there, follow the narrow but reasonably well-paved 10km country lane, which starts from c/Pou Nou in Artà and zigzags up through the hills

Hidden away in the hills 10km northwest of Artà, the **Ermita de Betlem** is a secluded hermitage, whose huddle of stone buildings occupies a sumptuous craggy setting. The hermitage was founded in 1805 on land whose abundant game had long made it popular as a hunting ground – King Jaume II had set it aside for his pleasure in the early fourteenth century – but the local landowner clearly had a change of heart, bringing in the monks, no doubt on the understanding that he was storing up treasure in heaven. The *ermita* now stands at the end of a cypress-lined path and its most interesting structure is the **church**, whose ponderous frame holds a batch of crude religious paintings and a faded fresco on the ceiling. The *ermita's* only facility is a small shop (with uncertain opening hours), which sells religious trinkets and postcards, but there's more than enough compensation in the panoramic views out across the Badía d'Alcúdia.

ARRIVAL AND INFORMATION
ARTÀ AND AROUND

By bus Buses to and from Artà stop beside the Ma-15 on the southern edge of the town centre. From the bus stops, it's a couple of hundred metres west to the foot of the main street – c/Ciutat and its continuation, c/Antoni Blanes. Destinations Cala Rajada (every 1–2hr; 30min); Capdepera (every 1–2hr; 20min); Colònia de Sant Pere (Mon–Fri 4 daily; 25min; advance reservations required on

617 36 53 65); Manacor (every 1–2hr; 1hr); Palma (every 1–2hr; 1hr 50min); Port d'Alcúdia (Mon–Sat 6 daily; 30min); Port de Pollença (Mon–Sat 2 daily; 1hr).

Tourist information The tourist office is in the town hall on Plaça de L'Ajuntament (Mon–Fri 10am–2pm; 971 82 97 78, artamallorca.travel).

ACCOMMODATION

Ca'n Moragues Pou Nou 12 971 82 95 09, canmoragues.com. In a handsome old house, this four-star hotel has eight comfortable rooms decorated in calming shades of yellow and cream. Some of the rooms overlook a courtyard garden with a small swimming pool and sauna – two ground-floor rooms give directly onto the garden, the others are upstairs. **€160**

★**Casal d'Artà** c/Rafael Blanes 19 971 82 91 63, casaldarta.de. Overlooking Plaça de L'Ajuntament, the *Casal d'Artà* is sited in an immaculately restored, three-storey former merchant's mansion dating from the 1930s.

It still has much of the original decor – stained glass, wooden ceilings, decorative ironwork, tiled walls and antique furniture, including several four-poster beds. There's a charming sun terrace on the roof too, and the owners are a fount of local knowledge. **€100**

El Encinar Carretera Artà–Son Servera (Ma-4041), Km3 971 18 38 60 or 639 38 59 74, elencinardearta.com. This handsomely restored and immaculately maintained country estate occupies an ideal spot 'twixt town and beach, about 5km from Artà on the Ma-4041 road to Son Servera. Sited in an airily

MARKET, SINEU (P.165) >

modernized old manor house, the eleven traditionally decorated rooms ooze atmosphere, and the facilities include a pool, restaurant and lush garden. Closed Nov–Feb. €135

★**Hotel Forn Nou** c/Centre 7 ☎971 82 92 46, ⊛fornnou-arta.com. Opened in 2012, *Forn Nou* is petite, chic and stylish – and it has a prime location, occupying an attractive corner house right in the centre. The rooms are finished to a high standard, and the ground floor houses an excellent restaurant (see below). Owner Toni is an attentive and friendly host and the hotel also boasts the best roof-terrace bar in town. €100

Jardi d'Artà Boutique-Hotel c/Abeurador 21 ☎971 83 52 30, ⊛hotel-arta.com. Slick and stylish deluxe hotel in a sympathetically modernized early nineteenth-century townhouse. Has twelve rooms and suites decorated in country-house style, a spa, an outside pool, charming gardens with views over town, and its own restaurant. Closed early Nov to late March. €155

Hotel Sant Salvador c/Pou Nou 26 ☎971 82 95 55, ⊛santsalvador.com. Once a grand *Modernista* mansion, the *Sant Salvador* is now a luxury hotel with an interior decorated in vibrant Almodóvar colours. Six of the eight rooms – each decorated in a different style, and some with jacuzzis – have balconies overlooking the town, and the hotel organizes beach excursions, picnics and other events for guests. €180

EATING AND DRINKING

Café Parisien c/Ciutat 18 ☎971 83 54 40. A boho little café-restaurant with distressed sea-blue furniture and a shaded courtyard garden at the back. Their tasty and reasonably priced soups, salads and Italian-influenced dishes are based on what is fresh in the market. Mains average €15; no cards. Daily 10am–11pm.

Ca Nostra c/Des Tren 1 ☎971 83 62 93, ⊛ca-nostra.es. A down-to-earth restaurant near the ring road that is a local favourite at lunchtimes. Main courses cost between €9 and €12, and the grilled fish is particularly good. Daily 9am–4pm & 6.30–11.30pm.

Ca'n Sion c/Cuitat 22 ☎971 82 92 48, ⊛restaurante-cansion.com. Smart, modern restaurant offering a tasty range of Spanish/Mallorcan tapas and full meals – try, for example, the mushrooms with pepper sauce or the home-made chicken croquettes. Main courses hover around €15, tapas €10. Tues–Sun 7–10pm, plus Wed 10am–3pm.

Forn Nou c/Centre 7 ☎971 82 92 46, ⊛fornnou-arta.com. Two restaurant options here at this small hotel (see above) – eat either on the roof terrace with views over town or inside in the neat and trim dining room. A well-considered three-course set menu is the order of the day (€25), starting off with the likes of marinated salmon in citrus fruits with wasabi mayonnaise. Reservations advised. Daily 6–11pm.

Mar de Vins c/Antoni Blanes 34 ☎662 03 04 60. In the town centre, *Mar de Vins* is a brightly coloured, friendly little café-bar ideal for midday tapas and a glass of wine. The menu (tapas from €8) is lively and creative – oxtail stew and avocado salad with soya dressing are typical. Has a large patio area that is perfect for whiling away a hot afternoon. Mon–Sat 10am–11pm.

Sa Grípia c/Rosa 1, off Plaça de L'Ajuntament ☎971 83 69 25. Relaxed, popular and informal café-restaurant occupying an ancient courtyard with an arched loggia at the back. The menu is strong on Mallorcan dishes and wines – and the fish of the day is usually excellent. Mains from €15. Reservations advised. Mon–Sat 9am–11.30pm.

Sa Tafona de Son Fang Carretera Artà–Ermita Betlem, km1.5 ☎971 82 95 91, ⊛satafona.com. In this attractive galleried *finca*, which once housed an ancient oil press (*tafona*), you'll find a good range of Mallorcan dishes – they're particularly proud of their charcoal-grilled meat and fish (from €18). About 2km northwest of Artà, on the road to the Ermita de Betlem. Daily except Wed noon–4pm & 7–11pm.

Colònia de Sant Pere

A low-key resort and one-time fishing village, **COLÒNIA DE SANT PERE** strings along the seashore with the Badía d'Alcúdia in front and the stern escarpments of the Massís d'Artà behind. Founded in 1881, the village is no more than a few blocks wide, its plain, low-rise modern buildings set behind a pocket-sized sandy **beach**, and although a flurry of recent building work has festooned the place with villa complexes, local planning laws at least prohibit the construction of houses more than two storeys high. It's all very informal and laidback – perfect for families with young children – and this, along with the setting, is its charm, but perhaps mainly as a day-trip destination: there are currently no hotels or *hostales* here, so to stay you have to book a villa or apartment.

ARRIVAL AND DEPARTURE

By bus Buses from Artà, about 13km away, arrive and depart from the bus stop on Plaça Bassa d'en Fasol, on the southwest side of the village centre and a 2min walk from

ACCOMMODATION AND EATING

Blau Mari Polígon de la Mar s/n ☎ 971 58 94 07, ⓦ restauranteblaumari.es. First-rate seafood restaurants line up along Colònia de Sant Pere's waterfront – this is one of the best, and has been for many a year. Eat inside or outside on the terrace. House specialities include lobster and black-rice paella, and mains start at €15. March–Oct Mon–Fri 10am–11pm, Sat & Sun 11am–2pm.

COLÒNIA DE SANT PERE

the seashore.

Destinations Artà (Mon–Fri 4 daily; 25min; advance reservations required on ☎ 617 36 53 65).

★ **Es Vivers** Polígon de la Mar 27 ☎ 971 58 94 78, ⓦ esvivers.com. Smart, family-run seafront restaurant, where they pride themselves on using the best of local and seasonal ingredients – and it shows in the tastiness of the food: try the grilled fish or the pasta. Has a well-appointed outside terrace and a lounge bar serving cocktails. Mains start at €20. Reservations recommended in the evenings. April–Nov daily 11am–11.30pm.

Capdepera

Spied across the valley from the west or south, the crenellated walls dominating **CAPDEPERA**, a tiny village 8km east of Artà and 3km west of Cala Rajada, look too pristine to be true. Yet the triangular fortifications are genuine enough, built in the fourteenth century by the Mallorcan king Sancho to protect the coast from pirates. The village, snuggled below the walls, contains a pleasant medley of old houses, its slender main square, **Plaça de L'Orient**, acting as a prelude to the steep steps up to the medieval fortress. The best time to visit is during the three-day **medieval market**, held in the third week of May. The locals dress up in medieval costumes and the entire town is jam-packed with people sampling local food, crafts and music.

4

Castell de Capdepera

Carrer Major s/n • Daily: April–Sept 9am–7.30pm; Oct–March 9am–4.45pm • €2 • ☎ 971 55 64 79, ⓦ www.castellcapdepera.com

The steps that lead up from Capdepera's Plaça de L'Orient are the most agreeable way to reach the **Castell de Capdepera**, but you can also follow the signs and drive up narrow c/Major. Flowering cacti give the fortress a special allure in late May and June, but it's a beguiling place at any time, with more than 400m of walls equipped with a parapet walkway and sheltering attractive terraced gardens. At the top of the fortress, **Nostra Senyora de la Esperança** (Our Lady of Good Hope) is the quaintest of Gothic churches, its aisle-less, vaulted frame furnished with outside steps that lead up behind the bell gable to a flat roof, from where the views are simply superb.

ARRIVAL AND DEPARTURE

By bus Buses stop on Plaça Constitució, just off the main street and a 3min walk from Plaça de L'Orient, just to the east.

Destinations Artà (every 1–2hr; 20min); Cala Rajada (every 1–2hr; 10min); Canyamel (May–Oct Mon–Sat every

CAPDEPERA

1–2hr, Sun 2 daily; 10min); Coves d'Artà (Mon–Sat 2 daily; 15min); Manacor (every 1–2hr; 40min); Palma (every 1–2hr; 1hr 30min); Port d'Alcúdia (Mon–Sat 6 daily; 50min); Port de Pollença (Mon–Sat 2 daily; 1hr 25min); Porto Cristo (every 1–2hr; 50min).

ACCOMMODATION AND EATING

La Fragua c/Es Pla d'en Coset 3 ☎ 971 81 94 03. Capdepera has several excellent restaurants, the pick being *La Fragua*, an intimate spot where they serve steak and other grilled specialities. It's located just off Plaça de L'Orient, on the way up towards the castle steps. Mains from €17. Daily: May–Aug noon–3pm & 6.30–11pm;

Sept–April Tues–Sun noon–3pm & 6.30–9pm.
Pizzeria Kikinda Plaça de L'Orient 4 ☎ 971 56 30 14. Several run-of-the-mill cafés line up on the town's main square – this is the best, serving good-value pizzas, pastas and salads from €9. Tues–Sun 6.30–10pm.
Son Barbassa Cala Mesquida 07580 ☎ 971 56 57 76,

Ⓦ sonbarbassa.com. There's nowhere to stay in Capdepera itself, but it's only about 3.5km north on the Cala Mesquida road to this first-rate *finca*, *Son Barbassa*, a carefully restored sixteenth-century rural estate complete with watchtower. There are twelve stylish rooms here as well as a spa and a pool with beautiful views over the valley and back across to Capdepera. They also have a very good restaurant (daily 12.30–3pm & 7.30–10pm) serving fresh vegetables from the hotel garden, with mains from €17. **€250**

Cala Rajada

Awash with cafés, bars and hotels, vibrant **CALA RAJADA**, a favourite with German tourists, lies on the southerly side of a stubby headland in the northeast corner of Mallorca. The town centre, an unassuming patchwork of low-rise modern buildings, is hardly prepossessing, but it is neat and trim, and around the town is a wild and rocky coastline, all backed by pine-clad hills and sheltering a series of delightful **beaches**.

Cala Rajada was once a fishing village, but there's little evidence of this today, and the **harbour** is now used by pleasure boats and overlooked by restaurants. From the harbour, **walkways** extend along the headland's south coast. To the southwest, past the busiest part of town, it takes about ten to fifteen minutes to stroll round to **Platja Son Moll**, a slender arc of sand overlooked by Goliath-like hotels. Alternatively, it's a pleasant ten-minute stroll east from the harbour to **Cala Gat**, a narrow cove beach tucked tight against the steep, wooded coastline. The beach is far from undiscovered – there's a bar and at times it gets decidedly crowded – but it's an especially attractive spot all the same.

Sa Torre Cega

C/Joan March 2, off c/Elíonor Servera • Guided tours (advance reservations required): Feb–April Wed & Sat 11am & 12.30pm, Fri 11am; May–Nov Wed, Thurs & Fri 10.30am & noon, Sat & Sun 11am & 6pm • €4.50 • ☎ 689 02 73 53, Ⓦ fundacionbmarch.es

Just to the northeast of the main harbour is **Sa Torre Cega**, the house and gardens laid out for the tobacco baron Joan March (see box, p.55) in the 1910s, but subsequently remodelled on several later occasions. The estate takes its name – "Blind Tower" – from the watchtower that once occupied the site and was incorporated, after much tinkering, into the lavish *Modernista* mansion that stands here today. Guided tours explore parts of the house and the lovely terraced gardens, with their scattering of modern sculptures.

Cap de Capdepera

Beyond Sa Torre Cega, **c/Elíonor Servera** twists steeply up through the pine woods to reach, after about 1km, the bony headlands and lighthouse of the **Cap de Capdepera**, Mallorca's most easterly point. The lighthouse, a folksy-looking affair with a bright-white tower, is not open to the public, but there are great views out along the coast from its immediate surroundings.

Cala Agulla

North of Cala Rajada, c/L'Agulla crosses the promontory to hit the north coast at **Cala Agulla**. The approach road, some 2km of tourist tackiness, is of little appeal, but the **beach**, a vast curve of bright golden sand, is big enough to accommodate hundreds of bronzing pectorals with plenty of space to spare. The further you walk – and there are signed and shaded footpaths through the pine woods to assist you – the more privacy you'll get.

ARRIVAL AND DEPARTURE   **CALA RAJADA**

By bus Most buses to Cala Rajada loop through the resort, with the most central stop being close to the intersection of c/Juan Sebastian Elcano and c/Bustamante.

Destinations Artà (every 1–2hr; 30min); Canyamel

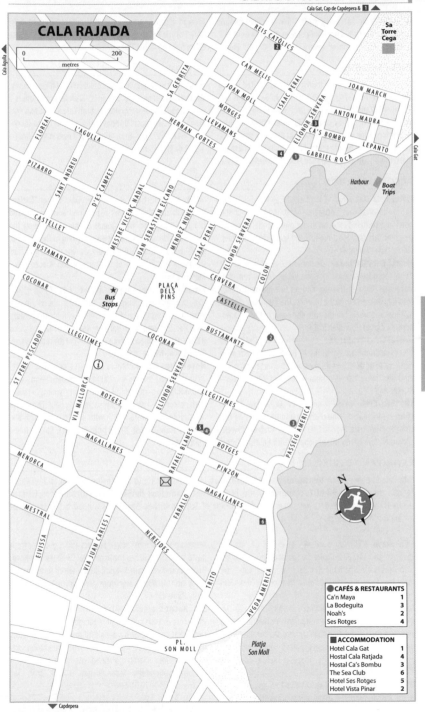

CALA RAJADA

Cala Gat, Cap de Capdepera & **1** ▲

0 — 200
metres

CALA RAJADA

Cala Agulla

REIS CATÒLICS **2**

Sa Torre Cega

CAN MELIS

SA GERRETA

JOAN MOLL

ISAAC PERAL

JOAN MARCH

MONGES

ELIONOR SERVERA

ANTONI MAURA

FLOREAL

L'AGULLA

HERNAN CORTES

LLEVAMANS

CA'S BOMBU **3**

LEPANTO

PIZARRO

SANT ANDREU

D'ES CAMBET

4 **1** GABRIEL ROCA

Cala Gat

Harbour

Boat Trips

CASTELLET

MESTRE VICENÇ NADAL

JUAN SEBASTIAN ELCANO

MENDEZ NUÑEZ

ISAAC PERAL

ELIONOR SERVERA

BUSTAMANTE

COCONAR

★ Bus Stops

PLAÇA DELS PINS

CERVERA

COLON

CASTELLET

ST PÈRE PESCADOR

LLEGITIMES

COCONAR

BUSTAMANTE **3**

ⓘ

ELIONOR SERVERA

LLEGITIMES

VIA MALLORCA

ROTGES

PASSEIG AMERICA

3

MAGALLANES

5 **4**

RAFAEL BLANES

ROTGES

MENORCA

PINZON

MESTRAL

VIA JUAN CARLES I

FARALLO

MAGALLANES

EIVISSA

NEREIDES

6

TRITO

N

AVGDA AMERICA

PL. SON MOLL

Platja Son Moll

Capdepera

● CAFÉS & RESTAURANTS

Ca'n Maya	1
La Bodeguita	3
Noah's	2
Ses Rotges	4

■ ACCOMMODATION

Hotel Cala Gat	1
Hostal Cala Ratjada	4
Hostal Ca's Bombu	3
The Sea Club	6
Hotel Ses Rotges	5
Hotel Vista Pinar	2

4

(May–Oct Mon–Sat every 1–2hr, Sun 2 daily; 20min); Capdepera (every 1–2hr; 10min); Coves d'Artà (Mon–Sat 2 daily; 25min); Manacor (every 1–2hr; 50min); Palma (every 1–2hr; 1hr 40min); Port d'Alcúdia (Mon–Sat 6 daily; 1hr); Port de Pollença (Mon–Sat 2 daily; 1hr 35min); Porto Cristo (every 1–2hr; 1hr).

INFORMATION

Tourist information The tourist office is located at Via Mallorca 36 (Mon–Fri 9am–1.30pm & 2.30–5.30pm, Sat 9.30am–1.30pm; March–Oct also Sun 10am–1.30pm; ☎ 971 81 94 67). They can supply an excellent range of local information including restaurant lists, bus schedules, details of car and bicycle rental firms, and free town maps marked with all accommodation. They also sell a popular, though not very detailed, pamphlet on local hiking routes.

Boat trips Creuers Illa Balear (🌐 illabalear.com) offers a wide range of summer boat trips from Cala Rajada to points along the east coast. Options include Porto Cristo (May–Sept 1–2 daily; €25 return) and the Coves d'Artà (May–Sept 1 daily; €15 return).

ACCOMMODATION

Hotel Cala Gat Avgda Cala Gat s/n ☎ 971 56 31 66, 🌐 hotelcalagat.com. Attractive and modern four-star hotel in a secluded location in the pine woods above the beach of Cala Gat. Most rooms have sea-facing balconies. Closed Nov–March. €160

Hostal Cala Ratjada c/Llevamans 2 ☎ 971 56 32 02, 🌐 hostalcalaratjada.com. Good-value, family-run one-star *hostal*, close to the port and set in a pleasant white-stucco building with rustic touches. The 30 rooms may be minimal and small, but they are also some of the cheapest in town. Closed Nov–March. €40

Hostal Ca's Bombu c/Elíonor Servera 86 ☎ 971 56 32 03, 🌐 casbombu.com. Homely place kitted out in a rustic style with lots of dark wood, 50 spartan rooms, a pool and large bar. It's great value, too. Closed Nov–March. €45

The Sea Club Avgda America 27 ☎ 971 56 33 10, 🌐 the-seaclub.com. One of the first hotel resorts on this stretch of the coast, *The Sea Club* is a comfortable and well-appointed family-run affair, popular with English visitors and known affectionately as "little Gibraltar" or "Chelsea Arts Club sur Med". It has maintained a warm, relaxed family atmosphere, with guests dining en masse on the front veranda each evening before retiring to the convivial poolside bar to party. Book early, as repeat custom keeps the place full for most of the high season. Closed Nov–March. €150

Hotel Ses Rotges c/Rafael Blanes 21 ☎ 971 56 31 08, 🌐 sesrotges.com. Engaging three-star hotel in an attractively restored and modernized eighteenth-century villa. Has 23 rooms, each decorated in traditional style, and it's in a good location just out of earshot of the main square. Closed Nov–March. €120

Hotel Vista Pinar c/Reis Catòlics 11 ☎ 971 56 37 51, 🌐 hotelvistapinar.com. Large, adequate and very affordable two-star hotel with ninety rooms – most with balconies – and its own swimming pool. The rooms are simple but comfortable, with all the usual facilities, and the hotel is just 200m from the port. Closed Nov–March. €45

EATING AND DRINKING

Cala Rajada heaves with **restaurants**, **cafés and bars**, particularly on and around the seafront and c/Elíonor Servera, the main boulevard. Competition is fierce, but most restaurants have similar menus with something German – sauerkraut and sausages, for instance – plus a range of Spanish dishes. Seafood is a good bet in the better restaurants around the port.

Ca'n Maya c/Elíonor Servera 80 ☎ 971 56 40 35, 🌐 canmaya.com. First choice for seafood, this upmarket place serves up superb main courses for around €30 – try their excellent paella and *arroz marinera*. Tues–Sun noon–4pm & 7–11pm.

La Bodeguita Passeig America 14 ☎ 971 81 90 62, 🌐 labodeguita.es. Inviting restaurant located in an old villa near the seashore on the southern side of the resort. Huge plates piled with meats, pastas and salads, with prices ranging from €15–25. There's a leafy garden too. Daily 9am–midnight.

Noah's Passeig America 2 ☎ 971 81 81 25, 🌐 cafenoahs .com. Just beyond the main tourist traps, this café-bar serves up very decent mixed platters and is good for fresh pasta salads; it also has the occasional DJ on the weekend. Happy hour lasts from 5–8pm, during which time you can enjoy one of *Noah's* signature premium gin and tonics. Daily 9am–late.

Ses Rotges c/Rafael Blanes 21 ☎ 971 56 31 08, 🌐 sesrotges.com. Generally regarded as the best restaurant in town, with a delightful courtyard terrace, this relaxing place offers a well-conceived menu featuring such delights as loin of lamb marinated with herbs, polenta and seasonal vegetables. Mains begin at €30. Mon–Sat 1–3pm & 7.30–10.30pm.

Coves d'Artà

Carretera Coves de s'Ermita s/n • Daily: April–June & Oct 10am–6pm; July–Sept 10am–7pm; Nov–March 10am–4pm • 40min tours every 30min • €14; children (7–12Y) €7 • ☎ 971 84 12 93, ⓦ cuevasdearta.com

The succession of coves, caves and beaches notching the seashore between Cala Rajada and Cala Millor begins promisingly with the memorable **Coves d'Artà** (often in Castilian, "Cuevas de Artà"), which are approached up a wide stairway that leads to a yawning hole high in the cliffs above the bay. This is the pick of the numerous cave systems of eastern Mallorca, its sequence of cavernous chambers, studded with stalagmites and stalactites, extending 450m into the rock face. Artificial lighting exaggerates the bizarre shapes of the caverns and their accretions, especially in the **Hall of Flags**, where stalactites up to 50m long hang in the shape of partly unfurled flags.

The Coves d'Artà have had a chequered history. During the Reconquista, a thousand Moorish refugees from Artà were smoked out from here to be slaughtered by Catalan soldiers waiting outside. In the nineteenth century, touring the caves for their scientific interest became fashionable – Jules Verne was particularly impressed – and, today, tour guides give a complete geological description of the caves in several languages (including English) as you wander the illuminated abyss. Allow about forty minutes for the visit, more if the usual queues are long.

ARRIVAL AND DEPARTURE   COVES D'ARTÀ

By car The caves are reached along the first major turning off the main coastal road (the Ma-4040), just south of Capdepera.

By bus Buses to the Coves d'Artà run from Canyamel (Mon–Sat 2 daily; 15min), Capdepera (Mon–Sat 2 daily; 15min) and Cala Rajada (Mon–Sat 2 daily; 25min).

By boat Boat trips run to the caves from Cala Rajada (May–Sept 1 daily; €15, not including admission).

Canyamel

CANYAMEL, just south along the coast from Cala Rajada, divides into two distinct sections, a tedious *urbanització* development to the south and an attractive, pocket-sized cove resort to the north. At the resort, a scramble of low-rise modern villas and a couple of hotels are draped around a handsome, pine-backed sandy **beach** in sight of a pair of rocky headlands – a perfect spot for a few hours' sunbathing.

ARRIVAL AND DEPARTURE   CANYAMEL

By bus Buses stop on Via Melesigeni, on the south side of the resort and a couple of minutes' walk from the seafront.
Destinations Cala Rajada (Mon–Sat 2 daily; 40min); Capdepera (Mon–Sat 2 daily; 30min); Coves d'Artà (Mon–Sat 2 daily; 15min).

ACCOMMODATION AND EATING

Can Simoneta Carretera Artà-Canyamel Km8 ☎ 971 81 61 10, ⓦ cansimoneta.com. Attractively sited on a cliff with panoramic sea views, the deluxe *Can Simoneta* is located between the *platja* and the *urbanització* – follow the signs from the main roundabout as you approach Canyamel. The five-star hotel is divided between two nineteenth-century buildings, elegantly decorated in white and beige tints and with all the mod cons you could want. Adults only. €400

Universal Hotel Laguna Via Costa i Llobera s/n ☎ 971 84 11 50, ⓦ universalhotels.es. Perched on the edge of the beach, this well-maintained, three-star hotel occupies a medium-sized modern block, and has an outside pool and its own restaurant. Closed Nov–April. €100

Porto Cristo

Workaday **PORTO CRISTO** prospered in the early days of the tourist boom, sprouting a string of hotels and *hostales*, but thereafter it was eclipsed by the mega-resorts that

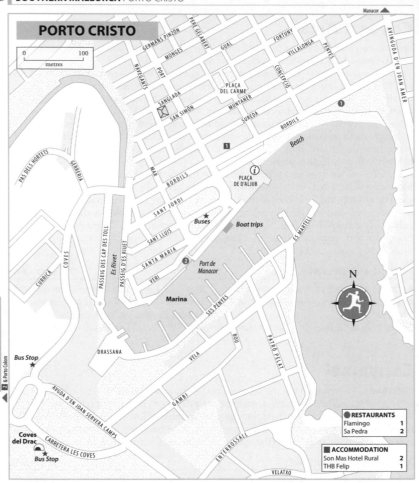

sprang up along the neighbouring coastline, with Cala Millor being a case in point. Don't be deceived by the jam of tourist buses clogging Porto Cristo's streets; they're usually on their way to the nearby Coves del Drac, the town's principal attraction, and few of their occupants will actually be staying here, which is understandable enough, though the town does possess a kind of low-key charm.

Porto Cristo's origins are uncertain, but it was definitely in existence by the thirteenth century, when it served as the fishing harbour and seaport of Manacor – it boasts one of the most sheltered harbours on the east coast. Nothing remains of the medieval settlement, however, and today the **town centre**, which climbs the hill behind the harbour, consists of high-sided terraced buildings mostly dating from the late nineteenth and early twentieth centuries. The town has its own **beach**, which is fine enough for sunbathing – though the swimming isn't great – and this is handily located right in the centre, tucked close to the entrance to the harbour. The **harbour** itself is a narrow V-shaped channel that accommodates a marina and lies at the mouth of the oily-green River Es Rivet, which serves as the town centre's southern perimeter.

Coves del Drac

Carretera Les Coves s/n • 1hr guided tours: mid-March to Oct on the hour 10am–5pm; Nov to mid-March at 10.45am, noon, 2pm & 3.30pm • €14.50 • ☎ 971 82 07 53, ⓦ cuevasdeldrach.com • The caves are a 10–15min walk south of Porto Cristo's harbourfront; direct buses run from several resorts and towns, including Palma (Mon–Sat 7 daily, Sun 3 daily; 1hr 15min)

Locals had known of the **Coves del Drac** ("Dragon's Caves"; "Cuevas del Drach" in Castilian) for hundreds of years, but it was the Austrian archduke Ludwig Salvator (see p.110) who recruited French geologists to explore and map them in 1896; they discovered four huge chambers that penetrated the coast's limestone cliffs for a distance of around 2km. The eccentric shapes of the myriad **stalactites and stalagmites** that the Frenchmen saw adorning each chamber immediately invited comparison with more familiar objects. As the leader of the French team, Edouard Martel, wrote, "On all sides, everywhere, in front and behind, as far as the eye can see, marble cascades, organ pipes, lace draperies, pendants of multi-faceted gems hang suspended from the walls and roof." Since the French exploration, the caves have been thoroughly **commercialized**. The present complex accommodates a giant car park, ticket office and restaurant, behind which lurk the gardens that lead to the flight of steps down to the caves – be prepared to queue, especially on summer weekends.

The tour

Inside the caves, rainwater has dripped and drizzled through the soft limestone to create innumerable concretions of calcium carbonate – many of which are illuminated. The multilingual tour guides shunt you past formations such as "the Buddha", "the Pagoda" and "the Snowy Mountain" as well as magnificent icicle-like stalactites; some are snowy white, while others have picked up hints of orange and red from the rocks they hang off. The *tour de force* is the larger of the two **subterranean lakes**, at 177m long, 40m wide and up to 12m deep, one of the largest underground lakes in the world. The lake's translucent waters flicker with reflected colours, while a small group of musicians drifts by in a boat. At the end of the tour, some visitors leave on foot, but you can also take a brief boat ride (included in the admission price) across part of the lake.

ARRIVAL AND INFORMATION   PORTO CRISTO

By bus The main coastal road (the Ma-4014 and Ma-4023) passes along Porto Cristo's harbourfront. Long-distance buses stop right in the centre of town above the harbour on c/Sant Lluís.

Destinations Alcúdia (Mon–Sat 1 daily; 1hr 50min); Artà (Mon–Sat 1 daily; 1hr); Cala Rajada (every 1–2hr; 1hr); Capdepera (every 1–2hr; 50min); Manacor (Mon–Sat 7 daily, Sun 3 daily; 1hr); Palma (Mon–Sat 7 daily, Sun 3 daily; 1hr 20min); Port de Pollença (Mon–Sat 1 daily; 2hr).

Tourist information The tourist office is bang in the centre of town on Plaça de l'Aljub (Mon–Fri 9am–3pm; ☎ 971 84 91 26, ⓦ visitmanacor.com).

ACCOMMODATION, EATING AND DRINKING

Flamingo c/Bordils s/n ☎ 971 82 22 59, ⓦ flamingo-portocristo.es. Arguably the best restaurant in town and certainly the one with the best location, perched on a rocky outcrop high above the beach. Serves up delicious home-made paellas and seafood – the steamed mussels are especially good. The cartoon decor is odd but charming, and the owner, Pepe, is a gruff but affectionate giant of a man who welcomes you with open arms. Mains average

PORTO CRISTO'S REPUBLICAN LANDING

In August 1936, Porto Cristo was the site of a **Republican landing** designed to capture Mallorca from Franco's Falangists. The campaign was a fiasco: the Republicans disembarked more than seven thousand men and quickly established a long and deep bridgehead, but their commanders, surprised by their initial success, didn't know what to do next. The Nationalists counterattacked and, supported by the Italian air force, soon had the Republicans dashing back to the coast. Barcelona Radio put on a brave face, announcing, "The heroic Catalan columns have returned from Mallorca after a magnificent action. Not a single man suffered from the effects of the embarkation."

€20. Daily 10am–midnight.

Sa Pedra c/Veri 4 ☎ 971 82 09 32, ⊛ restaurantsapedra .com. An upmarket place that serves up tasty seafood on a terrace overlooking the harbour; a typical main course will set you back around €20. Daily except Tues noon–4pm & 7–11pm.

Son Mas Hotel Rural Camí de Son Mas s/n, Carretera Porto Cristo–Porto Colom ☎ 971 55 87 55, ⊛ sonmas .com. Set in its own grounds and located in a sympathetically renovated farmhouse dating back to the seventeenth century, this four-star hotel has sixteen stylish suites, a climatized pool, sauna, spa and restaurant. To get there, follow the Ma-4014 towards Porto Colom for about 4km and turn right into the Camí de Son Mas; the hotel is signposted from here. **€325**

THB Felip c/Bordils 41 ☎ 971 82 07 50, ⊛ thbhotels .com. Routine, four-star chain hotel in a big old balconied building overlooking the main road and the harbour. The interior has been revamped in modern style and the rooms are neat and trim. Ask for a harbour view – and a room on one of the top floors to elude the noise of the traffic. Competitively priced. **€110**

Felanitx and around

With a population of just 17,000, small-town **FELANITX**, some 15km south of Manacor, is an industrious sort of place, producing wine, ceramics and pearls. Few would say the town is beautiful, but it does have a certain charm, its tangle of narrow streets lined with a selection of handsome old houses, mostly dating from the eighteenth and nineteenth centuries. The best time to visit is on Sunday morning, when a lively fresh produce and craft **market** takes over much of the centre. In particular, look out for the capers (Catalan *tapères*; Castilian *alcaparras*), produced locally and sold by size: the smallest are the most flavoursome, either as *nonpareilles* (up to 7mm) or *surfines* (7–8mm). Felanitx is also a convenient pit stop on the way to both the hilltop **Santuari de Sant Salvador**, a former monastery offering simple accommodation, and the ruined **Castell de Santueri** nearby.

Plaça Sa Font

The finest building in Felanitx is the church of **Sant Miquel**, whose soaring, honey-gold facade boasts a dramatic statue of St Michael, shown triumphant with a cringing devil at his feet. The church overlooks one of Felanitx's main squares, **Plaça Sa Font**, where, in an unusual arrangement, a wide and rather grand flight of stone steps digs down below street level to reach the **Font de Santa Margalida**, once the municipal well and now a water fountain. The church stands on a hillock and its easterly supporting wall shadows **c/Major**. Everything looks secure today, but in 1844 the wall collapsed, killing over four hundred people in the worst disaster to hit the town since the days of pirate attack – a **plaque** on c/Major commemorates the dead.

Santuari de Sant Salvador

Puig de Sant Salvador s/n • Daily 10am–5pm • Free • ☎ 971 51 52 60, ⊛ santsalvadorhotel.com • The sanctuary is a 15min drive from Felanitx: head east towards Porto Colom (Ma-4010) and after 2km take the signposted, 5km-long sideroad that snakes up the mountain; the driving is easy, the road in good condition

One of the more scenic portions of the **Serres de Llevant** mountain range lies within easy striking distance of Felanitx. The prime attraction here is the **Santuari de Sant Salvador**, whose assorted buildings stretch along a slender ridge at the top of the 509m-high Puig de Sant Salvador. The Santuari was founded in the fourteenth century in an attempt to stave off a further visitation of the Black Death, which had mauled Felanitx in 1348. It seemed to work, but the original buildings were demolished long ago and the present structure, a strikingly handsome fortress-like complex perched on the edge of the ridge, dates from the early eighteenth century. Inside, beyond the strongly fortified gatehouse, ancient vaulted corridors lead to the **church**, which shelters a much-venerated image of the Virgin Mary. Dominating the other end of the ridge is a gargantuan **statue of Christ the King** on top of a

CLOCKWISE FROM TOP CALA MONDRAGÓ (P.187); SEAFOOD; SINEU (P.165) >

massive plinth. Erected in 1934 and visible for miles around, it's possibly the island's ugliest landmark, though the views across Mallorca from beside the statue are fabulous. Sant Salvador was the last of Mallorca's monasteries to lose its monks – the final ones moved out in the early 1990s – and thereafter visitors were initially lodged in the old cells, though there are much more comfortable lodgings here today (see below).

The custodians at the Santuari should be able to point you towards the **footpath** that leads south across the hills to the Castell de Santueri (see below), about 4km away. The route is fairly easy to follow and the going isn't difficult, although it's still advisable to have a walking map and stout shoes. The path meanders through a pretty landscape of dry-stone walls, flowering shrubs and copses of almond and carob trees, and takes about 90 minutes to complete.

Castell de Santueri

Camí des Castell s/n • Mid-April to Sept daily 10am–6.30pm • €4 • ☎ 691 22 36 79, ⓦ santueri.org • From Felanitx, drive south on the Santanyí road for about 2km, then take the signed, narrow, bumpy and occasionally nerve-jangling 5km country lane that leads up to the castle; you can also walk here from the Santuari de Sant Salvador (see p.184)

Plastered onto a rocky hilltop about 7km south of Felanitx, the imposing ramparts of the **Castell de Santueri** date from the fourteenth century, though it was the Moors who built the first stronghold here several centuries earlier. Apart from the walls and the gateway, there's not much to see, but you can wander the bumpy scrubland behind the ramparts and enjoy the panoramic views. Curiously enough, local legend insists that **Christopher Columbus** was conceived in the castle, the result of a coupling between a local servant girl, Margalida Colom, and an imprisoned baron, Prince Carl of Viana – and it may well be true.

ARRIVAL AND DEPARTURE   FELANITX AND AROUND

By bus Buses connecting Felanitx with Palma, Manacor and Cala d'Or pull in at Passeig Ernest Mestre 8, a couple of minutes' walk north of Plaça d'Espanya, just to the west of Plaça Sa Font.

Destinations Cala d'Or (Mon–Fri 4 daily; 30min); Manacor (Mon–Fri 4 daily; 15min); Palma (5–8 daily; 1hr 10min).

ACCOMMODATION AND EATING

★ **Petit Hotel Hostatgería Sant Salvador** Santuari de Sant Salvador, Puig de Sant Salvador s/n ☎ 971 51 52 60, ⓦ santsalvadorhotel.com. Completed fairly recently, the former monastery's new wing offers 24 sparse but comfortable and modern guest bedrooms, all en suite and most with stunning views. Breakfast is served in an ancient vaulted room, but phone ahead if you require lunch or dinner: there is a café and restaurant, but there are no set hours. All in all, Sant Salvador makes a tranquil and economical base, though you will need your own transport to get here – and to get away again. **€60**

Porto Petro

Beginning to the east of Felanitx, the pretty little fishing villages that once studded the secluded coves of Mallorca's east coast have been overwhelmed by a tide of tourist development that stretches south almost without interruption from the bays of Cales de Mallorca to the **Cala d'Or**. The beaches are good and there are scores of restaurants and hotels to choose from, but only when you reach **PORTO PETRO**, just south of Cala d'Or, does the tourist pace relent, the lack of a beach here acting as a restraint to intensive development. Porto Petro's old fishing harbour has been turned into a marina, and villas dot the gentle, wooded hillsides, but even so it remains a quiet and tranquil spot, with the only real activity being the promenade round the crystal waters of its tongue-shaped cove. Perhaps surprisingly, the village's old and tiny centre, perched on the headland above the marina, is still identifiable too, its cluster of whitewashed houses recalling the days when it served as Santanyí's seaport.

ARRIVAL AND DEPARTURE

PORTO PETRO

By bus Buses pull in beside the waterfront on Passeig d'es Port.
Destinations Cala Mondragó (Mon–Sat 5 daily; 15min);

Palma (May–Oct every 1–2hr; Nov–April 3–5 daily; 1hr 30min); Santanyí (May–Oct every 1–2hr; Nov–April 3–5 daily; 20min).

EATING

Ca'n Martina Passeig d'es Port 56 ☎971 65 75 17. Porto Petro has several very good, moderately priced, harbourside restaurants, of which the *Ca'n Martina*, by the main dock, is one of the best: it's the place to go for a particularly delicious paella (€15 per person). Daily 9am–11pm.

Es Bergant Passeig d'es Port 39 ☎971 64 84 00. Unpretentious modern restaurant down by the harbour where they specialize in seafood prepared in Mallorcan and Spanish style. Spicy octopus and grilled squid are two especially popular dishes. Mains average €18. It is a busy spot, so reserve ahead or arrive early. Daily noon–11pm.

Mondragó Parc Natural

Park Open access • Free, but parking €5 • **Ses Fonts de n'Alis visitor centre** Carretera Cala Mondragó s/n • Daily 9am–4pm • ☎971 18 10 22, ⓦ en.balearsnatura.com

Mondragó Parc Natural, starting about 2.5km southwest of Porto Petro, protects a small but diverse slice of the east coast – around two thousand acres of wetland, farmland, beach, pine and scrub. There are two **car parks** to aim for, both signposted from the Ma-19, the road between Porto Petro and Santanyí: the better target is the **Ses Fonts de n'Alis** car park, about 500m from the tiny resort of Cala Mondragó (see below), which can also be reached direct from Porto Petro along a country road – just follow the signs. The other car park, **S'Amarador**, is on the low-lying headland south across the cove from Cala Mondragó. The park is latticed with footpaths and country lanes, and you can pick up a (rather poor) **map** from the **Fonts de n'Alis visitor centre**, beside the Fonts de n'Alis car park. This shows the park's four hiking trails: all are easy loops, two of forty minutes, two of thirty, though the signposting is patchy. Among them, the orange route is pleasant enough, giving good views of the bay and access to a small secluded beach: if you can't spot a sign, just keep the sea on your right-hand side and you shouldn't go far wrong.

Cala Mondragó

Delightful **CALA MONDRAGÓ** is one of Mallorca's prettiest and smallest resorts. There was some development here before the creation of the Mondragó Parc Natural in 1990, but it's all very low-key and barely disturbs the cove's beauty, its twin prongs framed by low, pine-clad cliffs and holding a pair of sandy beaches beside crystal-clear waters. Predictably, the cove's "unspoilt" reputation and safe bathing act as a magnet for sun-lovers from around and about, but you can escape the crowds by staying the night.

ARRIVAL AND DEPARTURE

CALA MONDRAGÓ

By bus Buses from Cala d'Or (Mon–Sat 5 daily; 45min) and Porto Petro (Mon–Sat 5 daily; 15min) pull in at the bottom

of the hill, just next to Cala Mondragó beach.

ACCOMMODATION AND EATING

★**Hostal Condemar** Carretera Cala Mondragó s/n ☎971 65 77 56, ⓦ hostalcondemar.com. An enticing and very economical *hostal* in a small-scale modern block about 200m from the beach. Most of the 45 rooms, which are decorated in plain traditional style, have sea-view balconies and there's an outside pool. Closed Nov–March. **€90**

Hotel Playa Mondragó Carretera Cala Mondragó s/n ☎971 65 77 52, ⓦ playamondrago.com. A friendly, family-run modern block with simple but attractive rooms. Breakfast is taken in the garden courtyard, adjacent to the swimming pool. Closed Nov–March. **€90**

Santanyí and around

Taking its name from a shortened version of "Santi Annini" (the Lamb of God), the crossroads town of **SANTANYÍ**, about 12km west of Porto Petro, has long guarded the island's southeastern approaches, a role that has cost it dear. Corsairs ransacked the place time and time again, prompting a medieval German traveller to bemoan their fate: "The Saracens constantly arrive in their ships, carry away prisoners, torment them and use them as slaves or sell them for money." In hope, rather more than belief, the townsfolk attempted to protect themselves by fortifying Santanyí and, although it didn't do them much good, one of the proudest of the town's medieval gates, **Sa Porta Murada**, has survived in good condition just to the west of the main square, **Plaça Major**. Nonetheless, it's Santanyí's narrow alleys, squeezed between high-sided sandstone houses, that are its main appeal, along with **Sant Andreu Apòstol**, just to the south of Plaça Major, a bulky, eighteenth-century pile that incorporates a finely worked early Gothic chapel, the **Capella del Roser**, a thirteenth-century survivor from the first church built on the site.

Cala Santanyí

From Santanyí, it's just a little under 4km southeast to **CALA SANTANYÍ**, an attractive little resort with a medium-sized, sandy **beach** at the end of a steep-sided, heavily wooded gulch. The development here is quite restrained, which makes it a relaxing spot for a swim and a bit of sunbathing.

4

ARRIVAL AND DEPARTURE
SANTANYÍ AND AROUND

By bus Buses pull in beside the Ma-19, on the northern edge of Santanyí on – or metres from – Plaça Ramon Llull. Destinations Cala Figuera (May–Oct Mon–Sat 3 daily; Nov–April Mon–Fri 1 daily; 20min); Cala Santanyí (May–Oct Mon–Sat 3 daily; Nov–April Mon–Fri 1 daily; 10min); Colònia de Sant Jordi (2–4 daily; 20min); Manacor (Mon–Fri 3 daily; 1hr 10min); Palma (2–4 daily; 1hr 30min); Porto Petro (May–Oct every 1–2hr; Nov–April 3–5 daily; 20min).

ACCOMMODATION, EATING AND DRINKING

Es Cantonet Plaça d'en F. Bernareggi 2 ☎ 971 16 34 07, ⓦ es-cantonet.net. In an old townhouse, this smart restaurant offers tasty main courses (€10–20). The menu changes seasonally and includes Mallorcan dishes as well as a roundup of other Mediterranean cuisines with Asian flourishes. It's located on the southwestern edge of the town centre on the road to Colònia de Sant Jordi (Ma-6100). Mon–Sat 6.30–11.30pm.

Finca Hotel Rural Es Turó Camí de Cas Perets s/n ☎ 971 64 95 31, ⓦ esturo.com. A classic *finca*, which has been tastefully converted into an immaculate, luxury modern hotel, all bright-white walls, wood-beam ceilings and tiled floors. It's located on a gentle hill 2.5km to the north of (and signposted from) the hamlet of Ses Salines, which is itself 8.5km west of Santanyí. **€150**

Sa Botiga c/Roser 2 ☎ 971 16 30 15, ⓦ sabotiga-santanyi.com. This creatively decorated, German-run café and restaurant offers a varied menu, featuring local, seasonal ingredients from seafood through to fancy salads. A café during the day, it switches to its restaurant menu at 6pm with mains starting at €13. C/Roser runs west from Plaça Major. Mon–Sat 9am–10pm, Sun 11.30am–10pm.

Sa Cova Plaça Major 30 ☎ 638 01 34 53. The pick of the cafés and bars on Santanyí's main square, *Sa Cova* is a groovy little place painted in cheerful, psychedelic colours and with a tiny stage hosting regular live music. Daily 10am–late.

Hotel Santanyí Plaça Constitució 7 ☎ 971 64 22 14, ⓦ hotel-santanyi.com. In an old stone townhouse, this four-star hotel has seven pleasantly modern rooms and a roof terrace with wide views. Plaça Constitució adjoins Plaça Major right in the centre of town. **€145**

Cap de Ses Salines

At the southern tip of Mallorca, about 15km from Santanyí, the wind-buffeted **Cap de Ses Salines** is a bleak, brush-covered headland edged by coastal pine woods. The **lighthouse** at the end of the road is closed to the public, but it is possible to scramble out along the surrounding coastline, which has an eerie sense of barren desolation. Thekla larks and stone curlews can often be seen here on the cape, while gulls, terns and shearwaters glide about offshore, benefiting from the winds which, when they're up, can make the place intolerable. You can also park your car near the lighthouse and stroll northwest along the seashore to the wide, shallow bay and deserted sandy beach of the **Platja des Caragol**: it's an easy walk of around thirty minutes each way.

Colònia de Sant Jordi and around

The highlight of Mallorca's south coast has to be **COLÒNIA DE SANT JORDI**, a curious and most enjoyable amalgamation of tourist settlement and old seaport, located just 15km southwest of Santanyí. It was the neighbouring saltpans that brought a degree of prosperity to Colònia in medieval times, and although it's tourism that now brings in most of the money, salt is still exported in large quantities. Inevitably, Colònia has expanded with the tourists, and today its wide streets pattern a substantial and irregularly shaped headland that pokes its knobbly head out into the ocean. In the middle of the headland lies the principal square, the unremarkable **Plaça Constitució**, while a new(ish) and really rather glitzy tourist zone has sprung up on the west side of town, with hotels and villas besieging the **Platja d'Estanys**, whose gleaming sands curve round a dune-edged cove. Much more amenable, however, is the **harbour**, on the northeast side of the headland. Here you'll find the best restaurants, the older and more reasonably priced hotels, a pair of sandy beaches and the boats to the offshore **Cabrera National Park** (see p.192). Colònia is also within easy driving distance of one of Mallorca's most famous beaches, **Es Trenc**.

The harbour

Colònia de Sant Jordi's old **harbour** is the most diverting part of town, its ensemble of early twentieth-century balconied houses and hotels draped around a handsome, horseshoe-shaped bay. There's nothing special to look at, but it's a relaxing spot with a handful of restaurants, fishing smacks, a marina and a slim, sandy beach, the **Platja d'es Port**. From here, it's a five-minute walk along the footpath north round the bay to the slender, low-lying headland that accommodates the extensive sands of the **Platja d'es Dolç** – a perfect spot to soak up the sun.

Cabrera National Park visitor centre

c/Enginyer Gabriel Roca s/n • Daily: Feb to mid-June & mid-Sept to Dec 9.30am–2pm & 3–6pm; mid-June to mid-Sept 10am–2pm & 3–11pm • Last admission 1hr before closing • €8 • ☎ 971 65 62 82, ⓦ cvcabrera.es

It's hard to make much sense of the new and fancy **Cabrera National Park visitor centre**, which occupies a large and conspicuous watchtower-like structure on Colònia's harbourfront. Frankly, the centre does not do much to illuminate Cabrera – you are much better off actually going there (see p.192) – though at least the subterranean aquarium is of more than passing interest.

Es Trenc

Es Trenc is about 6km from Colònia de Sant Jordi: head north out of town for 0.5km and turn left at the roundabout towards Campos; after another 2.8km, take the signed left turn and follow the country lane leading across the saltpans and wetlands to the large car park (€6) at the east end of the beach

A few kilometres west of Colònia de Sant Jordi is **Es Trenc**, a 4km strip of sandy beach that extends as far as the eye can see. It's neither unknown nor unspoilt, but the crowds are easily absorbed except at the height of the season, and development is

4

See Ses Salines, Campos, Santanyí & Es Trenc

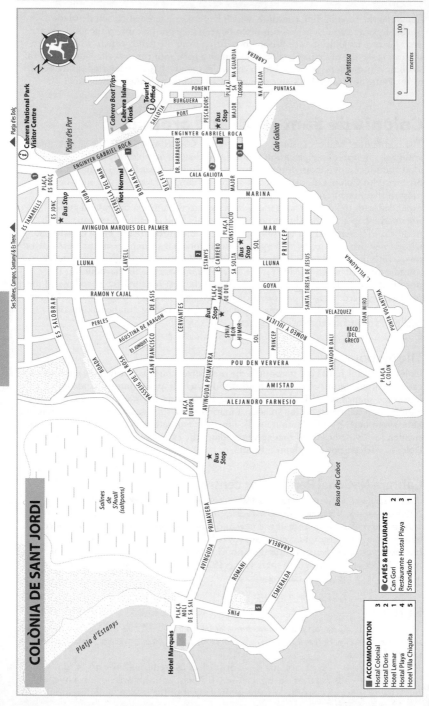

COLÒNIA DE SANT JORDI

Platja d'Estanys

Salines de S'Avall (saltpans)

Bossa d'es Cabot

PLAÇA MOLÍ DE SA SAL

Hotel Marquès

PINS

ROMANÍ

AVINGUDA PRIMAVERA

ESMERALDA

CARABELA

Bus Stop

PLAÇA EUROPA

AVINGUDA PRIMAVERA

ALEJANDRO FARNESIO

AMISTAD

POU DEN VERVERA

ES SALOBRAR

RONDA

PASSEIG DE LA ROSA

ES JONQUET

SAN FRANCISCO

AGUSTINA DE ARAGON

PERLÉS

RAMON Y CAJAL

LLUNA

CLAVELL

DE ASIS

CERVANTES

PLAÇA MARE DE DEU

SINIA BON HUMOR

SOL

PRINCEP

ROMEO Y JULIETA

SALVADOR DALI

VELAZQUEZ

JOAN MIRO

RECO DEL GRECO

PLAÇA C. COLON

PUNTA VOLANTINA

SANTA TERESA DE JESUS

Bus Stop

SOL

GOYA

LLUNA

SA SOLTA

ES CARRERO

ESTANYS

PLAÇA CONSTITUCIÓ

MAR

PRINCEP

MARINA

L. VILLALONGA

AVINGUDA MARQUES DEL PALMER

ES JONC

AUBA

ESTRELLA DEL MAR

BONANÇA

DELFIN

DR. BARRAQUER

CALA GALIOTA

MAJOR

Cala Galiota

ENGINYER GABRIEL ROCA

PESCADORS

PORT

BURGUERA

SALIOTA

PONENT

PLAÇA SA TORRE

NA GUARDIA

NA PELADA

PUNTASA

Sa Puntassa

CABRERA

Bus Stop

Bus Stop

Bus Stop

PLAÇA ES DÓLÇ

ES TAMARELLS

Platja d'es Port

Platja d'es Dólç

Cabrera National Park Visitor Centre

Cabrera Boat Trips

Cabrera Island Kiosk

Tourist Office

Not Normal

ENGINYER GABRIEL ROCA

0   100   metres

■ ACCOMMODATION

Hostal Colonial	3
Hostal Doris	2
Hotel Lemar	1
Hotel Playa	4
Hotel Villa Chiquita	5

● CAFÉS & RESTAURANTS

Can Gori	2
Restaurante Hostal Playa	3
Strandkorb	1

virtually nonexistent. The east end of the beach, near the car park, is far more appealing than the western portion, **Ses Covetes**, which is blotched by improvised shacks and drinks stalls.

Several **footpaths** lead from Es Trenc beach into the saltpans, the **Salines de Llevant**, which are known for their birdlife (see box, pp.266–267), but it's not a good area to explore on foot: the scenery is boring, it's smelly, and for much of the year insects are a menace. It's much better to drive or cycle along the maze-like network of narrow country lanes that traverse the saltpans, stopping anywhere that looks promising.

ARRIVAL AND INFORMATION   COLÒNIA DE SANT JORDI AND AROUND

By bus Buses to Colònia de Sant Jordi loop through the resort; the nearest stop to the harbour is on Avgda Marques del Palmer, at the corner of c/Jonc.
Destinations Manacor (Mon–Fri 3 daily; 1hr 30min); Palma (Mon–Sat every 2hr, Sun 3 daily; 1hr); Santanyí

(2–4 daily; 20min).
Tourist information Colònia tourist office is located right on the harbourfront (daily except Tues 10am–1pm & 4.30–6.30pm; ☎ 971 65 60 73, ⓦ www.ajsessalines.net).

GETTING AROUND

By train During the season, a toy-town *mini-tren* shuttles around Colònia every hour or two (May–Oct daily 9.30am–1.30pm & 4.30–10pm).
By taxi The resort's biggest and best taxi company is Taxi Jaime (☎ 630 36 62 02).

By bike Cycling in the flatlands around the resort is a popular pastime; the tourist office has information on local bike rental outlets, or you can try Not Normal, c/Bonança 6 (April–Oct daily 9am–7pm; ☎ 601 28 30 25).

ACCOMMODATION

Hostal Colonial c/Enginyer Gabriel Roca 9 ☎ 971 65 61 82, ⓦ hostal-colonial.com. Very agreeable, family-run one-star *hostal* with eight frugal but entirely adequate modern rooms, each of which has a small terrace or balcony. It's just 50m from the seashore, and there's a great ice-cream parlour downstairs, too. Closed Dec–Feb. **€80**
Hostal Doris c/Estanys 56 ☎ 971 65 51 47, ⓦ i75526 .wix.com/hostal-doris. Right in the centre of Colònia, on a narrow side street, this family-owned *hostal* has ten double rooms and three apartments, some with balconies; each is modern and plainly decorated. The breakfasts are good and the atmosphere noticeably convivial. **€80**
Hotel Lemar c/Bonança 1 ☎ 971 65 51 78, ⓦ hotel lemar.com. Likeable three-star hotel in a well-kept modern block overlooking the harbour. The 90-odd rooms are neat and trim and most have balconies, though it's best to specify you want a room at the front, otherwise you'll be struggling for a view of anything in particular. Closed Nov to mid-April. **€110**

★**Hostal Playa** c/Major 25 ☎ 971 65 52 56, ⓦ restauranteplaya.com. About a 5min walk from the main harbour, this appealing little family-run place has seven double rooms, four of which – and these are the ones you want – have a balcony looking out over the sea as it laps against the beach to the rear of the *hostal*. The rooms are pretty basic, but quite large, and the public area is delightfully old-fashioned with lots of wood, old photos and plates stuck on the walls. Breakfast is served on a pretty, sea-facing patio terrace, which doubles as a restaurant (see p.192). **€40**
Hotel Villa Chiquita c/Esmeralda 14 ☎ 971 65 51 21, ⓦ hotelvillachiquita.com. This smart and well-tended hotel occupies a rambling, *pueblo*-style modern villa in the tourist zone at the west end of Avgda Primavera. It has a good-looking garden, with lots of exotic cacti, and eighteen smartly decorated en-suite rooms. Closed Nov–Jan. **€200**

4

BIRDLIFE OF THE SALTPANS

The saltpans backing the beach at Es Trenc – the **Salines de Llevant** – and the surrounding farms and scrubland support a wide variety of **birdlife**. Residents such as marsh harriers, kestrels, spotted crakes, fan-tailed warblers and hoopoes make a visit enjoyable at any time of year, but the best time to come is in spring when hundreds of migrants arrive from Africa. Commonly seen in spring are avocets, little ringed plovers, little egrets, common sandpipers, little stints, black-tailed godwits, collared pratincoles and black terns.

EATING AND DRINKING

A string of **restaurants** lines up along the harbour, but everything is still pleasantly low-key and small-scale. The big gastronomic deal is the seafood, but here, in a town with its own fishing fleet, portions are substantial and often as not you get the whole fish rather than a slice. Bear in mind that things get busy from around 8pm, but close down early, by about 10.30pm.

Can Gori c/Estanys 21 ☎971 65 64 69. A favourite, no-frills local hangout with cheap beer, tasty tapas – fried squid, green pepper, spicy sausages and so forth – plus very pleasant service. Not the place for an intimate dinner perhaps, but still a great spot for a quick bite and a slice of island life. Daily 8am–1am.

Restaurante Hostal Playa c/Major 25 ☎971 65 52 56. The restaurant of the eponymous *hostal* (see p.191) may lack a little delicacy, but there's no complaining about the food: fish and more fish prepared in the traditional Mallorcan manner. Eat inside or out the back on the sea-facing patio-terrace. Main courses average €20–25. Easter–Oct Mon 7.30–10pm, Tues–Sun noon–3.30pm & 7.30–10pm.

★**Strandkorb** c/Enginyer Gabriel Roca 95 ☎971 65 52 99. On a pleasant little square just off the harbourfront, this excellent, very informal restaurant, with its long L-shaped pavement terrace, serves good, wholesome Spanish-Catalan food in generous portions and at affordable prices: the grilled hake costs just €15. Tues–Sun noon–10pm.

Cabrera National Park

The **Illa de Cabrera** ("Goat Island") is a bumpy, scrub-covered chunk of rock lying just 18km offshore from Colònia de Sant Jordi. Largely bare, almost entirely uninhabited and no more than 7km wide and 5km long, it's actually the largest of a cluster of islets that comprise the Cabrera archipelago. The most significant hint of Cabrera's eventful past is its protective **castle**, whose battered medieval walls are plonked on a hill above the island's supremely sheltered harbour. Otherwise, Pliny claimed Cabrera to have been the birthplace of Hannibal; medieval pirates hunkered down here to plan future raids; and during the Napoleonic Wars, the Spanish stuck nine thousand French prisoners of war on the island and promptly forgot about them – two-thirds died from starvation and disease during their four-year captivity. More recently, Joan March (see box, p.55) may well have sold illicit fuel here to passing German U-boats during World War II and, later still, the island was taken over by Franco's armed forces – before ultimately winning protected status as the **Parc Nacional de l'Arxipèlag de Cabrera** in 1991.

The island

The excursion from Colònia de Sant Jordi to Cabrera starts with a short voyage to the island. On the final stretch, the boat nudges round a hostile-looking headland to enter the harbour, **Es Port** – a narrow finger of calm water edged by hills and equipped with a tiny jetty. National Park personnel meet the boat to advise about what visitors can do and where – some parts of Cabrera are out of bounds – and there's a small park **information office** by the jetty too (see opposite). The most popular excursion is the stiff, thirty-minute hoof up the path to the ruins of the **castle**, which perches high up on Cabrera's west coast. The views from the fortress back to Mallorca are magnificent, and many sorts of **birds** can be seen gliding round the sea cliffs, including Manx and Cory's shearwaters and the rare Audouin's gulls, as well as peregrine falcons and shags. It is, however, the blue-underbellied **Lilford's wall lizard** that really steals the show: take time to have a (bring-your-own) drink down by the jetty, where you can tempt the Lilford's lizards out from the scrub with pieces of fruit.

As an alternative to the castle, it's an easy fifteen-minute walk round the harbour to **Sa Plageta beach**, from where you can head inland to the sombre **memorial** commemorating the French dead: the path to the memorial begins at Sa Plageta and takes about twenty minutes to walk in each direction. Beyond the memorial is a

museum (park staff can advise on its limited opening hours), sited in a former wine cellar and grain warehouse, which traces the history of Cabrera via a ragbag of archeological finds recovered from the island and its surrounding waters. On the return journey, most boats bob across the bay to visit **Sa Cova Blava** (Blue Grotto), sailing right into the cave through the 50m-wide entrance and on into the yawning chamber beyond. The grotto reaches a height of 160m and is suffused by the bluish light from which it gets its name; you can swim here too.

ARRIVAL AND INFORMATION

CABRERA NATIONAL PARK

By boat The harbourfront kiosk in Colònia de Sant Jordi (☎971 64 90 34, ⓦexcursionsacabrera.es) takes reservations for boat trips over to Cabrera island. There are two boats to choose from: an open-deck, 12-passenger speedboat or a covered, larger vessel which takes up to 50 passengers. There is a variety of excursions on offer, from cruises right round the island to guided nature walks on Cabrera; most excursions last six or seven hours and cost €40–50. Note that there are no sailings between November and March. On excursions where the boat goes straight to Cabrera, the speedboat takes 35min to complete the journey, the covered boat 45min.

Tourist information The park information office is beside Cabrera harbour (May–Oct daily 8am–2pm & 4–8pm; ☎630 98 23 63). The best source of online information on Cabrera – and all the other nature reserves and parks in the Balearics – is ⓦen.balearsnatura.com.

ACCOMMODATION

Refugi de Cabrera Cabrera ☎971 65 62 82, ⓦcvcabrera.es. One of the old military buildings near the dock has been turned into simple, hostel-style accommodation with 24 beds in 12 en-suite rooms. There is a microwave and a fridge, but guests need to bring their own food and drink. The maximum stay is two nights and advance booking is required, either online or in person at the Cabrera National Park visitor centre in Colònia de Sant Jordi (see p.189). Closed Dec–Jan. **€60**

4

Menorca

200 Maó

210 Port de Maó

214 Southeast Menorca

216 The northeast coast

221 Central Menorca

231 Ciutadella

240 Around Ciutadella

FORNELLS

5

Menorca

Second largest of the Balearic islands, boomerang-shaped Menorca stretches west from the enormous natural harbour of Maó to the smaller port of Ciutadella, a distance of just 45km. Each of these two small towns, which together hold around seventy percent of the population, has preserved much of its eighteenth- and early nineteenth-century appearance, though Ciutadella's mazy centre, with its grand mansions and Gothic cathedral, has the aesthetic edge over Maó's plainer, more mercantile architecture. Running through the rustic interior between the two is the main Me-1 highway, which spines the island, linking a trio of pocket-sized market towns – Alaior, Es Mercadal and Ferreries – and connecting with a sequence of side roads that branch off to the resorts and beaches that notch the north and south coasts.

The **Me-1 highway** acts as a rough dividing line between Menorca's two distinct geological areas. In the **north**, sandstone predominates, giving a red tint to the low hills that roll out towards the surf-battered coastline, with its myriad coves and inlets. It's here you'll find the lovely fishing village and mini-resort of **Fornells**; the bare and solitary **Cap de Favàritx**; the rearing cliffs and handsome beaches of the **Cap de Cavalleria**; and, a little inland, the rich birdlife of the **Parc Natural s'Albufera des Grau**. To the **south** of the highway all is limestone, with low-lying flatlands punctuated by bulging hills and fringed by a cove-studded coastline. Wooded ravines gouge through this southern zone, becoming deeper and more dramatic as you travel west – especially around the pleasant little town of **Es Migjorn Gran** and at **Cala Galdana**, a popular resort set beneath severe, pine-clad sea cliffs. The south coast also holds the island's best beaches, some developed – like **Son Bou** – others relatively untouched, such as **Cala Turqueta** and **Cala Macarella**. Straddling the two zones is **Monte Toro**, Menorca's highest peak, where the panoramic views reveal the topography of the island to dramatic effect.

The island's varied terrain is sprinkled with farmsteads that bear witness to an **agriculture** which, before much of it was killed off by urbanization/modernization, had become highly advanced. A **dry-stone wall** (*tanca*) protected every field and prevented the **Tramuntana**, the vicious north wind, from tearing away the topsoil. Even olive trees had their roots individually protected in little stone wells, while compact stone **ziggurats** sheltered cattle from both the wind and the blazing sun. Nowadays, many of the fields lie barren, but the walls and ziggurats survive, as do many of the old twisted **gates** made from olive branches.

Tourism Menorca-style: reserves and conservation p.199
Barbarossa gets rough p.203
Menorca's Talayotic sites p.206
Gastronomic accidents: Maó and mayo p.208
Boat trips from Maó – and the islands of Port de Maó p.212
Clubbing at the cliff-face: the Cova d'en Xoroi p.215
A day's hike: Es Grau to Sa Torreta p.216

Indecision off the Cape: Favàritx and Admiral Byng p.219
Richard Kane and the Camí d'en Kane p.222
Five great Menorcan beaches p.224
A day's hike: Es Migjorn Gran to the coast p.226
Coastal walks around Cala Galdana p.229
Hiking the island: the Camí de Cavalls p.241

CAP DE FAVÀRITX

Highlights

❶ Maó The labyrinthine lanes and alleys of Menorca's engaging capital ramble along the top of a ridge, high above its deep and long harbour. **See p.200**

❷ Talatí de Dalt One of the most satisfying of Menorca's many prehistoric remains, in a charming rustic setting just outside Maó. **See p.206**

❸ Cap de Favàritx A wind-stripped headland where a solitary lighthouse shines out over a lunar-like landscape of tightly layered slate. **See p.218**

❹ Monte Toro Menorca's highest point, offering wonderful views over the whole of the island. **See p.225**

❺ Ciutadella The island's prettiest town, its compact centre an inordinately appealing maze of handsome stone buildings culminating in a delightful Gothic cathedral. **See p.231**

❻ Cala Turqueta Menorca has a clutch of unspoilt cove beaches and this is one of the finest, with a band of fine white sand set between wooded limestone cliffs and crystal-clear waters. **See p.242**

HIGHLIGHTS ARE MARKED ON THE MAP ON P.198

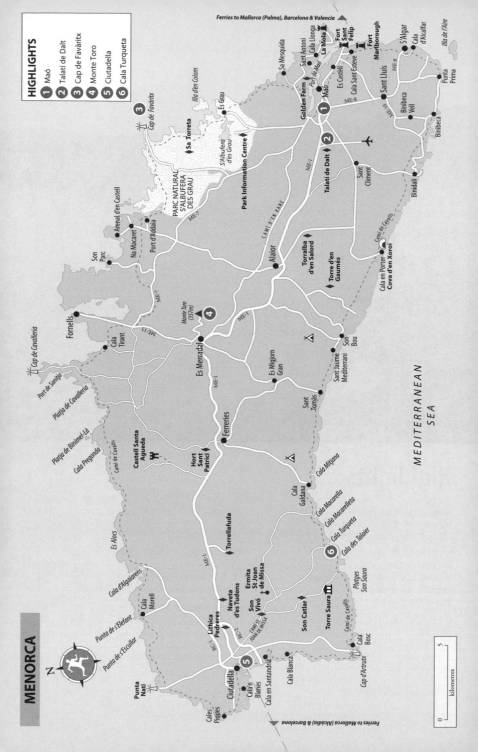

TOURISM MENORCA-STYLE: RESERVES AND CONSERVATION

By design, Menorca's **tourist development** is largely confined to individual coves and bays, and only among the sprawling villa villages in the southeast corner of the island has it become at all overpowering. Neither is it likely to spread: determined to protect their island from the worst excesses of the tourist industry, the Menorcans have clearly demarcated **development zones** and have also created a chain of **conservation areas** that protect around forty percent of the island. It was this far-sighted plan that prompted UNESCO to declare Menorca a **Biosphere Reserve** in 1993. The islanders have been especially keen to protect their undeveloped beaches, bringing both them and their immediate hinterland into public ownership as speedily as possible. To this end, the old mule and military track that encircles the island has been turned into a long-distance footpath, the **Camí de Cavalls** (see box, p.241).

The landscape is further cluttered by scores of prehistoric stone monuments, mostly dating from the second millennium BC. Perhaps surprisingly, considering this widespread physical evidence, little is known of Menorca's early settlers and there has been endless academic debate about exactly what means what. The most common remains are **talayots**, cone-shaped mounds of stone that may or may not have been watchtowers. It's from these *talayots* that the prehistoric Talayotic Period is named, running from 2500 to 123 BC, when the Romans arrived. Four of the finest Talayotic sites are **Talatí de Dalt**, just outside Maó, **Torre d'en Gaumés**, near Alaior, **Torrellafuda**, just off the Me-1 on the approach to Ciutadella, and the **Naveta d'es Tudons**, also near Ciutadella. Very different are the remains left by the British, who captured Menorca in 1708 during the War of the Spanish Succession and held it – with one or two interruptions – until 1802. The British planted fortifications along Maó's deep-water port, the **Port de Maó**, and one of them, the intriguing **Fort Marlborough**, has survived in fine fettle – as has the nearby Spanish fortress of **La Mola**.

Nowadays, Menorca's **tourist industry** rules the economic roost, but it has its singularities. It's dominated by the British, who account for around sixty percent of the island's visitors, and it's focused on holiday homes and package tours, with a strong sideline in activity holidays from walking to diving. It's also very **seasonal**: outside April/May to October, many restaurants, cafés and hotels close and the bus network is reduced to a skeleton service.

ARRIVAL AND DEPARTURE MENORCA

BY PLANE

Menorca airport Menorca's international airport (see p.207) is located just 5km southwest of the capital, Maó. The airport is a smart, compact affair with car rental outlets, ATMs, currency exchange facilities and a tourist office.

AIRPORT INFORMATION

Tourist information The tourist office (daily 8am–8.30pm; ☎ 971 15 71 15) in the arrivals hall issues free island maps and has a selection of free literature, including *Menorca Weekly*, a leaflet detailing forthcoming events, and *Menorca Explorer*, a general information booklet which contains simple maps of every town on the island as well as all sorts of listings.

TRANSPORT FROM THE AIRPORT

By bus There is a frequent bus service between Menorca airport and Maó bus station, just off Plaça S'Esplanada

(June–Sept daily every 30min, 6am–10pm; Oct–May daily every 30min, 6am–8pm; 15min). Single tickets cost €2.65. At Maó bus station, you can pick up buses to every part of the island (see p.207). Alternatively, Shuttle Menorca (April–Oct; ☎ 971 36 99 92, ⓦ shuttlemenorca.com) offers affordable minibus transfers between the airport and a wide range of destinations. Single fares average around €12.

By taxi A taxi between the airport to Maó costs about €12; taxi rates are controlled and a list of island-wide fares is available from the tourist office in the Arrivals Hall.

BY FERRY

Ferries and catamarans Boats to Menorca from the other Balearic islands and mainland Spain mostly dock at Maó's ferry terminal (see p.207), immediately below the centre of town, but there's also a limited range of services to and from Ciutadella (p.238). For details of routes and sample fares, see Basics (p.22 & p.23).

5

GETTING AROUND

By bus There's an excellent year-round bus service running along the Me-1 between Maó and Ciutadella, linking all the larger towns of the interior – Alaior, Es Mercadal and Ferreries. There's also a reasonably good year-round service to the smaller towns to the north and south of the Me-1, including Sant Lluís, Fornells and Es Migjorn Gran. The island's coastal resorts are all easy to reach by bus in the tourist season, usually from April to October, but out of season there's either a skeleton service, or no service at all. Bus timetables are available online at ⓦ menorca.tib.org.

By taxi Taxi rates are controlled and a list of islandwide fares is available from any tourist office.

By bicycle Most of the island's resorts, as well as Maó and Ciutadella, have bike rental outlets. Prices begin at about €12 a day.

By car Big-name car rental companies line up at Menorca airport, including Europcar (☎ 971 36 64 00) and National Asea (☎ 971 36 62 13). The airport tourist office (see p.199) has a complete islandwide list.

Maó

Despite its status as island capital, **MAÓ** (in Castilian, Mahón) has a sociable, small-town feel – the population is just 29,000 – and wandering around its ancient centre, with its long-established cafés and dinky little shops, is a relaxing and enjoyable way to pass a few hours. Nowadays, most visitors approach Maó from its landward side, but this gives the wrong impression. Thanks to its position beside the largest natural harbour in the Mediterranean, the town has always been a port and it's only from the **waterfront** that the logic of the place becomes apparent, its centre crowding the crest of a steep ridge that stands tall against the south side of the harbour. From this angle, Maó is beautiful, its well-worn houses stacked up high and interrupted by fragments of the old city walls and the occasional church.

Spreading along the top of the ridge, the **town centre** possesses two cultural highlights, the Churrigueresque chapel in the church of **St Francesc** and the assorted bygones and curios of the **Centre d'Art i d'Història Hernández Sanz**, but all told it's the general flavour of the area that appeals rather than any individual sight. The icing on the cake is the centre's striking and unusual hybrid **architecture**: tall, monumental Spanish mansions stand cheek by jowl with classical Georgian sash-windowed townhouses, elegant reminders of the British occupation. Below the centre, down by the harbour, you might also enjoy visiting **Xoriguer gin distillery**, where you can sample as many of the island's liquors as you can brave, or you might consider venturing a little further afield to see the substantial Talayotic remains of **Talatí de Dalt**, just west of town along the Me-1.

Port it may be, but there's no seamy side to Maó. **Nightlife** is limited to a few bars and clubs near the ferry terminal, and the harbourfront's main draw is its long string of **restaurants and cafés**, which attract tourists in their droves – though few stay the night, preferring the purpose-built resorts close by. As a result, Maó has surprisingly few *hostales* and hotels, which means that you can base yourself here and – if you avoid the waterfront – escape the tourist throng with the greatest of ease.

Plaça Espanya

From behind the ferry terminal, a graceful stone **stairway** and a narrow, twisting street – the Costa de Ses Voltes – tangle together as they climb up the hill to emerge in the middle of the old town at **Plaça Espanya**, which is overlooked by a handsome medley of high-sided houses. Here also, on the north side of the square, is an amenable little **fish market** (see p.209) dating from the 1920s and plonked on top of a sturdy bastion that was originally part of the Renaissance city wall. This mighty zigzag of fortifications, bridges and gates once encased the whole city and replaced the city's medieval walls, sections of which also survive and are clearly visible from the foot of Costa de Ses Voltes. Work on the new Renaissance walls started under

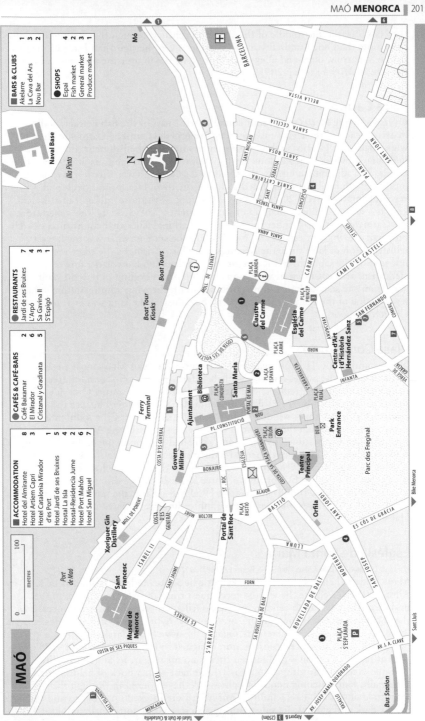

MAÓ

ACCOMMODATION

Hotel del Almirante	8
Hotel Artiem Capri	3
Hotel Catalonia Mirador d'es Port	1
Hotel Jardí de ses Bruixes	5
Hostal La Isla	4
Hostal-Residència Jume	2
Hotel Port Mahón	6
Hotel San Miguel	7

● CAFÉS & CAFÉ-BARS

Café Baixamar	2
El Mirador	6
Cristanal y Gradinata	5

● RESTAURANTS

Jardí de ses Bruixes	7
L'Arpó	4
Sa Gavina II	3
S'Espigó	1

■ BARS & CLUBS

Akelarre	1
La Cava del Ars	3
Nou Bar	2

● SHOPS

Espai	4
Fish market	2
General market	3
Produce market	1

5

the Habsburgs in the middle of the sixteenth century, though the chain of bastions took more than one hundred years to complete. On the right-hand side of the fish market a narrow, dead-end alley offers fine views down over the port and is home to the café *El Mirador* (see p.209).

Plaça Carme

Overshadowing **Plaça Carme**, immediately to the east of the fish market, is the massive facade of the eighteenth-century **Església del Carme**, a Carmelite church whose barn-like interior is almost entirely devoid of embellishment, though the high altar is worth a second look for its intricately carved tableaux and trumpeting angels. The adjoining cloisters, the **Claustre del Carme**, have, after long service as the municipal courts, been refurbished to house the town's fresh meat, fruit and vegetable **market** (see p.209) whose stalls – along with those selling tourist knick-knacks – are set against a platoon of vaulted arches. The cloisters were taken from the Carmelites in 1837 under the terms of a national edict that confiscated church property, passing vast estates and buildings to the state in what was the largest redistribution of land since the Reconquista. Unsurprisingly, the edict was bitterly resented by the Church, but it caught the popular mood, a volatile mix of anti-clericalism and self-interest, with many small farmers hoping to buy the confiscated land from the state at knock-down prices. Later right-wing administrations did return some of the ecclesiastical property, but most of the land was lost to the Church for good.

Plaça Constitució

Narrow and particularly pretty, **Plaça Constitució** is one of Maó's most engaging squares, where the horses and riders of the *Mare de déu de Gràcia* fiesta (see p.33) congregate in early September – hence the modern equine statue. One side of the square is dominated by the **Església de Santa Maria** (see below), but it's the genteel arcades, bull's-eye upper windows and wrought-iron grilles of the **Ajuntament** (Town Hall) that catch the attention. Built by the Spanish, the Ajuntament was subsequently occupied by the island's colonial governors, including Richard Kane (see box, p.222), who donated its distinctive clock. Kane also had portraits of King George III and Queen Charlotte hung in the entrance hall, but these were replaced long ago by portraits of three Spanish kings, Alfonso XIII (1886–1941), Carlos III (1716–88) and Carlos IV (1748–1819), the last two sporting the flamingo-like noses that centuries of inbreeding accentuated among the Spanish Habsburgs.

Església de Santa Maria

Plaça de la Constitució 3 • Daily 7.30am–1pm & 6–8.30pm • €2 • ☎ 971 36 22 78

Maó's principal church, the sterling **Església de Santa Maria** was founded in 1287 by Alfonso III to celebrate the island's reconquest from the Moors. Rebuilt in the middle of the eighteenth century and remodelled on several subsequent occasions, the church's **exterior** is an enjoyable architectural hybrid, its Gothic features encased within later Neoclassical accretions. Inside, the **nave** is all Catalan Gothic, a hangar-like, single-vaulted construction designed to make the **high altar** visible to the entire congregation – and indeed there's no missing it, its larger-than-life Baroque excesses featuring the Virgin Triumphant with a flock of helpful cherubs. Originally, kaleidoscopic floods of light would have poured in through the multitude of stained-glass windows, but most were bricked up ages ago and the nave is now dark and gloomy, its side-vaulting also scarred by some really rather ugly

5

in-fill arches. More in keeping with the original design are the truncated **transepts**, which sport intricate stuccowork with another flock of cherubs peering out from a swirling, decorative undergrowth. The church's pride and joy is its **organ**, a monumental piece of woodwork filling out the elevated gallery above the south entrance. The instrument, with its trumpeting angels and three thousand pipes, was made in Austria in 1810 and lugged across half of Europe at the height of the Napoleonic Wars. Britain's Admiral Collingwood helped with the move, probably as a crafty piece of appeasement: defiance of their new Protestant masters had played a large part in the locals' decision to revamp the church during the British occupation.

Carrer Isabel II

Running west from Plaça Constitució, long and slender **Carrer Isabel II** is distinguished by its Georgian architecture, all handsome wooden doors and fancy fanlights, sash windows, bay windows and ornate ironwork. This was once the heart of the British administration, as recalled by today's military governor's house, the eighteenth-century **Govern Militar**, about halfway along, with its elaborate paintwork and shaded, colonial-style arcades.

There's a useful – and extremely pleasant – short cut down to the harbour from c/Isabel II along **Costa d'es General**, an alley at the foot of c/Rector Mort. This alley tunnels through the old city wall before snaking its way down the cliff to the waterfront below.

The Església de St Francesc

Plaça Monestir • Daily 10am–12.30pm & 5–7pm • Free • ☎ 971 36 25 55

At the end of c/Isabel II, the Baroque facade of the **Església de St Francesc** appears as a cliff-face of pale stone rising high above the rounded, Romanesque arches of its doorway. The church was a long time in the making, its construction spread over the late seventeenth and eighteenth centuries following the razing of the town by the piratical Hayreddin Barbarossa in 1535 (see box below). Inside, the strong lines of the Gothic **nave** are disturbed by some clumsy stucco panelling around the shallow side-chapels, but there's aesthetic compensation in the impressive roof vaulting, not to mention the heavy-duty **high altar**. The latter is flanked by paintings depicting scenes from the lives of the Virgin Mary and St Francis, each and every one of them designed to edify the (illiterate) congregation. Tucked away off the north side of the nave, there's also the **Capella de la Concepció** (Chapel of the Immaculate Conception), an octagonal wonderland of light-white stone decorated with garlanded vines and roses in the full flourish of the Churrigueresque style. Completed in 1752, the chapel is attributed to Francesc Herrara, the painter, engraver and architect who trained in Rome and worked in Menorca before moving on to Palma in Mallorca.

BARBAROSSA GETS ROUGH

Born on Lesbos, the son of an Ottoman soldier, **Hizir Barbarossa** (c.1473–1547) cut his nautical spurs early, making a good living from the sea trade of the eastern Mediterranean with a bit of piracy on the side. By 1505, he had established a series of fortified bases in today's Algeria and Tunisia, and from here he proceeded to attack Christian shipping, ransoming his prisoners or selling them into slavery. It was then that the struggle for control of the western Mediterranean between the Ottomans and the Habsburgs gave him another business opportunity: the Sultan paid him handsomely for lending a helping hand and the **sacking of Maó** was a prime result. Barbarossa died in 1547, but the war lasted for another twenty years or so, until the Turkish fleet was annihilated at the Battle of Lepanto in 1571.

5

Museu de Menorca

Avgda Doctor Guàrdia s/n • April–Oct Tues–Sat 10am–2pm & 6–8.30pm, Sun 10am–2pm; Nov–March Mon–Fri 9.30am–2pm, Sat & Sun 10am–2pm • €2.40 • ☎ 971 35 09 55

The old monastic buildings adjacent to the Església de St Francesc now accommodate the **Museu de Menorca**, the island's largest museum. The collection is spread over three levels, with temporary exhibitions on the ground floor and the permanent collection up above. A visit begins with the old Franciscan **cloister** that abuts the museum, its sturdy pillars and vaulted aisles dating back to the early eighteenth century and illustrating the high point of the Menorcan Baroque.

The first floor

The **first floor** holds a wide range of prehistoric artefacts, beginning with bits and pieces left by the Neolithic pastoralists who were well established here by about 4000 BC. Then it's on to the **Talayotic period** (2500–123 BC), where the earlier items – household objects and the like – are pretty crude, unlike the later pieces, which exhibit considerable sophistication both in home-made goods and in the use of imported items. In particular, look out for the dainty, rather quizzical-looking **bronze bull**, probably of fifth-century Phoenician manufacture and found at Torralba d'en Salord (see p.223), and a small Egyptian bronze of **Imhotep** unearthed at Torre d'en Gaumés (see p.223). These key exhibits reflect the final flourishing of Talayotic culture when Menorca became a major port of call for ships sailing through the Mediterranean, particularly between Italy and Spain. The first floor is rounded off by an enjoyable sample of Roman pottery, including a number of whopping amphorae.

The second floor

The permanent collection continues on the **second floor**, where a series of displays gallops unconvincingly through the Moorish period up to 1900. Among the items on display is a medieval stone cross retrieved from the ruins of a long-gone castle; a batch of paintings of Maó harbour; a handsome assortment of majolica pottery; and several small features on island skills and crafts: the making of costume jewellery, silver purses, boats and shoes. Look out also for the whimsical wooden figurines (*vellons*) carved in the likeness of various island notables by two local carpenters, the scurrilous Monjo brothers, in the late nineteenth century.

Plaça Bastió

From the Museu de Menorca, it's a hop and jump to **Plaça Bastió**, a pleasant piazza holding Maó's one remaining medieval gateway, the **Portal de Sant Roc**, a sturdy affair of roughly hewn stone comprising two turrets, a connecting arch and a projecting parapet. The gateway is named after St Roch, a fourteenth-century hermit who was popular hereabouts as a talisman to ward off the plague: Christian legend asserted that he both recovered from a bout of the plague and cured fellow sufferers, a good recommendation at a time when every city in Europe feared an outbreak.

Carrer Hannover and around

Running up from Plaça Constitució, Maó's steeply sloping **main street** is the commercial heart of the old town, flanked by family shops and tiny piazzas. Different parts of the street bear different names, but the longest portions are **Costa de sa Placa** (Hannover) and **c/Moreres**, which is where you'll spy a dinky bust-on-a-plinth of Maó's **Mateu Josep Orfila** (1787–1853), to all intents and purposes the founder of modern toxicology. It takes five to ten minutes to walk from one end of the main street to the other and you emerge at **Plaça S'Esplanada**, the humdrum main square.

Centre d'Art i d'Història Hernández Sanz

c/Anunciva y 2 • Mon–Sat except Tues 10am–1.30pm & 6–8pm, Sun 10am–1.30pm • Free • ☎ 971 35 65 23

5

Inhabiting the former mansion of the Oliver family, who made their money from military supplies, the **Centre d'Art i d'Història Hernández Sanz** is something of a hotch potch, its disparate collection spread over three floors. The **ground floor** displays the mansion itself to fine advantage, especially its handsome interior staircase and Italianate murals, and here also is a section devoted to the Oliver family in particular and the Mahonese bourgeoisie in general. A further section traces the evolution of Maó as a port with a collection of vintage maps, and yet another – perhaps the most interesting of the lot – is devoted to **British Menorca**. Here you'll find a sort of "speaking clock" of Menorcan words and phrases derived from the English language, as well as a vitriolic British cartoon entitled *The English Lion Dismember'd*: Menorca had been returned to Spain by the Treaty of Amiens in 1802 and this clearly infuriated the cartoonist, who shows the English lion with one of his paws chopped off – the offending paw shaped like Menorca. Here also are a couple of historical paintings by **Joan Chiesa** (1754–1833), recording, in precise detail, the comings and goings of the British army, including the final evacuation of Maó in 1802. Little is known of this Chiesa, but he was related to a one-time Spanish governor of the island, **Giuseppe Chiesa** (1720–89), whose (very similar) paintings are also displayed in this section.

Upstairs, and of lesser interest, is a section devoted to eighteenth- and nineteenth-century Menorca, with lots of cameos of islanders in traditional costume; as well as more maps; a feature on the historian **Hernández Sanz**, whose idiosyncratic connoisseur's collection is the core of what is on display today; and temporary displays of modern, mostly local, art.

The quayside

Below Maó's town centre stretches the 3km-long **quayside**, in the middle of which is Maó's ferry terminal. To the west of the terminal, beyond a few bars, restaurants and the Xoriguer gin distillery (see below), the waterfront is occupied by the town's small fishing fleet and a mini-marina, and then comes an industrial area, which extends round the murky waters at the head of the inlet. To the east, it's a couple of hundred metres to the departure point for **boat tours** of Port de Maó (see box, p.212) and another short stroll to **Mô**, the pint-sized mermaid created by local sculptor Leonardo Lucarini. Mô announces the start of the town's **main marina**, an elongated affair where flashy chrome yachts face a string of restaurants, bars and cafés. By day, the half-hour stroll east along the quayside is tame verging on boring; at night, with tourists converging on the restaurants, it's rather more animated.

Xoriguer gin distillery

Moll de Ponent 91 • June–Sept Mon–Fri 8am–7pm, Sat 9am–1pm; Oct–May Mon–Fri 9am–1pm & 4–7pm • Free • ☎ 971 36 21 97, Ⓦ xoriguer.es

From Maó's ferry terminal, it's a couple of minutes' walk west to the **Xoriguer gin distillery** showroom, where you can help yourself to free samples of gin, various liqueurs and other spirits. Multilingual labels give details of all the different types, and there are some pretty obscure examples, such as **calent**, a sweet, brown liqueur with aniseed, wine, saffron and cinnamon; and **palo**, a liquorice-flavoured spirit supposedly of Phoenician provenance. The lime-green **hierbas**, a favourite local tipple, is a sweet and sticky liqueur, partly made from camomile collected on the headlands of La Mola (see p.212). In all its various guises, the main spirit is **gin** with *pomada*, a gin cocktail with lemonade, pretty much Menorca's national drink. British sailors first brought gin to Menorca in the late eighteenth century, but a local businessman, a certain Beltran, obtained the recipe in obscure circumstances

5

and started making the stuff himself. Nowadays, Xoriguer is the most popular island brand, mostly sold in modern versions of the earthenware bottles once used by British sailors and known locally as *canecas*. Here at the showroom, a litre of Xoriguer gin costs about €12.

Talatí de Dalt

May–Oct daily 10am–8pm; Nov–April open access • May–Oct €4; Nov–April free • ⓦ descobreixmenorca.com • The site is 4km west of Maó centre, just south off the Me-1 highway, and is not served by public transport; if you're driving along the Me-1, watch for the sign and then follow a narrow lane that reaches the site after 300m

Of the several Talayotic sites in the vicinity of Maó, easily the pick is the rusticated remains of **Talatí de Dalt**. Partly enclosed by a Cyclopean wall, the site features an imposing *taula* set within a circular precinct. The *taula* here appears to be propped up by a second T-shaped pillar, though it's generally agreed that this is the result of an accidental fall, rather than by prehistoric design. Next to the *taula* are the heaped stones of the main **talayot**, and just beyond are three **subterranean chambers** with columns and flagstones forming several rough roofs. These three chambers, which

---

MENORCA'S TALAYOTIC SITES

Menorca's **Talayotic sites** conform to a common pattern, though as you might expect there are marked differences in their state of repair. The tallest structure on each site is generally the **talayot** (from *atalaya*, Arabic for "watchtower"), a cone-shaped mound between 5m and 10m high, built of stone but without mortar or cement. There are dozens of ruined *talayots* on Menorca and the detail of their original design varies from site to site: some are solid, others contain one or more chambers. Most are found in and around settlements, but there are solitary examples too. Such diversity has generated considerable academic debate about their original purpose, with scholars suggesting variously that they were built for defence, as dwellings for chieftains, as burial sites or as storehouses. Popular belief has it that they functioned as **watchtowers**, but it's a theory few experts accept: they have no interior stairway, for example, and only a handful are found along the coast. Even so, no one has come up with a more convincing explanation. The mystery of the *talayots*, which are also found on Mallorca, is compounded by their uniqueness. The only Mediterranean structures they vaguely resemble are the Nuragh towers on Sardinia, though a Sardinian kinship is but one of several options, with Egypt, Crete and Greece also posited as possible influences.

These *talayots* are often positioned a few metres from a **taula**, a T-shaped structure comprising two huge stones up to 4.5m high. Some sites may contain several *talayots*, but there's rarely more than one *taula*, and this almost always sits in the middle of a **circular enclosure** whose perimeter is (or was) marked by a low wall. Archeologists have unearthed objects in these enclosures and the remains of firepits have been found against the perimeter wall. These discoveries imply a **religious function**, though there is insufficient evidence to justify referring to the enclosures as "shrines". There's general agreement, however, that the *taula* and its enclosure formed the public part of the settlement, and on many sites the remains of family dwellings surround them. Finally, Menorca also holds a number of **navetas**, stone-slab constructions shaped like inverted loaf tins and dating from between 1400 and 800 BC. Many have false ceilings, and although you can stand up inside, they were clearly not living spaces, but rather communal tombs, or ossuaries. The prime example is the **Naveta d'es Tudons**, outside Ciutadella. *Navetas* are never found in the same place as the *talayots* and *taulas*.

Archeologists divide the **Talayotic period** into several different eras, but as far as the non-specialist is concerned, the only significant difference between the various phases is the, **perimeter wall**, a dry-stone affair often several metres high and made up of large stones. These Cyclopean walls were for defence and reflect an increase in piracy across the western Mediterranean: the earlier settlements lack them, while the later ones – from around 1000 BC – do have them. There's more on the Talayotic period in Contexts (see p.246).

5

date from the very end of the Talayotic period, abut an inner courtyard and are much more sophisticated in construction than the earlier prehistoric dwellings that dot the rest of the site. Their exact function is not known, but there's no doubt that the *taula* was the village centrepiece, and probably the focus of religious ceremonies too. The site's rural setting is also charming – olive and carob trees abound and a tribe of hogs roots around the undergrowth.

ARRIVAL AND DEPARTURE   MAÓ

BY PLANE

Menorca airport Menorca's international airport (see p.199) is located just 5km southwest of Maó. A frequent bus service links the airport with Maó bus station, just off Plaça S'Esplanada (June–Sept daily every 30min, 6am–10pm; Oct–May daily every 30min, 6am–8pm; 15min); single tickets cost €2.65. A taxi from the airport to Maó costs about €12.

BY FERRY

Maó ferry terminal The terminal is located directly beneath the town centre, though ferries sometimes moor on the other (north) side of the harbour, a 10- to 15min walk away. From the ferry terminal, it's a brief walk up the wide stone stairway of Costa de Ses Voltes to Plaça Espanya and the oldest part of town. For details of ferry and catamaran routes, as well as prices, consult Basics (see p.22 & p.23).

BY BUS

Maó bus station Long-distance buses arrive and depart from the Estació d'Autobuses, off Avgda Josep Anselm Clavé, a couple of minutes' walk from the main square, Plaça S'Esplanada. Bus timetables are available online at ⓦmenorca.tib.org.
Destinations Alaior (Mon–Fri every 30min–1hr, Sat & Sun every 1–2hr; 10min); Cala Galdana (May–Oct 2 daily; Nov–April Mon–Sat 2 daily; 50min); Ciutadella (Mon–Fri every 30min–1hr, Sat & Sun every 1–2hr; 1hr); Es Castell (every

30–60min; 10min); Es Grau (mid-June to mid-Sept 4 daily; 20min); Es Mercadal (Mon–Fri every 30min–1hr, Sat & Sun every 1–2hr; 25min); Es Migjorn Gran (May–Sept Mon–Sat 6 daily, Sun 4 daily; Nov–April Mon–Sat 4 daily; 30min); Ferreries (Mon–Fri every 30min–1hr, Sat & Sun every 1–2hr; 35min); Fornells (mid-June to mid-Sept Mon–Sat 8 daily, Sun 4 daily; mid-Sept to mid-June 2 daily; 35min); Sant Lluís (hourly; 10min); Sant Tomàs (May–Sept Mon–Sat 6 daily, Sun 4 daily; Nov–April Mon–Sat 4 daily; 1hr); Son Bou (May–Oct every 1–2hr, but no Sun service in May & Oct; 45min).

BY CAR

Driving into Maó The ring road encircling Maó makes driving in easy enough, though the narrow lanes and complicated one-way system of the old town, which stretches from Plaça S'Esplanada to Plaça Espanya, are well-nigh impossible to negotiate and you're better off parking on the periphery.
Parking On-street parking is metered during shopping hours (Mon–Fri 9am–2pm & 4.30–7.30pm, Sat 9am–2pm) with a maximum stay of two hours (€1.60); at other times, it's free. Note that if the time you've paid for overlaps into a free period, your ticket will be valid for the time you've got left when the next restricted period begins. On-street parking spaces can, however, be hard to find, and the easier option is to head for a car park: the underground car park below Plaça S'Esplanada, is the largest and convenient for the town centre (Mon–Sat 8.30am–11.30pm; €2.40–2.60/hr).

GETTING AROUND

By bus Local buses (every 30min; single tickets €2.65) link the bus station with the harbour and ferry terminal via the inner ring road.
By bicycle Bike Menorca, out on the ring road to the southeast of the centre at Avgda Francesc Femenias 44

(☎971 35 37 98, ⓦbikemenorca.com), rents out road and mountain bikes from €14/day.
By taxi There are taxi ranks on Plaça S'Esplanada, at the bus station and on Plaça Espanya; alternatively, phone Radio Taxi Menorca on ☎971 36 71 11.

INFORMATION

Tourist information There's a tourist information desk at the airport (see p.199) and a main office down on Maó's harbourfront, metres from the ferry terminal at Moll de Llevant 2 (May–Oct daily 9am–8.30pm; Nov–April Mon–Fri 10am–1pm & 5–7.30pm, Sat 10am–1pm; ☎971 35 59 52, ⓦmenorca.es). There is also a seasonal office in a glass cube in the old town on Plaça Miranda (June–Sept Mon–Fri 9.30am–1.30pm & 5.30–8.30pm, Sat 9am–2pm). All

three will provide a free map of the island and leaflets on everything from beaches to bus timetables as well as a weekly events schedule. The main office also sells the best Menorca road map on the market – the *Mapa de Menorca* (1:75,000; €2.50) – and packs of information on the Camí des Cavalls long-distance footpath (see box, p.241). None of the three will help you find accommodation.

5

GASTRONOMIC ACCIDENTS: MAÓ AND MAYO

Maó has a curious place in culinary history as the birthplace of **mayonnaise** (*mahonesa*). Various legends, all of them involving the French, claim to identify its eighteenth-century inventor: take your pick from the chef of the French commander besieging Maó; a peasant woman dressing a salad for another French general; or a housekeeper disguising rancid meat from the tastebuds of a French officer. The French also changed the way the Menorcans bake their bread, while the British started the dairy industry and encouraged the roasting of meat.

ACCOMMODATION

Maó does not perhaps have the range of **accommodation** you might expect, but it does have a handful of inexpensive *hostales* close to the town centre and, although they are not especially inspiring, they're reasonable enough and convenient – unlike Maó's smarter **hotels**, which are – with one bijou exception – stuck out on the edge of town.

Hotel del Almirante Carretera Maó (Me-2) ⊕971 36 27 00, ⓦhoteldelalmirante.com. About 2km east of Maó beside (and signed from) the coastal road to Es Castell, this maroon and cream Georgian house was once the residence of British admiral Lord Collingwood. The delightful lobby is crammed with ancient bygones, and although the traditional bedrooms beyond are modest, all are perfectly adequate. The garden terrace is especially attractive, there's an outside pool and views down along the Maó inlet. Package-tour operators use the place, but there are often vacancies. From the town centre, take a taxi or the Es Castell bus and ask to be dropped off. Closed Nov–April. €110

Hotel Artiem Capri c/Sant Esteve 8 ⊕971 36 14 00, ⓦartiemhotels.com. Enjoyable and really rather friendly four-star hotel in a modern block that's handily located near the old centre of Maó, just a couple of minutes' walk west of Plaça S'Esplanada. The pleasant, large-ish rooms have been given a splash of colour and style over the past few years, and most have spacious balconies. The hotel also has a rooftop spa and pool. €80

Hotel Catalonia Mirador d'es Port c/Dalt Vilanova 1 ⊕971 36 00 16, ⓦhoteles-catalonia.com. This well-equipped, three-star chain hotel, with its own pool and gardens, occupies a modern block perched on a hill, about a 15min walk west of Plaça Bastió. The interior is kitted out in brisk minimalist style and many of the bedrooms have balconies with harbour views. €80

★**Hotel Jardí de ses Bruixes** c/San Fernando 26 ⊕971 36 31 66, ⓦhotelsesbruixes.com. Bijou hotel occupying a handsome old Spanish townhouse, complete with courtyard. The rooms vary considerably in size, but they are all immaculately turned out in a sort of John-Lewis-meets-country-house style. One has a splendid balcony, a reminder of its days as the home of a local merchant, while the attic rooms have bull's-eye windows and beamed ceilings. There's an excellent restaurant here, too (see opposite). €140

Hostal La Isla c/Santa Caterina 4 ⊕971 36 64 92, ⓦhostal-laisla.com. Rooms at this amenable one-star *hostal* may be on the small side, but they are reasonably attractive and comfortable, and all have private bathroom and TV. There's a bar and restaurant downstairs. €50

Hostal-residencia Jume c/Concepció 6 ⊕971 36 32 66, ⓦhostaljume.com. Centrally located on a narrow side street, this large, old-fashioned, one-star *hostal* occupies a five-storey modern block and has thirty or so frugal en-suite rooms. €60

Hotel Port Mahón Avgda Port de Maó s/n ⊕902 09 11 47, ⓦsethotels.com. Attractive, colonial-style four-star in a superb ridge-top location above the harbour and with grand views down along the Maó inlet. There's an outside swimming pool and a patio café, plus each of the eighty-odd rooms is kitted out in smart, modern style with air conditioning. It takes about 20min to walk to the hotel from the town centre or you can get there via the harbour and a steep flight of steps; you can also get here by local city bus (see p.207). €140

Hotel San Miguel c/Comercio 26 ⊕971 36 40 59, ⓦhotelsanmiguelmenorca.com. Somewhat austere from the outside, this three-star hotel has sixteen rooms of modern demeanour – nothing special, but comfortable enough. It's located on a dull side street a few minutes' south of Plaça Espanya. €80

EATING AND DRINKING

Most of Maó's **restaurants** are dotted along the town's elongated quayside and, although standards vary considerably, there are several first-rate places here. The town centre, on the other hand, has yet to make much of a gastronomic impact, with its assorted **cafés** and **café-bars** long on local atmosphere and short on tip-top food, though things are beginning to change and improve.

CAFÉS AND CAFÉ-BARS

Café Baixamar Moll de Ponent 17 ☎971 36 58 96, ⓦcafebaixamar.es. An attractively decorated little café-bar, with old-fashioned mirrors and pastel paintwork, serving tasty traditional Menorcan snacks – island cheese and sausage, for example – from as little as €5. Good wines, too. Perfect for a snack before a trip on one of the sightseeing boats from the nearby quay. Daily: May–Oct 9am–1am; Nov–April noon–11pm.

El Mirador Plaça Espanya 2 ☎971 35 21 07. Located footsteps from the fish market – and just off the main stairway leading from the harbour to the town centre – this appealing little café-bar offers a good range of snacks and tapas (from €5), and has superb views over the harbour from its terrace. Jazz is the favoured background music with occasional live gigs. Mon–Sat noon–midnight.

Cristanal y Gradinata c/Isabel II, 1 ☎971 36 33 16. Tucked away in the old town, this easy-going café is an attractively decorated little place whose speciality is *manolitos*, mini *boccadillos* with a variety of fillings – try the sausage. Snacks from €5. Mon–Fri 9am–3pm & 7–10pm, Sat noon–3pm & 7–10pm.

RESTAURANTS

★**Jardí de ses Bruixes** c/San Fernando 26 ☎971 36 31 66, ⓦhotelsesbruixes.com. This delightful hotel (see opposite) has a first-rate restaurant, where the menu is a canny combination of Spanish and Italian dishes. Home-made pastas are a key feature, though it's perhaps the risottos which really get the tastebuds humming. Eat inside in the ornate dining room or outside in the courtyard. Mains from €15. Tues–Sat 1–3.30pm & 7.30–10pm.

L'Arpó Moll de Llevant 124 ☎971 36 98 44. Unlike many of its quayside neighbours, this long-established restaurant has not jazzed itself up, but although the decor may be routinely modern, they serve an outstanding range of seafood – probably the widest selection in town. Attentive and friendly service too. Mains from €18. April–Oct daily 1–4pm & 5–11pm; Nov–March hours vary – call ahead.

★**Sa Gavina II** Moll de Llevant 157 ☎971 35 06 91. With its neat, modern decor and dinky little pavement terrace, this harbourside café-restaurant serves absolutely delicious (and substantial) tapas, including meatballs in tomato sauce and ravioli stuffed with spinach. No microwaved food here, and electric-fast service too. Tapas average €8. April–Oct daily 1–11pm, kitchen 1–4pm & 6–11pm; Nov–March hours vary – call ahead.

S'Espigó Moll de Llevant 267 ☎971 36 99 09, ⓦsespigo .com. Well-regarded, family-run restaurant that does a great line in both steaks and seafood – try, for example, the red peppers stuffed with seafood or the baked sea bream. Mains average €20. April–Oct daily 1–3.30pm & 8–11.30pm; Nov–March Tues–Sat 1–3.30pm & 8–11pm, Sun 1–3.30pm; closed Jan.

BARS AND NIGHTLIFE

Akelarre Moll de Ponent 41 ☎971 36 85 20. Opposite the ferry terminal, down on the waterfront at the foot of the old city walls, this is probably the best – and certainly the most fashionable – bar in town, occupying an attractively renovated ground-floor vault with stone walls and a miniature garden-cum-terrace at the back. Jazz and smooth modern sounds form the backdrop, with occasional live acts. No website, but they do have a Facebook page. Usually Mon–Thurs 7pm–3am, Fri–Sun 3pm–4am.

La Cava del Ars Plaça Príncep 12 ☎971 35 18 79, ⓦlacavadelars.com. This cellar space has been retro-fitted as a bar and small concert space that is very popular with twenty-somethings. They also do food, especially tapas (from €4), and great cocktails. Daily 6pm–3am.

Nou Bar c/Nou 1 ☎971 36 55 00, ⓦbarnou.com. This ground-floor café, with its leather armchairs and gloomy lighting, is a dog-eared sort of place much favoured and flavoured by the locals. Standing room only whenever there's a major festival – as there often is. Daily 6–11.30pm.

SHOPPING

Espai c/Cos de Gràcia 14 ☎971 36 34 07, ⓦespai14 .com. Friendly little bookshop with a reasonably good selection of Spanish/Catalan novels. They also sell a few English-language guidebooks and have a small selection of Menorca road maps, though the main tourist office down on the harbour (see p.207) has a wider selection of both road and hiking maps. Mon–Fri 9am–1.30pm & 5–8pm, Sat 10am–2pm.

Fish market Plaça Espanya. In a pretty little 1920s building, the fish market is the place to come for fresh seafood, mostly – but not exclusively – caught locally. The market shares its premises with a number of food stores

selling local produce, especially cheese. Mon–Sat 9am–2pm.

General market Plaça S'Esplanada. Popular with tourists, Maó's main square is home to a twice-weekly general market, mostly clothes and assorted trinkets with a few food stalls thrown in for good measure. Tues & Sat 9am–2pm.

Produce market Plaça Carme. Housed in the old cloisters of the Església del Carme (see p.202), Mao's biggest and best market has around eighty stalls selling all things Balearic – from wine and cheese through to sausages and oils. Daily 8.30am–9pm.

5

DIRECTORY

Banks Banks and ATMs are dotted along the main street between Plaça Espanya and Plaça S'Esplanada. The Sa Nostra bank has an ATM at c/Moreres 26, in between c/Bastió and c/Lluna.

Pharmacies Among several centrally located pharmacies, Farmacia Pons is on the main drag at c/Moreres 4 (Mon–Fri 9am–8.30pm, Sat 9am–2pm; ☎ 971 36 48 46).

Post office The central *correu* is at c/Bonaire 15, near Plaça Bastió (Mon–Fri 8.30am–8.30pm; Sat 9.30am–1pm).

Port de Maó

Port de Maó, as Menorcans term the whole of the extended inlet that links Maó with the Mediterranean, is one of the finest natural harbours in the world. More than 5km long and up to 1km wide, the channel also boasts the narrowest of deep-sea entrances, strategic blessings that have long made it an object of nautical desire. The high admiral of the Holy Roman Emperor Charles V quipped that "June, July, August and Mahon are the best ports in the Mediterranean", and after Barbarossa's destruction of Maó in 1535, the emperor finally took the hint and had the harbour fortified. Later, the British eyed the port as both a forward base for Gibraltar and a lookout against the French naval squadron in Toulon. Using the War of the Spanish Succession as an excuse, the British decided to occupy Menorca in 1708 and, with the odd interruption, stayed in control until 1802, pouring vast resources into the harbour defences – fortifications which the Spanish have since updated and remodelled on several occasions.

Both shores – as well as a trio of mid-channel islets (see box, p.212) – bear witness to all this military activity and are pockmarked by ruined fortifications, thick-walled affairs hugging the contours of the coast. The **north shore** comprises a hilly promontory that nudges out into the ocean, protecting the channel from the insistent northerly wind, the Tramuntana. The promontory's steep terrain has deterred the islanders from settling here, and although recent development has spawned a couple of suburbs, the north shore's key feature is the nineteenth-century fortress of **La Mola**, which sprawls over the headland at its very tip, some 7km from Maó. The highlights of Port de Maó's **south shore** are the unusual subterranean fortress of **Fort Marlborough** and **Cala Sant Esteve**, the pretty fishing village where it is located. Of lesser interest is the former garrison town of **Es Castell**, purpose-built by the English in the 1770s.

Golden Farm
No public access · Ⓦ sanantoniomenorca.com

From the traffic island at the west end of Maó's harbour, a byroad soon leaves the town behind, threading over leafy hills as it slips its way along Port de Maó's **north shore**. After 3km or so, the road passes below the **Golden Farm**, a fine old mansion in the British colonial style, which perches conspicuously on the hillside overlooking the inlet. The house is actually seen to best advantage when approached from the east, and only then can you spy its grand portico, whose two arcaded galleries dominate the south (Maó) side of the house. The upper gallery – the balcony – is equipped with a delicate balustrade and classical deities decorate the tympanum, a trio of languorous figures in vaguely erotic poses.

The mansion may well have been **Admiral Nelson**'s headquarters, albeit briefly, during the island's third British occupation (1798–1802), and there's all sorts of folkloric tittle-tattle alluding to romantic trysts here between Nelson and his mistress, **Emma Hamilton**. In fact, Nelson was much too concerned with events in Naples, where the Hamiltons were ensconced, and did his best to avoid visiting Menorca at all – he only came here once or twice for a couple of days apiece despite it being crucial for Britain's naval control of the Mediterranean. In July 1799, his

5

superior, Lord Keith, mustered his fleet at Port de Maó to resist a possible French attack and ordered Nelson to join him. Nelson refused point-blank, writing to the Admiralty, "I am fully aware of the act I have committed, but, sensible of my loyal intentions, I am prepared for any fate which may await my disobedience." The Admiralty let it go – a good job considering Trafalgar was just round the corner – and Keith ranted and raved in vain.

La Mola

Carretera de la Mola s/n • May Tues–Sun 10am–6pm; June–Sept daily 10am–8pm; Oct–April Tues–Sun 10am–2pm • €8 • ☎ 971 36 40 40, ⓦ fortalesalamola.com • There are no buses, but there is a water taxi service from Maó (see box below)

East of Golden Farm, the road along Port de Maó's northern shore weaves over a stretch of wind-raked heathland before it approaches the causeway leading over to the imposing fortifications of **La Mola** – with the zigzag walls of the **Illa del Llatzeret** (see box below) off to the right. Visitors to La Mola proceed over the causeway, carrying on for another 600m or so until they reach the car park in sight of the main gate, the **Porta de la Reina** (Queen's Gate), named after Queen Isabel II of Spain (1830–1904), during whose chaotic reign the fortress was constructed. La Mola's

---

BOAT TRIPS FROM MAÓ – AND THE ISLANDS OF PORT DE MAÓ

A **boat trip** is the only way to get close to the **three islets** that dot the Port de Maó inlet – four if you count the most westerly, tiny **Illa Pinto** (no public access), a naval base which sits opposite Maó's boat dock and is attached to the north shore by a causeway. The first of the islands to the east of Illa Pinto is the **Illa del Rei** (ⓦ islahospitalmenorca.org), whose dilapidated buildings once accommodated a military hospital. This was also where Alfonso III landed at the start of his successful invasion of Muslim Menorca in 1287. Next comes pocket-sized **Illa Quarentena**, a pancake-flat islet that has been used variously as a quarantine station and a naval base. Finally, the larger **Illa del Llatzeret** is the site of a former hospital for infectious diseases, which remained in service until 1917. The sturdy, late eighteenth-century stone walls surrounding Llatzeret were built for the daftest of reasons: the Spanish Secretary of State was convinced that contagion could be carried into town by the wind, so he had the walls built high and thick to keep the germs inside. Internal walls separated patients suffering different diseases for precisely the same reason. Llatzeret was only separated from the mainland in 1900 when a canal was cut on its landward side to provide a more sheltered route to the daunting **La Mola** fortress (see above).

BOAT TRIPS ALONG THE PORT DE MAÓ

Departing from the dock near the foot of **Maó's** Costa de Ses Voltes, various companies run regular **boat trips along the Port de Maó**, with the standard tour comprising an hour-long scoot down and around the inlet for €12 per person. Frequency depends on the season: from May to October there are departures every hour or so, whereas in January there are only a handful of sailings every week, if any at all. Almost all the boats have glass bottoms for underwater viewing. Of the three main companies, each of which has a harbourside ticket kiosk, **Yellow Catamarans** (☎ 639 67 63 51, ⓦ yellowcatamarans.com) is as good as any. They also offer longer tours, the pick of which sails right down the inlet before exploring some of Menorca's eastern shore (April–Oct 1–2 weekly; €25).

WATER TAXIS TO LA MOLA

A reliable **water taxi** service (April–Oct Mon–Sat 9.30am–8.30pm; ☎ 616 42 88 91, ⓦ watertaximenorca.com) links Maó's harbourfront with the massive La Mola fortress (see above), located right down the inlet at the tip of the north shore. A single fare costs €9, return €12, and advance reservations of at least a couple of hours are required. The same company also offers longer trips, with a cruise down the inlet and along Menorca's east coast (2–3hr; €80) being the pick of the crop; again, advance reservations are required. The departure point for the water-taxi service is something of a moveable feast, but currently it's from the pontoon at the *Restaurante La Minerva*, just to the east of the main boat dock at Moll de Llevant 87.

assorted stone walls and gun emplacements, which take two or three hours to explore properly, dominate the spatulate headland. The stronghold was built to protect Spain's Mediterranean coast from the French and British, with construction beginning on the fortress in 1850 and continuing for 25 years. Most of the effort went into the remarkable **landward defences**, whose tiers of complementary bastions, ditches and subterranean gun batteries were designed to resist the most intensive of artillery bombardments. In the event, it was hardly put to use: La Mola was built on the assumption that naval guns had a limited elevation, but when the British, among others, armed their ships with guns that could be elevated (and therefore lob shells over the walls) the fortress became immediately obsolete and no-one ever bothered to attack – hence its excellent state of repair.

Es Castell

Tucked in tight against Port de Maó's **south shore** just 3km from Maó, the gridiron streets of **ES CASTELL** were laid out by the British, who installed a garrison here, in what they christened Georgetown, in the 1770s. After the British left, the town changed its name, but kept its military character, retaining a garrison till very recently. As it always has been, the town centre is ranged around **Plaça S'Esplanada**, the old parade ground-cum-plaza, whose elongated barracks and Georgian-style town hall, with its stumpy, toy-town clock tower, bear witness to the British influence. The same British heritage is amplified in the cramped and narrow streets edging the square, where sash windows, doors with glass fanlights, and wrought-iron grilles adorn many of the older houses. It only takes half an hour or so to explore the centre, including a stroll down c/Stuart, which leads from the main square to the **harbour**, a pleasant spot occupying the thumb-shaped cove of **Cales Fonts**.

ARRIVAL AND DEPARTURE   ES CASTELL

By bus Buses from Maó to Es Castell (every 30–60min; 10min) stop just off the Me-2 at the end of c/Victori, which leads north to Plaça S'Esplanada, a 4min walk away.

ACCOMMODATION

Hotel Carlos III c/Carlos III, 2 ☎ 971 36 31 00, ⓦ artiemhotels.com. Above the seashore on the north side of Es Castell, this pleasant three-star hotel, with its sleek and spacious rooms decorated in whites and greys, occupies a prime location and comes complete with outside pool and expansive terrace. The better rooms have inlet-facing balconies. Lots of personality throughout, evident in unique touches such as lobby jazz on weekend evenings and printed recipes for organic Menorcan dishes left on your pillow during the day. Adults only. **€80**

Fort Sant Felip

Carretera Sant Felip s/n • Guided tours only: June–Sept Thurs & Sun at 10am; Oct, Nov & March–May Sat at 10am • €5 • ☎ 971 36 21 00, ⓦ museomilitarmenorca.com

Beyond Es Castell, the main coastal road continues down towards the mouth of Port de Maó before veering right for Sant Lluís (see p.214). Keeping straight, you soon pass the turning for Cala Sant Esteve (see p.214), from where it's a further 300m or so to the gates of a *zona militar*. This restricted military area sprawls over the bumpy headland that guards the inlet's southerly entrance, and it was here that the Emperor Charles V built an imposing star-shaped fortress in the 1550s, naming it **Fort Sant Felip** after his son, later Philip II. Once Menorca's greatest stronghold, the fort was adapted by the British, who controlled the seaway from the multitude of subterranean gun batteries they and their predecessors had carved in the soft sandstone. Unfortunately, this irritated the Spanish so much that once Menorca was returned to them in 1782 they promptly destroyed the fort in a fit of pique – a rather misguided move since the lack of defences allowed the British to recapture the island with the greatest of ease just a few years later.

5

Today, next to nothing survives, save the most fragmentary of ruins above ground with several old Spanish and British gun galleries and tunnels down below.

Cala Sant Esteve

From Fort Sant Felip, it's about 1.5km to **CALA SANT ESTEVE**, an extraordinarily picturesque little village, where old fishermen's houses necklace a slender cove with a turquoise sea lapping against crumbly cliffs. There's nowhere to stay and nothing much of a beach, but the village is home to the intriguing **Fort Marlborough**.

Fort Marlborough

Cala Sant Esteve • April & Oct–Nov Tues–Sun 9.30am–2.30pm; May–Sept Mon 9.30am–4.30pm, Tues–Sat 9.30am–8pm • €3 • ☎ 971 36 04 62 • Parking at the beginning of Cala Sant Esteve, a 10min walk away

Towards the far end of Cala Sant Esteve, on the south side of the cove, is **Fort Marlborough**, easily the most interesting of the assorted fortifications inhabiting Port de Maó. Named after one of Britain's most talented generals, Sir John Churchill, the Duke of Marlborough, the fort is an intricate, largely subterranean affair, built by the British to guard the southern approach to Fort Sant Felip between 1710 and 1726 and substantially reinforced sixty years later. The fort begins with a long **gallery** dug into the soft rock with counter-galleries cut at right angles to detect enemy attempts to mine into the fortress. In addition, the main gallery encircles an **interior moat** – dry now, but once filled with water – and is equipped with gun slits that would have been used to fire on intruders negotiating the moat from every angle imaginable. In turn, the moat encircles a small fortified hillock, the most protected part of the fortress and once the site of an **artillery battery** that had this stretch of the coast in its sights. The fort was besieged twice – by the French in 1756 and the Spanish in 1781 – and although it was captured on both occasions, it was only after a prolonged assault. One of the advantages of this type of fortress was that it could tie up a large enemy force for weeks, and yet required a minuscule garrison – the British installed just sixty men here.

Southeast Menorca

Bounded by the road between Maó and Cala en Porter, **southeast Menorca** consists of a low-lying limestone plateau, fringed by a rocky shoreline with a string of craggy coves. This part of the island has been extensively developed with a sequence of low-rise villa-villages gobbling up large chunks of land. It's difficult to be enthusiastic, especially in **Cala en Porter**, the biggest and perhaps the ugliest *urbanització* of the lot, though earlier developments, principally the attractive resort of **Cala d'Alcalfar**, which flanks an especially pretty cove, are much more appealing. Away from the coast, the interior is dotted with holiday homes, but it's all very discreet and for the most part this remains an agricultural landscape crisscrossed by country lanes and dotted with tiny villages, plus one town – mildly diverting **Sant Lluís**.

Sant Lluís

Just 5km south from Maó along the Me-8, trim **SANT LLUÍS** is a one-square, one-church, one-horse town of brightly whitewashed terraced houses. As at Es Castell (see p.213), the town's gridiron street plan betrays its colonial origins: on this occasion, it was a French commander, the Duc de Richelieu, who built Sant Lluís to house his Breton sailors in the 1750s, naming the new settlement after the thirteenth-century King Louis IX, who was beatified for his part in the Crusades. The French connection is further recalled by the three coats of arms carved on the west front of the large whitewashed **church** – those of the royal household and two French governors.

CLUBBING AT THE CLIFF-FACE: THE COVA D'EN XOROI

Sprawling **Cala en Porter** may be an unappetizing *urbanització*, but it does possess one of the island's most popular attractions, the **Cova d'en Xoroi**, c/Sa Cova 2, a large cave set in the cliff-face high above the ocean with a dramatic stairway leading to the entrance from the clifftop up above. During the day, the cave is open to visitors (daily: May & Oct from 3pm; June–Sept from 11.30am; €8 including one soft drink), but at night it really comes into its own as a **nightclub** (May–Sept Fri–Sun 11pm–5am; ☎ 971 37 72 36, ⓦ covadenxoroi.com), showcasing some big-name DJs and offering some oh-so-sophisticated cocktails; check the website to see who is on and when.

The cave is also the subject of one of the island's best-known – and least savoury – **folk tales**. Legend has it that a shipwrecked Moor named **Xoroi** (literally, "One Ear") hid out here, raiding local farms for food. Bored and lonely, he then kidnapped a local virgin – the so-called "Flower of Alaior" – and imprisoned her in his cave. Eventually, Xoroi's refuge was discovered when locals picked up his tracks back to the cave after a freak snowstorm. Cornered, Xoroi committed suicide by throwing himself into the ocean, while the girl, and the children she'd borne, were taken back to Alaior, where presumably they tried to live happily ever after.

ARRIVAL AND DEPARTURE   SANT LLUÍS

By bus Buses from Maó to Sant Lluís (hourly; 10min) stick to the main road (the Me-8) running along the east edge of town – and a couple hundred metres from the main street, c/Sant Lluís; get off at the c/Duc de Crillon stop.

ACCOMMODATION AND EATING

Hotel Rural Biniarroca Camí Vell 57, Sant Lluís ☎ 971 15 00 59, ⓦ biniarroca.com. In an attractively renovated old *finca*, this smart hotel has eighteen comfortable guest rooms decorated in a straightforward modern manner, but with retro flourishes. There's an outside pool, especially lovely gardens, and a first-rate restaurant (daily noon–3pm & 7–10.30pm; reservations required), where the menu features home- and island-grown ingredients; mains start at €20. The hotel is located just to the north of Sant Lluís and is signed from the Me-6. Closed mid-Oct to April. **€170**

Cala d'Alcalfar

Located about 5km southeast of Sant Lluís via the Me-8, **CALA D'ALCALFAR** is perhaps the most agreeable of the resorts sprinkled over southeast Menorca, comprising little more than a smattering of holiday homes and old fishermen's cottages set beside an inlet of flat-topped cliffs and a turquoise sea. Here development is restrained, and you can enjoy the sandy beach, then stroll out across the surrounding headlands, one of which has its own **Martello tower**, built by the Spanish in the 1780s.

ARRIVAL AND DEPARTURE   CALA D'ALCALFAR

By bus Buses to Cala d'Alcalfar from both Maó (May–Oct Mon–Fri 7 daily; 15min) and Sant Lluís (May–Oct Mon–Fri 7 daily; 5min) stop on c/Ample, on the north side of the cove and about 200m east of the *Hostal Xuroy*.

ACCOMMODATION

Alcaufar Vell Carretera Alcalfar km8 ☎ 971 15 18 74, ⓦ alcaufarvell.com. This delightful fifteenth-century stone farmhouse, just off the Me-8 about 2km northwest of Cala d'Alcalfar, has been boutique-ified to become one of Menorca's most atmospheric hotels. The 21 rooms are simple, awash with whitewashed stone and adobe-coloured tiles, and some of them have pitched roofs and beamed ceilings, but all have jacuzzi-style baths. **€305**

Hostal Xuroy c/Llevant 1 ☎ 971 15 18 20, ⓦ xuroy menorca.com. The main footpath down to Cala d'Alcalfar's beach runs through the family-run *Hostal Xuroy*, a pleasant two-star establishment with forty-odd spick-and-span (but basic) modern rooms, the pick of which have sea-facing balconies; it's a popular spot, so advance reservations are advised. Closed Nov–April. **€110**

5

The northeast coast

Stretching out between Es Grau and the Cap de Cavalleria, Menorca's **northeast coast** holds some of the island's prettiest scenery, its craggy coves, islets and headlands rarely rattled by the developers, as the harsh prevailing wind – the Tramuntana – makes life a tad too blustery for sun-seeking packagers. There are developed coves for sure – and four of them contain substantial villa resorts – but these are the exceptions rather than the rule, and for the most part this stretch of coast remains delightfully pristine.

Much of the northeast coast is readily reached via the enjoyable, 25km-long **Me-7**, linking Maó and Fornells. This runs alongside cultivated fields protected by great stands of trees, with the low hills that form the backbone of the interior bumping away into the distance. At regular intervals you can turn-off towards the seashore, with the first turning to the northwest of Maó taking you to both the hamlet of **Es Grau**, the starting point for a delightful two- to three-hour hike along the coast, and the **Parc Natural s'Albufera des Grau**, whose freshwater lake is noted for its birdlife. The next major turning – just beyond the Camí d'en Kane (see p.222) – clips north to the windy bleakness of the **Cap de Favàritx**, and the two turnings after that head north again for the four big villa resorts hereabouts – Port d'Addaia, Na Macaret, Arenal d'en Castell and Son Parc. Much more rewarding, however, is **Fornells**, whose bayside location and more measured development have made it one of the most appealing resorts on the island, with a batch of excellent restaurants to boot. There's no **beach** to speak of at

---

A DAY'S HIKE: ES GRAU TO SA TORRETA

Circular • 9km • 150m ascent • 3hr–3hr 30min • Easy • Trailhead GPS: +39° 56′ 56.99″, +4° 16′ 3.26″

This **coastal walk** takes you from the small resort of Es Grau along one of the wildest sections of the Menorcan seaboard, with a circular detour inland past the S'Albufera lagoon to visit the Talayotic complex of Sa Torreta, one of the most remote prehistoric sites on the island. The going is mainly easy and largely along well-marked tracks, with only one modest ascent towards the highest point of the walk at Sa Torreta farm. Note that some of the gates on the route are inscribed "*Propriedad Privato*" (private property): you can safely ignore these signs, but make sure that you keep to the tracks.

THE HIKE

Starting at the tarmac car park (and bus stop) at the entrance to **Es Grau**, walk round the large sandy beach and follow the path on the far side as it climbs up onto the low cliffs. At the top, ignore the well-defined track that heads off left and continue straight on, descending very sharply, then follow the path as it bears right until you see a solitary white house ahead. About 50m before you reach the house, a path branches off uphill to the left. Follow this to the top of the hill, with the low-slung **Illa d'en Colom** (island) off the coast directly ahead, after which the path swings left, giving expansive views of the rugged coast beyond, without a single sign of human habitation to be seen until, about 50m further on, the **lighthouse** on Cap de Favàritx hoves into view. As soon as you see the lighthouse, watch out for the path that descends to your right. Clamber down this path, past a curious little stone shelter built into the cliff side, then continue leftwards along the coast, which is clothed in wild maquis, comprising low, convoluted clumps of mastic and wild olive dotted with spiky pincushions of *Launaea cervicornis*. Aim about 45 degrees left of the **Martello tower** ahead, keeping left of the bare, rocky headland to your right, and follow any of the various paths that cross the maquis to reach the small bay of **Fondejador des Llanes**, a tiny, driftwood-covered cove, plus a longer, sandier inlet immediately beyond.

Follow the path directly above the beach, which is waymarked with posts inscribed "Camí de Cavalls" (see box, p.241), to a wall with a gap. Twenty metres beyond this is a small sandy clearing that accommodates a large information board relating to Cala Tamarells, a neighbouring beach. Bear left at the end of the clearing, following a path for a few more

A DAY'S HIKE: ES GRAU TO SA TORRETA

Taula and Talayot
Sa Torreta Farm
Cala Sa Torreta
Stone Building
Martello Tower
Es Colomar
Tamarells des Nord
Information Board
Illa d'en Colom
Fondejador des Llanes
75m
57m
57m
White House
MEDITERRANEAN SEA
N
S'Albufera d'es Grau
Es Grau
Bus Stop
- - - - Hiking route
0   500
metres

5

metres to reach a wide track (remember this point carefully for later on). Turn left and follow the track inland as it climbs up and then downhill through a beautifully secluded valley. After 750m the track gradually swings right and you have your first proper view of the **S'Albufera des Grau lagoon** (see p.218) to your left, one of Menorca's richest ornithological sites. The track slaloms right and gradually ascends for a further 1km, climbing steadily uphill (ignore the couple of subsidiary paths which head off to the left). The island's highest point, 357m **Monte Toro** (see p.225), now becomes visible in the distance as you ascend, while near the top to your left there's an overgrown and impassable walled track, typical of many of the island's abandoned donkey trails.

Go through a Menorcan-style gate to reach a T-junction, then go left to arrive at the farmhouse of **Sa Torreta**. Go through another gate, then turn right and walk 100m to a second T-junction. Go left here through a third gate. After 25m you'll pass a large circular threshing floor on your left, with Sa Torreta's **taula** and **talayot** now visible ahead. Just past the threshing floor, go through the gap in the wall on your right and cross the field to reach the walled Talayotic enclosure, one of the least-visited prehistoric sites on Menorca, and one of the few on the northern side of the island. The fine 4m *taula* and partly collapsed *talayot* here are proof of the longevity of Menorca's megalithic culture, postdating earlier examples by as much as a thousand years.

You're now at the highest point of the walk, with grand views down to the coast below. Retrace your steps past the threshing floor and back to the (third) gate, then turn left, continuing on along the main track for 1km downhill (ignoring a prominent left turn just before you rejoin the seafront) through a Menorcan-style gate to reach **Cala Sa Torreta**, a remote, scrub-covered beach littered with dried seaweed and sea-borne rubbish – not much good for swimming, though the clump of Aleppo pines behind the beach is a pleasant spot for a picnic and some birdwatching.

The track continues behind the beach to reach a fork. Go left here and past a small stone building, then across a small headland back towards the small bay of **Tamarells des Nord** and the Martello tower which you saw earlier. Here the path swings away from the shore. Walk inland on the track and continue for about 500m until you reach the narrow path on your left leading back to the sandy clearing with the Cala Tamarells information board. From this point retrace your steps back to Es Grau.

5

Fornells, but the resort does makes a great base for visiting some of the more remote cove beaches nearby, most memorably the **Platja de Cavalleria** or, at more of a stretch, **Cala Pregonda**.

Es Grau

Neat and trim, the hamlet of **ES GRAU** shunts up against a wide, horseshoe-shaped bay, where scrub and sand dunes fringe a vaguely unenticing arc of greyish sand that's interrupted by a faint stream trickling out into the bay – the only outlet for the lake at the heart of the **Parc Natural S'Albufera des Grau** (see below). The shallow waters of Es Grau are ideal for children, however, and at weekends the handful of bars and restaurants that dot the main street are crowded with holidaying Mahonese; the village is also a handy starting point for a day-hike to Sa Torreta (see p.216).

Parc Natural S'Albufera des Grau

Carretera de Maó a Es Grau, km3.5 • **Park** Daily dawn to dusk • Free • **Information centre** April–Oct Tues–Thurs 9am–7pm, Fri–Mon 9am–3pm; Nov–March Tues–Thurs 9am–5pm, Fri–Mon 9am–3pm • ☎ 971 17 77 05, ⓦ en.balearsnatura.com

The scrub-covered dunes behind Es Grau's beach form the eastern periphery of an expanse of dunes encircling the freshwater lagoon of **S'Albufera des Grau**. Only 2km from east to west and a couple of hundred metres wide, the lagoon was once fished for bass, grey mullet and eels – a real island delicacy – but fishing and hunting have been banned since the creation of the **Parc Natural S'Albufera des Grau** in the 1990s. The park boasts a varied terrain, including dunes (which are glued together by a combination of Aleppo pine, marram grass and beach thistle), and wetland, concentrated at the west end of the lake and containing patches of saltworts and rushes. Not surprisingly, the lagoon and its surroundings are rich in birdlife, attracting thousands of migrant birds in spring and autumn.

The well-maintained **access road** into the park begins about 2.5km back from Es Grau on the road towards Maó. Just 1.5km long, this skims past a scattering of villas before reaching the **park information centre**. Beyond here, veer left at the fork and keep going until you reach the **mini car park**, from where clearly marked paths run along the lake's southern shore. It's easy walking and the scenery is gentle on the eye, with the blue of the lake set against the rolling greens and yellows of the dunes. Birders – both casual and enthusiasts – should aim for **Es Prat**, the large patch of wetland at the west end of the lake. You would be best to bring binoculars; for more on Menorca's birds, see Contexts (p.266).

ARRIVAL AND DEPARTURE   ES GRAU

Buses Buses from Maó (mid-June to mid-Sept 4 daily; 20min) pull in at the bus stop on the approach road to Es Grau, about 4min from the village itself.

EATING AND DRINKING

Bar Es Grau Plaça des Mestre Jaume 13 ☎ 626 47 67 27. The hamlet's most popular place to eat is this low-key, café-cum-snack bar, whose shaded terrace perches on the water's edge at the start of the village. Avoid the pizza; order a salad (about €6). Daily 9.30am–11pm.

Tamarindos Passeig Des Tamarell 14 ☎ 971 35 94 20,

ⓦ barrestarantetamarindos.es. Es Grau is short of restaurants, but this waterside spot does something to fill the gastronomic gap – a cosy little place where you should stick to the seafood; main courses average €18. Daily: May & Oct 7–9pm; June–Sept noon–4pm & 7–10.30pm.

Cap de Favàritx

Heading northwest on the Me-7 from the Es Grau turning, it's a short hop to the right turn for the solitary **Cap de Favàritx**. At first, the road to the cape cuts along a wide valley and slips through dumpy little hills, but before long the landscape becomes barer

5

INDECISION OFF THE CAPE: FAVÀRITX AND ADMIRAL BYNG

In 1756, the **Cap de Favàritx** witnessed one of the British navy's more embarrassing moments when **Admiral Byng** (1704–57) anchored his fleet off here for no particular reason. The French had besieged the British garrison at Fort Sant Felip (see p.213) at the start of the Seven Years' War and Byng had been dispatched to Menorca to save the day. Instead, he dillied and dallied, allegedly reading and re-reading the Admiralty's instruction book, and managed to get caught with his nautical trousers down when the French fleet turned up off Cap de Favàritx too. The resulting battle was an inconclusive affair, but Byng faint-heartedly withdrew to Gibraltar, abandoning the British garrison to its fate. Back in London, the prime minister, the Duke of Newcastle, fumed: "He shall be tried immediately; he shall be hanged directly" – and proceeded to carry out his threat, if not exactly to the letter. On his return, Byng was court-martialled and shot by firing squad on his own flagship in Portsmouth harbour, an event which famously prompted **Voltaire** to remark in *Candide* that the British needed to shoot an admiral now and again "pour encourager les autres".

– and the grass gives way to succulents and bare rock. At the cape itself, just 8km from the Me-7, even the succulents can't survive and the **lighthouse** shines out over a bare lunar-like landscape of tightly layered, crumbly slate. The lighthouse is closed to the public, but the views out over the coast are dramatic and you can pick your way along the adjacent rocks, though if the wind is up (as it often is) this isn't much fun. The lighthouse itself was erected in 1922 and is one of the earliest buildings on Menorca to be made of concrete.

Fornells

FORNELLS, about 25km northwest of Maó, may be expanding in some haste, with modern villas trailing over its immediate surroundings, but in essence it remains a classically pretty fishing village at the mouth of a long and chubby bay. The place has been popular with visitors for years, above all for its **seafood restaurants**, whose speciality, *caldereta de llagosta* (*langosta* in Castilian), is a fabulously tasty – if wincingly expensive (think €70) – lobster stew. Fornells also possesses a wild setting with austere, rocky headlands rising to its north and east, their vegetation stripped right down by winter storms and ocean spray. This bleak terrain envelops various **fortifications** – evidence of the harbour's past importance – with the earliest begun in the late seventeenth century to ward against the threat of Arab and Turkish corsairs and including the battered remains of the **Castell de Sant Antoni** (open access; free), by the bay in the centre of the village. Later, the British went further, constructing a string of mini-forts, and then posting a garrison. One of the British commanders here exceeded his military brief, turning a local chapel into a tavern and incurring the disapproval of fellow officer John Armstrong: "In the Temple of Bacchus, no bounds are set to their [the soldiers'] Debauches and such a quantity of Wine is daily swallowed down, as would stagger Credulity itself." Quite – but there again, there wasn't much else to keep the poor old squaddies occupied.

Torre de Fornells

April–Oct Mon–Thurs 10am–3pm, Fri–Sun 10am–3.30pm • €3 • 📞 971 36 86 78

Of the several remaining British fortifications in and around Fornells, only the **Torre de Fornells** is easy to reach, perched on a bare and windy headland at the northern end of the village and approached up a wide walkway. The short haul up to this imposing circular watchtower is worth the effort as the views over the coast are panoramic.

ARRIVAL AND DEPARTURE   FORNELLS

By bus The bus stop for services to and from Fornells is on c/Verge del Carme, one block in from the waterfront and a 2min walk south of the main square – Plaça S'Algaret – via the pedestrianized c/Rosari.

5

Destinations Es Mercadal (mid-June to mid-Sept Mon–Sat 8 daily, Sun 3 daily; mid-Sept to mid-June Mon–Sat 2 daily; 15min); Maó (mid-June to mid-Sept Mon–Sat 8 daily, Sun 4 daily; mid-Sept to mid-June Mon–Sat 2 daily; 35min).

By car Parking can be a pain: the long approach road leading into Fornells is often jam-packed, but there's nearly always space in the large car park up the hill to the west of the main square: just follow the signs.

ACTIVITIES

The village's sweeping inlet provides ideal conditions for **scuba diving** – the coastline around here offers the best diving in Menorca – and **windsurfing**, as evidenced by the flocks of windsurfers periodically scooting across the calm waters at the southern end of the bay as you approach Fornells.

Aventura Náutica Passeig Marítim 41 ☎609 67 09 96, ⓦaventuranauticamenorca.es. Aventura Náutica, just south of the centre along the waterfront, organizes speedboat excursions round the north coast with snorkelling and swimming part of the deal. Prices start from €60, which includes refreshments and snorkelling equipment hire.
Diving Center Fornells ☎971 37 64 31, ⓦdiving fornells.com. The Diving Center Fornells, on the waterfront towards the south end of the village, rents out equipment and organizes diving courses for both novice and

experienced divers. Dives, including full equipment rental, start from €60 in high season; open-water diving courses cost €450 in high season. Advance reservations for courses and equipment are strongly advised, though 24hr is usually enough except at the height of the season.
Wind Fornells ☎664 33 58 01, ⓦwindfornells.com. Wind Fornells, located beside the bay towards the southern edge of the village, offers windsurfing tuition to both novices and more experienced hands, and teaches sailing skills too. Two-hour windsurfing courses start at around €80.

ACCOMMODATION

Hostal La Palma Plaça S'Algaret 3 ☎971 37 66 34, ⓦhostallapalma.com. Pleasant, neat little two-star *hostal*, with simple but cheerfully bright and colourful en-suite rooms. There's also an outside pool, and they have larger apartments for longer stays. Closed Nov–March. **€90**

Hostal S'Algaret Plaça S'Algaret 7 ☎971 37 65 52, ⓦhostal-salgaret.com. Straightforward two-star *hostal* with some thirty guest rooms, all en suite and decorated in brisk modern style, plus a small outside pool. Closed Nov–March **€90**

EATING AND DRINKING

Es Cranc c/Escoles 31 ☎971 37 64 42. A 5min walk north of Plaça S'Algaret, along the pedestrianized main street and just past the church, this popular and very informal, canteen-style restaurant offers a wide variety of fish dishes served in whopping portions. The daily specials, featuring such delights as hake and chips, are a snip at around €15, but although they do serve a *caldereta de llagosta* (€69), it tastes better elsewhere. Reservations advised. April to mid-Nov daily 1–3.30pm & 7.30–10.30pm.
Es Port c/Riera 5 ☎971 37 64 03. On the waterfront, just south of Plaça S'Algaret, this relaxed and easy-going restaurant with its traditional decor specializes in a magnificent *caldereta de llagosta* (€75). Reservations advised. April–Oct Tues–Sun 1–4pm & 8–11pm.
★**Sa Llagosta** c/Gabriel Gelabert 12 ☎971 37 65 66.

This cosy little restaurant, in a sympathetically converted old fisherman's house just along the waterfront from Plaça S'Algarete, has a small but select menu with the emphasis on local dishes and ingredients. The portions may be petite but the flavours are delicious, with each dish carefully prepared and presented. Main courses average around €25, though the *caldereta de llagosta* will cost you €75. Reservations advised. April–Oct daily 1–4pm & 7.30–11pm.
Sa Proa Passeig Marítim 13 ☎971 37 65 97. Cosy, modern restaurant, on the waterfront just south of Plaça S'Algaret, that offers a wide-ranging menu, including pizzas and an inventive range of seafood dishes; the fish risotto is especially tasty, as is the goat's cheese salad. Mains start at €18. April–Oct daily 12.30–11pm.

Cap de Cavalleria peninsula

Fornells is within comfortable striking distance of the knobbly peninsula that pokes out into the Mediterranean as far as the **Cap de Cavalleria**, Menorca's northernmost point. The road there begins at the staggered crossroads just 3km south of Fornells, where the Me-15 (from Es Mercadal) intersects with the Me-7 (from Maó). From the junction, a signposted turning leads west down a pretty country lane through a charming landscape of old stone walls and scattered farmsteads. After about 3km, keep straight on at the intersection and proceed for another kilometre or so to the signposted right-turn that leads north to the cape, running past the **car park** for several north-coast beaches (see below) on the way.

Port de Sanitja
About 1km beyond the car park for the Cap de Cavalleria's beaches, the road swings up and round to offer long-distance views of the cape with the foreground revealing a long and slender inlet, the **Port de Sanitja**, whose sheltered waters, once the harbour for the small but important Roman settlement of **Sanisera**, are flanked by low scrub. Dating from 123 BC, Sanisera was built on the ruins of an earlier Phoenician settlement, this combined history being quite enough to encourage several archeological digs, though there's nothing to see here today.

Cap de Cavalleria
The **Cap de Cavalleria** itself, which is named after the *cavalleries* (baronial estates) into which the island was divided after the Reconquista, is a bleak and wind-buffeted hunk of rock with 90m-high sea cliffs topped by a lonely **lighthouse** (*far*; no access). If you're lucky you'll glimpse some of the Balearic shearwaters that congregate here – a recent environmental project to restore their habitat has boosted their numbers.

Cap de Cavalleria beaches
The large dirt car park beside the road on the way to the cape marks the start of the 500m-long **footpath** – part of the Camí de Cavalls (see box, p.241) – that leads to the **Platja de Cavalleria**, a long, wide and very appealing double-curved beach of reddish sand framed by low-lying hills. There's rarely much of a crowd here, but you can continue west along the Camí de Cavalls to even more secluded coves. The two obvious targets are the **Platja de Binimel-Là**, a shale beach about 2.8km further west, where the waters are clear and good for swimming and snorkelling, though seaweed can be a problem; and, 2km further along, **Cala Pregonda**, a seastack-studded bay with a wide sandy beach. On all these beaches, there are no facilities – so bring your own food and drink.

Central Menorca

In between Maó and Ciutadella, **central Menorca** is the agricultural heart of the island, its rippling hills and rolling plains speckled with scores of whitewashed farmsteads. Things aren't, perhaps, quite as good as they once were – witness the many unkempt fields – but it's still possible to make a good living on the land and many Menorcans still do. The countryside also carries the myriad marks of past agrarian endeavours in its **dry-stone walls** and stone **ziggurats** (*barraques*), which were built to shelter cattle from wind and sun, and is liberally sprinkled with **Talayotic sites** in various states of disrepair.

By accident or design, the four little towns of the interior – Alaior, Es Mercadal, Ferreries and Es Migjorn Gran – have escaped full-on modernization and each holds an attractive ensemble of antique houses dating back to the eighteenth century, sometimes longer. First-up as you head west from Maó – either along the main road, the **Me-1**, or the more rusticated **Camí d'en Kane** – is the hilltop town of **Alaior**, which is itself close to two of the island's most extensive prehistoric sites, **Torralba d'en Salord** and **Torre d'en Gaumés**. Further west still is **Es Mercadal**, a hamlet in the shadow of **Monte Toro**, the island's highest peak, from where there are wonderful views. From Es Mercadal, it's a short journey southwest to **Es Migjorn Gran**, a pleasant if unremarkable little town that is the starting point for an excellent two- to three-hour hike down the **Barranc de Binigaus** (see box, p.226), while nearby lurks another big resort, **Sant Tomàs**. Back on the Me-1, you'll soon reach

5

RICHARD KANE AND THE CAMÍ D'EN KANE

In 1712, during the first British occupation of the island, **Richard Kane** (1662–1736) was appointed **Lieutenant-Governor of Menorca**, a post he held – with one or two brief interruptions – until the year of his death. When Kane arrived in Menorca, he found a dispirited and impoverished population governed from Ciutadella by a reactionary oligarchy. His initial preoccupation was with the island's **food supply**, which was woefully inadequate. He introduced new and improved strains of seed corn and had livestock imported from England – hence the Friesian cattle that remain the mainstay of the island's cheese-making industry. Meanwhile, a tax on alcohol provided cash to improve the port facilities at Maó and build the first **road** right across the island. Much of this road, the **Camí d'en Kane**, has since disappeared beneath newer versions, but part of it – from just north of Maó to Es Mercadal – has survived and now serves as a scenic alternative to the Me-1.

Kane's innovations were not at all to the taste of the Menorcan aristocracy, who, holed up in Ciutadella, were further offended when Kane moved the capital to Maó. They bombarded London with complaints, eventually inducing a formal governmental response in an open letter to the islanders entitled "A Vindication of Colonel Kane". Most Menorcans, however, seem to have welcomed Kane's benevolent administration – except in **religious matters**, where the governor caused great offence by holding Protestant services for his troops in Catholic churches. That apart, there's little doubt that, by the time of his death, Kane was a widely respected figure, whose endeavours were ill-served by the colonial indifference of many of his successors.

Ferreries, the fourth of the towns of the interior, from where it's a short hop south to **Cala Galdana**, an attractive resort of manageable proportions that's within easy hiking distance of several isolated **cove beaches**, most notably **Cala Macarella** and **Cala Turqueta**.

Alaior

ALAIOR, an old market town some 12km from Maó, has long been a nucleus of the island's dairy industry, but in recent years it has also become something of a manufacturing centre, its tangle of new – and newish – buildings spreading formlessly across the flat land north of the Me-1. This modern part of town is uninspiring, but beyond, about 1km up a steep hill, is the more appealing **old centre**, whose rabbit warren of narrow lanes and alleys surrounds the parish church of **Santa Eulalia**, on c/Retxats, a splendid edifice of fortress-like proportions built between 1674 and 1690. The church's main doorway is a Baroque extravagance, its exuberant scrollwork dripping with fruits and fronds, while the facade above accommodates a rose window and a pair of balustrades. Beyond the church – just up the hill to the northwest along bendy c/Angel – a mini-watchtower is plonked on top of the **Munt de l'Angel**, a hill from where you can look out over the countryside. From c/Angel, it's also a few metres north to the old town's main square, **Plaça Nova**, an attractive piazza flanked by pastel-painted civic buildings of considerable age.

The best time to be in Alaior is the second weekend of August, when the town lets loose with the **Festa de Sant Llorenç**, a drunken knees-up with displays of horsemanship. At its climax, a procession of horses tears through the packed town square, bucking and rearing, with their riders clinging on for dear life. Although no one seems to get hurt, you might enjoy the spectacle more from the safety of a balcony.

ARRIVAL AND DEPARTURE   ALAIOR

By bus Buses to Alaior loop through the southern edge of town, stopping on Carretera Nova at the foot of c/Miguel de Cervantes; from here, it's a steep (and convoluted) 500m haul north to the church of Santa Eulalia.
Destinations Maó (Mon–Fri every 30min–1hr, Sat & Sun every 1–2hr; 10min); Cala Galdana (April, May & Oct

Mon–Sat 2 daily; June–Sept 2 daily; 40min); Ciutadella (Mon–Fri every 30min–1hr, Sat & Sun every 1–2hr; 50min); Es Mercadal (Mon–Fri every 30min–1hr, Sat & Sun every 1–2hr; 15min); Es Migjorn Gran (May–Sept Mon–Sat 6 daily, Sun 4 daily; Nov–April Mon–Sat 4 daily; 20min); Ferreries (Mon–Fri every 30min–1hr, Sat & Sun every 1–2hr; 25min); Sant Tomàs (May–Sept Mon–Sat 6 daily, Sun 4 daily; Nov–April Mon–Sat 4 daily; 35min); Son Bou (May–Oct every 1–2hr, but no Sun service in May & Oct; 35min).

ACTIVITIES

Balearic Outdoor Holidays Alaior ✆ 0800 072 4832, ⊕ balearicoutdoorholidays.com. This family-owned outfit offers an outstanding range of week-long guided holidays, from birdwatching to painting, hiking and cycling. Their main focus is Menorca, where a week-long hiking tour costs in the region of €950–1100, and they operate from late April to mid-June and from early September to mid-October, with the occasional New Year extra. Hiking tours are geared to suit most levels of fitness and the majority involve the use of sections of the Camí de Cavalls, the long-distance footpath that encircles the island (see box, p.241). They provide all the necessary equipment, including coffee, tea and drinking water en route. Day-hikes (around €60 per person) are also available by prior arrangement; book well ahead of time.

Torralba d'en Salord

Carretera Alaior a Cala en Porter • April, May & Oct Mon–Sat 10am–6pm; June–Sept Mon–Sat 10am–8pm; Nov–March Mon–Fri 10am–2pm • €4, but free Nov–March • ⊕ descobreixmenorca.com • The site is 3km southeast of Alaior beside the road to Cala en Porter, but isn't served by public transport

One of the island's more extensive Talayotic settlements, **Torralba d'en Salord** is muddled by the old (and disused) Cala en Porter road, which slices right through the site, and by the modern stone walls built alongside both the old and new roads. From the car park, signs direct you around the remains of a **talayot**, just beyond which is the **taula**, one of the best preserved on the island. The rectangular enclosure surrounding it is also in good condition, and has been the subject of much conjecture by archeologists, who discovered that several of the recesses contained large fire pits, which may well have been used for the ritual slaughter of animals. It was, however, the unearthing of a tiny **bronze bull**, now in Maó's Museu de Menorca (see p.204), that really got the experts going. The theory was that the Menorcans (in common with several other prehistoric Mediterranean peoples) venerated the bull, with the *taula* being a stylized representation of a bull's head. The argument continues to this day. Beyond the *taula*, the signed trail circumnavigates the remainder of the site, which contains a confusion of stone remains, none of them especially revealing. The most noteworthy are the battered remains of a second **talayot** just next to the *taula*, and an underground chamber roofed with stone slabs.

Torre d'en Gaumés

Carretera Son Bou s/n • **Site** April, May & Oct Tues–Sat 9.30am–6pm, Sun–Mon 9.30am–3pm; June–Sept Tues–Sat 9.30am–8pm, Sun–Mon 9.30am–3pm; Nov–March daily dawn to dusk • €3, but free Nov–March • **Visitor centre** April–Oct Tues–Sun 9.30am–2pm • ⊕ descobreixmenorca.com • There's no public transport to the site; to get there by car take the Son Bou turning off the Me-1 at Alaior & then, after about 2.5km, veer left at the signposted fork

A visit to **Torre d'en Gaumés**, a rambling Talayotic settlement about 3.5km southwest of Alaior, begins at the pocket-sized **visitor centre**, where they show two short if eminently missable films on Talayotic life. From here, it's about 800m to the site itself, where the higher part – the area near the entrance – possesses three **talayots**, the largest of which is next to a broken-down **taula** in the centre of a walled, horseshoe-shaped enclosure. Together, the *taula* and the enclosure form what is presumed to have been the public part of the village, and it was here that archeologists unearthed a little bronze figure of the Egyptian god of knowledge, **Imhotep**, now in the Museu de Menorca in Maó (see p.204), a discovery that reinforced the theory that these enclosures possessed religious significance. In the

5

lower part of the settlement, there are the scant remains of several more houses, another walled enclosure and a comparatively sophisticated storage chamber – the subterranean *Sala Hipostila*. Here also are the clearly discernible remains of a **water collection system**, in which rainwater was channelled down the hillside between a series of shallow, artificial indentations to end up in underground cisterns and a cave. The latter had previously served as a funerary chamber – the site was inhabited and continually modified well into Roman times.

Son Bou and Sant Jaume Mediterrani

The coastal resort of **SON BOU**, located roughly 7km southwest of Alaior, boasts an extensive **cave complex**, cut into the cliff-face above the final part of the approach road. There are also the foundations of an early **Christian basilica**, set behind the beach at the east end of the resort, but these pale in comparison to the **beach**, a whopping pale-gold strand some 3km long and 40m wide. This is Menorca's longest beach, and behind it has mushroomed a massive tourist complex of skyscraper hotels and villa-villages that spreads west into the twin resort of **SANT JAUME MEDITERRANI**. The sand shelves gently into the sea, but the bathing isn't quite as safe as it appears: ocean currents are hazardous, particularly when the wind picks up, and you should watch for the green and red flags. The beach accommodates several bars, and **watersports equipment** is widely available – everything from jet-skis, snorkels and windsurfing boards down to sunloungers and pedalos. The development is at its crassest – and crowds at their worst – towards the east end of the beach, while bathing is much better to the west: here a strip of dune-fringed, marshy scrubland runs behind the strand, providing the shoreline with some much-needed protection and pushing the villa developments 1km or so inland.

ARRIVAL AND DEPARTURE   SON BOU AND SANT JAUME MEDITERRANI

By bus Buses to Son Bou and Sant Jaume Mediterrani travel along the road behind the beach with several stops on the way. The principal bus service is to Alaior (May–Oct daily every 1–2hr, but no Sun service in May & Oct; 35min) and Maó (May–Oct daily every 1–2hr, but no Sun service in May & Oct; 45min).

ACCOMMODATION

Sol Milanos/Sol Pingüinos Platja de Son Bou ☏ 971 37 12 00, ⊕ melia.com. Alongside each other, these two high-rise hotels boast 600 rooms between them and share facilities, including sun terraces, trampolines, outside pools, bars and restaurants. Neither has the most fashionable of rooms and they do tend to have bland white bathrooms, but they're acceptable enough, and half the rooms have small balconies with sea views – so ask for one of these. Closed mid-Oct to April. **€80**

Camping Son Bou Carretera St Jaume-Torre Solí, km3.5 ☏ 971 37 27 27, ⊕ campingsonbou.com. One of Menorca's rare campsites, the *Son Bou* is located on the more westerly of the two access roads linking the Me-1 with Sant Jaume Mediterrani. It's a well-equipped campsite with several hundred pitches set among the pine woods, as well as its own swimming pool, sports area, laundry and supermarket. Closed Oct– March. Tent pitch for two people with vehicle **€35**; cabin **€75**

FIVE GREAT MENORCAN BEACHES

Platja de Cavalleria See p.221
Son Bou See above
Cala Turqueta See p.242
Cala Macarella See p.242
Cala d'Algaiarens See p.243

Es Mercadal

ES MERCADAL, 9km northwest of Alaior along the Me-1, sits at the very centre of the island. Another old market town, it's an amiable sort of place whose antique centre of whitewashed houses and well-kept allotments is now edged by modern houses of a neat and trim demeanour. At the heart of the town, the minuscule main square, **Plaça Constitució**, has a couple of sleepy cafés and is a few paces from the Ruritanian **Ajuntament** (Town Hall), at c/Major 16, where locals come to shoot the breeze. That's just about it for sights unless, that is, you're bound for the summit of **Monte Toro**, which looms over the east side of town (see below).

ARRIVAL AND DEPARTURE	ES MERCADAL
By bus Es Mercadal's main bus stop is on Avgda Mestre Gari, just off the Me-1 on the southern edge of town, a 5min walk from Plaça Constitució: walk straight down Avgda Mestre Gari and its continuation, c/Nou. Destinations Alaior (Mon–Fri every 30min–1hr, Sat & Sun every 1–2hr; 15min); Cala Galdana (April, May & Oct	Mon–Sat 2 daily; June–Sept 2 daily; 25min); Ciutadella (Mon–Fri every 30min–1hr, Sat & Sun every 1–2hr; 35min); Es Migjorn Gran (April, May & Oct Mon–Sat 4 daily; June–Sept 4 daily; 15min); Es Mercadal (Mon–Fri every 30min–1hr, Sat & Sun every 1–2hr; 10min); Maó (Mon–Fri every 30min–1hr, Sat & Sun every 1–2hr; 25min).

ACCOMMODATION	
Hostal Jeni c/Mirada del Toro 81 **☎** 971 37 50 59, ⓦ hostaljeni.com. In a brightly decorated modern building, this *hostal* has fifty-odd spick-and-span en-suite bedrooms, as well as a swimming pool and sauna. It's	situated on the south side of the town centre just off the Me-1 – and about 100m from the bus stop. Tasty breakfast buffet, too. **€90**

Monte Toro

Es Mercadal is the starting point for the ascent of **MONTE TORO**, a steep 3.2km climb along a serpentine but easily driveable road. At 357m, the summit is the island's highest point and it offers wonderful **views**: on a good day you can see almost the whole of the island; in inclement weather, you can still see at least as far as Fornells. From this lofty vantage point, Menorca's **geological division** becomes apparent: to the north, Devonian rock (mostly reddish sandstone) supports a hilly, sparsely populated landscape edged by a ragged coastline; to the south, limestone predominates in a rippling, wooded plain that boasts the island's best farmland and, as it approaches the south coast, its deepest wooded gorges (*barrancs*).

It's likely that the **name of the hill** is derived from the Moorish al-Thor ("high point"), though the medieval Church invented an alternative etymology: in predictable fashion, this involves villagers (or monks) spotting a mysterious light on the mountain and, on closer investigation, being confronted by a bull (*toro*) which, lo and behold, obligingly leads them to a miracle-making statue of the Virgin. Whatever the truth, a statue of the Virgin – the **Verge del Toro** – was installed in a shrine here in the thirteenth century and Monte Toro has been a place of pilgrimage ever since. The ceremonial highlight is on the first Sunday of May, when the **Festa de la Verge del Toro** (Festival of the Virgin of the Bull) begins with a special Mass on the summit of Monte Toro and continues with a knees-up down in Es Mercadal.

The Augustinians added a **monastery** to the original hilltop shrine in the seventeenth century, but fearful islanders soon interrupted their monkish reveries by building a small **fortress** here against the threat of an Ottoman invasion. Bits of both the fort and the monastery survive, the former in a square stone **tower** that now stands forlorn and neglected, the latter incorporated within the present complex of buildings, where, flanking a cobbled courtyard, you'll find a couple of gift shops, a terrace café, a restaurant and the old monastery church, the **Santuari del Toro**. But there aren't any monks – they left decades ago. High above the complex stands a **statue of Christ the Redeemer**, erected in honour of those Menorcans who died in a grubby colonial war launched by Spain in Morocco in the 1920s.

5

A DAY'S HIKE: ES MIGJORN GRAN TO THE COAST

Circular • 8km • 150m ascent • 3hr–3hr 30min • Moderate • Trailhead GPS: +39° 56′ 58.42″, +4° 3′ 2.57″

Despite its modest dimensions, Menorca packs a surprising diversity into its landscape. One of the island's most unexpected topographical features are the dramatic limestone **gorges**, or *barrancs*, which score the southern coast, running from the hills inland down to the sea. Starting in the inland village of **Es Migjorn Gran**, this walk follows one of these gorges, the **Barranc de Binigaus**, down to the coast near Sant Tomàs, passing through an area rich in Talayotic remains and impressive natural limestone formations.

The **walk starts** on the edge of Es Migjorn Gran at the **car park** outside the municipal sports stadium (Camp Municipal d'Esports), by the town's main roundabout. From here, walk along the right-hand side of the main road (Avgda del Mar) in the direction of Sant Tomàs as far as the **Bar S'Auba**. Turn right up the hill along Avgda David Russell and continue to the T-junction with the Escola Publica in front of you and turn left – a total distance of about 450m.

The first half of the walk follows the road that you are now on. After a short while, it becomes a stony track, meandering slowly downhill towards the coast. The road starts by running picturesquely between limestone walls flanked by handsome old Aleppo pines, an old enclosure housing the substantial remains of two *talayots*, and a cemetery. Some 200m further on you'll pass another *talayot* on your right, followed by an attractive ensemble of white houses and Menorcan-style gates. Continue for a further 1km, passing enclosures littered with limestone boulders, until you reach the attractive old whitewashed farmstead of *Binigaus Vell*.

Just past here you'll have your first sight of the sea. The path continues for a further 750m, with the dramatic limestone formations of the **Barranc de Binigaus** coming into view on your left. Beyond here, the track passes through an intricate but overgrown system of terraces and enclosures before climbing past a potholed limestone outcrop to reach the brow of the hill. Two more *talayots* are now visible to your left; the land hereabouts holds an incredible jumble of natural, prehistoric and more recent agricultural stone-working, with the Barranc de Binigaus issuing into the sea via a narrow defile – your eventual goal – far ahead and below.

Descend through a Menorcan-style gate to the farmhouse of **Binigaus Nou**, a striking baronial-looking structure. About 50m before a second farm gate, turn right off the track onto a narrow path signed **Cova-y-Platja**. This leads to an unusual (but strangely unsigned) Talayotic **hypostyle chamber** and a fine view of the limestone cliffs of a secondary arm of the *barranc* behind. From the chamber continue along the path to rejoin the track. From here, the track hairpins down into the *barranc* beneath high walls of limestone and then proceeds past further wildly overgrown agricultural terracing before reaching the bottom of the hill at a Menorcan-style gate opposite a path signposted to the Cova dels Coloms.

The route continues along this path to the *cova* (cave). If you want to make the brief **detour to the coast**, walk through the gate ahead and continue straight on for 150m to reach the sea next to an old gun emplacement buried in the dunes and covered in windswept vegetation. If you're in need of refreshment, detour left here and walk along the beach for 750m to reach the resort of **Sant Tomàs** (see p.228). Back on the main route, head along the path signposted to the Cova dels Coloms. This path gradually ascends back into the *barranc* for 1km through woodland before reaching a large dry-stone wall and a fork. Head right here, along the narrowing gorge and beneath increasingly impressive limestone cliffs, scored with caves, until, after a further 750m, you reach a gap in another large wall marked with a splash of red paint. Pass through the gap and then bear left – ignoring the path going straight ahead – up a narrow path through thick woodland for about 500m, where you need to look out for a narrow side path joining acutely from the right. Take this side path and follow it uphill for 20m and then turn left up a zigzagging stone terrace to reach the **Cova dels Coloms** – a huge natural cave, impressive for its size if nothing else (the copious graffiti and overpowering smell of guano are less appealing).

Retrace your steps to the main path and turn right. After a few metres the path climbs to the left and becomes boulder strewn. It then zigzags up out of the gorge and returns you to the original track that you came down on at a point between Binigaus Vell and Binigaus Nou. Turn right and retrace your steps uphill to **Es Migjorn Gran** (see opposite).

The Santuari del Toro

The **Santuari del Toro** is entered via a low and deep stone porch decorated with flowers and shrubs. Inside, the barrel-vaulted nave is a modest, truncated affair dating from 1595, its gloominess partly dispelled by a central dome. The most prominent feature is the gaudy 1940s high altarpiece, whose fancy woodwork swarms with cherubs and frames the much-venerated **Verge del Toro**, depicting the crowned Virgin holding Jesus in her arms with the enterprising bull of folkloric fame at her feet. The statue is typical of the so-called black Catalan Madonnas, made either from black-stained wood or dark stone.

Es Migjorn Gran

Trailing along a low ridge amid intricate terraced fields, **ES MIGJORN GRAN** ("great southerly wind") is a sleepy little hamlet that lies some 7km southwest of Es Mercadel. One of several settlements founded on the island in the eighteenth century, it is the only one not to have been laid out by foreigners and, consequently, the gridiron streets of the likes of Es Castell are replaced by a more organic layout, the

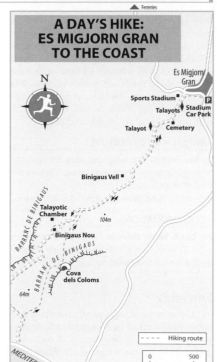

A DAY'S HIKE: ES MIGJORN GRAN TO THE COAST

5

houses of the old agricultural workers straggling along the elongated main street, c/Major, as it curves through town. While the village hardly sets the pulse racing, it is a peaceful and relaxing spot and it is also the starting point for an excellent hike (see opposite).

ARRIVAL AND DEPARTURE
ES MIGJORN GRAN

By bus Buses pull in beside the roundabout on the bypass (the Me-18) on the southeast side of Es Migjorn Gran, a 5min walk from c/Major.

Destinations Alaior (May–Sept Mon–Sat 6 daily, Sun 4 daily; Nov–April Mon–Sat 4 daily; 20min); Ciutadella (Mon–Fri 2 daily; 35min); Es Mercadal (April, May & Oct Mon–Sat 4 daily; June–Sept 4 daily; 15min); Ferreries (Mon–Fri 3 daily; 20min); Maó (May–Sept Mon–Sat 6 daily, Sun 4 daily; Nov–April Mon–Sat 4 daily; 30min); Sant Tomàs (May–Sept Mon–Sat 6 daily, Sun 4 daily; Nov–April Mon–Sat 4 daily; 15min).

ACCOMMODATION AND EATING

★**Fonda S'Engolidor** c/Major 3 ☎971 37 01 93, ⓦsengolidor.es. This small, family-run hotel-cum-B&B, in an attractively restored old terrace house, has five extremely cosy guest rooms decorated in a bright and breezy style, with a scattering of bygones to catch the eye. It's located on the main street towards the west (Ferreries) end of town and is also home to an excellent restaurant (see below). Closed Nov–April. **€80**

Hotel Rural Binigaus Vell c/Camí de Sa Mala Garba ☎971 05 40 50, ⓦbinigausvell.es. One of the swankiest places to stay on the entire island – and definitely worthy of the term boutique – this whitewashed *hotel rural* occupies an

immaculately renovated old farmhouse. The rooms have very high ceilings and spacious baths, and the best are built into the stone that once made up the stables. Every mod con, which is reflected in the price. Just 1km southwest of Es Migjorn Gran. **€240**

★**S'Engolidor** c/Major 3 ☎971 37 01 93, ⓦsengolidor .es. On the ground floor of the *Fonda* (see above), this is a smashing little restaurant, where the emphasis is on traditional Menorcan cuisine with mains around €19. The restaurant has a charming, (summer-only) courtyard garden with views over a wooded gorge; reservations are strongly advised. Tues–Fri 7–11pm, Sat & Sun 1–4pm & 7–11pm.

5

Sant Tomàs

South of Es Migjorn Gran, the road scuttles along a wooded ravine that leads down to the south coast and the really rather crass hotel and apartment buildings of **SANT TOMÀS**. The resort's saving grace is its inviting 3km-long sandy **beach**, very similar to that of Son Bou, a couple of headlands away to the east. The road reaches the shore halfway along the beach, which is called **Platja Sant Adeodat** to the west and **Platja Sant Tomàs** to the east. The latter is easily the more congested, and it's here you'll find the resort's high-rise hotels, as well as your choice of **watersports** facilities, including windsurfing boards, jet-skis and pedalos.

ARRIVAL AND DEPARTURE   SANT TOMÀS

By bus Buses to Sant Tomàs scoot along the seafront boulevard, stopping – among several places – in front of the *Hotel Nelson*.

Destinations Alaior (May–Sept Mon–Sat 6 daily, Sun 4

daily; Nov–April Mon–Sat 4 daily; 35min); Es Migjorn Gran (May–Sept Mon–Sat 6 daily, Sun 4 daily; Nov–April Mon–Sat 4 daily; 15min); Maó (May–Sept Mon–Sat 6 daily, Sun 4 daily; Nov–April Mon–Sat 4 daily; 1hr).

ACCOMMODATION

Sol Beach House Menorca Platja Sant Tomàs s/n ☎ 971 37 00 50, ⓦ melia.com. Smart and modern high-rise four-star hotel, overlooking the beach and with all the

facilities you might expect, including outside pools. The rooms are briskly modern – and very chain – but most have sea-facing balconies. Closed Nov–April. **€150**

Ferreries

Tucked into a hollow beneath a steep hill, **FERRERIES** is an unassuming little town, about 8km west of Es Mercadal, whose ancient whitewashed houses flank and frame a batch of narrow, sloping streets. A surprise here is the pagoda-like piece of modern sculpture in the main square, the **Plaça Espanya**, while just up the hill at the back of the *plaça* – up along c/Fred – stands the neatly shuttered **Ajuntament**, primly facing the parish church of **Sant Bartomeu**, a largely eighteenth-century edifice with an 1884-vintage belfry tacked onto the top. The liveliest time to be here is on Saturday morning, when a small food and crafts **market** (9am–1pm) is held on Plaça Espanya.

Jaime Mascaró Factory Shop

Carretera General s/n • Mon–Sat 9.30am–8pm • ☎ 971 37 38 37, ⓦ mascaro.com

Ferreries has a long history as a centre of Menorca's shoe-making industry, and although the cottage-cobblers of yesteryear are long gone, the town is still home to a big-name shoe manufacturer, **Jaime Mascaró**. They have a large factory shop here, about 1km or so east of the town centre along the main drag (Carretera General) on what was formerly the Me-1, though this now loops round the town to the north.

Hort Sant Patrici

Camí de Sant Patrici s/n • May–Sept Mon–Sat 9am–1pm & 4.30–8pm; Oct–April Mon–Fri 9am–1pm & 4–6pm, Sat 9am–1pm • Free • Guided tours on Tues, Thurs & Sat at 10am with advance reservations recommended • ☎ 971 37 34 85, ⓦ santpatrici.com • There's no public transport; to get there follow the signs from the Me-1 as it swings round the northern edge of Ferreries

In a pleasant rural setting just to the north of Ferreries, the enterprising **Hort Sant Patrici** comprises an assortment of farm buildings surrounding a good-looking *hacienda*, all set in attractive gardens. The main deal here is the locally produced **Menorcan cheese**: this is the most enjoyable of the several cheese-making plants open to the public on the island and the place is well set up for visitors, who can watch cheese being made at the factory, buy it at the shop and pop into the cheese museum. You can also stroll the well-maintained gardens, eat at the restaurant, drop by the winery – Patrici has its own vineyard – and stay here at the *Ca Na Xini* hotel (see opposite). As for the **cheese**, which is known generically as **Queso Mahon** after the island capital from where it was traditionally exported, it's a richly textured, white,

5

semi-fat cheese made from pasteurized cow's milk with a touch of ewe's milk added for extra flavour. It's sold at four different stages of maturity, either *tierno* (young), *semi-curado* (semi-mature), *curado* (mature) or *añejo* (very mature).

ARRIVAL AND DEPARTURE
FERRERIES

By bus Buses to Ferreries cut through the northern edge of the town centre, stopping in front of the *Nou Vimpi* café, a 4min walk from Plaça Espanya via Avgda Verge del Toro.
Destinations Alaior (Mon–Fri every 30min–1hr, Sat & Sun every 1–2hr; 25min); Cala Galdana (April, May & Oct Mon–Sat 6 daily; June–Sept 5–6 daily; 15min); Ciutadella

(Mon–Fri every 30min–1hr, Sat & Sun every 1–2hr 25min); Es Mercadal (Mon–Fri every 30min–1hr, Sat & Sun every 1–2hr; 10min); Es Migjorn Gran (Mon–Fri 3 daily; 20min); Maó (Mon–Fri every 30min–1hr, Sat & Sun every 1–2hr; 35min).

ACCOMMODATION AND EATING

Ca Na Xini Camí de Sant Patrici s/n ☎971 37 45 12, ⓦ canaxini.com. A self-styled "boutique" hotel of minimalist design, shoehorned into the bright and cheerful old manor house of the Hort Sant Patrici estate (see opposite). There are just eight guest rooms here, all with shades of white and cream to the fore. Two-night minimum stay applies for most of the year. No children. **€220**

Hotel Loar Avgda Verge del Toro 2 ☎971 37 41 81, ⓦ loarferreries.com. This straightforward three-star hotel occupies a four-storey modern block right in the centre of town. There's a pleasant rooftop pool and terrace, and although the rooms are decoratively uninspired, they are

comfortable and functional. **€50**

Nou Vimpi Plaça del Princep Joan Carles 5 ☎971 37 31 99. Something of a local institution, this popular café-bar serves a tasty range of tapas (from €4) and has a large terrace at the front beside the town bus stop. Daily 6am–11.30pm.

Hotel Ses Sucreres Sant Joan 13 ☎971 37 41 92, ⓦ hotelsessucreres.com. Formerly a village candle shop, this cosy three-star hotel has just six rooms of modest demeanour, but with local paintings hanging on the walls. It's all very nicely done – indeed it's charming. In the centre of the village, the briefest of walks from Plaça Espanya. **€140**

Cala Galdana

The bustling resort of **CALA GALDANA**, 9km south of Ferreries, occupies what was once a much-loved beauty spot, its clutter of high-rises and low-rises disfiguring – at least in part – a once-beautiful cove framed by wooded, limestone cliffs. More positively, the curving sandy **beach** and its pint-sized rocky promontory are still very appealing; the resort boasts several good hotels; you can rent all sorts of **watersports** equipment, from pedalos and water scooters to windsurfing boards and snorkelling tackle; and you can escape the crowds by hiking west or east along the coast to more secluded coves (see box below).

ARRIVAL AND DEPARTURE
CALA GALDANA

By bus Buses to Cala Galdana stop in the centre of the resort on Passatge Riu, a brief stroll from the beach.

Destinations Alaior (April, May & Oct Mon–Sat 2 daily; June–Sept 2 daily; 40min); Ciutadella (April, May & Oct

---

COASTAL WALKS AROUND CALA GALDANA

There are several exquisite **cove beaches** within easy walking distance of **Cala Galdana** via the **Camí de Cavalls** (see box, p.241). The most obvious choice is **Cala Mitjana** (no facilities), just 1km to the east, a broad strip of sand set at the back of a chubby little cove with wooded cliffs to either side. One favourite sport here is jumping into the crystal-clear waters from the surrounding cliffs. It's reached via a 30min walk along a footpath that begins at the Plaça Na Gran car park, near the main entrance to the *Hotel Melia Gavilanes* (see p.230).

Heading west from Cala Galdana, it takes about an hour to walk to **Cala Macarella** and a few minutes more to get to the neighbouring **Cala Macarelleta** (see p.242): climb the steps opposite the large *Hotel Artiem Audax*, which stands near the beach at the west end of the resort, and keep going along the path. Continuing west along the coast from Cala Macarella on the Camí de Cavalls, it takes about 2hr to walk to the next major beach, **Cala Turqueta** (see p.242).

5

Mon–Sat 6 daily; June–Sept 5–6 daily; 40min); Es Mercadal (April, May & Oct Mon–Sat 2 daily; June–Sept 2 daily; 25min); Ferreries (April, May & Oct Mon–Sat 6 daily; June–Sept 5–6 daily; 15min); Maó (April, May & Oct Mon–Sat 2 daily; June–Sept 2 daily; 50min).

ACCOMMODATION

Camping S'Atalaia Carretera Cala Galdana, km4.5 ☎ 971 37 42 32, ⓦ campingsatalaia.com. This medium-sized campsite has a full battery of amenities, including an outdoor swimming pool, a café, a laundry and a supermarket. It's a popular spot, not least because pine trees shade much of the site, so advance reservations are advised. The campsite is located about 3km from Cala Galdana, beside the road from Ferreries, and there is a bus stop outside – but be sure to let the driver know you want to get off here, otherwise you will go whizzing by. Pitch prices include vehicle and electrical hook-up. Closed Oct–March. Two-person pitch €30

Melia Gavilanes Avgda Sa Punta s/n ☎ 971 15 45 45, ⓦ melia.com. Cala Galdana has four large chain hotels, the pick of which is this four-star, set in its own verdant grounds and built against the cliffs that frame the beach. The hotel has every facility, from air conditioning and swimming pools to satellite TV, and most of the attractive, modern guest rooms have sea-facing balconies. Closed Nov–April. €180

Torrellafuda

Open access • Free • ⓦ descobreixmenorca.com • The site is just south of the Me-1, 8km from Ferreries & 9km from Ciutadella; take the clearly signed, 800m-long dirt road from the Me-1

Travelling west from Ferreries, the Me-1 soon leaves the central hills behind for the flatlands that herald Ciutadella. These are dotted with some of the island's more important prehistoric sites, the first one of real significance being **Torrellafuda**. From the car park, it's a brief walk to the site, where a particularly well-preserved *talayot* stands close to the *taula*, which is hidden away in a little wooded dell. The rustic setting is delightful – and it's a perfect spot for a picnic.

Naveta d'es Tudons

Easter–Oct Mon 9am–2.30pm, Tues–Sun 9am–8.30pm; Nov–Easter open access • €2, but free Nov–Easter • ⓦ descobreixmenorca.com • To get to the site, take the turning off the Me-1, almost 3km west of the Torrellafuda turning & 5km east of Ciutadella

Standing in a field a short stroll from the Me-1, the conspicuous **Naveta d'es Tudons** is easily the best-preserved *naveta* on the island. Seven metres high and 14m long, it consists of massive stone blocks slotted together using a sophisticated dry-stone technique. The narrow entrance on the west side leads into a small antechamber, which was once sealed off by a stone slab; beyond lies the main chamber where the bones of the dead were stashed away after the flesh had been removed. Folkloric memories of the *navetas'* original purpose survived into modern times – Menorcans were loath to go near these odd-looking and solitary monuments until well into the nineteenth century.

Lithica Pedreres de S'hostal

Camí Vell, km1 s/n • May–Oct Mon–Sat 9.30am–2.30pm & 4.30–8.30pm, Sun 9.30am–2.30pm; Nov–April daily 9.30am–2.30pm • €5, free Nov–March • ☎ 971 48 15 78, ⓦ lithica.es • The site is clearly signed from the outer ring road (the RC-2), just south of the main Me-1

One of the island's more unusual sights, the **Lithica Pedreres de S'hostal** occupies a former quarry on the edge of Ciutadella, some 2km to the east of town. Stone was quarried here for several centuries, only ending in 1994, and the old workings are now open to the public. From the ticket office, you descend to the old quarry floor, where you can wander among a labyrinth of giant stone stacks cut to all sorts of fanciful shapes. It was long the custom for the quarrymen to plant gardens in some of their old workings and there's a lovely verdant garden here today, shaded by orange and almond trees, as well as a stone maze and an open-air theatre, which is used for live performances.

Ciutadella

Like Maó, **CIUTADELLA** sits high above the sea, but here navigation into its old city-centre harbour is far more difficult, up a narrow channel too slender for all but the smallest of cargo ships. Nonetheless, despite this nautical inconvenience, Ciutadella was the island's capital right up until the eighteenth century, when it was usurped by Maó, initiating a long period of economic stagnation which only ended with the tourist boom of the last decades. One happy consequence of this stagnation is evident today in Ciutadella's compact **town centre**, which has barely been touched by modern development, its narrow, cobbled streets flanked by old and distinguished mansions and a fine set of Baroque and Gothic churches, all very much in the grand Spanish tradition. An ambitious renovation programme has further enhanced the centre, restoring most of the old stone facades to their honey-coloured best, and although it's the whole ensemble that gives Ciutadella its appeal, rather than any specific sight, the **Cathedral** is a real Gothic highlight and stately **Plaça d'es Born** is undoubtedly the Balearics' finest piazza. All in all, it's a lovely place to stay, and nothing else on Menorca

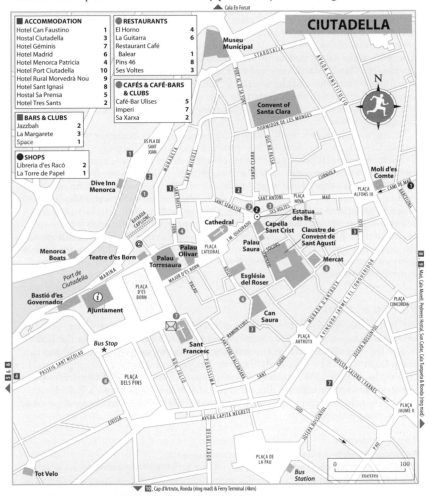

5

rivals the evening *passeig* (promenade), when the townsfolk amble the narrow streets of the centre, dropping in on pavement cafés as the sun sets. Allow at least a couple of days – the town has several good **places to stay** and several excellent **restaurants** – more if you seek out one of the beguiling **cove beaches** within easy striking distance: there are several wonderful spots to choose from, but **Cala Turqueta** and **Cala Macarella** are probably the pick of the bunch. Save time also for the prehistoric sites hereabouts, especially **Naveta d'es Tudons** (see p.230) and **Son Catlar** (see p.241).

Brief history

Chosen by the **Romans**, adopted by the **Moors** (as Medina Minurka) and then rebuilt by the **Catalans** during the Reconquista, Ciutadella was razed by Turkish corsairs in 1558, a brutal episode that was actually something of an accident. The Ottomans had dispatched 15,000 soldiers and 150 warships west to assist their French allies against the Habsburgs. With no particular place to go, the Turks rolled around the Mediterranean for a few weeks and, after deciding Maó wasn't worth the candle, they happened on Ciutadella, where the garrison numbered just forty. For the locals, the results of the assault were cataclysmic. The **Turks** carried off some three thousand captives – around eighty percent of the population – transporting them to the slave markets of Istanbul, and when the new Spanish governor arrived, he was forced to live in a cave. As news spread of the disaster, the pope organized a European whip-round and, with the money in his bag, an intrepid Menorcan doctor, one **Marcos Martí**, ventured east to buy the slaves back. Martí was remarkably successful and the returning hostages, together with the survivors of the assault, determinedly **rebuilt Ciutadella** in grand style. They refortified the town centre and then, reassured, set about adorning it with fine stone churches and sweeping mansions.

Throughout the seventeenth century, Menorca's leading **landowners** chewed the cud in Ciutadella, confident of their position and power. They were, however, in for a shock: the colonial powers of the eighteenth century had little time for the town's feeble port when compared with Maó's magnificent inlet, and the **British** simply – and abruptly – moved the capital to Maó in 1722. Thereafter, Maó flourished as a trading centre, while Ciutadella hit the skids, though the bulk of the Menorcan aristocracy decided to stay exactly where they were. As a result, the island's foreign rulers pretty much left them to stew in their own very Catholic juice – an increasingly redundant, landowning class far from the wheels of mercantile power. Bypassed and ignored by just about everyone, Ciutadella slipped into a long-lasting economic reverie that has, by coincidence, preserved the town's old and beautiful centre as if in aspic.

Plaça d'es Born

Primarily a nineteenth-century creation, **Plaça d'es Born** is a handsome affair whose centrepiece is a soaring **obelisk** commemorating the futile defence against the Turks in 1558. The obelisk's original Latin inscription, penned by the politician and historian **Josep Quadrado** (1819–96), reads "Here we fought until death for our religion and our country in the year 1558." Such grandiose poppycock was typical of Quadrado, then the region's most prominent politician and leader of the reactionary Catholic Union, which bombarded Madrid with complaints and petitions whenever the local governor did anything progressive.

The Ajuntament

Plaça d'es Born 15 • No public access, except for ground-floor tourist office (see p.238)

The Plaça d'es Born is flanked by several notable buildings, beginning on its western side with the **Ajuntament** (Town Hall), whose early nineteenth-century arches and crenellations mimic Moorish style, purposely recalling the time when the site was occupied by the Wali's *alcázar* (palace), which was razed to the ground after the Reconquista.

Teatre d'es Born

Plaça d'es Born 19

On the Plaça d'es Born's north side, architectural pride of place goes to the **Teatre d'es Born**, a neat, late nineteenth-century structure built to salvage some municipal pride: the merchants of Maó had just completed their opera house, so the oligarchs of Ciutadella promptly followed suit – though they weren't quite as energetic when it came to getting people to perform here and the building lay neglected for years. It's now reopened as a cinema.

The Palau Torresaura

Plaça d'es Born

The northeast corner of the Plaça d'es Born is dominated by the sweeping lines of the **Palau Torresaura**, built in the nineteenth century, but looking far older, and the grandest of several aristocratic mansions edging the plaza. Embellished by two handsome loggias, its frontage proclaims the family coat of arms above a large wooden door leading into a spacious courtyard. The antique interior, however, is off limits – like most of its neighbours, the house is still owner-occupied.

Església de St Francesc

c/Purissima s/n • Core hours Mon–Sat 9am–1pm • Free

The **Església de St Francesc**, standing in the southeast corner of the square, is a clean-lined, unpretentious structure whose hybrid architecture reflects the island's ups and downs. The original church was constructed shortly after the Reconquista, and it was here in 1301 that Jaume II met his nobles to parcel up Menorca into the feudal estates – the *Cavalleries* (from *cavaller*, the Catalan for baron) – that cemented his kingdom. In 1558, the Turks fired the church, but it was rebuilt to the original specifications in the 1590s, with further embellishments added later: the Baroque side door in the eighteenth century, the dome in the nineteenth. Like most of Ciutadella's churches, Republicans ransacked the place during the Spanish Civil War, but bits and pieces have survived, notably a motley crew of polychromatic saints. There's a further reminder of the war above the confessional at the transept, where you'll spot a black-and-white photograph and memorial to **Juan Huguet Cordona**, a young priest who was killed by the Republicans in 1936, earning him the church's accolade as a martyr.

The Cathedral

Plaça Catedral s/n • Core hours Mon–Sat 10am–4pm • €3, free when unattended in winter; combined ticket with Sant Agustí (see p.235) €5 • ☎ 971 35 65 23

The handsome **Catedral** (Cathedral) was built by Jaume II on the site of the chief mosque in the fourteenth century, but was subsequently remodelled after the Turkish onslaught of 1558. During the rebuilding, the flying buttresses of the original version were partly encased within a thick stone wall to guard against future attack, a modification that gives the cathedral its distinctive appearance today. The Gothic **side door** – on the south side of the church – was, however, left intact, its arching columns decorated with strange-looking beasts and the coats of arms of Aragón and Ciutadella, all surmounted by a delicate carving of the Magi honouring the infant Christ. Another survivor was the set of fierce-looking **gargoyles** that decorates the buttresses at roof level. The principal (west) **entrance** was added much later, in 1813, its flashy Neoclassical portico contrasting with the rest of the church and the intricate rose window above.

5

The interior

Inside, light filters through the stained glass of the narrow, lofty windows to bathe part of the **nave and high altar** in an ethereal glow. There's also a sequence of glitzy Baroque **side chapels**, though these look mediocre when compared with the beautifully carved stonework of the chapel just off the top left-hand corner of the nave. Most of the church's old furnishings and fittings were destroyed when the Republicans took control of Menorca during the Civil War – there are photos of the destruction on display in the **sacristy** and **vestry** at the back of the church among a scattering of ecclesiastical baubles, vestments, chalices, reliquaries and so forth. There was good reason for this outburst of anti-clericalism. Though the British had made Maó the island's capital in 1722, Ciutadella remained Menorca's ecclesiastical centre and, almost without exception, its resident Catholic hierarchy were rich and reactionary in equal measure. The priesthood enthusiastically proclaimed its support for the officers of the Maó garrison when the latter declared for Franco in July 1936, but this turned out to be a major gaffe. The bulk of the garrison stayed loyal to the Republic and, allied with local left-wing groups, they captured the rebels, shot their leaders and savaged Ciutadella's main churches as retribution.

Palau Olivar

Plaça de la Catedral 8 • Daily: May, Sept & Oct 10am–2pm; June–Aug 10am–3pm & 7–9pm • €3 • ☎ 647 63 44 87

Directly opposite the cathedral's main entrance is the **Palau Olivar**, whose stern, eighteenth-century facade is partly relieved by a pair of miniature balconies fronted by wrought-iron grilles. The mansion is still in private hands, but during the summer it's usually open to the public, who can wander through a set of formal rooms with family portraits and a mishmash of period furniture. In 1707, the house witnessed one of the town's crueller episodes, when a reclusive mother and daughter who worked and lived here were accused of witchcraft. Found guilty on palpably potty charges, the older woman was sent to prison for life, and the younger was executed – by any standard, a heavy price to pay for not joining in the town's social life.

Església del Roser

c/Roser • Hours vary with exhibitions, but core hours Mon–Sat 10.30am–1.30pm & 5.30–8.30pm • Free • ☎ 971 38 35 63

Dating from the seventeenth century, the **Església del Roser** is fronted by a hulking Churrigueresque facade, whose quartet of pillars is festooned with intricate tracery. The church was the subject of bitter controversy when the British governor Richard Kane (see p.222) commandeered it for Church of England services, which was not at all to the liking of the Dominican friars who owned the place. Now deconsecrated, the church's interior has been covered in cream paint and is used for temporary exhibitions of contemporary, mostly local, art and crafts.

Carrer Josep Maria Quadrodo

Plaça Catedral fades east into **c/Josep Maria Quadrado**, one section of the narrow main street that cuts right across the old town and the spot where – near the corner with c/ Seminari – you'll spy a perky bronze effigy of a lamb stuck on a column. The lamb concerned, the **Estatua des Be**, which symbolizes the Lamb of God, carries a flag bearing the cross of St John the Baptist and is a reminder of Ciutadella's biggest shindig, the Festa de Sant Joan (see p.33). Beyond the lamb, the next stretch of c/J.M. Quardodo is crimped by a block of whitewashed vaulted arches, **Ses Voltes**, distinctly Moorish in inspiration and a suitable setting for a string of busy shops and cafés. Further on is **Plaça Nova**, an attractive little square edged by popular pavement cafés, and then it's onto **Plaça Alfons III**, where you leave the cramped alleys of the old town behind.

Carrer Seminari

At the north end of **c/Seminari**, just metres from the cathedral, it's hard to miss the flamboyant facade of the **Capella del Sant Crist** (no fixed opening hours; free), a Baroque extravaganza with garlands of fruit and a pair of gargoyle-like faces. Inside, the intimate nave supports an octagonal stone dome and is also home to a charming if unattributed medieval panel painting depicting three local saints of obscure significance. Overseeing proceedings from above the high altar is an effigy of the crucified Christ, which is supposed to have dripped with sweat in 1661 and remains a popular object of devotion even today.

Next door to the church is a savings bank that occupies part of the **Palau Saura**, built in grand style by the British for a Menorcan aristocrat, Joan Miquel Saura, in return for his help in planning their successful invasion of 1708: a life-long opponent of the Spanish Bourbons, Saura took full advantage of the British occupation to take revenge on his Menorcan enemies; the British turned a blind eye.

Claustre de Convent de Sant Agustí

c/Seminari 7 • May–Oct Mon–Sat 10am–4pm • €3, combined ticket with Cathedral (see p.233) €5 • ☎ 971 48 12 97

The mildly enjoyable **Claustre de Convent de Sant Agustí** (Cloister and Convent of St Augustine) is tucked away behind an elongated perimeter wall, a sober, stone affair interrupted by two doorways – one for the cloisters and the museum, the other for the church, which was deconsecrated long ago. This old church doorway is surmounted by the most bizarre of sculpted cameos, depicting the Virgin Mary armed with a cudgel and standing menacingly over a cringing, cat-like dragon-devil.

The cloisters and museum

Sant Agustí's well-preserved **cloisters** are an exercise in Baroque symmetry, their vaulted aisles sporting a neat set of coats of arms and religious motifs. The rooms surrounding the cloisters now accommodate a modest **museum**, a hotchpotch of a collection which begins with an assortment of Talayotic and early classical archeological finds, most memorably a selection of small and delicate effigies. Among them is a superbly crafted miniature bull and a similarly exquisite little mermaid (*sirena*), almost certainly Greek bronzes dating from the fifth century BC.

A further room is devoted to the Impressionistic paintings of Ciutadella's **Pere Daura** (1896–1976). Daura concentrated on still-lifes, landscapes and village scenes, but as a one-time Communist and Republican soldier, he was obliged to leave Spain after Franco seized power, spending most of his later life in France and the USA. Look out also for the paintings of **José Roberto Torrent** (1904–90). The son of a cobbler, Torrent is usually regarded as Ciutadella's finest painter, a prolific and versatile artist who began with deftly coloured Menorcan landscapes in the Realist tradition. Later, in the 1960s, his paintings became more expressionistic, rendering island scenes in striking colours and shapes, but perhaps his most evocative work was produced in his old age with paintings of infirmity, loneliness and isolation.

Moving on, the vaulted **refectory** is a good-looking chamber with some dreadful eighteenth-century religious paintings; finally, on the left-hand side of the cloister, is the domed and single-aisled **Església dels Socors**, whose standard-issue Baroque decoration culminates in an extraordinarily artless high altar.

The market

Plaça Francesc Netto & Plaça Llibertat • Mon–Sat 9am–2pm

Ciutadella's principal **market** (*mercat*) rambles over two miniature squares, Plaça Francesc Netto and Plaça Llibertat. This is another delightful corner of the old town, where fresh fruit, vegetable, meat and fish stalls mingle with lively and inexpensive cafés selling the freshest of *ensaimadas*. The fish stalls occupy a dinky

5

little structure of 1895; the rest fill out a slender arcaded gallery that was constructed thirty years before as part of a municipal drive to clean up the town's food supply.

Convent of Santa Clara

c/Santa Clara • No public access

From c/J.M. Quadrado, a long, straight street – c/Santa Clara – slices north, hemmed in by the walls of old aristocratic palaces. At the top is the **Convent of Santa Clara**, a mundanely modern incarnation of a centuries-old foundation. In 1749, this was the site of a scandal that had tongues clacking from Ciutadella to Maó. During the night, three young women hopped over the convent wall and placed themselves under the protection of their British boyfriends. Even worse, as far as the local clergy were concerned, they wanted to turn Protestant and marry their men. In this delicate situation, **Governor Blakeney** had the room where the women were staying sealed up by a priest every night. But he refused to send them back to the convent and allowed the weddings to go ahead, thereby compounding a religious animosity that had begun in the days of Richard Kane.

Museu Municipal

c/Portal de Sa Font s/n • May–Sept Tues–Sat 10am–2pm & 6–9pm; Oct–April Tues–Sat 10am–2pm • €2.50, free on Wed • ☎ 971 38 02 97, 🌐 ajciutadella.org

The **Museu Municipal** occupies part of the old city fortifications, a massive bastion overlooking a slender ravine that had, until it was redirected, a river running along its base and on into the harbour. The museum consists of a long vaulted chamber that is mostly given over to a wide range of archeological artefacts, primarily a substantial collection of **Talayotic remains**, featuring finds garnered from all over the island. Each cabinet is clearly labelled in Catalan (a free English guide is available at reception), but the displays are not chronological, which unfortunately tends to confuse matters.

The **earlier pieces**, dating from around 1500 to 700 BC, include many examples of crudely crafted beakers and tumblers as well as a set of **six skulls**, which appear to have been subjected to some form of brain surgery, though no one is sure quite how or why. **Later work** – from around 700 BC – reveals a far greater degree of sophistication, both in terms of kitchenware, with bowls and tumblers particularly common, and bronze weaponry. From this later period, which ended with the arrival of the Romans in 123 BC, comes most of the (imported) jewellery, whose fine detail and miniature size suggest a Carthaginian origin.

Carrer Sa Muradeta and the harbour

Beginning beside the Museu Municipal, **Carrer Sa Muradeta** provides pleasant views over a ravine as it cuts down towards the Plaça d'es Born. As you near the square, a wide flight of steps – the **Baixada Capllonc** – bounces down to the harbour, where yachts and fishing smacks bob around in front of a series of waterside restaurants, with the old town walls forming a scenic background. The **harbour** is as flat as a millpond almost all of the time, but every so often, for reasons that remain obscure, it is subjected to a violent disturbance, the **Rissaga**. This begins with sudden changes to the sea level and is followed by a dramatic rush of water into the harbour before normality returns. The last great Rissaga took place in 1984 and submerged the harbourside beneath 2m of water, giving everyone an almighty shock.

FORNELLS (P.219) >

5

ARRIVAL AND DEPARTURE

By bus Buses from Maó and points east pull into the bus station on Plaça de La Pau, on the south side of the centre – and a 5–10min walk from Placa d'es Born. Buses from the tourist resorts of the west coast stop right in the centre, on the north side of Plaça dels Pins.

Destinations Alaior (Mon–Fri every 30min–1hr, Sat & Sun every 1–2hr; 50min); Cala Galdana (April, May & Oct Mon–Sat 6 daily; June–Sept 5–6 daily; 40min); Cala Morell (May–Oct 3–4 daily; 20min); Es Mercadal (Mon–Fri every 30min–1hr, Sat & Sun every 1–2hr; 35min); Es Migjorn Gran (Mon–Fri 2 daily; 35min); Ferreries (Mon–Fri every 30min–1hr, Sat & Sun every 1–2hr; 25min); Maó (Mon–Fri every 30min–1hr, Sat & Sun every 1–2hr; 1hr).

By ferry Car ferries and catamarans from Barcelona and Mallorca's Port d'Alcúdia dock at the Son Blanc ferry port, located at the western end of the outer ring road (the RC-2), about 4km south of the town centre. Bus #63 runs from Son Blanc to the centre of town, stopping on the north side of Plaça dels Pins. Its timetable matches ferry arrivals and departures and the journey time is about 15min. A taxi costs around €8. For ferry company details and routings,

see Basics (p.22, 23); tickets are available direct from the operators at the ferry terminal, but it's easier to buy them online. Note that Menorca's car rental companies do not allow their vehicles to leave the island.

By car If you're driving into Ciutadella from the east, there's no missing the inner ring road, which, under various names – principally Avgda Jaume I El Conqueridor and Avgda Negrete – encircles the old town. Approaching on the main road from the east (the Me-1), turn left when you reach the T-junction and keep going until you reach its conclusion on Plaça dels Pins. Driving east out of Ciutadella is more difficult as the last stretch of the Me-1 is westbound only; the solution is to use the outer ring road – just follow the signs. This outer ring road is named the RC-1 north of the Me-1 and the RC-2 to the south.

Parking Most of the town centre is pedestrianized, but you can pretty much guarantee there will be vacant on-street parking spaces on Passeig Sant Nicolau, which runs west from Plaça dels Pins at the end of the inner ring road.

GETTING AROUND

Bicycle and moped rental There are several bicycle and moped rental companies in Ciutadella, but one of the most reliable is Tot Velo, just west of Plaça dels Pins at c/Eivissa 59 (Mon–Fri 9.30am–1.30pm & 5–8.30pm & Sat 10am–1.30pm; ☎971 48 11 48, ⓦtotvelo.com). They rent bikes from €12/day.

Car rental The resorts of Menorca's west coast are

sprinkled with big-name car rental companies, including Europcar, in Cala en Blanes (May–Oct; ☎971 38 94 90). The tourist office (see below) has a complete list.

By taxi There's a taxi stand on Plaça dels Pins. Alternatively, call ☎971 48 22 22. The (regulated) taxi fare from Ciutadella to Menorca airport is about €55.

INFORMATION AND ACTIVITIES

Tourist information The main tourist office is located inside the town hall – the Ajuntament – at Plaça d'es Born 15 (May–Oct Mon–Sat 9.30am–8.30pm, Sun 9.30am–3pm; Nov–April Mon–Fri 9am–2pm & 4–8pm, Sat 9.30am–1.30pm; ☎971 48 41 55, ⓦajciutadella .org). It has a good range of information on Menorca as a whole and Ciutadella in particular, including bus timetables, ferry schedules, lists of *hostales* and hotels and free maps, but doesn't help with finding accommodation.

Boat rental Menorca Boats, down on the harbour at Passeig Moll 78 (☎609 61 19 58, ⓦmenorcaboats.com),

rents out all manner of speed boats. Prices begin at a hefty €350/ day in high season, €170 in low.

Diving Dive Inn Menorca, down near the harbour at Es Pla de Sant Joan 10 (☎651 64 43 19, ⓦdiveinnmenorca.com), organizes a wide range of deep-sea diving trips out amid the crystal-clear waters of the west coast. Introductory, day-long sessions start at €240 (Oct–May €190).

Horseriding Cavalls Son Àngel, Camí de Cala Morell-Algaiarens, km1 (☎609 83 39 02, ⓦcavallssonangel.com), specializes in horseriding excursions – anything from a quick, hour-long trot (€25) to a five-day expedition. Many of their excursions use the Camí de Cavalls (see box, p.241).

ACCOMMODATION

IN THE CENTRE

Hotel Can Faustino c/Sant Rafel 9 ☎971 48 91 93, ⓦcanfaustino.com. Super-deluxe hotel in a beautifully renovated old mansion in a great location, just a couple of minutes' walk from the Cathedral. The rooms are slick and modern – think creams and browns – with every mod con, and some have terraces overlooking the hotel's gardens

with and without city views. Naturally, there's a spa and naturally the hotel is expensive, but not perhaps as expensive as you might expect. **€180**

Hostal Ciutadella c/Sant Eloi 10 ☎971 38 34 62, ⓦalojarseenmenorca.com. Well-maintained, two-star *hostal* in a pleasantly updated older building on a side street off Plaça Alfons III. Has around twenty small and modest but comfortable rooms, each decorated in shades of yellow and brown. **€90**

★**Hotel Géminis** c/Josepa Rossinyol 4 ☎ 971 38 46 44, ⓦ hotelgeminismenorca.com. Distinctively painted in pink and white, this well-tended, comfortable two-star hotel has thirty rooms, each decorated in bright if somewhat frugal modern style. The rooms at the front have Art Deco-style balconies and overlook a quiet suburban street; those at the back overlook a small pool and courtyard. To get there, walk a few paces down c/Mossèn J. Salord i Farnés from the ring road and watch for the archway on the right; go through the arch and the hotel's on the right. Closed Nov–March. **€90**

Hotel Madrid c/Madrid 60 ☎ 971 38 03 28, ⓦ hotel madridmenorca.com. Located near the ocean, a 20min walk west of the town centre, the one-star *Madrid* comprises 22 reasonably comfortable if somewhat spartan rooms in a run-of-the-mill villa-style building with an outside pool. To get there, follow Passeig Sant Nicolau from the Plaça dels Pins, take the fourth turning on the left (c/Saragossa) and you'll soon hit c/Madrid – just a block and a half east of the hotel. Closed Nov–April. **€65**

Hotel Menorca Patricia Passeig Sant Nicolau 90 ☎ 971 38 55 11, ⓦ hotelmenorcapatricia.com. Smart, modern three-star popular with business folk and in a great location, a few minutes' walk from the town centre. The 44 comfortable, well-appointed rooms come with all facilities, the only downer being the lack of a sea view – though the best rooms have rooftop balconies with wide vistas over the town centre. There's also an outside swimming pool. **€95**

Hotel Port Ciutadella Passeig Marítim 36 ☎ 971 48 25 20, ⓦ sethotels.com. A 15min walk southwest of Plaça dels Pins, this smart and ultra-modern four-star hotel has a cleverly designed outside pool and around one hundred brightly decorated bedrooms with all mod cons. To get there head south on c/Mallorca and turn right at the roundabout at the end. Closed Nov–April. **€150**

★**Hostal Sa Prensa** c/Madrid 70 ☎ 971 38 26 98, ⓦ saprensa.com. Close to the rocky seashore at the end of c/Madrid, a 20min walk west of the centre, this neat and trim, villa-like, one-star *hostal* has eight straightforward, modern bedrooms, four of which have balconies and sea views. To get there, follow the directions for the *Hotel Madrid* (see above) and carry on for a further 200m or so towards the seashore. **€85**

Hotel Tres Sants c/Sant Cristòfol 2 ☎ 971 48 22 08, ⓦ grupelcarme.com. One of a small chain, this boutique hotel (with a fancy website) offers just eight light and airy modern rooms in an extensively renovated eighteenth-century townhouse that was built on top of the island's first Christian church. There are pleasant views from the terrace, and breakfasts are delicious. Minimum three-night stay during the peak season. **€220**

OUT OF THE CITY

★**Hotel Rural Morvedrà Nou** Camí Sant Joan de Misa, km7 ☎ 971 35 95 21, ⓦ morvedranou.es. In a rural location, about 6km south of Ciutadella on the way to the cove beaches of the south coast (see p.240), this delightful hotel occupies a sympathetically converted stone farmhouse set in its own gardens. The nineteen guest rooms are decorated in an unfussy manner and come complete with beamed ceilings and old stone walls. There is an outside pool, too, plus extremely helpful staff. Closed Nov–March. **€200**

Hotel Sant Ignasi Camí de Sant Ignasi s/n ☎ 971 38 55 75, ⓦ santignasi.com. This handsome seventeenth-century manor house has been tastefully converted into an immaculate hotel. Each of the 25 bedrooms is decorated in a style that blends with the original building, and there are gardens and an outside pool. It's located in a rural setting about 4km northeast of Ciutadella – and clearly signposted (down a very narrow 1.5km-long lane) from the road to Cala Morell. Closed mid-Oct to April. **€200**

EATING AND DRINKING

For an early **breakfast** the best place to go is the market (*mercat*) on Plaça Llibertat, where a couple of simple cafés serve coffee and fresh pastries. Later in the day, around **lunchtime**, aim for c/J.M. Quadrado or Plaça Nova, which together hold a good selection of inexpensive café-bars offering tapas and light meals. In the **evening**, most tourists make a beeline for the **restaurants** that line up along the harbourside, but – with the odd exception – you're better off seeking out the better-value places among the side streets near Plaça d'es Born. Incidentally, although the outside terraces on the harbourside restaurants look enticing, the nautical activity along the waterfront can be deafening.

CAFÉS AND CAFÉ-BARS

Café-Bar Ulises Plaça Llibertat s/n ☎ 971 38 00 31. This easy-going and very fashionable café-bar, in the heart of the city market, has loads of atmosphere (think white-plank wooden flooring, cabinets of old wine and spirit bottles) and is popular with a youngish local clientele. Offers a tasty range of pastries and tortillas in the morning, more substantial main courses (from €10) in the

later, and lots of drinks plus (turned-down) house music/jazz at night – as well as the occasional live concert. Mon–Sat 8am–late.

Imperi Plaça d'es Born 5 ☎ 971 38 22 20. Green-shuttered, neatly turned out café-bar offering good (Illy) coffee, snacks and cakes (from €4). Abutting the main square, its tiny terrace is a fine spot to observe the milling crowd. Daily 7am–midnight.

5

Sa Xarxa c/Sebastià 3 ☎ 971 48 03 23. Agreeable café-bar serving a good line in tapas and snacks, all at inexpensive prices (from €6). Its pavement terrace is set just off the main drag, which means it's a good place to watch the evening *passeig/paseo*. Daily 10am–11pm.

RESTAURANTS

El Horno c/Forn 12 ☎ 971 38 07 67. Smart and neat cellar restaurant near the northeast corner of Plaça d'es Born featuring a canny combination of Menorcan and French dishes. Try the rabbit or the mussels. Mains average a very competitive €14. Daily 7–11pm.

★ **La Guitarra** c/Nostra Senyora dels Dolors 1 ☎ 971 38 13 55. Located a short walk from the cathedral in an old cellar, whose stone walls sport a scattering of agricultural antiques, this is arguably the best restaurant in town, a family-run affair featuring the very best of Menorcan cuisine with main courses, such as rabbit with onions, averaging an extremely reasonable €15; neither should you miss the traditional *trempó* (salad) for just €8. Mon–Sat 11.30am–3.30pm & 7.15–11pm.

Pins 46 Plaça dels Pins 46 ☎ 971 48 16 74, ⓦ cafebalear .com. In an immaculately modernized old townhouse, this smart restaurant – one of a small local chain – offers a well-chosen menu featuring such delights as lobster with onion or grilled local prawns. Mains start at €18 and you can eat either inside or outside in the garden courtyard at the back and the pavement terrace at the front. Daily 11am–midnight.

Restaurant Café Balear Es Pla de Sant Joan 15 ☎ 971 38 00 05, ⓦ cafebalear.com. Part of a small chain, this appealing restaurant sits at the back of the harbour by the bridge – at a safe distance from the chuntering boats. The waterside terrace is the best place to eat, but there are tables inside too. The food is first-rate, with shellfish and fish the big deals – go for the swordfish carpaccio if it's available – though the steaks are good too. Main courses average €20. Reservations advised. May–Oct Mon–Sat 12.30–4pm & 7.30–11.30pm.

Ses Voltes Ses Voltes 16, c/J.M. Quadrado ☎ 971 38 14 98, ⓦ recibaria.com. This casual café-restaurant serves tapas, salads, baguettes and pizzas – try the delicious mozzarella with tomatoes, local sausage and honey. Set across two floors, it has comfy benches, and funky art on the walls, and just about everything on the menu is under €5. Daily 9am–midnight.

NIGHTLIFE

BARS AND CLUBS

Jazzbah Es Pla de Sant Joan 3 ☎ 971 48 29 53. This cool indoor/outdoor bar is one of Menorca's best places for a night out. It has several individual spaces with live music, and DJs when the bands have the night off. A large dance space means lots of regular parties. No website, but they are on Facebook. Note that hours can vary. Fri & Sat 11pm–6am.

La Margarete Sant Joan 6 ☎ 971 48 20 97, ⓦ lamargarete.flavors.me. In the town centre, near Plaça d'Artrutx, this is a hip and groovy garden bar with a young, mainly local clientele and regular DJs playing out in the open air. Daily 9pm–3.30am.

Space Pla de Sant Joan 15 ⓦ spacemenorca.com. This portside version of the renowned Ibiza club brings high-powered sound systems, fancy lighting and great DJs to Ciutadella. There is a well-appointed terrace with lounge seating up the stairs from the main dance floor. Hours vary – check website for details.

SHOPPING

Libreria d'es Racó c/J.M. Quadrado 40 ☎ 971 38 19 62. Right in the centre of town, this busy newsagent is an Aladdin's cave of a place stocked high with books, magazines and toys, and selling a limited range of island road maps. Mon–Sat 10am–2pm & 5.30–7.30pm.

La Torre de Papel Camí de Maó 46 ☎ 971 38 66 81. The best bookshop in town, offering a first-rate selection of contemporary Spanish (and Catalan) literature. Also sells a good range of used books, though few are in English. Mon–Sat 10am–2pm & 5.30–8.30pm.

DIRECTORY

Banks ATMs are dotted all over the town centre and there's one at the Banca March, Plaça d'es Born 10.

Pharmacies There are a number of downtown pharmacies, including *Farmàcia Cavaller*, at Plaça Catedral 7 (Mon–Fri 9am–1pm & 5–8pm; ☎ 971 38 00 83).

Post office The main *correu* is handily located at Plaça d'es Born 9 (Mon–Fri 8.30am–2.30pm, Sat 9.30am–1pm).

Around Ciutadella

One of Ciutadella's real charms is its proximity to the string of pristine **cove beaches** that notch the island's **southern shore**. There are several to choose from, but perhaps the most memorable are **Cala Turqueta** and **Cala Macarella**, both of which can be

---

HIKING THE ISLAND: THE CAMÍ DE CAVALLS

With great forethought, the Menorcans have restored and revived the **Camí de Cavalls** (Wcamidecavalls360.com), the old agricultural and military footpath that runs right round the island's coast for a distance of 185km. For the most part the hiking is fairly easy and the coastal views splendid – though the northern portion is a tad wilder and more challenging – and on the way the *Camí* passes dozens of **beaches**, some developed, others not. Particularly delightful stretches include Cala Galdana (see box, p.229) to Cala Turqueta (see p.242) on the south coast, and Cala Morell (see p.242) to Cala d'Algaiarens (see p.243) and Es Alocs on the north, with the latter stretch negotiating a string of short but steep hills. The **Camí de Cavalls Guidebook** (€18), on sale at Maó's quayside tourist office (see p.207), provides detailed descriptions of every section, and can be used in conjunction with a (fairly rudimentary) box of maps (€16), also on sale here.

---

reached via the **Camí de Sant Joan de Missa**, a country lane which runs southeast from Ciutadella's outer ring road (the RC-2). "Pristine" does not, however, necessarily mean uncrowded: sometimes they are and sometimes they are not – and it's hard to predict when, though summer weekends usually see them at their busiest. It's also a good idea to take your own food and water: most of the beaches have impromptu beach-bars of some description, but you can't bet your bottom dollar they will actually be open.

It's also a short hop from Ciutadella to the island's wild and windy **north shore**, where development is essentially limited to **Cala Morell**, a smart, modern resort that hugs a bleak and barren cove with a gritty beach, though the beach at nearby **Cala d'Algaiarens** is much more inviting. The **west coast** is different again: here, the pancake-flat and largely treeless coastal plain is edged by a long series of resorts that extend almost without interruption from Cales Piques in the north to Cap d'Artrutx, 15km away to the south. These resorts are, for the most part, neat and trim, modern and comfortable, but they are far from memorable, comprising villa-villages built in a sort of pan-Hispanic style with the occasional cove beach thrown in to the tourist stew. Finally, it's also worth noting that the long-distance **Camí de Cavalls** (see box, p.241) runs along the entire coast from Cala Galdana (see p.229) to Cala Morell, threading its way past a veritable brigade of cove beaches, including the ones described below.

Son Catlar

Open access • Free • Seasonal buses run between Ciutadella bus station and Son Catlar (early May to mid-June & late Sept to mid-Oct Mon–Sat 3 daily; mid-June to late Sept Mon–Sat hourly; 15min)

Deep in the countryside, about 7km south of Ciutadella, **Son Catlar** is the largest prehistoric settlement on Menorca, a sprawling set of ruins that are hard to decipher, but enjoyable all the same. To get there from Ciutadella's outer ring road (the RC-2), take the signed, cross-country **Camí de Sant Joan de Missa** southeast and, after about 3km, you reach the **Son Vivó farmhouse**, where the road branches into two: take the more westerly fork and, after another 3.2km, you'll reach Son Catlar, which was still expanding when the Romans arrived in force in 123 BC. The most impressive feature of this sprawling Talayotic village is its extraordinary **stone wall**, originally 3m high and made of massive blocks – the square towers were added later. Inside the walls, however, all is confusion. The widely scattered remains are largely incomprehensible and only the *taula* compound and the five battered *talayots* make much sense.

Platges Son Saura

Car park €5 • Seasonal buses run between Ciutadella bus station and the Platges Son Saura car park (early May to mid-June & late Sept to mid-Oct Mon–Sat 3 daily; mid-June to late Sept Mon–Sat hourly; 30min)

South of Son Catlar (see above), it's about 1.2km to the ornate gateway of the **Torre Saura farmhouse**, where the lane narrows and swings left for the final 2km jaunt down

5

to the large and distinctly scrawny car park. From here, it's just a 3min walk to the west side of a wide horseshoe-shaped cove, whose twin beaches make up the **Platges Son Saura**. Parts of the cove are often sticky with seaweed, but there is usually less of the stuff on the more sheltered western side, where pines fringe a wide arc of white sand. There are more facilities here than at most of its neighbours, including a summer beach bar (no set opening hours).

Cala Turqueta

Car park €5 · Seasonal buses run between Ciutadella bus station and Cala Turqueta (early May to mid-June & late Sept to mid-Oct Mon–Sat 3 daily; mid-June to late Sept Mon–Sat hourly; 30min)

Cala Turqueta, one of the island's most lauded beaches, is within easy striking distance of Ciutadella. Head southeast from Ciutadella's ring road (the RC-2) on the **Camí de Sant Joan de Missa**, and it's about 3km to the **Son Vivó farmhouse**, where the road forks: take the more easterly fork and it's a further 1.5km to the conspicuous **Ermita de St Joan de Missa**, a squat church with a dinky little bell tower. There's a signed fork here too – turn left for Cala Macarella and Cala Macarelleta (see below), but keep straight for Cala Turqueta. About 4.5km from the church, you turn at the sign, going through the gateway to cross the 500m-long dirt road that brings you to the car park. From here, it's a ten-minute walk to the *cala*, which fills out a handsome cove flanked by a heavily wooded limestone bluff. The **beach** is a sheltered horseshoe of white sand that slopes gently into the sea, making it ideal for bathing. It's a popular spot, so it's best to arrive early before the crowds, and although a beach bar sometimes appears, sometimes it doesn't – so bring your own food and water.

Calas Macarella and Macarelleta

From the **Ermita de St Joan de Missa** (see above), a country lane leads the 7.5km east, then south, to **Cala Macarella**, with the final portion of road twisting down through a deep wooded gorge before coming to a sudden halt at the first of two dirt car parks: one car park is free, but is a twenty-minute walk from the beach; the other costs €5 and is a five-minute walk from the beach. The beach itself is a hoop-shaped affair with a wooded limestone bluff behind and crystal-clear waters in front. In the unlikely event it's crowded – there is no bus service, but there is a beach bar – you can stroll round the bay along the signposted Camí de Cavalls footpath to **Cala Macarelleta**, smaller and possibly even prettier, and with the same formula of turquoise waters and limestone cliffs.

Cala Morell

Seasonal buses run between Ciutadella bus station and Cala Morell (mid-June to late Sept Mon–Sat hourly; early May to mid-June & late Sept to mid-Oct Mon–Sat 3 daily; 15min)

Signposted from Ciutadella's outer ring road (the RC-1), a well-surfaced country lane cuts northeast across a pastoral landscape bound for the small(ish) tourist settlement of **CALA MORELL**, just 8km from town. This is one of the island's more refined *urbanitzacions*, its *pueblo*-style villas – on streets named in Latin after the constellations – hugging a steep and rocky dog-legged bay. There's swimming off the rocky **beach** here, and you can also visit some of the old **caves** for which Cala Morell is noted, visible beside the road as you drive down into the resort. Dating from the late Bronze and Iron Ages, the caves form one of the largest prehistoric necropolises known in Europe, and are surprisingly sophisticated, with central pillars supporting the roofs and, in some instances, windows cut into the rock and classical designs carved in relief. No one owns the caves, so there's unlimited access – just scramble up from the road – but if you're after more than just a quick glimpse, bring your own torch.

North coast headlands

On the west side of Cala Morell, **c/Orio** slips north along the bay, but peters out to be replaced by a rough footpath that continues north along a bare and rocky promontory to the **Punta de S'Elefant** headland, which offers wide views over the surrounding coastline. This part of Menorca is wild and windswept with vegetation almost nonexistent, but only the truly adventurous will attempt the very difficult hike west from Cala Morell to the next headland along, the **Punta de S'Escullar**, the site of one of the largest colonies of Cory's shearwaters in the western Mediterranean, with thousands of birds returning to their cliffside burrows in the late afternoon throughout the summer.

Cala d'Algaiarens

Car park €5 • Seasonal buses run between Ciutadella bus station and Cala d'Algaiarens (early May to mid-June & late Sept to mid-Oct Mon–Sat 3 daily; mid-June to late Sept Mon–Sat hourly; 25min)

On the road from Ciutadella to Cala Morell, a signed turning leads east along a country lane to one of the north coast's best beaches, **Cala d'Algaiarens**. Well surfaced for the most part, the lane is alarmingly narrow in places, but the end car park is only a few minutes' walk from the **beach**, where low cliffs frame a wide arc of bright-white sand. The water deepens quite quickly off the beach and the currents can be strong, but there are no facilities, so the beach is usually very quiet.

WILD FLOWERS IN SPRING, MALLORCA

Contexts

245 History

264 Flora and fauna

272 Books

276 Language

285 Glossary

History

Mallorca and Menorca share similar but far from identical histories: the Romans and the Moors coveted and conquered them both, but the British were only interested in Maó's splendid harbour and the government in Madrid rarely gave two hoots about either. What the two islands do share is a long history of political and economic domination by a landowning elite, who were all too often absentees. Until the twentieth century, this caste presided over what was, to a large extent, a backward-looking, priest-ridden society, and many hated them for it: look at any old rural manor house, especially in Mallorca, and it will almost invariably be heavily fortified not so much from fear of invasion – though that was an issue – but more to keep the peasantry at bay.

Earliest peoples

The earliest inhabitants of the Balearics seem to have reached the islands from the Iberian peninsula, and carbon dating of remains indicates that human occupation was well established by 2800/2600 BC in Mallorca, 2300 in Menorca. The discovery of pottery, flints and animal horns fashioned into tools suggests that these early people were **Neolithic pastoralists**, who supplemented their food supplies by hunting. A key part of their diet appears to have been *Myotragus balearicus*, a species of diminutive mountain goat unique to the islands and now extinct. Hundreds of these animals' skulls have been discovered and several are exhibited in the islands' larger museums. The frequency of these finds has encouraged some experts to assert that the *Myotragus* was actually domesticated, the principal evidence being the supposed remains of crude corrals on the coast of Mallorca near Deià, though this assertion is now largely discredited.

Cave dwellers

Why, or how, the earliest of these Neolithic peoples moved to the Balearic islands is unknown. Indeed, the first landfall may have been entirely accidental, made by early seafarers travelling along the shores of the Mediterranean – and part of a great wave of migration that is known to have taken place in the Neolithic period. Many of the oldest archeological finds have been discovered in natural **caves**, where it seems likely that these early settlers first sought shelter. Later, cave complexes were dug out of the soft limestone that occurs on both islands, comprising living quarters, usually circular and sometimes with a domed ceiling, as well as longer, straighter funerary chambers. These complexes represent the flourishing of what is commonly called the **Balearic cave**

2700 BC	2500 BC	1500 BC
Neolithic pastoralists roam Mallorca, colonizing Menorca about four centuries later	The Balearics' native goat, the diminutive *Myotragus balearicus*, becomes extinct, possibly through over-hunting	The islanders learn how to work bronze; the Talayotic period begins

culture – one good (and readily accessible) example is at the resort of **Cala Morell**, on Menorca (see p.242).

The Beaker people

The archeological evidence indicates that Balearic cave dwellers soon came into regular contact with other cultures: the Mediterranean, with its relatively calm and tide-free waters, has always acted as a ready conduit. One of the earliest of these outside influences was the **Beaker people**, whose artefacts have been found right across Western Europe. Named after their practice of burying their dead with pottery beakers, their presence on the Balearics has been indicated by the discovery of Beaker ware at Deià. The Beaker people also had knowledge of the use of **bronze**, an alloy of copper and tin, and they exported their bronze-working skills into the Balearics around 1500 BC. This technological revolution marked the end of the cave culture and the beginning of the Talayotic period.

The Talayotic period

The megalithic remains of the **Talayotic period**, which lasted until the arrival of the Romans in 123 BC, are strewn all over Mallorca and Menorca – though, surprisingly, there's no evidence of them on Ibiza. The structure that gives its name to the period is the **talayot**, a cone-shaped tower with a circular base between 5m and 10m in height. These *talayots* are commonly thought of as watchtowers, but this is unlikely and their actual function is unknown. What is clear is that by 1000 BC a relatively sophisticated, largely pastoral society had developed on both Mallorca and Menorca, with at least some of the islanders occupying the walled settlements that still dot the interior. The two best examples are **Torre d'en Gaumés** (see p.223), near Alaior on Menorca, where you can still inspect three *talayots* and the remains of several houses, and Mallorca's **Ses Païsses** (see p.172), a well-protected settlement of impressive proportions outside Artà. Both were occupied well into the Roman period.

Menorca's taulas and hypostyles

Talayotic culture reached dizzying heights on Menorca, and it's here you'll find the most enigmatic remains of the period. These are the **taulas** ("tables" in Catalan), T-shaped structures standing as high as 4m and consisting of two massive dressed stones. Their purpose is unknown, though many theories have been advanced. One early nineteenth-century writer believed that they were altars used for human sacrifice, but the height of most *taulas* makes this very unlikely – unless the islanders were on stilts. More intriguingly, some academics have argued that the "T" was a **stylized head of a bull**, an animal that was much venerated in many parts of the ancient Mediterranean, most notably in Minoan Crete. True or not, it seems probable that the enclosures that surround every *taula* had religious significance. This was confirmed during excavations at **Torralba d'en Salord** (see p.223), where archeologists discovered animal remains and pottery in side recesses of fireplaces, and concluded that these must have been ritual offerings. They also found a bronze sculpture of a bull, suggesting that cattle were, indeed, worshipped. Torralba d'en Salord is one of the many places where

1000 BC	900 BC	800 BC
Pirate attacks encourage the Talayotic peoples to move into walled settlements	Phoenicians use the Balearics as a trading station, bringing greater security to the islands	Greeks displace the Phoenicians as the dominant power in the Balearics

taulas and *talayots* stand cheek by jowl. Often the remains are too broken down to be of much interest, but three sites where you get a real sense what was once here are **Torrellafuda** (see p.230), **Torre d'en Gaumés** (see p.223) and at **Talatí de Dalt** (see p.206), which incorporates a *talayot*, a *taula* and several columned chambers or **hypostyles**. Partly dug out of the ground and roofed with massive slabs of stone, these hypostyles must have taken considerable effort to build, and may have been used for important gatherings, possibly of communal leaders.

Menorca's navetas

The other distinctive structure to be found only on Menorca is the **naveta**, made of roughly dressed, dry-stone blocks and looking like an inverted bread tin. Dating from the beginning of the Talayotic period, the **Naveta d'es Tudons**, near Ciutadella (see p.230), is the finest surviving example, but there are around 35 others sprinkled across the island. They were collective tombs, or, more correctly, ossuaries, where, after the flesh had been removed, the bones of the dead were placed along with some personal possessions such as jewellery, pottery and bone buttons. Curiously, the Menorcans gave the *navetas* a wide berth long after their original purpose was forgotten, until well into the twentieth century.

Phoenicians

Fearful of attack from the sea, the Talayotic people built their walled settlements a few kilometres inland. This pattern was, however, modified from around 900 BC, when the Balearics became a staging post for the **Phoenicians**, maritime traders from the eastern Mediterranean whose long voyages reached as far as Cornwall in southwest England. The Phoenicians made the islands safer and more secure and the Talayotic peoples ventured out from their walled settlements. According to the Roman historian Pliny, the Phoenicians established a large settlement at **Sanisera** on Menorca's north coast (see p.221), and archeologists have also discovered Phoenician artefacts at **Alcúdia** on Mallorca (see p.148). Yet, in general, very few Phoenician remains have been found on the Balearics – just a handful of bronze items, jewellery and pieces of coloured glass.

Greeks

The **Greeks** displaced the Phoenicians around 800 BC, as several city-states explored the western Mediterranean in search of trade and potential colonies. Like the Phoenicians, the Greeks appear to have used the Balearics primarily as a staging post, for no Greek buildings have survived on either Mallorca or Menorca. The absence of metal apparently made the islands unsuitable for long-term colonization, and the belligerence of the native population may have played a part too: the Greeks coined the islands' name, the "**Balearics**", which they derived from *ballein*, meaning "to throw from a sling". The islanders were adept at this form of warfare, and many early visitors were repelled with showers of polished sling-stones – though some historians dispute this theory, claiming rather that the name comes from the Baleri tribe of Sardinia.

700 BC	**3rd–2nd century BC**	**247 BC**
Carthaginians begin to colonize the Balearics	Carthage and Rome wrestle for control of the Iberian peninsula in the Punic Wars. Rome wins and mainland Spain is incorporated into the Roman Empire	Birth of Hannibal, the brilliant Carthaginian commander, possibly on Ibiza

The Carthaginian Empire

The Greeks were also discouraged from colonization by the growth of the **Carthaginian Empire**. The Phoenicians had established Carthage on the North African coast in 814 BC, and from this base they gradually extended their authority across the western Mediterranean. They began to colonize the Balearics in the seventh century BC and the islands were firmly under their control by the beginning of the third century BC, if not earlier. Little is known of the Carthaginian occupation except that they established several new settlements, such as Sanisera (see p.221) and Alcúdia (see p.148). It is also claimed that the Carthaginian general, **Hannibal**, was born on Cabrera island off Mallorca, though Ibiza and Malta claim this too.

In the third century BC, the expansion of the Carthaginian Empire up into the Iberian peninsula triggered two **Punic Wars** with Rome. In both of these wars the Balearics proved extremely valuable, first as stepping stones from the North African coast to the European mainland and second as a source of mercenaries. **Balearic slingers** (see box below) were highly valued and accompanied Hannibal and his elephants across the Alps in the Second Punic War, when (for reasons that remain obscure) the islanders refused gold and demanded payment in wine and women instead. After Hannibal's defeat by the Romans at the battle of Zama in 202 BC, Carthaginian power began to wane and they withdrew from Mallorca and Menorca, although they continued to have some influence over Ibiza for at least another seventy years.

The Romans

As the Carthaginians retreated so the **Romans** advanced, incorporating Ibiza within their empire after the final victory over Carthage in 146 BC. On Mallorca and Menorca, the islanders took advantage of the prolonged military chaos to profit from piracy, until finally, in 123 BC, the Romans, led by the consul Quintus Metellus,

---

BALEARIC SLINGERS

Quintus Metellus, the Roman commander who invaded Mallorca in 123 BC, had a healthy respect for the warlike qualities of the islanders in general and their skill with the **stone-throwing sling** in particular. He had good reason. The Carthaginians had been using Balearic mercenaries for many decades and the islanders had inflicted heavy casualties on the Roman legions throughout the Punic Wars. Consequently, Metellus went to great trouble to protect his men by erecting mammoth shields of hide along the decks of all his ships – a stratagem that worked extremely well.

Male islanders were trained to use the sling in childhood, and they could propel a stone with great accuracy and force sufficient to crush most shields and helmets. The slinger had three slings of different lengths, one held in the hand, another wrapped round the stomach and a third tied round the head. According to the historian **Diodorus Siculus** (90–30 BC), these **slingers** were a particularly disagreeable bunch: they often went naked, covering their bodies in a mixture of pig fat and olive oil; were inordinately fond of wine; were keen on female slaves; and rounded off their weddings with all the male guests having congress with the bride in descending order of age – before passing her over to the groom. This may be hogwash, however: Siculus was nothing if not biased.

---

146 BC	123 BC	5th century AD	425 AD
Final defeat of the Carthaginians by Rome	Rome seizes and then colonizes the Balearics	Roman Empire collapses and the Visigoths become Spain's dominant military force	The Germanic Vandals pour over the Balearics, destroying everything in their path

restored maritime order by occupying both islands. These victories earned Metellus the title "Balearico" from the Roman senate and two of the islands were given new names, Balearis Major (Mallorca) and Balearis Minor (Menorca).

For the next five hundred years all the Balearic islands were part of the Roman Empire. Among many developments, Roman colonists introduced viticulture, turning the Balearics into a wine-exporting area, and initiated olive-oil production from newly planted groves. As was their custom, the Romans consolidated their control of the islands by building roads and establishing towns. On Mallorca, they founded Pollentia (Alcúdia) in the north and Palmaria on the south coast, near the site of modern Palma, while on Menorca they developed Port Magonum (Maó) as an administrative centre with Sanisera – previously the site of a Phoenician trading post – becoming an important port. Initially, the Balearics were part of the Roman province of Tarraconensis (Tarragona), but in 404 AD the islands became a province in their own right with the name **Balearica**.

The Vandals and Byzantines

By the fifth century the Roman Empire was in decline, its defences unable to resist the westward-moving tribes of central Asia. The **Vandals**, one of these tribes, moved in on the Balearics in around 425 AD, ending Roman rule at a stroke. So thoroughgoing was the destruction they wrought that Roman remains are at a premium, the only significant ruins being those of Pollentia at **Alcúdia** (see p.150). One of the reasons for the ferocity of the attack was religious. The Vandals had been Christianized long before they reached the Mediterranean, but they were followers of the **Arian sect**. This interpretation of Christianity, founded by Arius, an Alexandrian priest, insisted that Christ the Son and God the Father were two distinct figures, not elements of the Trinity. To orthodox Christians, this seemed dangerously close to the pagan belief in a multiplicity of gods and, by the end of the fourth century AD, Arianism had been forcibly extirpated within the Roman Empire. However, the sect continued to flourish among the Germanic peoples of the Rhine, including the Vandals, who, armed with their "heretical" beliefs, had no religious truck with their new Balearic subjects, persecuting them with vim and gusto.

In 533 the Vandals were defeated in North Africa by the Byzantine general **Count Belisarius** – who was later to be the subject of a novel by one of Mallorca's adopted sons, Robert Graves. This brought the Balearics under **Byzantine** rule and, for a time, restored prosperity and stability. Nonetheless, the islands were too far removed from Constantinople to be of much imperial importance and, when the empire was threatened from the east at the end of the seventh century, they were abandoned in all but name.

The Moors

As the influence of Byzantium receded, so militarized Islam moved in to fill the vacuum. In 707–8 the **Moors** of North Africa conducted an extended raid against Mallorca, destroying its entire fleet and carrying away slaves and booty, and by 716 the Balearics' position had become even more vulnerable with the completion of the

711	**756**	**859**
Islamic Moors (Arabs and Berbers from North Africa) conquer almost all of mainland Spain	Abd ar-Rahman I proclaims the Emirate of Córdoba, confirming Moorish control over most of Spain	The Vikings raid the Balearics; more destruction ensues

Moorish conquest of Spain. In 798, the Balearics were again sacked by the Moors – who were still more interested in plunder than settlement – and in desperation the islanders appealed for help to **Charlemagne**, the Frankish Holy Roman Emperor. As emperor, Charlemagne was the military leader of Western Christendom (the pope was the spiritual leader), so the appeal signified the final severance of the Balearics' links with Byzantium and the East.

Charlemagne's attempt to protect the islands from the Moors met with some success, but the respite was only temporary. By the middle of the ninth century, the Christian position had deteriorated so badly that the Balearics were compelled to enter a non-aggression pact with the Moors, and, to add to the islanders' woes, the Balearics suffered a full-scale **Viking** raid in 859. Finally, at the beginning of the tenth century, the **emir of Córdoba** conquered both Menorca and Mallorca. Moorish rule lasted more than three hundred years, though internal political divisions among the Muslims meant that the islands experienced several different regimes.

Moorish rule – the Amortadhas

In the early eleventh century, the emirate of Córdoba collapsed and control passed to the *wali* (governor) of Denia, on the Spanish mainland. This administration allowed the Christians – who were known as **Mozarabs** – to practise their faith, and the islands prospered from their position at the heart of the trade routes between North Africa and Islamic Spain. In 1085, the Balearics became an independent emirate with a new dynasty of *walis*, from **Amortadha** in North Africa. The Amortadhas pursued a more aggressive foreign and domestic policy, raiding the towns of Catalonia and persecuting their Christian subjects. These actions blighted trade and thereby enraged the emergent city-states of Italy at a time when Christendom was fired by crusading zeal. Anticipating retaliation, the Amortadhas fortified Palma, which was known at this time as Medina Mayurka, and several mountain strongholds. The **Christian attack** came in 1114 when a grand Italian fleet – led by the ships of Pisa and supported by the pope as a mini-crusade – landed an army of 70,000 Catalan and Italian soldiers on Ibiza. The island was soon captured, but Mallorca, the crusaders' next target, proved a much more difficult proposition. Palma's coastal defences proved impregnable, so the Christians assaulted the landward defences instead, the concentric lines of the fortifications forcing them into a long series of bloody engagements. When the city finally fell, the invaders took a bitter revenge, slaughtering most of the surviving Muslim population. Yet, despite their victory, the Christians had neither the will nor the resources to consolidate their position and, loading their vessels with freed slaves and loot, they returned home.

The Almoravides

It took the Moors just two years to re-establish themselves on the islands, this time under the leadership of the **Almoravides**, a North African Berber tribe who had previously controlled southern Spain. The Almoravides proved to be tolerant and progressive rulers, and the Balearics prospered: agriculture improved, particularly through the development of irrigation, and trade expanded as commercial agreements were struck with the Italian cities of Genoa and Pisa. The Pisans – crusaders earlier in the century – defied a papal ban on trade with Muslims to finalize the deal; consciences

902–905	11th century	1162
The Moors conquer the Balearics. They introduce many new crops, including the orange, lemon, peach, apricot and fig	Moorish Spain disintegrates into squabbling *taifas*, or petty fiefdoms	Alfonso II unites the kingdoms of Aragón and Catalunya; the Reconquista (the re-conquest of Spain by Christians) picks up speed

could, it seems, be flexible even in the "devout" Middle Ages when access to the precious goods of the east (silks, carpets and spices) was the prize.

Jaume I and the Reconquista

In 1203, the Almoravides were supplanted by the **Almohad** dynasty, who attempted to forcibly convert the islands' Christian population to Islam. They also started raiding the mainland, an extraordinary miscalculation given that the kingdoms of Aragón and Catalunya had recently been united, thereby strengthening the Christian position in this part of Spain. The unification was a major step in the changing balance of power: with their forces combined, the Christians were able to launch the **Reconquista**, which was eventually to drive the Moors from the entire Iberian peninsula. Part of the Christian jigsaw was the Balearics and, in 1228, the emir of Mallorca imprudently antagonized the young **King Jaume I of Aragón and Catalunya** by seizing a couple of his ships. The king's advisers, with their eyes firmly fixed on the islands' wealth, determined to capitalize on the offence. They organized the first Balearic publicity evening, a feast at which the king was presented with a multitude of island delicacies and Catalan sailors told of the archipelago's prosperity. And so, insulted by the emir and persuaded by his nobility, Jaume I committed himself to a full-scale invasion.

The invasion of Mallorca

Jaume's expedition of 150 ships, 16,000 men and 1500 horses set sail for **Mallorca** in September 1229. The king had originally planned to land at Pollença, but adverse weather conditions forced the fleet further south and it eventually anchored off Sant Elm, where it must have given the solitary shepherd who lived there a terrific shock. The following day, the Catalans defeated the Moorish forces sent to oppose the landing and Jaume promptly pushed east, laying siege to Medina Mayurka. It took three months to breach the walls, but on December 31 the city finally fell and Jaume was hailed as "**El Conqueridor**".

The invasion of Ibiza

The cost of launching an invasion on this scale placed an enormous strain on the resources of a medieval monarch. With this in mind, Jaume subcontracted the capture of **Ibiza**, entering into an agreement in 1231 with the Crown Prince of Portugal, Don Pedro, and the count of Roussillon. In return for the capture of the island, the count and the prince were to be allowed to divide Ibiza between themselves, provided they acknowledged the suzerainty of Jaume. This project initially faltered, but was revived with the addition of the archbishop of Tarragona. The three allies captured Ibiza in 1235 and divided the spoils, although Don Pedro waived his rights and his share passed to Jaume.

The capture of Menorca

In the meantime, Jaume had acquired the overlordship of **Menorca**. Unable to afford another full-scale invasion, the king devised a cunning ruse. In 1232 he returned to Mallorca with just three galleys, which he dispatched to Menorca carrying envoys, while he camped out in the mountains above Capdepera on Mallorca. As night fell and

1229	1232	1298	1311
Jaume I of Aragón and Catalunya captures Mallorca from the Moors; a bloodbath follows	Jaume I seizes Menorca from the Moors	Accession of Jaume II as king of Mallorca and Menorca	Death of Jaume II; accession of Sancho

his envoys negotiated with the enemy, Jaume ordered the lighting of as many bonfires as possible to illuminate the sky and give the impression of a vast army. The stratagem worked and the next day, mindful of the bloodbath following the invasion of Mallorca, the Menorcan Moors capitulated. According to the king's own account, they informed his envoys that "they gave great thanks to God and to me for the message I had sent them for they knew well they could not long defend themselves against me".

The terms of the Reconquista

In Menorca, Jaume's terms were generous: the Moors handed over Ciutadella, their principal settlement, and a number of other strong points, but the new king acknowledged the Muslims as his subjects and appointed one of their leaders as his *rais* (governor). The retention of Moorish government in Menorca, albeit under the suzerainty of the king, was, however, in marked contrast to events on Mallorca. Here, the land was divided into eight blocs, with four passing to the king and the rest to his most trusted followers, who leased their holdings in the feudal fashion, granting land to tenants in return for military service. In 1230 Jaume consolidated his position in Mallorca by issuing the **Carta de Població** (People's Charter), guaranteeing equality before the law, an extremely progressive precept for the period. Furthermore, Mallorca was exempted from taxation to encourage Catalan immigration, and special rights were given to Jews resident on the island, a measure designed to stimulate trade. Twenty years later, Jaume also initiated a distinctive form of government for Mallorca, with a governing body of six **jurats** (adjudicators) – one from the nobility, two knights, two merchants and one peasant. At the end of each year the *jurats* elected their successors. This form of government remained in place until the sixteenth century.

The Balearic Kingdom in the thirteenth century

Jaume I died at Valencia in 1276. In his will he divided his kingdom between his two sons: **Pedro** received Catalunya, Aragón and Valencia, while **Jaume II** was bequeathed Montpellier, Roussillon and the Balearics. Jaume II was crowned in Mallorca on September 12, 1276, but the division infuriated **Pedro** as the Balearics stood astride the shipping route between Catalunya and Sicily, where his wife was queen. He forced his brother to become his vassal, but in response Jaume II secretly schemed with the French. Predictably enough, Pedro soon discovered his brother's treachery and promptly set about planning a full-blooded invasion. However, Pedro died before the assault could begin and it was left to his son, **Alfonso III**, to carry out his father's plans. Late in 1285, Alfonso's army captured Palma without too much trouble, which was just as well for its inhabitants: wherever Alfonso met with resistance – as he did later in the campaign at the castle of Alaró – he extracted a brutal revenge. Indeed, even by the standards of thirteenth-century Spain, Alfonso was considered excessively violent and the pope excommunicated him for his atrocities – but not for long.

Alfonso invades Menorca

With Mallorca secured and Jaume deposed, Alfonso turned his attention to **Menorca**, where he suspected the loyalty of the Moorish governor – the *rais* was allegedly in

1324	1349	1479
Death of Sancho and accession of Jaume III as king of Mallorca and Menorca	Aragôn invades the Balearics; the defeat and death of Jaume III, "The Rash", marks the end of Mallorcan and Menorcan independence	Castile and Aragón, the two pre-eminent Christian kingdoms, are united under Isabella I and Fernando V (*Los Reyes Católicos*)

conspiratorial contact with the Moors of North Africa. Alfonso's army landed on Menorca in January 1287 and decisively defeated the Moors just outside Maó. The Moors retreated to the hilltop fortress of Santa Agueda, but their resistance didn't amount to much and the whole island was Alfonso's within a few days. The king's treatment of the vanquished islanders was savage: those Muslims who were unable to buy their freedom were enslaved, and those who couldn't work as slaves – the old, the sick and the very young – were taken out to sea and thrown overboard. Alfonso rewarded the nobles who had accompanied him with grants of land and brought in hundreds of Catalan settlers. The capital, Medina Minurka, was renamed **Ciutadella**, and the island's mosques were temporarily converted to Christian usage, before being demolished and replaced.

The Balearic Kingdom in the fourteenth century

Alfonso's violent career was cut short by his death in 1291 at the age of 25. His successor was his brother, Jaume, also the king of Sicily. A more temperate man, Jaume conducted negotiations through the papacy that eventually led, in 1298, to the restoration of the partition envisaged by Jaume I: he himself presided over Catalunya, Aragón and Valencia, while his exiled uncle, **Jaume II**, ruled as king of Mallorca and Menorca, Montpellier and Roussillon. Restored to the Crown, Jaume II devoted a great deal of time to improving the commerce and administration of the Balearics. To stimulate trade, he established a weekly market in Palma, reissued the currency in gold and silver, and founded a string of inland towns, including Manacor, Felanitx, Llucmajor and Binissalem on Mallorca and Alaior and Es Mercadal on Menorca. Jaume II attended to God as well as mammon, and his reign saw the building of many churches and monasteries. In the same vein, the king also patronized **Ramon Llull** (see p.61), the Mallorcan poet, scholar and Franciscan friar, providing him with the finance to establish a monastic school near Valldemossa. Perhaps his most important act, though, was to grant menorca its own **Carta de Població**, which bestowed the same legal rights as the Mallorcans already enjoyed.

King Sancho

On his death in 1311, Jaume was succeeded by **Sancho**, his asthmatic son, who spent most of his time in his palace at Valldemossa, where the mountain air was to his liking. Nonetheless, Sancho did his job well, continuing the successful economic policies of his father and strengthening his fleet to protect his territories from North African pirates. Mallorca and Menorca boomed: Mallorca in particular had long served as the entrepôt between North Africa and Europe, its warehouses crammed with iron, figs, salt, oil and slaves, but in the early fourteenth century its industries – primarily shipbuilding and textiles – flourished. In 1325, the traveller Ramón Muntaner praised Palma as an "honoured city of greater wealth than any with the most businesslike inhabitants … of any city in the world". He may have been exaggerating, but not by much, and Palma's merchants were certainly inventive: spotting a gap in the market, they went into **crossbow-making**, and by 1380 they were exporting them by the boatload.

1492	1494	16th century
The fall of Granada, the last Moorish kingdom in Spain; Columbus reaches the Americas	The Treaty of Tordesillas divides the New World between Spain and Portugal	Spain emerges as a single political entity, with the Inquisition acting as a unifying force; the Balearics fall into economic decline

The end of independence

Internationally, Sancho worked hard to avoid entanglement in the growing antagonism between Aragón and France, but the islands' future still looked decidedly shaky when he died without issue in 1324. Theoretically, the islands should have passed to Aragón, but the local nobility moved fast to crown Sancho's ten-year-old nephew as **Jaume III**. Hoping to forestall Aragonese hostility, they then had him betrothed to the king of Aragón's five-year-old daughter, though in the long term this marriage did the new king little good. After he came of age, Jaume III's relations with his brother-in-law, **Pedro IV of Aragón**, soured and Pedro successfully invaded the Balearics in response to an alleged plot against him. Jaume fled to his mainland possessions and sold Montpellier to the French to raise money for an invasion. He landed on Mallorca in 1349, but was no match for Pedro, who defeated and killed him on the outskirts of Llucmajor. His son, the uncrowned **Jaume IV**, was also captured, and although he eventually escaped, he was never able to drum up sufficient support to threaten the Aragonese.

Unification with Spain

For a diversity of reasons the **unification** of the Balearics with Aragón – and their subsequent incorporation within Spain – proved a disaster for the islanders. In particular, the mainland connection meant the archipelago's nobility soon gravitated towards the Aragonese court, regarding their local estates as little more than sources of income to sustain their expensive lifestyles. More fundamentally, general economic trends moved firmly against the Balearics. After the fall of Constantinople to the Turks in 1453, the lucrative overland trade routes from the Mediterranean to the Far East were blocked and, just as bad, the Portuguese discovered the nautical route round the Cape of Good Hope to the Indies.

In 1479, **Fernando V of Aragón** married **Isabella I of Castile**, thereby uniting the two largest kingdoms in Spain, but yet again this was bad news for the islanders. The union brought mainland preoccupations and a centralized bureaucracy, which rendered the islands a provincial backwater – even more so when, following Columbus's reaching the Americas in 1492, the focus of European trade moved from the Mediterranean to the Atlantic seaboard almost at a stroke. The last commercial straw was the royal decree that forbade Catalunya and the Balearics from trading with the New World. By the start of the sixteenth century, the Balearics were starved of foreign currency and the islands' merchants had begun to leave, signalling a period of long-term economic decline.

Sixteenth-century decline

Political and economic difficulties destabilized the islands' social structures throughout the sixteenth century. The **Jews**, as useful scapegoats, focused some of the swirling antagonisms that perturbed the islands, but there were many other signs of discontent. The aristocracy was divided into warring factions, the country districts were set against the towns, and perhaps most destabilizing of all were high taxes and an unreliable grain supply. In Mallorca, this turbulence coalesced in an **armed uprising** of peasants and artisans in 1521. Organized in a **Germania**, or armed brotherhood, the insurrectionists seized control of Palma, whose nobles beat a hasty retreat to the safety of either Palma's

1519	1532	1556
Cortés lands in Mexico, seizing its capital two years later	Pizarro "discovers" Peru, capturing Cuzco the following year	Felipe II (Philip II) becomes king of Spain and wages unsuccessful war against Europe's Protestants

Castell de Bellver or the Alcúdia citadel – those who didn't move fast enough were slaughtered in the streets. The rebels soon captured the Bellver, and polished off the blue-bloods who had sought protection there, but Alcúdia held out until relieved. It was a long wait: only in 1523 did the forces of authority return under the command of **Emperor Charles V**, king of Spain, Habsburg Holy Roman Emperor and the grandson of Fernando and Isabella. Charles negotiated generous terms for the surrender of Palma, but once in possession of the city, promptly broke the agreement and ordered the execution of five hundred rebels, who were duly hung, drawn and quartered.

Pirate attacks

The Balearics witnessed other sixteenth-century horrors with the renewal of large-scale **naval raids** from North Africa. This upsurge of piratical activity was partly stimulated by the final expulsion of the Moors from Spain in 1492, and partly by the emergence of the Ottoman Turks as a Mediterranean superpower. Among many attacks, Muslim raiders ransacked Pollença (1531 and 1550), Alcúdia (1551), Valldemossa (1552), Andratx (1553) and Sóller (1561), while **Hayreddin Barbarossa** ravaged Menorca's Maó after a three-day siege in 1535. Hundreds of Menorcans were enslaved and carted off, prompting Charles V to construct the fort of Sant Felip to guard Maó harbour. Two decades later, the Turks returned and sacked Ciutadella, taking a further three thousand prisoners – about eighty percent of the city's population. Muslim incursions continued until the seventeenth century, but declined in frequency and intensity after a combined Italian and Spanish force destroyed the Turkish fleet at **Lepanto** in 1571.

The arrival of the British

The Balearics' woes continued throughout the **seventeenth century**. Trade remained stagnant, landowners failed to invest in their estates, and the population declined, a sorry state of affairs that was exacerbated by continued internal tensions. Palma, in particular, was plagued by **vendettas** between its aristocratic families, with the Canavall

---

DISCRIMINATION AND PREJUDICE: THE JEWS OF MALLORCA

For several centuries, Mallorca's large **Jewish** community, concentrated in Palma and Inca, played a crucial role in maintaining the island's money supply and sustaining trade with North Africa. In return, they were treated in that strangely contradictory manner that was common across much of medieval Europe, alternately courted and discriminated against. They were, for instance, expected to live in their own ghettos and wear a distinctive type of dress, but were also allowed (unlike their Christian neighbours) to divorce and re-marry. Predictably, they were often blamed for things over which they had no control, from famine to plague, and were intermittently subjected to **pogroms** like the ones in Palma in 1391 and again in 1435 (see p.60). They were also subject to the attentions of the **Holy Office of the Inquisition**, which set up shop in Palma in 1484 determined to impose orthodoxy on all of the island's citizenry. The Inquisitors bore down on the Jews, most of whom either left or chose the course of least resistance and converted to Christianity, though a small percentage were burnt to death. As late as the 1970s, the descendants of these converts still formed a distinct group of Palma gold- and silversmiths, but no such enclave exists today.

1588	1598	17th century
The English defeat Felipe II's Armada, all but eliminating Spain as a major sea power	Felipe II dies. His legacy is an enormous but bankrupt empire	Spain enters a period of precipitate military, economic and political decline. Cervantes publishes *Don Quixote* in 1605

and Canavant factions regularly involved in street battles and assassinations. By the 1630s the population problem had become so critical that Philip IV exempted the islands from the levies that raised men for Spain's armies, though this gain was offset by the loss of 15,000 Mallorcans to the **plague** in 1652.

A new development was the regular appearance of **British** vessels in the Mediterranean, a corollary of Britain's increasing share of the region's seaborne trade and the Royal Navy's commitment to protect its merchantmen from Algerian pirates. The British didn't have much use for Mallorca, and largely ignored it, but they were impressed by **Maó's splendid harbour**, a secure and sheltered deep-water anchorage where they first put in to take on water in 1621. Forty years later, Charles II of England formalized matters by instructing his ambassador to Spain to "request immediate permission for British ships to use Balearic ports and particularly Port Mahon" – and the Spanish king granted the request.

The British seize Menorca

For a time the British were simply content to "borrow" Maó, but their expanding commercial interests prompted a yearning for a more permanent arrangement. It was the dynastic **War of the Spanish Succession** (1701–14), fought over the vacant throne of Spain, which gave them their opportunity. A **British force invaded Menorca** in 1708 and, meeting tepid resistance, captured the island in a fortnight. Apart from the benefits of Maó harbour, Menorca was also an ideal spot from which to blockade the French naval base at Toulon, thereby preventing the union of the French Atlantic and Mediterranean fleets. In fact, Menorca was so useful to the British that they negotiated its retention at the **Treaty of Utrecht**, which both rounded off the war and formalized the island's **first period of British occupation**, which was to last from 1708 to 1756.

The colonial occupation of Menorca

Sir Richard Kane, Menorca's first significant British governor, was an energetic and capable man who strengthened the island as a military base and worked hard at improving its administration, facilities and economy. He built the first **road** across the island from Maó to Ciutadella and introduced improved strains of seed and livestock. Indeed, such were the benefits of British rule that during the first forty years of the occupation the production of wine, vegetables and chickens increased by five hundred percent. Relations between the occupying power and the islanders were generally good – though the Catholic clergy no doubt found it difficult to stomach the instruction to "pray for His Britannic Majesty".

The French interlude

The first phase of British domination ended when the **French** captured Menorca in 1756 at the start of the **Seven Years War**. Admiral Byng was dispatched to assist the beleaguered British garrison but, after a lacklustre encounter with a French squadron, he withdrew, leaving the British force with no option but to surrender. Byng's indifferent performance cost him his life: he was court-martialled and executed for cowardice, prompting Voltaire's famous aphorism that the English shoot their admirals "pour encourager les autres". The new French governor built the township of **Sant Lluís** (see p.214) to house

1701–14	1804	1805
Europe's nation states slug it out in the War of the Spanish Succession; Britain takes Menorca and Gibraltar	Napoleon is crowned Emperor of France; Spain assists him in his war against England	The British navy, under Nelson, destroys the Franco-Spanish fleet at the Battle of Trafalgar

his Breton sailors and, once again, the Menorcans adjusted to the occupying power without too much difficulty. In 1763, Britain regained Menorca in exchange for the Philippines and Cuba, which it had captured from France during the Seven Years War.

The second British occupation of Menorca

The **second period of British occupation** (1763–82) proved far less successful than the first. None of the governors were as adept as Kane, and their tendency to ignore the islanders undermined the Menorcans' trust in the British. The crunch came in 1781 when, with Britain at war with both Spain and France, Spain's Duc de Crillon landed on the island with eight thousand soldiers. In command of a much smaller force, the British governor, John Murray, withdrew to Fort Sant Felip, where he was promptly besieged. Crucially, the Menorcans decided to succour Crillon's Franco-Spanish army and, with this material support, they were able to starve the British into submission after eight long months; thereafter, Menorca temporarily reverted to Spain.

The third British occupation of Menorca

The **third and final period of British rule over Menorca** ran from 1798 to 1802, when the island was occupied for its value as a naval base in the Napoleonic Wars. Landing at Port d'Addaia, the British took just nine days – and suffered no casualties – in recapturing the island, helped in no small measure by the foolhardy destruction of Fort Sant Felip by the Spaniards in the mid-1780s. It seems that the Spanish high command did not believe they could defend the fortress, so they simply flattened it, thereby denying it to any colonial power – and, of course, making the island vulnerable in the process. The British finally relinquished all claims to Menorca in favour of Spain under the terms of the Treaty of Amiens in 1802.

Eighteenth-century Mallorca

Meanwhile **Mallorca**, lacking a harbour of any strategic significance, was having a much quieter time, though the islanders did choose the wrong side in the War of the Spanish Succession (1701–14). Most of Spain favoured the French candidate, Philip of Anjou, but Catalunya and Mallorca preferred the Austrian Habsburg Charles III, who was supported by Britain and the Netherlands. Philip won, and promptly proceeded to strip the island of its title of kingdom and remove many of its historic rights. Otherwise, Mallorca was left pretty much untouched by the European conflicts that

---

MENORCA: POETRY IN MOTION

In the seventeenth century, most British seamen were too busy with the mundane – avoiding the lash for one – to be poetic, but a certain **John Baltharpe** wrote reams, including this little ditty about Menorca:

Good this same is upon Minork
For shipping very useful 'gainst the Turk.
The King of Spain doth to our King it lend,
As in the line above to that same end.

1808–14	1811 onwards	19th century
Napoleon arrests the Spanish king and occupies Spain; this starts the War of Independence (or Peninsular War), pitting the French against the Spanish and their new-found allies, the British	The South American colonies assert their independence, detaching themselves from Spain one by one	Protracted conflict between liberals and monarchists leads to further Spanish decline

rippled around it, but even so it did not prosper. Instead it turned in on itself, becoming a caste- and priest-ridden backwater preoccupied with its own internal feuds. By the 1740s, however, this reactionary introspection was ruffled by more progressive elements, who introduced liberal and rationalist ideas into island society under the banner of the **Enlightenment**. Oddly enough, the ideological conflict between Conservatives and Liberals focused on Ramón Llull (see p.61), with the former keen to have him beatified, the latter eager to denigrate his complex mysticism. The traditionalists won, but the bitterness of the dispute combined with its length (1749–77) divided the middle class into hostile camps.

One other major change was Madrid's edict pronouncing **Castilian** as the official language of the Balearics in place of the local dialect of Catalan.

The nineteenth century

For both Mallorca and Menorca, the **nineteenth century** brought difficult times. Neglected and impoverished outposts, they were subject to droughts, famines and epidemics of cholera, bubonic plague and yellow fever. Consequently, the islanders became preoccupied with the art of survival rather than politics, and generally stayed out of the **Carlist** wars that raged between the Liberals and the Conservatives on the Spanish mainland. Nevertheless, the islanders were obliged to implement a Liberal decree of 1836, which suppressed all of Spain's larger convents and monasteries – hence George Sand and Frédéric Chopin's extended stay in a monk-free Valldemossa monastery (see p.111). The leading political figure of the period was the historian **Josep Quadrado**, who led the reactionary Catholic Union which bombarded Madrid with petitions and greeted every Conservative success with enthusiastic demonstrations. Otherwise, many islanders emigrated, some to Algeria after it was acquired by the French in 1830, others to Florida and California.

The early twentieth century

Matters began to improve at the beginning of the twentieth century, when **agriculture**, particularly almond cultivation, revived. Modern services, like gas and electricity, began to be installed and a regular steam-packet link was established between Mallorca and the mainland. Menorca also developed a thriving export industry in **footwear** thanks to the entrepreneurial Don Jeronimo Cabrisas, a Menorcan who had made his fortune in Cuba and later supplied many of the boots worn by the troops in World War I. Around this time too, a **revival of Catalan culture**, led by the middle classes of Barcelona, stirred the Balearic bourgeoisie. In Palma in particular, Catalunyan novelists and poets were lauded, Catalan political groupings were formed, and the town was adorned with a series of splendid *Modernista* buildings.

Yet the **politics** were dire: by 1910, the ruling elite was divided between Conservative and Liberal groupings, each of which had little time or tolerance for each other. This failure to create a political discourse mirrored developments in the rest of Spain, and both here and on the mainland chronic instability was to be the harbinger of the **military coup** that ushered in the right-wing dictatorship of General Primo de Rivera, who seized power on the Spanish mainland in 1923. Rivera stayed in power until

1923	1930	1936–39
General Primo de Rivera organizes a right-wing military coup and seizes control of Spain	Rivera dies and one of his key supporters, the Spanish king Alfonso XIII, abdicates the following year; the Republicans take control and Spain polarizes to the political left and right	Spanish Civil War. General Francisco Franco and his Fascists win and extract a terrible revenge

THE SPANISH CIVIL WAR AND ITS AFTERMATH

With Spain in political turmoil, **General Francisco Franco** (1892–1975), who was the commander of the Spanish army in Africa, took the opportunity to lead a right-wing military rebellion against the Republican government in Madrid. His **Nationalists** received substantial support from Hitler and Mussolini, while the **Republicans** secured only sporadic help from the Soviet Union, though they were also assisted by thousands of politically active volunteers, organized in the **International Brigades**. The Civil War was vicious and bloody, but the Nationalists eventually prevailed and Franco became the head of a **Fascist dictatorship**; Pope Pius XII congratulated him on his "Catholic victory". Not a man to show much mercy, Franco took bloody reprisals against his enemies and although no one knows for sure how many people died, it was certainly many thousands. After the death of Franco, no effort was made to hunt down his murderous thugs – part of an accommodation between left and right designed to stop Spain from degenerating into a cycle of political revenge. This accommodation is still in place, though there are periodic attempts to get issues reopened and establish exactly who did what to whom, where and when.

1930, but the Republic that followed his fall was to be short-lived, brought to an end by Franco in the Spanish Civil War.

The Balearics in the Civil War

During the **Spanish Civil War** (1936–39), Mallorca and Menorca supported opposing sides. General Goded made Mallorca an important base for the Fascists, but when General Bosch attempted to do the same on Menorca, his NCOs and men mutinied and, with the support of the civilian population, declared their support for the Republic. In the event – apart from a few bombing raids and an attempted Republican landing at Porto Cristo (see p.183) – the Balearics saw very little fighting. Nevertheless, the Menorcans were dangerously exposed towards the end of the war, when they were marooned as the last Republican stronghold. A peaceful conclusion was reached largely through the intervention of the British, who brokered the surrender of the island aboard HMS *Devonshire*. Franco's troops occupied Menorca in April 1939 and the *Devonshire* left with 450 Menorcan exiles.

The fledgling tourist industry

The rich and famous discovered Mallorca's charms from the middle of the nineteenth century – Jules Vernes, for one, liked to visit, and both Edward VII and the German Kaiser regularly cruised its waters. The high-water mark of this elitist tourist trade was reached in the 1930s when a wealthy Argentine, Adan Diehl, opened the *Hotel Formentor* (see p.148). Never knowingly outdone, Diehl advertised the hotel in lights on the Eiffel Tower and attracted guests such as Edward VIII, the Aga Khan and Winston Churchill – no mean guest list by any standard. From such small and privileged beginnings, the Balearics' **tourist industry** mushroomed at an extraordinary rate after World War II. In 1950, Mallorca had just one hundred registered hotels and

1939–75	1975	1976–82
Franco establishes a one-party state, backed up by stringent censorship and a vigorous secret police	Death of Franco; Juan Carlos, the grandson of Alfonso XIII and Franco's appointed successor, becomes king	Juan Carlos helps steer the country towards democracy, but there are to be no trials of Franco's thugs

boarding houses, but by 1972 the total had risen to more than 1600, and similarly the number of visitors to Menorca rose from 1500 in 1961 to half a million in 1973. It was an extraordinary phenomenon greatly assisted by the Franco regime's indifference to planning controls and regulations.

The late twentieth century

After the **death of Franco** in 1975, the prodigious pace of development accelerated across the Balearics, thereby further strengthening the local economy. One twist, however, was the relative price of real estate: traditionally, island landowners with coastal estates had given their younger children the poorer agricultural land near the seashore, but it was this land the developers wanted – and so younger siblings found their prospects transformed almost at a stroke. In more general terms, the burgeoning tourist economy pumped huge quantities of money into the Balearics, and by 1990 the archipelago had one of the highest per capita incomes in Spain, four times that of Extremadura for instance, and well above the EU average. There was also the small matter of **sex**: the Franco regime had attempted to enforce a strict moral code in which Spanish girls kept their bodies to themselves until they were married. Many of the arriving tourists had no such inhibitions – much to the delight of a legion of local men; it took a couple of decades for Spanish women to re-focus their sights – and their mores.

The Autonomous Communities

The Balearics also benefited from the political restructuring of Spain following the death of Franco. In 1978, the Spanish parliament, the Cortes, passed a **new constitution**, which reorganized the country on a federal basis and allowed for the establishment of regional Autonomous Communities – in theory if not altogether in practice. Four years later, Felipe González's Socialist Workers' Party – the **PSOE** – was elected to office with a huge majority and the promise of change and progress. The PSOE did not fulfil all its objectives, but it did make a serious attempt to deal with Spain's deep-seated separatist tendencies by negotiating a large degree of regional autonomy. In the Balearics, the upshot was the creation of the **Comunidad Autónoma de las Islas Baleares** in 1983; and although the demarcation of responsibilities between central and regional governments has proved immensely problematic, the islanders have used their new-found independence to good effect, asserting the primacy of their native Catalan language – now the main language of education – and exercising greater control of their economy.

Tourism: a new direction

In 1996, the PSOE was defeated in the Spanish **general election**, but although the new Conservative regime – led by the **Partido Popular (PP)** – had strong centralizing credentials, it was also reliant on the regionalists for its parliamentary majority. Consequently, the trend towards **decentralization** continued, with most government expenditure now coming under the control of the Autonomous Communities. In particular, the Balearic administration used these regionalized resources to upgrade a string of holiday resorts and modernize much of the archipelago's infrastructure. In

1981	**1985**	**1986**
Colonel Tejero and a group of Guardia Civil officers loyal to Franco's memory storm parliament, but the putsch soon collapses	Abortion legalized; Catholic priests are horrified	Rafael Nadal born in Manacor, Mallorca; Spain joins the EU

part this reflected a particular concern with Ibiza and Mallorca's somewhat tacky image and was accompanied by the imposition of **stricter building controls**, a number of environmental schemes and the spending of millions of pesetas on refurbishing the older, historical parts of Palma. On Menorca, the money also paid for the creation of a Parc Natural, protecting the wetlands of S'Albufera d'es Grau along with the adjacent coastline.

The Conservatives, in power in the Balearics after the elections of 1991, also made moves to curb tourist development, but in this they failed to keep pace with public sentiment – as exemplified by a string of large-scale **demonstrations** held during 1998 and 1999. The demonstrations focused on four primary and interrelated concerns: the spiralling cost of real estate, foreign ownership of land (some twenty percent of Mallorca was in foreign hands), untrammelled development and loutish behaviour in the budget resorts. This failure to keep abreast of popular feeling in the islands resulted in the defeat of the Conservatives in the **1999 regional elections**.

The twenty-first century

After the regional elections of 1999, the Balearics' Conservative administration was replaced by an **unwieldy alliance** of regionalists, socialists and greens committed to halting further tourist development in its tracks. As one of its spokesmen said: "We need to dignify the tourist sector, not promote it as the cheapest in Europe with the idea that you can come here and do whatever you like." Faced with an annual influx of around eleven million holidaymakers, few islanders disagreed, and the coalition made significant progress, though they came unstuck when the tourist industry hit (comparatively) hard times in 2002 with an eight percent drop in the number of visitors. The main reason for the decline was the economic travails of Germany, but Balearic anxieties focused on the so-called **tourist tax** imposed by the regional government in May 2002. The idea was to impose a modest tax on every visitor over twelve years of age and spend the money – potentially about thirty million euros a year – on **environmental improvements**. However, the tourist industry created a huge hullabaloo that undermined the Balearic administration, and the Conservatives, who had pledged to rescind the tax, were (just) returned to office in the **regional elections of 2003**. This was a major setback for the environmentalist cause at a time when Spain's regionalists were already losing ground to Madrid – the Conservatives had won a second **general election in 2000**, but this time with an overall majority in the Cortes, thus firmly sidelining the regionalists.

The PP rules the roost

After their 2003 election victory, the Conservative-led Balearic administration proved remarkably gung ho when it came to **development**, ignoring environmental concerns by embarking, for example, on a large-scale road-building programme in the belief that more roads create better motoring – never mind the disfiguring of agricultural land that this involved. Indeed, they even became quite evangelical in their desire for development, most notably supporting a mass demonstration in favour of the expansion of port facilities at Ciutadella – an expansion that Menorca's PSOE-led council strongly opposed. The PP Mayor of Andratx, one **Eugenio Hidalgo**, joined in

1999	2002	2003	2004
Spanish economy begins a nine-year boom	Spain abandons the peseta and adopts the euro	The Conservative (PP) government commits to the invasion of Iraq; huge protests ensue	Islamic terrorists bomb Madrid; Socialists win the general election and pull Spanish troops out of Iraq

> ## POLITICAL SURPRISES: THE SPANISH ELECTION OF 2004
>
> At the start of 2004, Spanish opinion polls showed solid public support for the **Partido Popular (PP)** government, suggesting that the **general election** scheduled for March would return them to office. Then, on March 11, three days before polling day, a series of bombs exploded on Madrid's commuter trains, killing 192 people and injuring almost two thousand more. Rashly, the PP leadership blamed the Basque terrorist/separatist group ETA for the explosions, believing, so it would seem, that this false accusation would deflect attention away from the real reason for the attack – Spain's support for the Iraq war (ninety percent of Spaniards had been against it) – just long enough for the votes to be counted. It didn't wash, and by the time the polls opened, many had come to believe that – as was subsequently proved to be the case – Islamic terrorists had blown up the trains. The voters vented their political spleen against the PP, giving the **PSOE** an unexpected victory; the new regime's first act was to announce the immediate withdrawal of Spanish troops from Iraq.

the development bonanza, but in his case there were shady dealings involving illegal construction permits – among much else – and in 2008, two years after the scandal broke, Hidalgo was sent to prison for four years. This was all very depressing, but nevertheless the PP still managed to garner more votes than any other party in the Balearic **regional elections of 2007**. The catch was that they didn't quite secure an overall majority, and their opponents united to form a new ruling PSOE-led coalition.

Recession and depression

In 2007, the new PSOE-led Balearic administration, under the leadership of **Francesc Antich**, put the brakes on the helter-skelter development of its predecessor, but its priorities were soon muddied and modified by the worldwide recession: in 2009, Spain's housing market took a nose dive and unemployment began to rise, while in the Balearics the number of tourists dropped by about ten percent, bringing many hotels to the point of bankruptcy. Antich and his colleagues were obliged to consider all sorts of stimulus packages and then, as if things weren't bad enough, ETA, the Basque separatist group, exploded a number of **bombs** on Mallorca in the summer of the same year.

For the next two years, Antich and his colleagues did their best to keep the Balearics afloat, but in 2011 grumpy islanders ejected the administration in favour of the Conservatives, with the PP securing an overall majority under the leadership of **José Ramón Bauzà**, a one-time pharmacist from Marratxí, just outside Palma. Later in the same year, the PP won Spain's national election under **Mariano Rajoy**, but in the event the success of the PP was to be short-lived.

Into the future

A fiscal conservative, Rajoy was keen on **austerity**, but most Spaniards found the economic medicine hard to stomach, especially when unemployment hit a staggering 28 percent. There were also other factors in the decline of PP's popularity, notably a series of corruption scandals and the re-emergence within the party's ranks of an aggressive Catholic conservatism, as expressed in proposals to severely limit abortion. In the Balearics in 2012, things got much worse for Bauzà when Madrid cut its

2005	2008	2009	2011
Same-sex marriage made legal in Spain, to the outrage of Catholic priests	The Spanish economy hits the buffers	A car bomb explodes in Palma Nova, the work of Basque separatists; no one is killed	Conservatives defeat the Socialists in the general election, but the austerity programme they impose stirs deep resentments

regional subsidy to the islands by 48 percent; Bauzà immediately hit the airwaves to protest, but since it was his fellow PP politicians who had imposed the cuts, few were convinced or impressed.

Yet, right across Spain, this change in the public mood had a very different effect to previous shifts in opinion: the increasing unpopularity of the PP did not give its traditional rival, the PSOE, the major lift it had expected, but rather boosted the regionalists and spawned a new anti-austerity, anti-corruption party, **Podemos**, who – from a standing start – took 15 percent of the vote in the Balearics regional election of 2015. Thus, in the Balearics as elsewhere, the PP was unseated by a leftist alliance of anti-austerity parties spearheaded by Podemos. Quite how this new configuration will evolve is anyone's bet – and it's certainly possible that in the foreseeable future Catalunya will become an independent state, with the Balearics as a possible add-on. The former became much more likely in September 2015 when the separatists won the Catalunyan elections by something of a landslide – leaving Spain, as a political entity, at a veritable tipping point.

2012	2014	2015
Austerity and recession – but where is the king? Answer: he's hunting elephants in Botswana. Much derision follows	Both main parties – the PSOE and the PP – are increasingly mistrusted; support for anti-austerity coalition Podemos is on the rise	Spain in the melting pot: Podemos makes major electoral gains, as do the separatists of Catalunya

Flora and fauna

Despite their reputation as overdeveloped, package-holiday hotspots, Menorca and more especially Mallorca have much to offer birders and botanists alike. Separated from the Iberian peninsula some fifty million years ago, the Balearic archipelago has evolved (at least in part) its own distinctive flora and fauna, with further variations between each of the islands. Among the wildlife, it's the raptors inhabiting the mountains of northwest Mallorca – particularly the black vulture – that attract much of the attention, but there are other pleasures too, especially the migratory birds that gather on the islands' saltpans and marshes in April and May and from mid-September to early October. The islands are also justifiably famous for their fabulous range of wild flowers and flowering shrubs.

The account below serves as a general introduction, and covers several important birding sites, cross-referenced to the descriptions given throughout the Guide. For more specialist information, we have also listed some recommended **field guides** (p.275).

Habitats

The Balearic islands are a continuation of the Andalucian mountains of the Iberian peninsula, from which they are separated by a submarine trench never less than 80km wide and up to 1500m deep. **Mallorca** comprises three distinct geographical areas, with two ranges of predominantly limestone mountains/hills falling either side of a central plain, **Es Pla**. The **Serra de Tramuntana** dominates Mallorca's northwest coast and comprises a slim, 90km range of wooded hills and rocky peaks, all fringed by tiny coves and precipitous sea cliffs; it reaches its highest point at Puig Major (1447m). Also edged by sea cliffs is the **Serres de Llevant**, a range of more modest hills that runs parallel to the island's east shore and rises to 509m at the Santuari de Sant Salvador.

Menorca has less topographical diversity, dividing into two distinct but not dramatically different zones. The **northern half** of the island comprises rolling sandstone uplands punctuated by wide, shallow valleys and occasional peaks, the highest of which is Monte Toro at 357m. To the **south** lie undulating limestone lowlands and deeper valleys. Steep sea cliffs and scores of rocky coves trim the island's north and south shores.

Mallorca and Menorca share a temperate Mediterranean **climate**, with winter frosts a rarity, but there are significant differences between the two. The Serra de Tramuntana protects the rest of Mallorca from the prevailing winds that blow from the north and also catches most of the rain. Menorca, on the other hand, has no mountain barrier to protect it from the cold dry wind (the Tramuntana) that buffets the island from the north, giving much of the island's vegetation a wind-blown look, and obliging farmers to protect their crops with stone walls.

GOB – A VOICE FOR PRESERVATION

The threat to the islands' flora and fauna from developers has spawned an influential conservation group, **GOB** (Grup Balear d'Ornitologia i Defensa de la Naturalesa; ⓦgobmallorca .com), which has launched several successful campaigns in recent years. It helped save the S'Albufera wetlands from further development; played a leading role in the black vulture re-establishment programme; successfully lobbied to increase the penalties for shooting protected birds; and won its fight to protect and preserve Cabrera island.

HOOPOE

Mallorcan flora

The characteristic terrain of Mallorca up to around 700m is **garrigue**, partly forested open scrubland where the island's native trees – Aleppo pines, wild olives, holm oaks, carobs and dwarf palms – intermingle with imported species like ash, elm and poplar. Between 700m and 950m, the *garrigue* gives way to **maquis**, a scrubland of rosemary, laurel, myrtle and broom interspersed with swaths of bracken. Higher still is a rocky terrain that can only support the sparsest of vegetation, such as an assortment of hardy grasses and low-growth rosemary.

Across much of the island, this indigenous vegetation has been destroyed by cultivation. However, the **Aleppo pine** and the evergreen **holm oak** – which traditionally supplied acorns for pigs, wood for charcoal and bark for tanning – are still common, as is the **carob tree**, which prefers the hottest and driest parts of the island. Arguably the archipelago's most handsome tree, the carob boasts leaves of varying greenness and bears conspicuous fruits – large pods that start green, but ripen to black-brown. The **dwarf palm**, with its sharp lance-like foliage, is concentrated around Pollença, Alcúdia and Andratx. The **wild olive** is comparatively rare (and may not be indigenous), but the cultivated variety, which boasts silver-grey foliage and can grow up to 10m in height, is endemic and was long a mainstay of the local economy. There are also **orange** and **lemon** orchards around Sóller and innumerable **almond trees**, whose pink and white blossoms adorn much of the island in late January and early February.

Mallorca has a wonderful variety of **flowering shrubs**. There are too many to list here in any detail, but look out for the deep blue flowers of the **rosemary**; the reddish bloom of the **lentisk** (or mastic tree); the bright yellow **broom** which begins blossoming in March; the many types of **tree heather**; and the autumn-flowering **strawberry tree**, found especially around Ca'n Picafort. **Rockroses** are also widely distributed, the most common members of the group being the spring-flowering, grey-leafed cistus, with its velvety leaves and pink flowers, and the narrow-leafed cistus whose bloom is white.

Wild flowers and plants

In spring and autumn the fields, verges, woods and cliffs of Mallorca brim with **wild flowers**. There are several hundred species and only in the depths of winter – from November to January – are all of them dormant. Well-known flowers include marigolds, daisies, violets, yellow primroses, gladioli, poppies, hyacinths, several kinds

SELECTED BIRDS OF MALLORCA AND MENORCA

The list below describes many of the most distinctive **birds** to be found on Mallorca and/or Menorca. We have given the English name, followed in italics by the Latin, a useful cross-reference for those without a field guide.

Serin (*Serinus serinus*). Menorca. Winter visitor. Tiny, green-and-yellow canary-like bird of the finch family, with characteristic buoyant flight. Seen in almost any habitat.

Fan-tailed warbler (*Cisticola juncidis*). Mallorca & Menorca. Very common breeding resident. Typical small brown bird, but with very distinctive "zit-zit-zit" song, usually uttered in flight. Prefers wetland areas.

Nightingale (*Luscinia megarhynchos*). Mallorca & Menorca. Common breeding summer visitor. Rich-brown-coloured, robin-like bird with rich, vigorous and varied song. Prefers to sing from deep inside small bushes, often out of sight.

Wryneck (*Jynx torquilla*). Mallorca & Menorca. Mallorca: breeding resident. Menorca: spring, autumn and winter visitor. Medium-sized member of the woodpecker family with a complex pattern of brown, grey and lilac plumage. Favours olive groves.

Hoopoe (*Upupa epops*). Mallorca & Menorca. Common breeding resident. Pigeon-sized, pinky-brown bird with black head-crest. Named after its distinctive "upupu upupu" call. Its wings sport a complex black and white barring, creating a striking sight when in flight. Favours open areas with some trees nearby for nesting.

Black vulture (*Aegypius monachus*). Mallorca. Breeding resident only in the northern mountains. Massive, dark, powerful and solitary raptor with a wingspan approaching 3m. The most distinctive of the islands' birds. Faced extinction in the 1980s, but a concerted conservation effort has raised the population considerably.

Booted eagle (*Hieraaetus pennatus*). Mallorca & Menorca. Resident breeder. A small and very agile eagle, similar in size to a buzzard. Prefers the mountains, but happily hunts over scrub and grasslands too.

Eleonora's falcon (*Falco eleonorae*). Mallorca & Menorca. Mallorca: fairly common breeding summer visitor. Menorca: spring and autumn migrant. Dark, slim, elegant falcon. Hunts small birds and large insects with fantastic speed and agility. Often seen hunting insects near water.

Rock thrush (*Monticola saxatilis*). Mallorca & Menorca. Mallorca: breeding summer visitor. Menorca: spring and autumn migrant. Beautifully coloured rock- and quarry-loving thrush. Males have a pale blue head and orangey-red breast and tail. Females are a less distinctive brown and cream.

Blue rock thrush (*Monticola solitarius*). Mallorca & Menorca. Common breeding resident. Blue-coloured thrush, recalling a deep-blue starling. Can be found in any rugged, rocky areas at any time of year.

Firecrest (*Regulus ignicapillus*). Mallorca & Menorca. Common breeding resident. The smallest bird on the islands. This tiny pale green bird is named after its vivid orange-and-yellow crown. Abundant in any woodland.

Crossbill (*Loxia curvirostra*). Mallorca. Abundant breeding resident. The vivid red males and the lemon-green females of this bulky finch have an unusual crossed bill and a distinctive parrot-like appearance. The bill is adapted to extract seeds from pine cones.

Marmora's warbler (*Sylvia sarda*). Mallorca. Common breeding resident. A small blue-ish grey warbler with a long, often-upright tail and distinctive red eye ring. Prefers the bushy cover of the coastal lowlands.

Purple gallinule (*Porphyrio porphyrio*). Mallorca. Breeding resident only at Mallorca's S'Albufera. This purple-blue oddity was reintroduced to its marshland habitat at S'Albufera in 1991. It is now well established. Its incredibly long feet and swollen red bill make this hen-like bird very distinctive.

Little egret (*Egretta garzetta*). Mallorca & Menorca. Mallorca: breeding resident. Menorca: spring and autumn migrant. Long-legged, elegant white wading bird. In summer has beautiful long white plumes trailing from the back of its head. Breeds at S'Albufera only. A wetland specialist, though well adapted to treetop life.

Little bittern (*Ixobrychus minutes*). Menorca. Spring and autumn visitor. Secretive wetland specialist. This is the smallest member of the heron family breeding in Europe, at little more than 30cm tall. The male is an attractive pink-cream colour with contrasting black wings and cap. Males advertise themselves with a far-carrying gruff basal note, repeated regularly.

Purple heron (*Ardea purpurea*). Mallorca. Breeding summer visitor. Large, slender heron fond of reed beds. The male plumage has beautiful purple and rich-brown tones. Despite its size it can be rather elusive, hiding deep inside the reeds.

Black-winged stilt (*Himantopus himantopus*). Mallorca & Menorca. Mallorca: common breeding resident; Menorca: summer visitor. Incredibly long-legged black-and-white wader. Its medium size is somewhat extended by its long, straight, fine red bill. Can appear anywhere there is mud, but particularly common on saltpans.

Kentish plover (*Charadrius alexandrinus*). Mallorca & Menorca. Mallorca: common breeding resident. Menorca: spring and autumn visitor. Small, delicate wader of saltpans and marshes. Its pale-brown upper body contrasts with its gleaming white head-collar and underparts.

Cetti's warbler (*Cettia cetti*). Mallorca & Menorca. Very common breeding resident. This rather nondescript, chunky, wren-like warbler prefers dense thickets close to water. It possesses an astonishingly loud explosive song: "chet-chet-chet-chetchetchet".

Scops owl (*Otus scops*). Mallorca & Menorca. Common breeding resident. This tiny owl (just 20cm tall) is stubbornly nocturnal. At night, its plaintive "tyoo" note is repeated every few seconds often for long (monotonous) periods. Groves, plantations, small clumps of trees, conifer woodland and gardens can host this bird.

Greater flamingo (*Phoenicopterus ruber*). Mallorca & Menorca. Winter/spring visitor in small numbers. The unmistakable silhouette of this leggy wader with roseate wings, bill and legs can be seen on any wetland in spring. In winter, it's confined to the southern reaches of Mallorca – especially the S'Albufera wetland.

Great white egret (*Egretta alba*). Mallorca & Menorca. Winter visitor. This marshland specialist is really just a large version of the commoner little egret – an all-white, tall, elegant heron.

Audouin's gull (*Larus audouinii*). Mallorca & Menorca. Resident breeder. This rare gull favours the rocky coastline of both islands. It's the size and light-grey colour of a typical "seagull" but boasts a splendid red bill. Unfortunately it takes three years for birds to reach this adult plumage and prior to this they are much less distinctive.

Bee-eater (*Merops apiaster*). Mallorca & Menorca. Mallorca: common spring visitor, rare summer breeder. Menorca: breeding summer visitor. A brightly coloured, medium-sized bird, with a slim body, long pointed wings and slightly de-curved bill. It has a distinctive green, orange, yellow and blue plumage, and an instantly recognizable bubbling "pruuk" call. It prefers open, relatively flat, rugged countryside.

Egyptian vulture (*Neophron percnopterus*). Mallorca & Menorca. Mallorca: rare migrant. Menorca: breeding resident. Medium-sized raptor with small, rather pointed protruding head and featherless face. Wings held flat when soaring.

Cattle egret (*Bubulcus ibis*). Mallorca & Menorca. Mainly winter visitor. This small heron-like wader frequents the larger Balearic marshes. In winter it is white, but is distinguished from the little egret by its stubby all-yellow bill and stockier gait.

Night heron (*Nycticorax nycticorax*). Mallorca & Menorca. Mallorca: small resident population, increasing in summer with migrants. Menorca: spring and autumn migrant. Adults of this stocky, medium-sized heron are an attractive combination of black, grey and white. In contrast, younger birds up to three years old are a rather nondescript brown with cream speckling. This water bird is most active at night or dawn and dusk. By day they roost in the tree canopy or in large bushes.

Stone curlew (*Burhinus oedicnemus*). Mallorca & Menorca. Resident breeder, more common in summer. Thick-set wader that prefers dry rolling countryside to mud. Has a large, yellow, almost reptilian eye. Largely dull brown with some darker streaking, but with distinctive, long yellow legs. When in flight, its striking black-and-white wings become apparent.

Cory's shearwater (*Calonectris diomedea*). Mallorca & Menorca. Common breeder on offshore islands, but seen regularly all along the coast from March to August. Fairly large seabird. Like all shearwaters, this bird flies close to the sea's surface with stiff outstretched wings. Its size (nearly half a metre long with a wingspan of more than a metre) and pattern of flight are its most distinctive features as its plumage is rather boring. At sea it appears dark-backed and dirty-white below. A close view should reveal some yellow on the bill and a white eye ring. Thousands breed on offshore islands across the Balearics.

of cyclamen, the resinous St John's wort with its crinkled deep-green leaves and, abundant in the pine woods near the sea and in the mountains, many types of orchid. Two common mountain plants are the pampas-like grass **Ampelodesmos mauritanica**, giant clumps of which cover the hillsides, and a local variety of the sarsaparilla, **Smilax balearica**, which flourishes in limestone crevices where its sharp thorns are something of a hazard for walkers. Other common and prominent plants are the giant-sized **agave** (century plant), an imported amaryllid with huge spear-shaped, leathery leaves of blue-grey coloration, which produces a massive flower spike after ten years (just before it dies). There's also the distinctive **asphodel**, whose tall spikes sport clusters of pink or white flowers from April to June. The asphodel grows on overgrazed or infertile land and shoemakers once used its starch-rich tubers to make glue. Another common sight is the **prickly pear**, traditionally grown behind peasants' houses as a windbreak and toilet wall. A versatile plant, the prickly pear has a smell that deflects insects (hence its use around toilets) and its fruit is easy to make into pig food or jam.

Finally, many islanders maintain splendid **gardens** and here you'll see species that flourish throughout the Mediterranean, most famously bougainvilleas, oleanders, geraniums and hibiscus.

Mallorcan birds

Mallorca's diverse **birdlife** has attracted ornithologists for decades. The island boasts a whole batch of resident Mediterranean specialists and these are supplemented by migrating flocks of North European birds that descend on the island in their thousands during the spring and autumn. Crimping the northwest coast, the limestone **Serra de Tramuntana** mountains are a haven for birds of prey. The massive **black vulture** is the real star here. This rare and impressive resident raptor, with its near 3m wingspan, breeds in small numbers, but its size means there's a reasonable chance of a sighting. The Puig Roig area, near Lluc (see p.133) is an excellent place to see this vulture, but note that during late spring and summer there are sometimes access restrictions to the bird's active sea cliff nesting areas. The **booted eagle** is another mountain highlight, and there's a supporting cast of ospreys, red kites, Eleonora's falcons, kestrels and peregrines.

The **Embassament de Cúber**, or Cúber Reservoir (see p.131), just west of Lluc, provides a natural amphitheatre from where up to ten **bird of prey** species can be seen, including ospreys and red-footed falcons hunting over the water itself. The colourful **rock thrush** breeds in the quarry just west of the reservoir dam and on the nearby crags.

Seabirds

The **sea cliffs** of Mallorca's western coast are the breeding grounds of shearwaters, Mediterranean shag, storm petrels and Audouin's gulls. The most impressive seabird colonies are in the **Parc Natural de Sa Dragonera**, an island fastness off Sant Elm (see p.123), which is home to all these birds as well as several dozen pairs of Eleonora's falcons. The district's seabirds may also be viewed from **La Trapa**, a small headland nature reserve of pristine coastal *garrigue*. The reserve is about an hour's walk north of Sant Elm, but the going is fairly tough. A similarly good spot for seabirds is the **Cap de Formentor** (see p.146), at the other end of the island, from where a wide range of birds patrols the neighbouring bays of Pollença and Alcúdia.

Scrubland birds

Characteristic birds of Mallorca's **scrubland** can be found around the **Embassament de Cúber** (Cúber Reservoir), including a variety of warblers and small songbirds, such as nightingales, larks, pipits and chats. Another area of rich scrubland is the **Vall de Bóquer** (see p.145), near Pollença. Thoughtless development has harmed the olive groves and almond orchards at the base of the valley, but the Bóquer remains a migration hotspot, its pine avenues and denser wooded slopes hosting firecrests and crossbills among more familiar woodland birds like tits and wood pigeons. If you venture to the north end of the valley, you should be rewarded with the colourful delights of Marmora's warbler and the blue rock thrush. In spring, hundreds of bee-eaters can be heard and seen in and around the valley, as these stunning birds move through to breed elsewhere in the Mediterranean.

Wetland birds

Wetlands are a magnet for birds in the arid climate of the Mediterranean. Mallorca boasts the most important birdwatching spot in the whole of the Balearics in the marshes of the **Parc Natural de S'Albufera** (see p.156). Here, resident species are augmented by hundreds of **migrating birds**, which visit to find fresh water after their long journey north or south. Among scores of species, the shorter grasses shelter moorhens, coots, crakes and the reintroduced purple gallinule, while the reeds hide healthy numbers of several species of heron, bittern and egret as well as the occasional flamingo. A wide variety of small **wading birds** visit the marsh too, including the distinctively long-legged black-winged stilt and the abundant Kentish plover. The **open water** is popular with ducks, while in spring large numbers of terns may be seen. In winter the variety of duck species increases and kingfishers are common.

This rich birdlife attracts **birds of prey** and this is as good a place as any to see ospreys and marsh harriers. In addition, more than one hundred Eleonora's falcons have been seen together over the marsh in spring. Among the **smaller birds**, the spring dusk and dawn choruses provided by wetland warblers such as Cetti's, moustached and great reed are unforgettable. Neither is the sound of birds restricted to the daytime. At night, listen for the plaintive single note of the scops owl against a backdrop of warblers, crakes and crickets. The scops owl can also be heard in the south of the island, usually preferring almond groves and olive clumps.

Birds of the saltpan

Generally speaking, the south of Mallorca is not as rich in birdlife as other parts of the island, the main exception being the **saltpan** habitat of the **Salines de Llevant**, near Colònia de Sant Jordi (see p.191). Here, a wide variety of migrant wading birds, wintering duck and small flocks of wintering flamingoes and cranes can be seen. The site also has a breeding flock of more than a hundred black-winged stilts in summer and the abundance of prey attracts raptors, most frequently marsh harriers, kestrels and ospreys. The pans also host terns and Audouin's gulls: this red-billed gull is a Mediterranean specialist, and, although favouring the southern saltpans, it can be spied at many coastal spots.

Birds of the central plain

The country lanes that lattice Mallorca's **central plain**, Es Pla, have their own distinctive birdlife. In spring and summer, the calls and songs of small birds like serins, corn buntings and Sardinian warblers and the ubiquitous fan-tailed warbler create a busy backdrop to hot, lazy afternoons. Nightingales seem to be everywhere and their rich song leaves a lasting impression. In the shade of the abundant olive groves, the subtly plumaged wryneck can be found all year, often sharing this ancient landscape with the hoopoe.

Other Mallorcan fauna

Mallorca's surviving **mammals** are an uninspiring bunch. The wild boar and red fox were eliminated early in the twentieth century, leaving a motley crew of mountain goats, wild sheep, pine martens, genets, weasels and feral cats, as well as commonplace smaller mammals such as hedgehogs, rabbits, hares and shrews.

As far as **reptiles** go, there are four types of snake – all hard to see – and two species of gecko (or broad-toed lizard): the lowland-living wall gecko and the mountain-dwelling disc-fingered version. With any luck, you'll spot them as they heat up in the sun, but they move fast since warm gecko is a tasty morsel for many a bird. Off the south coast of Mallorca, the island of Cabrera (see p.192) has a large concentration of another lizard, the rare, blue-bellied **Lilford's wall lizard**.

Among **amphibians**, Mallorca has a healthy frog population, concentrated in its marshlands but also surviving in its mountain pools (up to around 800m). There are also three types of toad, of which the **Mallorcan midwife toad**, hanging on in the northern corner of the island, is the rarest and strangest. With no natural predators, its evolution involved a reduction in fecundity (it produces only a quarter of the number of eggs laid by its mainland relative) and the loss of its poison glands. This was fair enough until someone introduced the viperine snake to the island and, in the ensuing slaughter, the midwife toads were all but wiped out – only about five hundred pairs remain.

Common **insects** include grasshoppers and cicadas, whose summertime chirping is so evocative of warm Mediterranean nights, as well as more than two hundred species of moth and around thirty types of **butterfly**. Some of the more striking butterflies are red admirals, which are seen in winter, and the clouded yellows and painted ladies of spring. One of the more unusual species is the two-tailed pasha, a splendidly marked gold-and-bronze butterfly that flits around the coast in spring and late summer, especially in the vicinity of strawberry trees.

Menorcan flora

The indigenous vegetation in Menorca, which is far flatter than its larger neighbour, is almost all **garrigue** (partly forested scrubland), though intensive cultivation has reduced the original forest cover to a fraction of its former size – nowadays only about fifteen percent of the island is wooded. Native trees are the holm oak, the dwarf palm, the carob and, commonest of all, the **Aleppo pine**, which has bright green spines, silvery twigs and ruddy-brown cones. Olive trees are endemic and illustrate the effects of the prevailing Tramuntana, with grove upon grove almost bent double under the force of the wind.

Menorca's soils nourish a superb range of **flowering shrubs** and **wild flowers**. There is less variety than on Mallorca, but the islands have many species in common. In addition, Menorca boasts a handful of species entirely to itself, the most distinguished of them being the dwarf shrub **Daphne rodriquezii**, a purple-flowering evergreen, present on the cliffs of the northeast coast. In addition, the cliffs of much of the coast have a flora uniquely adapted to the combination of limestone yet saline soils. Here, **aromatic inula**, a shrubby perennial with clusters of yellow flowers, grows beside the **common caper**, with its red pods and purple seeds, and the **sea aster**.

Menorcan birds

The varied **birdlife** of Menorca includes birds of prey, wetland specialists, seabirds, waders and characteristic Mediterranean warblers, larks and pipits, but perhaps the most striking feature is the tameness of many of the birds – presumably because shooting birds is less popular here than in almost any other part of the Mediterranean.

There are several ornithological hotspots, but wherever you are **birds of prey** should be evident. Of these, the Egyptian vulture is the most impressive; there are around a hundred of them, the only resident population in Europe. Red kites, booted eagles and ospreys can also be seen year-round, joined by marsh and hen harriers in winter. Peregrines, kestrels and, in winter, sparrowhawks are also common, although in spring and autumn several others – such as the honey buzzard and black kite – may appear. **Monte Toro** (see p.225) on Menorca is as good a vantage point for birds of prey as any.

Birds of S'Albufera lake

Menorca's **best birdwatching spot** is the marshland, reeds and *garrigue* fringing **S'Albufera** lake near Es Grau (see p.218), which is itself part of the larger Parc Natural S'Albufera des Grau that extends north to Cap de Favaritx. The lake and its environs are popular with herons and egrets, the most elegant of **wetland birds**. Over the course of a year, little and cattle egrets, and purple, grey, night and squacco herons can all be seen too. **Booted eagles** are also common, flying over the area, while the muddy parts of the marsh attract many **smaller waders** in spring and the leggy black-winged stilt in summer. The lake itself hosts several thousand **ducks** in winter. The nearby **pine woodland**, next to the beach at Es Grau, is used by night herons that rest high in the trees by day and then move onto the marsh at dusk. Also **at dusk**, listen out for the plaintive single note of the scops owl against a backdrop of warblers, crakes and crickets; and, most strikingly, the rich-toned song of the nightingale. The tiny firecrest is common in the woodland, and in the spring this whole area comes alive with hundreds of migrants.

Birds of Cala Tirant and Son Bou

There are smaller marshes elsewhere on Menorca that are very good for birds. The wetland at **Son Bou** (see p.224) holds the island's largest reed bed, and the characteristic species of such a rich habitat are the noisy great reed warbler, moustached warbler and Cetti's warbler. The wetland at **Cala Tirant**, near Fornells, can be just as prolific, and the sandy area just inland of the beach is a first-rate place to see the spectacular bee-eater, which breeds in several small colonies on the island.

Birds of the Cap de Cavalleria

The **Cap de Cavalleria** (see p.220), at the northern tip of Menorca, attracts the curious-looking stone curlew, and several larks and pipits, while ospreys can often be seen fishing in the cape's **Port de Sanitja** (see p.221). Another special Balearic bird is the distinctive red-billed Audouin's gull, one of the world's rarest. A good place to see these is just off the coast by the lighthouse at the end of **Cap de Cavalleria**, where Mediterranean shags and shearwaters are also regularly seen.

Birds of the Algendar Gorge

The lush vegetation in the bottom of the **Algendar Gorge**, just inland from **Cala Galdana** (see p. 229), is a magnet for small birds and a perfect setting to hear nightingales and the short explosive song of Cetti's warbler. Above the gorge, booted eagles, Egyptian vultures and Alpine swifts gather to nest. The ravine also attracts a wonderful array of butterflies.

Birds of the Punta de S'Escullar

The barren, stony landscape of the northwest coast may seem an unpromising environment, but **Punta de S'Escullar** is the site of one of the largest colonies of Cory's shearwaters in the western Mediterranean. Thousands return to their cliffside burrows in the late afternoon throughout the summer. This rugged terrain also hosts the attractive blue rock thrush and migrant chats, wheatears and black redstarts. Pallid swifts and crag martins also breed on the cliffs.

Other Menorcan fauna

Menorca's **mammals** are a low-key bunch, an undistinguished assortment of weasels, feral cats, hedgehogs, rabbits, hares, mice and shrews. The one highlight is the island's **reptiles**. Of the four species of Balearic lizard, Menorca has three. There are two types of **wall lizard** – a green, black and blue version of Lilford's, and the olive-green and black-striped Italian lizard – as well as the Moroccan rock lizard, with olive skin or reticulated blue-green coloration.

Common **insects** include grasshoppers and cicadas as well as more than a hundred species of moth and around thirty types of **butterfly**. Three of the more striking butterflies are red admirals, which are seen in winter, and the clouded yellows and painted ladies, seen in spring.

Books

Most of the books listed below are in print and in paperback, and those that are out of print (o/p) should be easy to track down either in secondhand bookshops or online. Titles marked with the ★ symbol are especially recommended. One excellent specialist source of books about Spain is Paul Orssich (ⓦorssich.com), who focus on rare, used and out-of-print books.

GENERAL BACKGROUND

Phil Ball *Morbo: The Story of Spanish Football*. Excellent account of the history of Spanish football from its nineteenth-century beginnings with the British workers at the mines of Río Tinto in Huelva. Has sections on the golden years of Real Madrid; the dark days of Franco; and the stunning World and European Cup victories of recent years. Ever-present as a backdrop is the ferocious rivalry or *morbo* – political, historical, regional and linguistic – which has driven the Spanish game since its birth. Essential reading for every football aficionado visiting (or even thinking about visiting) Spain.

★**R. J. Buswell** *Mallorca and Tourism: History, Economy and Environment (Aspects of Tourism)*. One of a series investigating the effects of tourism on particular areas/regions, this intriguing and scholarly book is well argued and well researched, with pieces on just about everything you can think of – from the growth of mass tourism

through to golf and hiking.

★**Lucia Graves** *A Woman Unknown: Voices from a Spanish Life*. This moving memoir, by Robert Graves's daughter, is a succinct and thoughtful exploration of a life in between cultures – English and Mallorcan/Spanish. No one has better explored the deadening psychological weight of Franco's regime.

David Huelin (ed.) *Folk Tales of Mallorca*. The nineteenth-century priest and academic Mossèn Antoni Alcover spent decades collecting Mallorcan folk tales and this is a wide selection of them, running to almost 400 pages. They range from the intensely religious through to parable and proverb, but many reveal an unpleasant edge to rural island life, both vindictive and mean-spirited. Makes for intriguing background material, but unfortunately particular places on the island are never mentioned or described.

TRAVELOGUES

Sir John Carr *Descriptive Travels in the Southern and Eastern Parts of Spain and the Balearic Islands* (o/p). Written in 1811, and very much a period piece, Carr's detailed description of Mallorca is both well written and entertaining, though his anti-Semitism – the British consul in Palma was Jewish – is hard to bear.

★**Brian Dendle & Shelby Thacker** *British Travellers in Mallorca in the Nineteenth Century: An Anthology of Texts*. There are perhaps no outstanding contributors in this anthology, but the overall picture is intriguing and informative in equal measure: the engineer E.G. Bartholomew took a liking to stewed hedgehog ("dainty fat little joints"), and the aristocrat Sir John Carr raved about the Jardins d'Alfàbia and was welcomed in style by the grandees of La Granja.

Lucy McCauley (ed.) *Travelers' Tales Spain: True Stories*. It would be hard to better this anthology of writing on Spain, which gathers its short stories and journalism from the 1980s and 1990s – the book was published in 2002.

Featured authors include Gabriel García Márquez, Colm Tóibín and Louis de Bernières, whose "Seeing Red", on the tomato-throwing festival of Buñol, is worth the purchase price alone, and there's also the striking "In a Majorcan Garden" by Jill Burberry.

George Sand *A Winter in Majorca*. Accompanied by her lover, Frédéric Chopin, Sand spent the winter of 1838–39 on Mallorca, holed up in the monastery of Valldemossa. These are her recollections, often barbed and sharp-tongued – and very critical of the islanders. Always available at Valldemossa monastery (see p.111).

Gordon West *Jogging Round Majorca*. This gentle, humorous account of an extended journey around Mallorca by Gordon and Mary West in the 1920s vividly portrays the island's pre-tourist life and times. The trip had nothing to do with running – "jogging" here refers to their leisurely progress. West's book lay forgotten for decades until a BBC radio presenter, Leonard Pearcey, stumbled across it in a secondhand bookshop and subsequently read extracts on air.

HISTORY AND POLITICS

Michael Baigent & Richard Leigh *The Inquisition*. Trenchant trawl through the history of this infamous institution – from medieval beginnings to gradual collapse.

Particularly good on the Inquisition's relationship with the papacy.

Antony Beevor *The Battle for Spain: The Spanish Civil War*.

Long before Beevor hit the headlines with *Stalingrad*, he was ploughing his historical furrow – and this competent synopsis of the Civil War, running to more than six hundred pages and published in 2007, had its genesis in the 1980s.
Roger Collins *The Arab Conquest of Spain 710–97*. Much-lauded, enjoyably concise study documenting the Moorish invasion of Spain and the significant influence the conquered Visigoths had on early Muslim rule. There are also two companion titles by the same author, *Visigothic Spain 409–711* and *Caliphs and Kings: Spain, 796–1031*, each of which contains an intriguing insight into what is an oft-neglected corner of Spanish history.
★**J.H. Elliott** *Imperial Spain 1469–1716*. The best introduction to Spain's "golden age" – academically respected as well as being a gripping yarn. Also see his erudite *The Revolt of the Catalans: A Study in the Decline of Spain 1598–1640* (o/p), though this comes in at a whopping 648 pages.
John Hooper *The New Spaniards*. This excellent, authoritative portrait of post-Franco Spain was first written by *The Guardian*'s former Spanish correspondent in the 1980s and published in a revised edition in 2006. It is one of the best possible introductions to modern Spain.
★**Henry Kamen** *The Spanish Inquisition: An Historical Revision*. A highly respected examination of the Inquisition and the long shadow it cast across Spanish history. There's also Kamen's *Philip of Spain*, the first full-length English-language biography of Felipe II, the ruler most closely associated with the Inquisition; the intriguing *Imagining Spain: Historical Myth and National Identity*; and the scholarly *Spain's Road to Empire: The Making of a World Power (1492–1763)*.
Bruce Laurie *Life of Richard Kane: Britain's First Lieutenant Governor of Minorca* (o/p). Detailed (290-page) historical biography, which also provides a fascinating insight into eighteenth-century Menorca.
George Orwell *Homage to Catalonia*. Stirring account of Orwell's participation in – and early enthusiasm for – leftist revolution in Barcelona, followed by his growing disillusionment with the factional fighting that divided the Republican forces during the Civil War.
★**Geoffrey Parker** *The Army of Flanders and the Spanish Road (1567–1659)*. Sounds dry and academic, but this fascinating book gives a marvellous insight into the morals, manners and organization of the Spanish army, at the time the most feared and mutinous in Europe.
William D. Phillips, Jr *A Concise History of Spain*. There is a veritable platoon of books on the history of Spain, but this is the pick, the whole historical tale unravelled in 360 pages. Published in 2010 by Cambridge University Press.
Paul Preston *Franco: A Biography*. A penetrating – and monumental – biography of Franco and his regime, which provides as clear a picture as any of how he won the Civil War and survived in power so long. The same author's *Spanish Civil War: Reaction, Revolution and Revenge* is a compelling introduction to the subject and is more accessible for the general reader than Hugh Thomas's work (see below). Preston has also written a similarly authoritative account of the life and times of the Spanish king entitled *Juan Carlos: Steering Spain from Dictatorship to Democracy*, exploring in depth how Carlos helped move the country from beneath the long shadow of Franco. In 2012, Preston returned to similar themes in *The Spanish Holocaust: Inquisition and Extermination in Twentieth-Century Spain*, making use of newly available material to demonstrate that terror on an industrial scale was a key part of Franco's policy. Preston's latest work, *The Last Stalinist: The Life of Santiago Carrillo*, is a detailed biography of one of Spain's leading Communists.
Hugh Thomas *The Spanish Civil War*. Exhaustively researched and brilliantly detailed account of both the war and the complex political manoeuvrings surrounding it. Includes a small section on Mallorca. First published in 1961, it remains the classic text on the subject.
Giles Tremlett *Ghosts of Spain: Travels Through a Country's Hidden Past*. Tremlett (formerly the UK *Guardian*'s Madrid correspondent) digs into the untold story of Spain's Civil War dead and the collective conspiracy of silence surrounding the war's terrors; he then goes on to peel away the layers of the post-Franco era to present an enthralling and often disturbing study of contemporary Spain – warts and all. Published in 2012.

RELIGION

Anthony Bonner (ed.) *Doctor Illuminatus: A Ramon Llull Reader* (o/p). A selection from the lengthy and heavy-going treatises on mysticism and Christian zeal written by Llull, the thirteenth-century Mallorcan scholar and philosopher (see p.61). Llull's works were some of the first to be written in Catalan, but are not for the faint-hearted. A more manageable introduction to Llull is provided by Henry Carrigan (see below).
Henry Carrigan Jr (ed.) *Romancing God: Contemplating the Beloved* (o/p). Billed as a "Christian Classic", this 120-page book serves as a useful introduction to the collected thoughts of Mallorca's own Ramon Llull (see box, p.61).

ART AND ARCHITECTURE

Iria Candela *Miró* Immaculately illustrated, 80-page exploration of the life, times and artistic inspirations and aspiration of Joan Miró. Published by Tate in 2011.
Barbara Catoir *Miró on Mallorca* (o/p). Lavishly illustrated book covering Miró's lengthy residence in Cala Major, just outside Palma. There's discussion of the work Miró produced in this period and of his thoughts on the island as a whole. A little too hagiographical for some

tastes, perhaps – and could do with an update (it was published in 1995).

Gijs van Hensbergen *Gaudí: The Biography*. A worthy biography of one of the world's most distinctive architects, with Van Hensbergen putting substantial flesh on the man while placing his work firmly in context.

Janis Mink *Miró*. Recently reprinted, this beautifully illustrated book tracks through the artist's life and times.

The text is perhaps a tad ponderous, but there are lots of interesting quotations and, at 96 pages, you're not drowned in detail.

Rainer Zerbest *Gaudí: The Complete Buildings*. If you ever wondered why critics make such a fuss over Gaudí, then this book illustrates why – the man revealed in all his architectural virtuosity. Published in 2005 by Taschen.

LITERATURE

Agatha Christie *Problem at Pollensa Bay*. Among her many attributes, Agatha Christie (1890–1976) was a pioneering world traveller, who spent long periods of time in the Middle East working on archeological digs alongside her husband Max Mallowan. Christie visited Mallorca on several occasions and the entertaining tale that gives this collection of short stories its title is redolent of the days when only the well-heeled visited the island.

Ernest Hemingway *The Sun Also Rises* and *For Whom the Bell Tolls*. Hemingway remains a big part of the American myth of Spain – *The Sun Also Rises* contains some lyrically beautiful writing, while the latter – set in the Civil War – is a good deal more laboured. Hemingway also published two books on bullfighting, the better of which is the enthusiastic *Death in the Afternoon* (1932).

Roderic Jeffries *Sun, Sea and Murder*. London-born and now a Mallorca resident, Jeffries (b.1926) has turned out a number of murder-mysteries set in Mallorca, with Inspector Alvarez as his protagonist cop. Other novels in the Alvarez series include *A Question of Motive* and *Murder, Majorcan Style*.

Sian Mackay *Rafael's Wings*. Mackay knows contemporary Mallorca like the back of her hand and, although the drama at the centre of the book doesn't work too well, there's all sorts of interesting stuff on the island, its customs and predicaments.

Javier Marias *Tomorrow in the Battle Think on Me*. There are many who rate Marias (b.1951) as Spain's finest contemporary novelist – and the evidence is here in this searching, psychological thriller with its study of the human capacity for concealment and confession. Several other Marias novels are also available in English translation, including *A Heart So White*, *All Souls* and *The Infatuations*.

★Manuel Vázquez Montalbán *Murder in the Central Committee*; *An Olympic Death*; *The Angst-ridden Executive*; *Off Side*. Original and wonderfully entertaining tales by the man who was, until his untimely death in 2003, Spain's most popular crime-thriller writer. A long-time member of the Communist Party and Barcelona resident, Montalbán became a well-known journalist in post-Franco Spain; his great creation was the gourmand private detective Pepe

Carvalho. If this quartet of titles whets your appetite, move on to *Southern Seas* and a world of disillusioned Communists, tawdry sex and nouvelle cuisine – Montalbán's trademark ingredients – but don't bother with his very disappointing *The Man of My Life*.

Quim Monzó *The Enormity of the Tragedy*. A much-lauded Barcelona journalist and novelist, Monzó's absurdist take on contemporary Spain is hard to resist. This particular work deals with a trumpet player who wakes up with a permanent erection – and oh what calamities ensue.

Baltasar Porcel i Pujol *The Emperor or the Eye of the Cyclone*. Born in Andratx, Porcel (1937–2009) is commonly regarded as the most accomplished of Mallorca's modern novelists, turning out over twenty novels – some set in the Balearics, others not. None of his works is currently in print and in translation, but this particular novel (*Emperador O El Ojo Del Ciclon*) – perhaps his best – has been slated for publication in English. It deals with the Napoleonic prisoners held for many years on the island of Cabrera (see p.192).

Carme Riera *In the Last Blue*. Born in Palma in 1948, Riera is a well-known and prolific writer, but this is the only one of her works currently in print and in translation. It is set in seventeenth-century Mallorca at a time when the Inquisition is in full throttle, hunting down the island's Jews. Riera follows a group of terrified Jews as they try to escape persecution, but to no avail.

Llorenç Villalonga *The Dolls' Room*. Subtle if somewhat laboured portrait of nobility in decline in nineteenth-century Mallorca. Villalonga (1897–1980) was Mallorca's most prominent writer for several decades and his old house in Binissalem is now a museum (see p.163).

Helen Walsh *The Lemon Grove*. Oo-er, sultry times up in Deià. Passionate stirrings around the pool after the arrival of the "beautiful and reckless" Nathan; keep those Speedos on!

Carlos Ruiz Zafón *The Angel's Game*. One of the fastest-selling books in Spanish publishing history, this lengthy novel is an idiosyncratic mix of supernatural thriller-chiller and murder-mystery, set in the backstreets of Barcelona in the early twentieth century. If you liked this, try Zafón's most recent Gothic-meets-Magic-Realism novel, *Marina*.

CONTEMPORARY EXPAT TALES

Elena Davis *Witches, Oranges and Slingers: Half a Century on Mallorca*. Some expats may breeze in and out, but not

Elena Davis, a New Yorker who first visited the island in 1955 – and stayed after falling in love with Sóller. The long perspective makes her 200-page memoir particularly engaging.

William Graves *Wild Olives: Life in Mallorca with Robert Graves*. A son of Robert Graves, William was born in 1940 and spent much of his childhood in Palma and Deià, sufficient inspiration for these mildly diverting accounts of his Mallorcan contemporaries. The book's real focus, however, is his troubled family life and his difficult relationship with his father.

Peter Kerr *Snowball Oranges: One Mallorcan Winter*. Scottish farmer moves to a farmhouse in Mallorca – and loves it. In fact, he loves it so much that he goes on to write *Manana, Manana: One Mallorcan Summer; Viva Mallorca! One Mallorcan Autumn*; and *A Basketful of Snowflakes: One Mallorcan Spring*. But, all good things come to an end, and here it is *From Paella to Porridge: A Farewell to Mallorca and a Scottish Adventure*.

Chuck Maisel *Majorca, Paradise Not Lost: Living the Dream on a Spanish Island*. More tales of expat lives and rural idylls – this time one is a painter, the other a writer.

Anna Nicholas *A Lizard in my Luggage*. Racy tale of the author's breathless escape from PR hell in Mayfair to sun-kissed evenings in rural Mallorca. The first of a quintet – *Cat on a Hot Tiled Roof; Goats from a Small Island; Donkeys on My Doorstep* and *A Bull on the Beach* are the other four – which all plough a similarly entertaining furrow. The last, in which she and her family attempt to be as self-sufficient as possible, discusses the whys and wherefores with local cheese makers, shepherds and honey makers. The sixth in the series, *A Chorus of Cockerels*, is due for release in June 2016. Full marks to Nicholas for getting to know the island and its inhabitants so well. Easily the pick of this expat genre.

FOOD AND DRINK

Vicky Bennison *The Taste of a Place – Mallorca*. Enjoyable, well-illustrated book giving the lowdown on Mallorcan food and wine – not so much where to eat it, but more what it is like and where to buy it. Recipes too. Published in 2003, it could, however, do with an update.

Tomás Graves *Bread & Oil: A Celebration of Majorcan Culture*. Written by a son of Robert Graves, this intriguing and entertaining book explores Mallorca via its palate, with sections on what the islanders eat and how the ingredients

end up where they do. Adopting a similar approach, but with music in mind, is the same author's *Tuning up at Dawn: A Memoir of Music and Majorca*.

Jan Read *Wines of Spain*. Encyclopedic but still pocketable guide to the classic and emerging wines of Spain by a leading authority. Includes maps, vintages and vineyards and has an eight-page chapter devoted to the Balearic and Canary islands. First published in 1983, it was last updated in 2005.

FLORA AND FAUNA

Anthony Bonner *Plants of the Balearic Islands*. The only book on this subject currently in print, last published in 2004.

Michael Eppinger *Field Guide to the Wild Flowers of Britain and Europe*. Published in 2006, this is the most recent field guide on this subject.

Dave Gosney *Finding Birds in Mallorca*. A detailed guide to the best birding sites on Mallorca with supplementary DVD and smartphone app, the latter providing the most up-to-date information regarding bird sightings. Needs to be used with a field guide for bird identification. Published in 2012.

Christopher Grey-Wilson et al *Wild Flowers of the Mediterranean*. Excellent, comprehensive field guide. Published in 2004.

Enric Ramos *The Birds of Menorca*. More of a bird report than a field guide, this details the status of all bird species known on the island. It is aimed at the enthusiast, but still provides useful information about what to spot and where. Last published in 2000.

Lars Svensson et al *Collins Bird Guide: The Most Complete Field Guide to the Birds of Britain and Europe*. The definitive European birding field guide. Published in US as *Birds of Europe*. Second edition published in 2010.

SPECIALIST HIKING GUIDES

Discovery Walking Guides This British company produces a number of relevant hiking guides, including *Walk Mallorca*, detailing 53 walks with maps; *Walk Mallorca Tour & Trail Map*, which covers the key hiking areas; and *Walk Menorca*, describing 44 walks with maps. All three come with a complete set of GPS waypoints (available as downloadable gpx files), which allows for route inputting directly into a navigation device. The

guides are supplemented by clear 1:40,000 maps. These publications are the best on the market, but they are almost impossible to find on Mallorca or Menorca, so get them beforehand.

June Parker *Walking in Mallorca*. Refreshed in 2006, this popular, long-established hiking guide covers all the island's classic walks and has a GR221-specific companion guide, *Trekking through Mallorca* by Paddy Dillon.

Language

In recent decades the Balearics have attracted thousands of migrants from the rest of western Europe and today German, English, Catalan and Spanish are all widely spoken. Traditionally, the islanders are bilingual, speaking Castilian (Spanish) and their local dialect of the Catalan language – *Mallorquín* or *Menorquín* – with equal facility. *Català* (Catalan) has been the islanders' everyday language since the absorption of the Balearics into the medieval Kingdom of Aragón and Catalunya in the thirteenth century; Castilian, on the other hand, was imposed much later as the official language of government and business at the instigation of Madrid – and with special rigour by Franco. Almost inevitably, therefore, Spain's recent move towards regional autonomy has been accompanied by the islanders' re-assertion of Catalan as their official language. The most obvious sign of this has been the change of all the old Castilian town and street names into their Catalan equivalents.

On paper, **Catalan** looks like a cross between French and Spanish and is generally easy to understand if you know those two languages, although when it is spoken it has a very harsh sound and is surprisingly hard to come to grips with. To assist, there are several **Catalan-English/English-Catalan dictionary and phrasebooks** on the market, the pick being the one published by Hippocrene books (ⓦhippocrene books.com). **Spanish phrasebooks and dictionaries** are, by comparison, fairly commonplace, with the most user-friendly being Rough Guides' *Spanish Phrasebook*.

Catalan

When **Franco** came to power in 1939, *Català* publishing houses, bookshops and libraries were raided and their books destroyed. Furthermore, throughout his dictatorship Franco excluded Catalan from the radio, TV, daily press and, most importantly, the schools, which is why many older people cannot read or write *Català* even if they speak it all the time. Since Franco's death in 1975, however, the Balearic islanders have reasserted the primacy of Catalan as their language of choice, though the emigration of thousands of mainland Spaniards to the islands means that Castilian is the dominant language in around forty percent of Balearic households.

    Català is a Romance language, stemming from Latin and more directly from medieval Provençal, and is spoken by more than six million people in the Balearics, Catalunya, part of Aragón, most of Valencia, Andorra and parts of the French Pyrenees; it is thus much more widely used than several better-known languages such as Danish, Finnish and Norwegian. While Spaniards in the rest of the country often belittle it by saying that to get a *Català* word you just cut a Castilian one in half (which is often true), in fact the grammar is much more complicated than Castilian and there are eight vowel sounds, three more than in Castilian.

Getting by in Mallorca and Menorca

Although Catalan is the preferred **language** of most islanders, you'll almost always get by perfectly well if you speak Castilian (Spanish), as long as you're aware of the use of Catalan in timetables and so forth. Once you get into it, Castilian is one of the easiest languages there is, the rules of pronunciation pretty straightforward and strictly observed. You'll find some basic pronunciation rules below for both Catalan and Castilian, and a selection of words and phrases in both languages. Castilian is certainly easier to pronounce, but don't be afraid to try Catalan, especially in the more out-of-the-way places – you'll generally get a good reception if you at least try communicating in the local language.

Castilian (Spanish): a few rules

Unless there's an accent, words ending in d, l, r and z are **stressed** on the last syllable, all others on the second to last. All **vowels** are pure and short; combinations have predictable results.

A somewhere between back and father.
E as in get.
I as in police.
O as in hot.
U as in rule.
C is lisped before E and I, hard otherwise: cerca is pronounced "thairka".
CH is pronounced as in English.
G is a guttural H sound (like the ch in loch) before E or I, a hard G elsewhere: gigante is pronounced "higante".
H is always silent.
J is the same sound as a guttural G: jamón is pronounced "hamon".
LL sounds like an English Y: tortilla is pronounced "torteeya".
N as in English, unless it has a tilde (ñ) over it, when it becomes NY: mañana sounds like "man-yaana".
QU is pronounced like an English K.
R is rolled, **RR** doubly so.
V sounds more like B, vino becoming "beano".
X has an S sound before consonants, a KS sound before vowels.
Z is the same as a soft C, so cerveza is pronounced "thairvaitha".

Catalan: a few rules

With *Català*, don't be tempted to use the few rules of Castilian pronunciation you may know – in particular the soft Spanish Z and C don't apply, so unlike in the rest of Spain it's not "Barthelona" but "Barcelona", as in English.

A as in hat if stressed, as in alone when unstressed.
E varies, but usually as in get.
I as in police.
IG sounds like the "**tch**" in the English scratch: lleig (ugly) is pronounced "yeah-tch".
O varies, but usually as in hot.
U lies somewhere between put and rule.
Ç sounds like an English S: plaça is pronounced "plassa".
C followed by an E or I is soft; otherwise hard.
G followed by E or I is like the "zh" in Zhivago; otherwise hard.
H is always silent.
J as in the French "Jean".
LL sounds like an English Y or LY, like the "yuh" sound in "million".

N as in English, though before F or V it sometimes sounds like an M.
NY replaces the Castilian Ñ.
QU before E or I sounds like K; before A or O as in "quit".
R is rolled, but only at the start of a word; at the end it's often silent.
T is pronounced as in English, though sometimes it sounds like a D, as in viatge or dotze.
TX is like the English CH.
V at the start of a word sounds like B; in all other positions it's a soft F sound.
W is pronounced like a B/V.
X is like SH in most words, though in some, like exit, it sounds like an X.
Z is like the English Z.

Useful words and phrases

BASICS

ENGLISH	CASTILIAN	CATALAN
Yes, No, OK	Sí, No, Vale	*Sí, No, Val*
Please, Thank you	Por favor, Gracias	*Per favor, Gràcies*
Where, When	Dónde, Cuándo	*On, Quan*
What, How much	Qué, Cuánto	*Què, Quant*
Here, There	Aquí, Allí, Allá	*Aquí, Allí, Allà*
This, That	Esto, Eso	*Això, Allò*
Now, Later	Ahora, Más tarde	*Ara, Més tard*
Open, Closed	Abierto/a, Cerrado/a	*Obert, Tancat*
With, Without	Con, Sin	*Amb, Sense*
Good, Bad	Buen(o)/a, Mal(o)/a	*Bo(na), Dolent(a)*
Big, Small	Gran(de), Pequeño/a	*Gran, Petit(a)*
Cheap, Expensive	Barato/a, Caro/a	*Barat(a), Car(a)*
Hot, Cold	Caliente, Frío/a	*Calent(a), Fred(a)*
More, Less	Más, Menos	*Més, Menys*
Today, Tomorrow	Hoy, Mañana	*Avui, Demà*
Yesterday	Ayer	*Ahir*
Day before yesterday	Anteayer	*Abans-d'ahir*
Next week	La semana que viene	*La setmana que ve*
Next month	El mes que viene	*El mes que ve*

GREETINGS AND RESPONSES

ENGLISH	CASTILIAN	CATALAN
Hello, Goodbye	Hola, Adiós	*Hola, Adéu*
Good morning	Buenos días	*Bon dia*
Good afternoon/night	Buenas tardes/noches	*Bona tarda/nit*
See you later	Hasta luego	*Fins després*
Sorry	Lo siento/discúlpeme	*Ho sento*
Excuse me	Con permiso/perdón	*Perdoni*
How are you?	¿Cómo está (usted)?	*Com va?*
I (don't) understand	(No) Entiendo	*(No) Ho entenc*
Not at all/You're welcome	De nada	*De res*
Do you speak English?	¿Habla (usted) inglés?	*Parla anglès?*
I (don't) speak	(No) Hablo Español	*(No) Parlo Català*
My name is...	Me llamo...	*Em dic...*
What's your name?	¿Cómo se llama usted?	*Com es diu?*
I am English	Soy inglés/esa	*Sóc anglès/esa*
Scottish	escocés/esa	*escocès/esa*
Australian	australiano/a	*australià/ana*

Canadian	canadiense/a	canadenc(a)
American	americano/a	americà/ana
Irish	irlandés/esa	irlandès/esa
Welsh	galés/esa	gallès/esa

HOTELS AND TRANSPORT

ENGLISH	CASTILIAN	CATALAN
I want	Quiero	Vull (pronounced "fwee")
I'd like	Quisiera	Voldria
Do you know...?	¿Sabe...?	Vostès saben...?
I don't know	No sé	No sé
There is (is there?)	(¿)Hay(?)	Hi ha(?)
Give me...	Deme...	Doneu-me...
Do you have...?	¿Tiene...?	Té...?
...the time	...la hora	...l'hora
...a room	...una habitación	...alguna habitació
...with two beds/double bed	...con dos camas/cama matrimonial	...amb dos llits/llit per dues persones
...with shower/bath	...con ducha/baño	...amb dutxa/bany
for one person (two people)	para una persona (dos personas)	per a una persona (dues persones)
for one night (one week)	para una noche (una semana)	per una nit (una setmana)
It's fine, how much is it?	Está bien, ¿cuánto es?	Esta bé, quant és?
It's too expensive	Es demasiado caro	És massa car
Don't you have anything cheaper?	¿No tiene algo más barato?	En té de més bon preu?
Can one...?	¿Se puede...?	Es pot...?
...camp (near) here?	¿...acampar aquí (cerca)?	...acampar a la vora?
It's not very far	No es muy lejos	No és gaire lluny
How do I get to...?	¿Por dónde se va a...?	Per anar a...?
Left, right, straight on	Izquierda, derecha, todo recto	A l'esquerra, a la dreta, tot recte
Where is...?	¿Dónde está...?	On és...?
...the bus station	...la estación de autobuses	...l'estació de autobuses
...the bus stop	...la parada	...la parada
...the railway station	...la estación de ferrocarril	...l'estació
...the nearest bank	...el banco más cercano	...el banc més a prop
...the post office	...el correo/la oficina de correos	...l'oficina de correus
...the toilet	...el baño/aseo/servicio	...la toaleta
Where does the bus to... leave from?	¿De dónde sale el autobús para...?	De on surt el autobús a...…?
Is this the train for Barcelona?	¿Es este el tren para Barcelona?	Aquest tren va a Barcelona?
I'd like a (return) ticket to...	Quisiera un billete (de ida y... vuelta) para	Voldria un bitllet (d'anar i tornar) a...
What time does it leave (arrive in...)?	¿A qué hora sale (llega a...)?	A quina hora surt (arriba a...)?
What is there to eat?	¿Qué hay para comer?	Què hi ha per menjar?
What's that?	¿Qué es eso?	Què és això?

DAYS OF THE WEEK

ENGLISH	CASTILIAN	CATALAN
Monday	lunes	dilluns
Tuesday	martes	dimarts
Wednesday	miércoles	dimecres
Thursday	jueves	dijous
Friday	viernes	divendres
Saturday	sábado	dissabte
Sunday	domingo	diumenge

MONTHS OF THE YEAR

ENGLISH	CASTILIAN	CATALAN
January	enero	*gener*
February	febrero	*febrer*
March	marzo	*març*
April	abril	*abril*
May	mayo	*maig*
June	junio	*juny*
July	julio	*juliol*
August	agosto	*agost*
September	septiembre	*setembre*
October	octubre	*octubre*
November	noviembre	*novembre*
December	diciembre	*desembre*

NUMBERS

ENGLISH	CASTILIAN	CATALAN
1	un/uno/una	*un(a)*
2	dos	*dos (dues)*
3	tres	*tres*
4	cuatro	*quatre*
5	cinco	*cinc*
6	seis	*sis*
7	siete	*set*
8	ocho	*vuit*
9	nueve	*nou*
10	diez	*deu*
11	once	*onze*
12	doce	*dotze*
13	trece	*tretze*
14	catorce	*catorze*
15	quince	*quinze*
16	dieciséis	*setze*
17	diecisiete	*disset*
18	dieciocho	*divuit*
19	diecinueve	*dinou*
20	veinte	*vint*
21	veintiuno	*vint-i-un*
30	treinta	*trenta*
40	cuarenta	*quaranta*
50	cincuenta	*cinquanta*
60	sesenta	*seixanta*
70	setenta	*setanta*
80	ochenta	*vuitanta*
90	noventa	*novanta*
100	cien(to)	*cent*
101	ciento uno	*cent un*
102	ciento dos	*cent dos (dues)*
200	doscientos	*dos-cents (dues-centes)*
500	quinientos	*cinc-cents*
1000	mil	*mil*
2000	dos mil	*dos mil*

Food and drink

In this section we have provided a reasonably extensive **Castilian and Catalan menu reader**, though most restaurants, cafés and bars have **multilingual menus**, with English, Catalan and Castilian almost always three of the options. The main exceptions are out in the countryside, where there may only be a Catalan menu or maybe no menu at all, in which case the waiter will rattle off the day's dishes in Catalan – or sometimes Castilian.

BASICS

ENGLISH	CASTILIAN	CATALAN
Bread	Pan	Pa
Butter	Mantequilla	Mantega
Cheese	Queso	Formatge
Eggs	Huevos	Ous
Fruit	Fruta	Fruita
Garlic	Ajo	All
Oil	Aceite	Oli
Pepper	Pimienta	Pebre
Rice	Arroz	Arròs
Salt	Sal	Sal
Sugar	Azúcar	Sucre
Vinegar	Vinagre	Vinagre
Vegetables	Verduras/Legumbres	Verdures/Llegumes
To have breakfast	Desayunar	Esmorzar
To have lunch	Almorzar	Dinar
To have dinner	Sopar	Cenar
Menu	Carta	Menú
Bottle	Botella	Ampolla
Glass	Vaso	Got
Fork	Tenedor	Forquilla
Knife	Cuchillo	Ganivet
Spoon	Cuchara	Cullera
Table	Mesa	Taula
The bill/check	La cuenta	El compte
Grilled	A la brasa	A la planxa
Fried	Frit	Fregit
Stuffed/rolled	Relleno	Farcit
Casserole	Guisado	Guisat
Roast	Asado	Rostit

FRUIT (FRUITA) AND VEGETABLES (VERDURES/LLEGUMES)

ENGLISH	CASTILIAN	CATALAN
Apple	Manzana	Poma
Asparagus	Espárragos	Espàrrecs
Aubergine/eggplant	Berenjenas	Albergínies
Banana	Plátano	Plàtan
Carrots	Zanahorias	Pastanagues
Cucumber	Pepino	Concombre
Grapes	Uvas	Raïm
Melon	Melón	Meló
Mushrooms	Champiñones	Xampinyons (also bolets, setes)
Onions	Cebollas	Cebes
Orange	Naranja	Taronja

Peach	Melocotón	*Préssec*
Pear	Pera	*Pera*
Peas	Arvejas	*Pèsols*
Pineapple	Piña	*Pinya*
Potatoes	Patatas	*Patates*
Strawberries	Fresas	*Maduixes*
Tomatoes	Tomates	*Tomàquets*

BOCADILLOS (SANDWICH) FILLINGS

ENGLISH	CASTILIAN	CATALAN
Catalan sausage	Butifarra	*Butifarra*
Cheese	Queso	*Formatge*
Cooked ham	Jamón York	*Cuixot dolç*
Cured ham	Jamón serrano	*Pernil salat*
Loin of pork	Lomo	*Llom*
Omelette	Tortilla	*Truita*
Salami	Salami	*Salami*
Sausage	Salchichón	*Salxitxó*
Spicy sausage	Chorizo	*Xoriç*
Tuna	Atún	*Tonyina*

TAPAS AND RACIONES

ENGLISH	CASTILIAN	CATALAN
Anchovies	Boquerones	*Anxoves*
Stew	Cocido	*Bollit*
Squid, usually deep-fried in rings	Calamares	*Calamars*
Squid in ink	Calamares en su tinta	*Calamars amb tinta*
Snails, often served in a spicy/ curry sauce	Caracoles	*Cargols*
Cockles (shellfish)	Berberechos	*Cargols de mar*
Whole baby squid	Chipirones	*Calamarins*
Meat in tomato sauce	Carne en salsa	*Carn amb salsa*
Fish or chicken croquette	Croqueta	*Croqueta*
Fish or meat pasty	Empanadilla	*Empanada petita*
Russian salad (diced vegetables in mayonnaise)	Ensaladilla	*Ensalada russa*
Aubergine (eggplant) and pepper salad	Escalibada	*Escalibada*
Broad beans	Habas	*Faves*
Beans with ham	Habas con jamón	*Faves amb cuixot*
Liver	Hígado	*Fetge*
Prawns	Gambas	*Gambes*
Mussels (either steamed, or served with diced tomatoes and onion)	Mejillones	*Musclos*
Razor clams	Navajas	*Navallas*
Olives	Aceitunas	*Olives*
Hard-boiled egg	Huevo cocido	*Ou bollit*
Bread, rubbed with tomato and oil	Pan con tomate	*Pa amb tomàquet*
Potatoes in garlic mayonnaise	Patatas alioli	*Patates amb all i oli*
Fried potato cubes with spicy sauce and mayonnaise	Patatas bravas	*Patates cohentes*
Meatballs, usually in sauce	Albóndigas	*Pilotes*
Kebab	Pincho moruno	*Pinxo*

Octopus	Pulpo	*Pop*
Sweet (bell) peppers	Pimientos	*Prebes*
Kidneys in sherry	Riñones al jerez	*Ronyons amb xeres*
Sardines	Sardinas	*Sardines*
Cuttlefish	Sepia	*Sípia*
Tripe	Callos	*Tripa*
Potato omelette	Tortilla española	*Truita espanyola*
Plain omelette	Tortilla francesa	*Truita francesa*
Pepper, potato, pumpkin and aubergine (eggplant) stew with tomato purée	Tumbet	*Tumbet*
Mushrooms, usually fried in garlic	Champiñones	*Xampinyons*
Spicy sausage	Chorizo	*Xoriç*

SELECTED BALEARIC DISHES AND SPECIALITIES

Many of the specialities that follow come from the Balearics' shared history with Catalunya. The more elaborate fish and meat dishes are usually limited to the fancier restaurants.

SAUCES

Allioli	Garlic mayonnaise
Salsa mahonesa	Mayonnaise
Salsa romesco	Spicy tomato and wine sauce to accompany fish (from Tarragona)

SOUPS (SOPA), STARTERS AND SALADS (AMANIDA)

Amanida catalana	Salad with sliced meat and cheese
Carn d'olla	Mixed meat soup
Entremesos	Starter of mixed meat and cheese
Escalivada	Aubergine/eggplant, pepper and onion salad
Escudella	Mixed vegetable soup
Espinacs a la Catalana	Spinach with raisins and pine nuts
Esqueixada	Dried cod salad with peppers, tomatoes, onions and olives
Fideus a la cassola	Baked vermicelli with meat
Llenties guisades	Stewed lentils
Pa amb oli	Bread rubbed with olive oil, eaten with ham, cheese or fruit
Samfaina	Ratatouille-like stew of onions, peppers, aubergine/eggplant and tomato
Sopa d'all	Garlic soup
Sopas mallorquínas	Vegetable soup, sometimes with meat and chickpeas (garbanzos)
Truita (d'alls tendres; de xampinyons; de patates)	Omelette/tortilla (with garlic; with mushrooms; with potato). Be sure you're ordering omelette (tortilla), not trout (which is also truita).

RICE DISHES

Arròs a banda	Rice with seafood, the rice served separately
Arròs a la marinera	Paella: rice with seafood and saffron
Arròs negre	"Black rice", cooked with squid ink
Paella a la Catalana	Mixed meat and seafood paella, sometimes distinguished from a seafood paella by being called Paella a Valencia

MEAT (CARN)

Albergínies en es forn	Aubergines/eggplants stuffed with grilled meat
Botifarra amb mongetes	Spicy blood sausage with white beans
Conill (all i oli)	Rabbit (with garlic mayonnaise)
Escaldum	Chicken and potato stew in an almond sauce
Estofat de vedella	Veal stew

Fetge	Liver
Fricandó	Veal casserole
Frito mallorquín	Pigs' offal, potatoes and onions cooked with oil
Mandonguilles	Meatballs, usually in a sauce with peas
Perdius a la vinagreta	Partridge in vinegar gravy
Pollastre (farcit; amb gambas; al cava)	Chicken (stuffed; with prawns; cooked in sparkling wine)
Porc (rostit)	Pork (roast)
Sobrasada	Finely minced pork sausage, flavoured with paprika

FISH (PEIX) AND SHELLFISH (MARISC)

Bacallà (amb samfaina)	Dried cod (with ratatouille)
Caldereta de llagosta	Lobster stew
Cloïsses	Clams, often steamed
Espinagada de Sa Pobla	Turnover filled with spinach and eel
Greixonera de peix	Menorcan fish stew, cooked in an earthenware casserole
Guisat de peix	Fish and shellfish stew
Llagosta (amb pollastre)	Lobster (with chicken in a rich sauce)
Lluç	Hake, either fried or grilled
Musclos al vapor	Steamed mussels
Pop	Octopus
Rap a l'all cremat	Monkfish with creamed garlic sauce
Sarsuela	Fish and shellfish stew
Suquet	Fish casserole
Truita	Trout (sometimes stuffed with ham, a la Navarre)

DESSERTS (POSTRES) AND PASTRIES (PASTAS)

Cocaroll	Pastry containing vegetables and fish
Crema Catalana	Crème caramel, with caramelized sugar topping
Ensaimada	Flaky spiral pastry, often with fillings such as cabello de ángel (sweetened citrus rind)
Mel i mató	Curd cheese and honey
Postres de músic	Cake of dried fruit and nuts
Turrón	Almond fudge
Xurros	Deep-fried doughnut sticks (served with hot chocolate)

DRINKING

ENGLISH	CASTILIAN	CATALAN
Water	Agua	*Aigua*
Mineral water	Agua mineral	*Aigua mineral*
(sparkling)	(con gas)	*(amb gas)*
(still)	(sin gas)	*(sense gas)*
Milk	Leche	*Llet*
Juice	Zumo	*Suc*
Tiger-nut drink	Horchata	*Orxata*
Coffee	Café	*Café*
Espresso	Café solo	*Café sol*
White coffee	Café con leche	*Café amb llet*
Decaff	Descafeinado	*Descafeinat*
Tea	Té	*Te*
Drinking chocolate	Chocolate	*Xocolata*
Beer	Cerveza	*Cervesa*
Wine	Vino	*Vi*
Champagne/Sparkling wine	Champán/Cava	*Xampan/Cava*

Glossary

GLOSSARY OF CATALAN TERMS

Ajuntament Town Hall
Albufera Lagoon (and surrounding wetlands)
Altar major High altar
Aparcament Parking
Avinguda (Avgda) Avenue
Badía Bay
Barranc Ravine
Barroc Baroque
Basílica Catholic church with honorific privileges
Cala Small bay, cove
Camí Way or road
Ca'n At the house of (contraction of casa and en)
Capella Chapel
Carrer (c/) Street
Carretera Road, highway
Castell Castle
Celler Cellar, or a bar in a cellar
Claustre Cloister
Coll Col, mountain pass
Convent Convent, nunnery or monastery
Correu Post office
Coves Caves
Església Church
Ermita Hermitage
Estany Small lake
Festa Festival
Finca Estate or farmhouse
Font Water fountain or spring
Gòtic Gothic
Illa Island
Jardí Garden
Llac Lake
Mercat Market
Mirador Watchtower or viewpoint
Modernisme Literally "modernism", the Catalan form
  of Art Nouveau, whose most famous exponent was
  Antoni Gaudí; adjective "*Modernista*"
Monestir Monastery
Mozarabe A Christian subject of a medieval Moorish
  ruler; hence **Mozarabic**, a colourful
  building style that reveals both Christian and Moor-
  ish influences
Mudéjar A Moorish subject of a medieval Christian

ruler. Also a style of architecture developed by Moor-
ish craftsmen working for Christians, characterized by
painted woodwork with strong colours and complex
geometrical patterns; revived between the 1890s and
1930s and blended with Art Nouveau
Museu Museum
Nostra Senyora The Virgin Mary ("Our Lady")
Oficina d'Informació Turistica Tourist office
Palau Palace, mansion or manor house
Parc Park
Passeig Boulevard; the evening stroll along it
Pic Summit
Plaça Square
Platja Beach
Pont Bridge
Port Harbour, port
Porta Door, gate
Puig Hill, mountain
Rambla Avenue or boulevard
Reconquista The Christian Reconquest of Spain from
  the Moors beginning in the ninth century and culmi-
  nating in the capture of Granada in 1492
Rei King
Reial Royal
Reina Queen
Reixa Iron screen or grille, usually in front of a window
Renaixença Rebirth, often used to describe the Catalan
  cultural revival at the end of the nineteenth and
  beginning of the twentieth centuries. Architecturally,
  this was expressed as *Modernisme*
Retaule Retable, a wooden ornamental panel behind
  an altar
Riu River
Romeria Pilgrimage or gathering at a shrine
Salinas Saltpans
Santuari Sanctuary
Sant/a Saint
Serra Mountain range
Talayot Cone-shaped prehistoric tower
Taula T-shaped prehistoric megalithic structure
Torrent Stream or river (usually dry in summer)
Urbanització Modern estate development
Vall Valley

GLOSSARY OF ENGLISH ART AND ARCHITECTURAL TERMS

Ambulatory Interior covered passage around the
  outer edge of the choir in the chancel of a church
Apse Semicircular protrusion (usually) at the east end
  of a church

Art Deco Geometrical style of art and architecture
  popular in the 1930s
Art Nouveau Style of art, architecture and design
  based on highly stylized vegetal forms. Particularly

popular in Mallorca in the early part of the twentieth century – where it is normally referred to as *Modernisme* (see above)

Balustrade An ornamental rail, running, almost invariably, along the top of a building

Baroque The art and architecture of the Counter-Reformation, dating from around 1600 onwards. Distinguished by its ornate exuberance and (at its best) complex but harmonious spatial arrangement of interiors. Some elements – particularly its gaudiness – remained popular in the Balearics well into the twentieth century

Caryatid A sculptured female figure used as a column

Chancel The eastern part of a church, often separated from the nave by a screen; contains the choir and ambulatory

Churrigueresque Fancifully ornate form of Baroque named after its leading exponents, the Spaniard José Churriguera (1650–1723) and his extended family

Classical Architectural style incorporating Greek and Roman elements – pillars, domes, colonnades and so on – at its height in the seventeenth century and revived, as Neoclassical, in the eighteenth

Clerestory Upper storey of a church, incorporating the windows

Cyclopean Prehistoric style of dry-stone masonry comprising boulders of irregular form

Fresco Wall painting – durable through application to wet plaster

Gothic Architectural style of the thirteenth to sixteenth centuries, characterized by pointed arches, rib vaulting, flying buttresses and a general emphasis on verticality

Majolica A type of glazed pottery (see p.135)

Nave Main body of a church

Neoclassical Architectural style derived from Greek and Roman elements – pillars, domes, colonnades and so on – that was popular in the late eighteenth and nineteenth centuries

Plateresque Elaborately decorative Renaissance architectural style, named for its resemblance to silversmiths' work (*platería*)

Renaissance That period of European history – beginning in Italy in the fourteenth century – that marks the end of the medieval and the beginning of the early modern era. It is defined, among many criteria, by an increase in classical scholarship, geographical discovery, the rise of secular values and the growth of individualism; the term is also applied to the art and architecture of the period

Retable Altarpiece

Romanesque Early medieval architecture distinguished by squat forms, rounded arches and naive sculpture

Stucco Marble-based plaster used to embellish ceilings, etc

Transept Arms of a cross-shaped church, placed at ninety degrees to nave and chancel

Triptych Carved or painted work on three panels

Tympanum Sculpted, usually recessed, panel above a door

Vault An arched ceiling or roof

Small print and index

288 Small print

290 About the author

292 Index

299 Map symbols

Rough Guide credits

Editor: Polly Thomas
Layout: Pradeep Thapliyal
Cartography: Swati Handoo
Picture editor: Aude Vauconsant
Proofreader: Jan McCann
Managing editor: Monica Woods
Assistant editor: Divya Grace Mathew
Production: Jimmy Lao

Cover photo research: Nicole Newman, Aude Vauconsant
Editorial assistant: Freya Godfrey
Senior pre-press designer: Dan May
Programme manager: Gareth Lowe
Publisher: Keith Drew
Publishing director: Georgina Dee

Publishing information

This seventh edition published April 2016 by
Rough Guides Ltd,
80 Strand, London WC2R 0RL
11, Community Centre, Panchsheel Park,
New Delhi 110017, India
Distributed by Penguin Random House
Penguin Books Ltd, 80 Strand, London WC2R 0RL
Penguin Group (USA), 345 Hudson Street, NY 10014, USA
Penguin Group (Australia), 250 Camberwell Road,
Camberwell, Victoria 3124, Australia
Penguin Group (NZ), 67 Apollo Drive, Mairangi Bay,
Auckland 1310, New Zealand
Penguin Group (South Africa), Block D, Rosebank Office
Park, 181 Jan Smuts Avenue, Parktown North, Gauteng,
South Africa 2193
Rough Guides is represented in Canada by DK Canada, 320
Front Street West, Suite 1400, Toronto, Ontario M5V 3B6
Printed in Singapore
© Phil Lee 2016
Maps © Rough Guides

Help us update

We've gone to a lot of effort to ensure that the seventh edition of **The Rough Guide to Mallorca & Menorca** is accurate and up-to-date. However, things change – places get "discovered", opening hours are notoriously fickle, restaurants and rooms raise prices or lower standards. If you feel we've got it wrong or left something out, we'd like to know, and if you can remember the address, the price, the hours, the phone number, so much the better.

Please send your comments with the subject line **"Rough Guide Mallorca & Menorca Update"** to mail@uk.roughguides.com. We'll credit all contributions and send a copy of the next edition (or any other Rough Guide if you prefer) for the very best emails.

Find more travel information, connect with fellow travellers and plan your trip on ⓦroughguides.com.

Readers' updates

Thanks to all the readers who have taken the time to write in with comments and suggestions (and apologies if we've inadvertently omitted or misspelt anyone's name):

Jim Ainsworth; Roger Berkley; Peter Bettess; Joan B. Bonnín; Al Bottomley; Christopher Bowers; Derek Brampton; Mr Brown; Christopher Budd; Philip Burnard; Richard Buswell; Tom Coley; Stephan Conradi; Malcolm Curtis; Rosie Davies; Padraig & Barbara Doyle; William J. Drake; Maria Escandell; Diana Godden; Jackie Herbst; John Ireland; Carl Jackson; Coloma Jaume; Mike Kerr; Titia Ketelaar; Thomas Leppard; Leticia Lope; Carmela Lo Presti; Frances McCann; Yvonne McFarlane; M.J.D. Mackenzie; Fiona McLean; Richard McLellan; Ian McNichol; Judy Mallett; S.F.A. Martin; Eric Milesi; Andy Mitter; Jorge Moreno; Jean Mountfield; Clive Paul; Andy & Carol Pead; Gerard Platt; Karolina Roziecka; Jacopo Rumi; Alan & Claire Russell; Aleix Smartínez; Peter Tasker; David Taylor; Judy Taylor; Ronald Turnbull; Jason Umlah; Erik Vloeberghs; Judith Weller; Paul Westlake; Claire Woodward-Nutt.

ABOUT THE AUTHOR

Phil Lee loves spending time in Mallorca and Menorca, two of his favourite destinations. Phil has been writing for Rough Guides for well over twenty years and his other books in the series include Norway, Belgium & Luxembourg, Amsterdam, England, and the Netherlands. He lives in Nottingham, where he was born and raised.

Acknowledgements

Phil Lee: A big thank you to my editor, Polly Thomas, for her hard work and attention to detail in the preparation of this new edition of *The Rough Guide to Mallorca & Menorca*. Special thanks also to Maria Peterson for her translation skills in sorting out lots of bits and pieces; Ferran of the *Hotel Dalt Murada* for his excellent advice, hospitality and assistance in Palma; Antonia Pascual for her tips and hints in Estellencs; Richard Strutt, hiking guide extraordinaire, for his opinions and advice; James Hiscock for his hospitality and help with the wine recommendations; Flavio Mirabella of the delightful *Hotel Aimia* in Port de Sóller; Neil McQuillian of the Rough Guide team for his Palma recommendations; and the author Anna Nicholas for pointing me in the right directions in Sóller and for her enjoyable and enthusiastic conversation.

Photo credits

All photos © Rough Guides except the following:
(Key: t-top; c-centre; b-bottom; l-left; r-right)

Index

Maps are marked in grey

A

accommodation................26–28
accommodation prices............26
addresses.......................24
Admiral Byng....................219
agave...........................268
agrotourism.....................27
airports
  Mallorca......................69
  Menorca................199, 207
  Palma.........................69
Alaior.........................222
Alaró..........................105
Albarca valley.................134
Alcúdia........................148
Alcúdia.................... 149
Alcúdia, Badía d'......... 151–156
Alcúdia bay............... 151–156
Alcúdia peninsula....... 151–154
Aleppo pine.............. 265, 270
Alfàbia, Jardins d'............100
Alfonso III....................252
Algaida........................169
Almohads, the..................251
Almoravides, the...............250
Amortadhas, the................250
Andratx........................122
Anglada Camarasa, Hermen....66
Antich, Francesc...............262
Aqualand........................85
aquarium, Palma.................85
Archduke Ludwig Salvator
.... 110, 111
Arenal d'en Castell............216
art centre, Andratx............122
Artà.................... 172–176
Artà...................... 173
Artà, Massís d'................172
Artà caves.....................181
artificial pearls..............171
Artrutx, Cap d'................241
asphodel.......................268
ATMs............................39
Autonomous Communities,
  creation of..................260

B

Badía d'Alcúdia.......... 151–156
Badía de Palma.......... 78–85
Badía de Pollença....... 142–146

Balearic cuisine...............283
Balearic Outdoor Holidays
................................23, 223
banks...........................39
Banyalbufar....................120
Barbarossa, Hayreddin... 203, 255
Bardolet, José Coll............134
Barranc de Biniaraix...........99
Barranc de Binigaus............226
Bassa Blanca, Museu Sa........152
Bauzà, José Ramón..............262
BBC World Service..............32
beach sports....................34
beaches................10, 81, 109,
  154, 224
Beaker People..................246
beer............................31
Benàssar, Dionis...............138
Bendinat.......................83
Betlem, Ermita de..............174
bibliography............. 272–275
bicycle rental.................26
Biniaraix......................99
Binibona.......................136
Binigaus, Barranc de...........226
Binissalem.....................163
Binissalem............... 164
Biosphere Reserve, Menorca.199
birds..........................266
birdwatching
  books........................275
  in Mallorca..........268–269
  in Menorca...........270–271
black pig, Mallorcan...........78
black vulture.......6, 145, 266, 268
boat trips, Port de Maó........212
bocadillos...................29
Bodega José Luis Ferrer........164
bodegas......................30
bombs, Mallorca................262
Bonaire........................151
Bonany, Ermita de Nostra
  Senyora de...................167
books.................... 272–275
Bóquer valley..................145
botanical gardens, Sóller.......93
botanical gardens, Lluc.........135
brandy.........................31
British occupation, Menorca
................................255
Bunyola...................93, 103
bus contacts...................24
buses..........................23
Byng, Admiral..................219
Byzantines, the................249

C

Ca N'Alluny....................106
Ca'n Picafort............. 151, 154
Cabrera island, boats to.......193
Cabrera National Park..........192
Cabrera National Park
  visitor centre...............189
Cala Agulla....................178
Cala Bóquer....................145
Cala d'Alcalfar................215
Cala d'Algaiarens..............243
Cala Deià......................108
Cala d'Or......................186
Cala en Porter............. 214, 215
Cala Estellencs................121
Cala Fornells.............. 83, 84
Cala Galdana...................229
Cala Gat.......................178
Cala Macarella............ 229, 242
Cala Macarelleta.......... 229, 242
Cala Major................ 80, 84
Cala Mesquida.................177
Cala Mitjana...................229
Cala Mondragó..................187
Cala Morell....................242
Cala Piques....................241
Cala Pregonda..................221
Cala Rajada....................178
Cala Rajada.............. 179
Cala Sa Torreta................217
Cala Sant Esteve...............214
Cala Sant Vicenç...............141
Cala Sant Vicenç........ 141
Cala Santanyí..................188
Cala Tuent.....................132
Cala Turqueta............. 229, 242
Calderers de Sant Joan, Els
................................167
calent.......................205
Cales Fonts....................213
Calvià.........................82
Camí d'en Kane.................222
Camí de Cavalls...........35, 241
Camí de Sant Joan de Missa
.... 241, 242
Camp de Mar....................83
camping........................28
Can Boi, Deià................109
Can Prohom.....................92
Can Prunera Museu Modernista
................................93
Canada, Radio..................32
Canyamel......................181

canyoning 34
Cap d'Artrutx............................241
Cap de Capdepera 178
Cap de Cavalleria 220
Cap de Favàritx.........................218
Cap de Formentor 146
Cap de Ses Salines 188
Capdepera................................177
Capdepera, Cap de 178
car rental.................................... 25
Caragol, Platja des...................189
Carlists......................................258
carob tree.................................265
Carthaginians, the...................248
casas de huéspedes 26
Castell d'Alaró 104
Castell de Capdepera...............177
Castell de Santueri 186
Castilian............................ 276–284
Castilian menu reader
.... **281–284**
Catalan............................. 276–284
Catalan menu reader
.... **281–284**
catamarans
between Mallorca and Menorca
....23
company contacts, Spanish 22
from Ibiza..23
from mainland Spain 22
cava 30
Cavalleria, Cap de.....................220
Cavalls, Camí de.................35, 241
cave culture, Balearic 245
caves
Cala Morell.......................................242
Cova dels Coloms 226
Cova d'en Xoroi.............................215
Coves d'Artà....................................181
Coves del Drac 183
Son Bou...224
CCA Andratx Art Centre.........122
cellphones.................................. 39
cellers... 30
Centre d'Art I d'Història, Maó
....205
cervesa.. 31
Charlemagne 250
Charles V, Emperor...................255
cheese, Menorcan 228
cheese-making plant, Ferreries
....228
chemists..................................... 37
Chiesa, Giuseppe 205
Chiesa, Joan..............................205
childminding............................. 40
children, travelling with...........40
Chopin, Frédéric.......................111
Chopin concerts,
Valldemossa.........................114
Ciutadella 231–240
Ciutadella 231

Ciutadella ferry terminal.........238
Civil War, Spanish.....................259
climate.. 38
climate change............................ 21
coffee 32
cognac....................................... 31
Coll de Sóller 94
Colom, Illa d'en........................216
Colònia de Sant Jordi
.... **189–192**
Colònia de Sant Jordi 190
Colònia de Sant Pere...............176
Columbus, Christopher 186
condoms...................................... 37
conservation areas, Menorca
....199
Cornadors, Es 99
costs, average 36
Cova Blava, Sa...........................193
Cova d'en Xoroi 215
Cova dels Coloms 226
Coves d'Artà..............................181
Coves del Drac..........................183
Covetes, Ses..............................191
credit cards................................. 39
crime 36
crossbow-making.....................253
Cúber reservoir..........................131
Cura, Santuari de Nostra
Senyora de 170
currency exchange 38
cycling 25
Cyclopean walls 206

D

Daura, Pere................................235
Davallament, Pollença 33, 139
debit cards 39
Deià 105–109
Deià 106
Deià Archeological Museum
....107
Despuig, Cardinal Antonio
....69, 102
dictionaries 276
disabilities, travellers with.......41
diving, scuba 35, 220, 238
doctors 37
Douglas, Michael 110
Drac caves 183
Dragonera, Parc Natural de Sa
.... 22
drinks 29–32
driving in Mallorca and Menorca
.... 24
driving to the Balearics from
the UK.................................... 22

Dry-stone Route (GR221).........34,
91, 99, 122, 131
dwarf palm 265

E

eating and drinking 28–32
EEA reciprocal health
arrangements 37
EHIC 37
electricity 36
Els Calderers de Sant Joan
....167
email.. 38
Embassament de Cúber.........131
embassies, Spanish...................37
emergency number................... 36
ensaimada 28
entry requirements.................... 36
Ermita de Betlem 174
Ermita de la Victòria 151
Ermita de Nostra Senyora de
Bonany...................................167
Ermita de Nostra Senyora del
Puig.................................139, 140
Ermita de St Joan de Missa
....242
Es Castell...................................213
Es Cornadors 99
Es Grau 216, 218
Es Mercadal...............................224
Es Migjorn Gran 227
Es Pla...160
Es Portixol................................. 84
Es Prat.......................................218
Es Trenc 189
Escorca 133
Esporles.....................................119
Estellencs..................................121
ETA...262
EU reciprocal health
arrangements 37
Euro, the..................................... 38
Eurotunnel 22
exchange, currency 38
exchange rate............................ 38

F

fauna and flora............. 264–271
fauna and flora books..............275
Favàritx, Cap de.........................218
Felanitx......................................184
Fernando V.................................254
Ferrer, Bodega José Luis.........164
Ferrer, José 31
Ferreries 228

ferries
between Mallorca and Menorca
...................................23, 155
company contacts, Spanish...........22
from Alcúdia.................................155
from Ibiza..23
from mainland Spain......................22
from the UK.....................................22
ferry terminals
Ciutadella....................................238
Maó..207
Menorca.......................................199
Palma...70
festivals 32
field guides.....................................275
fincas...9, 27
flights
between Mallorca and Menorca...22
from Australia.................................21
from Canada...................................21
from Ibiza..22
from Ireland....................................21
from mainland Spain......................22
from New Zealand..........................21
from South Africa............................22
from the UK.....................................21
from the USA...................................21
flora and fauna............ 264–271
flora and fauna books...............275
flowers, wild 265, 270
fondas 26
food and drink menu reader
....**281–284**
Foradada, Sa..................................110
Formentor, Cap de 146
Formentor Hotel...........................148
Formentor peninsula 146
Fornalutx 99
Fornells..219
Fort Marlborough...........................214
Fort Sant Felip................................213
Franco..259
Franco, death of.............................260
Franja Roja 31
French occupation of Menorca
....256
Fundació Pilar i Joan Miró.......80
Fundació Yannick i Ben Jakober
....152
Fuster, Joan....................................114

G

gardens 93, 100, 102, 135
garrigue..............................265, 270
gas..24
Gaudí, Antoni...................................50
gay and lesbian travellers 38
gelaterias...31
Germania...254
gin 31

gin distillery, Maó.......................205
glassworks, Gordiola 168
glossaries
architectural terms.......................285
art terms.......................................285
Catalan terms...............................285
GOB (Grup Balear d'Ornitologia
i Defensa de la Naturalesa)
....264
Golden Farm..................................210
Gordiola glassworks 168
Gorg Blau...131
GR221
at Biniaraix.....................................99
at Gorg Blau.................................131
at Sant Elm...................................122
in Mallorca and Menorca 34
in Northern Mallorca 131
in Western Mallorca 91
Granja, La..118
Grau, Parc Natural S'Albufera des
....218
Graves, Robert 106, 107
Greeks, the.....................................247
Grup Balear d'Ornitologia i
Defensa de la Naturalesa
(GOB)...264

H

habitats 264
Hannibal...248
health..37
Hidalgo, Eugenio 261
Hidropark 155
hierbas 205
hikers' hostels.......................27
Castell d'Alaró...............................105
Deià...109
Northern Mallorca.........................131
Pont Romà....................................140
Port de Sóller..................................98
Son Amer.......................................135
Tossals Verds................................132
Western Mallorca...........................91
hikes
Alcúdia peninsula 152
Alcúdia peninsula 153
Barranc de Biniaraix 99
Cala Galdana................................229
Camí de Cavalls 241
Es Cornadors..................................99
Es Grau to Sa Torreta...........216–217
Es Grau to Sa Torreta 217
Es Migjorn Gran to the coast......226
Es Migjorn Gran to the coast
.... 227
La Trapa.......................................122
Port de Pollença to Cala Bóquer
....145
Port de Pollença to Cala Bóquer
(inset) 143

Serra de Tramuntana 91, 131
Valldemossa to Puig d'es Teix
....116–117
Valldemossa to Puig d'es Teix
.... 116
hiking 34, 142, 223
hiking books...................................275
hiking guides and maps 35
history........................... 245–263
holidays, public 39
holm oak...265
Homar, Catalina............................110
horseriding 34, 238
Hort de Sant Patrici, Menorca
....228
hospital treatment.......................37
hostal-residencias.................26, 27
hostales...26
Hostatgeria Castell d'Alaró
....105
hotels 26
hotels d'interior 27
hypostyles.....................................247

I

Illa d'en Colom..............................216
Illa de Cabrera................192–193
Illa del Llatzeret..........................212
Illa del Rei 212
Illa Pinto 212
Illa Quarentena...........................212
Illetes................................81, 84
Inca...165
information, tourist...................40
Inquisition, Spanish 255
insurance 37
inter-island ferries 23
inter-island flights 22
internet access................................38
Isabella I 254
Isabella II, Queen 102
itineraries 18
itineraries 19
IVA tax.....................................29, 36

J

Jaime Mascaró factory shop
....228
Jakober, Fundació Yannick i Ben
....152
Jardí Botànic, Sóller 93
Jardins d'Alfàbia.........................100
Jaume I..251
Jaume II...252
Jaume III...254

Jaume IV 254
Jews, the 60, 254, 255
José Ferrer 31

K

Kane, Camí d'en...........................222
Kane, Richard 202, 222, 256
Knights Templar 61

L

La Granja.......................................118
La Mola..212
La Trapa 122
language **276–284**
lesbian travellers......................... 38
LGBT travellers............................. 38
Lilfords wall lizard........... 192, 270
liqueur.. 31
Lithica Pedreres de S'hostal...230
lizard, Lilfords wall........... 192, 270
Llenaire Hotel 144
Llevant, Serres de 160, 172
Lluc monastery............................133
Llucalcari......................................109
Llucmajor......................................170
Llull, Ramon 61, 170, 253

M

Magaluf... 82
magazines...................................... 32
Mahon ....*see* Maó
mail.. 38
majolica..135
Mallorca & Menorca **5**
Mallorca airport 69
Mallorcan cuisine 283
Mallorcan midwife toad.........270
Mallorcan Primitives...........51, 53,
    59, 138
Mallorcan Walking Tours
    ....23, 142
Mallorcan wine............................ 31
Manacor.......................................171
Maó **200–210**
Maó 201
Maó, Port de **210–214**
Maó ferry terminal 207
maps, hiking 35
maps, road 38
maquis...265
Maravelles, Ses 84

March, Joan 54, 55, 178
Marineland.................................... 82
Marivent, Palacio de 80
markets, open-air 36
Marlborough, Fort......................214
Mascaró, Jaime 228
Massanella, Puig de 131
Massís d'Artà 172
Massís de Randa 169
Maura, Antoni 64
mayonnaise, origins of.............208
media, the 32
medical treatment 37
talayotic period 235, 236
talayotic sites 206
Menorca....................... **194–243**
Menorca............................... 198
Menorca, Museu de 204
Menorca airport 199, 207
Menorca & Mallorca 5
Menorcan cheese 228
Menorcan cuisine 283
menú del día 29
menu reader **281–284**
mercats 36
midwife toad................................270
Migjorn Gran, Es 227
Miquel Oliver wines................... 31
Mirador de la Creueta 146
Mirador de Ses Barques 131
Mirador Es Grau 121
Miramar...111
Miró, Joan 66, 67, 80, 91
mobile phones 39
Modernista, Can Prunera Museu
    93
Mola, General...............................66
Mola, La...212
monastery accommodation
    ....**27**
    Alcúdia peninsula 152
    Felanitx 186
    Lluc..135
    Northern Mallorca 131
    Petra..167
    Pollença 140
    Puig Randa 170
Mondragó Parc Natural...........187
Monestir de Nostra Senyora
    de Lluc 133
Monte Toro...................................225
Moors, the 249
mountain refuges, Mallorca 27
Mozarabs, the 250
Muleta Refugi............................. 98
Muro...157
Museu Balear de Ciències
    Naturals.................................... 93
Museu de Menorca 204
Museu Sa Bassa Blanca...........152
Myotragus balearicus 107

N

Na Macaret..................................216
Naveta d'es Tudons...................230
navetas 206, 247
Nelson, Admiral Horatio 210
Newman, Philip...........................138
newspapers 32
Northern Mallorca 126–157
Northern Mallorca 130

O

olive, wild 265
Oliver, Antoni Ribas 134
Oliver, Miquel 31
Orient...103
orxaterias 31

P

pa amb oli 29
Països, Ses....................................172
Palacio de Marivent 80
Palau Sancho, Valldemossa....114
PALMA....................................47–78
    Palma and around.................... 46
    Palma 48–49
    Central Palma 56–57
    accommodation 71–73
    airport 69
    Ajuntament................................ 62
    Antoni Maura, Avinguda d' 64
    aquarium..................................... 85
    Arc de L'Almudaina 60
    Argentina, Avinguda 66
    arrival.. 69
    art shops 77
    Avinguda d'Antoni Maura.............64
    Avinguda Jaume III.................. 65
    Baluard, Es 65
    banks... 78
    Banys Àrabs................................ 58
    bars, late-night.......................... 75
    bars, tapas 73
    Basílica de Sant Francesc 60
    beaches....................................... 81
    bike rental 71
    books... 77
    bus station 70
    buses 70, 71
    cafés 73
    Caixa Forum art gallery 66
    Can Alomar 62
    Can Balaguer 66
    Can Bordils 64
    Can Moner 65
    Can Oleza................................... 60
    Can Pavesi.................................. 65

Can Rei 67
Can Solleric 64
Can Vivot 64
car rental 71
Carrer Morei 60
Castell de Bellver 68
Cathedral 47–52
chemists 78
city pass 71
city tours 71
clothes shops 77
clubs 76
Consolat de Mar 68
consulates 78
Corte Inglés, El 77
craft shops 77
department stores 77
directory 78
drinking 73
driving 70
eating and drinking 73
El Corte Inglés 77
El Puig de Sant Pere 65
emergencies 78
EMT buses 71
Es Baluard museu d'art 65
Feixina, La 66
ferry terminal 70
food shops 77
football 76
Gaudí, Antoni 50
Gran Hotel 66
guided tours 71
harbourfront 68
horse and carriage rides 71
hotels 71
information 71
Jaume III, Avinguda 65
L'Àguila 67
La Feixina 66
library 78
Llotja, Sa 68
Llull, Ramon 61
Mà del Moro 65
Mallorcan Primitives 51, 53, 59
mansions 64
maps 77
March, Joan 54
markets 78
Morei, Carrer 60
Museu de la Catedral 51
Museu de Mallorca 58
Museu Diocesà 53
Museu Fundación Juan March......67
nightclubs 76
Old Town 58–64
ORA tickets 70
orientation 47
Palau de l'Almudaina 52
Palau March 54
Palma airport 69
Palma Aquarium 85
Palma ferry terminal 70
Palma Nova 82
Parc de la Mar 58
Parc Quarentena 68
parking 70
pass, city 71

Passeig d'es Born 62
Passeig Mallorca 65
performing arts 76
pharmacies 78
Plaça Cort 62
Plaça de la Reina 64
Plaça Major 67
Plaça Marquès del Palmer 67
Plaça Mercat 66
Plaça Weyler 66
Portella gateway 58
post office 78
Primitives, Mallorcan 51, 53, 59
railways 70
Ramon Llull 61
restaurants 74
Sa Llotja 68
Sant Francesc, Basilica de 60
Sant Jeroni, church of 62
Sant Miquel, church of 67
Sant Pere, El Puig de 65
Santa Eulalia, church of 60
shoe shops 77
shopping 77
tapas bars 73
taxis 71
Teatre Principal 76
Templar chapel 61
theatres 76
tourist offices 71
tours, guided 71
train stations 70
trains 70
transport 71
Unió, Carrer 66
walls, city 55
wine shops 77
Palma airport 69
Palma Aquarium 85
Palma ferry terminal 70
Palma Nova 82
palo 205
Parc Natural, Mondragó 187
Parc Natural de S'Albufera......156
Parc Natural de Sa Dragonera
123
Parc Natural S'Albufera des Grau
218
parks, regional and national
 ....34, 192
passports 36
pear, prickly 268
pearls, artificial 171
Pedra en Sec, Ruta de 34, 91, 99, 122, 131
Pedreres de S'hostal, Lithica..230
Pedro, King 252
Pedro IV 254
Peguera 83
Península de Formentor 146
pensions 26
Perlas Majorica 171
Petra 166
petrol 24
pharmacies 37

Phoenicians, the 247
phones 39
phrasebooks 276
phylloxera 31
Picasso, Pablo 66, 67, 91
pig, black Mallorcan 78
Pina 169
pinxtos 29
Platges Son Saura 241
Platja Cala Comtesa 81
Platja de Binimel-Là 221
Platja de Cavalleria 221
Platja de Formentor 146
Platja de Palma 84
Platja des Caragol 189
Platja Sant Adeodat 228
Platja Sant Tomàs 228
Platja Son Moll 178
Podemos 263
police 36
Pollença 136–141
Pollença 137
Pollença, Badía de 142–146
Pollença Bay 142–146
Pollentia Roman remains 150
pomada 205
Pont Romà Refugi 140
Port d'Addaia 216
Port d'Alcúdia 154
Port d'Alcúdia 155
Port d'Andratx 123
Port d'Andratx.................... 124
Port de Maó 210–214
Port de Maó boat trips 212
Port de Pollença........... 142–146
Port de Pollença................. 143
Port de Sanitja 221
Port de Sóller....................96–99
Port de Sóller 97
Port de Sóller tram 93
Port de Valldemossa 118
Portals Nous 81, 84
Portixol, Es 84
Porto Cristo 181–184
Porto Cristo 182
Porto Petro 186
post 38
prickly pear 268
Primitives, Mallorcan..........51, 53, 59, 138
Prohom, Can 92
public holidays 39
Puig d'es Teix 117
Puig de l'Àguila 141
Puig de Massanella 131
Puig Major 131
Puig Randa 170
Punic Wars, the 248
Punta de S'Elefant 243
Punta de S'Escullar 43

Q

Quadrado, Josep............ 232, 258
quarry................................230
Queso Mahon......................228

R

racions.................................29
radio..................................32
Radio Canada........................32
rail contacts, Mallorca &
    Menorca............................24
Rail Europe............................22
rainfall................................38
Raixa.................................102
Ramís, Juli.......................59, 114
Ramon Llull.....................61, 253
Randa................................169
Randa, Massís de 169
Reconquista, the...................251
refugis................................27
    Castell d'Alaró...................105
    Deià................................109
    Northern Mallorca 131
    Pont Romà........................140
    Port de Sóller.....................98
    Son Amer..........................135
    Tossals Verds.....................132
    Western Mallorca 91
riding, horse........................34
Rissaga, the.........................236
Roman remains, Alcúdia........150
Romans, the........................248
romerias..............................33
Rubió, Joan..........................92
Ruta de Pedra en Sec 34, 91,
    99, 122, 131

S

S'Albufera, Parc Natural de.....156
S'Albufera des Grau,
    Parc Natural 218
S'Arenal..............................84
S'Albufera des Grau........ 217, 218
S'Arracó.............................122
S'Atalaia campsite 230
S'Estaca.............................110
Sa Bassa Blanca, Museu..........152
Sa Calobra..........................132
Sa Dragonera, Parc Natural de
   123
Sa Foradada........................110
Sa Torre Cega 178
Sa Torreta...........................217

safety, personal 36
Sagrera, Guillermo 68
St James the Greater................163
Salines de Llevant 191
Salvator, Ludwig 110, 111
Sancho, King 253
Sand, George 111, 113, 272
sangria...................................31
Sanisera.......................... 221, 247
Sanitja, Port de 221
Sant Elm................................122
Sant Felip, Fort.......................213
Sant Jaume Mediterrani.........224
Sant Joan de Missa, Ermita de
   242
Sant Lluís.............................214
Sant Patrici, Hort de, cheese
    plant, Menorca 228
Sant Salvador, Santuari de
    (Felanitx) 184
Sant Salvador, Santuari de (Artà)
   172
Sant Tomàs...........................228
Santa Catalina Thomàs..........114
Santa Ponça............................82
Santanyí..............................188
Santuari de Gràcia.................170
Santuari de Nostra Senyora
    de Cura............................170
Santuari de Sant Honorat.......170
Santuari de Sant Salvador, Artà
   172
Santuari de Sant Salvador,
    Felanitx...........................184
Santueri, Castell de 186
SatNavs.................................25
sausages, Mallorcan 78
scuba diving............. 35, 220, 238
Selva...................................136
Serra, Junipero...................61, 166
Serra de Tramuntana hiking
    ....91, 131
Serres de Llevant 160, 172
Sert, Josep Maria 54
Ses Covetes..........................191
Ses Maravelles 84
Ses Països.............................172
Ses Salines, Cap de................188
sherry...................................31
shopping...............................35
shrubs, flowering....................265
Sineu..................................165
siurrels..................................77
slingers, Balearic 248
smoking.................................40
snorkelling, Fornells 220
Sóller................................91–96
Sóller..................................92
Sóller train.............................93
Sóller tunnel (Ma-11) 94

Sometimes.............................84
Son Amer..............................135
Son Bou...............................224
Son Catlar............................241
Son Marroig..........................109
Son Parc..............................216
Son Vivó........................ 241, 242
Southern Mallorca....... 158–193
Southern Mallorca............. 162
Spanish language....... 276–284
Spanish Civil War....................259
Spanish embassies...................37
Spanish Inquisition.................255
Spanish menu reader .. 281–284
sparkling wine, Spanish............30
speed limits 24
spirits...................................31
sports...................................34

T

Tafona de Son Fang, Sa 176
Talatí de Dalt.........................206
Talayotic period.......235, 236, 246
talayotic sites, Menorca..........206
talayots....................199, 206, 246
Tamarells des Nord 217
tapas.....................................29
taulas.............................. 206, 246
tavernas 30
taxes, local (IVA) 29, 36
taxis.....................................25
tea.......................................32
Teix, Puig d'es........................117
telephones.............................39
television...............................32
temperatures..........................38
Templar, Knights 61
Terra, Vin de la 31
terrorism..............................262
theme parks 82, 85, 155
Thomàs, Santa Catalina..........114
time zones..............................40
tipping...........................36, 40
toad, Mallorcan midwife.........270
Torralba d'en Salord................223
Torre Cega, Sa 178
Torre d'en Gaumés.................223
Torre de Fornells 219
Torre del Verger.....................120
Torre Nova............................82
Torre Saura...........................241
Torrellafuda..........................230
Torrent, José Roberto..............235
Torrent de Pareis.....................133
Tossals Verds.........................132
tour operators.........................23
tourist information....................40
tourist offices 40

train contacts, Mallorca & Menorca ... 24
train to Sóller ... 93
trains from the UK ... 22
trains in Mallorca ... 24
tram, Port de Sóller ... 93
Tramuntana Tours ... 23, 94, 97
Tramuntana, Serra de (hiking in) ... 91, 131
Trapa, La ... 122
travel agents ... 23
travel insurance ... 37
travellers' cheques ... 39
Trenc, Es ... 189
tunnel to Sóller (Ma-11) ... 94

V

Vall de Bóquer ... 145
Valldemossa ... 111–118
Valldemossa ... 112

Valldemossa Monastery ... 111–114
Vandals, the ... 249
vegan food ... 29
vegetarians ... 29
Victòria, Ermita de la ... 151
Vikings, the ... 250
Villalonga, Llorenç ... 163
Vin de la Terra ... 31
visas ... 36
Voice of America ... 32
vulture, black ... 6, 145, 266, 268

W

Waldren, Jacqueline ... 107
Waldren, William ... 107
walking ... 34, 142
walking books ... 275
walking guides and maps ... 35
walking trails ... 34

water parks ... 82, 85, 155
weather ... 38
websites, useful ... 40
Western Mallorca ... 86–125
Western Mallorca ... 90
Western Water Park ... 82
windsurfing ... 35, 220
wine, Mallorcan ... 31, 164
wine, Spanish ... 30

X

Xoriguer gin distillery ... 205
Xoroi, Cova d'en ... 215

Z

ziggurats ... 196

Map symbols

The symbols below are used on maps throughout the book

=====	Main road	◆ Point of interest	▲ Mountain peak	Church (town map)
=====	Minor road	⊠ Post office	⋒ Arch	Church (regional map)
▦	Pedestrian road	ⓘ Information office	∴ Ruins	Building
- - - -	Footpath	@ Internet access	∿ Hot springs	▦ Stately home
— -	Ferry	⛽ Petrol station	◠ Cave	Castle
───	Coastline	P Parking	⛺ Campsite	Fort
───	Wall	✛ Hospital	Lighthouse	♦ Museum
★	Bus stop	⚲ Monastery	Viewpoint	□ Park
✈	Airport	⊠ Gate/entrance	≍ Bridge	□ Beach

Listings key

■ Accommodation

● Café /restaurant/tapas bar

■ Bar/club/late-night bar

● Shop

Mallorcan *Walking* Tours

Mallorca lies at your feet waiting to be discovered

Guided Day Walks
With something for all abilities

Mallorcan Classic Trek
Guided and Self Guided
Both with vehicle assistance for your baggage

San Telmo Heaven *Tour in South West*

Hire a Guide service and Group Specialists
We've been sharing our passion for Mallorca
for more than 20yrs.

Tel: **+34 668 542 274**
richstrutt@hotmail.com
facebook.com/mallorcanwalking.tours

www.mallorcanwalkingtours.puertopollensa.com